BESIDE THE GOLDEN DOOR

Policy, Politics, and the Homeless

James D. Wright, Beth A. Rubin, and Joel A. Devine

D0061058

ALDINE DE GRUYTER

New York

About the Authors

James D. Wright is Charles and Leo Favot Professor of Human Relations, Department of Sociology, Tulane University. Dr. Wright is the author (or co-author) of over thirteen books including: *Address Unknown: The Homeless in America; Under the Gun: Weapons, Crime and Violence in America; Armed and Considered Dangerous: A Survey of Felons and Their Firearms; The State of the Masses, and The Greatest of Evils: Urban Poverty and the American Underclass* (all: Aldine de Gruyter).

Beth A. Rubin is Associate Professor, Department of Sociology, Tulane University. Dr. Rubin is the author of *Shifts in the Social Contract: Understanding Change in American Society* as well as numerous journal articles.

Joel A. Devine is Professor, Department of Sociology, Tulane University. Dr. Devine is the author of numerous journal articles, and co-author of *The Greatest of Evils: Urban Poverty and the American Underclass* (Aldine de Gruyter).

ALDINE DE GRUYTER
A division of Walter de Gruyter, Inc.
200 Saw Mill River Road
Hawthorne, New York 10532

This publication is printed on acid free paper ∞

Library of Congress Cataloging-in-Publication Data

Wright, James D.
    Beside the golden door : policy, politics, and the homeless / James D. Wright, Beth A. Rubin, and Joel A. Devine.
        p.   cm. — (Social institutions and social change)
    Includes bibliographical references and index.
    ISBN 0-202-30613-5 (cloth : alk. paper).— ISBN 0-202-30614-3 (pbk. : alk. paper)
    1. Homelessness—Government policy—United States.   2. Homelessness—United States—Public opinion.   3. Poor—Housing—United States.   4. Housing policy—United States.   5. Mental health policy—United States.   6. Public opinion—United States.   7. United States—Economic policy.   8. United States—Politics and government.   I. Rubin, Beth A., 1955–   .   II. Devine, Joel A., 1953–   .
III. Title.   IV. Series.
HV4505.W76   1998
363.5'96942'0973—dc21   97-52031
                                                                          CIP

Manufactured in the United States of America

10 9 8 7 6 5 4 3 2 1

To the memory of
Helen Loretta Moon Wright
1926–1995
and
Roberta Barbara White
1932–1989
and
Marc Berman
1954–1993

Give me your tired, your poor,
your huddled masses yearning to breathe free,
The wretched refuse of your teeming shore,
Send these, the **homeless,** *tempest-tost to me,*
I lift my lamp beside the golden door!

Emma Lazarus

Contents

For 6/29

For 6/29

Preface

Beside the Golden Door is based on papers, essays, and speeches that Wright and his colleagues have written since the publication in 1989 of *Address Unknown: The Homeless in America*. Much but not all of the material contained here has been published previously in one form or another; we have rewritten all of it in order to remove redundancies, improve the flow of the manuscript, correct factual errors, or sharpen the focus of our arguments.

Address Unknown contained Wright's thoughts on the problem of homelessness as of the mid-to-late 1980s; *Beside the Golden Door* updates the story through the middle 1990s. In some respects then, this book is an update ten years later. Like the earlier book, this one contains little or no material that would be inaccessible to the average undergraduate student or to a reasonably interested lay reader; that said, we think much that is contained here will prove useful as well to specialists in the topic of homelessness.

The critical reception afforded *Address Unknown* was generally positive and with a few exceptions it seems that most of the book has worn well. As such, there is relatively little overlap between the content of the earlier book and this one. The discussion of the number of the homeless in *Address Unknown* contains a few good guesses but is now otherwise passé. The treatment here is much more complete and tells the story of the Census Bureau's ill-fated effort to count the homeless in conjunction with the 1990 Census. There is also much more information about poverty and low-income housing in the present volume than in the earlier one.

The most controversial account of homelessness to have appeared in the last several years is the book by Baum and Burnes, *A Nation In Denial: The Truth about Homelessness* (1993). In contrast to the argument made in *Address Unknown* (and continued here), which locates the ultimate cause of homelessness in the rising rate of poverty and the continuing decline of low-income housing, Baum and Burnes argue that homelessness results from the various personal disabilities of the homeless themselves, specifically mental illness and alcohol and drug abuse. The thesis is hardly novel, but it has struck a responsive chord; "blaming the victim" has become rather a national pastime in our increasingly intolerant age. We take up various aspects of the Baum and Burnes analysis throughout our presentation, and as such, the treatment here of the so-called ADM disorders (alcohol, drug, and mental illness) is far more detailed and complete than the corresponding material from *Address Unknown*.

The thesis advanced in this book—also not novel—is that the emphasis on factors such as mental illness or substance abuse is descriptively accurate but fails as a causal account of the rise of homelessness as a social problem. Indeed, we think it is essentially pointless to cast the causal issue in either-or terms, as social structure *versus* individual deficiencies. The point argued in this volume is that the poverty and housing trends have created a situation where some people are destined to be homeless; personal factors such as mental illness or substance abuse are useful in predicting who those people will turn out to be. In brief, social structural developments put people at risk of homelessness; personal failings actualize that risk for specific individuals.

Federal policy toward the homeless in the 1990s is defined by the various provisions of the Stewart B. McKinney Homeless Assistance Act of 1987; the McKinney "story" is woven throughout the following text. One key provision of McKinney was the national system of Health Care for the Homeless (HCH) clinics that are now found in more than a hundred U.S. cities. The model for this clinic system was the 19-city HCH Demonstration Program funded principally by the Robert Wood Johnson Foundation and the Pew Charitable Trusts. It was the first author's good fortune to serve as principal investigator for the national evaluation of the HCH Demonstration Program. The evaluation was focused largely on the health consequences of being homeless (Wright and Weber 1987) and so the rather brief treatment of this topic in *Address Unknown* has been replaced with a much expanded discussion.

Finally, *Address Unknown* and much of the rest of the large literature on homelessness that has appeared in the last decade treats only the U.S. case and says little or nothing about the comparative dimensions of the problem. Contrary to what is sometimes implied in these discussions, homelessness is not just an urban issue nor is it uniquely an American issue. Certainly, homelessness has been endemic in various Third World societies for many decades; a comparison between the situation of homeless children in one such society, Honduras, and that of homeless children in the United States provides a disturbing indication of just how close to Third World conditions we have allowed ourselves to come. A wave of homelessness has also swept over the post-industrial societies of Western Europe in the last decade as well. The final chapters of this book review what we know about homelessness in its comparative dimensions and summarize what can be anticipated about the course of homelessness in the next century.

The subject matter addressed here has been dictated mainly by the various research projects Wright has undertaken since he came to Tulane in 1988. The HCH project was largely completed at the University of Massachusetts, but the final analysis of the data was not; many of the results of that analysis are summarized in the following chapters. The most accessible statement of the results of the HCH project is found in *Homelessness and Health* (Wright and Weber 1987), which was based on only the first (of three) years' worth of data; the update given here is based on the final analyses of the entire data set. Various parts of a more recent review of the literature dealing with the health behaviors of the homeless and the poor, written with Laurie Joyner, round out the statement on health and the homeless.

In 1990, Devine and Wright received a research contract from the Bureau of the Census to evaluate the implementation of S-Night in New Orleans; S-Night was the bureau's effort to count the nation's homeless population. Most of the material contained in Chapters 2 and 3 derives from our S-Night experiences. Those chapters also recount some of the controversies surrounding Rossi's effort to enumerate homeless people in Chicago in the mid-1980s, a project with which Wright was peripherally involved.

In 1991, Devine and Wright were funded by the National Institute of Alcohol Abuse and Alcoholism to establish a research-demonstration program that became known as the New Orleans Homeless Substance Abuser's Project (NOHSAP), a long-term residentially based alcohol and drug treatment and recovery program for homeless substance abusers in the New Orleans area. Research they did in connection with NOHSAP provides very useful descriptive data for a sample of 670 homeless alcoholics and drug addicts—a critically important and apparently growing subgroup within the larger homeless population. Much of the empirical material contained here on alcoholism and drug addiction as it pertains to the problem of homelessness is derived from these data. The NOHSAP experience also gives interesting data on the problems one encounters in looking to alcohol and drug treatment programs as a "solution" to the homelessness problem.

Also in the early 1990s, Rubin and Wright accepted an assignment to prepare a statement on the low-income housing situation for a Fannie Mae conference on housing and homelessness. The materials assembled in that assignment provide a convenient update of the low-income housing situation post–*Address Unknown* and appear in Chapter 4. Similarly, a review article that was solicited for *Societes Contemporaines* provides material that appears through the first four chapters.

Wright's interests in the comparative aspects of homelessness were initially stimulated by his involvement with *Proyecto Alternativos*, a community-based health education and primary health care project for street children in Tegucigalpa, Honduras, with which Wright has been affiliated since 1991. Although *Alternativos* is mostly a service delivery project, it has also provided some interesting research opportunities, the results of which we summarize in a later chapter.

Acknowledgments

We express gratitude to the various agencies and organizations that have funded our research on the homeless over the years: the Robert Wood Johnson Foundation, the Pew Charitable Trusts, the National Institute on Alcohol Abuse and Alcoholism, and the U.S. Bureau of the Census. We are also grateful to the following graduate students who have assisted at various stages of the editing: Lesley Reid, Krista Brumley, and Rebecca Matteo.

The material from which this book has been freely adapted is as follows:

(1) Wright, J. D. (1993). "The Homeless: Issues and Controversies." In *Introduction to Social Problems*, edited by C. Calhoun and G. Ritzer. New York: McGraw Hill.

(2) Wright, J. D., and J. A. Devine (1991). "No Fixed Address: The Nature of Homelessness in Contemporary America." *National Social Science Journal* 3(2, Spring):53–68.

(3) Wright, J. D., and J. A. Devine (1992). "Counting the Homeless: The Census Bureau's 'S-Night' in Five U.S. Cities." *Evaluation Review* 16(4, August):355–64.

(4) Devine, J. A., and J. D. Wright (1992). "Counting the Homeless: S-Night in New Orleans." *Evaluation Review* 16(4):409–17.

(5) Wright, J. D., and J. A. Devine (1995). "Housing Dynamics of Homeless Persons and Their Implications for Counting the Homeless." *American Journal of Orthopsychiatry* 65(3, July):320–29.

(6) Rubin, B. A., Wright, J. D., and J. A. Devine (1992). "Unhousing the Urban Poor: The Reagan Legacy." *Journal of Sociology and Social Welfare* 19(1, March): 111–47.

(7) Wright, J. D., and B. A. Rubin (1991). "Is Homelessness a Housing Problem?" *Housing Policy Debate* 2:937–56.

(8) Wright, J. D. (1991). "Poverty, Housing, Families, and Homelessness." Keynote Address, National Health Policy Forum, Washington, DC, 21 May.

(9) Rossi P. H., and J. D. Wright (1994). "Lost in the Streets: Homelessness in America." Featured review of A. S. Baum and D. W. Burnes, *A Nation In Denial: The Truth About Homelessness*, in *Contemporary Sociology* 23(1, January):41–42.

(10) Wright, J. D. (1994). "Is Mental Illness a Cause of Homelessness? No." Pp. 95–104 in *Controversial Issues in Mental Health*, edited by Stuart A. Kirk and Susan D. Einbinder. Boston: Allyn and Bacon.

(11) Devine J. A., and J. D. Wright (1997). "Losing the housing game: The levelling effects of substance abuse." *American Journal of Orthopsychiatry* 67(4):618–31.

(12) Wright, J. D., and J. A. Devine (1993). "Family Backgrounds and the Substance-Abusive Homeless: The New Orleans Experience." *Community Psychologist* 26(2):35–37.

(13) Wright, J. D., J. A. Devine, and N. Eddington (1993). "The New Orleans Homeless Substance Abusers Program." *Alcoholism Treatment Quarterly* 10(3–4):51–64.

(14) Devine J. A., J. D. Wright, and C. J. Brody (1995). "An Evaluation of an Alcohol and Drug Treatment Program for Homeless Substance Abusers." *Evaluation Review* 19(6, December):620–45.

(15) Wright, J. D. (1990). "Poor People, Poor Health: The Health Status of the Homeless." *Journal of Social Issues* 46(4):49–64.

(16) Wright, J. D., and L. Joyner (1995). "Health Behavior among the Homeless and the Poor." In *Handbook of Health Behavior Research*, edited by David S. Gochman. New York: Plenum.

(17) Wright, J. D. (1991). "Health and the Homeless Teenager: Evidence from the National Health Care for the Homeless Program." *Journal of Health and Social Policy* 2(Spring):15–35.

(18) Wright, J. D. (1991). "Children in and of the Streets: Health, Social Policy, and the Homeless Young." *American Journal of Diseases of Children* 145(5, May):516–19.

(19) Wright, J. D. (1993). "Homeless Children: Two Years Later." *American Journal of Diseases of Children* 147(May):518–19.

(20) Wright, J. D. (1991). "Poverty, Homelessness, Health, Nutrition, and Children." Chapter 4 in *Homeless Children and Youth: A New American Dilemma*, edited by Julee Kryder-Coe, Lester Salamon, and Janice Molnar. New Brunswick, NJ: Transaction.

(21) Wright, J. D. (1993). "Rural vs. Urban Homelessness in Louisiana." Presentation at the Third Annual Louisiana State Conference on Homelessness, Lafayette, LA, 11 October.

(22) Wright, J. D., M. Wittig, and D. C. Kaminsky (1993). "Street Children in North and Latin America: Preliminary Data from *Proyecto Alternativos* in Tegucigalpa and Some Comparisons with the U.S. Case." *Studies in Comparative International Development* 28(2, Summer):81–92.

(23) Wright, J. D., and A. Brayfield (1994). "Homelessness in the Post-Industrial Societies." Draft ms.

(24) Wright, J. D. (1993). "Homelessness:The Dust Bowl of the 1990s." Paper presented at the HUD Regional Conference on the Homeless, Dallas, Texas, 21 April.

(25) Wright, J. D. (1989). "Homelessness in the Remainder of the 20th Century." Plenary Address, National Association of Community Health Center's First Annual Homeless Health Care Conference, Arlington, Virginia, 6 October.

(26) Wright, J. D. (1993). Reviews of J. Blau, *The Visible Poor: Homelessness in the United States,* in *Social Service Review* 67(1, March):163–64; and M. Lang (1991). "Homelessness Amid Affluence: Structure and Paradox in the American Political Economy." *Contemporary Sociology* 20(1, January, 1991):76–77.

1

The Homeless
What Are the Issues? What Are
the Controversies?

Homelessness emerged as a significant social problem in the early 1980s. It became a major issue for discussion for the mass media, scholars and policymakers, and the general public throughout the decade. If nothing else, the rising tide of homelessness in the 1980s was a major media event. Every news outlet ran occasional obligatory pieces on homelessness, with the period between Thanksgiving and Christmas constituting the height of the season. Homelessness was the focus of at least two made-for-TV movies, another two commercial movies, and HBO's "Comic Relief," an annual fund-raiser now in its eighth year. News documentaries on the plight of the homeless appeared on NBC, ABC, CBS, and PBS; cover stories on the issue appeared in *Time*, *Newsweek*, the Sunday *New York Times Magazine*, and the Sunday *Boston Globe Magazine*. Washington potentates, joined by various celebrities, spent nights on steam grates in the nation's capital to dramatize the plight of the homeless. With the possible exception of AIDS, homelessness was probably the social problem of the 1980s.

Public interest in the issue was matched by the attentiveness of federal policymakers. Thus, Congress introduced some 32 separate bills addressing one or another aspect of homelessness in 1985 and considered a similar number in 1986. These various and sundry bills, if enacted, would have dispersed federal responsibility for the homeless over a wide range of agencies and departments, with separate and largely uncoordinated programs for homeless veterans, homeless families with children, homeless alcohol abusers, homeless teenagers, the homeless mentally ill, and so on. Congressman Henry Waxman of California was (and remains) perhaps the leading spokesman in Congress on the issue of homelessness. Distressed by the proliferation of uncoordinated bills, Waxman decided late in 1986 to submit omnibus legislation incorporating features from all the different legislative proposals then active. This legislation came to be known as the Stewart B. McKinney Homeless Assistance Act, in honor of the first (and so far only) member of Congress to die of AIDS.

Congress passed the McKinney Act and then President Reagan signed it into law in July 1987. It established a number of federally sponsored programs of assistance to the homeless and housed them in a number of different agencies: Housing and Urban Development (HUD), Health and Human Services (HHS), Labor, and Education. Coordination of programs across departments and agencies was made the responsibility of an Inter-Agency Task Force on the Homeless, which still exists today (as do most of the programs that McKinney created). Prior to McKinney, most of the national effort in behalf of the homeless arose from the private sector, principally the churches, and from local municipalities (nearly all big cities found it necessary to open large, city-funded overnight shelters for homeless people some time in the early 1980s). After McKinney, "the Feds" became major players in the homelessness arena.

Despite the various provisions of the McKinney Act, the problem of homelessness has, we believe, continued to worsen year after year (e.g., Burt 1992). In itself, this is scarcely surprising; most of the provisions of McKinney were intended to ameliorate the day-to-day living situations of homeless people, not to prevent new cases of homelessness from appearing on the streets or to eliminate the problem altogether. But political and public attention to the issue certainly began to fade after McKinney even if the problem itself did not.

For example, little was said about the homeless, one way or the other, in conjunction with the 1992 presidential campaign. Bush's platform promised only to continue the McKinney provisions more or less in their then-current form; Clinton finessed the issue by promising to convene a White House conference on the homeless if elected, a promise that as of this writing (late 1997) he has yet to keep. In the current vernacular, homelessness was a "hot button" topic at least through 1987; ten years later, many people and certainly many politicians look on it as "last decade's issue." The near-total fade-out of interest has been striking, although perhaps to be expected since the attention span of politicians rarely extends further than the next election.

Despite all the attention given to the issue in the 1980s, the public discussion of homelessness continues to be clouded by myths, misconceptions, and stereotypes that stand in the way of adequate understanding. Among the more prominent stereotypes are that the homeless are mostly crazy people who have been let loose from the state mental hospitals, or mostly broken-down alcoholics and drug addicts who can't hold a job, or welfare leeches content to get by on the dole, or people who for some reason have "chosen" to be homeless. Stuart Bykofsky described them in *Newsweek* magazine as the "drunk, the addicted, and the just plain shiftless" (1986), the implication being that most of the homeless could do better for themselves if they really wanted to, if they would just try harder.

There is, of course, an important element of truth in all of these stereotypes, but there is much in each of them that also seriously misleads. The fact is that all of these stereotypes are true of some homeless people, but that none of them is true of all homeless people. An essential point about the homeless is that they are a very diverse group of unfortunates; no easy catch phrase can adequately describe them all.

How many homeless people are there? How do they get to be homeless? Do people actually choose to be homeless? Is homelessness mainly a mental health or substance abuse problem? Or is the problem rooted in large-scale social-structural changes? Is homelessness a new problem? Is it a growing problem? And what, if anything, can be done to help?

A great deal of research in the last decade or so has attempted to answer these and related questions, much of it reviewed and summarized in the following pages. Indeed, when Wright began research on the homeless a decade ago, the published literature on the problem comprised a very thin stream of mimeographed research reports, a few newspaper articles, and occasional stray papers in out-of-the-way journals. Today, the shelf of homelessness research sags under the weight of several dozen monographs and several hundred research articles. Our working bibliography on the topic runs to more than 50 single-spaced pages with more than three-quarters of the entries published since 1985. Our aim here is to glean from this now-vast research literature a reliable portrait of today's homeless population, one accessible to nearly anyone with an interest in the issue.

One recent and controversial statement on the homeless is *A Nation In Denial: The Truth about Homelessness* (Baum and Burnes 1993), described as a "superb book" by Senator Bill Bradley and as "required reading" by ex-governor Mario Cuomo. Most recent book-length treatments of the issue (e.g., Blau 1992; Burt 1992; Lang 1989; Rossi 1990) stress that the homeless are a heterogeneous group victimized by larger social forces. Although all treatments acknowledge widespread mental illness and substance abuse among the homeless, most downplay the causal significance of these factors and focus instead on structural problems such as unemployment, inadequate low-income housing, rising poverty, and insufficient social welfare provisions as the principal explanations for the rise of homelessness in the United States.

Baum and Burnes spin quite a different tale. In their account, the vast
majority of the homeless, upwards of four in five, are mentally ill, substance abusive, or people with criminal records, and moreover, these
disabilities explain why people are homeless as well. Baum and Burnes
argue that people become homeless because they are disaffiliated, that is,
because they are cut off from social networks of family, friendship, and
work that provide the social "glue" in most people's lives; and that
people become disaffiliated (in this sense) because of the corrosive effects
of psychiatric illness, substance abuse, or legal troubles on social networks. Pointedly absent from this analysis is any recognition of social-
structural factors such as poverty, unemployment, or housing, which
(they argue) have been stridently but wrongly emphasized by zealous
advocates and fuzzy-headed researchers who find it ideologically convenient to deny some simple but very important truths.

In the Baum and Burnes account, this collective act of denial has obstructed the development of policies that would truly help the homeless.
They claim that the insistence of many advocates and researchers that
homelessness is fundamentally a housing problem is especially misguided and therefore reprehensible. More low-income housing, they argue, is not the solution because the lack of affordable housing is not the
cause. Only mental health and substance abuse treatment programs will
make a substantial dent in the homelessness problem.

The evidence they offer in favor of these propositions is of two sorts:
the authors' own extensive experience working with homeless people in
the Washington, D.C., area, and a wide, comprehensive review of the
social science and advocacy literature. In behalf of the Baum and Burnes
argument, we acknowledge that the pertinent evidence overwhelmingly
supports their conclusion that very large fractions of the homeless suffer
from physical, mental, and chemical dependency disorders and that these
personal deficiencies must therefore play some important role in the process by which people become homeless. Indeed, if one cumulates percentages across these various categories of disability, the sum always exceeds
half; in fact, the sum is usually on the order of 70 or 80%. And if one
expands the concept of disability to include such "deficits" as criminal
records, inadequate personal hygiene, subaverage intelligence, and so on
through a very long list, one soon reaches the point where essentially all
homeless people are included in the count.

Thus, these essential descriptive facts about the homeless are not in
serious dispute, at least not by capable, informed observers. As far as we
know, no advocate or researcher attempts to deny that mental illness is

more widespread among the homeless than among the domiciled population (although there is some dispute over just how "widespread" it is) or that homeless people are disproportionately alcoholic and drug-abusive. The issue here turns solely on whether these facts constitute an adequate explanation for the rise of homelessness over the past couple of decades.

Burt has pointed out that if mental illness and substance abuse are going to explain the large increase in the number of homeless people, then a minimum requirement would be evidence showing that mental illness and substance abuse are themselves more common ailments today than they were in the past, and there is precious little evidence to this effect. "Population rates of chronic or severe mental illness are very stable across time and place, including non-Western and less developed countries and cultures" (Burt 1992:108). Ditto substance abuse: "The proportion of alcohol abusers and alcoholics in the U.S. population has remained relatively constant at least since the late 1960s" (ibid.:109). As a matter of fact, aggregate consumption of alcohol has been declining in the U.S. population as a whole since the late 1970s. The trend in illicit drug consumption was also downward throughout the 1980s (Wright and Devine 1994:Chapter 2). It is therefore difficult to ascribe increasing homelessness to increasing mental illness or increasing alcohol and drug use because mental illness and substance abuse have apparently not been increasing. This alone is persuasive evidence that there must be more to the homelessness story than Baum and Burnes allow.

Burt also points out that if mental illness and substance abuse were indeed causally responsible for the rise of the "new homeless" (i.e., today's homeless), then we would expect to find more mental illness and substance abuse among the homeless of today than were found among the homeless of earlier eras, and this too is not consistent with the available evidence. To the contrary, "the presence of the mentally ill among skid row and homeless populations may have increased somewhat during the 1980s, but it is by no means a new phenomenon" (1992:109). Concerning substance abuse, "Stark (1987) summarizes twenty-three studies, conducted in every decade from the 1890s through the 1970s. Their findings are very similar to more recent studies . . . . Not too much has changed, it seems, with regard to the prevalence of alcohol problems among homeless populations in the United States" (ibid.:111).

The argument in this book is that an emphasis on personal defects as an explanation of homelessness diverts attention from more basic issues of housing, poverty, welfare, and public policy. To achieve a proper understanding of homelessness in contemporary American society, one must consider the problem in its larger social, political, and economic context. Ascribing the causes of homelessness to the personal deficiencies of homeless people is an unwarranted case of "blaming the victim" and should be avoided not because it is mean-spirited but because it is misleading. It tells part, but not the whole, of the story.

To summarize briefly, a variety of complex social system dislocations—an increasing rate of poverty, a deteriorating social "safety net," the steady loss of low-skill employment and low-income housing, and others—have created a situation in the inner cities (and in certain rural and small town areas as well) where some people are essentially destined to become homeless. In so many words, we now have more poor and otherwise marginalized people than we have affordable housing in which to accommodate them. These large scale social and economic developments put marginal people "at risk" of homelessness. And given that a pool of risk has been created, it comes as no great surprise that those within the pool who do become homeless are drawn heavily from the most vulnerable ranks of the poverty population—the ill, the addicted, and the socially disaffiliated—especially when the social welfare system has been systematically dismantled, leaving wide gaps into which the vulnerable can fall.

Analyses that focus on personal deficits of the homeless mistake the characteristics of people who are homeless for the causes of the homeless, and these are definitely not the same things. It mistakes the needs that homeless people have, which include mental health and substance abuse treatment, with the reasons they are homeless, which has more to do with poverty, housing, and related structural conditions than with personal disabilities and dysfunctions. Or such, in any case, is the argument we pursue here.

There is a further problem with that emphasis, which is that treatment programs for ADM disorders are demonstrably not very effective; they often function as revolving doors that produce short-term remission while clients remain in treatment but precious little in the way of long-lasting improvement. And one important reason why ADM treatment is not especially effective with homeless clients is that treatment rarely addresses the more fundamental social-structural issues of poverty, housing, welfare, and employment that lie at the heart of the matter.

Several dozen research-demonstration projects, funded through McKinney, have been undertaken in the last several years that have focussed on innovations in the provision of mental health and substance abuse treatment to homeless people. One generalization that emerges from this literature is that treatment for homeless people with ADM disorders is generally most effective when it is coupled with stable supportive housing. That is to say, stabilizing homeless people's housing situations appears more and more to be the essential first step in effectively addressing their psychiatric or substance abuse problems. So even if Baum and Burnes were right, it still would not get us off the housing hook and homelessness would still be a housing problem first and foremost.

A final problem with the emphasis on mental illness and substance abuse as the principal causal factors in homelessness is that it fails to acknowledge that the heterogeneity of the homeless is perhaps their most distinguishing characteristic. Many homeless people are mentally ill, but the majority are not. Probably half or more of the homeless do abuse alcohol and other drugs, but the other half do not. Some are indeed shiftless, but many have been brutally victimized by economic misfortune. A few may even choose to be homeless, but the vast majority live the way they do because they lack the resources needed to live in any other way.

There are, in short, many paths to homelessness these days, and it is misleading to emphasize any one factor or set of factors to the exclusion of others. Demythologizing the nature and circumstances of homelessness has been one principal accomplishment of the research of the last decade.

The problem of homelessness is not unique to the present day and age; to the contrary, we have witnessed periods of widespread homelessness throughout our history (Wright 1989a; Monkkonen 1984; Hopper and Hamburg 1984). Nor are we the only contemporary nation that confronts a substantial homelessness problem; the problem appears widespread throughout the advanced industrial societies (Friedrichs 1988; see also Chapter Thirteen). Still, homelessness seems especially anachronistic, even offensive, in contemporary American society and there are many, ourselves included, who see the persistence of homelessness into the 1990s (and no doubt beyond) as a blot on our national character. It would be convenient to think that homeless people themselves are to blame for their condition and that the problem could be magically solved with a few extra billions for expanded alcohol, drug, and psychiatric treatment. But when all is said and done, this line of explanation is altogether too self-serving to be correct.

THEORIES ABOUT HOMELESSNESS

As is obvious from the above discussion, numerous viewpoints or "theories" about homelessness have emerged over the past decade, all seeking to explain some aspect or feature of the problem. Before considering the major points of view in any depth, it proves useful to ask what, exactly, an adequate theory of homelessness would explain.

In general, theories in any field develop to provide an explanatory framework into which certain agreed-upon facts or observations can be integrated and thereby understood. But if we ask about the "agreed-upon facts" of homelessness that an adequate theory should explain, we actually come up with very little. As we show in the remainder of this chapter, there is little agreement on the definition, number or trends in the extent of homelessness.

In varying degrees, all theories of homelessness are theories about the causes of homelessness, that is, theories about what causes people to become homeless or theories about what has caused the number of homeless people to increase. The concept of "cause" is, however, fundamentally ambiguous. Consider a hypothetical case involving a fellow named Bill. Bill is a high school drop-out. Because of Bill's inadequate education, he has never held a steady job; rather, he has spent his adult lifetime doing various odd jobs, picking up temporary or seasonal work when available, hustling at other times. Because of his irregular and discontinuous employment history, Bill's routine weekly income is meager, and because his income is minimal, he is unable to afford his own apartment and lives instead with his older sister. Now, Bill drinks more than he should (this for a dozen different reasons) and because he drinks more than he should, he is frequently abusive and hard to get along with. Bill's sister is usually very tolerant in such matters, but because she has been having some problems at work, she comes home one Friday in a foul, ungenerous mood only to find Bill passed out on the couch. She decides that Bill's dependency and alcoholism are more than she can continue to take, and because of her decision, Bill is asked to leave. Bill spends Saturday looking for an apartment that he can afford, but because his income is so low and because there are very few units available to someone with Bill's income, he finds nothing and heads to the local shelter for homeless people instead, whereupon Bill effectively becomes a homeless person.

Given the scenario, what would we say is "the cause" of Bill's homelessness? Is he homeless because of his inadequate education, poor job history, and meager income? Yes. Is he homeless because he drinks too much? Yes. Is he homeless because his sister had a bad week at the office? Yes. Is he homeless because of a severe shortage of low income housing in his city? Yes. We might also say that Bill is homeless because his parents only had two children (so he had no other siblings to lean on when his sister had all she could take) or that he is homeless because all of his friends and social acquaintances are in situations similar to his (and are therefore unable to help him ride out rough times). We could even say that Bill is homeless because there is no national "right to housing" law that guarantees adequate housing to all citizens regardless of their ability to pay or that he is homeless because the need for Section Eight housing vouchers greatly exceeds the available supply or that he is homeless because former employers in his city have relocated their productive activities elsewhere or even that he is homeless because he lives in a society that tolerates homelessness among its members. Not much creativity is required to write dozens of sentences of the general form, "Bill is homeless because . . . ," each and every one of which would in some sense be true.

The point is not just that homelessness has multiple "causes" (even in a single specific case), although that is itself an important truth, but rather that there are different conceptions of *cause* that are sometimes used interchangeably and even indiscriminately. The question, "What causes homelessness?" depends less on the antecedents of homelessness than on what we mean by *cause*. Are we referring to proximal or ultimate causes? Necessary, sufficient, or predisposing conditions? Are we attracted to a particular causal factor or agent because it is indeed a universal antecedent of homelessness, or because it is a factor about which something could be done?

The tension in the theoretical literature is between personal defects and social-structural defects as "the" explanation for homelessness. We have already asserted that this need not be an either/or matter, although it is frequently presented as such. And we have also suggested an obvious and easy reconciliation: defects and dislocations of social structure (in the broad sense of the term) create a population at risk of homelessness; defects of persons determine who within the at-risk population actually becomes homeless. Which side of this coin one chooses to emphasize seems to depend more on predilection, taste, and ideology than on data, observations, or evidence. A truly adequate theory, it seems, would give a proper accounting of both sides.

Finally, a useful theory of homelessness would not only account for the facts of the case but also suggest something about how policymakers approached the problem. Even the most hard-bitten and punitive analysts grant that homelessness is a problem and that the quality of urban life would improve if there were fewer homeless people. The question is what (if anything) might be done to reduce the number of homeless people in our midst. In advance of any evidence, that nothing can be done is a plausible conclusion, but if that is *not* the conclusion, then an adequate theory will call attention to the social policy "leverage points" at which we might successfully intervene.

As is usually the case with theories of social problems, theories of homelessness fall along a conservative-liberal continuum. At the far right of this continuum is the theory that homeless people are homeless by choice, a view explicitly embraced by former president Ronald Reagan along with many others. The essence of this view is that it is a tough, competitive world out there and that success requires hard work and effort. Many people lack the energy or motivation to compete; thus, they do not compete, but rather they drift downward in the social structure until they hit bottom, which for our purposes means becoming homeless. Naturally, one's expectations (about life, relationships, living standards, and the like) are adjusted downward as well. In this view, the homeless are people who have voluntarily given up on the rat race of modern life in favor of the "freedom" inherent in a life on the streets; people are said to become homeless because they actively choose to be homeless in preference to the daily grind. Bykofsky's phrase, "the drunk, the addicted, and the just plain shiftless," comes quickly to mind. And the solution to homelessness is straightforward: Sober up, take a shower, get a job!

Many advocates and researchers, we included, reject this viewpoint (for reasons discussed at length later). But we are quick to admit that it contains an important element of truth. People do not actively choose to be homeless, yet it is certainly true that homeless people often make bad choices (or decisions) that eventuate in their becoming homeless and all that ensues. Over the past decade, we have chatted with, hung out with, or formally interviewed hundreds of homeless people, and it is a rare homeless person for whom "sober up, take a shower, get a job" would not be good advice. Although how they are going to sober up, where they are going to take that shower, and how they are going to find a job would, of course, remain problematic, it is still good advice. The "homeless by choice" theory is a clear example of "blaming the victim," but sometimes the victims deserve a share of the blame, and in this homelessness is no exception.

Many activists, researchers, and service providers are less interested in blaming the victims than in pitying, assisting, and ultimately curing them. In this view, which occupies the center of the left-right continuum, the various defects of homeless people—for example, their mental and physical illnesses, their substance abuse—are less moral failings than diseases that require diagnosis and treatment. This viewpoint is shared rather widely in the service provider community (mainly because it posits more services as the solution). If the various "disorders" of the homeless could be identified and properly treated, then damaged social networks would heal, damaged people would improve, and eventually no one would be homeless. People become homeless, in this view, because of inadequate services and will only become unhomeless when services are expanded and improved.

Many proponents of these sentiments look on the deinstitutionalization of the mentally ill as a critical factor in producing our current homelessness problem and as the classic case in point. All societies at all times and places inevitably harbor large numbers of psychiatrically disturbed individuals. Throughout most of the twentieth century, the United States dealt with this issue through large state mental hospitals where homeless people were housed, treated, warehoused, ignored—take your pick. For various reasons, the mental health community—among others—decided that these large mental hospitals did not provide optimal conditions for improvement or treatment, and thus began the move to deinstitutionalize the mentally ill. This change in the nature of the services provided to mentally ill persons put large numbers of them back into the communities, and despite the original intention (to establish a vast network of community-based mental health services, walk-in clinics, crisis intervention services, halfway houses, and the like), most communities proved ultimately to lack the services mentally ill people living outside institutions would need. Thus, many of the mentally ill became homeless and will remain homeless until the necessary mental health services are created. Lack of proper services, that is, caused the problem, and only more and better services will solve it.

A similar dynamic pushed the alcohol- and drug-addicted out of institutions and into streets. At one time, drunkenness was considered a moral failing and society dealt with the problem by locking up public inebriates in the drunk tank. Once the idea that addiction is a disease became firmly established, the drunk tank came to be seen as punitive and counterproductive: that is, drunks did not need a safe, secure place to sleep it off; rather, they and their disorders required treatment services. Baum and Burnes refer to this as the "decriminalization of alcoholism." The need for treatment, however, easily outstrips the supply of treatment slots, and so many of the drunk and the addicted become homeless and will remain homeless until adequate treatment for their disorders is made available. This is what Baum and Burnes refer to as "the truth about homelessness." Everything else is perseverance.

To put a point on the differences between the "homeless by choice" and "inadequate services" theories of homelessness, no proponent of the latter would consider that people become mentally ill, alcoholic, or addicted by "choice." Again, these are not seen as moral failings but as diseases that people "catch" through no direct fault of their own. So while there are some descriptive similarities between the two views, the general tenor and, most assuredly, the policy implications are very different.

Herewith, a summary of the "inadequate services" view by its most notable recent proponents:

> In marked contrast to many current analysts of homelessness, we do not consider major social, economic, and political forces to be at the root of today's homelessness. Inadequate housing, poverty, unemployment, declining social benefits and governmental cutbacks have disastrous consequences for the poor and disadvantaged of America, but the homeless suffer from more immediate problems that prevent them from maintaining themselves in stable housing, from working, and from utilizing social benefits. If left untreated, these problems lead to isolation and alienation, misery, serious physical health problems, and early death. The effects of alcoholism, drug addiction, and/or mental illness are the precipitating cause of the downward spiral that ends with the disconnection from a society that stigmatizes the people who suffer from these diseases. (Baum and Burnes 1993:170)

Or as they have it in an earlier passage,

> Focussing solely on affordable housing without first addressing the disabling conditions of the vast majority of the homeless is analogous to simply providing a walking cane to someone who has suffered a broken foot without first resetting the bones in the foot and encasing the foot in a cast. (ibid.:138)

We have already sketched some of the reasons why this line of analysis is not adequate as a causal account of homelessness; it also fails as a model for intervention. The "inadequate services" theory of homelessness entails three propositions, only one of which is unambiguously true. The first proposition is that the homeless are comprised mostly of "defective" people (true). The second proposition is that services and treatment programs can cure these "defects" (probably not true). And the third proposition is that if these "defects" of homeless people were cured, there would be no homelessness (also probably not true). Proposition 2 embraces a much greater faith in the efficacy of alcohol, drug, and mental health treatment than the evidence warrants. As far as Proposition 3 is concerned, it will suffice for now only to note that while happy, sober, well-adjusted homeless people would be a definite improvement over degraded, besotted, mentally impaired homeless people, happy, sober, well-adjusted homeless people would still be homeless.

Services for the homeless have expanded exponentially over the last decade, so much so that there is a vast cadre of social workers, health professionals, case managers, outreach workers, alcohol and drug counselors, and the like whose livelihood and professional identities now depend on the existence of homeless people to receive the services being offered. Despite this vast expansion, it remains true that the range of services normally available to homeless people remains inadequate by nearly any reasonable standard. Within this cadre, services have come to be seen as ends in themselves, rather than means to some higher end (e.g., independent, self-supporting, productive adults). Thus, service providers consider it a success when they can get a homeless client enrolled in a drug treatment program, knowing full well that the outcome of treatment in the large majority of cases is relapse and a near-instantaneous return to the streets.

A third viewpoint, the social-structural, or political-economic view of homelessness (the viewpoint of the authors of this book), argues that trends in urban political economies have created structural conditions that literally destine some people to be homeless. Various social and economic developments (mainly though not exclusively in the urban areas) have created an "underclass" that is ill-suited to compete in the new economy. Increasingly concentrated urban poverty and the steady erosion of low-income communities and neighborhoods have created a large pool of people at risk for all manner of degradation and marginalization, including the loss of their housing. Stated simply, in the last two decades, the cities have come to contain more poor people and fewer units of low-income housing. Once these trend lines crossed, homelessness was the inevitable consequence.

These social-structural conditions exist independently of the level of psychiatric disturbance or chemical dependency within the population. That the people made homeless by these conditions are disproportionately drawn from the ranks of the chemically dependent or mentally ill is an important but contingent truth. That is, mentally ill and addicted people do not become homeless because of their defects but rather because these defects render them most vulnerable to these larger social-structural developments. Returning to the Baum and Burnes metaphor, proponents of the structural theory of homelessness would maintain that social services represent the walking stick (the palliative) and more low-income housing represents the cast (the cure).

Conservative theories of homelessness blame the victims; centrist or services-oriented theories want to repair the victims; social-structural theories want to eliminate the social, political, and economic forces that victimize people in the first place.

Social-structural theories are not all of a piece. Some analysts (such as those of this book) have emphasized the housing aspects of the situation; others (such as Peter Rossi) emphasize the income aspects; still others focus on the deterioration of welfare-state safety nets, on certain demographic and ecological transformations, or on issues of employment. Some of the analysts who work in this tradition have been relentlessly (and needlessly) hostile to any suggestion that mental illness or chemical dependencies play any important role in producing the contemporary homelessness problem; such emphases are said to "medicalize" what is essentially a social (not a medical) problem. Thus, Snow (Baker, Anderson, and Martin 1986; Snow, Baker, and Anderson 1989) has consistently argued that the prevalence of mental illness among the homeless has been exaggerated; others have made similar claims with respect to alcohol and drug addiction. Just how widespread these disorders are among the homeless is taken up in detail in later chapters; for now, we wish only to note that *any* level of psychiatric disturbance or chemical dependency among the homeless is compatible with the social-structural theory. From the social-structural viewpoint, that is, prevalence rates of the various ADM disorders are interesting but not germane; nothing of theoretical importance follows from these rates one way or the other.

WHO ARE THE HOMELESS?
SOCIAL AND DEMOGRAPHIC CHARACTERISTICS

To many people, homelessness is an abstraction or simply an annoyance. To the homeless themselves, however, it is a fact of existence, a way of life that is relentless in its humiliation of the flesh and spirit. It is nearly impossible to express in words what it means to be homeless or to be so poor that even taking care of the basic necessities of life is a daily struggle. Two recent ethnographies bear mention here for their touching evocation of homeless lives, Jonathan Kozol's *Rachel and Her Children* (1988) and Elliot Liebow's *Tell Them Who I Am* (1993). Both portray the human faces of homelessness much more adequately than any of the more quantitative research reviewed here.

What does the research of the past decade about the essential descriptive characteristics of the homeless teach us? As we have already stressed, we have learned, first and foremost, that they are a very diverse group of people: men and women, adults and children, young and old, black and white, lucid and deranged. To speak, therefore, of "the" homeless is itself somewhat misleading because it suggests a unity of kind that is not observed empirically. The homeless display a diversity of kind that is matched by a diversity of problems, circumstances, and social service needs.

We have also learned that relatively few of the homeless are chronically homeless (Wright and Weber 1987; Sosin, Piliavin, and Westerfelt 1990). Indeed, only a quarter to a third would be considered chronically or permanently homeless in the sense that they become homeless at some finite point in their lives and then remain homeless forever after. The majority, rather, are episodically homeless, that is, they become homeless now and again, with the episodes of literal homelessness punctuated by periods of more or less stable housing situations (Piliavin and Sosin 1987–1988). And of course, many homeless people on any given night are recently homeless for the first time, such that no pattern is yet established.

The importance of this observation requires some amplification because it is a point to which we return again and again throughout these pages. Chronicity is part of the stereotype of homelessness in part because it is often convenient to think of "the" homeless as a fixed, stable, identifiable group within the larger population. The very question of how many homeless people there are itself presupposes a fixed, stable population of homeless people that can then be counted. Homelessness, however, is less a state or condition than a process of social marginalization that often produces untoward housing outcomes. People who are homeless today may have housing tomorrow, and of course vice versa. Thus, "the" population of homeless people is ever-changing; its composition is dynamic, not static.

One obvious implication of the high rate of episodic homelessness is that the number of people destined to experience an episode of homelessness over any extended time period is larger, and probably quite a bit larger, than the number of people who happen to be homeless on any particular day. In statistical terminology, this is the difference between a point-prevalence and a period-prevalence estimate (see, e.g., Culhane, Dejowski, Ibanez, Needham, and Macchia 1994), the latter always the larger number unless the population of things being counted is absolute, fixed and stable. As we shall see, much of the ongoing controversy over the number of the homeless derives from confusion on precisely this issue.

That most homelessness "these days" is of the episodic rather than chronic variety also has important policy implications. It implies, for example, that a large part of the solution to the homelessness problem is to prevent episodes of homelessness among the at-risk population, a far different matter than trying to attend to the multiple and often severe problems of chronically homeless individuals. By definition, episodically homeless people find themselves acceptably housed at least from time to time. An important goal of policy should therefore be to extend the periods during which this is the case.

What else have we learned about the social, demographic, and existential characteristics of the homeless? Dozens of studies report essentially descriptive data. Most of these studies are based on samples from single cities, and each city's homeless population is to some extent unique. Making due allowance for city-by-city variation, however, all recent studies report the same general patterns.

It is clear, for instance, that a sizable fraction of today's homeless are women, and that a smaller but still significant fraction are the children of homeless adults. Depending on the study, the proportion of women varies roughly between a quarter and a third; children under age 16 make up approximately another tenth. All told, then, women and children comprise roughly three-eighths of the total, the remainder being adult men. It has become a commonplace assertion that women and children represent the fastest growing subgroup within the homeless population, but this has been asserted far more regularly than it has been documented. There is, however, at least some evidence that the assertion is true.

Homeless women are themselves not a homogeneous group (Stoner 1983). One large and important subgroup is the lone, mentally ill women from whom the "bag lady" stereotype has been derived; they apparently constitute only about a third of the total (Wright 1988). Another quarter are women with dependent children in their care [of whom only about half receive Aid To Families with Dependent Children (AFDC)]; compared to other homeless women, the mothers are less likely to abuse alcohol or drugs, less likely to be mentally impaired, and more likely to be homeless strictly for economic reasons. Still a third group is homeless teenage girls, many of them runaways or throwaways fleeing abusive family situations (Wright 1991; Shane 1987; Yates, MacKenzie, Pennbridge, and Cohen 1988). Obviously, the various types of homeless women have rather little in common other than their sex and their homelessness, although they are regularly discussed as though they too were somehow an undifferentiated group.

Most of the recent research on homeless children has focused on their mental and physical well-being. These studies paint a worrisome and depressing picture. Physical disorders of all sorts are dramatically more common among homeless children than among children in general (Wright 1990a). These include widespread lack of immunization, development and learning disorders of varying severity, anger, depression, anxiety, and uncertainty about life. The large numbers of homeless children in existence, and the range and severity of their problems, imply that the homelessness of the 21st century is already being created today.

Aside from the large proportion of women, the most surprising demographic fact about the homeless is that they are relatively young; the average age among homeless adults falls somewhere in the low to middle thirties in practically all studies. One common stereotype is that the homeless are an elderly population, but the elderly are in fact underrepresented, usually comprising less than 5% of the total in most studies. In the national population as a whole, about 12% are over age 65.

There are two hypotheses about the apparent deficit of elderly homeless, both no doubt true to some extent. First, once people turn 65, they become eligible for a range of benefits (subsidized elderly housing, Medicare, Social Security benefits, etc.) that may be adequate to get them and keep them off the streets (Rossi and Wright 1987). Second, the rate of mortality among the homeless is sufficiently high that relatively few of them may ever survive to age 65 in the first place; indeed, the average age of death for homeless men appears to be in the early fifties (Wright and Weber 1987; Hibbs, Benner, Klugman, Spencer, Macchia, Mellinger, and Fife 1994).

Although apparently underrepresented, the elderly homeless comprise a uniquely vulnerable subgroup and one with highly specialized housing and service needs; recent studies that address these issues include Cohen, Teresi, and Holmes (1988), Damrosch and Strasser (1988), Doolin (1986), and Kutza and Keigher (1991).

The relatively young average age of homeless adults suggests that an important but unappreciated factor in the rise of the "new homeless" is the maturation of the so-called baby boom generations, the immensely large cohorts of persons born in the postwar era (roughly 1947 to 1964). The youngest baby-boomers are just turning 30; the oldest are in their early 50s. These cohorts have created problems sequentially in every institution they have touched on their way through the life cycle. Today, the baby-boomers are in the housing market. The more successful have come to be known as yuppies (young urban professionals), and it is their numbers, their purchasing power, and their housing preferences that have been responsible at least in part for gentrification and for the sharp increase in housing costs, particularly in the urban areas.

The baby boom was not, however, just a middle-class phenomenon. Poverty families also bore large numbers of children during the postwar years, and these children are also moving through the life cycle. Unlike the yuppies, college was not in the future for most of the baby boom children of the poor, and neither was middle-class employment in the expanding professional, technical, and service sectors of the economy. These children are now independent of their parental households; they are out on their own and facing serious employment shortages and a consequent inability to compete successfully in an ever-more-expensive housing market. These, in short, are "yuffies"—young urban failures, whose numbers are partly responsible for the increasing poverty rate and who are sharply overrepresented among the "new homeless."

The racial and ethnic composition of the homeless closely mirrors that of the underlying poverty population in each city, but there is no doubt that racial and ethnic minorities are heavily overrepresented (First, Roth, and Arewa 1988). In the 19-city HCH data (Wright and Weber 1987), 45% of the homeless were white, 40% black, 11% Hispanic, 2% American Indian, and 1% Asian, with the remainder in the "other" category. In a national sample of soup kitchen and shelter users (Burt and Cohen 1989b), about 58% were nonwhite, very similar to the result in the 19-city sample. In some cities (e.g., Washington, D.C., New Orleans), of course, the proportion of African-Americans among the homeless exceeds 80%.

Other demographic findings of some significance: First, more than half the homeless appear to have graduated from high school; some have even had a few years of college education. Among the men, about a third are veterans of the U.S. armed services (Robertson 1987). Most homeless people (70% or more in most studies) are indigenous to their current state of residence, despite the presumption among many that they are a highly transient group. About a quarter of the men have felony convictions, a much lower percentage than most people would expect (see also Gelberg, Linn, and Leak 1988; Snow et al. 1989).

Granting that the homeless are a diverse group, most or all share three essential characteristics. First, the homeless are drawn mostly from the poverty population. In many studies, their monthly incomes average less than half the poverty line, although some prove to have surprisingly high incomes. Advocates for the homeless sometimes assert that many people are "only one paycheck away" from homelessness and that "these days" increasing numbers of formerly middle-class people are found among the ranks. In fact, very few homeless people come from middle-class backgrounds. Most were born into poverty and have been poor all their lives.

Second, homeless people exhibit very high rates of personal and social disabilities, including mental illness, substance abuse, and physical infirmities. Many advocates and some researchers try to belie the significance of these patterns. We agree that it is a mistake to focus on these factors as the primary causes of homelessness, but it would be foolish to deny that such disabilities are widespread among the homeless or that they present formidable barriers to successful reintegration into the larger society.

Finally, homeless people exhibit astonishingly high levels of estrangement (alienation or isolation) from family and social networks. Relatively few have ever married or remain in contact with their families of origin; most of the people within their social networks are other resource-poor homeless individuals much like themselves. The process of social disintegration is also one that apparently begins very early in the lives of the homeless; the outcome of this process is that homeless people rarely have access to the web of social relationships that most people can draw on to weather life's misfortunes.

Robert Frost wrote that "home is the place where, when you have to go there, they have to take you in"; by the same logic, to be homeless is to be without such a place. Almost everybody knows at least someone to whom they can turn in the face of catastrophe or exceptional need. The homeless are those of whom this cannot be said

HOW MANY HOMELESS?

The number of homeless people has been a controversial issue since 1984, when the Department of Housing and Urban Development (HUD) undertook the first nationwide estimate (HUD 1984). Based on local figures and some reasonable guesses, HUD concluded that the number of homeless people was between 200,000 and 300,000. Advocates for the homeless had been claiming that the number was at least several million and dismissed the HUD study as an effort orchestrated by a conservative administration to minimize the seriousness of the problem. In response, the advocates were accused of making up their numbers (e.g., Horowitz 1989). The controversy surrounding the 1990 U.S. Census effort to count the homeless provides ample evidence that the battle over numbers still rages.

Much of the controversy involves matters of definition and thus consists of little more than polemicists on both sides talking past one another. Defining homelessness is a complex and troublesome issue: absent an agreed-upon definition of homelessness, no count can possibly be definitive. It is easy to agree on the extremes of a definition, but there are many ambiguous cases at the margins. Estimates of the total number of homeless will vary by orders of magnitude depending on how one handles the definitional problem.

In order to count homeless people, researchers require precise definitions, which are by their nature exclusive. In contrast, advocates can make do with much looser, and therefore more inclusive, definitions. This difference alone explains to a considerable extent why scientifically credible attempts to count the homeless have, without exception, produced lower numbers than those the advocacy community promotes.

Cities applying for federal McKinney Act money are often compelled to provide an "estimate" of the local homeless population as part of their application. So-called windshield surveys are often used for this purpose, but they prove to be utterly without value. Many people who *look* homeless are not. Many people who *are* homeless do not look like they are. Many drunks sleeping it off on the park bench have a place to go once they sober up, etc. Driving around the seedier sections of a city counting the number of "apparently" homeless people does not constitute legitimate evidence for anything.

Defining homelessness would seem simple enough but is not. An especially ambiguous case concerns persons who are temporarily doubled up with family members or friends, the so-called hidden homeless. If a person has recently been evicted and is staying with friends until a new apartment is found, should that count as a case of homelessness or not?

Counting the number of people who sleep in overnight shelters for the homeless (the sheltered homeless) is relatively easy, although not without problems. Counting the street homeless—those who do not use temporary shelter but sleep outdoors or in public places—is much more difficult. Counting the hidden homeless is nearly impossible. Many estimates of the number of homeless people begin with a count of the sheltered homeless and then make an assumption about their numbers relative to those who sleep on the streets. Some have argued that the ratio of street homeless to sheltered homeless is as high as 10 to 1, but this is largely an unstudied topic, and where it has been studied, the ratio is usually on the order of 1 or 2 to 1.

Even after a decade of research, there is only a rough, tentative agreement on the number of homeless people—somewhere between half a million and three-quarters of a million of them in the United States on any given night (e.g., Burt 1992; Kondratas 1991). This, of course, is the point-prevalence estimate, and what it implies about the period-prevalence of homelessness is even less clear. Based on evidence concerning the frequency and duration of episodes of homelessness among individuals who are not chronically homeless, some researchers have estimated that the number of people who are homeless at least once in the course of a year is three to five times higher than the number who are homeless at any one time (Rossi, Wright, Fisher, and Willis 1987; Vernez, Burnham, McGlynn, Trude, and Mittman 1988). The agreed upon one night count of between 500,000 and 750,000 homeless suggests that the number of Americans destined to be homeless at least once in an average year is between 1.5 million and 3.75 million. The number destined to be homeless at least once in a 5- or 10-year period would presumably be higher still.

IS HOMELESSNESS A NEW PROBLEM?

Some people seem to believe that the current homelessness problem is unprecedented in American history, but homelessness has surfaced as a significant problem many times in the past. Indeed, homeless people founded American society. The inscription at the base of the Statue of Liberty invites the world to "send these, the homeless, tempest-tost to me. I lift my lamp beside the golden door." In the 19th and early 20th centuries, hundreds of thousands of homeless immigrants passed through Ellis Island and into the nation's heartland to populate the cities and build a modern society.

From the 1950s to the present day, homeless people have rarely been seen as builders of nations. More commonly, they have been dismissed or vilified as derelicts and bums, hopeless alcoholics, insane or otherwise dangerous people, or social parasites deserving of contempt—in short, as beyond help, responsible for their own misery, or socially unworthy (Hopper and Hamburg 1984). To the extent that this depiction has recently changed, it is because of the seemingly sudden appearance in the streets and shelters of what has been called the "new homeless"— homeless young men, women, children, and whole families, groups that society has traditionally obligated itself to protect. Broken-down drunks can be ignored, but the rise of the "new homeless" struck many observers as a clear signal that something had gone very seriously wrong.

Granted that the homeless have been with us throughout history, how do the "new homeless" (i.e., today's homeless) differ from those of times past? Rossi (1989, 1990) has provided a detailed comparison. One significant point of contrast is that today's homeless apparently suffer from a more severe form of housing deprivation than did their counterparts 20 or 30 years ago. Bogue's 1958 (1963) study in Chicago found that of the estimated 12,000 homeless, only about 100 actually slept on the streets, with most of the remainder spending their nights in cheap flophouses. In Rossi's 1986 survey of Chicago, nearly half the homeless slept outdoors. Thus, nearly all the old homeless found nightly shelter; today they do not.

The difference is due to the nearly total disappearance of flophouses in Chicago and elsewhere (Hoch and Slayton 1989). The housing function of the single room occupancy (SRO) hotel has been taken over by large overnight shelters for the homeless. But many homeless persons avoid these dangerous and unappealing places, are denied access because of drunkenness or other behavioral problems, or are turned away because the shelters are filled. The result is a sizable group of homeless persons who must live in the streets.

A second major difference, one to which we alluded earlier, is the presence of sizable numbers of women and children among today's homeless (McChesney 1990; Kryder-Coe, Salamon, and Molnar 1991. Bogue found that in 1958 women accounted for no more than 3% of Chicago's skid row population; today, about a third of the homeless are adult women and about 10 to 15% are children and youth under age 18. A third important contrast, also noted above, is that the elderly have disappeared almost entirely from the ranks of the homeless. Studies in the 1950s and 1960s routinely reported the average age of homeless persons to be in the middle 50s, in contrast to an average today somewhere in the 30s.

Two further differences between the old homeless and the new stand out. First, today's homeless are economically much worse off. In 1958, Bogue estimated the average annual income of Chicago's homeless to be $1,058; Rossi's estimate for 1986 was $1,198. Converted to constant dollars, the average income of today's homeless is barely a third of the income of the homeless in 1958. Second, the old homeless were mostly white: 70% in Bahr and Caplow's (1973) study of the Bowery and 82% in Bogue's (1963) study of Chicago. Among the new homeless, racial and ethnic minorities are heavily overrepresented.

These transformations in the nature of homelessness are apparently quite recent. In the mid-1980s, Wright and his colleagues reviewed medical records of homeless men seen in a health clinic at the New York City Men's Shelter, in the very heart of the Bowery, for the period 1969 through 1984 (Wright et al. 1987). Among the men seen in the early years of this period (1969–1972), almost half (49%) were white, 49% were documented alcohol or drug abusers, and the average age was 44 years. Among men seen at the end of the period (1981–1984), only 15% were white, only 28% were documented alcohol or drug abusers, and the average age was 36 years.

It is appropriate to speak of the "new homeless," then, not because homelessness is a new problem in the larger historical sweep of things but because of the dramatic transformation in the nature of the homeless population that has occurred in the past two decades. Today's homeless are not only old, broken-down alcoholic Skid Row men; rather, they are surprisingly young, relatively well educated, dominated by racial and ethnic minorities, and distressingly large numbers of them are homeless women, homeless children, and homeless families. Understandings that may have been adequate in the 1950s or 1960s are clearly not adequate today. In earlier decades, homelessness could perhaps have been understood as arising from the personal problems of a relative handful of needy, defective, lost souls. Today, we are talking about some hundreds of thousands of people whose collective miseries bespeak fundamental disarticulations in the political economy of the nation.

IS HOMELESSNESS A GROWING PROBLEM?

Since the number of homeless people is not known precisely, it is difficult to say for sure whether that number is increasing or decreasing. Based on indirect indicators such as the use of shelters and soup kitchens, however, it appears that the size of the homeless population increased dramatically throughout the 1980s and into the early 1990s.

Evidence through the early 1980s was reviewed in some detail by the U.S. General Accounting Office; the conclusion at that time was as follows:

> In summary, no one knows how many homeless people there are in America because of the many difficulties [in] locating and counting them. As a result, there is considerable disagreement over the size of the homeless population. However, there is agreement in the studies we reviewed and among shelter providers, researchers, and agency officials we interviewed that the homeless population is growing. Current estimates of annual increases in the growth of homelessness vary between 10 and 38 percent. (1985:12–13)

More recent evidence on the upward trend in homelessness supports the GAO conclusions. City to city, annual increases in the size of the homeless population are reported to be between 20 and 30%. Newly opened facilities for the homeless are rapidly filled to capacity; to illustrate, the 1988 client load in the 109 McKinney Act–funded HCH clinics exceeded the projected client load by more than 15% (Lewin-ICF 1989). A study by the U.S. Conference of Mayors in 1986 of 25 major U.S. cities concluded that in 22 of the 25, homelessness had indeed increased. There has been a parallel increase in the numbers seeking food from soup kitchens, food banks, and the like (Freeman and Hall 1986; Burt 1992). None of these data are definitive but they all point to the same conclusion: the homeless population has been growing.

Burt has produced the definitive study on the growth in homelessness in the 1980s: "These increases occurred in every region of the country, in cities from 100,000 to over 1 million in population, and even in relatively prosperous suburbs of primary cities. Both numbers and rates increased almost threefold" from 1981 to 1989 (1992:139).

IS HOMELESSNESS A MENTAL HEALTH OR SUBSTANCE ABUSE PROBLEM?

Baum and Burnes are scarcely alone in arguing that most homelessness results from mental illness and substance abuse. We have already acknowledged the exceptional rate at which the ADM disorders occur among the homeless. But to conclude that many homeless people are psychiatrically ill or chemically dependent is not to conclude that people are homeless because of these disorders.

Although there is some controversy about the true prevalence of mental illness among the homeless, the consensus in the literature is that about a third suffer from clinically significant psychiatric illness (e.g., Institute of Medicine 1988; Lamb 1984; Tessler and Dennis 1989), and while this is a much higher rate of mental illness than that found in the domiciled population, it also leaves a large majority—two-thirds—who are not psychiatrically disabled and whose homelessness must therefore result from other factors.

Since only about a third of the homeless are mentally ill, can one conclude that homelessness is at least one-third a mental health problem? We believe that even this proposition is fundamentally misleading. Many of the homeless are also hungry, but no one suggests that they are homeless because of their hunger. The more logical conclusion is that many mentally ill people have housing needs that are not adequately addressed, and they therefore become homeless in disproportionate numbers.

This is not just a point of semantics. If homelessness were actually caused by mental illness, then more and better mental health treatment would presumably lower the number of homeless people. If, in contrast, the fundamental issue is housing, then more and better mental health treatment would only reduce the prevalence of psychiatric symptoms among people sleeping in the shelters and living in the streets. As we indicated earlier in this chapter, this is exactly the difference between well-adjusted homeless people and no homeless people at all.

After mental illness, alcohol and drug abuse are the most commonly cited "causes" of homelessness; indeed, the alcoholic Skid Row bum is probably the most common stereotype of homeless people these days

(Stark 1987). In the past few years, concerns with drugs other than alcohol, especially crack cocaine, have also surfaced in discussions of the homeless. This image of the broken-down homeless alcoholic (or drug addict) is not entirely without foundation. "In whatever setting homeless adults are studied, alcoholism is the most frequent single disorder diagnosed" (Institute of Medicine 1988:60).

The rate of alcohol abuse among the U.S. population as a whole is not known to any useful degree of precision; most experts in the field use a "rule of thumb" of about 10% (Fisk 1984; Institute of Medicine 1988:60). Assuming this value is indicative, alcohol abuse is four or five times more widespread among the homeless than among the domiciled population. But again, to say that half of the homeless abuse alcohol is not to say that half are homeless because of their alcohol problems. In at least some cases, alcohol abuse is the consequence of homelessness, not the cause. In one study in Los Angeles, in fact, about a quarter of homeless alcoholics had only begun drinking heavily after their first episode of homelessness (Koegel and Burnham 1987).

There are many published analyses of homeless alcoholics. A particularly detailed and useful contribution is that of Roth and Bean (1985). The study is based on a sample of 979 homeless persons, of whom 204 (21%) had been drinking "some" or "a lot" in the month prior to the interview and who had sought help for their drinking problems at some time in the past. These 204 problem drinkers differed in many respects from the remainder of the sample. Demographically, they were disproportionately male, white, and old. As would be expected, they also had troubled marital histories (more likely than the remainder to be divorced or separated), more run-ins with the law, and higher rates of psychiatric impairment. They tended also to have been homeless and to have been unemployed for longer periods than the remainder of the sample, were more transient, and were more socially isolated. Finally, by self-report, they also showed higher levels of physical ill health. These data support the image of the homeless alcohol abuser as multiply disadvantaged and as exhibiting disproportionately high rates of poor physical, mental, and social health (see also Koegel and Burnham 1987; Fisher and Breakey 1987 Ropers and Boyer 1987a; Wright 1989b).

There are fewer studies of homeless abuse of drugs other than alcohol, but there is reason to believe that drug use and abuse in this population has increased quite dramatically in the last decade. Problems with drugs other than alcohol are significantly more common among the younger homeless, especially among those in their teens and early 20s; in particular, the rate of "crack" addiction seems to be increasing quickly. One important indicator of the extent of the drug problem among the homeless is that the rate of HIV infection is starkly elevated compared to the background level, by at least an order of magnitude (Wright 1990b).

As with psychiatric disturbance, rates of alcoholism and drug dependence among the homeless are very high, reliably estimated at 50 or 60% (Wright and Weber 1987; Fisher and Breakey 1987; Koegel and Burnham 1987). However, here too we are left with 40 or 50% who are not substance abusers and whose homelessness must result from other factors. As with mental illness, it is misleading to conclude from the high rate of substance abuse among the homeless that homelessness is mainly an alcohol and drug problem and therefore not a housing or income problem. The more logical conclusion, again, is that alcohol- and drug-abusive poor people have great difficulties maintaining their hold on acceptable housing and therefore become homeless in disproportionate numbers.

To say that the homeless mentally ill and substance-abusive need housing, first and foremost, is not to say that housing is all they need. Their housing needs are entangled with their needs for treatment, and their needs for treatment are themselves not unitary. The substance-abusive need assistance in overcoming their addictions; the mentally ill need treatment for their psychiatric illnesses; both groups need case management, job training and placement services, supported work environments, counseling in money management and social skills, and retraining in acts of daily living such as bathing, personal hygiene, and dress. But none of this can happen in the absence of some solution to their housing problems. The goal of policy should not be just to produce sane, sober, well-kempt homeless people, but to be rid of the condition of homelessness once and for all, and this is not something treatment alone can accomplish.

DO PEOPLE "CHOOSE" TO BE HOMELESS?

The essence of the conservative theory of homelessness is that many (or most) homeless people have chosen to be homeless, that they have voluntarily forgone the rat race of modern society for the unfettered romance and adventure of life in the streets. No credible analyst takes this prejudice the least bit seriously, but the viewpoint surfaces with sufficient regularity in discussions with students and others that it bears at least a few passing comments.

For reasons that will soon become obvious, we refer to the "homeless by choice" view as the "Let's Make a Deal" theory of homelessness. "Let's

Make a Deal" is a popular game show. At the end of the show, the most successful contestants are asked to choose one of three doors, each of them winning the prize behind the door they choose. Behind one of the doors might be a new luxury car; behind another, a trip to some exotic destination; and behind the third, something worthless and silly, such as a can of pork and beans. Suppose, now, that a contestant chooses Door Number One and "wins" the can of pork and beans. Would we then say that this contestant actually chose the can of beans in preference to the car or the vacation? Of course not. If the contestant had been able to foresee the consequences of his or her choice, he or she would certainly have made a different decision.

All things considered, "Let's Make a Deal" is not a bad metaphor for life. All people, day in and day out, confront choices that they have to make but whose consequences they cannot anticipate. It is a mistake to confuse the choice with the unforeseen consequences of the choice. So too with the homeless. All homeless people have faced critical turning points, or decisions, that went the wrong way and whose unforeseen, unintended, and unchosen consequence was an episode or even a life of homelessness. This is not to say that people choose to be homeless, but rather that homelessness is often the result of choices whose consequences could not be predicted.

There is, of course, an important sense in which people "choose" to take a hit on the crack pipe and thereby commence a lifelong addiction to drugs, "choose" not to show up for work and thereby lose their jobs, or "choose" to get into an argument with a formerly supportive family member and thereby burn their sole remaining bridge to stable housing. And it is also true that any of these "choices," and thousands more, can lead quite directly to homelessness. Likewise, young people "choose" to be sexually active and pregnancies, sexually transmitted infections, and even AIDS sometimes follow directly from that choice. But surely there is an important difference between "choosing" to have sex and "choosing" to have AIDS.

The principal evidence in favor of the "Let's Make a Deal" theory of homelessness is that many homeless people, when interviewed, will say they are happy enough with their lives and circumstances; in these interviews, many will even stress some positive features of being homeless—the freedom, the adventure of living on the edge, and the like. But there is every difference between accommodating to the cards life has dealt you and actually being happy with the hand. When homeless people say they are "satisfied" with being homeless, what they mean is that they are unable to conceive of an attainable alternative, not that a life of homelessness is positively preferable to such alternatives as may exist.

Consider what a homeless person would choose by choosing to be homeless. The rate of AIDS infection among the homeless exceeds that among the general population by roughly a factor of 10, the rate of sexual assault on homeless women exceeds that on women in general by a factor of 20, the rate of tuberculosis among the homeless exceeds that among the general population by a factor of perhaps 100, and the average age of death for homeless men is around 53 years old versus a "normal" life expectancy of more than 70 (see Chapter 8). One does not "choose" to sleep in the gutters, scavenge food from dumpsters, or forgo 20 years of life expectancy, however directly that existence may have followed from other choices and decisions.

THE POLITICAL ECONOMY OF HOMELESSNESS: POVERTY AND HOUSING

There is little doubt that homelessness is a complex and multifaceted problem. We can begin to get a handle on this complexity, however, by stating an obvious point. Homeless people are people without housing; therefore, the ultimate cause of the problem is an insufficient supply of housing suitable to the needs of homeless people. Since the homeless are generally the poorest of the poor, this means an insufficient supply of housing that very poor people can afford.

Homeless people themselves readily identify the lack of housing and the lack of money to acquire housing as the source of their troubles. Ball and Havassy (1984) asked a sample of mentally disturbed homeless people in San Francisco to identify "the most important issues you face or problems you have trying to make it in San Francisco or generally in life." The most common response was "no place to live indoors" (mentioned by 94%), followed by "no money" (mentioned by 88%). No other response was chosen by as much as half the sample.

The loss of low-income housing over the past decade has been substantial. Between the late 1970s and the early 1980s, the number of low-income units in 12 of the 20 largest American cities dropped from 1.6 million units to 1.1 million units, a decline of about 30%. This trend continued throughout the 1980s and into the 1990s. In the same period and cities, the number of poor people rose from about 2.5 million to 3.4 million, an increase of 36% (Wright and Lam 1987) and this trend has also continued. Nationwide, the poverty rate increased sharply in the early 1980s, peaked in 1983 (at 15.4%), and has hovered around the 1983 peak ever since; the most recent (1993) poverty rate (15.2%) rivals the 1983 peak. Right now there are nearly 40 million Americans at or below the official poverty line (Devine and Wright 1993). The sharp increases in poverty in the 1980s were accompanied by equally sharp losses in affordable housing. The net result has been more and more poor people and fewer and fewer units in which to house them, and that has spelled more homelessness (Rubin, Wright, and Devine 1992).

Thus, the quick answer to the question, Why are people homeless? is that they are too poor to afford the little low-income housing there is and that available programs of relief and assistance cannot make up the difference. The solution to homelessness is less poverty and more low-income housing; everything else treats the symptoms of homelessness but not the root causes.

The increasing rate of poverty and the dwindling supply of low-income housing did not "just happen." Joel Blau has argued that the homelessness problem has resulted largely from the policy decisions and ideological agenda of the Reagan and Bush administrations, an agenda whose first priority was the upward transfer of income (Blau 1992). The success of this effort is attested to by the increasing share of national income now going to the most affluent fifth of the population. Inevitably, in an era of economic stagnation, making rich people richer requires making poor people poorer, and the poverty of the poor deepened in the Reagan-Bush years as the wealth of the affluent increased. Taking still more from those who have the least has in turn caused many to become homeless.

As American competitiveness in the world economy suffered and as the economy shifted from an industrial base to a service base, the means available to make the rich richer became more limited; the business-led effort of the 1980s to contain or reduce wages was the obvious solution and one to which the administration happily agreed. Following the "principle of less eligibility"—the axiom that welfare must pay less than work—the containment or reduction of wages further required steep cutbacks in social welfare programs. "From the outset, the Reagan administration . . . sought to reduce the entire social wage" (Blau 1992:49). This reduction entailed the elimination of many programs, sharp reductions in benefit levels, and a tightening of eligibility standards. The net result was that "middle income people ran harder to stay in place, the working poor tried not to lose too much ground, and those at the bottom of the income scale struggled to retain their housing" (ibid.:x), often without success. Of course, Congress's and the Clinton administration's complete dismantling of AFDC has completed the process.

Blau raises an interesting question: "Why has every level of government persisted in carrying out wasteful short-term policies [to ameliorate homelessness], when the cumulative social costs of these policies undoubtedly exceed the expense of providing permanent, affordable housing? The answer is that a more adequate solution to homelessness would conflict with the underlying principles of the U.S. economy: private profit, self-sufficiency through work, and the commodification of basic human needs such as food, housing, and medical care" (ibid.:177).

Clearly, the government could build, operate, and subsidize low-income housing so that no one would be forced to be homeless, but that would usurp the prerogatives of the real estate industry; thus, people will remain homeless precisely because little or no profit can be made by providing housing to the poor. The government could offset market failures by providing income guarantees, housing subsidies, and essential services, but such programs set a bad example by undermining the relationship between work and material well-being, "which is, along with the concept of private profit, perhaps the underlying principle of a market economy" (ibid.:179). In the final analysis, poverty, hunger, and homelessness persist because the conservative agenda of two administrations granted capital the unrestricted right to accumulate regardless of the social costs. One enduring legacy of those years, given recent reductions in that deficit, has been the systematic discrediting and dismantling of the welfare state. At no time since the early 20th century has the state's role in providing some sort of safety net for the least disadvantaged in society been so attenuated. The outlook for the future, therefore, is unquestionably pessimistic.

2

Counting the Homeless

Once homelessness had become a highly visible social problem, the question more or less immediately arose as to just how many homeless people there were. As the problem intensified, it became increasingly apparent that the federal government would soon be forced to respond; some knowledge about the number of the homeless was therefore necessary in order to set the appropriate magnitude for a federal intervention.

As we indicated in Chapter 1, the opening salvo in the "numbers controversy" was fired in a 1984 report to the secretary of the Department of Housing and Urban Development (HUD 1984). Based on "informed judgment" and shelter capacity in a number of large cities, the HUD report estimated that there were some 250,000 to 350,000 homeless people in the nation, barely a tenth the numbers then being claimed by the advocacy community.

The HUD number, of course, was immediately dismissed by many outraged advocates and nonadvocates alike. The commitment of the Reagan administration to the issue of homelessness was obviously in some doubt and it seemed altogether too convenient for HUD to conclude that there were only a few hundred thousand homeless people out there. Mitch Snyder, the best known of the homeless advocates, sued HUD for negligence in the production of the report; Snyder's numbers, in turn, were dismissed as fraudulent by some (Horowitz 1989) and passionately defended by others. A decade later, the issue remains unresolved [see, for example, the winter 1994 issue of *Housing Policy Debate* (5:2)].

The same scenario was played out in a number of cities, always with the same general result. Someone would undertake to count the number of homeless people in a city; the effort would produce a number much lower than local advocates expected; the counting effort would be dismissed as flawed or even politically motivated. Rossi's effort to count the homeless in Chicago (Rossi et al. 1987) produced an estimate of only about 3,000 literally homeless people; advocates and service providers in the city had been suggesting a count in the range of 12,000 to 15,000; Robinson's (1985) count in Washington, D.C., turned up fewer than half the expected number; likewise in a number of other cities, where the ensuing controversy was often bitter.

COUNTING THE HOMELESS IN CHICAGO:
A CAUTIONARY TALE

The Chicago "episode" bears recounting in some detail first, because it provides a convenient illustration of the many thorny issues that have to be resolved in trying to count homeless people, and second, because it is a useful case study in the often strained relationship between advocacy and scientific research.

Results from the Chicago study were summarized in a report by Rossi and associates entitled *The Condition of the Homeless in Chicago* (1986) and in an article published in *Science* (Rossi et al. 1987). Although the report covered a very wide range of topics and issues, the principal point of controversy was Rossi's estimates of the number of homeless people. The report gave a range of estimates of both the nightly and the annual homeless population, each derived from various underlying assumptions [some of them "foolishly heroic," as Rossi has said in a recent article (1994)].

The Chicago study defined the homeless on any given night as persons either (1) found in the shelters and other facilities set up to deal with homeless people, or (2) found on the streets with no normal residence to which they could go. To produce a count, Rossi began by obtaining a list of every shelter in the city, of which there were 28, and then sent field workers to each of those shelters on designated nights to enumerate the persons found there. This gave an estimate of the size of the sheltered homeless population.

To obtain an estimate of the size of the street homeless population, the study began by taking a stratified probability sample of Chicago blocks (stratified by advocates and Chicago police according to the likely num ber of homeless persons who would be found there). Field workers were sent to each sampled block between the hours of midnight and 6:00 A.M. to scour the streets for homeless people. Every place where a person might be found in the sampled blocks was systematically searched: this included cars, hallways of apartment buildings, basements and roofs, abandoned buildings, etc. Interviewers were instructed to continue searching until they either encountered a locked door or were prevented from going further, for example, by the landlord of a building.

Every person found in this process—whether clean or dirty, drunk or sober, awake or asleep—was then interviewed to determine whether they met the study's criteria for homelessness. Careful counts were kept of the numbers of homeless found in each sampled block; working backwards from the sampling design and the known total number of blocks, Rossi was able to produce a statistically unbiased estimate of the size of the street homeless population. Added to the shelter numbers, this gave an estimate of the total number of homeless persons on a designated night.

The counting operation was actually undertaken twice, once in fall 1985 and again in winter 1986. Both waves were similar and so were the results. Estimates of the nightly homeless population in Chicago ranged from 1,600 to 3,100, with 2,300 as the "best guess" figure; estimates of the annual homeless population ranged from about 4,500 to 8,800, with 7,000 as a "best guess" figure.

All these estimates were substantially lower than the numbers being cited in the advocacy community, where the rule of thumb was that the Chicago homeless population numbered somewhere in the range of 12,000 to 25,000. Advocates quickly denounced Rossi's numbers as "ludicrous" (see "Agencies Rally Around Homeless, Hit Study" 1986).

Setting aside mere assertion or aggrieved protestation, one may ask about the actual evidence available in Chicago at the time that would have suggested a true number of homeless people an order of magnitude higher than any of Rossi's estimates. As it turned out, the "12,000 to 25,000" figure was not derived from any empirical evidence whatsoever; it was a conveniently large number that the advocates in Chicago had talked one another into. When the advocates were asked where this number came from, the answer was that these were the numbers given for Chicago in the infamous 1984 HUD report; when the people who produced that report were asked where the numbers came from, the answer was that these were the figures that had been given to them by the Chicago advocacy community. A very thorough search never did disclose the ultimate origins of the rule-of-thumb figures; they are best described as a convenient fiction. And yet, through a process of mutual citation and what William James called "the will to believe," these fictions came to be taken as hard facts.

One independent piece of evidence—in fact, the only independent piece of real evidence ever cited in the controversy—was that the total case load in Chicago's HCH project amounted to about 2,000 people in the first year. This number was cited, for example, in the Chicago *Tribune* to sustain the conclusion that Rossi's numbers were "ludicrous" (i.e., "laughably absurd"). It was apparently thought inconceivable that the Chicago HCH project could have seen 2,000 clients in a year if there were only 2,300 homeless people on a typical night.

But is this really "inconceivable?" Rossi's estimate of the annual homeless population in Chicago was on the order of 7,000; all else equal, the HCH case load of 2,000 would imply that the HCH project provided services to 29% of the city's homeless. And while this level of coverage might seem high, it is certainly not ludicrously high, least of all when the HCH coverage in some of the project cities appeared close to 100%.

This illustrates the first important point about counting the homeless, which is that the time frame is critical. Point-prevalence (or one-night) estimates are always much lower than period-prevalence (monthly or yearly) estimates simply because homelessness is not a static condition. The comparison between Rossi's one-night figure of 2,300 and the Chicago HCH project's annual case load was misleading, even sophistic.

There are many good reasons to believe that HCH coverage in Chicago could easily have been as high as a quarter to a third of the total annual homeless population. First, HCH represented a cost-free good to homeless people and had been designed so as to promote maximum accessibility and usage. According to data from both Rossi's survey and from the HCH client files, about two-thirds of the Chicago homeless received some sort of public assistance, and in comparison to what a homeless person would have needed to do to receive these forms of assistance, receiving assistance through HCH would have been ridiculously simple. If, as the data suggest, two-thirds of the HCH clients in Chicago had successfully gotten themselves enrolled in one or another benefit program (none of them designed to be especially accessible to homeless persons), then it is entirely possible that a quarter to a third of the homeless had availed themselves of a free service designed from the very beginning to be maximally accessible to homeless persons.

The proper comparison with Rossi's point-prevalence estimate might be the *daily* case load in the Chicago HCH project, which averaged 15–25 clients per day over the first year of operation. If Rossi's point-prevalence estimate of 2,300 is taken seriously, the implication is that the HCH project saw about 1% of the total homeless population of the city each day, and that surely does not seem like a ludicrous or inconceivable number.

There is also the definitional issue that is somewhat different. One of the many strengths of Rossi's study is that it was absolutely clear on the exact definition of "homelessness" used to produce the counts. As we indicated earlier, to be homeless for purposes of Rossi's study, a person had either to be (1) in a shelter for the homeless or (2) out on the streets or in other public places between midnight and 6:00 A.M.. This is plainly a very strict definition of homelessness. It excludes those who are marginally housed, for example, in flophouses, cheap hotels, or SROs. It also excludes any persons who normally have no place to live but were fortunate enough to find temporary housing on the nights when the study was done. Other classes of arguably homeless persons were also excluded, in most cases because there was no way to include them given the resources at hand. Because of these exclusions, it is obvious that Rossi's figures were at best an estimate of the size of the truly *hard-core* homeless population of Chicago, as the report itself acknowledged (Rossi 1986:58).

Now, if one wishes to compare this number with that one, the essential first step is to compare the definitions that go into the production of those two numbers, to make sure that both numbers are in fact counting the same thing. What, then, were the eligibility criteria used in the Chicago HCH project to ensure that only homeless people were included in the client data? In fact, there were no eligibility criteria in use at any time during the project. As in most other HCH cities, persons in need were offered services whether they were truly "homeless" or not. HCH was not "health care for the *homeless*" so much as health care for the homeless, the near homeless, the marginally housed, the obviously destitute, those of shabby appearance, and more or less anyone else who looked like they needed health care that they could not afford.

Given the program's accessibility goals, the lack of strict eligibility criteria is certainly understandable, but it cannot be assumed that every HCH client would satisfy a literal definition of homelessness. Rephrasing the point, the number of people who satisfy a very loose or nonexistent and intentionally inclusive definition of "homelessness" is, of necessity, very much larger than the size of the population who would meet a definition of homelessness more narrowly conceived. The Chicago HCH project provided services to both the hard-core homeless population of the city and some fraction of a far larger poverty population whose existence was clearly on the margins of society whether they happened to have a relatively stable housing situation or not.

Some direct evidence on the point can again be obtained from the Chicago HCH client data. The Chicago project employed a "Health Screening Tool" that was used as an intake interview; one of the items included in the interview was whether the client had "a regular place to stay." In the instruction manual that accompanied the tool, a "regular place to stay" was defined as "an apartment, room, or house that is available to the patient for ten consecutive months." Clearly, anyone who had a "regular place to stay" by this definition would have been excluded from Rossi's definition of homelessness. Remarkably, more than a third

(34.6%) of the Chicago HCH clients did have a regular place to stay by this definition.

Suppose, finally, that the implicit and more inclusive HCH definition of homelessness had been employed by Rossi in estimating the size of the homeless population. Since the data just reviewed suggest that about two-thirds of the HCH clients would meet Rossi's definition and one-third of them would not, the implication is that the size of the homeless population using the less strict definition would be half again as large as the size of the homeless population using the more strict definition. So, rather than 7,000 homeless in a year, the estimate would become 10,500, close to the lower boundary of the advocates' "rule of thumb" numbers.

What lessons does the Chicago episode teach us? Two seem especially important. First, since homelessness is not a static or chronic condition, there can be very large differences between the point-prevalence and period-prevalence estimates; the wider the "period," the larger the discrepancy. Thus, there is some consensus in the research community that the number of homeless people on any given day is somewhere between 500,000 and a million; and yet there is also evidence that as many as 7 million distinct individuals experienced at least one episode of homelessness in a recent five-year period (Link et al. 1993). There is no fundamental contradiction between these two numbers; the difference only implies that the homeless population "turns over" on relatively short time scales, which is obvious in any case from data on the recent housing histories of homeless people (see the next chapter).

Second, how one defines "homelessness" makes all the difference. To researchers, precise (and therefore exclusive) definitions are essential. There is no other way to proceed. To advocates, however, homelessness is less a state or condition than a metaphor for urban poverty in its most extreme manifestation; to them precise definition is a conceptual nicety but is otherwise not terribly important.

The definitional issue is by no means simply a scholastic one. In a fundamental sense, a definition of homelessness is, ipso facto, a statement as to what should constitute the floor of housing adequacy below which no member of society should be permitted to fall. But surely, homelessness implies something more serious than just "inadequately housed." If we took poor people living in objectively inadequate housing as the criterion for homelessness, then our definition would demarcate virtually the entire poverty population of the country.

It is relatively obvious that "the total number of the homeless," whether in Chicago or in the nation as a whole, is of necessity a "soft," ambiguous number that probably cannot be known with a high degree of precision. In addition to problems of definition and time frame, there are all the other uncertainties inherent in the research process, the uncertainties of sampling, measurement error, and related factors. No matter how inclusive the definition and how systematic the search, it is also obvious that the homeless are a mobile, even nomadic and certainly hard-to-locate group, and so the possibility is always open that large numbers of them may have been missed in the counting effort. No study can provide a definitive count of the size of the homeless population; the best one can hope for is a more or less plausible count with known uncertainties.

"More or less plausible" is, in turn, an extremely relative matter. Among social scientists, there are agreed-upon criteria of plausibility, including such things as how well the sample was designed and executed, the diligence and care taken with the field operations, the conceptualization of the problem at the front end of the research, and the sophistication of the data analysis. Many tend, however, to have a different criterion of research plausibility: A piece of research is plausible only if it produces results consistent with an a priori worldview, if the results accord with one's conventional wisdom. In this view, the results of research therefore fall into two categories: the category of things that were known to be true all along, and the category of things that cannot possibly be true. Needless to say, such a mind-set tends to render research pointless.

Advocates for any cause prefer big numbers over little numbers, often because their principal loyalty is to the issue, not necessarily to the conduct of high-quality research; advocacy research is often intended to persuade, not to inform. Homelessness is by no means the only issue area where these tendencies appear.

HOW MANY HOMELESS?

In the middle and late 1980s, a number of national conferences on counting the homeless were convened, always with palpable tensions among the participants. Advocates who agreed to participate in these conferences were certain that there were a lot more homeless people out there than the researchers had ever been able to enumerate. Most researchers who attended the conferences were prepared to believe this but wanted to know just where all the "missing" homeless were. From this tension derived the notion of the "hidden homeless": persons illegally doubled or tripled up with family and friends, those who preferred for legal or other reasons to remain out of sight, homeless people who were temporarily institutionalized (in jails, prisons, hospitals, etc.), and those who routinely spent their nights in places where enumerators never looked.

Once the notion of the "hidden homeless" entered the vocabulary of the debate, any hope for a definitive count was lost. Since all of these are plausible points—no researcher would be so brazen as to claim to have counted *everyone*—it soon became customary to describe literal counts of the homeless as lower boundary estimates and to make upward statistical adjustments to produce "best guess" estimates. (No one has yet produced an upper boundary since in at least some of the more expansive definitions of homelessness, the category demarcates nearly the entire poverty population of the country, some 40 million people.) This custom produced an uneasy truce between advocates and researchers. Researchers could (and do) say that there are at least X number of homeless (in a city, a state, or in the nation) and quite possibly more than X; advocates in turn could (and do) say, truthfully, that the estimated X does not rule out a true number very much larger than X.

By the end of the 1980s, most studies were converging on an X for the nation as a whole in the middle to high hundreds of thousands— somewhere, that is, between a half-million and a million literally homeless people in the United States on a typical night (for an overview of research on this point, see Burt 1992; Kondratas 1991; Wright 1989a). A well-known Urban Institute study (Burt and Cohen 1989a) projected 567,000 to 600,000 homeless people, with a proviso that the projection is "probably on the high end, based on our desire to err on the side of generosity . . . to avoid getting into the same kinds of binds that HUD had gotten into before" (quoted in Kondratas 1991:7). The conservative analyst William Tucker projected a number of "about 700,000" in an influential (1987) article; a 1990 Congressional Budget Office estimate was also around 700,000. Thus, there was an emergent if somewhat apprehensive consensus at the end of the decade that the number of the homeless was probably more than a half-million but less than a million. This was still many fewer homeless people than many believed there to be, but it was a number that at least some advocates (e.g., Dolbeare 1991) and some members of the research community had more or less agreed to live with.

THE 1990 CENSUS

Throughout the era of the "numbers controversy," it was known to all participants that the 1990 federal census of the population would also attempt to enumerate at least some of the homeless in some cities. This most recent effort to count homeless people took place on the night and early morning of March 20–21, 1990, so-called "S-Night" (S stands for "shelter and street"). Between 6:00 P.M. and midnight on March 20, Census teams entered all known shelters for the homeless to enumerate homeless persons sleeping or staying indoors. From 2:00 to 4:00 A.M. the next morning, the enumerators attempted to count homeless persons out on the streets. Finally, later that morning enumerators tried to locate persons occupying abandoned buildings. The apparent hope, at least among some, was that the shelter, street, and abandoned building enumerations would yield some estimate of the number of the homeless in America, or at least provide firm empirical data from which such an estimate might be constructed. (For further detail on the S-Night methodology, see Taueber and Siegel 1991.)

During the week of April 8, 1991, the Census released its S-Night results; only 228,621 homeless people were counted, or quite a bit less than half the "best guess" estimates that had become customary by the end of the 1980s. Indeed, this was fewer homeless people than the HUD report had estimated in 1984! Thus, the number of homeless once again became controversial.

If the Census count is even approximately complete or accurate, it would imply that the research community had (inadvertently or otherwise) allowed its "best guess" to creep unjustifiably upward to satisfy or placate the advocates—a disturbing example, perhaps, of research being held hostage to political agendas. Alternatively, it is certainly possible that the S-Night number is an undercount by a factor of two or more and that the consensus "best guess" remains the more plausible estimate. In the remainder of this chapter and the next, we discuss a range of evidence bearing on the second of these possibilities.

It is fairly obvious that staff researchers in the Bureau of the Census do not consider the 1990 S-Night results as anything close to a "final word" on the number of homeless; indeed, a press release from the Bureau accompanying the release of the S-Night results cautioned that "S-Night was not intended to, and did not, produce a count of the 'homeless' population of the country." With characteristic caution (or, as some have suggested, uncharacteristic caution even by the Bureau's high standards), the release was accompanied by all the necessary caveats, exceptions, and conditions—in the hope (however innocent) that the number would be taken for what it is, not misinterpreted or distorted into something it is not. But the history of controversial numbers gives little reason for optimism on this score, and it is an easy wager that the Census number will ultimately be reified by all contenders. As a rule, the Census is considerably more cautious about its numbers than are the people who use those numbers for their own ends.

THE S-NIGHT EXPERIMENTS

The Census's S-Night operation was studied in close detail in five cities by five different groups of investigators; the cities were New York, Chicago, Los Angeles, Phoenix, and New Orleans. Wright and Devine undertook the New Orleans version of the S-Night assessment; we draw heavily on that case, although similar results were reported by all five teams. We further note for the record that the general design for these S-Night assessments and the money necessary to implement them came from the Bureau of the Census itself. The Census yields to no one in its concern over the adequacy of its procedures.

All five of the S-Night evaluations were similar in design and intent, although there were also important differences among the studies that we do not discuss here. (For further detail on all five S-Night experiments see the August, 1992, issue of *Evaluation Review*.) Among the contracted activities, for example, researchers initially compiled their own independent lists of local shelters for the homeless. These inventories were subsequently compared against shelter lists developed earlier by the Census's district offices in conjunction with local municipal authorities, in the hope of compiling the most exhaustive possible list of shelters.

Rossi's experience in Chicago and similar experiences in other cities have shown that counting the sheltered homeless is not especially problematic. Most of the (large) uncertainty in estimating the number of homeless people pertains to counting the street component. Thus, the primary activity of each of the five teams was to undertake research bearing on the general methodological adequacy of the early morning street count. This entailed the hiring, training, and supervision of approximately 60 persons to be deployed as observers ("decoys") within certain designated sections of each city. The number and exact placement of the observation teams (the decoys) were not supposed to be known to the Census district office nor to the enumerators who actually conducted the street count, although the district offices (if not the enumerators) were aware that an S-Night study was being conducted.

The objective of the experiment was transparent and simple. As the Census enumeration teams combed their assigned areas, they would be expected to encounter and enumerate the S-Night decoys as well as "real" homeless people. Enumerators were instructed to approach and enumerate *everyone* they encountered (in their predesignated sites) out on the streets between 2:00 and 4:00 A.M. (whether "apparently homeless" or not). Since the investigators would know who the decoys were (and how many of them were out there), any enumerated decoys could be subtracted from the city totals later. Since the decoys were deployed in areas researchers thought the homeless frequented, during the time the enumeration was taking place, then the number of decoys actually found and enumerated would give a direct indication of the adequacy of the Census counting effort (assuming, of course, that the list of predesignated enumeration sites was itself adequate, a problematic assumption in several of the cities).

To provide further independent details, observers in each city were also to take note of the number of persons they observed in predesignated sites on the street, whether those persons appeared to be homeless or not, and whether they observed those people being counted by the Census teams. Observers also took note of other factors that might have had a bearing on the count, for example, weather conditions or police presence. Upon exiting the street, each observer was debriefed and questioned regarding these and other relevant matters.

Finally, coming at the problem from the other side, the research contracts also required interviews of samples of actual homeless persons after S-Night was over, to see how many of them had been enumerated and to gauge their awareness of and attitudes about the Census effort.

S-NIGHT RESULTS: AN OVERVIEW

As would be anticipated, the S-Night *shelter* count appears to have been reasonably complete in all five cities, although even here there were some nontrivial problems (many pertaining to the question, What constitutes a "shelter?") Among homeless persons interviewed after S-Night, most who had spent S-night in a conventional shelter recalled having been enumerated. So in shelters that the Census knew about, the count was apparently thorough.

In contrast, the S-Night street count was seriously incomplete. Among the five cities, the "hit rate" (the proportion of decoys definitely located and enumerated by the Census) varied from 22 to 66%; thus, the counting effort apparently missed a third of the target population in the best case and nearly four-fifths in the worst case. Reasons for this vary from city to city owing to (possibly) unique local factors, but as many investigators have learned, enumerating street people is a formidable undertaking and the 1990 Census effort was at least as problematic as its several precursor studies had been.

Some of the problems in the enumeration effort were common to all five cities, among them the following:

1. *Shelter Lists and Definition.* The Census definition of a shelter for the homeless was all emergency public and private shelters with sleeping facilities; hotels or motels costing $12.00 or less per night or funded either by the local government or private organizations that house homeless persons or families; excluding facilities for abused women (Schwede and Salo 1991). Conventional shelters and flophouses meeting these criteria and servicing respectably large numbers of homeless people were easy to list and then enumerate in all five cities. But in each city one can also find "quasi-shelters" and other "informal" overnight establishments that provide shelter for the homeless but are either not covered by the Census definition or that no one knew about before S-Night began. Many churches, for example, allow a few homeless people to spend their nights in the vestibule or elsewhere in the church; in at least one case, the emergency room of the local public hospital functions, in effect, as a large overnight shelter for the homeless. Although the shelter count appears to have been relatively complete, problems of definition and subsequent enumeration were encountered even here.

2. *Site Selection.* The deployment of S-Night observers ("decoys") in all five cities was restricted to predesignated areas of the city that the Census, working with local authorities, had identified as "high-density" homeless areas. In essence, the S-Night street enumeration was restricted to homeless persons who spent the night somewhere in these predesignated areas; street people outside those areas were not enumerated. Since Census S-Night resources were themselves limited, coverage of entire cities was clearly out of the question; at the same time, the restricted nature and number of sites that were in fact searched strictly limited the completeness of the count in all five cities. It also became obvious in several cities that the sites to be searched had been so designated because of a large daytime presence of homeless people; where homeless people spend their days and where they spend their nights are not necessarily the same places.

3. *Intentional Avoidance.* In the weeks preceding S-Night, newspapers in a number of cities printed articles indicating that many of the homeless would purposely attempt to avoid enumeration on S-Night. A few well-known advocates for the homeless, such as the late Mitch Snyder, urged a policy of noncooperation, apparently feeling that any

count would be a substantial undercount that would lead to an "official" understatement of the dimensions of the problem and to further reductions in funding for homeless programs. On the other hand, the National Coalition for the Homeless endorsed the S-Night operation and urged cooperation. Did knowledge of the S-Night enumeration stimulate avoidance behavior among the homeless, as Snyder counseled? All five experiments investigated this issue; intentional avoidance was apparently a problem in some cities, although not in all of them.

4. Census Protocol. S-Night decoys in all cities reported numerous violations of the stated Census protocol. For example, observers were occasionally asked, "Are you homeless?" even though the protocol specifically disallowed this question. (The idea was to enumerate all persons found on the streets regardless of their apparent homelessness.) Also, sleeping persons were sometimes awakened (they were to be enumerated but not awakened), some double-counting took place, privacy act sheets were not always distributed, etc. Most of these violations are not especially serious but they do indicate among the enumerators a certain indifference to the procedures they were instructed to follow.

More seriously, observers in all five cities reported seeing at least some street people who were apparently never approached by Census workers and who therefore never appeared in the enumeration. Many of these unenumerated homeless were in the predesignated sites where the Census was searching; many others were in sites that were not searched in the first place but rather in contiguous sites. All five experiments concluded, unambiguously, that there were more homeless people out there on the streets than the enumerators ever found or counted.

Observers in several cities reported that the census enumerators seemed extremely hesitant and fearful while they were out on the street. This is scarcely a surprise; no one would be very comfortable out on the streets of any of the five cities between 2:00 and 4:00 in the morning. Still, the evident hesitance of the enumeration teams to expose themselves to possible risk does not increase one's confidence in the aggressiveness or completeness of the enumeration. It is also obvious that many enumerators substituted their own subjective evaluations about who looked homeless for actual enumeration.

S-NIGHT IN NEW ORLEANS

The S-Night experiment in New Orleans was broadly similar to those undertaken elsewhere, and since it is the one with which we are most familiar, we consider it here in greater detail. Of the five cities, New Orleans is the smallest and most geographically compact, and one would expect the S-Night enumeration to have been more complete in New Orleans than in the other cities. This expectation was confirmed: more "decoys" were located and enumerated in New Orleans than in any of the four other cities. Still, even in this "best case," the Census located and counted only 19 of the 29 teams of decoys that we had deployed, for a "hit rate" of 65.5%. Even granting the assumptions upon which the S-night street count was based, the undercount, especially of street homeless, was evidently substantial.

It is arguable that our decoys (or those in other cities) did not look sufficiently "homeless" to attract the attention or interest of the enumerators, but they were joined in the streets that evening by numerous (evidently) homeless people who were never seen, approached, or counted by the Census teams. Also, among the homeless persons we interviewed the following morning, not one who had spent the night out-of-doors reported having been enumerated. The count of homeless persons in shelters appears to have been reasonably complete (within some limits discussed later), but the count of street people was seriously flawed. Rossi's search for street people in Chicago was much more thorough and aggressive than the S-Night search in New Orleans (and in the other four cities).

THE SHELTER COUNT IN NEW ORLEANS

Compared to the street count, the S-Night shelter count was reasonably complete, although even here there were some problems. Among homeless persons interviewed the morning after S-Night, all but one who had spent the night in a shelter recalled definitely having been enumerated, and the final person was simply "not sure." In New Orleans shelters that the Census knew about, the count was apparently quite thorough.

The list of shelters used by the Census had been developed over the previous year in consultation with municipal authorities and the homeless advocacy community. The size and compactness of New Orleans, the concentration of shelters within a small geographical area, the relative dearth of local social services, and the long-standing cooperative relationship between city officials and homeless advocates all facilitated the generation of a relatively comprehensive list.

Our effort to compile an independent shelter list added little to what the Census already knew. The local Coalition for the Homeless had recently been instrumental in developing what is known as the "freeze plan," whereby extra shelter space is activated when the temperature drops below freezing (not common in New Orleans, but not unheard of). Working out the details of the "freeze plan" required a complete compilation of existing shelter capacity, a compilation that was very current and available to the Census as well as to us. So far as "normal" shelters for the homeless are concerned, the list employed by the Census for the S-Night shelter enumeration was accurate and exhaustive as nearly as we could tell.

The Census definition of a "shelter" for the homeless was meant to include commercial establishments such as flophouse hotels. No a priori list of these establishments existed and we were not confident about our ability to compile such a list, so we made a special effort to identify qualifying commercial establishments. However, this effort proved unsuccessful. Like many cities, New Orleans has witnessed the virtual disappearance of the once-common flophouses. As recently as 1984, there were several cheap hotels in and around the city's Warehouse District. The changing economics of shipping, urban land use, and, specifically, the urban renewal brought about by the 1984 World's Fair have made New Orleans flophouses largely a thing of the past. The few relatively cheap hotels that remain tend to charge nightly room rates somewhat higher than the Census cutoff ($15 to $20 per night). Thus, we included no cheap flophouses on the list we supplied to the Census.

The difficulties of accurately listing flophouse hotels is amply illustrated by one establishment about whose existence we only learned after S-Night was completed, a hotel in the downtown area that charges a mere $5 per night. This establishment cannot be found in the phone book and, indeed, does not even have a listed phone number. None of our contacts had ever even heard of this facility. The advocates pointed out that when such facilities are known to the homeless, they are usually avoided because they are more expensive than the "real" shelters, there is no voucher system that will offset the cost, and they are correctly perceived to be unsafe environments that cater mainly to drug dealers and prostitutes. And as a matter of fact, we became aware of this facility only because it was mentioned in the local paper in connection with a homicide that had occurred on the premises. How many of these "shadow" hotels exist around the city, and how many homeless people sleep there on any given night, remains anybody's guess.

Interviews with homeless persons the following morning also revealed an informal sector to the commercial facilities of which we were not previously aware. The reference here is to businesses, typically small, out-of-the-way bars or "drinking clubs," that are not technically "shelters" or flophouse hotels and that do not have conventional sleeping facilities but that do allow homeless clients to sleep there overnight. The Census definition would not include this sort of establishment as a place of lodging; nonetheless, homeless people regularly spend the night in them, curled up in a booth or sprawled out on the floor or an available pool table. Importantly, this behavior is not covert or illicit; it is condoned by the proprietor.

Here too, the number of such establishments and the number of homeless people who frequent them are unknown. Our sources suggest that these informal lodges serve as a regular hangout and a not infrequent source of shelter. In some respects, these establishments are more like private clubs than commercial taverns. A fairly regular set of homeless patrons purchase liquor (and food if available), even running tabs against any regular source of income such as a disability check, and simply crash there for the night. It is not likely that these clubs represent a numerically large portion of the total overnight shelter available to the homeless, although they certainly might. Our point is only that homeless persons in New Orleans who do frequent these clubs would not have been included in the S-Night enumeration, whatever their numbers.

Whether similar "homeless clubs" exist in other cities we cannot say. It seems unlikely that New Orleans is completely unique in this respect, although local regulation of business in general and bars in particular truly pales in comparison to a Northeastern norm. Many bars in New Orleans, for example, remain open 24 hours a day, and the enforcement of health, fire, and building codes in the city is notoriously lax.

In addition to shelters, flophouse hotels, and other "conventional" sources of lodging, the homeless also often spend their nights in public facilities such as bus stations, airport terminals, and subway stations. Most of these sorts of public facilities were included in the S-Night enumeration, but one important omission also came to light during our interviews with homeless persons the following morning. In New Orleans, sizable numbers of homeless people spend their nights at the emergency room of Charity Hospital, the only public hospital providing indigent health care in the city. The waiting room at the ER has seats for several hundred persons and it is not uncommon to sit for many hours before receiving attention. Most homeless people that we have interviewed admitted to spending at least an occasional night there; given this and the seating capacity, it is likely that Charity is in effect the second largest shelter for the homeless in the city. The number of homeless who spent S-Night at Charity is, however, unknown, as Charity did not appear on the Census list of shelters or public places to search.

What is the total effect of these various omissions on the overall shelter count? Unfortunately, one cannot know. If the "shadow" flophouses were numerous, then presumably more people would know about them, and so this is probably the least serious problem with the shelter count. Also, even assuming some turnover during the night, the total number of homeless passing through Charity on any given night could not be more than a few hundred. The number of informal "lodges" is completely unknown. All in all, it is easy to imagine these problems causing a net undercount well in the hundreds, although probably not in the thousands. At the same time, the total capacity of "normal" shelters in the city is fewer than a thousand beds, and so as a proportion of the sheltered homeless, an undercount of several hundred is by no means trivial.

THE STREET COUNT IN NEW ORLEANS

Still, there is very little doubt that the shelter enumeration was more complete and more reliable than the street count. We alluded earlier to the principal result, that Census workers located and enumerated only 19 of our 29 decoy teams. Details of this result follow.

We began with a list of 19 specific sites (or nodes) within the Central Business District of the city that had been provided to us by the field supervisor of the local Census district office. Each "site" was the center point of a four-by-four-block grid, except when a site abutted some natural boundary such as the Mississippi River. Critically, these 19 grids had been previously chosen by the Census, in conjunction with local officials and advocates, as the areas of highest homeless concentration in the city and thus as the areas where the S-Night street sweep would be taken. No effort was made to enumerate homeless people anywhere in the city outside these 19 grids.

With the possible exception of one area (to the immediate north of the French Quarter), the 19 grids represent a reasonably thorough coverage of the high-density, homeless-frequented, downtown and near-downtown areas of the city, at least during the daytime hours. A daytime reconnaissance taken the week before S-Night found large numbers of apparently homeless people in each of the 19 sites. There are less dense nodes of concentration in the Uptown section of the city that were not included in the S-Night sweep, and no effort was made to locate any "scattered-site" homeless (persons spending the night out-of-doors in places around town where the homeless do not normally congregate). Certainly, it was reasonable to expect, a priori, that a large fraction of the street homeless of the city would be found somewhere in the 19 areas that were searched, but since these were the only places searched, S-Night cannot tell us how large that fraction is, the first of many serious limitations.

We laid out the nineteen grids on a map and then reconnoitered each one during daylight hours the week before S-Night, looking for specific places to deploy our decoy teams within each grid. Our personnel were sufficient to create 29 two-person teams, so several grids had multiple teams deployed within them. Thus, on S-Night, we had 29 teams comprised of 58 total people located in precisely those areas where the Census would be searching for the homeless. In addition, we also had two roving drive-by teams that continuously checked on our observation teams and noted general conditions in and around the 29 specific sample sites.

The 58 observers were recruited from three distinct sources. Roughly one-sixth were sociology graduate students. Another third were formerly homeless individuals recruited from a local long-term substance abuse treatment program; about half of this group were veterans of the armed services. The remaining observers were community organizers recruited from a local community action agency. Except for the graduate students, all of our observers were streetwise persons who could be trusted to handle themselves in what was a potentially dangerous situation. Half were black, two were Hispanic, and one was Native American; the rest were Caucasian. Approximately two-thirds were male; ages ranged from 18 to 50. Team assignments were made across rather than within the three groups of recruits where possible. All observers were paid, sworn in as temporary employees of the Census, and provided with a three-hour training session covering unobtrusive observation, census protocol, and safety procedures.

The training program stressed that trainers repeat several key points again just prior to deployment on S-Night itself. First, observers were to remain within their assigned grids at all times during the two hours, although they were free to move around within their sites if they wished. Second, contrary to their expectations, they were not supposed to "pretend" they were homeless. Most showed up for S-Night dressed in casual street clothes; some looked rather shabby, none looked like tourists. Finally, they were not to do anything either to attract or avoid the Census enumerators; if approached, they were to answer any questions asked of them openly and honestly. In essence, our observing teams were instructed to sit, stand, or walk around in their assigned areas, making mental notes as to conditions, other people in their area, presence of police, presence of Census enumeration teams, etc.

Although the forecast included the possibility of rain, S-Night was clear, relatively dry for a subtropical climate, but unusually chilly by New Orleans standards. Whereas the local normal minimum daily temperature during March is 51.6 degrees Fahrenheit, the temperature dipped into the low 40s on this particular occasion, with a brisk wind. As a consequence, shelters probably had a higher than normal utilization and a smaller proportion of the homeless population remained on the streets. Whether for this or other reasons, the number of homeless people in evidence in the observation sites was definitely fewer on S-Night itself than it had been in the daytime reconnaissance undertaken the previous week.

In contrast to the situation in several other cities, most advocates and social service workers in New Orleans urged their homeless clients to cooperate with the Census on the grounds that everyone's interests would be best served by the most complete count possible. In turn, our interviews the following morning did not uncover a single homeless individual who said he or she had intentionally evaded enumeration. In New Orleans at least, intentional evasion does not appear to have been a serious problem.

Alternatively, many of the homeless have very good reasons to "lay low" at night—not specifically to elude the Census, but to avoid the police, thugs, and others that would constitute a potential threat to their well-being. This generalized avoidance strategy was poignantly expressed by a one-legged homeless man we interviewed that morning. This extremely vulnerable individual reported numerous occasions when he had been robbed and beaten while sleeping in the streets. The logical adaptation to the evident risk would be either to "buddy up" or to find a place to sleep where the thugs would not normally think to look; our one-legged informant solved his problem by sleeping in trees! A concerted effort to escape victimization would also cause one to elude the more benign purposes of Census enumerators as well, even if that was not the intention.

Most of the homeless we have interviewed (on the morning following S-Night and since) have had similar stories to relate. In fact, the question itself is often a source of some incredulity, as if it were stupid even to ask whether one sought safe, out-of-the-way places to spend the night. Common strategies include sleeping within the protected confines of dumpsters, under abandoned vehicles, beneath shrubbery, in protected, non-visible doorways, or even up in a tree—anything that would afford an added measure of security in an uncertain and hostile environment. The S-Night search procedures would have uncovered very few (if any) of the homeless who adopted such avoidance tactics. Unfortunately, we do not have good evidence upon which to calculate the frequency of this kind of avoidance behavior, but it is certainly of some significance that none of the persons we interviewed who had spent the previous night out-of-doors reported having been enumerated by the Census.

Summarizing briefly, there are many (but it is not clear how many) homeless people who sleep in areas of the city where the Census did not search, and none of them would have been included in the street count. Even in areas where the Census did search, many homeless people would have been missed not through intentional evasion of the Census but through intentional evasion of threats to their physical well-being. What, then, can be said about homeless people who were in the areas where the Census was looking and who were not sleeping in locations that would cause them to be overlooked?

The preceding, of course, defines the conditions that obtained for our 29 observer teams; based on the "hit rate" given earlier, we would guess that the Census missed roughly a third even of these presumably easy-to-count homeless people. This guess is consistent with the information reported in the observer debriefings. Our observers reported numerous instances of readily visible and apparently homeless persons who were entirely overlooked by the Census teams working in the area. As an extreme case in point, one of our teams was positioned in a site near the Mississippi River, at the edge of a wide, block-long median strip in the middle of a street. Much of the perimeter of this median strip is heavily landscaped with shrubbery, with open lawn and benches inside the perimeter. Our observers reported that a team of Census enumerators indeed walked past this area but failed to enumerate either them (the team itself, which was sitting in open view on the perimeter) or any of the estimated 20 homeless people camped out on the benches and grass inside the perimeter. Similar if less dramatic oversights were reported by a number of our teams.

A further complication in the S-Night enumeration is that individuals do not necessarily remain in one place all night. One of the drive-by teams, for example, observed the same solitary individual wandering through a number of different observation sites during the early morning hours. Was this person ever counted? Was he counted more than once? Similarly, one homeless person we interviewed the following morning began his night at the bus station, was rousted by security, made his way over to a nearby park, and ended the night "crashing" at Charity Hospital. His route from the bus station to the hospital took him through roughly a half-dozen of the Census enumeration sites, but according to him he was never counted.

Our observers also took note of numerous violations of the stated Census enumeration procedures. For example, several observers who were approached by the Census were asked, "Are you homeless?" The protocol was to enumerate all people out on the streets in the stipulated times and areas; enumerators were specifically instructed not to ask whether people were homeless. The rationale for this, incidentally, was a concern in the Bureau that people would be threatened or embarrassed by such a direct question and would therefore deny their homelessness, thus causing an undercount. For what it is worth, we asked the homeless people we interviewed how they would respond to the question, "Are you homeless?" None indicated the least bit of discomfort with the query or any evident embarrassment about what is, after all, a rather obvious condition of their existence.

Most problematic, a number of the Census enumeration teams appeared extremely hesitant and fearful to our observers (and to observers in the other four cities). Our drive-by teams reported that the enumerators "stuck out like sore thumbs." The apparent result was fairly widespread avoidance by the enumerators both of our observers and of the truly homeless. Given the conditions and time when the enumeration was done, this is surely understandable; our teams witnessed countless drug deals, solicitations of prostitution, police shakedowns, and all the rest of the activities one would expect at night on the streets of any major city. However understandable, it does not cause one to be confident in the diligence of the enumeration effort.

One final problem worthy of note is that New Orleans is very much a late-night city. Homeless people will definitely be found on the streets of the French Quarter at 3:00 in the morning. So too will vacationing tourists and conventioneers. Compounding the problem, sizable fractions of both groups will be staggering drunk. Strict adherence to the stated Census protocols would have resulted in the enumeration of numerous boozy doctors and businessmen, a problem that was avoided because the Census enumerators apparently used their own subjective evaluations about who "looked" homeless in deciding whom to approach. The problem with this, of course, is that not all homeless people actually look like they are homeless, and many of the people who "look" homeless in fact are not.

Some of the problems with S-Night in New Orleans are unique to the city; most of them are not. If anything, the conditions present in New Orleans would lead one to expect a more (not less) complete count that was obtained in the other cities. Thus, the S-Night result in New Orleans (and elsewhere) makes it nearly certain that the national S-Night count cannot be taken in itself as a reliable or accurate indicator of the number of the homeless, least of all the street component. We probably learned more from S-Night about counting the homeless than we learned about the homeless count.

Still, the disparity between the S-Night count of 228,000 homeless people and the consensus "best guess" guess in the literature, a half million to a million homeless people, is sufficiently wide to warrant a closer look. Having said what there is to be said about "counting the homeless," let us consider why the homeless cannot be counted in the first place.

3

Why the Homeless Can't
Be Counted

S-Night is only the most recent of a large number of efforts to count the homeless in various cities or states, all more or less unsatisfactory. For all the effort that has been spent trying to count the homeless, it proves useful to consider the many reasons why they cannot be counted.

As we mentioned earlier, S-Night results were released with an important but often-overlooked caveat: "S-Night was not intended to, and did not, produce a count of the 'homeless' population of the country" (*U.S. Department of Commerce News* 1991). The S-Night count totaled 228,372 homeless people. Of these, 178,638 were enumerated in shelters and the remaining 49,734 were enumerated in various street locations. Needless to say, many people—advocates and researchers alike—have looked on these numbers with suspicion, as they are considerably less than half the estimates that had become customary by the end of the 1980s. Thus, despite the bureau's many caveats about the S-Night effort, the number of the homeless remains controversial; indeed, the bureau has been in court defending its S-Night procedures against the grievances of the advocacy community.

There are two important factors that might have caused S-Night to undercount homeless people. The first, to which Chapter 2 alludes, is the number of homeless people who in fact spent S-Night in places where they might have been counted by the Census but were not. The second and for present purposes more important factor is the number of homeless people who spent S-Night in places where the Census would never have looked for them in the first place. We can refer to these two groups as the uncounted and the uncountable, respectively.

THE UNCOUNTED HOMELESS

How complete and reliable was the S-Night count? How many persons who spent the night in places where the Census looked for them—e.g., in the shelters, on the streets, or in abandoned buildings—were actually found and enumerated by the Census? As we have just discussed, S-Night experiments designed to answer exactly these questions were undertaken in Chicago (Edin 1992), New York (Hopper 1992), Los Angeles (Cousineau and Ward 1992), Phoenix (Stark 1992), and New Orleans (Devine and Wright 1992). Results from all five experiments suggested that the S-Night shelter count was reasonably complete. It is obviously impossible to be precise in such matters, but for purposes of the calculations undertaken in this chapter, we simply assume that the shelter count was 90% complete, which seems a reasonable assumption.

In contrast, as Chapter 2 shows, the S-Night street count was seriously incomplete, although just how incomplete is yet to be determined. Direct evidence on the incompleteness of the count comes from the five S-Night experiments, but there is indirect evidence that is even more compelling and that provides a most convenient starting point for the material covered in this chapter. This "indirect" evidence is that the S-Night street count of 49,734 is implausibly low given the shelter count of 178,638.

The immediate implication of this result is that the sheltered homeless are 3.6 times more numerous than the street homeless (178,636/49,734 = 3.6). No other study of which we are aware has concluded that the number of sheltered homeless exceeds the number of street homeless, much less by a factor of three or four. In fact, nearly all other studies conclude that there are at least as many street homeless as sheltered homeless, and perhaps several times more. If the true ratio is indeed on the order of 1:1 (a relatively conservative assumption given findings reported in the literature), then the Census "should" have found at least as many street homeless as sheltered homeless, i.e., a couple of hundred thousand of them. By this standard, the Census enumeration of roughly 50,000 street homeless amounts to only about a quarter of those who "should" have been found.

Although it may seem inconceivable that the Census actually missed three-quarters of its target street population, this figure is quite consistent with the results from the S-Night experiments. The best S-Night result was a "hit rate" of 66% in New Orleans, but as we discussed in Chapter 2, one would have expected a better rate in New Orleans than in the other cities. In the Chicago experiment, the observers actually saw Census enumerators in only one-third of the predesignated enumeration sites and among 18 homeless people interviewed the following morning, only 5 (28%) believed that they had been counted (Edin 1992:365). In Los Angeles, the S-Night data suggest that between 59 and 70% of the target population was missed (Cousineau and Ward 1992:389); in Phoenix, only 30% of the seeded "decoys" believed that they were counted. Thus, with the partial exception of the New Orleans result, results from the other S-Night experiments are entirely consistent with the conclusion that the Census enumerators missed perhaps three quarters of otherwise countable homeless people who were on the streets that morning.

What, then, does the S-Night count of 228,372 homeless people tell us about the true number of "countable" homeless people in the country? If, as we have assumed, the shelter count was about 90% complete, then the best guess about the size of the sheltered homeless population is 178,638/0.9 = 198,500, or roughly 200,000. And if there are indeed as many street as sheltered homeless (i.e., if the S-Night street undercount was in fact as severe as the experimental data suggest), then the total "countable" homeless population is twice the sheltered homeless population, i.e., on the order of 400,000. This conclusion is consistent not only with the direct results of the S-Night experiments but also with independent research on the ratio of sheltered to street homeless.

HOUSING DYNAMICS AND THE "UNCOUNTABLE" HOMELESS

Homelessness is frequently considered to be, or commonly stereotyped as, a chronic or long-term condition such that people tend to stay homeless more or less indefinitely once they have become homeless for the first time. But as the discussion in Chapter 1 made obvious, most homeless people are episodically homeless, that is, they become homeless from time to time in response to short-term changes in their social, psychological, or economic circumstances. Thus, it is less literally "houselessness" than a high level of housing instability or housing marginality that seems to define the condition of homelessness most accurately. In the 19-city HCH study, about half the homeless exhibited this episodic pattern, a quarter were considered chronically homeless, and the remaining quarter were recently homeless for the first time.

The housing dynamics of homeless people obviously complicate any effort to count them, S-Night certainly included. Homeless people, for instance, might temporarily "double up" with family and friends for short periods; if that period of doubling-up happened to span S-Night, then they would not have been counted in either the shelter or street enumeration. Or they may have found a room for the night in an inexpensive flophouse (but one charging more than the S-Night cutoff of $12), or "crashed" with some friends, or spent the night with a "john," or in a crack house or shooting gallery. Otherwise-homeless people who happened to spend S-Night in places or locations where the S-Night enumerators never even intended to look comprise the theoretically "uncountable" proportion of the homeless population, because the S-Night enumeration procedures would never have included them no matter how thoroughly or diligently those procedures were followed. A cash windfall, an extended period of sobriety, or a sympathetic sister would all be sufficient in at least some cases to get a homeless person off the streets for a bit and thus out of the view of the S-Night operation.

To round out the S-Night picture, we therefore need data on the numbers of homeless people who would have spent S-Night in some sort of situation or location that would have rendered them theoretically uncountable in the sense described above, i.e., data on the actual housing dynamics of a sample of homeless people. These data are available for a sample of 670 homeless crack addicts and alcoholics in New Orleans, all of them participants in the New Orleans Homeless Substance Abusers Project (NOHSAP; described in detail in later chapters).

NOHSAP was an alcohol and drug treatment program for homeless people; clients were given a very lengthy baseline interview on their second or third day in treatment. Among the many items of information obtained during baseline was a reconstructed 60-day housing history, from which the following data were derived. Although one might well be suspicious of the accuracy with which the prior 60 days could be recalled by homeless addicts on their second or third day off the streets, the test-retest reliabilities for these data were actually quite high (Joyner 1992).

The categories of recently, episodically, and chronically homeless are useful in emphasizing the often transitory and marginalized nature of the homeless condition but they are, nonetheless, arbitrary demarcations in a continuum of housing histories that homeless people experience. There is no obvious answer to the question, How long do people have to be homeless before they can be considered chronically homeless? Or to the question, how many interruptions in the condition of homelessness have to occur before a person should be considered episodically homeless? Still, it is obvious that the recent housing histories of chronically, episodically, and recently homeless people might be very different, and these differences therefore need to be taken into account in parsing their possible effects on the completeness of the S-Night homeless count.

The total number of times homeless in the lifetime (number of homeless episodes) varies in the NOHSAP sample from 1 (62%) to 50 or more (5%); even in the past five years, the number of episodes varies from 1 (66%) to 25 (4%). Likewise, the elapsed time between the first episode of homelessness and the present varies from a few days or weeks up to 34 years (mean = 3.9 years). If one cross-tabulates the number of episodes with the elapsed time, there are at least some cases in every cell.

The "recently homeless" are easy enough to identify in these data; they are persons who have only experienced one or two episodes of homelessness, all within the past year. This group represents 45% of the 609 clients with nonmissing data on the component variables. It is also obvious that clients who have experienced only one episode of homeless that has lasted for two or more years can be considered chronically homeless; that is, they became homeless just once and have been homeless for some years ever since. This group comprises another 19% of the sample. The remaining clients (34% of the total) were divided into "chronic" and "episodic" categories, depending on whether their total time homeless over the lifetime was half or more (chronic) or less than half (episodic) of the total years available to have been homeless since the year they first became homeless. By these admittedly arbitrary standards, 45% of the NOHSAP clients were first-time homeless, 23% were episodically homeless, and 32% were chronically homeless. Compared to other studies of homeless people (e.g., Wright 1989a), the first-time homeless are apparently overrepresented in these data and the episodically homeless are underrepresented. Table 3.1 shows various aspects of the sample's homelessness history according to these three categories.

The recently homeless are disproportionately women (29 vs. 22% and 19% for the other two groups), consistent with the common depiction of homeless women as the "new homeless." Alcoholics are overrepresented among the episodic and chronic groups; crack addicts are overrepresented among the recently homeless. Average ages are about identical in all three groups. Average lifetime episodes of homelessness are just over 1 for the recently homeless, just over 4 for the episodically homeless, and just over 8 for the chronically homeless. Total months of homelessness average 2 for the recently homeless, 12 for the episodically homeless, and 46 for the chronically homeless. The average episodically homeless person in these data first became homeless 8 years ago and in 4 episodes of homelessness has accumulated a total of about 1 year of life on the streets; the average chronically homeless person, in contrast, first became home-

Table 3.1.   The Recently, Episodically, and Chronically Homeless: Baseline Data
from the New Orleans Homeless Substance Abusers Project

	Recently Homeless	*Episodically Homeless*	*Chronically Homeless*
N [a]	273	141	196
Gender composition			
Male	71	78	81
Female	29	22	19
Average age	32	33	33
Percentage with alcohol as primary substance problem	9	32	28
Percentage with crack as primary substance problem	86	65	68
Average life-time episodes of homelessness	1.1	4.4	8.1
Average episodes of homelessness, last five years	1.1	2.9	4.7
Elapsed number of years since 1st episode	0.6	8.0	5.2
Total months of accumulated homelessness	2.0	11.9	46.1
60-Day Housing Histories of NOHSAP Clients: Average Number of Days Spent in Each Place			
Indoor public place	0.3	0.6	0.8
Bus or streetcar	0.0	0.1	0.1
Abandoned building	3.0	3.5	4.7
Car or other vehicle	2.1	1.6	1.9
The street, outdoors	8.0	6.6	11.7
Emergency shelter	2.7	3.9	6.8
Hotel or motel	1.7	1.8	1.4
Own SRO room	0.4	1.3	0.6
Someone else's SRO room	0.7	0.2	0.0
Own apartment or house	6.3	8.5	2.0
Parents / guardian's place	9.4	5.7	3.9
Someone else's place (n.e.c.)	16.5	14.4	12.6
Boarding house, board-and-care	0.0	0.0	0.2
Transitional housing	0.1	0.2	0.0
Group home	0.0	0.0	0.1
Long-term ADF facility	0.0	0.4	0.0
Charity Hospital	1.9	1.8	1.9
Other hospital	0.3	0.5	0.3
Nursing home	0.0	0.0	0.1

(continued)

Table 3.1. Continued

	Recently Homeless	Episodically Homeless	Chronically Homeless
Treatment, recovery program	0.4	1.6	1.5
Jail or prison	1.2	2.9	3.4
Corrections halfway house	0.1	0.0	0.0
Drink house, juke joint, etc.	0.2	0.4	0.3
Crack house	3.4	2.8	4.6
Nights with a john	0.4	0.2	0.2
Other	0.4	0.4	0.6
Sum of means	59.5	59.4	59.7

[a] Intermittently missing data are omitted item by item.

less about 5 years ago and in 8 spells of homelessness has accumulated nearly 4 years of time on the streets. All of these patterns are, of course, as one would expect given the definitions employed in creating these three groups.

The baseline survey contained a long series of questions on each client's living arrangements just prior to the onset of the current episode of homelessness. As might be expected, the recently homeless were somewhat more likely (31%) than the episodically (18%) or chronically (21%) homeless to have been living with parents or guardians before the current episode, but otherwise these questions revealed no large or interesting differences among the three groups. The same was true of another long sequence concerning who respondents were living with before the current episode (alone, with parents, with spouses or sexual partners, etc.).

Yet a third lengthy sequence asked about the circumstances and events that precipitated the current episode of homelessness; subgroup differences in the responses were generally insignificant but the marginal results are of interest. By far the most commonly mentioned "precipitant" was the client's drug and alcohol abuse, cited by 81% of the sample. Various "relationship" problems were also prominent in the responses: 36% said that they had simply been "kicked out," 36% said that someone they had been depending on for support ended their support, and 46% cited marital or familial conflicts or divorce as a precipitating factor. Inevitably, strictly economic factors were also implicated: 24% mentioned loss of a job, 10% mentioned the loss of other income, 50% mentioned increased living expenses, and 11% mentioned eviction as precipitating factors. No other factor was mentioned by as many as 10%. Thus, as in virtually every other study of the homeless ever published, alcohol and drugs, familial estrangement, and poverty emerge unambiguously as the proximate causes of homelessness.

A final relevant question sequence attempted to reconstruct the client's housing history for the 60 days prior to entry into treatment (Table 3.1). Here too, the subgroup differences were generally modest although all were in the expected direction. The chronically homeless, for example, spent more nights in homeless shelters (average = 6.8 nights) than either the episodically homeless (3.9 nights) or the first-timers (2.7 nights); likewise, the chronically homeless spent more nights sleeping out of doors (11.7 nights vs. 6.6 and 8.0 nights for the episodically homeless and first-timers, respectively). In contrast, the first-timers spent more of their recent nights with parents (9.4 vs. 5.7 and 3.9 for the episodic and chronic) or friends (16.5, 14.4, and 12.6 nights, respectively). Also of some interest are the average nights of the previous 60 spent in jail (1.2, 2.9, and 3.4, respectively), in crack houses (3.4, 2.8, and 4.6), and in abandoned buildings (3.0, 3.5, and 4.7), the sums in each case equaling or exceeding the nights spent in homeless shelters (an indicator of the grossly inadequate shelter provisions available in New Orleans, whose total shelter capacity amounts to fewer than 1,000 beds).

These 60-day housing histories, of course, bear directly on the S-Night count. As the count was actually implemented in New Orleans, the Census enumerators could have potentially counted homeless people who were sleeping in indoor public places (bus stations and the like), in abandoned buildings or in cars, out on the streets or in other outdoor places (assuming they were not concealed places), in emergency overnight shelters, and in very cheap SRO rooms. Summing over these six categories, the average recently homeless person in the NOHSAP sample spent 16.5 of the previous 60 nights sleeping in a location that would have made him or her potentially countable in S-Night (28% of the available nights); the average episodically homeless person spent 17.5 (29%) of the 60 nights sleeping in potentially countable places; and the average chronically homeless person spent 26.5 (44%) of the 60 nights sleeping in potentially countable places. Thus, even if the Census had managed to count all the homeless people who were "out there" and theoretically countable, the actual housing dynamics of homeless people would have caused very large numbers of them to be missed.

The housing history data also bear on the ratio of street to sheltered homeless. If we define "street homeless" as people who sleep in indoor public places, buses, streetcars, abandoned buildings, cars, and all "street and outdoor places," and define the "sheltered homeless" as people who sleep in emergency shelters, then the ratio of street to sheltered homeless is 4.96 for the recently homeless, 3.18 for the episodically homeless, and

2.8 for the chronically homeless. Based on these data, the 1:1 ratio assumed here is obviously very conservative. This is also further evidence that the 49,734 street homeless enumerated in S-Night can only be a very small fraction of the total street population; there is simply no independent evidence in any source to suggest that the sheltered homeless are more numerous than the street homeless, and a great deal of evidence to suggest precisely the opposite.

One final point suggested by the housing history data is that the street homeless and sheltered homeless are not distinct populations; nearly all the homeless people in this sample spend at least an occasional night in an emergency shelter and nearly all of them also occasionally sleep out-of-doors. Which homeless people are considered "sheltered homeless" depends a great deal on who makes it to the shelter line first.

For purposes of a few final calculations, we assume that the relative proportions of recently, episodically, and chronically homeless people are about those reported in Wright's (1989a) 16-city study, i.e., one-half episodically homeless, one-quarter recently homeless, and one-quarter chronically homeless. We have also used the "corrected" S-Night figure, 400,000 countable homeless people, as the base; thus, we assume that among the 400,000 are 200,000 episodically homeless people and 100,000 each recently and chronically homeless people.

By the above estimates, the 200,000 episodically homeless people who were theoretically countable in S-Night are but 29% of the total number of episodically homeless people (since episodically homeless people only spend 29% of their nights in places that would have made them theoretically countable); the 100,000 theoretically countable recently homeless people are but 28% of the total of recently homeless people; and the 100,000 theoretically countable chronically homeless people are but 44% of their true total. Simple arithmetic then gives a best guess of 1,300,000 homeless people as of the S-Night date—about 400,000 theoretically countable homeless people (of whom only 228,000 were actually counted) and an additional 900,000 or so whose sleeping locations on an average night—hotel or motel rooms, prisons, jails and other institutions, apartments and houses of friends, family, and acquaintances, and the like—made them essentially uncountable in practically any conceivable method of enumeration. Thus, by the logic and evidence presented here, the actual S-Night count of 228,000 is not inconsistent with any estimated number of homeless people up to and including 1,300,000, a number that also amply exceeds the rough consensus of a total homeless count in the high hundreds of thousands as of the end of the 1980s.

It is, of course, possible that the recent housing histories of homeless crack addicts and alcoholics in New Orleans do not generalize to the national homeless population. A particular concern in this connection is the severely inadequate supply of shelter beds in the New Orleans area. On the other hand, a shortage of shelter beds is not exactly an uncommon problem in American cities. If we assume that the national homeless population spends *twice* as many nights in overnight shelters as do the New Orleans homeless, then the "percentage of nights in theoretically countable locations" increases to 32% for the recently homeless, 36% for the episodically homeless, and 56% for the chronically homeless, and the overall best guess figure declines to $(100,000/0.32) + (200,000/0.36) + (100,000/0.56) = 1,046,000$ total homeless people. If we further subtract from this total the estimated number of recently homeless people (312,500) on the grounds that they may not have yet been homeless when S-Night took place, we are left with 734,000 homeless people, approximately the consensus value in the recent literature.

CONCLUSIONS

S-Night missed large numbers of the homeless, as the Census Bureau is itself quick to admit. The ensuing undercount has two distinct components. First, there is an uncounted component consisting of homeless people who spent S-Night in a place or situation where they could theoretically have been counted but were not. Relatively few homeless people who spent S-Night in an overnight shelter fall into this category but the large majority of street homeless do, some three-quarters of them by our estimate. Taking this large uncounted stratum into account raises the estimate of the number of the homeless from 228,000 to about 400,000.

Then second, the actual housing dynamics of homeless people are such as to put many of them in sleeping locations on any given night where they would not be enumerated in any counting effort, no matter how aggressively it was conducted. These are what we have called the uncountable homeless, and our data suggest that there may have been as many as 600,000 to 900,000 of them on the night S-Night took place, depending on what assumptions one is willing to make about the generalizability of the New Orleans data.

The fact of the matter is that the literally homeless population, particularly the episodic component, spends relatively few nights sleeping in overnight shelters, in public places, or in street locations that would make them theoretically enumerable. As befits highly marginalized people, most bounce around from place to place, spending a few nights in the shelters, a few nights on the streets, a few nights with family and friends—in short, a few nights here and a few nights there. That being the case, one despairs of ever finding an enumeration procedure that would actually count a large fraction of them; it is, nonetheless, a virtual certainty that S-Night did not. By the logic and evidence presented here, S-Night probably enumerated fewer than one in three (using 734,000 as the base), and may have enumerated fewer than one in five (using 1,300,000 as the base), of the nation's one-night literally homeless population.

Given the episodic nature of much homelessness, trying to count the homeless is a little like trying to count the number of flies in a house whose windows and doors are wide open. At any one moment, there is a definite number of flies in the house and that number is theoretically countable. Practically speaking, however, the rapid movement of flies in and out means that no count can be definitive or even very useful. Likewise, while there is some finite and theoretically countable number of literally homeless people in the United States at any one time, they are but a fraction of a much larger number of persons who are at risk of homelessness and who are destined to be homeless at some other time. In this sense, the number of flies or of homeless people is a less pertinent question than the transition probabilities that govern movement in and out of the condition being counted.

Extending the metaphor one further step, the flies-in-the-open-house problem obviously cannot be solved just by swatting flies; one must first shut the windows and doors. So too one cannot solve the problem of homelessness by addressing the problems of people who happen to be homeless this day, this week, or this year. Actually solving the problem requires some way of preventing the at-risk population from becoming homeless in the first place.

4

Poverty, Housing, and Homelessness

In Chapter 1, we mentioned some results from an early-1980s survey of homeless people in San Francisco, who were asked to identify "the most important issues you face or problems you have trying to make it in San Francisco or generally in life" (Ball and Havassy 1984). The most common responses were "no place to live indoors" (mentioned by 94%), followed by "no money" (mentioned by 88%). No other response was chosen by as much as half the sample. At a sufficiently abstract level, the connections between poverty, the housing supply, and homelessness may be dim. At the level where life is lived, the connections seem stunningly obvious.

Obvious or not, there has been a concerted effort to discount or deny that there is any important connection between homelessness, poverty, and the low-income housing supply—some by conservative commentators who seem congenitally incapable of owning up to any flaw in the American social condition and some by more centrist analysts who seem to fear that any serious discussion of social-structural determinants will divert attention or funds from the service programs they favor. We are particularly intrigued by the line of argumentation positing that homelessness is fundamentally a problem of mental illness, substance abuse, and related personal deficiencies and therefore it cannot a problem of housing, income, and social structure, as though it must be one or the other rather than both.

As we have discussed, rates of personal deficiencies and disabilities of various sorts are admittedly very high among practically any sample of homeless people. But why is this fact thought to imply that homelessness is therefore an alcohol, drug, or mental health problem and not a housing problem? By what evidence or logic does an emphasis on the housing connection qualify as an act of collective "denial," as Baum and Burnes insist? If the loss of low-income housing in the 1980s and 1990s is not directly and causally responsible for the rising tide of homelessness, it has surely been an important contributing factor and has provided the social-structural backdrop against which other factors operate.

The conservative point of view in these matters is conveniently summarized in a piece by Randall Filer (1990), "What We Really Know About the Homeless?" Filer's general argument is that homelessness is not nearly so serious as many have come to believe and that programs of assistance to the homeless may actually create (and certainly worsen) the homelessness problem. Like many others, he views welfare benefits, AFDC, housing subsidies, and other elements of the "citizen wage" as a threat to the market because these programs reward the poor for being poor and the homeless for being homeless. "The more generous he programs for the homeless are, the greater this number [of homeless] will be as people respond to the incentives created" (Filer 1990). So far as the link to low-income housing is concerned, he remarks that "despite the implication of the word 'homeless,' we know almost nothing about the connection between homelessness and housing markets. There is no reliable evidence that homelessness is more extensive in cities with tight housing markets."

A noted advocate for the homeless, Robert Hayes, has said that the three main causes of homelessness are "housing, housing, and housing." In turn, analysts such as Baum and Burnes or Filer deny (or doubt) that housing is an important part of the issue. That both views exist simultaneously suggests at once that there are ideological as well as empirical factors at play. The ideological issue is transparent: it is whether homeless people themselves or the larger society are responsible for the homeless problem.

Is it true that "we know almost nothing" about the relationship between homelessness and the low-income housing situation? No: We know full well that there is a relationship between housing markets and homelessness; otherwise, the very concept of homelessness itself has no practical meaning. In a fundamental sense, to deny that homelessness is a housing problem is to deny that true homelessness exists.

It is also apparent that Filer's sentiments were shared by President Reagan and President Bush throughout their administrations and were, indeed, institutionalized in budgets and policies that in the final analysis exacerbated the homelessness problem. By far the most complete and telling statement on this point is Joel Blau's *The Visible Poor* (1992). As a result of the Republican posture toward housing and poverty issues, the homeless situation was much worse at the end of the 1980s than it had been at the beginning (Burt 1992), and so unhousing the urban poor is a lamentable but enduring legacy of that decade.

THE URBAN POVERTY SITUATION

We have already summarized the general thrust of our argument. Recent developments in the political economy of the cities have marginalized increasingly large sectors of the urban poverty population; that coupled with continued increases in housing costs and a continuing decline in the supply of low-income housing have put an increasingly large segment of the urban poverty population at risk of homelessness. The contribution of social structure to the contemporary homelessness problem has been to create and expand this population at risk; in other words, that is the specific sense in which it could be said that social-structural factors are causally related to homelessness.

The causal question here is analogous to the question of whether unprotected sex "causes" AIDS. There is certainly a sense in which the answer to this question is no, since infection with the HIV virus is what causes AIDS. But unprotected sex increases one's risk of contracting the HIV virus and subsequently AIDS, so the causal chain is straightforward. HIV virus is the proximal cause of AIDS; factors that increase one's risk of contracting the HIV virus are in turn the ultimate causes of AIDS.

So too with homelessness. Social-structural factors such as poverty and a dwindling supply of low-cost housing are rarely the proximal causes of homelessness, i.e., they are not the homelessness "virus." But they *are* the factors that increase the susceptibility of the at-risk population to whatever that homelessness "virus" is. To maintain that social-structural factors are not a cause of homelessness is rather like maintaining that unprotected sex does not cause AIDS (because the HIV virus causes AIDS) or that improper sanitation does not cause tuberculosis (because bacilli cause tuberculosis) or that smoking does not cause coronary heart disease (because the build-up of plaque in the coronary vessels causes coronary heart disease).

Granting, then, that any particular individual can become homeless for any of a thousand different reasons, what have been the major risk factors that have increased the susceptibility of the urban population to this "disease"? Let us begin with a discussion of recent changes in the poverty situation, changes that have been more fully described elsewhere (Devine and Wright 1993). In this connection, there are four specific trends of interest:

1. The Poverty Population Is Growing. The first and perhaps most important fact about the poor "these days" is that there are somewhat more of them than there used to be. Trends in the poverty rate have been closely monitored since the federal government first settled on an "official" definition of poverty in the early 1960s. In general, the official aggregate poverty rate declined throughout the 1960s, held constant (more or less) in the 1970s, and then once again began to increase sharply in the early 1980s, reaching a post-1960s peak of 15.2% in 1983. Thereafter, poverty once again declined slowly and steadily for six years, though it never fell below 12.8 (in 1989), a figure still higher than at any point in the 1970s. With the recession of the early 1990s, poverty once again racheted upward, hitting a recent high mark of 15.1% (and 39.3 million people) in 1993, whence it has slowly declined in conjunction with the recent economic expansion. Nonetheless, by 1996 the number and percentage of impoverished Americans remains at 36.5 million persons and 13.7%, respectively (U.S. Bureau of the Census 1997).

In short, as poverty ebbs and flows with the rhythms of economic expansions and contractions, it tends to plateau at somewhat higher levels than before. In 1980 (or in other words, at about the time homelessness began to be seen as a serious and possibly growing problem), there were an estimated 29.2 million Americans living below the poverty line. Since then, and depending on the exact year in question, the number of the poor has increased two and one-half times to 10 million people, representing millions of additional persons who are now at risk for all the things that poverty can bring, including the loss of one's housing.

The number of the poor fluctuates within fairly narrow limits from year to year. In the ten years from 1970 to 1979, the average number of poor persons each year was 24.7 million. In the decade of the 1980s, the average number of poor people increased to 32.6 million, and in the seven years of the 1990s for which data are presently available (1990–1996), the average was 36.6 million (see Table 4.1). So, despite recent decreases during the 1994–1996 years, there are almost 3 million more poor in mid-decade than there were at the start of the decade.

While some of this increase stems from the fact that the resident population of the United States has increased by almost 60 million people since 1970, it is also true that the rate of poverty has also tended to drift upward since the early 1980s, though these trends are somewhat more erratic and less decisive. Just to round out the picture, however, Table 4.2 presents the average poverty rates (percentage of persons falling below the poverty line) by decade.

As the population as a whole has become more urban, so too has the poverty population. In 1980, about 62% of the poor lived in metropolitan areas and about 36% lived in the central cities of those metropolitan areas. In 1996, three-quarters of the poor (77%) lived in metropolitan areas and

Table 4.1. Persons in Poverty, U.S., 1990–1996

Year	Number in (Millions)	Percentage	Change from Previous Year (Millions)
1990	33.6	13.5	2.1
1991	35.7	14.2	2.1
1992	36.9	14.5	1.2
1993	39.3	15.1	2.4
1994	38.1	14.5	−1.2
1995	36.4	13.8	−1.7
1996	36.5	13.7	0.1
Average	36.6	14.2	+1.5

43% lived in the central cities. Between 1980 and 1996, the metropolitan poverty population increased from 18.0 million to 28.2 million and the central city poverty population increased from 10.6 million to 15.6 million.

If we focus, therefore, on the period from 1980 to 1996, we derive the picture shown in Table 4.3.

Thus it is clear that the increase in the metropolitan poor (10.2 million) is larger than the increase in the total number of the poor (7.3 million), which implies (correctly) that the number of poor people living outside the metropolitan areas has declined. In other words, the increasing number of persons living in poverty since 1980 has been exclusively a metropolitan (urban) development. About two-thirds of the total growth in the poverty population has occurred specifically in the central cities (i.e., 5 million/7.3 million = 0.68).

Our first conclusion, that we state with a high degree of certainty is that the size of the poverty population, and especially the size of the urban poverty population, has dramatically increased. For present purposes, the size of the poverty population is a more relevant consideration than the poverty rates because it is the absolute size of the poverty population that dictates the number of persons at risk for homelessness. Still, it is clear that the poverty rates as well as the number of the poor tended generally to increase in the 1980s and 1990s.

Table 4.2. Average Poverty Rates (Percentage), U.S., by Decade

	Average	High Value	Low Value
1960–1969	17.5	22.2 (1960)	12.1 (1969)
1970–1979	11.8	12.6 (1970)	11.1 (1973)
1980–1989	13.8	15.2 (1983)	12.8 (1989)
1990–1997	14.2	15.1 (1993)	13.5 (1990)

Table 4.3. Change in Numbers of Poor (Millions), U.S., 1980–1996

Total number of the poor in 1980	29.2
Total number of the poor in 1996	36.5
Increase in total poor from 1980–1996	7.3
Total number of metropolitan poor in 1980	18.0
Total number of metropolitan poor in 1996	28.2
Increase in metropolitan poor from 1980–1996	10.2
Total number of central city poor in 1980	10.6
Total number of central city poor in 1996	15.6
Increase in central city poor from 1980–1992	5.0

2. *The Poverty of the Poor Is Deepening.* That "the poor are getting poorer" has been the theme of countless media accounts over the last decade. Unlike much staple media fare, this theme seems to have some basis in fact, although the trends are not as dramatic as those just recounted.

One commonly used measure of income inequality is the distribution of income by income quintiles. If the poor are getting poorer, then the share of income going to the bottom income quintile should register some decline, and as a matter of fact, it does. In 1970, the bottom fifth of the U.S. (family) income distribution accounted for 5.4% of total national income, and in 1996, 4.2%—which amounts to a proportional income loss of 22.2%. Over the same time span, the share of total income going to the most affluent fifth of families increased from 40.9 to 46.8%, a proportional increase of 14.4%. (Note: the drop in household income is even more dramatic than the reported change in the family income distribution.) Joel Blau (1992) refers to these trends as "the upward transfer of income" and describes this "upward transfer" as a specific ideological priority of the Reagan and Bush administrations.

Another useful indicator is what is called the "income deficit." For any specific family or individual, the income deficit is the difference between that family's (or person's) income and the corresponding poverty line. If the poor are getting poorer, then we should see some increase in the average income deficits, and again we do:

Twenty years ago, the four-person poverty cut-off was $6,191 (1977 dollars) and the mean income deficit for poverty *families* was $2,177 (also 1977 dollars). Thus, in 1977, the income deficit for families was $2,177/$6,191 = 35% of the four-person poverty standard. In other words, the average incomes of poor families in 1977 were about 65% of the four-person poverty standard. In 1992, the four-person poverty standard was $14,335 (1992 dollars) and the mean income deficit for poverty families was $5,751 (1992 dollars), so by 1992, the income deficit had risen to 40% of the four-person poverty standard (or in other words, the average incomes of poor families had fallen to about 60% of the four-person poverty line). The change in this measure is not dramatic but it is in the direction implied by the argument that the poor are getting poorer.

The picture for unrelated individuals is somewhat sharper. In 1977 the mean income deficit for unrelated individuals ($1,188) amounted to 36% of the single-person poverty standard ($3,267); by 1992, the mean deficit ($3,218) was 45% of the single-person poverty standard ($7,143). Rephrased, in 1977 the average poor single individual (i.e., not living within a family) enjoyed an income that was about 64% of the poverty standard, and in 1992, 55%. This evident deterioration in the income situation of unrelated individuals is especially pertinent to the argument we advance here, because homeless people come overwhelmingly from this category.

We can also work directly with the average incomes of the poor rather than the income deficits (all figures in then-current dollars). Table 4.4 shows that the average incomes of the poor are getting progressively further away from the corresponding poverty standard. Here too, the trend is by no means pronounced but definitely in the "right" direction.

As a final measure of the depth of poverty, we can consider the number of people (or families) whose incomes are at or below 50% of the corresponding poverty standard, a commonly employed measure of "extreme" poverty. The argument that the poor are getting poorer would imply that the proportion of the poor at or below the standard for extreme

Table 4.4. Mean Income as Percentage of Poverty Line, Families and Unrelated Individuals, 1970–1992

Poverty Families	Mean Income	Four-Person Poverty Line	Mean Income as % of Poverty Line
1970	$2,211	$ 3,944	54.1
1980	4,451	8,494	52.4
1990	6,927	13,359	51.8
1992	7,127	14,335	49.7
Unrelated Individuals	Mean Income	One-Person Poverty Line	Mean Income as % of Poverty Line
1970	$1,098	$ 1,947	56.4
1980	2,431	4,234	57.4
1990	3,703	6,800	54.5
1992	3,840	7,299	52.6

Table 4.5. Trend in Poverty (%), 1975–
1995

1975	29.7
1980	33.6
1985	37.5
1990	38.4
1995	38.2

poverty has risen, and again, it has. Data on those at or below 50% of the
poverty standard are only available since 1975. In that year, these extremely poor persons numbered 7.7 million out of a total 1975 poverty
population of 25.9 million, or 29.7% of the total. Two decades later, 13.9
million out of 36.4 million total poor were below 50% of the poverty
standard. In five-year increments, the trend has been as shown in Table
4.5. These are perhaps the clearest data available to illustrate the deteriorating economic circumstances of the nation's poverty population. The
"extremely poor" now comprise nearly two-fifths of the total poor, a
proportion than has generally shifted upward since these data were first
reported. The acceleration of this trend in the first half of the 1980s is
perhaps especially notable.

3. The Chronicity of Poverty Is Increasing. Although we tend to think
of poverty as a permanent (or chronic) condition, there is in fact considerable movement of specific persons and families back and forth across the
poverty line from year to year. Persons and households who are poor this
year, that is, may or may not be poor next year. Thus, just as much
homelessness is episodic rather than chronic, so too is much poverty.

Episodic poverty is made possible in the first instance because at any
one time there are large numbers of people and families who, although
not poor by the official poverty standard, are nonetheless very close to
poverty. Data for 1992 provide a convenient illustration. In that year, the
official poverty rate was 14.5%. The percentage of persons at or beneath
125% of the poverty line, however, was 19.4% and the percentage at or
beneath 150% of the poverty line was 24.1%, nearly a quarter of the U.S.
population. Persons and families close to but above poverty in one year
can be easily driven down into poverty in the next, either by economic
misfortunes or changes in family composition. And likewise, persons and
families near to but still beneath the poverty standard in one year can be
driven up above the poverty line in the next. Thus, the "barrier" between
poor and near-poor is highly permeable.

The good news, therefore, is that poverty is not a permanent (or even necessarily long-term) condition for many of the poor. The bad news is that the proportion of the poor for whom poverty *is* a more or less permanent (or at least long-term) condition is growing (e.g., Devine and Wright 1993:Chapter 5). The chronically poor—those who tend to be beneath poverty year after year—have come to comprise an increasingly large fraction of the total poverty population.

Unfortunately, the evidence in favor of this point is not straightforward. Most of the complexity derives from the lack of an agreed-upon standard for what constitutes "chronic" poverty. Suppose we were to consider income and income dynamics over the span of a decade. A family that was beneath the poverty line in each of the ten years would obviously be considered chronically poor, and likewise, a family that was beneath poverty in only one or two of the ten years and above poverty in the remaining years would be considered episodically poor. But how about a family that was below the poverty line in five of the years and above it in the other five? Are they chronic or episodic? Since there is no obvious or agreed-upon answer to this question (since, in other words, the choice of a standard for chronic poverty is inevitably arbitrary), it is not possible to state an exact percentage of the poor who are chronically poor or track that percentage over the decades.

Devine and Wright handled the problem by taking 20 years worth of data (1969–1989) from the Panel Survey of Income Dynamics (PSID). They used 2-, 3-, 4-, and 5-year windows as time frames and every conceivable standard for chronic poverty as measures. For example, in the analyses of the 5-year windows, they examined the trends separately for those who had been poor in 3 of the 5 years, 4 of the 5 years, and all 5 of the 5 years. What they discovered is that regardless of the window or time frame employed and regardless of the standard for chronicity, the proportion of the poor who qualified as chronically poor had increased. Another way to phrase the same conclusion is that the average length of poverty episodes has been growing—that is, poor people "these days" tend to spend more years below the poverty line than poor people did in earlier decades.

4. *The Spatial and Social Isolation of the Poor Is Increasing.* Many analysts of the 1980s remarked upon the increasing "ghettoization" of the poor, particularly the urban poor (e.g., Danziger and Gottschalk 1987; Ricketts and Mincy 1988; Ricketts and Sawhill 1988). The key evidence in favor of this proposition was an increase from 1970 to 1980 in the proportion of the urban poor who lived in "poverty areas," that is to say, in census tracts where 20% or more of the residents were beneath the pover-

ty level. The implication of this increase was that the urban poverty population was coming to be increasingly concentrated in a relatively small number of impoverished neighborhoods with exceptionally high rates of all the social pathologies with which poverty is associated: deteriorating physical conditions, substandard housing, high rates of crime, violence, and drug abuse, elevated rates of teen pregnancy and female heads of households, high levels of welfare dependency, high rates of homelessness, and all the rest. The further implication was that the urban poor were becoming progressively more isolated from the rest of society, not just spatially and economically, but also socially.

Corresponding data from the 1990 Census are now available and make it possible to analyze the concentration of urban (or inner-city) poverty over two decades (Kasarda 1993). Kasarda's analysis focuses on developments in the nation's 100 largest central cities, which in 1990 contained a total of 14,214 census tracts. (Census tracts are arbitrary geographical demarcations used by the Census to identify what are colloquially known as "neighborhoods." Census tracts typically contain about 1,500 households and 4,000–5,000 residents.)

Kasarda categorizes census tracts according to the following criteria:

Poverty tracts are tracts where at least 20% of the residents fall below the official poverty level.

Extreme poverty tracts are tracts where at least 40% of the residents fall below the poverty level.

Distressed neighborhoods are census tracts that "simultaneously exhibit disproportionately high levels of poverty, joblessness, female-headed families, and welfare receipt" (ibid.:256).

Severely distressed neighborhoods are distressed neighborhoods that also have "exceptionally high teenage school drop-out rates" (ibid.). (See ibid.:256–57) for the theoretical rationale behind the chosen criteria.)

Trends over two decades in the 100 largest central cities were as shown in Table 4.6: "A fundamental conclusion to be drawn from [these data] is that poverty neighborhoods became a more prominent feature of urban space in 1990" (ibid.:258). The growth of poverty tracts and extreme poverty tracts implies not only that the number of the urban poor has been increasing (as above) but that the spatial concentration of urban poverty is also increasing. One would be hard-pressed to find a more dramatic statement on what has happened to urban America over the past 20 years than these four simple lines of data.

Kasarda also presents useful data on the poverty populations of the 100 cities (Table 4.7): The first line of data confirms an earlier point about

Table 4.6. Trends in Census Tracts over Two Decades in 100 Largest Central Cities

Percentage of All Tracts That Are:	1970	1980	1990
Poverty Tracts	27.3	34.2	39.4
Extreme Poverty Tracts	6.0	9.7	13.7
Distressed Tracts	2.4	11.0	13.0
Severely Distressed Tracts	1.3	4.1	4.0

Source: Kasarda (1993:Table 1).

the increasing rate of poverty in the inner cities; the remainder of the table shows the increasing proportion of the inner-city poor living in poverty ghettoes. In most cases, the trends from 1970 to 1980 are sharper than those from 1980 to 1990; in fact, from 1980 to 1990 there was a marginal decrease in the percentage of the urban poor living in "extremely distressed" tracts. With that exception, however, all the other trends are very definitely in the direction implied by the "increasing concentration" argument.

Kasarda concludes, "This analysis has shown that while there have been some striking individual city turnarounds, poverty concentration and neighborhood distress continued to worsen in our major cities between 1980 and 1990" (ibid.:281). Other analysts have concluded likewise. An analysis of the segregation of the poor in the 100 largest metropolitan areas shows that "on average, the poor became somewhat more segregated between 1970 and 1990 in the nation's 100 largest metropolitan areas" (Abramson and Tobin 1995:59). Among many others reaching essentially the same conclusion are Jargowsky (1994) and Massey and Eggers (1990, 1993).

To conclude, all in all there seems little doubt that recent trends in the cities have provided exceptionally fertile ground for the growth of the homeless population. The increasing size of the urban poverty population puts more people at risk for everything with which poverty is associated;

Table 4.7. Poverty Populations in Census Tracts of the 100 Largest Cities

	1970	1980	1990
Overall Poverty Rate (%)	14.5	16.7	18.3
Poor in Poverty Tracts (%)	55.1	63.8	68.8
Poor in Extreme Poverty Tracts (%)	16.5	22.5	28.2
Poor in Distressed Tracts (%)	6.6	27.0	28.1
Poor in Extremely Distressed Tracts (%)	4.3	9.5	8.6

Source: Kasarda (1993:Table 1).

the increasing depth, chronicity, and concentration of poverty increase the magnitude of risk. The net result is more people at higher risk, and that— it seems to us—has spelled more homelessness. When analysts such as Baum and Burnes opine that "we do not consider major social, economic, and political forces to be at the root of today's homelessness" (1993:170) one wonders who is in "denial" and who is telling the "truth."

We suggested earlier the potential utility of public health metaphors for understanding the relationships among personal factors, social-structural factors, and homelessness. Let us suppose that health workers have observed a definite increase in active tuberculosis cases in a specified geographical location. These workers have also noted that within that specified location, there are more people living in progressively less sanitary conditions—more overcrowding, unclean water, piles of litter, garbage, and excrement, and the like. Knowing quite a bit about how tuberculosis is transmitted, what conclusions would these health workers reach?

Public health experts would agree that three conclusions are justified:

1. The increasing number of people living in progressively less sanitary conditions *caused* the increase in active tuberculosis. This conclusion would be in order even if the number of active TB cases were a very small fraction of the population at risk.
2. Every person with active tuberculosis would, of course, require treatment, but successful treatment of all the active cases would not prevent new cases from appearing. Thus, "treatment" per se does not, will not, and cannot solve the problem.
3. If we were inclined actually to solve this TB problem, we would have to intervene directly in the risk factors in order to prevent new cases from appearing, that is, we would have to reduce the size of the population at risk or increase the level of sanitation, or both. The need for these preventative measures would exist independently of the level of treatment provided to persons with active TB infections.

This situation is exactly analogous to the homeless situation in the cities. Burt and many others have shown a "definite increase" in cases of active homelessness. The material so far discussed in this chapter likewise shows a definite increase in the size of the population at risk of homelessness (i.e., more poverty) and a commensurate increase in the magnitude or severity of that risk (deeper, more chronic, and more concentrated poverty). And the same three essential conclusions are in order: The increasing magnitude and severity of risk have caused the increase in active cases; the active cases need (and deserve) treatment but more and better treatment for the active cases will not prevent new cases from appearing; the only real solution to the outbreak is to halt, then to reverse, and ultimately to eliminate the trends in the major risk factors.

There seems no end to the factors cited by various analysts to explain the growth of homelessness in the 1980s and 1990s, but nearly all of them are pertinent mainly to the extent that they contribute to (or derive from) one or more of the four major trends in the urban poverty situation discussed above. Jencks provides a useful illustration. "The spread of homelessness in the 1980s," he writes, "had many causes: declining job opportunities for unskilled men, political restrictions on the creation of new flophouses, the increase in single motherhood, the erosion of the purchasing power of welfare recipients, and continuing changes in state mental-health policies" (1994:42). Concerning the continuation of the trends into the 1990s, he adds "the invention of crack" and improvements in the shelter system as important factors.

But why would any of these developments lead to more homelessness? Declining job opportunities for the unskilled are relevant because they have increased the size of the poverty population (and thus, the population at risk for homelessness). Single motherhood is relevant because it increases the risk of poverty and also the depth of poverty (as fixed resources must be stretched to support additional people). The erosion in the purchasing power of welfare is relevant because it increases the depth and chronicity of poverty. Drug addiction is relevant because it too can increase the depth and chronicity of poverty and also because it contributes to the deterioration of poor urban neighborhoods. And so on.

The other factors Jencks mentions—state mental health policy, the loss of flophouses, and the expansion of services for the homeless—are more complicated. As the mentally ill are concerned, at-risk mentally ill people from impoverished backgrounds who were deinstitutionalized in the 1970s or 1980s were "returned" to neighborhoods, communities, and families that were progressively less able to support them than they would have been at some time in the past, so even here, recent developments in the poverty situation have been germane (an issue to which we return in Chapter 6).

The argument that improved shelter for the homeless (or, more generally, expansions in the quantity and quality of services available to the homeless) can itself increase the number of the homeless is explicit in the Randall Filer piece discussed earlier in this chapter and is taken up by Jencks in some detail. If adequate shelter is available, households may be less inclined to accommodate their marginal adult members and correspondingly more likely to turn these members out. In this sense, "new shelters also attract some people who would otherwise be living with friends or relatives in conventional housing" (Jencks 1994:42).

True enough! But this argument presupposes (1) marginal people who are only housed in the first place through the generosity of family and friends and (2) some limits, whether emotional or financial, to that generosity. New shelters suck marginally housed people into homelessness only if there are marginally housed people to begin with (i.e., a population at risk). Why would people "otherwise be living with family and friends" except that they are unable to afford their own place to begin with? This argument makes sense only if there are ever-more marginal (and marginally housed) people and ever-tighter constraints on the generosity of their families and friends. And those, we suggest, have been the unmistakable consequences of the poverty trends we have been discussing.

There is a further wrinkle to Jencks's argument, namely, that improved shelters "lure" people out of conventional housing "when moving to a shelter improves their chances of getting permanently subsidized housing." He explains: "About two million single-parent families currently live in someone else's home. Most would prefer living in a place of their own, but they can only afford one if they get some kind of subsidy. Since there are not enough federally subsidized units . . . , there is always a waiting list. Federal law gives priority to certain kinds of applicants, including the homeless" (ibid.:42). Thus, being homeless (or, what amounts to the same thing, moving into a shelter for the homeless) can dramatically reduce the waiting time for a housing subsidy.

Again, the argument is true enough, so long as we add that most of those two million people are living in someone else's home because they are too poor to afford their own place and that the waiting lists for subsidized housing are always long because the need for subsidized housing is very much greater than the supply.

More generally, we can say that people will "choose" to live in shelters for the homeless (which amounts to saying that they will "choose" to be homeless) whenever living in a homeless shelter beats the alternative. Although there are some notable exceptions, shelters in the United States are for the most part Spartan accommodations at best and filthy, roach-infested, dangerous, and unhealthy at worst. If there are indeed some people who actively prefer living in the shelters to the alternative (and, of course, there are), this says a great deal about the degradation and desperation inherent in the alternatives they face.

LOW-INCOME HOUSING

Jencks's comments about the doubled-up population and his analysis of "political restrictions on the creation of new flophouses" raises the second major topic to be addressed in this chapter, namely, the supply of low-income housing. It is obvious that the poverty trends so far recounted would not necessarily have led to an increase in homelessness if the supply and cost of low-income housing had somehow kept pace, that is, if there were more low-income units to accommodate the increasing number of the poor and if the cost per unit had declined to accommodate increasingly lower poverty incomes. But for the most part, the housing trends were in precisely the opposite direction.

Unfortunately, there is no agreed-upon standard or criterion for "low-income" or "affordable" housing comparable to the federally defined poverty line, so while recent trends in poverty can be documented by looking up a line of data in the *Statistical Abstract*, recent trends in the low-income housing situation cannot. Rather, one must piece together relevant data from a number of different sources, none of them entirely satisfactory.

HOUSING AND URBAN DEVELOPMENT (HUD) PROGRAMS

Ferrara (1990:539) has pointed to increasing levels of federal expenditures to aid the homeless in the 1980s as evidence of the Republican willingness to address the homeless problem. For example, he notes that HUD expenditures increased from $12.5 billion in 1980 to an estimated $22.8 billion in 1990. What Ferrara does not say is that these figures are not expenditures on low-income housing programs or on the homeless; they are, rather, total HUD expenditures on all housing subsidy programs. The 1990 HUD payout specifically for low-income housing programs was about $1.6 billion, nowhere near the $22.8 billion figure Ferrara cites.

Nonetheless, Ferrara makes a useful point. Throughout the 1980s, advocates for the homeless made a concerted effort to convince HUD that homelessness fell within the agency's purview, and by the latter half of the decade, this effort began to bear fruit. Under the provisions of the

McKinney Act, in fact, HUD was designated as the lead agency for homeless programs (significantly, not Health and Human Services). If homelessness is not really a housing problem, then why have three successive administrations insisted that the Department of Housing and Urban Development head up the federal effort?

HUD expenditures on low-income public housing programs and low-rent public housing loans more than doubled in the 1980s, as Ferrara mentions, although a correction for inflation would make the apparent increase less impressive. But it is also true that only a share of the total HUD budget is spent on housing subsidies for the poor, and that an even smaller share is spent on the subsidized construction of new low-income housing. Specific expenditures to provide low-cost housing for the poor have been quite considerably less than anything Ferrara suggests.

By far the largest share of the HUD effort in behalf of poor households is in Section 8 housing vouchers, which have only a tenuous and indirect relationship to the low-income housing supply. As expenditures on housing vouchers have increased, the federal commitment to the subsidized construction of new low-income housing has declined. One result is that many poor people who are fortunate enough to receive Section 8 vouchers have to give them back because they are unable to locate an acceptable Section 8 unit. The problem with housing vouchers is that you can't rent units that aren't there.

Expenditures specifically on the *homeless* poor or on facilities to assist the homeless were not tallied as a separate category in any of HUD's documents prior to 1987. In 1987, $15,000,000 was appropriated for this purpose; no figure for the actual outlay is provided. Also, in 1988, within the category of Policy Development and Research Expenditures, there was an outlay of $2,661,000 for "supplemental assistance or facilities to assist the homeless." To be sure, HUD expenditures on the homeless increased in 1988 and thereafter, under the provisions of the McKinney Act, about which more later.

Ferrara also remarks that the total number of families assisted by HUD programs increased from 3.1 million in 1980 to 4.4 million in 1990, which is true. But it is also true that the size of the poverty population fluctuated between 35 and 40 million people throughout the decade, and so it is obvious that HUD coverage of households in need is very limited, whatever the total number of households receiving assistance. Data from the Center for Budget and Policy Priorities (Shapiro and Greenstein 1988) show state-by-state subsidy (or coverage) rates for the very low-income renter population (not the total poverty population); the coverage is almost never above 50% and nationwide averages less than a third. It can also be noted that Ferrara's figures include nonpoverty households who receive HUD housing assistance, for example, the elderly (among whom the poverty rate has been declining and who now enjoy the lowest poverty rate of any age group in the nation).

By far the largest and most aggressive federal effort on behalf of the homeless is the McKinney Act, enacted in 1987. Under the terms of this act, HUD has spent more than $200 million on the Supportive Housing Demonstration Program, an expenditure frequently cited as evidence of the Reagan and Bush administrations' willingness to address the housing problems of the homeless (e.g., ACCESS 1990). Other housing provisions within the act have provided roughly $80 million to subsidize more than 2,000 single room occupancy (SRO) hotels for a decade, have funded the opening and operation of a number of emergency shelters for the homeless, and so on. The supportive housing program was a particular source of pride because it was intended to provide housing geared to the unique and diverse needs of subgroups within the homeless population (the alcoholic, the mentally ill), a pet theme of then–HUD secretary Jack Kemp.

Close examination of the budgetary outlays from the McKinney Act reveals, however, that relatively little has gone to the provision of permanent low-income housing. Much of it is targeted toward other purposes and populations. In 1987, to illustrate, a total of $80 million was appropriated for the supportive housing program. Of that $80 million, $20 million went to transitional housing for homeless families, not to permanent low-cost housing. In 1988, $100 million was authorized for the program but only $65 million was appropriated and of that, $20 million was again for transitional, not permanent housing. As is apparent in the budgetary outlays, most of the McKinney housing money has been spent in marginal ameliorations of the worst aspects of the housing situation of the homeless (shelters, SROs, transitional programs, etc.); very little is invested in adding permanent units to the low-income housing supply (Rubin et al. 1992).

FEDERAL HOUSING POLICY

Despite the self-congratulatory claims of Ferraro and others, the homelessness problem worsened in the 1980s and the federal response did very little to dampen the trend. While some monies were being spent on low-income housing and on programs specifically for the homeless, the broader housing policies of the Reagan-Bush years easily undid what good these programs might otherwise have accomplished.

In brief, housing policy in the 1980s was two-pronged: tax subsidies to underwrite the housing costs of upper income groups (mainly through the provision of the tax code that allows homeowners to deduct mortgage interest and property tax payments) and a largely unrestricted private market for lower-income groups. This approach to housing policy was ideologically consistent with the overall Reagan-Bush agenda of deregulation, privatization, and liberation of the "invisible hand," as was the evident consequence: the institutionalization of the private market as the solution to an inadequate low-income housing supply.

Sadly, the private market has few if any incentives to provide low-income housing; there is much more money to be made in housing the affluent than in housing the poor. Privatizing the low-income housing market means in essence that the federal government has abnegated its responsibility to guarantee to all citizens a minimum standard of housing adequacy.

Part of Reagan's reluctance to provide housing to the homeless stemmed from his well-known belief that many homeless people are homeless by choice. A related theme in the administration was that housing conditions reflect cultural problems or preferences specific to certain ethnic groups. Regarding the doubling-up that is associated with a housing squeeze (Mutchler and Krivo 1989), Philip Abrams of HUD suggested that it is "characteristic of Hispanic communities, irrelevant to their social and economic conditions . . . . It is a cultural preference, I am told" (quoted in Momeni 1990:136). Even if true, which is unlikely, the relevance of this comment is uncertain since Hispanics comprise well less than a twentieth of the total homeless population.

IF NOT HOUSING, WHAT?

The question whether homelessness is "really" a housing problem is perhaps best approached by asking, If homelessness is not a housing problem, then what kind of problem might it be? Most observers agree that the number of homeless people in the cities increased significantly in the 1980s. What besides a dwindling low-income housing supply would suffice to account for the trend? Even if one concluded that homelessness is not *just* a housing problem, there seems little doubt that inadequate low-cost housing must have had something to do with the problem, and it is useful to ask just what that something is.

Superficially, the answer to the question whether homelessness is a housing problem is both clearly yes and obviously no. On the one hand, homeless people, by definition, lack acceptable, customary housing and must sleep in the streets, double up with friends and family, or avail themselves of temporary overnight shelter. The lack of acceptable housing, in short, is implied in the very definition of homelessness. On the other hand, one can argue that housing is not the real problem since there is plenty of housing to go around. The problem, rather, is that homeless people cannot afford the housing that is otherwise available to people of sufficient means (Heatherly and Pines 1989). In this sense, homelessness is not a housing problem but a money problem; the root causes are poverty, unemployment and underemployment, inadequate wages, and the insufficient income provisions of the welfare state (Rossi 1989, 1990).

It is, of course, foolish to pose the question in these either-or terms. The more useful question concerns the intersection of housing and economics and can be phrased thus: To what extent is the problem of homelessness caused by an insufficient supply of housing of the sort that homeless people need and could afford to live in?

Housing and money are by no means the only problems homeless people face. Many are mentally ill, many more are chemically dependent, some are physically disabled, most are profoundly estranged from family and friends. These disabilities are of critical importance in specifying exactly what kind of housing problem homelessness is, but they do not negate the principal conclusion, that the fundamental need is for housing.

The 1980s witnessed an impressive outpouring of research on who the homeless are, how they got to be homeless, and what could or should be done to help. This research (summarized in Chapter 1) has pointed to three common characteristics of homeless people: extreme poverty, high rates of personal disability, and high levels of familial and social estrangement. Does acknowledgement of these facts therefore suggest that homelessness is *not* a housing problem, but rather a poverty problem, a disabilities problem, and an estrangement problem? Surely not: rather, these facts explain *why* homelessness is a housing problem at its very core.

Consider first the now commonplace research finding that homeless people are often estranged from family and friends (see also Chapter 5). The housing implication of this fact is that they are rarely able to draw on kin and friend networks to sustain them through periods of social, economic, or psychological crisis. Most people who found themselves in a near-homeless or proto-homeless condition would have people to whom they could turn to help them "get back on their feet." In general, this is a resource that homeless people lack.

The estrangement problem is of two very different sorts, the two sorts well-illustrated in certain findings from Rossi's survey of the homeless in Chicago. Homeless persons in that survey were asked whether they would like to return to their families, and if so, whether they thought their families would take them in. In general, the men said they would like to return but knew they would not be welcome; the women had no wish to return in the first place. Thus, the estranged are either family rejects who have exhausted the patience or resources of their kin networks, or family leavers fleeing a domestic situation so troubling and so abusive that life on the streets becomes the preferred alternative. (We discuss still other forms of familial estrangement in the next chapter.)

Many of the family rejects, of course, have been expelled because of their alcohol and drug abuse or because of other personal problems (chronic unemployment, troubles with the law, etc.) If their rejection is not to lead to homelessness, then their need is for rooming or boarding houses (or SRO rooms) appropriate to single individuals of limited means. Absent a sufficient supply of such units, they end up on the streets. The family leavers have different housing needs: sanctuaries, battered women's programs, halfway houses, and transitional programs, all coupled with social and psychological services to address their troubled histories.

The role that family and kin networks play in housing the poor is not usually appreciated. Data from the city of Chicago provide an illustration. There are approximately 100,000 general assistance recipients in the city. Most are single, unaffiliated, nonwhite males—in short, extremely poor persons who do not qualify for AFDC, Supplemental Security Income (SSI), Social Security Disability Insurance (SSDI), or other forms of welfare. A study of general assistance recipients by Stagner and Richman found that half resided with family or friends; absent this housing assistance, as many as 50,000 additional Chicagoans could well be homeless (Stagner and Richman 1985). Given this result, the surprise is not that there are so many homeless people but that there are so few.

Likewise, the high rates of mental illness and substance abuse among the homeless indicate that many mentally ill and substance-abusive people have unique, specialized housing needs that are not being adequately addressed, and they are therefore homeless. Obviously, the housing needs of mentally ill or substance-abusive homeless people are very different from the housing needs of other homeless persons or of the poor in general. But to say that these groups have unique or specialized housing needs does not refute the viewpoint that homelessness is a housing problem; it merely helps to specify what kind of housing problem it is.

SKID ROW

Estranged, impoverished, and otherwise defective homeless men and women have existed in all times and places throughout American history; this aspect of the larger homeless problem is scarcely new. In times past, however, most urban areas contained a social system that provided for their housing and other needs, the system called skid row. Skid row areas, of course, continue to exist; indeed, it is one of the places where the homeless tend to concentrate in most cities. But if skid row areas continue to exist, the skid row social system has all but disappeared, and this has posed a formidable housing problem for the homeless alcoholic, drug abusive, or mentally ill poor (Hoch and Slayton 1989).

There were many significant elements to the old skid row social system, but two are of particular interest: the flophouses, rooming houses, missions, and such that provided extremely cheap housing to the skid row population, and the day labor outlets that provided casual employment. The employment provided through day labor outlets was largely unskilled work; loading and unloading trucks, trains, and boats was perhaps the most common. And the income to be earned through such work was also minimal. At the same time, the flops were extremely cheap, and cheap meals were also widely available. In those times and in this particular social system, one could pick up a dollar or two a day working at casual labor, and, more to the point, get by on a dollar or two a day. It was unquestionably a poverty existence, but it provided some level of nutrition and housing, even for the impoverished, the psychiatrically impaired, and the alcohol-dependent.

The SRO hotels and the flophouses, of course, have largely disappeared, victims of urban renewal, gentrification, and the "revitalization" of downtown. Hartman and Zigas estimate that these processes have resulted in a loss of over a million units of SRO housing in the past two decades (Hartman and Zigas 1989; see also Kasinitz 1984; Huttman 1989). Some of the city-by-city figures are of interest: In San Francisco, 18% of the existing SRO units were destroyed or converted in a four-year period in the late 1970s, with further losses since. Similarly, in New York City there was an overall 60% loss of SRO hotel rooms between 1975 and 1981. The number of New York hotels charging less than $50 per week declined from 298 to 131 in that period; of those dropping out of the price range, the majority are no longer even hotels and have been converted to other uses, mainly to condominiums. Denver lost 29 of its 45 SRO hotels between 1971 and 1981, Seattle lost 15,000 units of SRO housing from 1960 to 1981, and San Diego lost 1,247 units between 1976 and 1984 (Hoch and

Slayton 1989:175). The loss of SRO housing was described as "a nation-wide trend" even in the late 1970s (Special Committee on Aging 1978), a trend that has doubtlessly accelerated since.

With the loss of the flophouses has also come the disappearance of day labor outlets. Most of the work once done in this fashion has been mechanized; many hundreds of thousands of day labor opportunities were wiped out by the invention and widespread adoption of the forklift truck, containerized shipping, and, of course, the unions. The unionization of the construction and stevedore industries in particular has made day labor in these sectors obsolete. The function formerly served by the day labor outlets has been assumed by large "temporary help" corporations such as Manpower. These are sanitized temporary help outlets located far from the skid row areas; they are no longer part of the skid row social system, at least not in most North American cities.

Thus, the flops and the SROs of skid row are largely gone, their housing function having been taken over by the large temporary overnight shelters that now exist in nearly every city. Opportunities for casual day labor are also largely gone, the income function of casual labor having been replaced by scavenging from trash cans and by panhandling. The social system of skid row, in short, has been replaced by the disorganized existence of homelessness, and nowhere has this been more problematic than among the alcoholic, the drug-abusive, and the mentally impaired. With the "housing of last resort" now decimated, the disabled poor—at least, many of them—end up living literally in the streets.

POVERTY AND LOW-INCOME HOUSING:
THE LEGACY OF THE 1980s

On average, the homeless are extremely poor, so poor that the poverty line would represent a standard of affluence to many of them. Thus, even if we could successfully stabilize the mentally ill homeless, adequately treat the alcoholic and drug-addicted homeless, or reintegrate the estranged homeless with their families and friends, in most cases they would still be poor. And, as poor people, they would then face the same housing problem that all poor people face: namely, an insufficient and dwindling supply of low-income housing. This is the ultimate sense in which homelessness is a housing problem: namely, that there is not enough cheap housing to go around.

That low-income housing was disappearing was fairly obvious even early in the 1980s (Wright and Lam 1987) and has become even more obvious since. A comparison of the number of units renting for less than $250 a month (30% of a $10,000 annual income) and the number of households with annual incomes under $10,000 reveals that in 1985 there were 4 million fewer units than renter households needing units, with the discrepancy between the number of poor families and the number of very low–income rental units evident in every state. The shortage was lowest in West Virginia (11%), highest in California (268%), and nationwide stood at 94%. By the mid-1980s, in other words, there were very nearly twice as many very low-income renter households as there were low-cost units to accommodate them. The decade that has transpired since has witnessed no improvement but rather further deterioration in the low-income housing supply; one recent compilation of relevant data on the point can be found in Timmer, Eitzen, and Talley (1994).

The actual housing situation is no doubt worse than even these grim figures suggest. The count of very low–income units given in the previous paragraph apparently contains as many as 800,000 vacancies, nearly 20% of the total supply (Hartman and Zigas 1989). Among other things, high vacancy rates often indicate inadequate living conditions; many of these units are vacant because they have been condemned. The number of truly livable low-income housing units available in the market is apparently not known, but is surely less than the total units tallied above.

Despite the evident gap between need and supply, HUD funding levels for subsidized housing assistance declined sharply from 1980 to 1989. In 1980, the funding for this purpose stood at $26.6 billion, and in 1989, $7.4 billion. In recent years, the number of additional families receiving assistance has been less than 100,000 per annum, despite a poverty population around 40 million. In contrast to frequent claims that HUD played a major role in solving the housing crisis through an infusion of funds into the system, HUD officials have indicated that they are "backing out of the business of housing" (ACCESS 1990). The hope among many advocates for the homeless, that the Clinton administration would reverse these trends, has gone unrealized.

These recent downward trends in the federal obligation to subsidize the construction of low-income housing reverse a historical commitment dating to 1937, when the government undertook its first public housing program (Hartman and Zigas 1989; Levitan 1985). The 1937 program provided federal subsidies to amortize the cost of building low-cost housing, was administered by local housing boards, and was highly restrictive in eligibility. The Housing Act of 1949 established a national goal of upgrading and augmenting the general housing stock so that every American would have a "decent home and suitable living environment." Throughout much of the postwar period, the housing industry was highly productive, the concern over "inadequate housing" referred to the quality, not quantity, of available units, and the number of relatively affordable suburban single-family units steadily increased.

The Housing Act of 1968 set a goal of 26 million new units over the next decade, 6 million of them targeted to low-income households (Hartman and Zigas 1989:8). The goal was not met; thereafter the government refrained from setting specific numerical housing goals. The 1980s witnessed lowered housing production levels across the board and a sharp diminution in the federal low-income housing effort. To be sure, national housing policy has always been market determined, and that has always worked fairly well for moderate- to upper-income groups. That the market does not work particularly well for lower-income groups has been recognized in federal housing policy since the depression. This half-century of recognition notwithstanding, during the Reagan and Bush administrations, housing policy for the poor was market-based with a vengeance, much to the overall detriment of the low-income housing supply.

What happened to the low-income housing stock? A market- based policy implies that the private sector will invest in options that generate the most profit in the shortest time. The essential "high-profit" housing developments of the 1980s were abandonment, arson, gentrification, conversion, and displacement. Despite the growing poverty population and the enhanced need for low-income housing, the decade witnessed considerable loss of low-income housing through arson and abandonment, outright destruction through urban renewal and downtown "revitalization," and a great deal more conversion of low-income to upper-income units through the process of gentrification (Carliner 1987; Dolbeare 1988; Hope and Young 1986; Lang 1989). In general, "demolition, rehabilitation, abandonment, and condominium conversion have lessened the number of low-rent housing units in most major cities" (Huttman 1989).

Throughout the 1980s and 1990s, gentrification has resulted in a dramatic decline in housing for society's most impoverished citizens. Gentrification inverts the normal flow of housing (Carliner 1987:121–22). The classical model of housing "replacement" suggests that as more affluent families expand into new housing in previously undeveloped areas, they abandon older housing, which then becomes available to the poor. This can be fairly called the trickle-down theory of low-income housing. With increased numbers of affluent households seeking older, urban housing to renovate, however, the "trickling" process reverses and fewer low-income units are the result. Some estimate that gentrification and related processes resulted in a loss of over a million SRO units in the 1970s and 1980s (Hartman and Zigas 1989:6).

As we have already stated, SROs have always served as the "housing of last resort" for the most marginal members of the urban poverty population (Kasinitz 1984; Hoch and Slayton 1989; Huttman 1989). Despite the evident need for housing of this general sort, the SROs continue to decline. While these forms of housing are less than pleasant, their loss, as we indicated several pages above, has been considerable, as have the consequences. Ironically, in one city, 1,800 SRO units were converted for temporary use by the city's Department of Social Services. Huttman also reports that in some instances SROs have been converted to upscale tourist hotels or to expensive apartment buildings.

Unfortunately, the destruction of SROs is only part of a larger process of displacement. Based on data from the Annual Housing Survey, Huttman estimates that somewhere between 1.7 and 2.4 million persons are being displaced annually through outright destruction of units. Razed units are predominantly low-income units; replacement units frequently are not. For example, in 1987 there were 346,500 new apartments built nationwide. Of these, only 23,900 (7%) rented for less than $350 a month. The median rent for new units constructed in 1987 was nearly $550 per month, well beyond the reach of low-income families and hopelessly beyond the reach of the homeless poor.

Another part of the displacement process is condominium conversion. From 1970 to 1979, about 370,000 low-income units were converted to condominia, a trend that surely continued into the 1980s and since. Conversion to condominia usually doubles the rent and about two-thirds of the previous occupants of converted units move out (Hope and Young 1986:107).

Thus, downtown "revitalization" has been a mixed blessing. On the one hand, the razing of rotted urban slums and their replacement by attractive boutiques, elegant restaurants, up-scale condominiums, and the like are positive developments, as is the ensuing increase in the urban tax base. At the same time, these processes have displaced large sectors of the poverty population and have destroyed much low-income housing. With few federal funds to subsidize replacement of lost low-income units, many of the displaced are permanently displaced, which is to say, homeless.

It is, of course, true that the federal government continues to subsidize the housing costs of the poor, mainly through the Section 8 housing voucher program. In order to qualify as a Section 8 unit, an apartment must rent for less than a designated "fair market value." At the same time, to prevent obvious abuses, the unit must also meet certain housing quality standards. Landlords providing such units receive what amounts to a guaranteed clientele whose rents are being paid by the federal government. In theory, Section 8 enhances the housing purchasing power (housing demand) of the poor and this should in turn cause landlords to increase the supply of eligible low-rent units, either via new construction or through renovation of existing units to bring them up to the mandated quality standards.

Perhaps the most serious problem with the Section 8 program is that the housing vouchers are not entitlements given to every qualifying family; there are a limited number of vouchers available each year and they are given mainly to AFDC recipients. Thus, only about a tenth of the poverty population is actually subsidized via Section 8. It is possible that more complete coverage of the poverty population would appreciably enhance the demand for low-income housing and thus elicit the necessary supply, but this has clearly not happened with the existing level of coverage. As matters stand, apartments good enough to satisfy the quality standard but cheap enough to satisfy the rent standard are few and far between, and nearly half the households who receive a Section 8 voucher in any given year must return it unused because an acceptable unit cannot be found.

With the supply of low-income housing continuing to shrink and the need continuing to grow, it is not surprising that the waiting lists for public housing have become prohibitively long. The U.S. Conference of Mayors recently surveyed public housing waiting lists in 27 large cities. The average waiting time from application to occupancy of a subsidized unit was 22 months. In Chicago, the average applicant will wait 10 years for a unit; in Washington, D.C., 8 years; in New York, 17 years; in Miami, 20 years (Daly 1989). The Conference of Mayor's survey also showed that waiting lists for assisted housing had been closed in 65% of the surveyed cities due to excess demand.

Although not commonly appreciated, federal subsidies for middle- and upper-middle-class housing actually dwarf the federal low-income housing subsidy. The major subsidy for the housing costs of the middle class is the tax provision that allows homeowners to write off mortgage interest from their taxable incomes. The 1986 tax reform act ruled out mortgage interest deductions for anything other than a person's primary residence, but this provision was easily circumvented by financing second or even third homes (and many other things as well) through negotiated remortgaging of the primary residence, the so-called "equity loans" that have become so popular.

Dolbeare (1988) has estimated that various homeowner tax deductions cost the federal treasury more in two years than the total federal outlay for subsidized low-income housing has cost over 50 years. Federal expenditures on low-income housing including public housing operating subsidies from 1937 through the 1987 fiscal year totaled $97 billion. In 1986 and 1987, the revenue lost through various homeowner tax deductions amounted to $102 billion.

Tucker (1987) has argued that rent control in many cities has depressed the supply of low-rent units and has therefore contributed to the homelessness problem. His evidence consists of a modest statistical correlation between the estimated number of homeless in a city and whether the city exercises rent control. It is rather difficult to take this analysis very seriously. First, the number of homeless people is not known with sufficient precision in any city to allow a compelling test of the hypothesis. Available estimates of the number of homeless frequently vary by an order of magnitude. Also, the analysis is strictly bivariate, with no possible confounding factors taken into account. It is a plausible surmise that artificially low rents depress the motivation to build new units and thus depress the low-income housing supply; it is also possible that rent control keeps housing within the means of persons and families who would otherwise be on the streets. Probably both processes occur simultaneously, but the evidence necessary to test for such effects is simply not available.

FINAL THOUGHTS ON POVERTY AND HOUSING

The general trend of the 1980s was more poor people competing for less low-income housing, a trend noted and remarked upon by many dozens of observers. The result has been a serious low-income housing "squeeze." According to Dolbeare, there were two low-income units for each low-income household in 1970, and two low-income households for each low-income unit in 1983. In 1975, about 4 million low-income renters paid more than 30% of their incomes for rent; in 1983, 16 million low-income renters paid more than 30% of their incomes for rent (Nelson 1990); in 1993, the figure had risen to nearly 70% of the total poverty population.

Most rental housing in the urban areas has come to be priced well beyond the means of the poor. But even poor people have to live somewhere and, increasingly, somewhere has meant on the streets. In the first instance, then, homelessness is unquestionably a housing problem in that the loss of low-income housing and the gain in the urban poverty population have created a situation where some are destined to be without housing. The implication is that we would face a formidable homelessness problem today even in the complete absence of mental illness, alco-hol and drug abuse, and all the other disabling conditions to which the homeless are prone.

As we suggested earlier, asking if homelessness is a housing problem is rather like asking whether bad luck is why people lose their money in Las Vegas. It is obvious that bad luck or insufficient skill cause some people to lose; likewise, good luck and skill are why some win. But the laws of probability and the rules of the game ensure that someone must lose, and indeed that the losers must outnumber the winners. That there must be more losers than winners has nothing to do with luck or skill; it is the rule by which the game itself is played.

And so too with homelessness. Recent trends in the poverty rate, in the concentration of the poor in the central cities, and in the low-income housing supply have created an urban housing "game" that some are destined to lose. Who in fact loses—given that some must lose—is an entirely separate issue, and we should not be surprised to learn that the losers in the housing game turn out to be the most disadvantaged and debilitated sectors of the poverty population: the mentally impaired, the physically disabled, the substance-abusive, the disaffiliated, and the estranged.

Is homelessness just a housing problem? Certainly not. There is a long list of contributing and complicating factors that we have discussed in order to specify just what the nature of the housing problem is. Still, an inadequate supply of low-income housing provides the backdrop against which these many other factors unfold. With a large and growing urban poverty population and an inadequate and shrinking supply of low-cost housing, the problem is destined to worsen and only more housing will make the final difference. Rephrased, if our goal is only to repair defective souls, housing need not concern us very much. If, on the other hand, our aim is to be rid of the condition of homelessness once and for all, then housing must concern us above all other things.

5

Families and Family Estrangement

Families are relevant to the story of American homelessness in the 1990s in a number of different ways. First, the concept of "homeless families" has been made to carry a great deal of political and symbolic weight. It is regularly asserted, for example, that homeless families are the fastest growing segment of the homeless population—an assertion frequently uttered but not frequently researched. Second, as we have suggested in numerous prior passages, estrangement from family is evidently an important part of the process by which people become homeless. These, then, are the topics of the present chapter: Who are these homeless families about whom so much has been written? And just what is the nature of the relationship between familial estrangement and homelessness?

HOMELESS FAMILIES

The rhetorical value of the concept of "homeless families" is easy to appreciate. "Home" and "family" are closely intertwined in our collective sensibility; families should have homes, and homes should contain families. Even the U.S. Census defines a family in part by the existence of a shared dwelling unit. The intimate connections between our concepts of "home" and "family" make the very notion of a "homeless family" especially anachronistic and therefore offensive. Broken-down skid row drunks and muttering schizophrenics are one thing, but homeless families are something else again. Is there anyone so mean-spirited that they would deny assistance or at least sympathy to a homeless family?

Just as Baum and Burnes have questioned the emphasis of many advocates on housing as a root cause of homelessness, the sociologist Dan

McMurry has also purported to expose the notion of homeless families as a myth created by myopic advocates and sentimental academics seeking to romanticize the homelessness issue. McMurry also joins with Baum and Burnes in his relentless hostility to Wright's previous work; see his review (1990) of *Address Unknown*: "a disappointment," "crippled by emotional baggage," and—our personal favorite—"Wright comes across as an empirical Mr. Rogers."

The essential observation from which McMurry's thesis derives is that intact husband-wife couples with dependent children in their care are very rarely found among the homeless. Indeed, most of the people to whom we refer as homeless families are actually single women with children, not husband-wife pairs. Usually, they are poor, inner-city, African-American women with children, which seems to add considerably to McMurry's indignation.

McMurry's thesis, articulated in an article in *Reader's Digest* (Bidinotto 1991), is that we (myopic advocates and sentimental academics such as ourselves) misleadingly call these people homeless "families" in order to create sympathy for them that they do not really deserve. And when we describe homeless "families" as the "fastest growing subgroup" within the larger homeless population, we also create more sympathy for the issue of homelessness than it deserves.

We acknowledge that most "homeless families" are indeed homeless single women with dependent children. One does occasionally encounter intact husband-wife-children family units among the homeless but they are relatively rare. In the alcohol and drug treatment program that we ran for homeless people in New Orleans, fewer than a tenth of the homeless families we dealt with were intact husband-wife pairs (with or without dependent children); the remaining nine-tenths were homeless women with kids. To our knowledge, no study reports a proportion of intact married couples among homeless families much higher than about 10%. So, yes, the large majority of homeless families are unmarried women with children.

Many people seem to be surprised by this fact and, like Dan McMurry, more than a little annoyed that they have somehow been misled by the homeless family "myth." But what is the difference between the mythical homeless family (toward which sympathy may be appropriately expressed) and the real homeless family (which, we gather, may be treated with contempt)? The principal difference is that in the latter case, we are talking about homeless women with children and in the former, about homeless women with husbands and children. Stripped to its essential core, McMurry's argument seems to be that it is OK to be sympathetic if there's a husband in the picture but otherwise not.

Since an intact husband-wife pair would seemingly have more resources upon which to draw than a single mother would have, and since
(therefore) we might normally be inclined to show more sympathy toward the latter than the former, the logic of the argument requires some
explication. It seems that the difference is mainly this:

If Mom, Dad, and the kids are all out on the streets and homeless, it
must be the result of some terrible misfortune that has befallen the male
breadwinner. Men, that is, should be sufficiently empowered to prevent
homelessness among their women and children, and when they cannot, it
is a pity.

If on the other hand it is just a mother with children and no husband in
sight, then the children must be the product of sexual promiscuity and
their homelessness must be the consequence of irresponsible women
bearing children they cannot support. To show pity would, perforce,
encourage behavior of which we disapprove; these women, that is, deserve to be homeless because they have had the audacity to bear children
without benefit of male partners.

Now, in fairness to McMurry and others of his ilk, when dewy-eyed
advocates for the homeless refer to homeless "families," the image they
hope to create is assuredly not that of unmarried, welfare-dependent,
crack-addicted teenaged women who are living in the streets with their
children because they use their AFDC payments to buy drugs rather than
pay rent. And there are very definitely more young girls of this description among the category of homeless families than there are intact
husband-wife pairs—of that, one may be certain. At the same time, anyone who is truly surprised that large numbers of single young women
with children have appeared among the ranks of the homeless can only
be described as innocent of recent trends in poverty in America, chief
among those trends being the so-called feminization of poverty about
which analysts and researchers have been writing for the last 30 years.

The essential facts are these:

1. The overall poverty rate in the U.S. population as a whole these
    days is right around 14–15%.
2. Among all families regardless of race or head of household status,
    the poverty rate is somewhat lower, right around a tenth; thus, the
    poverty rate is higher among unrelated individuals than among
    families.
3. Among *intact* husband-wife families, the poverty rate is only about
    half that of all families, i.e., about 1 in 20 instead of 1 in 10.
4. Among families *headed by women* (that is to say, among women
    with children but no husbands), the poverty rate is approximately

one in three and among families headed by black women, it is a bit more than one in two.

Thus we see that the poverty rate among female-headed households (regardless of race) is about five or six times the rate among intact husband-wife households. Women heading their own families confront a sharply elevated risk of being in poverty and, therefore, an equally elevated risk of anything that is associated with being in poverty, and that definitely includes being homeless. Most homeless families turn out to be husbandless women with children for the very simple reason that most poor families are also husbandless women with children.

It is easy to explain why female-headed households are grossly overrepresented among the poverty population, and thus among the homeless population. First, in an economy where family affluence often depends on the contributions of multiple wage earners, families with only a single potential wage earner are at an obvious and severe disadvantage. Women on their own, by definition, survive on a single income; most husband-wife pairs these days have two incomes to keep them out of poverty and off the streets—a powerful safeguard. Compounding the problem, wage rates for women average only about 65% of the wage rates of men; women remain heavily concentrated in traditionally low-paying "female" sectors of the labor force.

Many women with children have never been married; indeed, more than half the nonwhite babies born this year will be born to unmarried mothers. As we have already suggested, this fact seems to fuel some of Dan McMurry's rage against homeless women with kids. But married or not, these women do not get pregnant without the active complicity of male partners, and the most recent national study we have seen of the topic suggests that fewer than 4% of the unmarried fathers of these babies pay any child support at all. Even more disturbing is that only about a third of the mothers who *have* been married receive child support payments; nonpayment of child support by absent fathers is a national disgrace. In no small measure, the feminization of poverty (and of homelessness) is the result of abandonment by males.

A final factor in the feminization of poverty is that the real purchasing power of AFDC and most other welfare payments has been approximately halved by the inflation of the last three decades (Rossi 1989), in many states—Louisiana, for example—the average monthly AFDC payment is less than $200.

The net result of factors just enumerated is that women with dependent children (i.e., female-headed households) suffer from sharply elevated poverty rates—rates some five or more times the rate among intact husband-wife families. With the dismantling of AFDC, this situation will only worsen. Inevitably then, the risk of joining the homeless increases considerably and these women come to be sharply overrepresented among the homeless population. All of this is well-known to poverty specialists and has been for decades. So it is hard to see the sense in which any of it could be described as "myth."

As the material in the previous chapter has shown, the poor suffered mightily in the 1980s, and despite the general economic recovery in the early years of the Clinton administration, the 1990s have not been any better. The national poverty rate went up to 15.2% in 1993, which translates into just about 40 million Americans at or below the poverty line; the rate dropped somewhat, to 13.8%, in 1995. Poverty rates throughout the 1980s were generally higher than they had been in the 1970s, and the rates in the 1990s, so far, have been higher still. Is there any reason to expect that women were somehow exempt from these trends or from their consequences? And if not, then why would one be surprised or angered to learn that "homeless families" usually means homeless women with kids? It could scarcely be otherwise.

As the poverty of the central cities has deepened, the resources available to women and children from their family, kin, and social networks have also apparently declined. In decades past, it seems that most poor women with children had someone to whom they could turn in times of crisis to help them weather the storm and get back on their feet. This no longer appears to be true. The families and friends of the poor are also poor; many could not provide assistance even if they were otherwise inclined to do so. So imagine, if you will, a poor, black, young inner-city mother with a child or two, who is faced with an unexpected emergency, say, an unanticipated medical expense or an unforeseen repair bill. Eviction for nonpayment of rent is imminent. Where will this woman turn for the few hundred dollars she needs to keep herself and her children from becoming homeless?

Not to her family and friends. They too are poor and getting poorer and could not provide much help even if they wanted to. (As we see later, they also may not want to.) Certainly not to the labor force: Rates of unemployment in the central cities routinely approach or exceed 50%, and the few jobs that are available pay a minimum wage that will barely cover the cost of child care. Surely not to the children's father, who may only be a hypothesis in any case. And not to AFDC: Even when AFDC was an operative program, the average AFDC payment in most states would not even cover the cost of rent, much less the rent plus whatever emergency had put this woman into her current situation. Now that the Clinton administration has ended AFDC as a long-term solution to family poverty, the options are even fewer.

So what alternatives to homelessness are open to this woman? Prostitution? Thievery? Drug dealing? We might wish—along with Dan McMurry—that all these poor women would get jobs, get husbands, get sober, get a nice little house in the suburbs, get out from underfoot. Alas, that is not the world in which we live. Here in the real world, they get to be homeless.

There are roughly 4 million female-headed households below the poverty line in the United States today. Counting both the mothers and their children, this amounts to about 12 million persons living in poverty households headed by women. No one knows for sure just how many homeless people there are in the country at any given moment; let's say a million and let it go at that. And of these, about a quarter are women and children. So by these assumptions, the total number of homeless women and children on any given day would not be more than, say, 250,000 or so, this from a population at risk that numbers about 12 million. Thus, nearly *all* poor women with children find some way to avoid being homeless in spite of what must be considered rather long odds; it would be a useful contribution to learn more about how they actually do this.

FAMILY BACKGROUNDS AND FAMILIAL ESTRANGEMENT

One would expect families to play a critical role in helping impoverished or otherwise marginal persons maintain their hold on housing. There are people who simply do not have any living family members, but most people have parents, siblings, children, aunts, uncles, cousins, or other kin to whom they could turn in times of crisis or need. It therefore comes as no surprise that estrangement from families and other social networks tends to be a distinguishing feature of the homeless. If these people retained functioning kin networks, then presumably their networks would take them in and, perforce, they would not be homeless. Thus, the process of becoming homeless and the process of becoming familyless must be more or less the same process.

Most research on familial estrangement among the homeless has focused on the adult years. It is regularly reported, for example, that many homeless adults have never married and that divorce and separation are common among those who have, that many homeless adults have long since lost touch with any children they may have had, and that contact with parents, siblings, or other family members is infrequent, nonexistent, or troubled. Since the material we present later is derived from the NOHSAP sample, it is also worth noting that we would expect all these things to be even worse among the substance-abusive homeless than among others. As a matter of fact, we would probably assume that substance abuse itself is one major reason why the families of homeless people frequently want nothing further to do with them. Indeed, it is an explicit theme of critics such as Baum and Burnes that substance abuse causes homelessness via its direct effects on family estrangement.

The familial estrangement so evident among homeless adults, however, frequently has roots in family dysfunctions that date to the earliest childhood years, i.e., that have nothing at all to do with the behaviors of homeless adults. For example, a remarkably high percentage of homeless adults report having been reared in "broken homes," by single parents, by stepparents, in foster homes, or in institutional settings (e.g., Sosin et al. 1990); reports of physical, sexual, and emotional abuse as children are widespread, especially among homeless women (e.g., Burroughs, Bouma, O'Connor, and Smith 1990). In a deep sense, many homeless adults have been literally homeless and familyless since birth. Familial estrangement is less a disability that befalls young adults than a process of family dysfunction and isolation that can be traced to early childhood in many cases. Contrary to a common presupposition, family estrangement among the homeless is *not* an adult onset disorder.

Consistent with findings from many other studies, the NOHSAP sample (introduced initially in Chapter 3) displays a remarkable degree of current isolation and estrangement from family. Despite an average age in the 30s, more than half the sample (56%) have never married, fewer than a tenth (9%) are currently married, and the remainder are divorced or separated (or, for about 1%, widowed). Marital status is approximately the same for both men and women. Thus, the principal affinity attachment for most adults in this society—the family of procreation—is essentially missing for the vast majority of this sample. (The *family of procreation* is the family formed when persons marry; the *family of origin* is the family into which people are born.) Also of some interest, despite the marital status, the large majority have had children (69% of the men, 87% of the women). Most of the women who have had children report fairly regular contact with them (71% say they have "a lot" of contact with their children), but the same is true of only a minority of the fathers (43%). Thus, homeless adults of both genders are estranged from adult partners; homeless men are estranged even from their own children.

Some indication of estrangement from families of origin can be obtained from data on living arrangements prior to the first episode of homelessness. (It should be kept in mind that this "first episode" is also the current episode of homelessness for the majority of the NOHSAP sample.) Slightly more than a tenth of the respondents (13%) were living on their own just prior to the first experience of homelessness, another third (32%) were living with spouses or "quasi-spouse," and a handful (5%) were living with friends. Thus, about half were living either with a parent (36%) or with other relatives (14%). Given the average ages (low 30s) and the recency of the first homelessness episode for most of the sample, it is obvious that many of our respondents were dependent adults, largely unemployed and with significant substance abuse problems, who were domiciled rather than homeless at the time they first became homeless principally because of the generosity of their families of origin toward them. Once resources or patience wear thin, the ties of familial obligation or generosity are severed and another case of homelessness appears on the streets. Estrangement from the family of origin is evidently quite significant in the process by which at least half of our respondents became homeless in the first place.

The experiences of men and women differ in this connection, although the general patterns are similar. The women in the sample were less likely than the men to be living alone prior to the first homelessness episode (5 and 15%, respectively) and more likely to be living with a spouse (40 and 30%, respectively). For both groups but especially for the women, then, marital dissolution as well as estrangement from the family of origin is also part of the process of becoming homeless. Many of the women who were living with a spouse (or "quasi-spouse") prior to first becoming homeless no doubt became homeless "by choice," that is, came to prefer life on the streets over their abusive and otherwise unsatisfactory domestic situation. Many of the men, we suspect, were simply kicked out by their spouses (just as many of the men who were living within the families of origin were kicked out by their parents).

There are some useful details that can be added to the general portrait of isolation and social disaffiliation. The large majority of our respondents (75% of the men and 66% of the women) received no financial support or assistance from family or friends. Proportions on the order of 40% report having had significant problems in their relationship with their mothers, fathers, stepparents, and siblings at some point over the lifetime, and more than half (55%) report having had serious problems in their relationships with spouses or sexual partners. In the majority of cases, those reporting any "relationship" problems over the lifetime also report that those problems are ongoing and current.

Obviously, these data are not sufficient to decide whether people in the NOHSAP sample are estranged from their families (of origin or procreation) because they are homeless and drug-addicted, or whether they are homeless and drug-addicted because they are estranged from their families. Doubtlessly, both processes must operate to some extent; as we said earlier, the process of becoming homeless and that of becoming familyless must be largely the same. But whatever the pathways of cause and effect, it is clear that most homeless adults survive without benefit of the family networks of nurturance and support that most other people can fall back on to sustain them through periods of personal crisis.

In the respects so far discussed, our sample of substance-abusive homeless people in New Orleans differs little from the general homeless population; patterns of familial isolation, disaffiliation, and estrangement quite similar to those reported above are also routinely reported in nearly every published study of homeless people. And as we have also suggested, this could scarcely be otherwise: If homeless people were not estranged from familial networks, then their families would presumably take them in and there would be no reason for them to be homeless in the first place.

It is a mistake, however, to conclude from these commonplace findings that familial estrangement is a misfortune that befalls young adults and that eventuates in their becoming homeless. The emphasis on familial disaffiliation among the adult homeless suggests—incorrectly—that many of these unfortunate souls spent their early years in the context of a stable, supportive, nurturing home environment, that their ties to that environment were later disrupted (whether through periods of dependency, unemployment, alcohol and drug problems, or troubles with the law), and that as a consequence of that disruption, they ended up on the streets. The actual pattern observed in our results is that the process of disaffiliation and estrangement stretches back into the early childhood years, and thus that the "final break" that puts someone on the streets is less a disruption in an otherwise placid family situation than the culmination of a lifelong process.

The NOHSAP interview protocol contained a number of questions about respondents' family situations "when you were growing up," that is to say, during the formative childhood years. A slim majority (53%) report that the family of their early childhood consisted of both natural parents, of which we have more to say later. Thus, nearly half (47%) grew up in something other than the conventional mother-father-child family structure. The next largest group, comprising 22%, was raised by a single parent, the mother in almost all cases; another 12% were raised by a single natural parent and a stepparent. About a tenth (9%) were raised by nonparental relatives and 4% were raised in foster or adoptive homes. Thus, compared to the conventional middle-class American norm, the early childhood family situations of just under half the sample were in some sense irregular.

We do not mean to imply by this observation that the conventional mother-father-children family is somehow normatively superior to all others, that single parents, stepparents, or surrogate parents are incapable of providing an acceptable home life for children, or that anything short of being raised through one's childhood by both natural parents is somehow dysfunctional. What we do mean to imply is that the families of origin for nearly half our respondents were themselves unstable to at least some extent. In many or most of these cases, the family of origin is not a stable point of orientation but rather a moving target of affinity and affective ties.

Some indication of this instability surfaces in data on the marital statuses of our respondents' natural parents (a question asked of all respondents whether they were reared by both natural parents or in some other arrangement). Just over three-quarters (78%) reported that their natural parents were in fact married; the remainder reported that their natural parents were never married (19%) or that they simply did not know (3%). Of those whose natural parents *were* married, about three-quarters (73%) report that the marriage was ultimately dissolved through divorce or separation (or in a few cases by the death of a spouse). Thus, only 21% of our respondents had married parents whose marriages survived through to the respondent's adult years; the remainder experienced some "break" in the family structure at some point in their early lives. (All these patterns are effectively identical for males and females alike.) Remarkably, then, only about a tenth of these respondents were reared by two legally married parents whose marriages remained intact throughout the respondent's childhood; the immense majority were reared by parents who subsequently divorced or separated or who never married in the first place, by a single parent (with or without stepparents), by nonparental kin, or in foster or adoptive homes.

Respondents were also asked to characterize their early childhood as "happy," "so-so," or "unhappy." Half were "happy" as children, the remainder less than happy. Of some interest, the women were significantly less likely to report being happy than the men (42 to 52%, respectively). Many apparently had a great deal to be unhappy about. In the total sample, 15% reported being sexually abused as children, 25% reported physical abuse, and 42% reported some degree of emotional abuse. These proportions are significantly higher for women than for men in all cases. Among the women respondents only, 36% reported being physically abused as children, 42% had been sexually abused, and 58% had been emotionally abused. How these results compare with the experiences of other nonhomeless people is anybody's guess, but we can at least conclude that the structural instability indicated in the data on parents' marital statuses and early childhood living arrangements is matched by a great deal of interpersonal difficulty or outright abuse taking place between subsequently homeless children and their adult guardians during the early formative years.

Data on substance abuse among respondents' family members provides a final indicator of early family dysfunction. In the total sample, well more than half (58%) report substance-abusive fathers (among the women only, the figure is 68%), a quarter report substance-abusive mothers (among the women, it is 37%), two-thirds report substance-abusive siblings, and so on.

In sum, the lack of attachment to family and the ensuing absence of a familial "safety net" upon which persons can rely in times of crisis are frequently and correctly cited by many observers as an inherent part of the process by which people become homeless. It is wrong, however, to look on familial disaffiliation as an "adult onset" disorder. Nearly all of this sample of substance-abusive homeless adults in the New Orleans area were reared in structurally "irregular" family situations; "the" family of origin for most of our respondents is not some fixed point of reference or affection but rather a shifting, variable series of parents, stepparents, and other adults (some related, some not) who at various times served as guardians for our respondents during their early years. If we wished that, in some ideal world, homeless persons maintained a stable attachment to their families, we would also have to admit that in many cases it is not at all clear just who they should be attached to.

It is also obvious that the process of familial estrangement is a two-way street, that is, some homeless adults are estranged because of things they have done to family members but many are estranged by things that family members have done to them. Which is to say that homeless adults are as often the victims of the process of disaffiliation as they are the perpetrators. The structural instabilities in the families of origin are obviously compounded by high levels of substance abuse and child abuse such as those reported above.

The data thus suggest that for many homeless adults, familial estrangement is a process that begins essentially at birth. Evidence on early family backgrounds shows that familial ties are generally not resources that homeless people once possessed and subsequently lost, but rather resources that many homeless people have been without since their earliest childhood years. In a deep sense, today's homelessness has its roots in the family dysfunction of earlier generations.

6

Mental Illness and Substance Abuse

We have argued that homelessness is the logical consequence of increased poverty and decreased low-income housing, an argument others also make (e.g., Blau 1992; Fallis and Murray 1990; Jencks 1994; Timmer et al. 1994). Critics of this view, such as Baum and Burnes (1993), acknowledge the tightening of the low-income housing supply but point to other factors to explain the rising tide of homelessness. In this chapter we focus on what Baum and Burnes (1993) and other of their ilk view as the two most important of these factors: mental illness and substance abuse.

MENTAL ILLNESS

The argument has been made again and again that homelessness is largely either a mental health problem, caused in substantial measure by inadequate discharge planning during the process of deinstitutionalization and by other related changes in society's treatment of the mentally ill, or a substance abuse problem. Our argument, in contrast, is that homeless is fundamentally a housing problem and that the emphasis on these two factors as causative diverts attention from more basic issues of political economy that lie at the heart of the homeless dilemma.

There is, of course, no denying that the rate of psychiatric disorder is sharply elevated among the homeless compared to the domiciled population. Early in the current homelessness crisis, the published estimates of the percentage of homeless people who were mentally ill varied wildly, from about 10% on the low end to 90% on the high end. But over the past 10 years, empirically credible estimates have stabilized at about one in three. The proportion of homeless persons who are "mentally ill" in some clinically significant sense is one-third. This, of course, is more mental illness than one typically expects to find among a "normal" population, but if a third of the homeless are mentally ill, then two-thirds—the substantial majority—are not, and if the majority of the homeless are not mentally ill (at least not in any clinically significant sense), then mental illness cannot be a sufficient explanation for their homelessness.

Although we do not dispute the general finding that one homeless person in three has significant psychiatric problems, we do claim that the measurement (or diagnosis) of mental illness among the homeless is a formidable challenge. Estimates toward the low end of the range of results reported in prior studies are usually based on the records of mental health service providers, on cases of psychiatric hospitalization, and on related archival or documentary sources of data. Thus not all psychiatrically impaired people come at one or another point into the mental health care system. This may be more true of the mentally ill homeless than of the mentally ill in general; it is almost certainly more true today than at any previous point in the nation's history, now that institutionalization for psychiatric problems is assiduously avoided and that involuntary commitment to treatment is virtually impossible unless the person is an obvious "danger to self or others." Moreover, not everyone who does come under care leaves an identifiable trace in agency records, especially not in outpatient or crisis intervention programs. Thus, estimates based on hospital or clinical records most likely represent lower-boundary estimates, not "best guesses."

High-end estimates of the rate of mental illness among the homeless are usually based on some sort of diagnostic protocol contained within a larger questionnaire being administered to convenience samples of homeless people. Many of the questions these standardized assessment protocols contain are of dubious validity as indicators of psychiatric disease within a homeless context. Here, to illustrate, are some of the items used to tap "mental illness" in Rossi's survey of homeless people in Chicago (a survey in whose design Wright was involved):

> Do you feel unhappy about the way your life is going?
> Do you feel discouraged and worried about your future?
> Do you feel so tired and worn out at the end of the day that you cannot enjoy anything?

Rossi took these three items directly from well-known and widely used assessment protocols that were designed to measure symptoms of chronic depression (for the appropriate references, see Rossi et al. 1987:note 17). Certainly for the "normal," domiciled, middle-class population, these are good indicators of depression. In contrast, for a homeless person who sleeps in the gutters and scavenges his sustenance from garbage cans, these responses reflect a sane reaction to daily life. Were such a person to pronounce himself "happy" about the way his life "is going," we would quickly come to doubt his grasp on reality. Homeless people should feel "discouraged and worried" about their future. Uncertain and inadequate nutrition, irregular sleeping locations and arrangements, and a great deal of forced walking and standing in lines would make anyone feel "tired and worn out." And what comes at the end of homeless persons' days that they are supposed to enjoy? The point, rather an obvious one, is that a truly sane homeless person would have to answer yes to all of these questions.

Many of the apparently "crazy," "bizarre," or "abnormal" behavioral patterns homeless people exhibit are adaptations to the rigors and dangers of street or shelter existence, and should not be taken as signs of psychiatric impairment. Laypeople routinely mistake coping behavior among the homeless for mental illness (Redburn and Buss 1986). Rummaging in garbage cans for something to eat would strike most people as bizarre or "situationally inappropriate" to say the very least, but it is very sensible behavior if it is the only alternative to hunger. Urinating in public is repulsive and, again, bizarre to most, but in a nation that (unlike many advanced nations) does not routinely provide public restroom facilities, where else are the homeless to go? Lack of options accounts for as much, or more, of the apparently "crazy" behavior observed among the homeless as clinical psychiatric impairment. In fact, as Koegel, Burnam, and Farr (1990) indicate, the subsistence strategies homeless adults employ demonstrate considerable resilience, and this resilience is present, independent of the incidence of mental illness (Koegel et al. 1990).

Finally, concerning the inference of mental illness from a history of psychiatric hospitalization, it has become something of a truism among care providers for the homeless that the "never-institutionalized" mentally ill are now much more common than the "ever-institutionalized" mentally ill. They often ignore that the first waves of deinstitutionalization of the mentally ill in this country occurred in the 1950s and accelerated in the 1960s; by the middle 1970s, almost all of the people who were ever destined to be "deinstitutionalized" already had been. So as a direct contributing factor to the rise of homelessness in the 1980s, deinstitutionalization could not have been that important. Indeed, the proportion homeless specifically because they have recently been released from a mental hospital is not more than a tenth. Given the history, the concern these days is less with mentally ill people who have been inappropriately released from treatment than with those who were never brought into a system of treatment in the first place. Homeless mentally ill persons in their 20s or early 30s are very unlikely to have been institutionalized in the first place, and therefore equally unlikely ever to have been deinstitutionalized. Their lack of prior psychiatric treatment, however, speaks more to large-scale societal developments of the past three decades than to their level of psychiatric functioning.

Since we know, then, that one-third of the homeless are mentally ill, it makes sense to ask whether mental illness is not the cause of homelessness. Even this proposition is, we believe, fundamentally misleading; that is, it is simply incorrect to conclude that mentally ill homeless people are homeless because of their mental illness. The better conclusion is that many mentally ill people have housing needs that are not being adequately addressed, and they are therefore homeless. This point is one that runs through the research on homelessness; even the psychiatric community, which arguably has a vested interest in defining homelessness as a result of mental illness, has rejected this position. Cohen and Thompson, both members of a department of psychiatry, argue that the focus on psychiatric explanations "diverts attention from the real causes and necessary remedies" (1992:384). The real causes and remedies are related not to the mental illness of the homeless in their perspective, but rather to the lack of low-income housing and appropriate low-skill jobs. Similarly, Sosin and Grossman's (1991) comparison of homeless and formally domiciled mental patients also related contemporary homelessness to the lack of resources rather than mental health deficits.

Likewise, in a study of 700 New York families requesting shelter compared to 524 families randomly drawn from the New York public assistance cases, Shinn (1992) found that while a history of mental illness did, indeed, increase the risk of homelessness, it was the lack of affordable housing and prior victimization that caused the onset of homelessness.

Obviously, the housing needs of mentally ill homeless people are very different from the housing needs of other homeless persons or those of the poor in general, a point that was recognized at the beginning of the deinstitutionalization movement in the 1950s. This movement was based on the assumption that a large network of halfway houses, supported housing options, and community-based mental health centers would be provided. Although deinstitutionalization proceeded, very little of this network was put in place; as a result, many former mental patients were returned to their families and communities only to find that their families were unwilling or unable to provide for their care and that their communities lacked adequate provisions for their multifaceted needs.

Thus, the housing problem posed by the existence of large numbers of mentally ill homeless people is that the current supply of supported transitional and extended-care housing for the mentally disturbed is insufficient or, in many places, simply nonexistent; the absence of an ample supply of such housing is exactly why so many mentally ill people are homeless in the first place. The simple expedient of more flophouses or public housing projects cannot address the housing problems the mentally ill homeless face. Elliott and Krivo examined census data from the U.S. Census and from HUD in order to examine directly the determinants of homelessness. Their interest was in assessing the relative contributions of structural (poverty, availability of low-cost housing, economic conditions) versus personal factors (demographic characteristics and expenditures on mental health care). To their surprise, the most important predictors of the homelessness rate were the absence of low-income housing and the expenditures on mental health care. While indirect evidence at best, this study, because it is an aggregate-level analysis, makes clear that the "availability of residential services for the mentally ill and the economic conditions of areas have marked effects on homelessness rates" (1991:124). Adequate housing for this group requires on-site supportive social and psychiatric services, and since few could afford to pay rent, the necessary subsidies would be deep ones. These points, of course, only specify the nature of the housing problem that mentally ill homeless people face; they do not imply that the housing problem is of less causal significance than mental illness.

Also important are the "dually diagnosed" homeless who have recently begun to receive a great deal of research attention. These, of course, are the homeless who are both chemically dependent and mentally ill. Their unique problem resides in the fact that most alcohol and drug treatment programs refuse admission to persons with co-occurring psychiatric disorders (on the not unreasonable grounds that these programs are not properly equipped to deal with mental problems) and that most mental health programs refuse admission to those who are also drinking or using (on the same grounds). Thus, the dually diagnosed need the stabilizing residential care of the mentally ill and the alcohol- and drug-free living environment of the substance-abusive.

What is clear about the relationship between homelessness and mental illness is that people do not become homeless just because they are mentally ill. Mentally ill people become homeless because housing that satisfactorily meets their needs is in very short supply and because they do not have sufficient financial resources to translate their evident needs into a housing demand that would stimulate additions to the supply. In the absence of capable advocacy and case management, the homeless mentally ill fall easily through the cracks—and the housing "crack" is one that they have fallen through in distressingly large numbers. It is, of course, correct to say that the mentally ill homeless require more than just housing, but it is also correct to say that the absence of acceptable housing lies at the base of their problems.

Indeed, it is a fair judgment that until the housing situations of homeless mentally ill persons are stabilized, efforts to address their many other problems will be largely fruitless. By themselves, counseling, therapy, and psychotropic medication cannot compensate for the psychic anguish and mental disordering that results from life on the streets. In the absence of acceptable housing options along the lines sketched above, we cannot even adequately address the mental health problems of the homeless mentally ill, much less their housing, financial, and other problems.

Our argument that mental illness is not a cause of homelessness is not intended to deny or belittle the often profound psychiatric disabilities suffered by many homeless people. Any capable services program for the homeless must necessarily address these psychiatric difficulties. Many homeless people are also undernourished and a capable services package would also include food. That homeless people need to eat, however, does not mean that they are homeless because they are hungry. Likewise, many battered women prove, upon detailed examination, to be mentally ill; any program of services for battered women would, of course, include psychiatric counseling. But their need for psychiatric service surely does not imply that these women are battered because they are mentally ill.

In the remainder of this chapter, we address the second group of homeless who figure prominently in individual level explanations for homelessness: the substance- and alcohol-abusive.

SUBSTANCE ABUSE

Understanding the process by which an individual becomes (or stays) homeless necessitates exploring the interaction between personal factors and large-scale social-structural trends. As a means of explicating the process of becoming or staying homeless and of exploring the interaction between structural factors and personal disabilities, this chapter presents data on the housing dynamics and socioeconomic characteristics of a sample of 670 homeless substance abusers who participated in the New Orleans Homeless Substance Abusers Program (NOHSAP), a three-year, federally funded research demonstration project. By definition, all the people in this sample are either alcoholic or drug-abusive (mostly the latter); about a quarter also suffer from clinically significant psychiatric illness as well.

In a real sense, homelessness is a socioeconomic "status." We have, therefore, organized this section of the chapter according to the factors that dictate socioeconomic status in the larger population, specifically, education, employment, and income. In contrast to conventional wisdom, data from the NOHSAP sample reveal substantial diversity in educational and occupational attainment as well as in earnings, which is to say that homeless people, even homeless drug addicts, are not "all of a piece." Many homeless drug addicts have monthly incomes that put them well above the official federal poverty line (or such, in any case, is true in the data examined here). Nevertheless, drug consumption and dependence serve as socioeconomic "equalizers" that dissolve otherwise potentially critical differences in human capital and economic capacities; drug abuse "levels" otherwise important differences among the homeless. Likewise, drug abuse constitutes a critical mechanism that dissolves frequently tenuous familial ties and material support—thus rendering these individuals "losers" in the urban housing game despite their incomes and other human capital resources.

The research community estimates that the rate of alcohol abuse among the nation's homeless exceeds 40%; among homeless men, it is close to 50%. "In whatever setting homeless adults are studied, alcoholism is the most frequent single disorder diagnosed" (Institute of Medicine 1988:60). Numerous studies undertaken throughout the early 1980s—and thus predating crack cocaine—demonstrated that at least 15–30% of the homeless abused drugs other than alcohol (Shlay and Rossi 1992). More recent evidence since the late 1980s suggests dramatically higher rates of drug abuse and addiction. For instance the New York City Commission on the Homeless compiled data revealing that "66 percent of the single adults tested in New York's general-purpose shelters had traces of cocaine in their urine" (Jencks 1994:26). Jencks goes on to observe that while the New York data may well overstate the extent of drug use and abuse among the nation's homeless, other available evidence suggests that somewhere between a third and half of the homeless are frequent crack users. Consistent with this finding, the New Orleans Task Force on Hunger and Homelessness estimates that three-quarters of the city's homeless abuse alcohol, and that more than half abuse other drugs, most frequently crack. In sum, then, alcohol and drug abuse are arguably the most common health problems associated with homelessness, probably surpassing even mental illness in extent. The study we discuss below focused on that sector of the homeless.

THE NEW ORLEANS HOMELESS SUBSTANCE ABUSERS
PROGRAM (NOHSAP)

NOHSAP was a residentially based, adult resocialization, therapeutic intervention targeted to homeless alcoholics and drug abusers in the Greater New Orleans area. With a city population of about half a million and a metropolitan area population of approximately 1.3 million, New Orleans is the nation's 25th largest city. The city ranks second in its overall poverty rate and in the rate of child poverty for largest cities (see National Public Health and Hospital Institute 1995; Children's Defense Fund 1992); poverty in the city is heavily concentrated within the 70% black majority. Estimates of the size of the city's one-night homeless population vary from 5,000 to 12,000, of whom about 80% are African-Americans and about 25% are women.

NOHSAP saw its first clients in February 1991. Over the next two years almost 700 clients passed through the facility. Of these, 506 became "control" clients, meaning that they received only seven (or fewer) days of detoxification and were then released back to the streets. One hundred sixty-four clients were randomly assigned to (and accepted) "treatment," i.e., they were enrolled into one or more extended treatment programs ranging from 3 weeks to 12 months (mean time in treatment = 5 months). The data reported here are from the baseline interviews conducted during client's second or third day in detoxification ($N = 670$).

For the record, clients entered NOHSAP on referral from a local public hospital, so the operational definition of "substance abuser" for the program (and therefore for our research) is someone with an alcohol or drug problem sufficiently serious that the doctors and nurses at Charity Hospital felt that some sort of treatment was in order. Since terms such as "abuse" or "addiction" have never been clearly defined in the research (or treatment) literature (on this point, see Wright and Devine 1994), this definition seems as good as any.

CHARACTERISTICS OF NOHSAP CLIENTS

Social and demographic characteristics of the client sample closely mirror those reported in other studies of substance-abusive homeless people (Conrad, Hultman, and Lyons 1993; Koegel and Burnham 1987;

Wright 1989b). Respondents were overwhelmingly African-American (82.2%), relatively young (mean age = 34), and predominantly male (75.4%). About 90% were born and raised in Louisiana.

Almost a quarter (23%) of the clients reported having been hospitalized in a psychiatric facility at some time in their life. While inpatient psychiatric hospitalization is not an unambiguous or exhaustive indicator of mental health status, these data suggest that the rate of clinically significant mental illness was a bit less among NOHSAP clients than among the adult urban homeless in general. A slight majority (53%) of the clients were polysubstance-abusive; about half (47.6%) had alcohol problems; most (85%) were crack addicts; small proportions abused heroin and other illicit drugs. A quarter (27%) of the respondents had previous treatment for their alcohol problems, and more than half (54%) had prior treatment for their other drug problems. Thus, in the main, ours was a sample of multiply troubled, young, black, crack-addicted, homeless males. They are representative of some components of the urban underclass (Devine and Wright 1993).

Despite the many commonalities among this sample (race, age, substance abuse, and homelessness, to list the more important), NOHSAP clients prove rather remarkably diverse in educational and occupational attainment and in their monthly earnings. This diversity alone belies any simple explanation for their homelessness (as explained in more detail below); that is, NOHSAP clients were not homeless solely because of low educational or occupational attainments or even low incomes, since our sample was highly variable in all three of these human capital characteristics.

EDUCATION

One might expect any sample of homeless people to be homogeneously low on any measure of socioeconomic status, most of all since many observers have reported extreme poverty as a common trait among the homeless (e.g., Rossi et al. 1987; Burt and Cohen 1989a). However true this might be among homeless people in general, it is certainly not true among the homeless drug addicts in our sample. Focusing first on education, just over half of the NOHSAP clients (52%) completed 12 or more years of formal education; about one in seven had a year or two of college thereafter; the remainder (48%) dropped out before completing high school. The educational attainments were about equal for both men and women. Two-fifths of the men and a third of the women also completed some technical or vocational education beyond high school.

Many are surprised to learn that the majority of homeless persons have graduated from high school but this finding is a common one (for a review of previous studies, see Wright 1989a); in the National Health Care for the Homeless evaluation data (Wright and Weber 1987), for example, the proportion of homeless clients with a high school education or better was 53% ($N = 17,762$). In the national population as a whole (as of the 1990 Census) the proportion with a high school degree or better was 78%; among blacks only, 66%; and among the national poverty population, about 62% (U.S. Bureau of the Census 1994). We have not been able to locate equivalent figures for New Orleans as a whole or for the black or poverty populations of the city, but given the dropout rates characteristic of New Orleans public high schools (which in recent years have run upward of two-thirds), it is quite possible that the average NOHSAP client was somewhat better educated than the average indigent adult in the city. Thus, while the educational attainment of our sample was definitely lower than that of the U.S. population as a whole, it was only marginally lower than the attainments of the national poverty population and probably equivalent (or nearly so) to the average education of poor people in New Orleans.

It follows from these findings that low educational attainment does not explain why some people become homeless and others do not. Further analysis suggests that the problem may be less the amount of education homeless people receive than the return they get from their educational accomplishments. In a "normal" population of U.S. adults, the zero-order bivariate correlation between educational attainment and income is on the order of .4; in these data the correlation is only .05. Thus, homeless substance abusers of the sort we studied are apparently less able than other adults to translate their educational attainments into significant income (or employment) benefits. Just why this might be the case is a matter of speculation; one speculation is that chronic drug abuse erodes whatever advantage one's educational attainments might otherwise confer—precisely the sense in which we mean that substance abuse levels otherwise important socioeconomic differences among the homeless. (For what it is worth, and consistent with this speculation, education is weakly but positively correlated in these data with both the number of years using drugs and the dollars spent on drug use in the last month; also of some possible interest, education was positively associated with most treatment outcomes.)

EMPLOYMENT

Again in contrast to conventional expectation, a substantial majority of our clients (75%) had acquired something along the way that they were willing to describe as a "profession, skill, or trade," and so just as it is not quite right to describe them as "uneducated," so too is it wrong to describe them as entirely "unskilled." For the men, the "profession, skill, or trade" in question refers overwhelmingly to skilled (44%) or semiskilled (38%) blue-collar trades; the women were about equally divided between lower white-collar clerical and sales trades (46%) and semiskilled blue-collar labor (47%). A more detailed look at the specific trades in question suggests that many of these clients are ill-prepared for full participation in the high-skill sectors of the new economy; currently, the only growth sector in the New Orleans labor market is in the tourism industry and most of the new jobs in that sector are low-level "service" jobs for which the human capital requirements are rather minimal in the first place. The educational backgrounds and vocational skills of our sample, although definitely limited, were probably not much more limited than those of the average New Orleans labor force participant. It would be wrong to depict these people as entirely without human resources that they could use to secure decent jobs and modest but respectable standards of living.

As befits a group of relatively young adults with troubled life histories, however, the employment record was irregular and discontinuous, more or less regardless of any acquired skills, whether the frame of reference was last week, last month, last year, or the entire lifetime. Only about a tenth of the clients had been more or less continuously employed in the same line of work throughout their adult years. The usual pattern was to have held a number of different jobs (five or fewer for the modal respondent, more than five for about a third). Considering that the average respondent began living on his or her own at age 19 and is now about 34, the labor force history spans about 15 years; thus, even assuming continuous labor force participation, our average respondent holds any single job for not more than about 3 years. In fact, on the average, the longest full-time job ever held by NOHSAP males lasted 3.6 years, and by NOHSAP females, 2.4 years.

Looking at the employment pattern for the year prior to entry into the NOHSAP treatment program, only a quarter of the males and 14% of the females had regular full-time employment. The most common arrangement for the men (34%) was irregular employment (odd jobs, day labor, etc.) followed by unemployment (29%); more than half the women (52%)

were unemployed for most of the year. The most common arrangement in the week prior to entry into treatment was "just hanging out," reported by 42% of the men and 61% of the women. Only about 10% were working full-time in the week before entering treatment. The average man in the sample was paid for working only 6.5 days in the previous month; the average women, 1.8 days. Thus, the modal participant completed high school and has acquired some job skills, but has a highly irregular employment pattern.

Within this sample, the zero-order correlation between education and occupational skill level is .31, indicating that respondents' education does translate positively into subsequent job skills. However, relative skill level does not predict either work pattern or income. The correlations between occupational skill level and (1) days worked (during the past month), (2) work pattern over the past year (i.e., regular full-time, regular part-time, irregular employment, unemployment), (3) work-derived income, and (4) total income in the last month are .04, .02, .00, and .00, respectively. Again, even when homeless substance abusers do manage to accumulate some human capital, whether in the form of education or job skills, it does not pay off in the usual ways.

Why not? As above, the speculation is that chronic drug use diminishes the value of whatever human capital homeless addicts have otherwise attained, i.e., that substance abuse levels or reduces the effects of skill or education on well-being. Further analysis lends some indirect support to this proposition; the zero-order correlations between the number of days worked during the past month and the income derived from employment are consistently, positively, and significantly related to dollars spent on drugs and alcohol (during the past month), the number of days using drugs other than alcohol (during the past month), the number of years using drugs other than alcohol, and the number of days using alcohol (during the past month). Thus, in the aggregate, all that more employment or more income seems to buy substance abusive homeless people is more drugs—not socioeconomic advantage that might otherwise be invested in improving their housing or social conditions.

INCOME

While the average incomes of homeless people are well beneath the poverty line in any of a number of studies, it would be a mistake to presume that all or even most homeless substance abusers were entirely without monetary resources or that substantial variation does not exist within this "negatively privileged" group. While previously presented data on education and employment suggest a somewhat truncated distribution of life chances (relative to American society at large), they also make clear that there are substantial differences within this population. Presumably, these differences also would be manifested in variable incomes.

To understand income dynamics among the sample, the NOHSAP researchers invested considerable effort in eliciting reliable information on both sources and levels of income. Individuals were probed in detail about income from formal- and informal-sector employment, receipt of SSI, Food Stamps, and other transfers, receipt of money and goods from family and friends, panhandling, scavenging, prostitution, drug sales, etc. All questions referred to the 30 days preceding entry into NOHSAP. In addition, interviewers sought to gain information on the incidence of the activity and data on compensation-in-kind or trade as well as cash (Table 6.1 summarizes these data).

Due to the nature of the questions as well as the characteristics and condition of the clients, reliability could be problematic. There is, however, an encouraging literature on the reliability of self-report data among various samples of alcohol- and drug-abusive people (Babor, Stephens, and Marlatt 1987; Hesselbrock, Babor, Hesselbrock, Meyer, and Workman 1983; Sobell, Sobell, and Nirenberg 1988; Wolber, Carne, and Alexander 1990). Although one might expect (perhaps stereotypically) substance abusers to be dishonest or at least in denial about their problems, most studies find that these self-reports are generally valid and reliable, at least when clients are drug free, assured confidentiality, and are interviewed in a clinical research setting. Importantly, reliability analyses of the baseline interviews revealed high levels of veracity with these and other seemingly sensitive subjects (e.g., sexual and criminal activities). See Joyner, Wright, and Devine (1996) for details and data regarding the reliability studies.

For this sample, the largest share of income (on average) was derived from various illegal activities: petty crime, theft, drug dealing, and, for the women, prostitution. NOHSAP women averaged $410 from illegal income in the month before treatment; NOHSAP men averaged $393. These amounts represent 49 and 42% of total average monthly income, respectively.

Income from employment averaged $284 for the men and $70 for the women. For men, as noted, this was the income earned in 6.5 days of paid employment, and for women, it was the income earned in 1.8 days. The corresponding wage per day is therefore $44 for the men (or $5.46 per hour assuming an eight-hour work day) and $39 for the women ($4.86 per

Table 6.1.   Income Last Month, Levels, and Sources[a]

	Males ($)[c]	Females ($)[c]	Total Sample[b] $	Total Sample[b] Total (%)
Employment	284	70	230	47
% with zero income	44	81		53
Public transfers	67	199	99	37
% with zero income	67	51		63
Unemployment compensation	4	2	4	2
Public assistance, welfare	31	171	66	33
Pension, Social Security, SSDI	30	25	29	6
Private transfers[d]	49	89	59	37
% with zero income	64	59		63
Legal informal-sector income[e]	84	55	77	43
% with zero income	53	70		57
Panhandling	29	15	26	20
Sale or pawn of personal goods	53	40	50	24
Scavenging cans, other stuff	3	—	2	9
Illegal income	393	410	399	39
% with zero income	62	53		60
Other	49	14	40	13
% with zero income	85	93		87
Total income, all sources combined[f]	922	836	899	100

[a] Responses to the question, In the 30 days before you came here, how much money did you receive from the following sources?
[b] Cell entries are average (mean) reported amounts of income in dollars from each of the indicated sources; missing data are omitted item by item; "zero" income from any source is treated as a *nonmissing* value.
[c] Cell entries in the "Total" column show the sample mean and the percentage of the total sample who received *any* income from each of the indicated sources.
[d] Money received from mate, family, or friends.
[e] Money received from panhandling, scavenging, and pawning.
[f] Note: totals do not exactly sum due to rounding.

hour), somewhat although not dramatically higher than the minimum wage in both cases (the minimum wage in Louisiana was the federally mandated minimum, $4.25 per hour).

Among those whose total income placed them in the bottom quintile of the sample income distribution, employment earnings averaged only $18, while 75.9% reported zero money from employment. Regarding illegal income, 90.7% of those in the bottom quintile reported none and the average was therefore only $5. By contrast, only 41.8 and 23.5% of those in the top quintile reported zero income from employment and illegal activities, respectively. Average earnings among the upper fifth of the sample were $560 from employment and $1,551 from illegal activities.

Income in the previous month from all sources averaged $922 for the men and $836 for the women. For the entire sample, the mean was $899 and ranged from $0 to $11,247. These figures annualize to $10,788 in yearly income ($11,064 for the men and $10,032 for the women), and range from zero to almost $135,000, an income spread that captures better than 95% of the American household income distribution (U.S. Bureau of the Census 1993). In fact, slightly more than 2% of the homeless sample reported incomes sufficiently high that on an annualized basis they would be in the top quintile among American households.

These figures raised a certain amount of skepticism. The data and the associated reports on patterns of drug use and purchases reveal, however, that all but one of the 15 cases with annualized incomes of better than $58,000 proved quite plausible. In essence, this rather select group was running through several thousand dollars worth of drugs per week.

The annualized average income exceeds the federal poverty line for a single person; in fact, it exceeds the federal poverty line for two-person households. The 1992 poverty threshold for a single person (under 65 years of age) was $7,299; for a two-person household it was $9,443; and for a three-person household it was $11,186 (U.S. Bureau of the Census 1993; Devine and Wright 1993). How, then, in a city where the cost of housing is relatively low, can people have incomes above the poverty line and still be homeless? Addiction provides the short and simple answer: the average NOHSAP client was spending just under $600 per month on drugs and alcohol, 64% of the total income for men and 71% of the total income for women.

The monthly income figures we report here are much higher than the monthly income figures other studies of homeless persons report—some five times higher than the figures Rossi reports for homeless people in Chicago in the early 1980s and six times higher than the figures Burt and Cohen report in their national survey of soup kitchen and shelter users in the mid-1980s (Burt and Cohen 1989a; Rossi 1986). Both these studies, however, predate the crack epidemic of the late 1980s and early 1990s, which has created income opportunities in the urban underclass that formerly did not exist (e.g., Staley 1992). If one subtracts the large component of income due to various illegal activities, the resulting figures are somewhat closer to (although still higher than) the figures reported in previous research. Moreover, staff asked NOHSAP clients a very detailed series of questions with numerous probes concerning all their various sources of income over just the previous 30 days, including income from illegal sources, which might provide more accurate and reliable income data than a single question about "your average monthly income" such as that posed in most earlier surveys. (Note that neither the Rossi nor Burt-Cohen survey asks anything about illegal income, the largest single income component for the persons studied here.)

It is also true that averages of the sort we report above can be misleading. On the "average," NOHSAP clients earned $399 in illegal income in the month prior to entry into treatment, and yet 60% of the sample reported no income from illegal sources. Thus, the median income from all sources was lower than the mean income (and thus more in line with previous studies). The mean income figures reported above are also inflated somewhat by a few outliers that may or may not be credible.

Even with all the above allowances, however, the number of homeless persons in this sample with incomes sufficient to live an independent, nonhomeless existence was striking. We obviously do not wish to deny the extreme poverty of the homeless as a whole nor the role of extreme poverty in producing homelessness. Among the substance-abusive homeless in this study, however, there was unquestionably a sizable stratum who would not be homeless if they were paying landlords as much as they were paying their drug dealers.

The relationship between income and drug consumption in this sample was brutally simple: higher incomes (whatever the source) typically result in higher drug consumption (whatever the measure). Thus, monthly income is positively and significantly correlated with total days using drugs in the previous month ($r = .28$), with total years of drug abuse ($r = .13$), and, critically, with total dollars spent on drugs ($r = .69$). Thus, all that a high income buys the average homeless drug abuser is more drugs. To illustrate the magnitude of the effect, we regressed dollars spent on drugs in the last month on the last month's income and a range of control variables (days worked, education, race, age, gender, etc.). Over a number of different specifications, and with other factors held constant, the coefficient for monthly income was always right around .5 (and was always highly significant), which means that for every additional dollar of income in this sample, 50 cents goes to increased drug consumption. When we substitute the number of days using drugs (during the past month) as the dependent variable in otherwise the same models, the results were also significant and positive. The more money homeless addicts earn, in short, the more drugs they consume; here too, drug use levels incomes in that the net income (the total income minus the drug bill) was much less variable in this sample than gross income.

Furthermore, the drug (and alcohol) use patterns for our sample have quite a long history, such that the leveling effects have had plenty of time to do their damage. The average NOHSAP client started using alcohol and marijuana at about age 15 and first tried hard drugs at about age 21. Clients drinking alcohol to excess (56% of all clients) had been doing so for about 12 years and clients using crack cocaine (83% of all clients) had been doing so for about 5 years. Smokeable cocaine (crack) made its first appearance as an abused street drug in 1985 or 1986 (Akers 1992:122). In short, crack had only been around for 5 or 6 years when our clients entered treatment, and thus most of the crack addicts in the sample had been abusing crack for the entire period of the urban crack epidemic. Since the average client began drinking alcohol at age 15 and is now 34, the 12 years of regular, excessive alcohol use represent 63% of the total possible years since the onset of excessive drinking behavior; likewise, with the onset of hard drug use at age 21, the 5 years of crack use represent 38% of the total possible years. Most clients (69%) also reported some years (average = 8.8 years) of regular marijuana use (although many fewer were currently using marijuana); a substantial minority also reported some years of regular heroin use (11%, mean years of use = 6.6), hallucinogens (13%, mean years = 2.7), "downers" (13%, mean years = 3.5), and "uppers" (13%, mean years = 3.1). Adding years across categories of drugs, it is apparent that the average NOHSAP client had been abusing alcohol or drugs (or frequently both) for pretty much the entirety of his or her adult existence.

The NOHSAP income data suggest two additional points worthy of emphasis: First, many people think of the homeless as welfare "leeches" content to live off the dole. Unless one is a parent with dependent children and thus eligible for AFDC, or disabled and thus eligible for SSI or SSDI, it was very hard to be "welfare dependent" in Louisiana since the only other program for which our clients would nominally be eligible is Food Stamps. Including Food Stamps, SSI, SSDI, AFDC, and all other forms of public assistance, the average NOHSAP male received $67 in the month before treatment, and the average NOHSAP female, $199 (representing 7 and 24% of total monthly income, respectively). Overall, almost two-thirds of the NOHSAP clients (63%) received no money (or food stamps) from public assistance in the month prior to starting treatment; among those receiving *any* assistance, the average amount for the month was $198. Among the 222 NOHSAP clients receiving any welfare assistance, 99 (or 45%) received exactly $105 in the month prior to treatment. This happens to be the basic food stamp allotment for a single individual in the city; thus, the proportion of NOHSAP clients receiving any welfare assistance other than food stamps is about 18%. As a crude comparison, nationwide, about half of all homeless adults receive some sort of welfare assistance and the other half do not (Wright and Weber 1987). In New Orleans and elsewhere, the total contribution of "welfare" to the monthly income of homeless addicts proves to be fairly minimal. Now, of course, welfare reform has rendered even this amount impossible.

Second, only 20% of the NOHSAP clients reported any income from panhandling in the previous month; among those with any income from panhandling ($N = 137$), the average amount received was $124 ($107 if two implausible outliers are excluded)—this in sharp and definite contrast to the stereotypical view that most or all homeless people panhandle regularly and raise substantial amounts of cash in the process. We have seen anecdotal reports in the New Orleans media suggesting that many panhandlers clear literally hundreds of dollars a day from the activity; these data suggest that homeless panhandlers are lucky enough to clear $100 a month.

The income data also suggest two more general conclusions. First it is obvious that these people would not be nearly as poor if they were not spending upward of two-thirds of their total income on drugs. For this sample of homeless addicts, in short, there is no reasonable doubt that drugs keep poor people impoverished and keep homeless people homeless. When a sample of homeless substance abusers is averaging almost $600 per month in expenditures on drugs and alcohol, it is very hard to escape the conclusion that they are homeless, at least in substantial part, because of their drug and alcohol consumption, or alternatively, that they could afford not to be homeless if they chose to spend their money on rent instead of drugs.

At the same time, although it is true that the average monthly income for this sample exceeds the corresponding poverty line, this is only true because of the large sums of illegal income they report, and it is therefore a legitimate question whether the average incomes would be as high as they are were it not for the fact that many of these users are integrated into the traffic in narcotics. Thus, many of the people in our sample have access to higher than expected incomes precisely because they are involved in the narcotics business. And as a matter of fact, if this sample of homeless addicts both stopped using alcohol and drugs and ceased all illegal activities, the net result would be to leave them only marginally better off. The men would save $593 a month by getting and staying clean and sober but lose $390 a month in illegal income; overall, they would net a bit less than $7 extra per day. The women would gain $595, lose $410, and therefore net just over $6 extra per day. Thus, the net economic benefit to this sample of not being an addict and not being involved in criminal activity proves rather a pittance. And so it is not quite right to say that many of these people could choose not to be homeless if they spent their incomes on something other than drugs; being involved in drugs is, sad to say, what gives them access to relatively high incomes in the first place.

SUBSTANCE ABUSE AND HOUSING OUTCOMES

The circumstances of homelessness do not permanently exclude the substance-abusive homeless from stable housing; they do, however, more or less permanently marginalize them in the housing economy. Even when stably housed, their tenuous hold on resources (economic, social, or emotional) keeps them at high risk for future episodes of homelessness.

The point is an important one. The housing dynamic of homelessness is not a simple matter of being unable to afford rent, or of using up too many of one's resources in the support of a drug or alcohol habit. Drug and alcohol use and a wide range of other "personal" factors such as mental illness or criminal records combine to marginalize a large and growing stratum of the urban poverty population, i.e., to put them at risk of homelessness (vs. making them homeless, which is not the same thing). As in epidemiology, the prevalence of the "disease" of homelessness is less interesting and less relevant to policy than the distribution of risk factors for the disease. Personal attributes such as drug abuse and mental illness are relevant to the discussion of homelessness less as causal factors than as risk factors that increase marginalization, that therefore render tenuous a person's hold on (or claim to) resources, and that in the end increase the likelihood of unfavorable housing outcomes.

As an approach to the question of marginality, we constructed a heuristic model containing indicators of virtually all of the constructs implicated in the above discussion. Specifically, we regressed a measure of the number of days homeless during the preceding 60 days (our best measure of housing "marginality") on several measures of substance abuse (i.e., days using drugs other than alcohol during the past month, years using drugs other than alcohol, days using alcohol during the past month, years using alcohol, and dollars spent on drugs and alcohol during the past month); client scores on the ASI psychiatric composite; an index of family dysfunctionality (see Devine, Wright, and Joyner 1994); educational attainment (measured in years of education); days worked during the past month; total income; and several demographic controls (i.e., age, race, and gender). We consider this model heuristic inasmuch as it represents the proverbial empirical "kitchen sink" and is plagued by some collinearity.

Critically, despite these blemishes, the coefficient indexing the numbers of days using drugs in the past month is positive and significant. Days worked during the past month is also significant but negative as one would expect (i.e., employment diminishes days homeless; this despite the observation that other income often goes toward acquiring drugs). The only other measures achieving statistical significance are gender (males experience more days homeless than females) and age (the coefficient is positive). While hardly definitive, the results from this exercise do lend support to a principal observation of this chapter, namely, that drug abuse exerts a leveling effect and plays a critical role in the housing dynamics of homelessness; even among a sample all of whom are drug-abusive and homeless to some extent, those using the most drugs experience the least favorable housing outcomes.

CONCLUSIONS

Homeless people are not homogeneous; even homeless alcoholics and drug addicts and the mentally ill are not homogeneous. Contrary to stereotype, homeless drug abusers are very heterogeneous with respect to education, job history and skills, and incomes. The distinguishing socioeconomic feature of homeless people is not that they are all uneducated or unskilled, but that they are generally unable for a variety of reasons to translate any human capital advantages they may have accrued into improved social or housing situations. Substance abuse is a critical factor that tends to level the effects one might otherwise anticipate of these highly variable human capital attributes. The general pattern is that homeless substance abusers with more resources consume more drugs, and those with fewer resources consume less drugs; basically, everyone in our sample consumes as much drugs as the available resources allow.

Neither individual nor structural factors alone are sufficient to explain homelessness. As we have stressed, there is no reasonable doubt that many of the people in our sample would not be homeless if they spent their money on rent rather than drugs; at the same time, participation in the drug economy is what gives many in the sample access to higher than expected incomes in the first place. It does not follow, then, that if we were somehow able to get rid of all the drugs, the number of homeless people on the streets would decline; it does not even follow that the material well-being of the average person in our sample would improve. Many of the people we have studied would be highly marginalized whether they used drugs or not; in certain important respects, it is likely that they use drugs because they are socially, legally, and economically marginalized, not the reverse. The housing outcomes for marginalized homeless people are certainly complicated and worsened by their alcohol and drug use and mental illness, but it is marginality more than mental illness, alcohol, or drugs per se that serves as the root cause.

7

Why Alcohol and Drug Treatment
Is Not the Solution

The previous chapter presented data on clients who received services through the New Orleans Homeless Substance Abusers Project (NOHSAP). Here we discuss the project itself and what it suggests about "solving" the problem of homelessness through more and better alcohol and drug treatment. Summarizing briefly, we argued in Chapter 6 that commentators such as Baum and Burnes do not really understand the causes of homelessness; the present chapter argues that their suggested solutions won't work either.

NOHSAP was a program funded by the National Institute of Alcohol and Alcohol Abuse in a second round of funding of such programs. One of the key problems with programs funded in the first round was the dual and conflicting role of the program directors. Previously, the very people who had run the program had also been the evaluators. In the second round, the evaluators (here, Wright and Devine) were completely independent from the actual program implementation. This framework is important to understand as we outline what NOHSAP did and did not do. From the onset, it is clear that while this effort was one of the best to date, it remained deeply flawed in its implementation.

NOHSAP was designed to achieve four principal goals: (1) a drug- and alcohol-free existence, (2) residential stability, (3) economic independence, and (4) a reduction in family estrangement and an increase in general social functioning. The hope was to demonstrate that with proper, well-designed interventions, even homeless alcoholics and drug addicts could be successfully reintegrated into the larger society and become productive, functioning, independent adults. NOHSAP's successes and failures in achieving these goals say a great deal about the extent to which alcohol and drug treatment might be expected to "solve" the nation's homeless problem.

PROGRAM DESIGN

NOHSAP was designed as a three-phase intervention: (1) detoxification, (2) Transitional Care (TC), and (3) Extended Care / Independent Living (ECIL). Placement into TC and ECIL, the treatment conditions, was to be accomplished via randomization from a pool of clients clinically deemed eligible (see below, Randomization). Two separate detoxification programs were available: one for single adults without children and a second family program for intact husband-wife couples or women with children. Both were seven-day programs focused on sobering up, an introduction to AA and NA principles, twice-daily group meetings, some counseling, and limited assessment and case management. Clients who successfully completed detoxification and who were judged clinically suitable for further treatment comprised the pool from which NOHSAP researchers randomly chose TC clients.

Transitional Care (TC) was a 21-day program involving more extensive client assessment, greater case management, twice-daily group meetings, placement in an off-campus alcohol or drug group, and general reinforcement of any positive steps taken during detoxification. Clients successfully completing the TC program became eligible for the ECIL program, a 12-month program that continued and amplified all the interventions and strategies begun during TC and that was intended to add a GED program, job training, job placement, and other "adult living" programs. As it turned out, however, the program only provided the latter services sporadically, so in many respects ECIL was only a longer-term version of TC.

The general philosophy behind the NOHSAP intervention—and indeed behind all residential treatment programs—is that one cannot begin to address the alcohol and drug problems of homeless substance abusers until they are first stabilized residentially, that is, until they have a clean, secure, and comfortable place to live. The prevailing opinion among alcohol and drug professionals is that the key to successful treatment is to provide social and physical environments that value sobriety positively (Korenbaum and Burney 1987). This environment, needless to say, is not the one on the streets. Indeed, even acknowledging that many people are homeless precisely because of a pattern of chronic alcohol and drug abuse, drunkenness provides many positive benefits for a homeless person, and high rates of alcohol and drug abuse will continue to prevail among the homeless so long as this remains true. Thus, the NOHSAP services package was specifically designed to provide a residential environment where sobriety was the norm and where program participants and practitioners positively encouraged independent living.

Sobriety, like drunkenness is learned behavior and therefore requires practice; relapse is an inherent and unavoidable aspect of recovery (Brown 1985; Miller, Gorski, and Miller 1982). Through episodes of sobriety and relapse, the recovering abuser practices and then masters a substance-free life-style. One must first unlearn the dysfunctional behaviors of the past and then learn (or in many cases, relearn) more functional patterns of behavior for the present and future. Periods of relapse, while certainly not encouraged, were generally tolerated; treatment was not denied or halted when persons exhibited the patterns of behavior that caused them to need treatment in the first place.

Chronic alcohol and drug use often serves a range of positive functions for a homeless individual. Treatment programs that attempt to address the alcohol or drug issue without also addressing the more basic problems for which alcohol or drug abuse is the client's solution are doomed or, at best, ineffectual. To put it bluntly, homeless people have many good reasons for getting and staying drunk. NOHSAP tried to provide good reasons for them to get and stay sober.

There is little doubt that alcohol and drug abusers are, in general, the most seriously disabled subgroup within the homeless population. This is also the subgroup for whom employment or permanent long-term housing has traditionally been the least likely. It is easy to assume that these multiple disabilities are inherent to the homeless substance abuser and are therefore largely intractable. NOHSAP was, in its very essence, an experiment to test this proposition, to learn, in short, whether there is hope even for the most debilitated and problematic among the homeless.

TREATMENT ISSUES

The literature identifies many barriers to adequate treatment of homeless substance abusers. One of the most important is the co-occurrence of psychiatric disorders. The rate of psychiatric disorder is significantly higher among homeless substance abusers than among the homeless in general (Wright 1989b). What to do with homeless clients who are both alcohol- or drug-abusive and mentally ill has therefore been extremely problematic. One strength of NOHSAP was that mental health services as well as drug and alcohol treatment were essential program components, with both group and one-on-one therapy sessions offered to clients with these particular needs.

A second major treatment issue is the general lack of appropriate after-care and long-term rehabilitative services. Most existing programs available to homeless substance abusers consist of short-term detoxification coupled (perhaps) with some counseling or rehabilitation, followed by release back to the streets, which is to say, release to exactly the environment that stimulated or exacerbated their substance abuse in the first place. Thus, many homeless substance abusers have been detoxified and "rehabilitated" time after time, almost always at considerable expense and with very inconsiderable success.

There were other key treatment issues the program confronted. First, many clients were polysubstance-abusive ("garbage can addicts"), with crack plus alcohol the most common combination. There may well be some homeless people who are "pure" alcoholics or "pure" crack heads, but we saw very few of them.

There was an interesting normative structure surrounding that abuse. Many NOHSAP clients would freely admit to their cocaine addiction but deny that they had any problem with alcohol. Since alcohol is cheap, legal, and readily available, clients assumed that its use was socially sanctioned, even encouraged (especially in New Orleans). Since everyone drinks alcohol anyway, clients did not perceive it as a problem. The problem is that most crack addicts use large quantities of alcohol to come down off the crack high or to sustain them between crack highs, and as a matter of fact, probably 90% of the relapse from cocaine addiction is first to alcohol and then back to cocaine and other drugs. The important treatment issue here therefore lies in convincing clients that the habitual and irresponsible use of alcohol is every bit as deleterious to their physical, social, and economic well-being as their habitual and irresponsible use of crack.

EVALUATION DESIGN

NOHSAP enrolled its first clients in February 1991. Program development staff continuously enrolled clients in the research component of the program through April 1992, and over that 14-month period, and conducted baseline interviews with 670 homeless substance abusers. In all, 670 clients were baselined during the detox phase of treatment. Of these, 164 were eventually placed in one or both of the treatment conditions (TC only, $N = 107$; TC + ECIL, $N = 57$) and the remainder ($N = 506$) were released back to the streets after detox and constitute the controls. As the previous chapter suggests, the demographic profile of NOHSAP clients was broadly comparable to the overall profile of homeless people throughout the country. Staff scheduled follow-up interviews at 3, 6, 12, and 18 months subsequent to initiation of treatment; follow-up interviewing was halted in January 1993. Tracking clients for follow-up interviews was a formidable challenge; Wright, Allen, and Devine (1995) fully describe the methods the researchers used for that purpose.

The outcome evaluation focused on the 6-month follow-ups since it is well-known that relapse normally occurs in the first 6 months subsequent to treatment (Brown 1985; Gerstein and Harwood 1990). In order to maximize cases available for analysis and to minimize problems of attrition, we created a "synthetic 6-month master follow-up file" containing each client's baseline interview and the follow-up interview occurring closest in time to the 6-month anniversary of the client's release from treatment. The initiation of the client's treatment determined the original follow-up interviewing schedule. The synthetic 6-month follow-up data for control and TC treatment clients, whose total time in treatment was 1 month or less, came from the actual 6-month interview except when the 6-month follow-up was missing, in which case the evaluators used the follow-up interview that occurred nearest in time to the 6-month anniversary point. The client's follow-up interviews might be the 3-, 12-, or even 18-month interview. Clients in the ECIL program remained in treatment for periods ranging from less than 2 months to more than 12 months. Again, the evaluators always took the synthetic 6-month follow-up data for ECIL clients from the follow-up interview occurring closest in time to the 6-month anniversary of the client's termination from treatment. For clients completing ECIL, this was normally the 18-month follow-up interview; for clients who left ECIL prematurely, it could be either the 6-or the 12-month interview. In a few cases, the research staff conducted special follow-up interviews near the 6-month anniversary point.

As is obvious, the synthetic 6-month follow-up file contained data on every client with whom the staff ever conducted a follow-up interview, regardless of when the follow-up occurred. Of the 670 clients originally baselined, we have at least one follow-up interview for 620, or 93%. Although the procedures described above mean that any follow-up interview can be treated as the 6-month follow-up for purposes of the outcome analysis, the synthetic 6-month interview is in fact the actual 6-month interview in 86% of the cases, the 3-month interview in 6% of the cases, the 12-month interview in 5% of the cases, and the 18-month interview in the remaining 3%.

The overall design for the outcome evaluation was straightforward in theory. As indicated above, staff were supposed to screen clients completing each program phase for suitability for further treatment and then randomize them into or out of the next program phase. Randomization would assure initial equivalence between treatments and controls, aggressive tracking and follow-up would minimize attrition, and changes from baseline to follow-up in various well-known, standardized measures [specifically, the Addiction Severity Index (McLellan, Luborsky, Woody, and O'Brien 1980, McLellan et al. 1985; McGahan, Griffith, Parente, and McLellan 1991)] would provide valid outcome indicators. Thus, the design seemed to protect admirably against threats to internal validity (Cook and Campbell 1979). Since the control condition amounted to 7 days of detox followed by release back to the streets, which is the "customary treatment" usually made available to homeless and indigent substance abusers nationwide, the external validity of the design also seemed acceptable.

RANDOMIZATION

The plan at program start-up was to place every suitable client in the TC program until the program reached capacity and then to randomize clients into TC from the pool of detoxed eligibles thereafter. Program staff were to make a clinical assessment of suitability or eligibility for further treatment. By design, staff placed appropriate clients in an alternative program after detox so that NOHSAP resources would be reserved for those without a treatment alternative. In fact, however, out-placement was extremely rare.

The staff sought to use similar methods to place clients in the 20-bed, 12-month ECIL program with the added proviso that only those clients who had successfully completed TC would be eligible. As with TC, staff were to make initial placement to capacity on a nonrandom basis, and thereafter they were to determine entry into ECIL via randomization from the pool of staff-determined eligibles.

The randomization plan allowed clinical staff to "cream" the client stream by only placing the names of clients they considered sufficiently motivated or potentially likely to succeed on the selection lists. Given the ineffectiveness of most alcohol and drug treatment programs (Akers 1992), however, the research staff did not consider creaming to be a problem but an asset. Effective creaming would avoid squandering resources on unsuitable clients; moreover, randomizing from a pool of creamed clients would theoretically match treatments and controls on initial motivation, also an asset. Once the staff had determined lists of eligible clients, however, the principal investigators (Wright and Devine) did the random selection of clients from the lists.

Data on the actual randomization of clients into the two treatment groups showed, to our surprise and dismay, that only a third (32%) of the 164 clients who ever entered TC and a fourth (25%) of the 57 clients who ultimately went on to treatment in the ECIL program were actually randomized into their treatment statuses. If we exclude the first 24 (14%) and 20 (35%) clients in TC and ECIL, respectively (as per the design described above), the figures improve but only marginally. Even then, less than two-fifths of the TC (38%) and ECIL (38%) populations were placed in treatment by randomization.

Just how and why the NOHSAP clinical staff managed to subvert the randomization scheme is a long and complicated story (Devine et al. 1994). Basically, when randomization selected a "good" client for treatment, staff implemented the selection; otherwise they ignored it. This problem is common in program evaluations.

The failure of randomization raised obvious questions about the equivalence of treatment and control groups, and so the evaluators conducted an exhaustive analysis (ibid.). Although that analysis revealed some disturbing nonequivalences, there was a straightforward and easily handled demographic explanation. In brief, staff were more likely to select women for treatment than men. Among the 505 men who were baselined, 86% ended up in the control group and only 14% were placed in further treatment; among the 165 women who were baselined, 53% went into the control group and 47% were placed in further treatment. Thus, women were three times more likely than men to be selected for TC and ECIL.

With this large sex disparity held constant, the residual differences between treatments and controls generally disappeared. To illustrate, the zero-order comparison between treatments and controls showed that treatment clients had significantly more severe pretreatment employment problems than control clients had, but we knew from earlier descriptive analyses that female clients also had significantly more severe employment problems than males. With sex controlled, the treatment-control difference in employment problems became statistically insignificant (ibid.:27–40).

In like manner, we tested the significance of the baseline differences between treatments and controls on 557 baseline variables. This analysis revealed significant zero-order differences in 89 cases (or 16% of the comparisons examined). We then partialed out the known sex difference and reexamined the treatment-control difference on the 89 initially significant variables; with sex held constant, only 24 statistically significant differences remained. The analysis allowed the evaluation team to conclude that with sex held constant, the baseline equivalence of treatments and controls was sufficient to proceed with the outcome analysis.

The severe selection bias in favor of women, and especially women with children, is easy to understand and to justify. For nearly all NOHSAP clients, failure to be selected for TC or ECIL meant a return to life in the streets, a fact of which clinical staff were certainly aware. Given the choice between condemning a man or a woman to such an existence, most staff found it less troubling to condemn the man, and most certainly so if the woman also had dependent children in her care.

Clearly, the randomization design was compromised; nevertheless, the NOHSAP experiment remained largely intact because it maintained the essential equivalence of treatment and control groups (with sex held constant) (at least on the 500+ variables that we could inspect). The implication, incidentally, is that the much-vaunted "gut instinct" that our program staff liked to think told them which clients were promising and which clients were not (and which was clearly used instead of randomization to select clients for treatment in NOHSAP) was itself essentially random, at least in outcome.

ATTRITION

Nonrandom selection of clients for treatment and control conditions can threaten the Time 1 equivalence of treatment and control groups; differential attrition over time can likewise produce Time 2 differences that reflect methods artifacts rather than true experimental effects. Two different sorts of attrition were of concern in the NOHSAP experiment: research attrition and treatment attrition.

Research Attrition. As already reported, 670 clients were baselined and all but 50 of them had at least one follow-up interview, so the net research attrition amounted to $50/670 = 7\%$ of all cases. Wave by wave, of course, the attrition was higher, ranging from 15 to 33%.

In field experiments, the primary concern with attrition is usually whether there is a differential attrition rate for treatments and controls. In NOHSAP, this was not the case; essentially the program achieved identical net follow-up rates with both treatments and controls. Among the 670 baselined NOHSAP clients, 506 were in the control group and 164 were in one of the experimental conditions. Staff completed at least one follow-up interview with 468 of the controls (93%) and with 152 of the treatments (93%). We attribute this encouraging result to a tracking effort that anticipated that controls would be harder to follow and that therefore invested more resources in tracking the controls (Wright, Allen, and Devine 1995).

How do the 50 cases for whom we have no follow-up data differ from the 620 cases included in the outcome analysis? An extensive quantitative analysis based, again, on 500+ variables from the baseline survey showed no clear pattern of difference between the two groups, although the tracking effort seems to have been marginally less successful in locating white alcoholics (the "traditional" skid row homeless) than others. We also analyzed extensive field and tracking notes that were available for 42 of the 50 never-found clients; among the 42, 8 clients (or 19%) were known to have died and another nine clients (or 21%) were known to have moved out of state and were never reached by telephone for their follow-up interview. Thus, about 40% of the never-located clients were missing for good and known reasons; the remainder simply disappeared.

Treatment Attrition: Survival in Treatment. As we have already stated, detox was intended to be a 7-day program, TC theoretically added another 21 days of treatment, and the ECIL program could have added another 12 months. In fact, the actual time in treatment was highly variable from client to client. Among the 164 treatment clients, 107 (or 65%) exited the program after TC (TC only), and the remaining 57 went on to ECIL (TC + ECIL). For convenience, we refer to these two groups as TC and ECIL clients, respectively, emphasizing, however, that all 57 ECIL clients also went through the TC program.

Days in treatment (not including days in detox) averaged 20.0 days for TC clients but varied from 4 to 35 days (SD = 4.8 days). In fact, 14% of the TC clients actually completed 2 or fewer weeks of treatment whereas 12% completed more than the allotted 21 or 22 days.

In theory, ECIL clients could have received 21 days of TC treatment subsequent to detox and 365 days of ECIL treatment subsequent to TC, for a possible maximum of 386 days in treatment. In fact, among the 57 ECIL clients, days in treatment averaged only 166 (43% of the maximum; median days in treatment were only 135) and varied from 16 to 396 (SD = 109 days). Only three ECIL clients (5% of the total) actually completed 386 or more days in treatment.

Clients might have left either TC or ECIL prematurely for any number of reasons. Some clients were administratively discharged for disciplinary reasons, rules infractions, or relapse; some left prematurely of their own accord, against staff advice; some left because they (and staff) felt they were ready for reentry into the "real world." Clinical data on discharge statuses show that among the 57 ECIL clients, only 17 (or 30%) are considered to have graduated from the program. (Program staff never developed clear "graduation" criteria for either ECIL or TC; in fact, this lack was a source of considerable confusion among both clients and staff. And so it cannot be inferred that the 17 clients considered on the clinical side as ECIL graduates actually completed some fixed number of days in treatment.)

Detailed analyses of retention in treatment produced only marginally significant results. Given the strong initial selection bias in favor of women, the evaluators expected that sex would predict retention in treatment but it did not. Wright and Devine conducted multivariate statistical analyses of the data in order to assess the factors that would predict client retention. Thus, their dependent variable was total days in treatment and they considered the impact of a large number of variables (social and background characteristics, entering substance problem, drug use histories, homelessness histories, ASI composite scores, etc.). Race emerged as a marginally significant predictor (blacks averaged more days in treatment than whites), but other background variables such as age, gender, and religion were always insignificant. One variable concerning the client's homelessness history and a few variables reflecting clients' alcohol and drug histories were significant (or marginally significant) predictors of retention in treatment, but most were not. Among the several ASI composite scores, only the alcohol variable predicted retention in treatment; the other composites were insignificant in all analyses. Retention in treatment was not significantly related to any measure of psychological status, despite some studies showing that clients with moderate psychopathology are more readily retained in treatment than others (Joe et al. 1983; Joe, Simpson, and Hubbard 1991; McLellan 1983; McLellan, Luborsky, Woody, O'Brien, and Druley 1983).

The lack of any consistent pattern in the attrition-from-treatment analysis is fairly persuasive evidence that the clinical staff did not attempt to deal with the most troubled or problematic clients by finding reasons to terminate their treatment (which they certainly could have done). On the other hand, these findings leave unexplained a rather curious anomaly, namely, that so many ECIL clients left the program well in advance of their allotted 12 (or 13) months. This is an important substantive issue to which we return later.

PROCESS EVALUATION

A process evaluation is necessary in order to ensure that the treatment actually delivered bears some resemblance to the treatment-as-designed, which is frequently not the case (Rossi and Freeman 1989). As a reminder, Wright, Devine, and others were the evaluators of the program. They neither designed nor implemented it. This separation was central to NOHSAP's support and praise from the granting agency. They gathered NOHSAP process evaluation data over a one-year period during which a member of the research team was assigned on a part-time basis to monitor the program site. The data consist of extensive interviews conducted with all key members of the treatment staff during the year (including those who left the organization for whatever reason), ongoing formal and informal contact with clients in all three phases of the program, and field observations.

The process evaluation revealed that the subcontractor delivered a program similar to that envisioned in the original NOHSAP design but that there were significant deviations and problems in many areas. Some of these deviations and associated problems were sufficient to raise questions about the probable long-term effectiveness of the program.

The NOHSAP treatment philosophy was very much that addiction is a disease and that as addicts learn more about the nature of their disease, they will come more successfully to control their addictive behaviors. [The "disease model" of addiction is close to universally accepted among treatment specialists, although a number of scholars are beginning to question its utility; see Fingarette (1988) for a statement of the contrary position.] Thus, the NOHSAP interventions were meant to be educational and didactic. The evaluation team observed a number of NOHSAP group meetings as they occurred. These group meetings consisted mostly of talking and learning about addiction, of testimonials concerning how miserable addiction had made one's life, of confessionals about the pain and suffering that one's addiction had caused, and of hopeful panegyrics about a more sober future.

Most of the management and staff of NOHSAP were themselves recovering addicts. The advantage of their addiction histories—hardly a trivial one—is that they provided positive role models for our clients. But staffing an alcohol and drug program with recovering addicts can also be problematic, and this problem warrants a brief discussion.

In the worldview of recovering addicts, the key to success in treatment lies in changing the interior or spiritual self. Thus, NOHSAP treatment was focused more on talking about addiction, learning about the nature and process of addiction, and laying bare the inner self than on specific program elements such as educational or vocational training or life skills development. (In fairness, more educated clients did tend to respond more positively to the NOHSAP intervention, which lends some credence to the didactic or educational model of intervention.)

Since recovery requires spiritual transformation and an act of personal will, there is a tendency among addicts in recovery to individualize problems. In NOHSAP, this tendency surfaced as a disposition on the part of management and staff to dismiss day-to-day operational problems as the result of unrepentant addicts who were not "working their program." Thus, it was not uncommon for NOHSAP management to treat complaints from clients and staff as the aggrieved protestations of unhappy addicts rather than as signs of more basic organizational and operational problems. Instead of decisive intervention to resolve problems, management frequently invoked the organizational equivalent of the Serenity Prayer.

The basic implementation problem (one that recurred throughout the program) was a limited relationship between the formal organizational chart and the actual division of managerial labor and responsibility. Off-site management retained primary control of the program but responded slowly to day-to-day programmatic issues; likewise, on-site management (the NOHSAP directors) suffered from lack of direction, poorly defined authority and responsibility, and limited discretion to respond unilaterally to problems as they arose. In short, neither NOHSAP management nor clinical staff had precise job descriptions and behavioral protocols.

Staff concern over apparently capricious management decisions, major unresolved program issues, and serious financial difficulties that set in after the first year created an insecure organizational climate during the early months of 1992 that persisted through project close-out. Many staff members began openly to express concerns about the security of their jobs during this period. During the spring and summer of 1992, the deteriorating financial situation began noticeably to affect staff morale and productivity.

Despite the many problems, staff did implement to some degree most of the major components of the NOHSAP intervention the designers originally proposed. Nonetheless, that implementation deviated from the original plan in a number of ways. Those deviations raised questions about long-term program effectiveness:

1. The initial plan was to offer clinical follow-up to all TC and ECIL clients for up to two years after release but resource constraints prevented any serious implementation of this plan. The only clini-

cal follow-up ever offered was an aftercare group that was to meet once a week, but even this was underused.

2. While the program offered "case management" to all clients, the actual case management services staff provided varied dramatically over time and were never as proactive or aggressive in linking clients to services as the original proposal suggested they would be.

3. Finally, the original program featured job training and placement prominently, especially as components of the ECIL program, but only a few clients ever received these services and staff never mounted a programwide effort at vocational assessment, training, or placement.

The subcontractor organization for NOHSAP was remarkably non-bureaucratized and while that characteristics might seem appealing, in fact it generated a number of deep and abiding problems with the program along four dimensions. First, the program lacked explicit policies and procedures to guide the work of staff members. What procedures and policies did exist were only occasionally written and staff frequently ignored them. Similarly, the program director created few well-defined objectives and performance standards regarding the quantity and quality of services being delivered, which led to additional problems.

A second problem arose from the absence of consistent, routinized documentation and record-keeping. The absence of a reliable system of documentation made it impossible to monitor the progress of implementation in terms of the frequency, duration, and intensity of services or treatments delivered.

A third problem was the absence of internal mechanisms to monitor performance (i.e., a quality assurance or quality control function). The NOHSAP clinical operation never developed a formal system to link goals, objectives, program activities, and staff services in any coherent manner, much less a system that would allow close monitoring or fine-tuning of program performance over time or direct feedback on performance. The paucity of explicit procedural standards or expectations regarding service delivery led to a "let's make it up as we go along" attitude even among those in leadership positions. At best, broad programmatic goals guided the staff; they were never given specific guidelines about the behaviors, strategies, approaches, or techniques to follow in implementing program components. Thus, the delivery of basic services such as case management or psychiatric counseling was highly variable across time and person. Our impression is that many of these issues are quite common among alcohol and drug programs for the homeless.

Finally, the program director often hired NOHSAP staff without regard to their formal qualifications or credentials and frequently enough with no clear job description or training to guide their work. According to one NOHSAP manager that we interviewed, "We always seem to be putting the cart before the horse when it comes to hiring people. We hire them and even after they are on payroll we do not have a clear idea of what exactly they are going to do. We hire people because of our personal relationship with them and then too often they become a drain on the organization." Remarkably, despite these four problems with implementation, most clients were highly satisfied with their NOHSAP experience.

OUTCOME EVALUATION

A well-established technique for evaluating a treatment program's success in enabling participants to recover from addiction is through analysis of what practitioners call an Addiction Severity Index (ASI). Wright and Devine subsequently conducted an analysis of the program data to generate ASI composite scores. These scores (Fureman, Parikh, Bragg, and McLellan 1990; McGahan et al. 1991) provide a convenient way to summarize the effects of NOHSAP treatment in a number of different areas. The ASI scores are computed according to a standardized formula from variables contained in each section of the ASI and provide composite indicators of the extent or severity of a client's medical, employment, alcohol, drug, legal, psychiatric, and family/social problems. The ASI was developed specifically as an instrument that could be used to monitor recovery from addiction disorders.

Wright and Devine relied on regression analyses of the ASI composites in which the dependent variables are the composite scores in each area as measured at follow-up; the baseline composite score is entered among the regressor variables. Holding initial values constant, the regression coefficients for other regressors therefore represent the predicted change (from Time 1 to Time 2) in the composite score for a unit increase in the independent variable in question. For reasons discussed earlier, they held sex constant in all analyses.

The results of this analysis indicated the following:

1. Baseline ASI composite scores are positively and significantly related to follow-up ASI composite scores in all seven areas; the coefficient for employment problems is noticeably stronger than

the coefficients in the other areas (meaning that employment problems are generally more persistent from Time 1 to Time 2 than are problems in other areas).

2. Holding Time 1 values constant, sex is insignificant in five areas and shows a significant positive coefficient in the other two; in other words, the employment problems and family / social relationship problems of women tended to worsen (against their Time 1 values) in the six months following treatment.

3. The coefficients for the TC dummy are consistently negative (indicating positive outcomes) but very small in magnitude and never significant.

4. Net of all other variables, the coefficients for the variable representing shorter-than-average ECIL stays are sometimes positive and sometimes negative but hover around zero and are never significant.

5. The coefficients for longer-than-average ECIL stays are always negative (indicating positive outcomes), always larger in magnitude than the coefficients for the other treatment variables, and are statistically significant (at alpha = .10) in three cases: employment, alcohol problems, and familial and social relationships.

Thus, ECIL stays exceeding the median number of treatment days conferred moderate benefits on all indicators and sufficiently strong benefits to achieve statistical significance on three of seven indicators; TC stays and ECIL stays shorter than the median stay conferred no discernible benefit in any area.

The evaluators conducted extensive, more fine-grained outcome analyses almost invariably with results similar to those obtained on the ASI composites (Devine et al. 1994). For example, they asked clients during their follow-up interviews to tell how they were doing with sobriety, housing, employment, and family relationships. These self-reported outcome assessments rather faithfully reproduced the ASI composites analysis. ECIL stays exceeding the median number of treatment days conferred moderately strong benefits on all the self-reported indicators except familial reintegration; shorter ECIL stays seem to have conferred marginally positive income and employment benefits but no discernible or consistent benefit in other areas; TC stays conferred marginally positive benefits in terms of alcohol and drug relapse but no consistent benefit in any other area. In general, differences in these self-assessments between controls, TC clients, and short-term ECIL clients were modest or nonexistent; only long-term ECIL clients consistently reported better outcomes by statistically significant margins.

The ASI provides no measure of housing outcomes, but here too the general pattern of results was the same. In the period since release from treatment, more than half the control males (54%) had experienced at least one episode of homelessness and more than a quarter (26%) had been continuously homeless for the entire period. All other groups did better at avoiding homelessness than control males: the proportions who experienced at least one homeless episode were 23% of control females, 43% of TC males, 22% of TC females, 30% of short-term ECIL clients (regardless of gender), and 10% of long-term ECIL clients (again regardless of gender). In terms of avoiding homelessness altogether, women tended generally to do better than men and treatment groups tended generally to do better than control groups, although in the latter case the differences were large only for ECIL clients completing more than the median days in treatment. Again, neither TC nor a short-term ECIL stay appears to have conferred any strongly positive housing benefit, but a long-term ECIL stay apparently did.

Finally, more sophisticated econometric models undertaken to correct for possible selection biases owing to nonrandomization and attrition supported evidence findings of modest treatment success (see Devine, Brody, and Wright 1997). Detailed analyses of a large number of indicators of alcohol and drug relapse tended also to reproduce the ASI composites analysis. Throughout these analyses, all treatment clients did somewhat better, and long-term ECIL clients did significantly better, in regard to relapse to alcohol but not significantly better in avoiding relapse to other drugs.

CONCLUSION

The goal of NOHSAP was to demonstrate that it is possible to take homeless and impoverished drug addicts and turn them into responsible and productive adult citizens of the community. There is some, but only some, comfort in recognizing that this goal was very ambitious to begin with. The three-year history of NOHSAP is one of progressive downscaling of initial expectations. Analyses of the baseline data revealed that most NOHSAP clients came into the project with even deeper and more serious problems than we had anticipated. Results from the process evaluation showed that staff encountered many problems in the implementation of the project, and that the actual program-as-delivered was by no means as good as the program-as-designed. The program director's and

staff's failure to implement the randomization scheme made the evaluators anxious about whether the study would produce any useful outcome
data; the small numbers of clients the program retained in treatment
suggested that evaluators would have trouble discerning even fairly
strong effects.

The data did not sustain our initial optimism about NOHSAP but
neither did they confirm our subsequent cynicism. The process evaluation
confirmed that staff never fully or even partially implemented many of
the initially intended interventions. It is also clear, however, that
NOHSAP did provide housing and stable living conditions for many
homeless people and that the program was successful in creating a
strong, peer-supported residential and therapeutic community that valued sobriety, support, and respect for one another and that gave homeless addicts an opportunity to salvage their lives. While they were there,
the program was somewhat successful. Given our previous discussion of
the complex needs of the substance-abusive homeless, this program did
support the contention that a successful response requires a multidimen-
sional approach that tackles the drug and/or alcohol abuse, employment
deficiencies, and social support networks, and facilitates the stability of
existing family structure.

Likewise, the outcome evaluation confirmed that NOHSAP was only
partially successful in producing sober, stably housed, employed, self-
sufficient, socially functioning former addicts. In general, long-term ECIL
clients showed statistically significant if rather modest improvements in
several (but certainly not all) areas of functioning, and in a few cases, any
treatment appeared to confer some benefit compared to the control
group. Also, success was generally greater in the area of sobriety and
relapse than in the areas of housing, employment, or general social functioning. But to conclude that success was limited to only some clients and
to only some areas of functioning is not to deny that for at least those few
clients, NOHSAP was a highly beneficial experience.

The outcome evaluation showed that all treatment groups did better
than controls in avoiding relapse to alcohol, although the differences
were very modest in all cases except long-term ECIL clients. Since relapse
to alcohol is the most common form of relapse even for clients addicted to
other drugs, the generally positive treatment effects for alcohol relapse
must be scored as a significant program accomplishment. On the other
hand, the outcome data generally did not show even marginally significant treatment effects for relapse to drugs other than alcohol (although,
again, long-term ECIL clients tended to do slightly better than other
groups on most indicators). Do we therefore conclude that NOHSAP
failed in this critical area? Or do we have to conclude that crack is a

powerful, addictive drug and that even a long-term and rather intensive intervention at best loosens but rarely breaks the addiction?

NOHSAP was also only marginally successful in helping clients attain stable jobs, self-sufficient incomes, and acceptable housing. On the plus side, long-term ECIL clients did tend to do better in the areas of housing, employment, and income than did other groups, but on the minus side, these effects were rarely large and only occasionally significant. And certainly, part of the problem here was the failure of the program to fully implement the intended interventions in these areas. But at the same time, our clients had relatively meager human resources from which to draw in the first place, and the New Orleans housing and labor markets are hardly favorable for formerly homeless addicts in the early stages of their recovery. Again, is the right conclusion that NOHSAP failed to achieve these program goals or that the exogenous barriers essentially precluded success from the very beginning?

The "good" accomplished by NOHSAP inheres mostly in the more or less consistently positive effects observed among long-term ECIL clients; the "bad" is that these effects were rarely strong, not uniform in all areas of functioning, and generally not observed among TC or short-term ECIL clients. The "ugly" is that the program was never fully implemented as intended, and especially that it proved impossible to retain more than a handful of clients in treatment for more than the initial few months.

Why so many ECIL clients left ECIL prematurely is rather a mystery, and an important one. It is certainly possible that program-specific factors drove clients away, but the results of our exit questionnaires showed that most clients were highly satisfied with most aspects of the NOHSAP program. It is also possible that the clinical staff unloaded clients at the first sign of trouble, retaining only those deemed near-certain bets to succeed. But our analysis of retention in treatment suggested rather persuasively that the clinical staff did not attempt to deal with the most troubled or problematic clients by finding reasons to terminate their treatment.

We are left, then, largely by default, with the hypothesis that there is something intrinsic to the circumstances, personalities, or conditions of homeless addicts that precludes most of them from being retained in a treatment program for much more than a few months. As a matter of fact, there are relatively few studies of long-term (more than one-month) alcohol and drug treatment programs for any population of substance abusers, with the exception of long-term methadone maintenance programs for recovering heroin addicts; but the scarce literature available on the topic points unambiguously to long-term retention as a significant problem. Concerning long-term "therapeutic community" interventions similar to ECIL, "attrition from TCs is typically high—above the rates for methadone maintenance but below the rates for outpatient non-methadone treatment. Typically, about 15% of admissions will graduate after a continuous stay" (Gerstein and Harwood 1990:189). Thus, the disturbingly low retention of clients in ECIL is actually about average, or even a bit better than average, for interventions of this sort. Also, "the minimum retention necessary to yield improvement in long-term outcomes seems to be several months" (ibid.), also highly consistent with our outcome analysis.

If the substance abusing homeless require "minimum retention" of several months to receive beneficial long-term outcomes, and if the homeless addicts NOHSAP researchers studied are typical, then the conclusion is that programs cannot retain most homeless addicts in treatment long enough for treatment to do them much good. However discouraging this conclusion seems, it may well be correct, and if it is correct, then the proportion of homeless addicts that are in fact "recoverable," the proportion that can be turned into stable and productive citizens, may be not much more than a few percent. The reason why treatment will not "solve" the homeless problem, in short, is not because treatment is ineffective but because it is very difficult to design programs that successfully retain homeless substance abusers long enough for treatment to work.

The statistician John Tukey is reported to have said, "Anything worth doing is worth doing superficially." He did not intend this as a license to ignore research standards or proceed in a sloppy, haphazard manner, but rather as a reminder that effects of sufficient strength to be worth discussing are likely to make themselves heard over the background static. For all the problems NOHSAP generated on both the program and research sides, the principal lesson comes through with some clarity: homeless addicts whom a program can retain in a NOHSAP-style treatment program for more than a few months usually profit from the experience, but most homeless addicts cannot be so retained.

8

Health and Health Status

INTRODUCTION

We have stressed throughout that the rising tide of homelessness has resulted from a continuing decimation of the low-income housing supply coupled with recent increases in the number of poor and near-poor persons and families. Homeless people, however, do not live their lives at such high levels of abstraction. Their existence is dominated by a daily struggle for life's most rudimentary needs. Unmet health care needs top the list of needs, being surpassed only by food and shelter on the agenda of daily concern.

While no one would dispute the importance of research on the problems of homelessness in all of its aspects, the focus on health issues perhaps requires some explanation. Attention to physical health can and often does play an important role in addressing many other problems. Homeless people—youths or adults—are often simply too ill to place in employment or other counseling programs, too ill to stand in line while their applications for benefits are being processed, too ill to search for housing within their means. Extreme poverty and general estrangement from society and its institutions further limit access to conventional health care institutions.

The effects of poverty and homelessness on health are not lost on homeless people themselves. Ropers and Boyer (1987b) investigated the perceived health status of a sample of homeless individuals in Los Angeles. The proportion of homeless reporting themselves to be in "poor" health was 70% greater than the proportion among low-income respondents (family income under $10,000) in the National Health Interview Survey. Self-reported poor health was higher among respondents with chronic health conditions, among those who had recently seen a physi-

147

cian for an acute health problem, among those experiencing chronic depression, and among those with severe alcohol-dependence symptoms (ibid.:673). A large percentage of respondents also stated that their health had deteriorated since the onset of homelessness. Additional data on perceived health status among the homeless are reported in Altman et al. (1989), Burt and Cohen (1989a), and Rossi et al. (1987).

And, as we have made clear, all of the homeless are not adults. Among youths, poor health and especially chronic physical illness probably contribute to the cycle of poverty, whereby the homeless children of today become the destitute and homeless adults of tomorrow. This issue is, and should be, of particular concern. Recurring health problems of even minimal severity will disrupt school attendance and interfere with studying and homework activities; indeed, researchers have already documented the effects of homelessness on school performance and cognitive development among children (Bassuk and Rubin 1987; Bassuk, Rubin, and Lauriat 1986). Beyond undermining academic success, chronically poor health or physical disabilities will impede, if not preclude, normal labor force participation and may in turn foster welfare dependency. Thus, poor health is one mechanism by which homelessness reproduces itself across generations. For these reasons, while the focus of this chapter is on the health of the homeless, we are particularly concerned with the impact of health issues on homeless youth.

There is every reason to expect that homeless youth experience exceptionally widespread health problems, an expectation that is borne out by what little research exists. Yates et al. (1988) compared the health problems of 110 runaway youth in Los Angeles to those of 655 nonrunaway youth who had been seen in the same health clinics. Among the conclusions of the study were that "runaway street youth are at greater risk for a wide variety of medical problems and of health-compromising behaviors including suicide and depression, prostitution, and drug use" (p. 820). Yates et al. noted that more widespread among the runaway youth were genito-urinary problems, hepatitis, asthma, serious respiratory infections (pneumonia), lice, drug abuse, and trauma. In like fashion, Shane (1987) has reported data for 536 clients of agencies serving homeless, missing, and runaway youth in New Jersey. Here too, physical and mental health problems were widespread.

The report of the Institute of Medicine (1988) and the extensive body of health care research that report summarized (e.g., Brickner, Scharer, Conanon, Elvy, and Savarese 1985; Brickner, Scharer, Conanan, Saverese, and Scanlan 1990; Wright and Weber 1987) have made it plain that health and homelessness are linked together in at least three important ways. First, poor health, physical as well as mental, is often a cause of homelessness, especially when it involves disabilities severe enough to prevent work.

Second, poor health is often a consequence of homelessness. Indeed, it is hard to imagine a style of existence more profoundly deleterious to health than a life in the shelters or on the streets. Finally, whatever the pathways of cause and effect, homelessness greatly complicates the delivery of adequate health care.

In 1984, recognizing the often unmet health care needs of the homeless population, the Robert Wood Johnson Foundation and the Pew Charitable Trusts announced their National Health Care for the Homeless (HCH) initiative—a four-year, $25 million grant program that ultimately established HCH clinics in 19 U.S. cities. Part of the national evaluation of this program involved gathering and processing data on health and related social problems of clients seen in the 19 HCH clinics. Between program start-up in March 1985 and the end of data collection in December 1987, researchers gathered information on nearly 100,000 homeless and destitute people from all over the United States. This chapter summarizes the principal health findings for adults, adolescents, and children from this vast body of data and integrates it with other research speaking to the health of homeless adults and children.

PRIOR RESEARCH

The first book-length study of the topic summarized in detail relevant research on health aspects of homelessness through about 1984 (Brickner et al. 1985). In that study, Brickner concluded that "the medical disorders of the homeless are all the ills to which the flesh is heir, magnified by disordered living conditions, exposure to extremes of heat and cold, lack of protection from rain and snow, bizarre sleeping accommodations, and overcrowding in shelters. These factors are exacerbated by stress, psychiatric disorders, and sociopathic behavior patterns" (ibid:3). One could expand this list of risk factors more or less indefinitely: uncertain and often inadequate provisions for simple acts of daily hygiene, communal bathing and eating facilities, unsafe and unsanitary shelters [shelter living presents near-optimal conditions for the transmission of infectious and communicable disease (Gross and Rosenberg 1987)], exposure to the social environment of the streets, general debilitation and susceptibility to infection, inadequate diet, no access to a home medicine cabinet with its usual stock of palliatives, no place to go for bed rest, too much smoking and drinking, an absence of family networks and other support to fall back on in times of illness, crushing poverty, and no health insurance. It is, indeed, a safe assertion that no aspect of homelessness is actually good for a person's health.

At that time, it was sadly apparent that "the information base about health problems of the homeless is rudimentary (Brickner et al. 1985). Studies of derelicts have produced many a PhD thesis. In all this work, however, there is rarely a comment about health or disease. The same vacuum exists in the 957 pages of the 1982 *Congressional Hearings on Homelessness in America*" (ibid.:3–4).

The information base has developed considerably since 1984 and now consists of perhaps a half-dozen major studies and several scores of journal articles. In nearly all cases, the recent research has only confirmed Brickner's original findings. Subsequent chapters in the Brickner volume documented elevated incidences of many physical disorders among the homeless. Compounding these many health problems, of course, are high rates of alcohol abuse and mental illness (as we have demonstrated in previous chapters). The remainder of this chapter summarizes findings from the Health Care for the Homeless Demonstration Program and from the National Ambulatory Medical Care Program. Doing so provides a powerful picture of the extent of health problems the homeless face.

RESEARCH DESIGN AND PROCEDURES

A detailed account of the methods and procedures of the HCH research effort appears in Wright and Weber (1987) and of homeless teenagers in Wright (1989c). In all, 19 cities participated in the HCH demonstration program, but for technical reasons, this chapter excludes data from three of these cities. Programwide, between start-up and the end of data collection in December 1987, HCH clinics saw just under 100,000 homeless clients a total of nearly 300,000 times: 5% of those were teenagers between the ages of 13 and 19 years old. This chapter discusses analyses based on about 63,000 of these clients; this includes all teenagers who were HCH clients between start-up and data collected from 1985 to 1987.

The HCH client population is, in the first instance, a clinical population, consisting of homeless and destitute persons who, for whatever reason, sought health attention in the HCH clinics; thus, clients may differ from homeless people in general in any number of ways. There are, however, no gross differences between homeless people in general and HCH clients specifically on any variable we have examined. The average age, percentage female, percentage who are members of homeless families, percentage veterans, and most other demographic characteristics of

HCH clients are all essentially identical to the known characteristics of the larger homeless population. One evident reason for this similarity is the very aggressive outreach most of the 19 projects undertook; indeed, in cities where the calculation can be made, it appears that the local HCH projects reached between a quarter and a third of the total homeless populations of their respective cities each year.

While we are confident about those comparisons, there are some things the data do not tell us. We cannot, for instance, differentiate between homeless teenagers who are still living with their parent or parents and those who are already out "on their own." Limited analysis from the first year of program operation suggests that among younger teens (ages 13 and 14), a sizable fraction (about half) are still living under adult supervision, whereas nearly all of the older teens (ages 16 to 19) live independently. Likewise, we cannot distinguish runaways from nonrunaways in these data. We do know, however, that although the large majority of homeless adults are men, the heavy preponderance of males is true only among adults. At all ages under 20, males and females appear in the HCH data in nearly equal proportions. In fact, in the data the analyses retain, homeless teenagers ($N = 1,694$), females outnumber males by 57 to 43%. Slightly less than half the teenagers are white.

Most encounters with most clients generated information about health and related problems that researchers recorded on Contact Forms and submitted to the research team for coding, entry, and analysis. The Contact Forms were, in essence, medical progress notes. Registered nurses extracted all medical information from these notes.

In addition to the clinical data, the HCH project also obtained more detailed information about a sample of clients from case assessment questionnaires HCH care providers filled out (usually project nurses, social workers, or case managers). The research team drew samples from the Year I client base; care providers, usually working in teams, reviewed their files on each sampled client and answered a series of questions about the client's background, housing history, psychiatric condition, employment history, and the like. The study sampled about 1,400 clients in this manner, although the effective sample size on any given question is usually much smaller because of high rates of missing data.

Primary source data on the physical health problems of HCH clients appear in Wright and Weber (1987). For comparative purposes, we compare these data with data from the National Ambulatory Medical Care Survey (NAMCS), a survey of patients seen in ambulatory practice in 1985. NAMCS was based on a systematic random sample of clients seen in a probability sample of ambulatory care settings in a randomly stipulated week in 1985. These data were derived from a single visit to a doctor in a large urban area. The client, not the visit, was the unit of analysis. The homeless clients the HCH data include and the walk-in clients in the NAMCS data are both clinical populations. What is clear from the comparisons, however, is that the similarities stop there. The differences are extreme, the comparisons illustrative of the ways in which homelessness causes physical problems.

Wright (1989c) compared the health problems of homeless children during the first year of the HCH program to those of children included in the NAMCS. Nearly all disorders are more common among the homeless group. About 7% of the homeless children had scabies and lice infestations, for example, compared to 0.2% of the NAMCS children; upper respiratory infections were about twice as common, skin disorders four times as common, poor dentition ten times as common, etc. Homeless children were also more likely than normal children to suffer from chronic physical disorders.

The HCH data on children confirm all the patterns literature reports. The general configuration of illness among homeless children in general and among HCH children in particular is similar to that of children in general, although somewhat different than the configuration observed among homeless adults (acute disorders are more common, and chronic disorders less common, among the children than the adults). That is to say, the health problems homeless children face are not exotic or unusual disorders; they are, rather, the same health problems all children face. By far the most common disorders appearing among the children are minor upper respiratory infections, followed by minor skin ailments and ear disorders, then gastrointestinal problems, trauma, eye disorders, and lice infestations. In all these cases, differences in the rates of disorder between homeless boys and girls are relatively minor.

Differences between homeless children and children in general, in contrast, are often large and in some cases dramatically large. Although the general pattern of illness among homeless children is not atypical of children's illnesses in general, the comparative rates of occurrence are often inordinately elevated.

POOR HEALTH AS A CAUSE OF HOMELESSNESS

Throughout this book we have been addressing debates about the causes of homelessness. That question was also a concern in the HCH program. One of the topics the client survey covered dealt with care providers' assessments of the principal reasons why each client was homeless. Care providers were given "a list of factors that are sometimes involved in a person's becoming homeless" and asked to rate the importance of each factor in regard to the particular client in question. The survey included 22 possible factors (along with an open-ended "any other" option). Thus, these data are based on care provider judgments, not on the responses of homeless people themselves, whose viewpoint might be very different. Opinions, even professional opinions, about what causes homelessness are not the same as the causes of homelessness themselves.

Care providers' most frequently cited reason for homelessness, by far, was alcohol and drug abuse, mentioned as the single most important factor in the homelessness of 32% of the sample and as a major factor for an additional 22%. About 41% of the adult HCH clients were alcoholic and about 13% abused drugs other than alcohol, with considerable overlap between these two conditions (see Chapter 6). Both estimates are approximately in the middle of the range of results other studies of the era report. (More recent studies show much higher rates of drug abuse other than alcohol among today's homeless population.)

Also very prominent on the list of reasons for homelessness was chronic mental illness, which providers rated as the most important factor in the homelessness of 16% and as a major factor in the homelessness of an additional 18%. Several lines of evidence from the HCH evaluation converge on about one-third as the best estimate of the rate of mental illness among HCH clients, roughly the consensus value in the literature.

Chronic physical disorders place tenth on the list of reasons for homelessness, ahead of many of the more commonly discussed factors such as loss of entitlements or recent release from a mental or other institution. Overall, care providers cited poor physical health as the most important reason for the homelessness of about 3%, as a major factor for an additional 10%, and as a contributing factor for as many as 22%. Thus, as a cause of homelessness, poor physical health is surprisingly important.

We have consistently argued that viewing mental illness, alcoholism, and ill health as causes of homelessness is problematic; rather, these factors increase the vulnerability of certain segments of the population to the conditions (poverty, insufficient housing) that contribute to becoming homeless. Further analysis of these data showed clearly that employability provides the linkage between ill health on the one hand and homelessness on the other. Among those for whom poor physical health was cited as the single most important factor in homelessness, HCH staff also considered 54% not employable and 24% as probably not employable. In fact, HCH staff considered about 17% of the sampled HCH clients physically disabled and incapable of working, a figure that is consistent with independent estimates derived from the clinical data.

Among the 17% HCH staff judged physically incapable of work, incidentally, fewer than one in five received Social Security Disability Insurance (SSDI) payments, and fewer than half received either SSDI or Supplemental Security Income (SSI). It is plausible to assume, therefore, that the SSDI eligibility and benefit level rollbacks of March 1981 enhanced the importance of poor physical health as a reason for homelessness, at least to some extent (Bassuk 1984), a change that bodes poorly for the disabled in this era of further benefit retrenchment.

All told then, how many people are homeless because of health issues? Casting the net as broadly as possible (to include alcoholism, drug abuse, chronic mental illness, and chronic physical disorders) and including those for whom these factors are at least of minor importance, we end up with the conclusion that health issues of one or another sort are implicated to some extent in the homelessness of almost everybody. To be sure, an increasingly large number of people are homeless largely for strictly economic reasons, but even in these cases, ill health will also be a secondary contributor. At minimum, these data leave little doubt that attention to health issues is critical in both the analysis of homelessness and in the provision of needed services to homeless people.

HOMELESSNESS AS A CAUSE OF POOR HEALTH

That homelessness contributes both to acute and chronic disorders seems fairly obvious (if you sleep out of doors, you will probably get a lot of colds!), but some have objected to treating homelessness as a cause of chronic physical disorders of the sort we discuss below. In fact, homelessness causes chronic as well as acute disorders. For example, homelessness increases a person's exposure to infectious and communicable disorders and can therefore be a direct cause of diseases like tuberculosis. Medical science has demonstrated that severe stress can trigger genetic predispositions to many disorders (such as hypertension); homelessness is a severely stressful existence. Long periods of malnutrition, another condition frequently associated with homelessness, can cause some chronic disorders (such as anemia and various degenerative bone diseases). Homelessness, in short, is an important cause of acute and chronic medical problems.

1. Acute Physical Disorders

The most common acute ailments adult HCH clients presented were upper respiratory infections (33%), followed by traumas (25%) and minor skin ailments (15%). More serious skin ailments were also common (4%). All these disorders were much more widespread among HCH clients than among NAMCS patients (by factors ranging from 3 to 6), most likely resulting from overexposure to the environment that the homeless experience. Upper respiratory disorders of varying degrees of severity are endemic to homelessness and appeared among all subgroups in nearly equal proportions. In most cases they were treated with over-the-counter medications.

Lacerations and wounds were the most common of the traumas, followed by sprains, bruises, and fractures. Trauma of all types was more common among men than among women, and slightly more common among young than old, patterns that are probably linked to age and gender differences in aggressive behavior. Traumatic injury is among the top three or four presenting conditions in any health care outlet serving predominantly homeless people (Brickner et al. 1985, 1990; Institute of Medicine 1988; Wright and Weber 1987). "Homeless people are at high risk for traumatic injuries for a number of reasons. They are frequently victims of violent crimes such as rape, assault, and robbery" (Institute of Medicine 1988:44). To illustrate something of the dimensions of the problem, Kelly (1985) has reported that the rate of sexual assault against homeless women exceeds that of U.S. women in general by a factor of 20. Physical and sexual violence and exploitation are exceedingly common elements in the lives of homeless women and are, indeed, a major precipitating factor for homelessness among women (Buckner, Bassuk, and Zima 1993; Sullivan and Damrosch 1991; Hagen 1987; Bassuk 1993; Dail 1990; D'Ercole and Struening 1990; Milburn and D'Ercole 1991; Shinn, Knickman, and Weitzman 1991). According to D'Ercole and Struening (1990), "[W]omen in a New York shelter were 106 times more likely to be raped, 41 times more likely to be robbed, and 15 times more likely to be assaulted than were housed African-American women." A third of the homeless women interviewed by Hilfiker (1989) had been raped. Wood, Valdez, Hayashi, and Shen (1990) compared homeless mothers to poor but housed mothers in Los Angeles and found that homeless mothers more commonly reported spousal abuse (35 vs. 16%), child abuse (28 vs. 10%), drug use (43 vs. 30%), mental health problems (14 vs. 6%) and weaker support networks [see also Milburn and D'Ercole (1991) and Jackson-Wilson and Borgers (1993)]. Other subgroups among the homeless also face higher-than-average risks of traumatic injury due to intentional violence, among them homeless teens (Wright 1991; Yates et al. 1988), the homeless mentally ill (French 1987), and homeless alcoholics and drug addicts (Wright and Weber 1987).

The predominant acute disorders suffered by HCH youth are upper respiratory infections (~35%), traumas (~20%), and minor skin disorders (also ~20%). Infestations (lice and scabies), genito-urinary problems, and gastro-intestinal disorders were also quite common. In general, young homeless men have more acute disorders than young homeless women, although there are several important exceptions to this pattern, especially in regard to genito-urinary disorders. The males, particularly those over age 16, show exceptionally high rates of injuries, especially sprains and lacerations. Except for trauma, there were no consistent effects for age.

Comparisons with the rates of acute disorders among NAMCS youth show wide differentials in almost all cases. HCH youth are two or three times more likely to suffer minor respiratory infections than are NAMCS youth, about twice as likely to suffer serious respiratory infections, and many times more likely to suffer from genito-urinary disorders and skin ailments, both minor and severe. None of the acute disorders is more common among NAMCS than among HCH teens.

Lice infestations are the characteristic or prototypical acute health ailment of homeless persons regardless of age. These infestations are nearly nonexistent among NAMCS teens; in fact, there are only ten lice cases recorded among the more than 5,000 NAMCS youth contained in the analysis. In contrast, about 6% of the HCH youth are afflicted with this disorder, a differential on the order of 30 to 1.

In contrast, among NAMCS children, a mere 0.2% had lice infestations (this amounts to 13 cases of lice among 6,309 children), compared to more than 7% of the HCH children, a differential on the order of 35 to 1. Upper respiratory infections are twice as common among homeless children as among ambulatory children in general, skin disorders about four times as common, gastrointestinal disorders about three or four times as common, ear infections nearly twice as common, poor dentition more than ten times as common.

Children, clearly, are not immune to the deleterious effects of homelessness on physical health. That many of these children are over age 5 and therefore required to attend school, where their illnesses can then circulate to other children, is an additional point of concern.

Programwide, the daily project workload was heavily dominated by the treatment of these and related acute disorders. Based on care providers' characterizations of clients' primary medical problems, we judged about two-thirds were acute and the remaining one-third were chronic.

This situation is quite similar to that in regular ambulatory medical practice.

2. Chronic Physical Disorders

Among all HCH clients the program treated, 28% had at least one chronic physical disorder; among clients seen more than once (for whom the data are much more reliable), the figure was 37%; and among NAMCS patients, 27%. We thus infer that chronic physical disease, like chronic alcohol abuse and chronic mental illness, is also more common among the homeless than among the domiciled population. Chronic disorders (all types combined) were about equally common among HCH men and women and were also about equally common among nonwhites and whites. In contrast, the prevalence of these disorders increased sharply with age, reaching about 60% among those over 50. The proportion of HCH youth with any chronic physical disorder varies from 10 to 20% and averages about 18%. This rate is nearly twice the rate of chronic disease observed among NAMCS teens (just under 10%). Young homeless women are more prone to these disorders than young homeless men; obversely, older teens are more prone to them than younger teens, regardless of gender.

The principal chronic disorders the HCH projects treated were hypertension, arthritis and other musculoskeletal disorders, problems with dentition, gastro-intestinal ailments, peripheral vascular disease, neurological disorders, eye disorders, genito-urinary problems, ear disorders, and chronic obstructive pulmonary disease. For youth the most common chronic disorders were eye disorders, gastrointestinal disorders, ear problems, neurological impairments, and problems with dentition. Other chronic disorders definitely more prevalent among HCH than NAMCS youth include endocrine dysfunction, cardiac and vascular disease, and hypertension.

Among the chronic conditions, peripheral vascular and limb disorders are prototypical of the health problems of the homeless, again regardless of age (McBride and Mulcare 1985). As with the case of lice infestation, these problems are exceedingly rare among NAMCS youth and distressingly common among homeless youth. In the case of diagnosed peripheral vascular disease, the differential is on the order of 10 or 20 to 1.

Younger children also exhibited troubling rates of chronic physical disorders. About one in eight of the HCH children already have one or another chronic health condition: cardiac disease, anemia, peripheral vas-

cular disorders, neurological disorders, and the like. While the overall
rate of chronic physical disorder among homeless children is about the
same as that observed among ambulatory children in general, differences
in specific categories are substantial, among them endocrine disorders,
seizures, and cardiac and vascular disorders.

Pediatricians affiliated with the New York City Children's Health Project identified what they call a "homeless child syndrome," comprised of
"poverty related health problems, immunization delays, untreated or
under-treated acute and chronic illnesses, unrecognized disorders,
school, behavioral, and psychological problems, child abuse and neglect"
(*Homeless Child Syndrome* 1988). It would obviously be wrong to suggest
that all homeless children exhibit all aspects of this syndrome. At the
same time, most homeless children probably do exhibit one or more of
these problems and disorders; at the very least, they are more commonly
observed among homeless children than among children in general or
even poverty-level children.

Hypertension.   The Department of Community Medicine, St. Vincent's
Hospital and Medical Center of New York City conducted detailed exam-
inations of hypertension among the homeless. This research found abnormally elevated blood pressures in about a quarter to a third of the clients
screened, nearly twice the rate obtained in the HCH data. The difference
is due largely to the difference in the proportion of clients screened; they
did not test all HCH clients for hypertension. In both data sets, and in the
population at large, hypertension is more common among men than
women, more common among nonwhites than whites, and increases
sharply with age. The disorder is also very much more common among
alcohol abusers than nonabusers. In NAMCS, 6.5% of the patients are
hypertensive; thus, the homeless are some two to four times more likely
to suffer the disorder than the domiciled population. Moreover, though
alcohol abuse is certainly a major factor, it is not the sole cause. Even
among non-alcohol-abusing HCH men, the rate of hypertension exceeds
the NAMCS rate by an approximate factor of two.

Gastro-Intestinal Disorders.   Gastro-intestinal disorders include a wide
range of chronic and acute disorders and symptoms ranging from ulcers
and hernias to diarrhea and gastritis. Differences across subgroups are
minor. Here too, there is an obvious link to alcohol abuse, but the rates for
nonabusing HCH clients still exceed the NAMCS rate. Even setting aside
the alcoholics, the homeless are some two to three times more likely to
suffer these disorders than the domiciled ambulatory population.

Peripheral Vascular Disease. Peripheral vascular disease (PVD) is perhaps the characteristic chronic physical disorder associated with a homeless existence (McBride and Mulcare 1985). The category contains a wide range of specific disorders each sharing a common origin, namely, venous or arterial deficiencies in the extremities. In the HCH data, these disorders are somewhat more common among men and whites than among women and nonwhites, and like most chronic disorders, increase regularly with age. Compared to the NAMCS data, (PVD) is four to five times more common among the homeless than among the general ambulatory population.

The exceptionally high rate of PVD among the homeless is not primarily the result of alcohol abuse but results from life-style. Constant forced walking and the tendency to sleep with the legs in a dependent position causes blood and body fluids to pool in the extremities; this in turn requires higher venous pressures in order to return the blood through the circulatory system. Over a sufficient period of time, this behavior destroys the venous valves, leading to edema, thromboses, cellulitis, and ulceration. Poor hygiene and exposure to the environment further increase the possibility of infections. In the extreme case, gangrene and subsequent amputation ensue.

Poor Dentition. More than a tenth of HCH clients had poor dentition. This condition is probably an underestimate of the true rate of dental disorders since dental services were not directly available through most HCH facilities. These problems declined with age (presumably because the teeth are lost and are therefore no longer a problem); differences by gender and race were minor. The dental problems suffered by the homeless result from neglect of daily dental hygiene and inadequate dental attention over long periods.

Neurological Disorders. Neurological symptoms and disorders range in severity from migraine headaches and neuritis to Parkinson's disease, peripheral neuropathy, multiple sclerosis, and quadriplegia. Most of these conditions likely contributed to people becoming homeless and then the conditions of homelessness exacerbate the severity of the condition. The most common neurological disorders in this population were seizures, but these are treated as a separate category. Excluding seizures, these disorders were about equally widespread across all subgroups.

There is a strong link between seizure disorders and patterns of alcohol abuse. Seizures are three times more common among homeless alcoholics than nonalcoholics. Still, the rates of seizure disorders among the nondrinking homeless were much higher than the rate in the general ambulatory population.

Other Chronic Disorders.   Other chronic disorders that were considerably more widespread among the homeless than among NAMCS patients include anemia, ear disorders, liver disease, chronic obstructive pulmonary disease, and genito-urinary problems. The difference in liver disease is solely a function of alcohol abuse; among nondrinking homeless, the rate is not substantially higher than that observed in NAMCS. A few chronic disorders occur at approximately equal rates in both the HCH and NAMCS populations; these include cancer, diabetes and other endocrinological disorders, vision problems, stroke, and arthritis and related musculoskeletal ailments.

Pregnancy and Sexuality.   Though not chronic conditions, it is important to discuss pregnancy and sexuality. The increasing numbers of poor and homeless women have led to concerns about their use of various preventive health and family planning services. The pregnancy rate among homeless women is high compared to other groups of women. Pregnancy risk factors among socioeconomically disadvantaged women include "environmentally induced risk factors such as nutritional inadequacy, excessive stress, life-long medical under-service, inadequate housing and sanitation, and many medical conditions and diseases, both chronic and acute, such as genito-urinary tract infections and hypertension" (Geronimus 1986:1416). Enhanced behavioral risk factors in these populations include elevated rates of alcohol, drug, and tobacco abuse (Bassuk and Weinreb 1993). The effects of these risk factors on pregnancies among poor and homeless women are evident in the higher proportion of low-birthweight infants and much higher rates of infant mortality (Combs-Orme, Risley-Curtiss, and Taylor 1993; Hogue and Hargraves 1993; Collins and David 1990). Neglect of routine gynecological and prenatal care is also a common complicating factor (Chavkin, Kristal, Seabron, and Guigli 1987). The rate of pregnancy among homeless women is surprisingly high. Among all adult women seen more than once, 12.2% were pregnant at or since their first contact with HCH; in NAMCS, the figure is 7.1% (the physician sampling frame for NAMCS includes physicians in gynecological and obstetrical practice; see Wright 1989c; Bassuk and Weinreb 1993; Weitzman 1989). Likewise, the rate of pregnancy among HCH youth is astonishing. Among HCH girls aged 13–15, 14% were pregnant at or since their first contact with HCH; among those 16–19, the figure is 31%, the highest rate of pregnancy within any HCH age group. Corresponding figures for NAMCS girls are 1 and 9%, respectively. Further analysis showed no important differences in the rates of pregnancy according to race or ethnicity.

Pregnancy outcomes for these homeless teenage girls are unknown.

Among the 264 pregnancies represented in these data, 6 are known to have ended in miscarriage and 9 were ended by induced abortion, but the true rates of miscarriage and abortion are presumably much higher. It is also unknown what proportion of these pregnancies were consequences of rape, although the proportion is possibly quite high since the rate of sexual assault on homeless women is some 20 times that of the overall U.S. female population (Kelly 1985). ∅ or little birth control

3. Nutritional Disorders

Very little has been written about diet and nutrition among the homeless, whether youths or adults, and specific studies of dietary intake or nutritional deficiency disorders among homeless persons are essentially nonexistent. Unfortunately, the entire topic of hunger, malnutrition, and poverty has become so intensely politicized that the calm voice of science can barely be heard in the din. Some have claimed that an epidemic of hunger is sweeping across the poverty population of this country, a point of view that serious scientific research does not sustain (Graham 1985). Such evidence as there is suggests modest dietary deficiencies in some nutrients among poor as opposed to nonpoor persons, not wholesale hunger or malnutrition among the nation's poor.

Much of the research on poverty, children, and malnutrition is based on inferences from anthropomorphic data (specifically, age-by-weight-by-height measurements grouped by quintiles or percentiles), not on direct nutritional intake surveys or observations. Most studies based on such approaches (e.g., Scholl, Karp, Theophano, and Decker 1987; Shah, Kahan, and Krauser 1987) report weight-for-height abnormalities among poor children, but inherent genetic differences in biological growth potential are known to be a possible confounding factor. That the decreased growth observed among poor children results from nutritional deficiencies is therefore typically an inference from anthropomorphic differences; other environmental or genetic factors that might explain these differences are rarely examined in any depth.

There is a small literature focused on nutritional deficiency disorders among poor and nonpoor children. Iron deficiency anemias, for example, are more widespread among poor children than nonpoor children, both in Canada (Shah et al. 1987) and the United States (Singer 1982). Rickets (resulting from vitamin D deficiency) are also more common in poor than nonpoor children.

Direct studies of nutritional intakes and ensuing deficiencies are relatively rare. Shah et al. (1987) report data from the Nutrition Canada

Survey showing that mean intakes of all nutrients among children varied directly with family income level, with particularly pronounced differences in the intakes of vitamins A and C, folic acid (folate), and calcium. The authors suggest that "children of low-income families are usually fed lower-quality diets, which consist of more refined carbohydrates and fewer meats, fruits, and vegetables" (p. 486) and other research is consistent (Zee, DeLeon, Robertson, and Chen 1985; Wilton and Irvine 1983).

One can anticipate, nonetheless, that nutritional disorders would be relatively widespread among homeless persons regardless of age and, indeed, that is the condition of the homeless teens seen in HCH. Focusing first on the broad category of nutritional deficiency disorders (comprised overwhelmingly of malnutrition and the various vitamin deficiency diseases), not a single case appears among NAMCS teens; among HCH youth, the rates of these disorders vary from 1.1 to 3.6% and average about 2% overall. Obesity is also more common among HCH than NAMCS youth, regardless of age or gender. Thus, among the nutritional disorders, only anemia is about equally common in both groups.

Two percent of clients exhibited nutritional deficiencies (mainly malnutrition and vitamin deficiencies) (vs. fewer than 0.1% of the NAMCS patients). These disorders tended to increase slightly with age. Obesity was less common than malnutrition and is more widespread among women than men. (For additional information on nutritional status among homeless adults, see Laven and Brown 1985; Rauschenbach, Frongillo, Thompson, Andersen, and Spicer 1990; Thompson et al. 1988.) Nutritional deficiencies are found among about 2% of the HCH children and are virtually nonexistent among NAMCS children (there are only three cases of these disorders recorded in the NAMCS data). A very few studies have noted the disproportionate occurrence of nutritional deficiency disorders among homeless children. Wright (1989c) has reported that 2.2% of homeless children who received care during the first year of the HCH program were diagnosed with anemias; this is twice the rate for "normal" children seen in ambulatory pediatric clinics nationwide (see also Miller and Lin 1988). An additional 1.6% of the homeless children had nutritional deficiency disorders other than anemia (most of them vitamin deficiency disorders); among children in general, such deficiencies are practically nonexistent.

4. Infectious and Communicable Disorders

The health consequences of being homeless are borne primarily but not exclusively by homeless people themselves. Unlike most sick people, sick homeless people are not normally isolated from the healthy. They tend to remain in the shelters or in the streets, making frequent contact with others. To the extent that they are prone to infectious and communicable diseases, their illnesses threaten not only their own well-being but possibly the public health as well.

The principal population at risk from these and related disorders is largely other homeless people. The shelter system itself may well abet the transmission of infectious and communicable diseases (Gross and Rosenberg 1987), most of all in a population that tends to be malnourished and debilitated in any case. Most of the people who are made ill by contact with ill homeless people will thus be other homeless people.

Homeless people, however, are not quarantined inside the shelters. Many facilities serving homeless people are intentionally closed for part of the day, thus forcing the homeless to circulate among the larger population. The condition of homelessness itself is also not static; there is, rather, considerable "migration" into and out of the homeless condition over any extended time. The population placed at potential risk by infectious and communicable disease borne among the urban homeless, in short, is much larger than the homeless population itself.

We do not mean to suggest that homeless people should be isolated from the rest of the population in order to protect the healthy. The point rather is to emphasize the urgent need for thorough, aggressive screening of homeless people for communicable disorders and adequate medical treatment for those found to be afflicted. In the long run, of course, the solution to the health risks the condition of homelessness poses is to eradicate the condition itself.

Infectious and communicable disorders borne among the homeless range from the trivial to the profound. At any given time, about one HCH client in five, whether adult or teen, was afflicted with some infectious or communicable condition, a rate five or six times that observed among NAMCS patients. Most of these disorders were relatively minor (lice infestations, minor skin ailments, and the like), but also included within the category are much more serious illnesses such as AIDS, tuberculosis, and the various sexually transmitted venereal diseases; we discuss each below.

AIDS. There was evidence of active AIDS infections in 103 clients and HIV positivity in 66 additional clients. Among clients seen more than once, the corresponding numbers are 77 and 58. Taking the latter figures as the more indicative and converting to customary epidemiological rates, we estimate the rate of AIDS infection among homeless adults was approximately 230 cases per 100,000. And likewise, the estimated rate of

HIV positivity (not accompanied by active AIDS) among homeless adults is about 170 cases per 100,000.

In the 1985 NAMCS survey, there were 9 recorded cases of AIDS among 49,903 urban adult patients, which converts to about 18 AIDS infections per 100,000 adult ambulatory patients in the general U.S. population. Likewise, by the end of calendar year 1987 (when HCH data collection ceased), just under 50,000 AIDS cases had been reported to the Centers for Disease Control in Atlanta; the total population of the country in 1987 was about 241 million, which again gives an estimated national rate of AIDS infection on the order of 20 cases per 100,000. The rate of AIDS infection among the homeless therefore appears to exceed that of the general population by an order of magnitude.

Most of the HCH AIDS cases (69 of 77, or 90%) are young men and do not differ significantly by race. However, in the general population the rates are higher for nonwhites than for whites.

In that population, the primary vector for AIDS transmission is homosexual contact, with intravenous drug use a strong secondary vector (CDC 1987; Norman 1986). The pattern among the HCH AIDS cases was very different. Among the AIDS cases with documented risk factors ($N = 59$), 63% were known IV drug abusers with no history of homosexual contact (or prostitution), 27% were known homosexuals (or prostitutes) with no history of IV drug abuse, and 10% were both. The number of cases is obviously small, but the clear indication is that IV drug abuse is more important than homosexual contact in the transmission of AIDS among homeless men.

Even so, homosexual contact is a source, which raises concerns about sex practices. Although little is known about safe sex practices among the homeless, some data are available for a sample of homeless men in Miami (MMWR 1991b). Among the sexually active men in this sample ($N = 78$ men who had had sex at least once in the prior month), about 10% were exclusively homosexual and about half reported having used a condom on one or more occasions in the prior month. Trading drugs for sex or sex for drugs was relatively common. There is clear potential for many additional AIDS infections in this population. The emphasis to date has been on education and prevention, with "safe sex" and "clean needles." It is worth asking, however, just how successful a clean needles campaign will be in a population of IV drug abusers where the simple act of washing one's face and hands, not to mention one's "works," is highly problematic.

Even more chilling is the inaccessibility of treatments that *have* emerged. The AIDS "cocktail" of antivirals and protease inhibitors has demonstrated impressive, albeit mixed results in slowing if not actually stopping the spread of the disease for individuals who have been diagnosed with AIDS. The conditions of homelessness, however, make health care practitioners reluctant to prescribe the cocktail. It requires a very strict regimen of pill-taking timed with food. The concern is that failure to comply completely with the regimen will allow the virus to mutate and throw the health care community back to square one. For reasons we discuss below, therefore, the homeless are unlikely recipients of this possible life-saving mix.

Other Sexually Transmitted Venereal Diseases. The homeless are, on average, in their mid-thirties and as sexually active as the population in general. This factor contributes to the spread of sexually transmitted diseases. Overall, caregivers observed STDs in about 3% of the adult clients seen more than once, in 1.9% of the men and in 5.4% of the women. These infections were moderately more prevalent among nonwhites than whites and definitely more prevalent among the young than among the middle-aged and old. The rate of STD infection among the homeless was about twice that of the ambulatory population in general. STDs are more common among women than men at all ages, and more common among the young than among the old regardless of gender.

Prostitution is one of the avenues of STD transmission. The data documented it for only a very small fraction of the homeless teens; the true rate must be considerably higher than the documented rate. About 26% of the runaway youth in the Yates et al. (1988) study were involved in street prostitution (survival sex), which is consistent with impressionistic evidence from health care providers at many of the HCH sites. To correct any possible misconceptions on this score, street prostitution is relatively common among both homeless teenage females and homeless teenage males.

Tuberculosis. The rate of tuberculosis is arguably the single best indicator of the living conditions of the poor. Since the advent of anti-TB antibiotics in the 1950s, the rate of TB infection in the population as a whole has steadily declined year by year. In the early years of the 1980s, however, the rate of decline began to decrease, and the TB rate has leveled off in the years since, reversing a long historical trend. The apparent correspondence between the TB reversal and the upsurge in homelessness in the 1980s is probably not coincidental, especially given the rate of TB infection among the homeless reported here and in other studies. The HCH data contained 376 documented cases of active tuberculosis among all HCH adult clients and 326 among adult clients seen more than once. Again taking the latter as the most indicative, the estimated rate of TB infection was 968 cases per 100,000 homeless adults. In contrast, the rate of TB infection in the national population at large is about 9 per 100,000, and among the urban population, about 19 per 100,000 (CDC 1984).

Fewer than a fifth of the HCH clients ever seen were documentably screened for tuberculosis. Since tuberculosis "may cause few or no symptoms for decades" (McAdam et al. 1985), it is possible that our estimate, although strikingly higher than the national average, is, nonetheless, a substantial underestimate. St. Vincent's Hospital in New York City has run an aggressive TB screening program among its homeless clients for several years; active TB infections have been found in about 4% of all cases screened (ibid.). The CDC has also reported tuberculosis data for homeless persons in Boston; the reported rate for 1984 was 317 cases per 100,000 homeless (CDC 1985). There is, however, reason to believe that the CDC rate is based on an inflated denominator; a more recent estimate of the number of homeless people in Boston suggests that the true rate may be twice the reported rate. Thus, the rate of tuberculosis among the homeless is at least 25 times higher, and possibly hundreds of times higher, than the rate in the urban population generally.

In addition to these conditions, we note that morbidity among homeless children appears to be much more widespread than among children in general or among poor children in particular. Miller and Lin studied 158 homeless children in Seattle and reported that "although the majority of the children were considered to be in good or excellent health, the proportion whose health was described as 'fair' or 'poor' was four times higher than in the general U.S. pediatric population" (1988:671–672). These authors also remark a high prevalence of abnormal anthropometry and immunization delays within this population. Homeless children appear to overuse emergency room services, underuse preventive health services, and have far fewer dental visits compared to the general pediatric population. Similar results for homeless children in Boston have been reported by Bassuk et al. (1986), and for homeless children in New York by Alperstein, Rappaport, and Flanigan (1988).

Finally, there has been little research on mortality among the homeless. Three separate studies (Wright and Weber 1987; O'Connell et al. 1990; Alstrom, Lindelius, and Salum 1975) all report an average age of death for homeless men around 51 or 52 years old; one study of San Francisco homeless reports an average age at death of 41 years old (MMWR 1991a). It is fairly obvious that mortality among the homeless is astonishingly high. There is also evidence (Chavkin et al. 1987) that infant mortality is very high among children born to homeless women. Death by violent means and death secondary to alcohol and drug abuse appear to be grossly overrepresented among causes of death for homeless persons (Wright and Weber 1987). In any average recent year, about 1% of all deaths in the United States are due to homicide; among the deaths of homeless people investigated in Wright and Weber (1987:128), 26% were murders. Other studies of mortality among the homeless report similar results (e.g., MMWR 1991a:879).

Returning to data from the NOHSAP study is revealing. NOHSAP clients were asked how often they had been victimized by robbery, assault, rape, or forcible theft, how many times they had been beaten up, and how many times they had been stabbed with a knife or shot with a gun. Overall, 91% had experienced one or more of these victimizations (93% of the men, 90% of the women), usually on several occasions. The average woman in these data had been robbed 3 times in her life, assaulted or beaten up 14 times, raped 5 times, and shot at once; the average male had been shot at twice. Likewise, Gelberg and Linn (1989) report that 71% of their sample of homeless people in Los Angeles had been victimized by some crime in the previous year.

The pattern of violence against persons who eventually become homeless often begins in childhood (Wright and Devine 1993). Emotional, sexual, and physical abuse during childhood are common elements in the biographies of homeless people (Kennedy et al. 1990; Burroughs et al. 1990; Susser, Lin, Conover, and Struening 1991). Homeless women are also frequent victims of family violence; indeed, abusive mates are a leading risk factor for homelessness among women (Browne 1993; Goodman 1991).

The exceptional rate of violence against the homeless is a joint function of exposure and vulnerability. The streets (and to a lesser but still significant extent the shelters) are inherently dangerous places and so exposure to potentially violent situations is widespread (indeed, well-nigh universal). Some homeless people go to truly extraordinary lengths to protect themselves from the inherent dangers (e.g., keeping on the move all night long and sleeping during the day, sleeping up in trees, in dumpsters, or in other concealed places)—highly adaptive health behavior in this population. And many, of course, are in poor physical health, generally debilitated, mentally impaired, or impaired by alcohol and other drugs, so they are often easy targets. One might think that the homeless are protected to some extent by the fact that they possess practically nothing worth stealing, but Wright and Weber (1987) report one case where a homeless alcoholic man was beaten to death for a sack of aluminum cans, worth maybe $3 at the recycling center.

Premature mortality is apparently one important reason why the elderly (over age 65) are underrepresented among the homeless by approximately a factor of 4. Based on the research cited above, one of the "costs of being homeless" in America is roughly 20 years of life expectancy.

HOMELESSNESS AS A COMPLICATING FACTOR IN THE DELIVERY OF HEALTH CARE

Ill health is both a cause and a consequence of homelessness, and homelessness in turn greatly complicates the delivery of adequate health services. Chief among these complications are the many barriers to continuity of care. Programwide, HCH staff saw about half of the clients once and only once. Like the homeless in general, HCH clients are a highly transient, mobile population with whom continuous contact is nearly impossible in many cases, this despite the very aggressive outreach efforts that characterized all the HCH projects.

It would be wrong to suggest that these difficulties result in all cases from so-called "noncompliant" patients. Many homeless people are literally intimidated by customary health care settings; many have had bad experiences in such settings at previous times; many fear—often with good reason—anything that looks "official." Mutual trust is essential to continuity of care in any health care setting; among homeless people, trust is often a very hard-won commodity.

Homeless patients are notorious for breaking appointments and failing to appear for follow-up work. Health care professionals who lament this fact seldom appreciate that the average homeless person does not keep an appointment calendar where the follow-up information will be recorded. Moreover, "Please come back next Thursday" has meaning only if "Thursday" has meaning. If the days and weeks are little more than a continuous collage of disconnected experiences and forgotten conversations, "Come back next Thursday" may well have no meaning at all. What we sometimes forget is how tightly our own notions of time are tied to the routines of family and work. Lacking both, many homeless people have no sense of day, week, month, or year. They are often sensitive only to season.

Maintaining a follow-up schedule (getting to referrals, keeping appointments, and the like) requires access to transportation, which is routinely problematic for the homeless (Elvy 1985), a daily calendar in which appointment dates and times can be recorded, and sufficient free time to go to doctors' offices or clinics. One might think that "free time" would be the least of a homeless person's barriers, but this is much more problematic than many people realize. Perhaps the distinguishing feature of the daily existence of homeless people is that they are required to stand in line for practically everything. In many cities, for example, soup kitchen lines begin to form around 10:00 A.M. for the noon meal; if one is not in line early enough, the food may well be gone. A homeless person with a follow-up appointment scheduled at, say, 11:00 A.M. may have to choose between keeping the appointment and eating. And there are other lines in which to stand for the evening meal, a bed in the shelter, the clothing outlet, etc.

With no medicine cabinet in which to store medication, many homeless people carry their medications with them. After a few days of walking and sleeping with bottles of pills in the pocket, the pills are often ground down to a powder (Kinchen and Wright 1991). Under the circumstances of homelessness, bottles of medication are also often lost or stolen. Torres, Lefkowitz, Kales, and Brickner report that homeless AIDS patients frequently failed to complete antibiotic regimens "because they lost or could not afford to fill their prescriptions" (1987:780). Other compliance problems in this population were a greater tendency to exit the hospital against medical advice and to be lost to follow-up.

The homeless mentally ill and substance-abusive face special compliance problems. Both groups can (often do) have severe memory problems. Both groups have altered perceptions of pain and other somatic states, which can influence their motivation to be compliant. Many medications are strongly contraindicated with alcohol, and so homeless alcoholics frequently must choose between taking their medication and drinking, the latter very much a part and parcel of their daily existence, the former not.

For many homeless people, health care and treatment compliance are luxuries that assume priority only after the more pressing needs of daily existence have been satisfied—the needs to obtain food, find shelter, avoid predators, and the like. Given these far more pressing and immediate needs, it is little wonder that homeless people are frequently noncompliant. One study of referral keeping among homeless women in Seattle reported that "personal stresses and competing priorities, weighed against perceived medical urgency," were the major barriers (Schlosstein, St. Clair, and Connell 1991:279).

Even in the relatively infrequent case where health care practitioners can engage clients in a more or less continuous system of care, the material conditions of a homeless existence imperil the delivery of adequate health services. We have already discussed the ethical dilemmas health care practitioner face in the face of the AIDS "cocktail." We can make a similar point in the instance of managing diabetes within the context of homelessness. Diabetes is about as common among the homeless as among the general population. In the normal population, diabetics can effectively manage the disease by frequent blood or urine testing, tight dietary control, and daily insulin injections. But what can "tight dietary control" possibly mean to a person who takes his or her meals at the shelter or soup kitchen—or worse, eats whatever can be scavenged from street sources? Studies of the nutrient contents of soup kitchen meals show that they are adequate in terms of calories and major nutrients but are exceptionally high in sugars, salt, starches, and fat (Winick 1985). The standard soup kitchen diet, in short, is singularly inappropriate for a diabetic, but the alternative, no food at all, is clearly worse.

And what of the daily insulin injection? To turn a homeless diabetic loose on the streets with a supply of clean syringes would be to sign his or her death warrant or at least to invite criminal victimization. At the same time, having every homeless diabetic come to clinic for a daily insulin injection would clearly strain the resources of any health care facility.

A leading center of diabetes research in the United States, the Joslin Clinic in Boston, Massachusetts, advises diabetic patients to watch what they eat, see their doctor regularly, and "stay happy and try to avoid depression." This is obviously a tall order for any diabetic, whether homeless or not. To a homeless diabetic who eats what is available to eat and who sees a doctor irregularly if at all, it is an impossible, even absurd prescription.

It would be remiss not to conclude this discussion with a brief comment about noncompliance behavior among health professionals who treat the homeless and the poor. There is an increasingly large literature showing that uninsured (mostly indigent) patients tend to receive worse care than insured and more affluent patients, clear evidence of failure to comply with standard-of-care guidelines. One study of recurrent tuberculosis (Kopanoff, Snider, and Johnson 1988) reported that about 20% of the recurrent cases resulted from the fact that patients had no chemotherapy prescribed for their previous TB episode; another 20% resulted from inappropriate or inadequate therapy. A chart review for patients being treated in an outpatient STD clinic in a public hospital in Los Angeles found that 49 of 176 patients (28%) received care that failed to meet even the minimum quality-of-care criteria (Shekelle and Kosecoff 1992). When physicians judge patients to be "poorly motivated," they are four times more likely to relegate these patients to self-care than clients who are perceived to be motivated (McArtor et al. 1992).

Physician attitudes about indigent and homeless patients apparently underlie these patterns. One study of family practice residents found a majority who believed that "poor patients are more likely than others to miss appointments without canceling (73%), more likely to be late for appointments (51%), and less knowledgeable about their illnesses (80%)" (Price, Desmond, Snyder, and Kimmel 1988:615). A majority also felt the poor people are not likely to practice preventative health behaviors or to be compliant with medical regimens, and a substantial minority (41%)

believed that poor people simply care less about their health than more affluent people. If physicians believe that poor or homeless patients will be noncompliant and treat such patients on that basis, then this will surely increase the odds that their poor and homeless patients will in fact be noncompliant, a classic case of what is often called the self-fulfilling prophecy.

The experiences of the HCH clinics have taught us that what is true of diabetes is equally true of many other physical disorders. What is gained by sterile dressings on the wounds or leg ulcers of a man who sleeps in the gutter? What is the point of prescribing medication when many homeless people have trouble finding a drink of water with which to take their pills, or when the pills themselves are frequently ground down to dust after only a few days simply from being carried around in one's pocket? What is the point of recommending a low-salt diet to a homeless hypertensive when beans, hot dogs, and potato chips are the soup kitchen's daily fare? What, even, is the point of telling a homeless emphysemic woman to quit smoking when cigarettes are the woman's only remaining pleasure in this life?

HEALTH, HEALTH POLICY, AND THE HOMELESS

The major conclusion the HCH data suggest is that the homeless suffer from most disorders at an elevated and often exceptionally elevated rate. Some share of the effect is no doubt due to the unique demographic characteristics of the homeless (compared to the domiciled population); an even larger share results from the high rates of alcohol and drug abuse and mental illness. These points granted, the largest share of the difference results from the conditions of homelessness itself: first, the extreme poverty that characterizes this population, and secondarily the various life-style factors enumerated earlier. Persons denied adequate shelter are thereby exposed to a range of risk factors that are uniquely destructive of physical well-being.

A number of studies have shown that the homeless have an inordinate number of health problems but face many profound barriers to accessing health care. Most lack a regular source of medical care and most are also without health insurance, whether public or private, resulting in costly and inefficient overutilization of inpatient and emergency care services (Robertson and Cousineau 1986; Elvy 1985).

Robertson and Cousineau (1986) studied urban homeless adults in Los Angeles and found that less than half of those with a chronic medical problem had contacted a physician in the previous year about that problem; only 13% had a regular physician that they saw. Many said they did not see a doctor because they did not consider their problem sufficiently serious or felt that it could not be treated in any case. About a quarter cited no money or no health insurance as the reason. In these data, 81% reported having no health insurance coverage of any kind; 7% had Medicaid, 4% had Medicare, 5% had private insurance, and 2% had veterans health benefits. One in five had been hospitalized for a health problem during the previous year. Participants in this study were three times more likely to report themselves in fair or poor health, 50% more likely to report a physical health disability, and twice as likely to have been hospitalized in the previous year compared to national estimates for large cities.

Hilfiker (1989) reports that most homeless individuals cannot name a regular source of care and do not have health insurance either; therefore, they frequently turn to the emergency room when their health degenerates, an expensive and inefficient alternative to continuing primary care. He also reports that most homeless people also receive no public assistance and that benefit levels are generally inadequate for those who do. Nationwide, only about 20% of the homeless are covered under Medicaid or other forms of public insurance; even when this coverage is present, patients are often forced into second-rate public systems because private medicine has essentially abandoned the homeless and the poor (ibid.). In the same vein, 79% of homeless soup kitchen users studied by Bowering, Clancy, and Poppendieck (1991) did not have health insurance; similar results are reported by Aday, Fleming, and Anderson (1984).

The principal barrier to access to health care among the homeless is extreme poverty (Altman et al. 1989), but lack of money and insurance are not the only barriers. Wood, Hayward, Corey, Freeman, and Shapiro (1990) enumerate the general stresses of homelessness, preexisting family problems, and weak support networks as factors increasing the likelihood that homeless families will not seek or obtain access to the health and social service system, a system that is not especially user-friendly in any case, least of all to those without a fee source. Further, amidst the daily struggle for survival and the quest to meet even the most basic human needs, health is rarely a high-priority item (Kerner, Dusenbury, and Mandelblatt 1993).

This literature suggests three major classes of reasons why homeless people experience difficulties obtaining necessary medical care. First is the health care system itself and the manner in which health care practitioners traditionally deliver health care in this country. This category includes an inadequate supply of public health facilities, lack of providers for Medicaid patients, geographic factors that limit accessibility, and the forbidding and often unfriendly institutional settings in which care is typically delivered. Second are the many special and unique needs and circumstances of homeless people, their distraction from health concerns by more basic survival issues, the exceptional rates of morbidity, educational deficits, high rates of mental illness and substance abuse, etc. The final set of factors inheres in the attitudes of health professionals who frequently define homeless and indigent persons as unworthy or undesirable clients even when they happen to possess a fee source. This has been called the GOMER problem: Get Out of My Emergency Room.

There is also overwhelming evidence that the health care providers can overcome all these barriers. The national HCH demonstration project (Wright and Weber 1987) and the larger 109-city HCH program the Stewart B. McKinney Homeless Assistance Act created make that clear (Vicic 1991). Vicic points out that in the first year of the McKinney program, 231,000 homeless individuals saw health care workers a total of 783,000 times. This implies, first, that programs can bring homeless people into a system of health care if it is designed with the unique circumstances of homeless people in mind, and second, that programs can establish some level of continuity of care even among a transient, difficult-to-reach homeless population. The barriers, while formidable, are clearly not insurmountable.

Access to adequate health care is problematic for the poor in general, for poor children and youth in particular (Levey, MacDowell, and Levey 1986; Newacheck and Halfon 1986), and also for the homeless (Elvy 1985; Healthcare for the Homeless Coalition of Greater St. Louis 1986). Homeless youth face at least one additional barrier: in coming to the attention of anything that smacks of "officialdom," homeless teenagers face the risk of being declared wards of the state and thereby placed under foster care.

From the viewpoint of national health policy, it is advantageous to look on homelessness as a remediable condition of the environment that places a numerically large and growing portion of the urban poverty population at high health risk. Indeed, it is hard to conceive of a socially defined risk factor that is of greater consequence for a person's physical well-being. And yet, current national health policy with respect to the homeless is strongly oriented toward amelioration, not prevention. Through the auspices of the Stewart B. McKinney Homeless Assistance Act, we now have HCH clinics up and running in more than a hundred cities across the nation. What we do not have in place is a set of policies to prevent homelessness and thereby to avoid its negative health consequences.

Ameliorative programs such as those contained within the McKinney Act are certainly better than nothing. At the same time, it is obvious that a person cannot be physically, mentally, or socially healthy without a stable, secure, place in which to live. Among the many good reasons to "do something" about homelessness is that homelessness makes people ill; in the extreme case, it is a fatal condition.

CONCLUSIONS

We began this chapter arguing that the impact of health deprivation on homeless youth would illuminate the future in certain dire ways; we return to that point here. It is of some interest that the best available studies of the effects of poverty on child and teenage health report relatively slight differences in the prevalence of most disorders between poor and nonpoor children, whether chronic or acute (Egbuono and Starfield 1982; Newacheck and Starfield 1988). The larger differences are found in the ensuing consequences of disease. Differentials on the order of those reported here are not found anywhere in the published literature on poverty and child health. The evidently disproportionate rate of illness observed among homeless teens, in short, is not just a simple consequence of their impoverished circumstances. Homelessness is an independent and quite consequential risk factor in its own right.

Conventional notions of childhood and youth break down in the context of homelessness in that many chronological children and youth are forced to do very adult things. Homeless teenagers are often hard, savvy, and cynical beyond their years—tough kids on mean streets. At a time in life when the most pressing problems of many teens are acne and whom to invite to the high school prom, homeless teenagers are already out on their own, hustling and scavenging an existence, and worrying about where they will next eat or sleep. Many of them are already caught in a downward spiral of liquor, drugs, disease, and problems with the law. In many if not most cases, their chances to get back "on the right track" and to assume productive, independent social roles are already exceedingly remote.

Knowing how and to what extent homelessness affects the health of teenagers does not in itself tell us what needs to be done. Most of what has been done to date is along the lines of amelioration. There is an evident need to continue such programs: aggressive screening of homeless youth for health disorders, and proper treatment and health care once problems have been diagnosed. But here as in many other areas of public health, the only ultimate, long-term solution is to be found in prevention. The homeless teenagers of today are thus destined, at least in many cases, to be the homeless adults of the 21st century. The ensuing social costs are probably not calculable but are no doubt extremely high. We will avoid the negative consequences of homelessness on the health of youth only when we find a way to prevent teenagers from being homeless in the first place.

An aggressive, broad-scale federal assault on homelessness in all its various manifestations would easily add several tens of billions of dollars to the annual federal expenditure on housing, health, and human services. No one who follows the Washington scene would consider this the least bit likely anytime in this century. The prospects for community-based local programs are scarcely brighter, since most of the cities and states face budget problems every bit as serious as the federal problem. That would seem to leave the private sector as the most promising source for new programs, but the limit may well have been reached here as well. In fact, approximately three-quarters of the total national expenditure for assistance to the homeless already comes from the private sector, principally the churches. Thus, for the foreseeable future, we will have to content ourselves with programs of amelioration, such as those embodied in the Stewart B. McKinney Homeless Assistance Act, knowing full well that such measures do not and cannot provide any final solutions to this problem.

Thousands of children around the nation whose lives and futures are being destroyed by forces over which they have no control. "The Children's Defense Fund . . . has estimated that more children die each year from poverty-related causes than traffic fatalities and suicides combined" (Oberg 1987:568), and while this is very likely an exaggeration, it is an exaggeration that makes a point. It is a useful if troubling question to ask ourselves: What does the very existence of homeless children say about us as a nation? What image does this present to the world?

In February 1987, Wright had the opportunity to testify at hearings before the House Select Committee on Children, Youth, and Families, and to speak about the effects of homelessness on the physical health of children. Among the several witnesses present at the hearings was Yvette Diaz, a lovely 12-year-old Hispanic girl living with her mother and three siblings at one of the large welfare hotels in midtown Manhattan. Yvette is a charming young lady with an engaging smile and coal black shoulder-length hair, soft-spoken but firm in her opinions, and very sweet. In the course of her testimony, she remarked, "If I could have anything that I could want, I wish that we could have our own apartment in a nice clean building and a place that I could go outside to play in that is safe. I want that most of all for me and my family."

A clean place to live and a safe place to play do not seem like too much to ask. These are not the rapacious demands of some welfare-dependent drug addict but the plaintive wish of a young child to have those things that normal children have. In thinking about these hearings, we wonder: What kind of world is this, where such simple things can only be a dream to some children? As a kind and generous nation, are we truly prepared to let this continue?

9

Outside American Cities:
Rural and European Homelessness

Throughout this book we have looked at current homelessness exclusively in American urban terms. Most studies of the homeless deal with urban homeless populations, and most federal, state, and local programs of assistance for the homeless are targeted to the major urban areas. Despite this focus, nearly all recent studies acknowledge at least the existence of a homeless problem in the small-town and rural areas. Yet the rural homeless are, for all practical purposes, invisible—to researchers, public policymakers, and the public at large. Similarly, there have been parallel increases in homelessness throughout the advanced Western democracies. Advocates for the homeless have sometimes attempted to depict the issue as a uniquely American phenomenon, often with an explicit claim that "in no other advanced society would something like this be allowed to happen." The reality is that the structural changes that have transformed the U.S. economy have been global, and thus their negative impact has been global as well. Consequently, the numbers, trends, characteristics, public opinion, and social policy responses of the European experience with homelessness closely mirror that of the United States.

Our purpose in this chapter is to review in some depth one major study of rural poverty (First, Toomey, and Rice 1990) and three recent and relatively comprehensive reports on homelessness in Europe (Study Group on Homelessness 1993; Daly 1992, 1993) and to compare and contrast the homeless situation in Europe with that in the United States. A comparative perspective on the problem of homelessness sheds further light on the debate over the primacy of personal vs. structural explanation, and we have argued throughout that that approach is ultimately limited. Rather it is the interaction between these factors that is important. The discussion below does provide some interesting observations that are pertinent to that debate. It is clear, however, that there is a need for further comparative research on the homeless. Finally, in Chapter 10 we return to our concerns with homeless children. There, our comparison will be between Honduran street children and American homeless children.

We go first to the heartlands.

RURAL POVERTY

When we think about rural America, the image that springs to mind is a scenic countryside, with traditional communities that "take care of their own" or, in short, a simpler time—this, of course, in stark contrast to the alienation and outright hostility that we now commonly associate with the large urban areas. Acknowledging the existence of poverty and homelessness in the small towns and rural areas is difficult for many of us; it "challenges our belief in the way people in the small towns and rural areas live their lives" (First et al. 1990).

But, of course, poverty has not disappeared from the rural areas—not by any means. And since homelessness is the most extreme manifestation of poverty, we can safely assume that there is homelessness—no doubt a great deal of it—in the rural areas also. Since we know quite a bit more about rural poverty than about rural homelessness, we begin with some information on the poverty situation in the rural areas.

Unfortunately, any discussion of the rural poor is complicated by the frequent changes the federal government makes in its city-size categories and designations. In the 30 years since the government first began to keep systematic data on poverty, the city-size nomenclature has shifted from nonfarm/farm to urban/rural and then again to metropolitan/ nonmetropolitan. These changing designations (and the associated changes in definition and record keeping) attempt to capture developing qualitative differences in the meanings of terms such as *urban* and *rural* in an era of widespread urbanization, but they also greatly complicate comparisons over time. The labels *farm, rural,* and *nonmetropolitan* overlap to some degree, but they are not identical. Specifically, the farm population is defined as persons living in rural territories who derive some specified minimum of their income from the sale of agricultural products. The rural category consists of the farm population plus other nonfarm persons residing in nonurban areas. Finally, the nonmetropolitan population refers to all persons outside metropolitan statistical areas (MSAs)—it includes the farm population plus the rural population plus the populations of small cities and towns. (An MSA is a central city of at least 50,000 plus the surrounding county.)

These changing designations reflect the changing realities of economy and demography. Over time, the locus and activities of the U.S. population have shifted from rural areas and agricultural pursuits to an urbanized industrial life. Even more recently, we find evidence of important post-industrial economic transformations and accompanying population shifts within large-scale urban areas. Recent Censuses document the movement out of central cities into suburban and exurban regions.

(Farm) Poverty. As the farm population of the United States has decreased, so has the incidence of rural poverty. In 1990, only about 2% of the U.S. population remained "on the farm," and of that small percentage only about half were economically dependent on agriculture, the remainder being employed in a variety of nonfarm activities: factories, lumbering, mines, and so on. Each Census between 1940 and 1970 showed an absolute decline in the size of the rural or farm population; in the 1980 Census, however, the rural population increased by 5.6 million and a further increase was registered in the 1990 Census also. Most of this is exurban development rather than a return to the farm. Throughout the 70s, 80s, and 90s, the number of actual farms, farmers, and farm employees has continued its decline.

Not surprisingly, the economic fortunes of those who remain dependent on farming fluctuate dramatically with the vicissitudes of agricultural markets. Farm income also remains highly sensitive to interest rates. Consequently, farm poverty rates have historically been much higher (and more volatile) than nonfarm rates, although that has become less true in the past two decades.

The rate of farm poverty dropped dramatically from more than 50% in 1959 to about 11% in 1990. Even as late as 1967, the farm poverty rate was routinely twice that of the nonfarm rate; these days, the rates are very similar. This 75–80% reduction in farm poverty between 1959 and 1990, however, does not reflect a major turnaround in the economics of the family farm so much as a continuous replacement of small-scale, economically marginal family farming operations by large-scale agribusiness enterprises. In fact, the size of the farm population shrank from more than 15 million in 1959 to less than 5 million in 1990, even as the rate of agricultural productivity dramatically increased. Unable to "make it" in farming, 10 million people left altogether and half of those who remain are employed in nonfarm pursuits. Thus, the rate of poverty within the farm population has correspondingly plummeted.

Many authors lament the decline of the family farm. In the more romanticized versions, honest, hardworking yeomen are driven off the land by uncaring market forces and unscrupulous agribusiness operators. The rate of farm poverty in 1959—a bit more than half—should suffice to dispel this notion. In fact, for most of the 20th century, "family farming" was barely more than subsistence agriculture, characterized by hard work, long days, and deep economic privation. Many family farmers of the 30s, 40s, and 50s actively chose to leave the drudgery of farming for the alienating, but more lucrative returns that factory labor provided. It was a choice that was often accompanied by remarkable improvements in the family's standard of living.

The net result of the trends of the last three decades is that farm poverty now accounts for only 1.6% of all U.S. poverty, while it represented 20.3% of the poverty total in 1959. More concretely, there were 534,000 farm poor in 1990, nearly all of them living in families. On average, farm families are somewhat larger than U.S. families as a whole (3.59 vs. 3.19 persons). In general, the average family cash incomes of both the farming poor and nonpoor lag behind their nonfarm counterparts. For those on the farm, these figures are $5,214 and $31,560, respectively; among nonfarming families the corresponding figures are $5,868 and $36,680.

What do the farm poor look like? Among the 616,000 farm poor are 220,000 children under the age of 18 (36% of the total) and 65,000 senior citizens (11% of the total). Only 6% of the farm poor are black. At the same time, the incidence of poverty among black farmers is more than a third (33.9%); the corresponding rate for white farmers is 12.1%. Less than 5% of the farm poor live in female-headed households, and only 2.6% of the farm poor are children living in such households. These figures represent a sharp contrast with the nonfarm poor, where 37.7% live in female-headed households, and where 22% are children living in female-headed households.

Nonmetropolitan Area Poverty.   These days, when we speak of "rural poverty," we normally refer to the nonmetropolitan population, not the farming population per se. And while the farm population has diminished to 2% of the population, 22.4% of the U.S. population—more than 56 million people—live in nonmetropolitan areas—in the small cities and towns and rural areas. Since the 1970 Census, the population of nonmetropolitan areas has grown by almost 20% so as to comprise slightly more than a fifth of the national population. Despite this population growth, or perhaps because of it, the nonmetropolitan areas have a higher-than-average poverty rate of 16.3% and they contain about 27% of the nation's total poverty population.

Race and regional factors confound poverty in the nonmetropolitan population. First, the South is overrepresented: 44% of the non-metropolitan population resides in the South as compared to 34% of the overall U.S. population. Thus, some nonmetropolitan poverty is linked more to region than to city size. Within the South, the nonmetropolitan population is disproportionately black. In the nation as a whole, blacks comprise 12.4% of the total population, 9.4% of the nonmetropolitan population, and 29.3% of the poverty population. In the South, they comprise 20.3% of the nonmetropolitan population and 41.3% of the non-metropolitan poor. In fact, 96.8% of all poor nonmetropolitan blacks live in the South. Outside the South, the nonmetropolitan population is 96.3% white. Thus, as numerous authors have observed, small-town and rural poverty outside the South is almost exclusively a white phenomenon. Whites comprise 92% of the non-Southern nonmetropolitan poverty population. Despite generally dwindling differences between the South and non-South over time, the South continues to fare more poorly in many socioeconomic categories, and in the rate of poverty in the small-town and rural areas, the disparity exceeds 50%: 20.5% in the South vs. 13.0% elsewhere.

The age-dependent populations—children and the elderly—comprise approximately half of the poor in nonmetropolitan areas. Out of a total of 9.1 million nonmetropolitan poor, 3.4 million are children and an additional 1.3 million are elderly. The incidence of poverty among these two groups is 22.9 and 16.1%, respectively. The former rate runs about 10% ahead of the age-specific national rate, while the latter exceeds the age-specific national rate by almost a third.

Contrary to a common expectation, the overall poverty rate in non-metropolitan areas exceeds the metropolitan area rate. That is, the rate of poverty in small towns and rural areas is actually higher than the poverty rate in the big cities. This is true for blacks, Hispanics, and whites. Except for the Northeast, it is also true regionally. However, in the Midwest and West the nonmetropolitan poverty rate exceeds the metropolitan rate by only one or two percentage points, while the difference in the South is almost 50%. Overall, blacks comprise slightly less than a quarter (23.6%) of all nonmetropolitan poverty. In the South, however, the figure is 41.3%.

While the incidence of nonmetropolitan poverty in the South exceeds the rate in other nonmetropolitan areas, a comparison of mean family sizes and incomes of Southern vs. non-Southern non metropolitan poor families shows negligible differences. The family size difference amounts to 0.17 persons (poor Southern families in the small towns and rural areas are slightly larger) and the income difference amounts to $127 a year. Perhaps contrary to expectation, the mean family income of the black poor in nonmetropolitan areas is higher than the corresponding figure for poor whites. This difference is particularly pronounced in the South, where it exceeds $550, but this advantage is offset by the slightly higher average size of Southern nonmetropolitan poor black families.

RURAL HOMELESSNESS

Since the nature of poverty is somewhat different in the rural and in the urban areas, there are certain obvious ways in which one would expect urban homelessness to differ from rural homelessness. For example, poverty in the rural areas is not as tightly linked to female-headed households as it is in the urban areas. Most rural poverty therefore involves intact families (i.e., husband-wife dyads). The implication is that rural homelessness is more often family homelessness than is urban homelessness. Also, in the urban areas, poverty comes more and more tightly to be linked with race; thus, nationwide, more than half the urban homeless are nonwhite. The implication is that rural homelessness will not show the stark black-white differences that urban homelessness shows. Finally, since rural poverty is strongly overrepresented in the South, we can expect especially high rates of rural homelessness in the Southern states.

As in urban areas, the fundamental cause of growing rural poverty results from displacement (Fantasia and Isserman 1996). In the rural case, that displacement takes the form of farm foreclosures. In the 1980s, there were over 650,000 farm foreclosures. Roughly 2,000 farmers gave up farming every week. Moreover, rural unemployment and poverty also deepened due to declining employment and profitability in lumber and mining. In fact, Fantasia and Isserman's survey of homelessness indicates that while 18% of the homeless population live in rural America, 67% of all substandard housing is found there as well (ibid.:155–56).

As the research community comes to focus more on rural homelessness, what can we expect to find? There are a couple of studies that provide some clues. One of those is *Rural Homelessness in Ohio* (First et al. 1990). Among the key findings in that study:

1. Homelessness is a reality for a growing number of rural Americans, a situation that has received little or no attention in any quarter.
2. The rural homeless are less visible than the urban homeless because of the relative scarcity of social services and shelters to assist them or to respond to their needs. Thus, the rural homeless must rely more on relatives, friends, and traditional self-help strategies. "The increase (First et al. 1990:81) in the number of [rural homeless] has placed a significant strain on these traditional support systems."
3. In Ohio and presumably elsewhere, estimated rates of homelessness per 10,000 population were as high or higher in the rural areas as in the urban areas.
4. The urban homeless tend overwhelmingly to be men—upward of 75% in most studies. The rural homeless, in contrast, are divided about 50–50 between men and women. The rural homeless were much more likely than the urban homeless to be currently married; thus, as suggested above, rural homelessness tends more to be intact family homelessness than urban homelessness.
5. Rural homeless were more likely to be homeless strictly for economic reasons (job loss, eviction, etc.) than urban homeless, and were less likely to be homeless because of various personal disabilities such as mental illness or substance abuse. In Ohio, the estimated rate of mental illness among rural homeless was about half the estimated rate for urban homeless.
6. Inevitably, the rural homeless were much less likely to rely on shelters to meet their temporary housing needs. Most were currently staying with family or friends, in motels, or in cars. In the rural areas, homelessness often means being doubled or tripled up, more so (apparently) than in the urban areas. This is another reason why the rural homeless are relatively invisible.

Important conclusions the Ohio study suggests are first that homelessness is definitely not limited to the urban areas; some rural areas have even higher homelessness rates (just as many also have even higher poverty rates) than nearby urban areas. There are potentially important demographic differences between rural and urban homelessness: more women and more families in the rural areas compared to urban areas. Shelters and other social services for the homeless are severely underdeveloped in the rural areas. Lack of services contributes greatly to the invisibility of the problem and implies that the rural homeless must rely on traditional support systems (family, friends, church, community) rather than on federal, state, or local programs of assistance.

We shift our focus now from rural America to Europe. While the locale is changing, the story, essentially does not.

HOMELESSNESS IN EUROPE

Some level of official concern about the emergence of homelessness in Europe dates to at least 1985, when the Irish convened the first pan-European seminar on the homeless in Cork. A follow-up conference was held in Belgium the following year. In 1989, a pan-European Federation of National Organizations Working with the Homeless (FEANTSA) was formed and in 1991 the Commission of the European Communities gave FEANTSA the responsibility for implementing a European Observatory on Homelessness that would "explain homelessness as a European event" and "draw together the different strands of homelessness in the twelve member states" of the Commission (Harvey 1992).

The European Observatory on Homelessness has so far issued two reports: *European Homelessness: The Rising Tide* (Daly 1992) and *Abandoned: Profiles of Europe's Homeless People* (Daly 1993). The Study Group on Homelessness (SGH) of the Council of Europe released a third relevant document, *Homelessness: Social Cooperation in Europe,* in 1993 (the Council of Europe is comprised of 32 member nations). These three documents provide a fairly comprehensive overview of homelessness across a rather wide swath of Europe but have enjoyed extremely limited distribution in the United States. (We thank Maryse Marpsat of the Centre du Sociologie Urbaine in Paris for making these materials available.) We intend the detailed summaries that follow to impart some sense of European homelessness to the American audience.

Like many Americans who have familiarized themselves with the problems of the homeless in his country, European commentators on homelessness see the problem as a threat to their claim to membership in the community of civilized nations. The SGH report (1993:13) refers to homeless people as "the waste products of progress, at the leading edge of social exclusion, a blot on our planet." And from Harvey (1992): "Each single homeless person is a reminder to European governments and peoples of just how much is yet to be done before we can call ourselves civilized nations upholding the highest standards of human and civil rights."

ON DEFINITIONS AND NUMBERS

The Europeans, like the Americans, have struggled over the issue of how best to define homelessness and have also failed to achieve a satisfactory resolution. The European emphasis is more on social process than strictly on the loss of housing. "Homelessness thus reveals something far more essential than a personal situation typified by the lack of housing or income; it reveals a process of social exclusion" (SGH 1993:15). The SGH and FEANTSA both recognize a continuum of "homelessness" ranging from the literally homeless (persons sleeping out of doors) to the unsuitably housed. "Treating homelessness on a continuum emphasizes a number of factors about it. First, it is part of a social process, a matter not of individual choice but an outcome of social and economic forces" (Daly 1992:2). A key theme in the various European writings on the topic is that the homeless are not just people who have been excluded from suitable housing but those who have been excluded, in some fundamental sense, from full participation in civil society, a useful point fully applicable to American homeless as well.

In the U.S. debate over proper definition, a key issue has been the so-called hidden homeless, persons temporarily doubled or tripled up with family and friends. Interestingly, Finland is one of three member states in the Council of Europe that has legislated an official definition of homelessness (Ireland and the United Kingdom are the other two) and it specifically includes "persons temporarily accommodated by relatives or friends" (SGH 1993:22).

As for the total number of homeless people in Europe as a whole or in specific nations, "no country has reliable figures [although] few countries claim to have no homeless people" (ibid.:25). At least 12 members of the Commission of the European Communities keep fairly careful track of the number of persons who use shelters and other facilities for homeless people; a compilation of these data (Daly 1993:Table 1) suggests a minimum of 2.5 million homeless people in those 12 nations, or a rate of roughly 7.5 homeless per 1,000 inhabitants. The methods that produce these numbers are widely variable across the 12 nations and the possibility of some double-counting cannot be ruled out. But the results give at least a workable first approximation.

How does the American rate of homelessness compare to the European rate? The European data are compiled over the span of a year and therefore estimate the annual size of the homeless population, not the single-point-in-time population. Needless to say, the number of persons destined to be homeless at least once in the course of a year is much larger than the number who happen to be homeless on any given night. In the United States, recent estimates of the number of homeless people on any given night range roughly from a half-million to one million and the annual population of homeless people in the United States is estimated to be 3–5 times higher than the one-night population (Rossi et al. 1987). Taking the middle figures in these ranges, the annual U.S. homeless population is on the order of $750,000 \times 4 = 3$ million, which would be equivalent to an annual homeless rate of about 11 per 1,000 population. Given the inherent uncertainties in these figures, one might safely conclude that the U.S. rate is perhaps somewhat higher than the European rate, but not by very much. Proportionally speaking, there appear to be about as many homeless people in Europe as in the United States. (There is also evidence to suggest that the Canadian homelessness rate is on the same order of magnitude.)

Daly emphasizes that the 2.5 million figure should be treated as a minimum or lower-boundary estimate because it counts only the service-using homeless and not those homeless people who avoid shelters and other homeless facilities and also because it does not include the "hidden homeless," those doubled up with family or friends. Also excluded are what Daly calls the "potentially homeless," that is, "people who live in insecure living situations . . . and who are therefore at risk of losing their accommodations. It is estimated that this condition defines the living situation of some ten per cent of the Communities' population" (1993:4). Ten percent would not be a bad guess about the number of marginally housed or "potentially homeless" people in the United States either. For example, a recent estimate is that more than half the U.S. poor now spend more than 70% of their total income on rent alone; the current poverty rate is right around 15%. Daly guesses that the "true" count of literally homeless people in the nations of the Commission of the European Communities could well exceed 5 million. In terms of sheer numbers, then, the U.S. and European homeless problems are broadly similar.

Since current numbers of homeless people are known only imprecisely in all countries, it is hard to be definitive about the question of recent trends. The best source of information on homelessness trends in the United States in the 1980s is Burt (1992), who concludes that the number of homeless grew more or less continuously throughout the decade. Much the same is apparently true in Europe as well: "With few excep tions, the growth in the numbers of homeless people is universally acknowledged and is linked with a variety of social and economic factors" (SGH 1993:29).

Some of the factors implicated in the increasing numbers of homeless in Europe are common to all nations; others are specific to certain countries. For example, the collapse of the Soviet bloc and the reunification of Germany stimulated a substantial flow of European population from East to West that "significantly affected the social situation firstly in the Federal Republic of Germany and subsequently in the peripheral Eastern bloc countries" (ibid.). Something similar could be said to have exacerbated the homeless problem in the United States also, namely, the continuous flow of "undocumented aliens" into the United States and the more general flow of population from the Rust Belt to the Sun Belt areas (the latter said to be responsible for a great deal of the homelessness encountered in various Sun Belt cities such as Phoenix and Albuquerque).

A second country-specific factor we consider concerns differences in each of the European nations' welfare and housing policies. While this topic goes well beyond the scope of this discussion, we mention a few policies. The Finns, for example, have an explicitly stated policy of eliminating homelessness and, as a result of this policy, the number of homeless has apparently declined quite considerably in that country. This policy is in stark contrast to the situation in the United Kingdom, where the numbers of homeless people have apparently increased drastically. "In England, the number of requests for homelessness relief increased seven-fold between 1971 and 1986" (ibid.:30). The homeless problem in Germany is also apparently worsening dramatically as rents have risen markedly and "the number of affordable dwellings [i.e., low-income housing units] is declining by 100,000 per year" (ibid.).

CHARACTERISTICS OF THE EUROPEAN HOMELESS

Any number of sources have described social and demographic characteristics of homeless people in the United States. And here too, the European situation tends to mirror that of the United States. As in the United States, males comprise the majority of the homeless throughout Europe, but the fraction of women and children is relatively large (on the order of a quarter to a third) and apparently growing (Daly 1993:8). Also reproducing the U.S. pattern, the European homeless "are more likely either to have never been married or to be divorced or separated" than the population as a whole. In Europe as well as in the United States, the average age of the homeless is surprisingly young; in Europe, about 70% of the homeless are younger than 40. "A host of factors is responsible" for homelessness among youth, among them "the unfavorable employment situation for young people, the shortage of independent accommodation, a pattern of migration in which younger people predominate" (ibid.:9). Much the same can be and indeed has been said about homelessness among the young in the United States.

In the United States, homeless people are often stereotyped as transients moving around the country to seek more generous welfare arrangements or favorable climates; in contrast, practically every empirical study of this question has concluded that the large majority of homeless people were born in the state where they currently reside. And likewise in Europe: while immigrant populations have a higher risk of homelessness than nationals in nearly every country, "the vast majority of the recipients of [homeless] services in all countries are nationals" (ibid.).

Extreme poverty is a nearly universal characteristic of homeless persons in the United States (e.g., Rossi 1990) and again, the same is true in Europe (SGH 1993:43). Daly reports that the educational levels of homeless people throughout Europe are "generally low" and employment records "poor" (1993:11). "Whether for unemployment, ill health, or some form of pension, state payments are the mainstay of homeless people across the Communities" (ibid.:12). Here, at last, is one definite difference between homelessness in Europe and in the United States: in Europe, practically *every* homeless person receives some sort of state payment, whereas in the United States, only about half the homeless receive any governmental assistance or welfare support (e.g., Wright and Weber 1987).

Both Daly and the SGH acknowledge high incidences of poor physical and mental health among the homeless of Europe and, likewise, elevated levels of alcohol and drug abuse (Daly 1993:10–11; SGH 1993:44–46). As in the United States, estimates of the rate of mental illness among the European homeless vary widely but tend to fall in the range of 30 to 50%.

Deinstitutionalization of the mentally ill has been a trend in many European countries no less than in the United States and in both contexts it has "led many highly vulnerable people into homelessness" (SGH 1993:46). Again consonant with the American experience, mentally ill homeless people in Europe confront shortages of community-based psychiatric counseling services, job training and retraining programs, financial assistance measures, and sheltered housing options to promote independent community living. Lacking these necessary support services, the deinstitutionalized mentally ill "have been left to sort out housing for themselves" (ibid.).

Perhaps the best single indicator of physical health status is relative mortality. In one British study, the average age of death for a sample of homeless people was 47 years (Daly 1993:10); in one Swedish study, it was 54 years (Alstrom et al. 1975); and in a comparable U.S. study based on homeless populations in 16 large cities, it was 51 years (Wright and Weber 1987:Chapter 8). Throughout the contemporary Western world, the price of being homeless amounts to about 20 years of forgone life expectancy.

Unlike the oft-expressed American perspective that blames alcohol, mental illness, and self-indulgent substance abuse for the rise in homelessness, the European view tends to be somewhat more enlightened in this respect. Acknowledging that rates of alcohol and drug abuse are elevated among the European homeless, the SGH report counsels against any effort to impute causal significance to the fact:

> Thus, instead of homelessness being seen as the result of a social process which involves a deep sense of alienation that is often accompanied by such symptoms as psychiatric problems and undue reliance on drugs and alcohol, such symptoms are viewed as the causes of homelessness. In turn, this can lead to stereotypical images of homelessness, like that of the middle aged or elderly man who is thought to be homeless because he is an alcoholic. He is often called a "vagrant," and there are laws in a number of European countries making vagrancy a chargeable offense. This stereotype in no way matches the profile of those who are becoming homeless in Europe today. (SGH 1993:44–45)

CAUSES OF HOMELESSNESS

In Europe and in the United States, the causes of homelessness are both personal and structural or economic. As we have argued throughout this book, social, economic, and structural factors in the United States have created a housing game that some are destined to lose; personal factors identify disabilities or vulnerabilities that are useful in predicting who the losers in the housing game turn out to be. Among many large-scale structural factors that determine the rules of the housing game, the two most important are the increasing rate, depth, and chronicity of poverty in the American cities and the dwindling supply of low-income housing.

European commentators focus on the same structural factors as explaining the increasing rate of homelessness in Europe. "Economic crisis and the growth of unemployment over the last two decades in most European countries, with the consequent increase in poverty, are crucial underlying factors in the growth of homelessness" (SGH 1993:49). As in the United States, labor market restructuring and the precipitous loss of semiskilled and unskilled jobs have "seriously disadvantaged those with the lowest educational attainment and trained skills" (ibid). The picture on the housing side is complicated owing to the vastly different housing policies and practices that prevail in the various European nations; "however, one common feature can be identified: the lack of affordable housing" (ibid.; see also Daly 1993:17). The European low-income housing crisis is linked to at least four developments that have occurred to a varying extent across the continent (SGH 1993:50):

(1) A shrinking and increasingly expensive private rental sector (in the United States, this is known as "gentrification"); (2) reductions in state expenditures on public (or "social") housing, which has occurred in several European countries, as in the United States; (3) privatization of public rental housing (i.e., selling off of public units to private buyers); and (4) increasing rents charged to occupants of public housing, eviction of tenants who cannot afford the higher rents, and selection of new tenants on the basis of ability to pay. Although the terms of discussion are somewhat different, U.S. experts on the low-income housing problem will quickly see many similarities between the European and American situations.

The more personal or individual factors involved in homelessness are also quite similar on both sides of the Atlantic. The SGH report enumerates deinstitutionalization of both the mentally ill and prison populations, youth unemployment and alienation, family violence, more general familial and marital breakdown, increasingly strict eligibility criteria and reductions in benefit levels in various social welfare programs, and comparatively high rates of immigration as factors that have put increasing numbers of Europeans on the streets. As in the United States, then, increasing unemployment and poverty have combined with a declining supply of low-income or affordable housing to increase the overall risk of homelessness; mental illness, substance abuse, loss of welfare benefits, family instability, and a host of related factors have increased the size of the population vulnerable to that risk. Increasing homelessness has been the inevitable result.

SOCIAL POLICY

European policy toward the homeless varies wildly from nation to nation. "At one extreme are countries such as Belgium, Luxembourg, Spain, Portugal, Greece and Italy with little or no coordinated national policy on homelessness" (Daly 1992:7). The relative indifference of these nations to the plight of their homeless people may reflect a general underdevelopment of the social welfare state (Italy, Spain, Portugal), a lack of recognition that there is a homeless problem in a particular country (as in Greece, apparently), or the failure of national governments to assign any particular priority to their homeless problem.

At the other extreme, "France is an exemplar . . . , its coordinated, integrated and diversified program of measures for the homeless placing it on a plateau higher than all other member states in this domain of policy" (ibid.:8). The French homeless program is embedded in a broader effort to combat poverty and marginalization. The nation concedes its citizens' right to housing as a fundamental right of citizenship equivalent to the right to vote (a similar right to housing is acknowledged in the constitutions of the Netherlands, the Scandinavian countries, Portugal, and Spain, which lack coordinated policy toward the homeless, articulate housing as a citizenship right). Moreover, France indemnifies that right through financial incentives to the private sector to acquire and refurbish accommodations suitable to the low-income and homeless populations and through the provision of "psychological and other forms of support and confidence building as well as specific help to (re)enter the labor market" (ibid.). In other words, the French subsidize housing and jobs for their low-income, marginal, and homeless citizens, apparently with little concern over the disincentives these subsidies might produce or the untoward effects of an overly generous social wage.

The remaining countries of the Commission of the European Communities apparently fall somewhere between these two extremes. We noted Finnish policy earlier. Most European countries recognize some obligation to their homeless populations, but many fragment the homeless problem by identifying particular groups (e.g., families, children) as priorities for aid and thereby devaluating the needs of others (single people, women without children, etc.). The United Kingdom penalizes homeless people who are deemed to have left their previous abode voluntarily. Serious resources limitations apparently exist throughout the continent: "nowhere in the Communities at present could it be said that an abundance of resources is made available . . . to the homeless" (ibid.). Thus, as in the United States, many European nations have focused their efforts on crisis intervention through the provision of temporary overnight shelter rather than mount a concerted effort at prevention or long-term stabilization and reintegration.

As in the United States, both the public and private sectors provide services for the homeless in Europe. "Private provision dominates in practically all member states, on a two-thirds / one third ratio" (ibid.:9). In the United States, about three-quarters of the total effort in behalf of the homeless comes through the private sector, principally the churches, so again the U.S. and European situations are broadly similar. A final similarity worth noting: "in many cases [France a notable exception], the predominantly private character of services highlights the reluctance, if not the failure, of the state to become directly involved in this domain of social provision" (ibid.).

Based on a survey of some 3,800 homeless service providers in 13 different nations, Daly also concludes that the specific services homeless people receive varies considerably across Europe. Responding to basic needs for shelter, food, and clothing is a priority everywhere; across the entire sample of service providers, about 80% offered "basic needs" services along these lines. In some countries, these were essentially the only services available. Most service providers also offer information (e.g., about rights and entitlements, availability of programs and services). Services aimed at reintegration of the homeless were predictably less widespread. In a few cases (Denmark, Luxembourg, Belgium), nearly all providers offer reintegration services; in other cases (Ireland, Scotland, Spain, and Greece), such services are for all practical purposes nonexistent.

Although services alone will not solve the homeless problem, they can make the lives of homeless people more comfortable and less degrading. Daly identifies five problems with service provision that tend to be common across the European countries she surveyed: gaps in services, fragmentation of services, inadequacies or even contradictions in official policy, limited governmental commitment to the issue of homeless, and a general lack of cross-national collaboration or even information-sharing about the problem.

The SGH report makes the useful further observation that official national policy on the homeless is dictated to some important extent by how homelessness is conceptualized and defined. As we mentioned above, the British officially distinguish between voluntary (nonpriority) and involuntary (priority) homeless and thus compel local authorities "to recognize as homeless and accept as beneficiaries of welfare policies only persons with children, pregnant women and isolated individuals rendered vulnerable by age, physical or mental disability and illness, and then only after an inquiry to assess the present conditions of accommodation, the imminent risk of its loss and above all whether their homeless condition is intentional" (1993:58). Thus, the British posture tends to mirror that of the United States, where people who are homeless "by choice" are deemed unworthy.

The contrasting case is that of Finland, where the official definition of homelessness discards not only the traditional stereotypes of alcoholism, vagrancy, immigration, and the like but even the very notion of literal "rooflessness." Homelessness in Finland thus includes not only the literal homeless but also the hidden homeless (the doubled-up population) and essentially anyone else who is unsuitably or unacceptably housed. More so than any other European nation, the Finns define the problem of homelessness in social terms and therefore emphasize that "homelessness is a social problem, not a personal failure" (ibid.:59). This stance has removed the stigma of being homeless and has prompted the Finnish government to commit unambiguously to the total elimination of homelessness in their country as a national policy goal.

CONCLUSIONS

The comparisons in this chapter, between rural and urban, and American and European homelessness reveal striking parallels in cause but a remarkable variation in responses. "Homelessness is truly a European phenomenon in the sense that, while the extent varies across member states, homelessness exists in each to a significant degree. Moreover, the factors precipitating homelessness are similar across national boundaries" (Daly 1993:14). And so too across continents, or so it would seem. In the early to mid-1980s, homelessness arose as a significant social problem in the United States and practically all the nations of Europe as well. Every indication is that the problem has worsened on both sides of the Atlantic in each subsequent year.

Characteristics of homeless people seem more or less the same everywhere; key causal factors appear to be increasing unemployment, increasing impoverishment, and a dwindling supply of low-income housing in all countries. The broad similarities between the rural and urban and U.S. versus European homeless situations strongly suggest that structural factors related to the changing world economic order lie at the heart of the homeless problem in the post-industrial West, not the personal failings of specific homeless individuals.

10

Street Children in North and Latin America

As we have stressed throughout this volume, the 1980s witnessed a dramatic transformation in the character of homelessness in the United States and Europe. In previous decades the U.S. homeless were predominantly older, largely white, broken-down alcoholic men; today a very sizable fraction are women and children. As proportionally more women and children comprise the U.S. and European homeless, so have they come more and more to resemble the street populations of the so-called third world, where homelessness, family disorganization, exploitation, and abandonment among children have become increasingly important problems during the past decade.

The United Nations' Year of the Child and its Declaration on the Rights of Children focused much attention on the situation of street children in less developed countries throughout the world. That this situation is essentially intolerable goes without saying (Bromley and Gerry 1979; Lusk 1989); increasingly, one hears of violence directed toward street children, including police brutality, frequent imprisonment, and even (in at least one case) killings of *gaminismos* (street children) that are informally sanctioned and abetted by officials and the media (Agnelli 1986:18). In their haste to condemn these intolerable conditions in the less developed nations, however, many commentators in the more developed countries have all too easily forgotten that the conditions of children in their own countries have steadily deteriorated in the past decade. This chapter presents descriptive data on street children in Tegucigalpa, Honduras, and then contrasts their economic, social, and physical well-being with that of homeless children in the United States. Despite the many obvious differences between these two nations, the parallels among their homeless children are striking.

THE HONDURAN CONTEXT

Honduras is one of the poorest of the Central American nations, indeed, one of the poorest nations in the Western Hemisphere. This small, impoverished, and mountainous country has suffered the consequences of neighbors at civil war, corruption, hurricanes, military occupation, and foreign (U.S.) ownership of a great deal of its limited productive economy. The official unemployment rate in 1990 was 28%, inflation was nearly 4% a month, and foreign debt was almost $1,000 per capita—this in a country where per capita income is estimated to be only about $525 a year (Duggan 1990:104). Although rates of unemployment in excess of a quarter of the labor force invariably mean severe hardship for a large mass of the population, they are not uncommon in Latin America, especially when rural populations are included (Barry 1986; Krehm 1984; Stonich 1991).

Poor soil, ancient agricultural practices, and the "bright lights" of the cities have sent many rural dwellers in Honduras and elsewhere into the urban areas to seek a better standard of living; this has in turned fostered the development of what is called the "elastic household," where rural families send family members (frequently adolescent children) into the cities to supplement family incomes, which in rural Honduras amount on the average to less than $20 per month (Barry and Norsworthy 1990; Stonich 1991). Thus, temporary (and, often enough, permanent) migration is a common practice. Men often leave their communities and families to harvest fruit or coffee; women move to the cities, often with the children in tow, hoping to find domestic work.

Once in the city, living arrangements are often overcrowded households consisting of extended families of various loosely related members (parents, children, aunts and uncles, boyfriends, and others). The vast tracts of periurban areas that quickly develop offer affordable rent and perhaps electricity but rarely running water or plumbing. The widespread squalor that exists within these areas (or *barrios*) is now common on the fringes of cities throughout the developing world. Once seen as a "problem" that modernization would solve (Tumin 1964; Ward 1962), the *barrios* have actually provided a "solution" to low-income housing needs of the rural-to-urban migrant population (McGee 1984; Streeten 1989); they house (however inadequately) cheap laborers, and because they are illegal or, at best, quasi-legal, governments can and do limit the services, programs, improvements, and protection that they might otherwise have to provide.

The poverty of Honduras is evident everywhere, from its aging airport to the inadequate housing encountered throughout the capital city, Tegucigalpa. More than two-thirds of the population live below the third world poverty standard [United Nations (ECLA) 1989]. (The U.S. poverty line, which is now about $16,000 in annual income for a family of four, would be considered a standard of affluence in Honduras.)

As we have suggested, and in common with many Latin American countries, Honduras has witnessed a vast influx of population into its cities (mainly Tegucigalpa and San Pedro Sula) in the last decades, and this influx has put an exceptional strain on municipal resources and services. Housing conditions throughout the city are substandard and overcrowded; it is quite common for as many as seven or eight people to share a single room. As is also customary in nations where the rate of infant mortality is high (about 60–65 deaths per 1,000 live births in Honduras), birth rates are also very high; most fecund women will have a half-dozen children or more during their reproductive years. Children are an economic resource in Honduras and elsewhere in Latin America [each child, after all, represents an extra worker (Kahl 1988)] and it is therefore important that one have enough of them to ensure that a reasonable number survive infancy.

The high birth rate and influx of rural populations have brought immense numbers of children and young teenagers into the city; indeed, the overwhelming impression one gains in first visiting Tegucigalpa is that there are children everywhere. As passengers step off the plane, children descend upon them to beg for money, sell candies and gum, or offer to carry bags. Street vendors, some as young as three or four years old, work throughout the city's open-air markets; nearly every street corner will have a small gaggle of children just hanging around; bands of teens sniffing glue can be seen here and there. Current estimates are that more than half of the Honduran population is under age 19, a proportion that is destined to rise, given the high birth rate.

Because of the grossly substandard housing conditions that prevail throughout the city, the distinction between "homed" and "homeless" is by no means as obvious as it is in the United States. In the Honduran context, four wooden posts and a sheet of corrugated tin comprise a "home" not very far removed from the average housing stock available to the poor in the city. In the same vein, minimally acceptable housing by U.S. standards, such as the public housing projects, would qualify as comfortable middle-class housing in Honduras. The poverty there is so abject and so widespread, and the housing stock so degraded, that many of the people who have "housing" are barely distinguishable from those that do not.

Thus, in the Honduran context and elsewhere in the less developed world, reference is made more frequently to "street children" than to "homeless children," although as we see later, many street children in

Honduras are literally homeless. An alternative and often-encountered synonym is "children in especially irregular circumstances." In either case, the referent is to the very large number of young people in the less developed countries who, although of school age, are not in school (or if they attend school do so for only part of the day) and who spend the majority of their time in the streets and markets of the cities foraging for their existence in the informal sector of the economy. UNICEF estimates that there are some 40 million children around the globe who exist in these irregular, high-risk conditions; certainly, there are thousands of them in Tegucigalpa alone.

PROYECTO ALTERNATIVOS

Proyecto Alternativos is a health education and social services project that provides services to street children in Tegucigalpa. The project operates out of six principal sites and a number of auxiliary sites close to the primary sites. Five of the six are based in various open-air markets around the city; the sixth site is a recreation area in the center of the city frequented by street teens. Project activities in each site are of four primary sorts: health education, a feeding program for the otherwise undernourished, nonformal educational and recreational activities, and primary health care. Most recently, the project has introduced classes for parents of street children. A separate team (comprised of two street educators) assigned to each market site spend each day in their site, and three technical support teams (one team comprised of a doctor and nurse, the other two teams comprised of a psychologist and a social worker) circulate among the six sites weekly.

The United Nations defines a street child as "any girl or boy . . . for whom the street (in the widest sense of the word, including unoccupied dwellings, wasteland, etc.) has become his or her abode and / or source of livelihood; and who is inadequately protected, supervised, or directed by responsible adults" (Lusk 1989). UNICEF and *Proyecto Alternativos* make a further critical distinction between children "in" the street and children "of" the street. The former are boys and girls who work (usually for their mothers) as vendors in the markets or in some other market-based economic activity (carrying bags, begging, hauling away garbage, and the like); obviously, they retain some contact with their families and live, however loosely, with some degree of parental (or adult) supervision. The latter, in contrast, are mostly teenagers who are orphaned or whose families abandoned them or who have run away from their families, and who consider the streets themselves to be their home. True abandoned street children are too young to enter the legitimate labor force and too estranged from their families to participate in the family's economic activities; they pass their time by sniffing glue, by "hanging out," and in various forms of petty criminality. Thus, children in the streets are primarily market kids, and children of the streets are primarily abandoned street kids. The latter are truly "homeless" and (more to the point, perhaps) familyless; the former are not. Market children form an important part of the labor force of the informal economy and society tends therefore to tolerate them; society often regards abandoned street children, in contrast, as a nuisance at best, and as criminals or derelicts at worst.

Not being literally homeless, of course, does not make the market children any less needy nor their social situation any more acceptable. Indeed, the project we discuss below focused on preventative activities for this group. These are mostly children between 4 and 18 who may or may not attend school but rather spend the majority of their day helping their families earn a subsistence income. In the typical case, the mother will have a "fixed-site" stall in one of the markets, where she sells, say, onions or avocados. Her children in turn take small bags of the product and wander through the market looking for customers. When the child makes a sale, he or she returns to the mother's stall, turns in the money, and obtains another bag of produce, a process that continues for as long as the market is open. Other activities of the market children include caring for younger siblings (the number of six- and seven-year-olds one encounters in the markets with a toddler in tow is striking), running errands, shining shoes, begging, scavenging, carrying trash and garbage from the market stalls to the central dumping area, and more or less anything else that will earn them a little money (Bromley and Gerry 1979; Connolly 1990).

Remarkably, the small amounts that the market children earn through these labors frequently represent a significant portion of the family's income; in other words, the principal motive for this child labor arrangement is economic (not social or cultural). The minimum wage for the lowest category of Honduran worker is 12 *lempiras* per day—roughly $2.00. Many of the women in the market earn even less than the formal minimum wage. Industrious market children often earn several *lempiras* a day, obviously not a trivial contribution. Thus, in many cases, these children do not attend school because their families cannot afford to do without the extra income they provide. (Also, since most Honduran schools require parents to supply school uniforms and supplies, many of the families could not afford to send their children to school in any case.)

Since many of these children do not attend formal school, the health education classes the project offers represents their only structured classroomlike activity. Recently, these classes have focused on the prevention and treatment of cholera, the incidence of which has reached epidemic proportions in several Central and South American nations. Other health topics covered in these classes have dealt with AIDS, dental hygiene, tuberculosis, basic anatomy, diarrheal disease, respiratory infections, sexuality and reproduction, diet and nutrition, and skin disorders.

Nonformal educational activities supplement and reinforce the health education sessions. Sometimes these are simple coloring projects; sometimes they are quizzes on the health education materials; and sometimes they are just singing and dancing. The associated feeding programs are also based in the markets and provide balanced 1,100-calorie lunches to selected children whose nutritional status has been assessed as problematic. The project also provides primary health care in the community onsite by the doctor-nurse team. First aid, curative care, assessment, counseling, and prevention are the principal health care activities; children needing more extensive workups or care are taken to various public clinics and hospitals around the city, depending on location and need. All project staff promote follow-up. Finally, the project's psychologist and social worker minister to the emotional and social needs of the children and their families.

The research component of *Proyecto Alternativos* is designed to provide descriptive data on the children the project serves; a second goal is to generate data that allow a comparison of health and social problems of street children in Honduras with those of homeless children in the United States. The project developed two principal sources of data on the Honduran children: (1) baseline protocols completed for the clients by project case workers; the instrument is not administered as a questionnaire but rather is completed by the case worker from notes taken during several interviews with each child; and (2) data on health problems the project's clinical and field records generate. The first of these comprise 1,023 completed questionnaires that form the basis for the statistical information presented later.

CHILDREN IN AND OF THE STREETS OF TEGUCIGALPA

The children *Proyecto Alternativos* serves are very young; ages range from 1 to 22 years and average about 11 years. Children of the streets are older on average (mean age = 12.9 years) than market children (mean age = 10.3 years). Boys are more numerous than girls: among market children (N = 909), 54% are boys and 46% are girls; the street children (N = 110) are overwhelmingly boys (95%).

Among homeless adults in the United States, males predominate by roughly two to one; among homeless youth, males and females are represented in approximately equal proportions. As with the market children of Honduras, homeless preteens in the United States almost invariably live with a parent (in most cases, a mother), whereas homeless teenagers are typically out on their own, away from any consistent adult influence. The sex ratios, living and sleeping circumstances, and average ages of the various groups suggest that market children in Honduras are demographically comparable to homeless preteens in the United States, and that children of the street in Honduras are comparable to homeless U.S. adolescents. The strong preponderance of males among Honduran children of the street and among homeless U.S. adults is indicative of the matrilineal organization of poverty families in both nations, whereby young males are considerably more likely than young females to be "turned out" (kicked out or asked to go) once familial resources have been stretched past the limit.

A substantial majority of both groups are native Tegucigalpas, although nearly 40% of the children of the street (and 17% of the market children) are in-migrants from other regions of the country, reflective of the rural-to-urban population flow discussed earlier. One assumes that many of the in-migrating children of the street have fled abusive or otherwise unacceptable family situations whereas the in-migrating market children have come to the city with their families.

Other studies of street children in Bogotá and Guatemala City suggest that weak or disorganized family structures contribute a great deal to the problem. Whether resulting from the cultural disorientation rural migrants experience or the extreme material deprivation of the urban slum, the family's role as a protective and socializing force for children is diminished; for many older boys in particular, life in the streets becomes an adaptation to unbearable family conditions (Connolly 1990). Consistent with these earlier findings, the Honduran children also tend to come from large, disorganized family backgrounds. About 5% of the children of the streets and 2% of the market children are orphans; among the remainder, the average number of other persons living in the child's nuclear household is 5.3. Very few of the parents of these children are currently married (15% of the market kids; only 8% of the street kids); most are separated or divorced (45% of the total sample), or were never married in the first place (32%).

Family disorganization and estrangement are, of course, dramatically higher for the true abandoned street children than for the market children. Among the latter, case workers have assessed 78% as having good to excellent relations with their families; among the former, this is true of only 32%. Three-quarters of the children of the street but only a fifth of the market children exhibit symptoms of family dysfunction. Nearly 9 in 10 of the market children (86%) live with one or both of their parents; among children of the street, barely a third live with a parent and most (57%) live and sleep, literally, in the streets of the city. Two-thirds of the market kids have someone who takes care of and looks after them during the days (normally the mother, of course). This is true of only 13% of the children of the street, and in most cases (9 of 14) the caretaker is a brother or sister who is also in the streets. About half the market children attend school (many are too young to do so); 90% of the abandoned street children do not. Of those who have ever received formal schooling, almost all have completed three or fewer years. A bare majority (57%) can read and write at some level; the remainder cannot. Very few of these children (either category) are recent arrivals; 82% have been in or of the streets for more than a year.

A high degree of family disorganization also characterizes homeless persons in the United States. Among homeless adults, as among the parents of the Honduran children, few are married, many are separated and divorced, and many more never married in the first place. Recent studies suggest that perhaps as many as a third of the U.S. homeless grew up at least in part in the foster care system (e.g., Blau 1992); profound estrangement from the family of origin (and of procreation) is widespread. Thus in family background no less than in demographic characteristics, there are obvious similarities between the Honduran and U.S. cases.

Many analysts and commentators have ascribed the disorganization of the U.S. poverty family to the perverse incentives posed by the nation's welfare system, in particular Aid to Families with Dependent Children (AFDC), which is said to encourage out-of-wedlock pregnancy, high fertility, and female-headed households. It is of more than passing interest that there are equivalent rates of all these indicators of family "dysfunction" among the families of street children in Honduras, where there is a very limited welfare system and where nothing even remotely similar to AFDC exists. The similarity in outcome, in the context of very different structural conditions (presence or absence of welfare) suggests instead that severely restricted economic opportunities in both nations create a shortage of desirable males capable of helping to support a family, and that the women in both nations therefore do without husbands in fulfilling their pronatalist values.

As we suggested earlier, most of the market children's economic activities are based on the informal economy of the open-air market; average daily earnings per child (as reported to the interviewers) vary from as little as 20 *centavos* (about $0.04) to as much as 10 *lempiras* ($1.90). In nearly all cases, the earnings of the market children are shared with their families. In addition to general "market work," other activities include carrying things, running errands, and selling trinkets, gum, and candy. The children of the street support themselves mainly through begging (42%), carrying things for people (15%), and petty theft (12%); nearly all of them keep for themselves whatever money they earn.

Interviewer assessments of client functioning in a number of areas showed that about one client in six (16%) probably suffered fair to poor mental health, more than a third (36%) were in fair to poor physical health, and over 40% had significant nutritional deficiencies. In most cases, these assessments were more negative for the children of the street than the market children, but the differences were not large. The range and extent of health and social problems indicated in these data are scarcely surprising. As of the intake interview, doctors had not seen 5% of these children and another 51% had not been seen by a doctor or other health professional in more than a year. Their nutritional needs were also unmet; it is worth noting that only 59% of these children ate three meals a day on the average; about a third ate only two meals a day; 8% ate only one. Here, as in most other comparisons, the market children fared considerably better; among the abandoned street children, only 6% ate three meals a day. Despite these differences, it is of considerable interest that researchers have found second- and third-degree malnutrition only among the market children; they have seen no such cases among the children of the street. It also needs to be mentioned that in the Honduran context, the breakfast meal can consist of just coffee and bread and lunch or supper might be nothing but tortillas and salt. In most Latin American countries, definitely including Honduras, inadequate nutrition is so prevalent that most hospitals have special wings to care for malnourished and starving children (Lusk 1989). There are other conditions that undermine the life chances of these children.

Police have arrested about half the children of the street (but almost none of the market children); 4 in 10 have been in jail (15% of them many times). One in five of the abandoned street kids belongs to a street gang. More than half sniff glue (half regularly); 4 in 10 also drink alcohol at least occasionally; 6 in 10 smoke cigarettes; 1 in 5 smokes marijuana. (In contrast, substance abuse is nearly absent among the market children.) Thus, inhalants are the most commonly abused substance among abandoned street children in Honduras, as opposed to alcohol (and then crack) among homeless teens in the United States, but the overall rate of substance abuse is about the same in both contexts. As in the United States, street children in Honduras sniff glue because it is very cheap; the pharmacological effects are quite similar to those of alcohol. Sniffing glue, like getting drunk, diminishes pain, reduces fear, increases bravado, and suppresses hunger (Aptekar 1988; Janowsky 1991).

Further compounding the health and emotional difficulties of the abandoned street children is that many of them (44%) are sexually active (compared to only 5% of the market children). Almost all of the sexually active children of the street (85 percent; $N = 47$) have been treated for sexually transmitted diseases at least once (compared to only 40% of the sexually active market children; $N = 40$). More than a fifth of the sexually active children of the street also have engaged in prostitution.

Despite the many clear differences between children in and of the streets of Tegucigalpa and homeless children in U.S. cities, the health problems of the two groups are remarkably similar. Skin ailments, respiratory infections, trauma, and dental problems are the leading causes of morbidity in both contexts. As in the U.S. case, the diseases and disorders exhibited among these children are not unusual or exotic ailments for the most part; they are, rather, the characteristic diseases of childhood. But because of the degraded conditions of existence, they appear at abnormally high rates and intensities.

During a recent visit to the project, Wright observed the medical team treating six of the abandoned street children. Three of the children were being treated for trauma (two of them secondary to police-administered beatings the previous evening, the third a knife wound resulting from a fight), one had an upper respiratory infection, one had a severe case of head lice, and the sixth had come to see the doctor just because he was sad. A similar scene could be observed at HCH clinics anywhere in the United States.

Street children in all societies inhabit an exceptionally high-risk environment. Nutritional status and personal hygiene are generally poor; thus, many are debilitated and susceptible to infection. Life in the streets is an obvious risk factor for injuries and disorders due to exposure. Crowded and unsanitary living conditions present optimal vectors for the transmission of infectious and communicable disease. Air and noise pollution are extreme. Extreme poverty prevents customary treatment with over-the-counter palliatives such as aspirin, dermatological preparations, or cough syrup. All in all, there is scarcely any aspect of a street existence that does not imperil the physical health of children; this is equally true in Honduras, in the United States, and, one imagines, everywhere else.

The general theme that emerges in these data (consistent with the observations of our street educators and clinicians in Tegucigalpa) is that the social problems of the market children stem primarily from the extreme poverty of their families, whereas the social problems of the abandoned street children result from being essentially familyless in the first place. Neither situation is acceptable, of course, but there is little doubt that the abandoned street children are the more troubled group (and more comparable to homeless teens in U.S. cities). For the remainder of this chapter we turn to a brief discussion of the U.S. case (recognizing that the material echoes what we presented in previous chapters).

POVERTY, HOMELESSNESS, AND CHILD HEALTH IN THE UNITED STATES

There is little doubt that many of the health and nutritional problems of homeless children and youth in the United States result from the extreme poverty characteristic of the homeless population. Poverty rates, which had been high throughout the 1980s, jumped up even higher in the early years of the 1990s, reaching nearly 40 million poor people in the United States in 1993, when the number of households receiving Food Stamps was higher than at any time in the program's history. And, as has been true for many years, about 40% of the poor are children. The role of poverty in creating homelessness also implies that the recent increase in the number of homeless women (and therefore homeless children) is a consequence of the so-called feminization of poverty about which much has been written (Devine and Wright 1993; Duncan 1984; Ehrenreich and Piven 1984; Sidel 1996). In 1996, Sidel notes that women and children comprise almost 80% of all Americans living in poverty (ibid.:70). As a consequence, the poverty rate among U.S. children is almost twice that of adults: in 1996, 19.8% of those under age 18 were officially classified as poor; among those 18–64, the corresponding figure was 11.5% (U.S. Bureau of the Census 1997).

Not only is poverty increasing, the character of American poverty is changing. Historically, the large majority of the poor were episodically poor, that is, their incomes would fall below the official poverty line from time to time, reflecting short-term fluctuations in household composition or family economic circumstances. Today, we find that more and more families are chronically poor, that is, continuously beneath the poverty line year after year (Devine and Wright 1993). Also, this more obdurate chronic poverty, as in Honduras, is concentrated in central city poverty areas. All things considered, the poverty situation in the nation today is arguably worse than at any time since the mid 1960s and much closer to what we observe in third world countries like Honduras.

The recent trends in the poverty rate and other changes in the American family have begun to erode the social, economic, and physical well-being of children. Nationwide, a fifth of our children live in families below the poverty line; in several cities, this figure now approaches 50%. Children suffer the highest aggregate poverty rate of any age group in the U.S. population. This is especially true of children in female-headed households, now nearly a quarter of all children.

The effects of poverty and homelessness on the physical health of children are far-reaching. One stunning indicator of the deteriorating condition of children is the declining proportion of them who are covered by medical insurance. In 1996, 10.6 million, or 14.8% *of all children*, including 3.4 million (or 23.3%) of all *poor* children, were without health insurance. These data reflect the deepening poverty and hardship befalling the nation's children. In 1987, in contrast, 11.2 million or 17.8% of all children were uninsured (Cunningham and Monheit 1990). Even more precipitous was the decline in public insurance coverage among children in households with working single parents: in 1977, a third of these children were covered by public insurance (principally Medicaid), and in 1987, barely 13%. The reality of children in the United States is shockingly close to that of Honduran street children.

Among the most firmly established correlates in the epidemiological literature is that between poverty and infant mortality; indeed, "the correlation between poverty and high infant mortality rates is undisputed" (Miller 1985:35). Particulars vary from study to study, but poor infants appear to be between 60 and 300% less likely to survive the first year of life than are children born to more affluent mothers (Slesinger, Christenson, and Cautley 1986; Spurlock, Hinds, Skaggs, and Hernandez 1987; Nersesian, Petit, Shaper, Lemieux, and Naor 1985). The black-white difference in infant mortality is on the order of two to one; in fact, infant mortality among U.S. black babies exceeds the rate in Jamaica (Farley and Allen 1987:47).

Exactly what factors are implicated in the correlation between poverty and premature infant death is less certain: inadequate prenatal care, low birth weights, excessive smoking, drinking, and drug use among poor pregnant mothers, and earlier-than-average first births among poor mothers are among the most commonly cited factors (Dott and Fort 1975a, 1975b; Hardoy 1986).

Infant mortality in the United States has been declining among all socioeconomic groups for decades, but the rate of decline slowed abruptly in the 1980s, especially among poor mothers (Miller 1985; Sogunro 1987). It is now more or less universally conceded that the long-standing national goal of not more than nine infant deaths per 1,000 live births by the year 1990 (set in 1979 by the U.S. Public Health Service) will go unattained. Least of all will this laudable goal be attained among blacks, the poor, or the homeless, despite its already having been attained (or exceeded) in many nations around the world.

Poverty negatively affects morbidity as well as mortality among children, although evidence on the point is not entirely conclusive. An early review of the appropriate studies suggested that "in addition to higher infant mortality and child mortality, poor children have more disabilities, handicaps, dental caries, visual and hearing impairments, lead poisoning, and incomplete immunizations than nonpoor children" (Egbuono and Starfield 1982; Newburger, Newburger, and Richmond 1976). Other researchers have added anemia, chronic ear infections, learning disabilities, scabies and lice infestations, and increased suicide rates to this list (Shah et al. 1987).

Data from the National Health Survey (reported by Egbuono and Starfield) show approximately equal prevalences of most acute disorders among poor and nonpoor children, more severe sequelae of those acute disorders among the poor than the nonpoor, higher (but only slightly higher) rates of chronic disorders among the poor, and higher hospitalization rates for poor children (Egbuono and Starfield 1982:551). Analysis of the Child Health Supplement to the 1981 National Health Interview Survey (Newacheck and Starfield 1988) revealed similar results: while the reported prevalence of most disorders among children was approximately similar across income levels, poor children were more severely affected by their illnesses (as measured by bed days), were more likely to have multiple illnesses in the one-year span covered by the study, and utilized fewer physician services.

"Children living in poor households in the United States have traditionally received inadequate health services" (Gortmaker 1981:567) despite the widespread availability of Medicaid to poor children since 1967. The same can be said of other advanced industrial nations such as Canada (Shah et al. 1987) or Great Britain (Wadsworth 1988). The similarities to the conditions in Honduras are embarrassing. Inadequate access to appropriate care is perhaps the primary mechanism that links poverty to ill health among both children and adults (St. Peter, Newacheck, and Halfon 1992).

CONCLUSION

Children in and of the streets of Honduras and throughout the third world are the unwitting victims of large-scale economic and demographic dislocations that will not be resolved yet in this century or anytime soon in the next. Widespread poverty, inflation, high birth rates, continued periphery-to-core migration, rising unemployment, declining levels of aid from the developed world, and other factors have made and will continue to make street children a fixture throughout the cities of the third world. That fact is perhaps not surprising; more remarkably, homeless children have also become a fixture in U.S. cities (and elsewhere in the industrial world as well), and their economic, social, psychological, and physical conditions appear every bit as troubled as those of third world street children. There is, it appears, no special advantage in being extremely poor in a wealthy nation as opposed to being extremely poor in an impoverished one. Despite the many glaring differences between Honduras and the United States, the material, social, and medical circumstances of the very poorest and neediest children prove remarkably, even disturbingly similar in both nations.

Homeless street children suffer the burdens of disorganized and estranged family life—in Honduras and the United States. Homeless street children show exceptional levels of physical illness and mental anguish—in Honduras and the United States. Homeless street children are often underfed if not clinically malnourished—in Honduras and the United States. Homeless street children abuse drugs, prostitute themselves, scavenge for sustenance in the garbage, and become involved in crime—in Honduras and in the United States. In Latin America, street children are abused, victimized, and occasionally even killed by merchants and the police; in the United States, they kill one another (Aptekar 1994). Homelessness and extreme poverty are far more decisive in setting the conditions of life for children than national context or cultural differences. When we hold the situation of street children in Honduras up to the mirror, we see . . . ourselves. Nancy Boxill has likened this lamentable image to the "portrait of Dorian Gray . . . too awful to gaze upon, too costly to repair" (1990:4).

11

Homelessness in the Twenty-First Century

We much wish we could write a conclusion to this book that is filled with hope for the future, but we cannot. Recent developments in Washington and elsewhere do not bode well for a progressive solution to the problems we have raised throughout this book. There are few good reasons to believe that things are getting or will get any better, and many good reasons to believe that they will get much worse.

One of the truly important accomplishments of the research this book reviewed is the unambiguous, largely irrefutable demonstration that homelessness is indeed a poverty problem. The overall poverty rate in the decade of the 1980s was discernibly higher than it had been in the 1970s, especially in the large cities; in the 1990s the poverty problem is worsening. At the same time that the poverty population of the large cities is increasing, the supply of affordable low-income housing continues to decline. Despite the many residual controversies over the "numbers" issue, essentially everybody agrees that the number of homeless persons increased dramatically during the decade of the 1980s and is continuing to do so.

The consequence of all this is that we know full well what must be done to address the root causes of homelessness: more low-income housing, and less poverty. We do not mean to imply that this is all we need to do; clearly, the needs of homeless people often transcend their income and housing problems. Our point, rather, is that until we address the income and housing issues, everything else we try to do will be crisis intervention only and will not, indeed, cannot address the root problems. But where is the political leadership? What is necessary to prevent continuing homelessness in the next century?

A few simple calculations, based on defensible assumptions all around, will show just how hopeless the situation is. A reasonably aggressive federal intervention in the housing market, for example, one that

209

would arrest the loss of existing low-income units and add a reasonable number of new units to the supply through federally subsidized construction, would add perhaps $20 billion per year to HUD's low-income housing expenditure. That is roughly twice what the federal government now spends in all programs combined to subsidize the housing costs of the total national poverty population. No one in their right mind thinks we are going to spend $20 billion a year addressing the housing problems of homeless people. The Reagan administration left a legacy of massive federal debt and declining faith in government as an effective institution for progressive social change.

The picture is equally dismal on the income side of the equation. Peter Rossi has converted current welfare payment levels (for instance, AFDC) to 1968 dollars to show that the purchasing power of welfare today is only about half what is was 20 years ago. Twenty years ago, a welfare-dependent household could at least keep a roof over its head on the average welfare payment: this is obviously no longer the case. The immediate implication is that the government would need to approximately double welfare benefits of all sorts to restore them to their 1968-era values, and that certainly is not going to happen. Quite the contrary; now we have had welfare reform that has removed even this safety net from underneath the very poor.

Then there is the minimum wage, which was recently raised in two steps from $3.35 to $4.25 (1996) to $5.15 (1997) per hour. The increase restores only a tiny fraction of the purchasing power of the minimum wage lost to inflation since 1981 (when the wage was last raised). To indicate something of the absurdity of what we now call the "minimum" wage, we note that a person working 40 hours a week, 50 weeks a year, at the minimum wage and supporting a four-person household would be more than $5,000 a year below the official poverty line. A single mother working full time at the minimum wage and supporting two children would also still be more than $2,000 below it. To raise the minimum wage beyond the poverty level, in short, would require an increase to $6.26 per hour for a three-person household and an increase to $8.02 per hour for a four-person household, and this is also not going to happen. So the minimum wage will continue to be a subpoverty wage into the foreseeable future.

In the same vein, one might consider the problems that have been encountered in recent efforts to enhance the housing stock available to the poor, for example, the New Jersey Fair Share initiative analyzed in exquisite detail by Lang (1989). The heart of Lang's analysis consists of a series of case studies of various low-cost housing and shelter initiatives in various New Jersey localities. An extensive review of several such initiatives concludes that while local efforts are sometimes successful in restraining the cost of housing, "much of the cost savings has been absorbed by inflation resulting in a marginal effect on total housing costs" (ibid.:116). Indeed, the principal effect of most local low-cost housing initiatives has been to keep the price of housing "within the range of the suburban middle class and their upwardly mobile offspring," not to expand the housing options of the central city poor. Local efforts along these lines are therefore described as a fool's errand; there are no local solutions to national problems.

An evaluation of New Jersey's Fair Share initiative is a case study in how local low-income housing efforts fail. Fair Share originated as a state Supreme Court decision concerning the legality of exclusionary zoning. In brief, the Court ruled that local communities could not use exclusionary zoning to avoid their fair share of the responsibility for housing low-income people, that local communities "cannot foreclose the opportunity and . . . must affirmatively afford the opportunity for low and moderate income housing" (ibid.:121). Each local community was thereby obligated to provide low-cost housing for their fair-share portion of the regional low-income population.

The Fair Share ruling occurred nearly two decades ago, in 1975. Opposition from local communities, developers, real estate interests, and others led to endless interpretations, additional rulings, litigation, state housing legislation, and so on, but very little low- to moderate-income housing has been built. Indeed, the evidence suggests that the low-income housing problem has worsened in New Jersey since the Fair Share ruling was first issued. "[T]he number of attorneys and planners newly affluent as a result of this [Fair Share] opinion probably exceeds the number of formerly urban low and moderate income families with new . . . housing in the suburbs" (ibid.:133). And so it goes. From 1975 to the date of writing, about 2,000 affordable units of housing had been built, this against an estimated need for about 150,000 such units.

The problems of housing the poor, the destitute, and the homeless exceed the resources available to any single community and probably those of any single state. Thus, federal initiatives are essential. And yet, federal housing policy toward the poor is a shambles. A decade's advocacy in behalf of the homeless has produced only piecemeal ameliorative programs at the federal level, most of them located in the Department of Health and Human Services, not in the Department of Housing and Urban Development. Will another decade accomplish more? Probably not. "Still, efforts to craft a workable and just solution must go forward; not to make the attempt would be unthinkable" (ibid.:210).

As if all this were not bad enough, there are other less tangible but no less important developments afoot, all of which bode ill for the course of homelessness in the 1990s and beyond. First, there has been an unmistakable hardening of the spirit as it pertains to the nation's homeless population. Less and less are the homeless looked upon as unfortunate souls desperately in need of assistance; more and more are they regarded as detritus to be swept out of sight and out from underfoot. As evidence of this, witness the recent efforts in Los Angeles, New Orleans, and elsewhere to ban the sale of fortified wine in areas where homeless people congregate. No one expects this measure to help homeless alcoholics overcome their drinking problem, and that, of course, is not even the point. The point is to disperse them, make them go elsewhere, and take their problems with them in the process.

Wright was interviewed a few years ago by the local daily newspaper on the growing numbers of panhandlers in New Orleans's French Quarter. He took pains to explain that not all panhandlers in the Quarter were homeless people and, assuredly, that not all homeless people in the city panhandled in the Quarter. Wright also raised the question whether the occasional harassment of tourists by panhandlers was really at the heart of the problem, most of all in a city with the highest unemployment rate in the nation and where nearly half the population lives below the poverty line. Subsequent letters to the editor revealed extremely little enthusiasm for his views. One Quarter businessman was particularly adamant; in his view, all these drunks, vagrants, and panhandlers should be rounded up by the police and tossed in jail—this, mind you, in a city where drugs are sold openly in the projects because we lack both police resources and jail space to do anything about it.

Stuart Bykofsky, a reporter for the *Philadelphia Daily News*, referred to the homeless as "the drunk, the addicted, and the just plain shiftless" (in a 1986 article in *Newsweek*). Bykofsky reasoned that since homeless people live in the streets, and since the streets are maintained by the taxes he pays, then he, Bykofsky, is effectively their landlord. His solution was straightforward: "I want them evicted," he wrote. This is a hard, mean-spirited, but increasingly common attitude. Compassion and generosity toward the homeless are being replaced by a much more punitive, hard-bitten, uncaring mood.

Second, policymaking circles have begun to reveal an attitude that might be referred to as the "complacency of modest accomplishment." In Washington, this will arise as a subtle, often unstated, but nonetheless palpable opinion that we have already dealt with homelessness through the provisions of the McKinney Act, that homelessness was last year's issue, that the appropriate programs are in place and working, and that nothing more really can or even should be done. At the local level, officials express this attitude in a mayor's evident pride that the city has opened a new municipally funded shelter for the homeless or, in the extreme case, that some local outfit has received funding through the McKinney Act to deal with homelessness issues.

The tendency among policymakers, in short, is to mistake having done anything at all for having provided a sufficient response to the problem. After all, from a politician's viewpoint, a problem is "solved" once he or she is off the hook. In a deep sense, McKinney has left the federal government and many local communities off the hook of homelessness, and that is a very troubling development.

Third, and related to our second observation, political attention has been diverted from homelessness and related poverty issues by other, apparently more pressing concerns, chief among them crime, the "war on drugs," and—above all else—deficit reduction. Indeed, it is little short of astonishing just how quickly the crime and drug problems moved in on the political agenda, pushing every other social and human problem off to the sidelines. We do not mean to make light of the nation's crime and drug problems; at the same time, they are definitely not the only problems confronting us—not by any means. But they may well prove to be the only significant social problems that we choose to confront in the current political and fiscal environment. And needless to say, in an era of fixed or shrinking resources, money spent to fight crime and drugs is money no longer available to any other purpose.

Finally, we have begun to witness what can only be called the inevitable institutionalization of the homelessness problem. The attention homelessness received in the last decade has resulted in a vast cadre of shelter and soup kitchen operators, advocates, social workers, health care professionals, case managers, researchers, and others whose professional identities, job security, and personal values revolve around the homelessness issue. Already, we hear of turf battles between groups trying to protect their fiefdoms, sometimes even at the expense of the homeless people they are presumably trying to serve.

In some respects, of course, the institutionalization of the issue is a positive development—it means, after all, that some essential services are now in place. In other respects it is an inevitable development. But it may be a very dangerous and counterproductive development if it causes us to lose sight of the collective goal. And let there be no mistake: the goal is not to make the lives of homeless people more comfortable, healthier, or less degrading. The ultimate goal is to be rid of homelessness once and for all—in a word, to put homeless service providers, advocates, and researchers right out of business. And it is a rare organization indeed that can summon the courage to destroy its own reason for being.

Will the many organizations, agencies, associations, and groups that now exist to serve the needs of the homeless population be able to resist the organizational imperatives of survival? Are there not already strong vested interests in the perpetuation of the homeless problem? These dangers are clearly present. Whether they come to pass remains to be seen.

There is no doubt that homelessness costs us a lot of money and will cost us even more in the future, but no one is in a position to say exactly how high the costs are or will be. Part of the problem in trying to determine the costs is that most of the annual expenditure on problems of homelessness—about two-thirds of the total—is borne by the private sector, principally the churches, and most of the remainder is borne by state and local government, not by the federal government. So you cannot look up a line somewhere in the federal budget and state just what the total costs of homelessness are. The costs, though evidently high, are widely dispersed across 50 states, tens of thousands of municipalities, and hundreds of thousands of private charitable organizations.

The current costs of homelessness are not only dispersed across a large number of jurisdictions; they are also often indirect and hard to calculate. For example, research has shown that the rate of tuberculosis among the homeless is a hundred times or more the rate in the general population. There is no serious doubt that homelessness increases the number of persons at risk from this disease. What, then, does it cost local departments of public health across the nation to detect and treat the additional cases of tuberculosis that rising homelessness has caused? No one knows the exact cost, but we can be certain that it is not cheap.

Let us pose a series of rhetorical questions in the same vein: How many urbanites around the nation now customarily avoid certain downtown areas because of the large numbers of homeless people who gather there? And what is the dollar value of the trade and commerce that is thereby lost to businesses operating in those areas? How much lost tourism has there been in New York City now that there are, by some estimates, 30,000 or 40,000 homeless people strewn around the city?

What does it cost us collectively to operate the many tens of thousands of temporary shelters, soup kitchens, missions, drop-in centers, and such that have sprung up to address the needs of the nation's homeless? How much needless overutilization of public hospital emergency rooms could be avoided if the homeless were given adequate primary health care? What is the dollar value to society of the wasted human capital represented by the "tattered bundles of humanity" that now litter our streets and conscience? What is it worth to us economically when we enable the otherwise destitute and downtrodden to live productive, independent lives?

What price do we pay in the court of world opinion when our major newspapers run almost daily stories about America's homeless on the front page? What do we give up in negotiations with other countries over "human rights" when it is manifestly obvious to anyone that many of our own citizens do not enjoy decent housing, adequate nutrition, or suitable health care? It is probably not possible to assign a dollar value to any of these costs, but they are real costs just the same.

Finally, what is the cost we pay in our dignity as a nation when we let some of our own citizens sleep in the gutters and scavenge an existence from our garbage? What does it say about us as a free, democratic society when we are confronted with hundreds of thousands, maybe millions, of our fellow citizens trapped in the desperation and degradation of homelessness and do little except to throw up our arms and whine that the federal budget deficit rules out any genuine solution? Has our collective social conscience eroded so thoroughly that we are now prepared to let homelessness run its own course? It saddens and embarrasses us to suggest this as a very real possibility.

The Statue of Liberty stands in New York Harbor as the most visible and most symbolic message of what we intend for our nation to be in the eyes of the rest of the world. Inscribed at the base of that statue is the sonnet by Emma Lazarus that is reproduced at the beginning of this volume, one that invites the world to "send these, the homeless, tempest-tost to me, I lift my lamp beside the golden door." It is sadly obvious that as a nation we have let the golden door swing shut on hundreds of thousands of our own citizens. They sleep in the gutters and streets and temporary shelters of our cities, scavenging food, cans, and bottles from the trashcans, and all this for just one reason: *because we allow it to continue.* The most important "need" of homeless people—the wretched refuse of our own shores—is not more mental health counseling, alcohol and drug treatment programs, health care for the homeless clinics, or even more subsidized low-income housing, but to have the golden door kicked back open again.

References

"Agencies Rally Around Homeless, Hit Study" (1986). *Chicago Tribune,* 30 August.

Abramson, A., and M. Tobin (1995). "The Changing Geography of Metropolitan Opportunity: The Segregation of the Poor in U.S. Metropolitan Areas, 1970 to 1990." *Housing Policy Debate* 6(1):45–72.

ACCESS (1990). *Federal Monies Support Transitional and Permanent Housing.* Washington, DC: Author.

Aday, L., G. V. Fleming, and R. Anderson (1984). *Access to Medical Care in the US: Who Has It, Who Doesn't?* Chicago: Pluribus.

Agnelli, S. (1986). *Street Children: A Growing Urban Tragedy.* London: Weidenfeld and Nicolson.

Akers, R. L. (1992). *Drugs, Alcohol and Society: Social Structure, Process, and Policy.* Belmont, CA: Wadsworth.

Alperstein, G., C. Rappaport, and J. Flanigan (1988). "Health Problems of Homeless Children in New York City." *American Journal of Public Health* 78:1232–33.

Alstrom, C. H., R. Lindelius, and I. Salum (1975). "Mortality among Homeless Men." *British Journal of Addictions* 70:245–52.

Altman, D., E. L. Bassuk, W. R. Breakey, A. A. Fischer, C. R. Halpern, G. Smith, L. Stark, N. Stark, B. C. Vladeck, and P. Wolfe (1989). "Health Care for the Homeless." *Society* 26:4–5.

Aptekar, L. (1988). *Street Children of Cali.* Durham, NC: Duke University Press.

Aptekar, L. (1994). "Street Children in the Developing World: A Review of Their Condition." *Cross Cultural Research* 28:3:195–224.

Babor, T. F., R. S. Stephens, and A. Marlatt (1987). "Verbal Report Methods in Clinical Research on Alcoholism: Response Bias and Its Minimization." *Journal of Studies on Alcohol* 48:410–24.

Bahr, H., and T. Caplow (1973). *Old Men, Drunk and Sober.* New York: New York University Press.

Ball, J. F., and B. E. Havassy (1984). "A Survey of the Problems and Needs of Homeless Consumers of Acute Psychiatric Services," *Hospital and Community Psychiatry* 35:917–21.

217

Barry, T. (1986). *Guatemala: The Politics of Counterinsurgency.* Albuquerque, NM: Inter-Hemispheric Education Resource Center.

Barry, T., and K. Norsworthy (1990). *Honduras: A Country Guide.* Albuquerque, NM: Inter-Hemispheric Education Resource Center.

Bassuk, E. (1984). "The Homeless Problem." *Scientific American,* 251:40–45.

Bassuk, E. (1993). "Homeless Women-Economic and Social Issues: Introduction." *American Journal of Orthopsychiatry* 63:337–39.

Bassuk, E., and L. Rubin (1987). "Homeless Children: A Neglected Population." *American Journal of Orthopsychiatry* 57:279–86.

Bassuk, E., L. Rubin, and A. Lauriat (1986). "Characteristics of Sheltered Homeless Families." *American Journal of Public Health* 76:1097–1101.

Bassuk, E., and L. Weinreb (1993). "Homeless Pregnant Women: Two Generations at Risk." *American Journal of Orthopsychiatry* 63:348–57.

Baum, A. S., and D. W. Burnes (1993). *A Nation in Denial: The Truth about Homelessness.* Boulder, CO: Westview.

Bidinotto, R. J. (1991). "Myths about the Homeless". *Reader's Digest* 138(June):98–103.

Blau, J. (1992). *The Visible Poor: Homelessness in the United States.* New York: Oxford University Press.

Bogue, D. J. (1963). *Skid Row in American Cities.* Chicago: University of Chicago Community and Family Studies Center.

Bowering, J., K. L. Clancy, and J. Poppendieck (1991). "Characteristics of a Random Sample of Emergency Food Program Users in New York: II. Soup Kitchens." *American Journal of Public Health* 81:914–17.

Boxill, N. A. (1990). *Homeless Children: The Watchers and the Waiters.* New York: Haworth.

Brickner, P. W., L. K. Scharer, B. A. Conanon, A. Elvy, and M. Savarese (eds.) (1985). *Health Care of Homeless People.* New York: Springer.

Brickner, P. W., L. K. Scharer, B. A. Conanan, M. Saverese, and B. C. Scanlan (eds.) (1990). *Under the Safety Net: The Health and Social Welfare of the Homeless in the United States.* New York: Norton.

Bromley, R., and C. Gerry (1979). *Casual Work and Poverty in Third World Cities.* Chichester: Wiley.

Brown S. (1985). *Treating the Alcoholic: A Developmental Model of Recovery.* New York: Wiley.

Browne, A. (1993). "Family Violence and Homelessness: The Relevance of Trauma Histories in the Lives of Homeless Women." *American Journal of Orthopsychiatry* 63:370–83.

Buckner, J. C., E. L. Bassuk, and B. T. Zima (1993). "Mental Health Issues Affecting Homeless Women: Implications for Intervention." *American Journal of Orthopsychiatry* 63:385–99.

Burroughs, J., P. Bouma, E. O'Connor, and D. Smith (1990). "Health Concerns of Homeless Women." Chapter 9 in *Under the Safety Net: The Health and Social Welfare of the Homeless in the United States,* edited by P. W. Brickner, L. K. Scharer, B. A. Conanan, M. Saverese, and B. C. Scanlan. New York: Norton.

Burt, M. R. (1992). *Over the Edge: The Growth of Homelessness in America*. New York: Russell Sage Foundation.

Burt, M. R., and B. E. Cohen (1989a). *America's Homeless: Numbers, Characteristics, and Programs That Serve Them*. Washington, DC: Urban Institute.

Burt, M. R., and B. E. Cohen (1989b). "Differences among Homeless Single Women, Women with Children, and Single Men." *Social Problems* 36:508–24.

Bykofsky, S. (1986). "No Heart for the Homeless." *Newsweek*, 1 December.

Carliner, M. (1987). "Is Homelessness a Housing Problem?" Pp. 119–29 in *The Homeless in Contemporary Society*, edited by R. D. Bingham, R. E. Green, and S. B. White. Beverly Hills, CA: Sage.

Centers for Disease Control (1984). *Morbidity and Mortality Weekly Report* 34:299–305.

Centers for Disease Control (1985). *Morbidity and Mortality Weekly Report* 34:28.

Centers for Disease Control (1987). *Morbidity and Mortality Weekly Report* 36:524–25.

Chavkin, W., A. Kristal, C. Seabron, and P. E. Guigli (1987). "The Reproductive Experience of Women Living in Hotels for the Homeless in New York City." *New York State Journal of Medicine* 87:10–13.

Children's Defense Fund (1992). *The State of America's Children*. Washington, DC: Children's Defense Fund.

Cohen, C. I., J. Teresi, and D. Holmes (1988). "The Mental Health of Old Homeless Men." *Journal of the American Geriatric Society* 36:492–501.

Cohen, C. I., and K. S. Thompson (1992). "Psychiatry and the Homeless." *Biological Psychiatry* 32:383–86.

Collins, J. W., and R. J. David (1990). "The Differential Effect of Traditional Risk Factors on Infant Birthweight among Blacks and Whites in Chicago." *American Journal of Public Health* 80:679–81.

Combs-Orme, T., C. Risley-Curtiss, and R. Taylor (1993). "Predicting Birth Weight: Relative Importance of Sociodemographic, Medical, and Prenatal Care Variables." *Social Service Review* 67:617–30.

Connolly, M. (1990). "Adrift in the City: A Comparative Study of Street Children in Bogota, Columbia, and Guatemala City." Pp. 129–49 in *Homeless Children: The Watchers and the Waiters*, edited by N. A. Boxill. New York: Haworth.

Conrad, K. J., C. I. Hultman, and J. S. Lyons (1993). *Treatment of the Chemically Dependent Homeless: Theory and Implementation in Fourteen American Projects*. Binghamton, NY: Haworth.

Cook, T. D., and D. T. Campbell (1979). *Quasi-Experimentation: Design and Analysis Issues for Field Settings*. Chicago: Rand McNally.

Cousineau, M. R., and T. W. Ward (1992). "An Evaluation of the S-Night Street Enumeration of the Homeless in Los Angeles." *Evaluation Review* 16(4):389–99.

Culhane, D. P., E. F. Dejowski, J. Ibanez, E. Needham, and I. Macchia (1994). "Public Shelter Admission Rates in Philadelphia and New York City: The Implications of Turnover for Sheltered Population Counts." *Housing Policy Debate* 5:107–40.

Cunningham, P. J., and A. C. Monheit (1990). "Insuring the Children: A Decade of Change." *Health Affairs*, Winter:76–90.

D'Ercole, A., and E. Struening (1990). "Victimization among Homeless Women: Implications for Service Delivery." *Journal of Community Psychology* 18:141–52.

Dail, P. W. (1990). "The Psychosocial Context of Homeless Mothers with Young Children: Program and Policy Implications." *Child Welfare* 69:291–308.

Daly, G. (1989). "Programs Dealing with Homelessness in the United States, Canada and Britain." Pp. 133–52 in *Homelessness in the United States: Volume II: Data and Issues*, edited by J. A. Momeni. New York: Greenwood.

Daly, M. (1992). *European Homelessness: The Rising Tide*. Brussels: European Federation of National Organizations Working with the Homeless.

Daly, M. (1993). *Abandoned: Profiles of Europe's Homeless People*. Brussels: Commission of the European Communities.

Damrosch, S., and J. A. Strasser (1988). "The Homeless Elderly in America." *Journal of Gerontological Nursing* 14:26–29.

Danziger, S., and P. Gottschalk (1987). "Earnings Inequality, the Spatial Concentration of Poverty, and the Underclass." *American Economic Review* 77(May):211–15.

Devine, J. A., C. J. Brody, and J.D. Wright (1997). "Evaluating an Alcohol and Drug Treatment Program for the Homeless: An Economic Approach." *Evaluation and Program Planning* 20(2):205–15.

Devine, J. A., and J. D. Wright (1992). "Counting the Homeless: S-Night in New Orleans." *Evaluation Review* 16(4):409–17.

Devine, J. A., and J. D. Wright (1993). *The Greatest of Evils: Urban Poverty and the American Underclass*. Hawthorne, NY: Aldine de Gruyter.

Devine, J. A., J. D. Wright, and L. M. Joyner (1994). "Issues in Implementing Randomized Experiments in Field Settings: The New Orleans Homeless Substance Abuse Program." *New Directions for Program Evaluation* 63(fall):27–40.

Dolbeare, C. (1988). "The Low Income Housing Crisis and its Impact on Homelessness." Pp. 31–42 in *Assisting the Homeless: State and Local Responses in an Era of Limited Resources*, edited by J. Kincaid. Washington, DC: Advisory Commission on Intergovernmental Relations.

Dolbeare, C. (1991). "Federal Homeless Social Policies for the 1990s." Paper presented at the 1991 Fannie Mae Annual Housing Conference, Washington, DC.

Doolin, J. (1986). "Planning for the Special Needs of the Homeless Elderly." *Gerontologist* 26:229–31.

Dott, A. B., and A. T. Fort (1975a). "The Effect of Maternal Demographic Factors on Infant Mortality Rates." *American Journal of Obstetrics and Gynecology* 123:847–53.

Dott, A. B., and A. T. Fort (1975b). "The Effect of Availability and Utilization of Prenatal Care and Hospital Services on Infant Mortality Rates." *American Journal of Obstetrics and Gynecology* 123:854–60.

Duggan, P. (1990). "Yes, We Have Good Bananas." *Forbes* 145:104–13.

Duncan, G. (1984). *Years of Poverty, Years of Plenty*. Ann Arbor, MI: Institute for Social Research.

Edin, K. (1992). "Counting Chicago's Homeless: An Assessment of the Census Bureau's Street and Shelter Night." *Evaluation Review* 16(4):365–74.

Egbuono, L., and B. Starfield (1982). "Child Health and Social Status." *Pediatrics* 69(5):550–57.

Ehrenreich, B., and F. Piven (1984). "The Feminization of Poverty." *Dissent* 31:162–70.

Elliott, M., and L. J. Krivo (1991). "Structural Determinants of Homelessness in the United States." *Social Problems* 38(February):113–31.

Elvy, A. (1985). "Access to Care." Pp. 223–31 in *Health Care of Homeless People*, edited by P. W. Brickner, L. K. Scharer, B. A. Conanon, A. Elvy, and M. Savarese. New York: Springer.

Fallis, G., and A. Murray (1990). *Housing the Homeless and the Poor: New Partnerships among the Private, Public and Third Sectors.* Toronto: University of Toronto Press.

Fantasia, R., and M. Isserman (1996). "Homelessness: A Source Book." *Administration in Social Work* 20:97–98.

Farley, R., and W. Allen (1987). *The Color Line and the Quality of Life in America.* New York: Russell Sage Foundation.

Ferrara, P. J. (1990). "Letter: Federal Housing and Poverty." *Science* 248:538–39.

Filer, R. K. (1990). "What We Really Know about the Homeless." *Wall Street Journal*, 10 April, p. A24.

Fingarette, H. (1988). "Alcoholism: The Mythical Disease." *Public Interest* 91:3–22.

First, R. J., D. Roth, and B. D. Arewa (1988). "Homelessness: Understanding the Dimensions of the Problem for Minorities." *Social Work* 33:120–24.

First, R. J. Toomey, and J. Rice (1990). *Rural Homelessness in Ohio.* Columbus: Ohio State University, College of Social Work.

Fisher, P. W., and W. R. Breakey (1987). "Profile of Baltimore Homeless with Alcohol Problems." *Alcohol Health and Research World* 11(3, Spring):36–38.

Fisk, N. (1984). "Epidemiology of Alcohol Abuse and Alcoholism." *Alcohol Health and Research World* 9(1):4–7.

Freeman, R., and B. Hall (1986). "Permanent Homelessness in America." Unpublished mimeo, National Bureau of Economic Research, Washington, DC (August).

French, L. (1987). "Victimization of the Mentally Ill: An Unintended Consequence of Deinstitutionalization." *Social Work* (November–December):502–5.

Friedrichs, J. (ed.) (1988). *Affordable Housing and the Homeless.* Hawthorne, NY: Aldine de Gruyter.

Fureman, B., G. Parikh, A. Bragg, and A. T. McLellan (1990). *Addiction Severity Index: A Guide to Training and Supervising ASI Interviews Based on the Past Ten Years.* Philadelphia: University of Pennsylvania/Veterans Administration Center for Studies of Addiction.

GAO (U.S. General Accounting Office) (1985). *Homelessness: A Complex Problem and the Federal Response.* Washington, DC: Author.

Gelberg, L., and L. S. Linn (1989). "Assessing the Physical Health of Homeless Adults." *Journal of the American Medical Association* 262:1973–79.

Gelberg, L., L. S. Linn, and B. D. Leake (1988). "Mental Health, Alcohol, and Drug Use, and Criminal History Among Homeless Adults." *American Journal of Psychiatry* 145:191–96.

Geronimus, A. T. (1986). "The Effects of Race, Residence, and Prenatal Care on the Relationship of Maternal Age to Neonatal Mortality." *American Journal of Public Health* 76:1416–21.

Gerstein, D. R., and H. J. Harwood (1990). *Treating Drug Problems.* Washington: National Academy Press.

Goodman, L. A. (1991). "The Prevalence of Abuse among Homeless and Housed Poor Mothers: A Comparison Study." *American Journal of Orthopsychiatry* 61:489–500.

Gortmaker, S. L. (1981). "Medicaid and the Health Care of Children in Poverty and Near Poverty." *Medical Care* 19(6):567–82.

Graham, G. C. (1985). "Poverty, Hunger, Malnutrition, Prematurity, and Infant Mortality in the United States." *Pediatrics* 75:117–25.

Gross, T. P., and M. L. Rosenberg (1987). "Shelters for Battered Women and Their Children: An Under-Recognized Source of Communicable Disease Transmission." *American Journal of Public Health,* 77:1198–1201.

Hagen, J. L. (1987). "Gender and Homelessness." *Social Work* 32:312–16.

Hardoy, J. E. (1986). "Poverty Kills Children." *World Health* July:12–15.

Hartman, C., and B. Zigas (1989). "What's Wrong with the Housing Market." Paper presented to the Institute for Policy Studies, Conference on Homeless Children and Youth: Coping with a National Tragedy, Washington, D.C.

Harvey, B. (1992). "European Homelessness—The Rising Tide." In *European Homelessness: The Rising Tide,* edited by M. Daly. Brussels: Commission of the European Communities.

Healthcare for the Homeless Coalition of Greater St. Louis (1986). *Program Description* (mimeo). St. Louis: Author.

Heatherly, C. L., and B. Pines (eds.) (1989). *Mandate for Leadership III.* Washington, DC: Heritage Foundation.

Hesselbrock, M., T. F. Babor, V. Hesselbrock, R. E. Meyer, and K. Workman (1983). "Never Believe an Alcoholic? On the Validity of Self-Report Measures of Alcohol Dependence and Related Constructs." *International Journal of Addictions* 18:593–609.

Hibbs, J. R., L. Benner, L. Klugman, R. Spencer, I. Macchia, A. K. Mellinger, and D. Fife (1994). "Mortality in a Cohort of Homeless Adults in Philadelphia." *New England Journal of Medicine* 331(August 4):304–9.

Hilfiker, D. (1989). "Are We Comfortable with Homelessness?" *Journal of the American Medical Association* 262:1375–76.

Hoch, C., and R. A. Slayton (1989). *New Homeless and Old: Community and the Skid Row Hotel.* Philadelphia: Temple University Press.

Hogue, C. J. R., and M. A. Hargraves (1993). "Class, Race, and Infant Mortality in the United States." *American Journal of Public Health* 83:9–12.

Homeless Child Syndrome (1988). *Today's Child* 2:entire issue. [A publication of the New York City Children's Health Project.]

Hope, M., and J. Young (1986). "The Politics of Displacement: Sinking into Homelessness." Pp. 106–12 in *Housing the Homeless,* edited by J. Erickson and C. Wilhelm. Rutgers: Center for Urban Policy Research.

Hopper, K. (1992). "Counting the Homeless: S-Night in New York." *Evaluation Review* 16(4):376–88.

Hopper, K., and J. Hamburg (1984). *The Making of America's Homeless: From Skid Row to New Poor (1945–1984)*. Report prepared for the Institute of Social Welfare Research. New York City: Community Service Society.

Horowitz, C. (1989). "Mitch Snyder's Phony Numbers." *Policy Review* 50 (Summer).

HUD (U.S. Department of Housing and Urban Development) (1984). *A Report to the Secretary on the Homeless and Emergency Shelters*. Washington, DC: Office of Policy Development and Research.

Huttman, E. (1989). "Homelessness as a Long-Term Housing Problem." Pp. 81–94 in *Homelessness in the United States: Volume II: Data and Issues*, edited by J. A. Momeni. New York: Greenwood.

Institute of Medicine (1988). *Homelessness, Health, and Human Needs*. Washington, DC: National Academy Press.

Jackson-Wilson, A. G., and S. B. Borgers (1993). "Disaffiliation Revisited: A Comparison of Homeless and Nonhomeless Women's Perceptions of Family of Origin and Social Supports." *Sex Roles* 28:361–77.

Janowsky, E. (1991). *Street Children and Street Education in Guatemala City and Tegucigalpa, Honduras*. Unpublished master's thesis, Tulane School of Public Health, New Orleans, LA.

Jargowsky, P. A. (1994). "Ghetto Poverty among Blacks in the 1990s." *Journal of Policy Analysis and Management* 13(2):288–310.

Jencks, C. (1994). "The Homeless." *New York Review of Books* 41:20–27, 39–46.

Joe, G. W., D. D. Simpson, and R. L. Hubbard (1991). "Treatment Predictors of Tenure in Methadone Maintenance." *Journal of Substance Abuse* 3:73–84.

Joe, G. W., B. K. Singh, J. Garland, W. Lehman, S. B. Sells, and P. Seder (1983). "Retention in Outpatient Drug-Free Treatment Clinics." *Addictive Behaviors* 8:219–34.

Joyner, L., J. D. Wright, and J. A. Devine (1996). "Reliability and Validity of the Addictions Severity Index among Homeless Substance Misusers." *Substance Use & Misuse* 31(6):729–51.

Joyner, L. (1992). *An Assessment of the Reliability of the Addiction Severity Index (ASI) among Homeless Substance Abusers*. Unpublished master's thesis, Department of Sociology, Tulane University, New Orleans, LA.

Kahl, J. A. (1988). *Three Latin American Sociologists: Gino Germani, Pablo Gonzales Casanova, Fernando Henrique Cardoso*. New Brunswick, NJ: Transaction.

Kasarda, J. D. (1993). "Inner-City Concentrated Poverty and Neighborhood Distress: 1970 to 1990." *Housing Policy Debate* 4(3):253–302.

Kasinitz, P. (1986). "Gentrification and Homelessness: The SRO Occupant and the Inner City Revival." *Urban and Social Change Review* 17(Winter):9–14.

Kelly, J. T. (1985). "Trauma: With the Example of San Francisco's Shelter Programs." Pp. 77–91 in *Health Care of Homeless People,*, edited by P. W. Brickner, L. K. Scharer, B. A. Conanon, A. Elvy, and M. Savarese. New York: Springer.

Kennedy, J. T., J. Petrone, R. W. Deisher, J. Emerson, P. Heslop, D. Bastible, and M. Arkovitz (1990). "Health Care for Familyless, Runaway Street Kids." Pp. 82–

117 in *Under the Safety Net*, edited by P. W. Brickner, L. K. Scharer, B. A. Conanan, M. Saverese, and B. C. Scanlan. New York: Norton.

Kerner, J. F., L. Dusenbury, and J. S. Mandelblatt (1993). "Poverty and Cultural Diversity: Challenges for Health Promotion among the Medically Underserved." *Annual Review of Public Health* 14:355–77.

Kinchen, K., and J. D. Wright (1991). "Hypertension Management in the Health Care for the Homeless Clinics: Results from a Survey." *American Journal of Public Health* 81:1163–65.

Koegel,, P., and A. Burnam (1987). "Traditional and Non-Traditional Homeless Alcoholics," *Alcohol Health and Research World* 11(3, Spring):28–34.

Koegel, P., A. Burnam, and R. K. Farr (1990). "Subsistence Adaptation among Homeless Adults in the Inner City of Los Angeles." *Journal of Social Issues* 46(4):83–107.

Kondratas, A. (1991). "Estimates and Public Policy: The Politics of Numbers." Paper presented at the 1991 Fannie Mae Annual Housing Conference, Washington, DC (May).

Kopanoff, D. E., D. E. Snider, and M. Johnson (1988). "Recurrent Tuberculosis: Why Do Patients Develop Disease Again? A United States Public Health Service Cooperative Survey." *American Journal of Public Health* 78:30–33.

Korenbaum, S., and G. Burney (1987). "Program Planning for Alcohol-Free Living Centers." *Alcohol Health and Research World* 11:68–73.

Kozol, J. (1988). *Rachel and Her Children*. New York: Crown.

Krehm, W. (1984). *Democracies and Tyrannies of the Caribbean*. Westport, CT: Lawrence Hill.

Kryder-Coe, J., L. Salamon, and J. Molnar (eds.) (1991). *Homeless Children and Youth: A New American Dilemma*. New Brunswick, NJ: Transaction.

Kutza, E. A., and S. M. Keigher (1991). "The Elderly 'New Homeless': An Emerging Population at Risk." *Social Work* 36:288–93.

Lamb, H. R. (1984). "Deinstitutionalization and the Homeless Mentally Ill." *Hospital and Community Psychiatry* 35(9):899–907.

Lang, M. (1989). *Homelessness Amid Affluence: Structure and Paradox in the American Political Economy*. New York: Praeger.

Laven, G. T., and K. C. Brown (1985). "Nutritional Status of Men Attending A Soup Kitchen: A Pilot Study." *American Journal of Public Health* 75:875–78.

Levey, L. A., M. MacDowell, and S. Levey (1986). "Health Care of Poverty and Non-Poverty Children in Iowa." *American Journal of Public Health* 76:1000–3.

Levitan, S. (1985). *Programs in Aid of the Poor*. Baltimore: Johns Hopkins University Press.

Lewin-ICF (1989). *The Health Needs of the Homeless: A Report on Persons Served by the McKinney Act's Health Care for the Homeless Program*. Washington, DC: National Association of Community Health Centers.

Liebow, E. (1993). *Tell Them Who I Am: The Lives of Homeless Women*. New York: Penguin.

Link, B. G., E. Susser, A. Stueve, J. Phelan, R. Moore, and E. L. Struening (1993). "Reconsidering the Debate about the Numbers of Homeless People in the

United States." Paper read at the annual meetings of the American Public Health Association.

Lusk, M. W. (1989). "Street Children Programs in Latin America." *Journal of Sociology and Social Welfare* 16:55–77.

Massey, D. S., and M. L. Eggers (1990). "The Ecology of Inequality: Minorities and the Concentration of Poverty (1970–1980)." *American Journal of Sociology* 95(5):1153–88.

Massey, D. S., and M. L. Eggers (1993). "The Spatial Concentration of Affluence and Poverty during the 1970s." *Urban Affairs Quarterly* 29(2):299–315.

McAdam, J., P. W. Brickner, R. Glicksman, D. Edwards, B. Fallon, P. Yanowitch (1985). "Tuberculosis in the SRO/Homeless Population." Pp. 155–75 in *Health Care of Homeless People*, edited by P. W. Brickner, L. K. Scharer, B. A. Conanon, A. Elvy, and M. Savarese. New York: Springer.

McArtor, R. E., D. C. Iverson, D. E. Benken, V. J. Gilchrist, L. K. Dennis, and R. A. Broome (1992). "Physician Assessment of Patient Motivation: Influence on Disposition for Follow-up Care." *American Journal of Preventive Medicine* 8:147–49.

McBride, K., and R. Mulcare (1985). "Peripheral Vascular Disease among the Homeless." Pp. 121–29 in *Health Care of Homeless People*, edited by P. W. Brickner, L. K. Scharer, B. A. Conanon, A. Elvy, and M. Savarese. New York: Springer.

McChesney, K. Y. (1990). "Family Homelessness: A Systemic Problem." *Journal of Social Issues* 46:191–206.

McGahan, P., J. Griffith, R. Parente, and A. T. McLellan (1991). *Composite Scores from the ASI*. Washington, DC: NIDA Project DAO2254 and the Veterans Administration.

McGee, T. (1984). "Conservation and Dissolution in the Third World City." Pp. 107–26 in *Urbanism and Urbanization: Views, Aspects, and Dimensions*, edited by N. Iverson. Leiden, The Netherlands: E. J. Brill.

McLellan, A. T. (1983). "Patient Characteristics Associated with Outcome." In *Research on the Treatment of Narcotic Addiction: State of the Art*, edited by Cooper, Altman, Brown, and Czechowicz. Washington, DC: U.S. Government Printing Office.

McLellan, A. T., L. Luborsky, G. E. Woody, and C. P. O'Brien (1980). "An Improved Diagnostic Instrument for Substance Abuse Patients: The Addiction Severity Index." *Journal of Nervous and Mental Disease* 168:26–33.

McLellan, A. T., L. Luborsky, G. E. Woody, C. P. O'Brien, and K. A. Druley (1983). "Predicting Response to Alcohol and Drug Abuse Treatments." *Archives of General Psychiatry* 40:620–25.

McLellan, A. T., L. Luborsky, J. Cacciola, J. Griffith, F. Evans, H. L. Barr, and C. P. O'Brien (1985). "New Data from the Addiction Severity Index: Reliability and Validity in Three Centers." *Journal of Nervous and Mental Disease* 173:412–23.

McMurry, D. (1990). "Review of *Address Unknown*." *Social Forces* 69:331–33.

Milburn, N., and A. D'Ercole. 1991. "Homeless Women: Moving Toward a Comprehensive Model." *American Psychologist* 46:1161–69.

Miller, C. A. (1985). "Infant Mortality in the U.S." *Scientific American* 253(1):31–37.

Miller, D., and E. Lin. 1988. "Children in Sheltered Homeless Families: Reported Health Status and Use of Health Services." *Pediatrics* 81:668–73.

Miller, M., T. Gorski, and D. Miller (1982). *Learning to Live Again: A Guide for Recovery from Alcoholism*. Independence, MO: Independence.

Momeni, J. A. (1990). *Homelessness in the United States, Volume II: Data and Issues*. New York: Greenwood.

Monkkonen, E. H. (1984). *Walking to Work: Tramps in America, 1790–1935*. Lincoln: University of Nebraska Press.

Morbidity and Mortality Weekly Report (1991a). "Deaths Among Homeless Persons: San Francisco (1985–1990)." 40:877–80.

Morbidity and Mortality Weekly Report (1991b). "Characteristics and Risk Behaviors of Homeless Black Men Seeking Services from the Community Homeless Assistance Plan—Dade County, Florida, August 1991." 40:865–68.

Mutchler, J. E., and L. Krivo (1989). "Availability and Affordability: Household Adaptation Squeeze." *Social Forces* 68:241–61.

National Public Health and Hospital Institute (1995). *Urban Social Health: A Chart Book Profiling the Nation's One Hundred Largest Cities*. Washington, DC: Author.

Nelson, K. P. (1990). "Assisting Low Income Families: Policy Implications of Priority Housing Needs." Paper presented at the Annual Meetings of the American Sociological Association, Washington, DC.

Nersesian, W. S., M. Petit, R. Shaper, D. Lemieux, and E. Naor (1985). "Childhood Death and Poverty: A Study of All Childhood Deaths in Maine (1976 to 1980)." *Pediatrics* 75:1 (41–50).

Newacheck, P. W., and N. Halfon (1986). "Access to Ambulatory Care Services for Economically Disadvantaged Children." *Pediatrics* 78:813–19.

Newacheck, P. W., and B. Starfield (1988). "Morbidity and Use of Ambulatory Care Services among Poor and Nonpoor Children." *American Journal of Public Health* 78(8):927–33).

Newburger, E., C. Newburger, and J. Richmond (1976). "Child Health in America: Toward a Rational Public Policy." *Milbank Memorial Fund Quarterly* 54:249.

Norman, C. (1986). "Sex and Needles, Not Insects and Pigs, Spread AIDS in Florida Town." *Science* 234:415–17.

O'Connell, J. J., J. Summerfield, and F. R. Kellogg (1990). "The Homeless Elderly." Pp. 151–68 in *Under the Safety Net*, edited by P. W. Brickner, L. K. Scharer, B. A. Conanan, M. Saverese, and B. C. Scanlan. New York: Norton.

Oberg, C. (1987). "Pediatrics and Poverty." *Pediatrics* 79:567–68.

Piliavin, I., and M. Sosin (1987–1988). "Tracking the Homeless." *Focus* 10(4, Winter):20–24.

Price, J. H., S. M. Desmond, F. F. Snyder, and S. R. Kimmel (1988). "Perceptions of Family Practice Residents Regarding Health Care and Poor Patients." *Journal of Family Practice* 27:615–21.

Rauschenbach, B. S., E. A. Frongillo, F. E. Thompson, E. J. Y. Andersen, and D. A. Spicer (1990). "Dependency on Soup Kitchens in Urban Areas of New York State." *American Journal of Public Health* 80:57–60.

Redburn, F., and T. F. Buss (1986). "Beyond Shelter: The Homeless in the USA." *Cities* 4(1):63–69.

Ricketts, E. R., and R. B. Mincy (1988). "Growth of the Underclass." Changing Domestic Priorities Discussion Paper. Washington: Urban Institute.

Ricketts, E. R., and I. V. Sawhill (1988). "Defining and Measuring the Underclass." Changing Domestic Priorities Discussion Paper. Washington: Urban Institute.

Robertson, M. J. (1987). "Homeless Veterans: An Emerging Problem?" Pp. 64–81 in *The Homeless in Contemporary Society*, edited by R. D. Bingham, R. E. Green, and S. B. White. Beverly Hills, CA: Sage.

Robertson, M. J., and M. R. Cousineau (1986). "Health Status and Access to Health Services among the Urban Homeless." *American Journal of Public Health* 76:561–63.

Robinson, F. G. (1985). *Homeless People in the Nation's Capital*. Washington, DC: University of the District of Columbia, Center for Applied Research and Urban Policy.

Ropers, R. H., and R. Boyer (1987a). "Homelessness as a Health Risk." *Alcohol Health and Research World* 11(3, Spring):38–41.

Ropers, R. H., and R. Boyer (1987b). "Perceived Health Status among the New Urban Homeless." *Social Science and Medicine* 24:669–78.

Rossi, P. H. (1986). *The Condition of the Homeless*. Chicago: NORC.

Rossi, P. H. (1989). *Without Shelter: Homelessness in the 1980s*. New York: Priority.

Rossi, P. H. (1990). *Down and Out in America*. Chicago: University of Chicago Press.

Rossi, P. H. (1994). "Comment on Dennis P. Culhane et al.'s Public Shelter Admission Rates . . . " *Housing Policy Debate* 5:163–76.

Rossi, P. H., G. A. Fisher, and G. Willis (1986). *The Condition of the Homeless of Chicago*. Amherst, MA and Chicago: Social and Demographic Research Institute and NORC.

Rossi, P. H., and H. Freeman (1989). *Evaluation: A Systematic Approach*. Newbury Park, CA: Sage.

Rossi, P. H., and J. D. Wright (1987). "The Determinants of Homelessness," *Health Affairs* 6:19–32.

Rossi, P. H., J. D. Wright, G. Fisher, and G. Willis (1987). "The Urban Homeless: Estimating Composition and Size," *Science* 235(March 13):1336–41.

Roth, D., and J. Bean (1985). *Alcohol Problems and Homelessness: Findings from the Ohio Study*. Ohio Department of Mental Health, Office of Program Evaluation and Research (July).

Rubin, B. A., J. D. Wright, and J. A. Devine (1992). "Unhousing the Urban Poor: The Reagan Legacy." *Journal of Sociology and Social Welfare* 19:111–47.

Schlosstein, E., P. St. Clair, and F. Connell (1991). "Referral Keeping in Homeless Women." *Journal of Community Health* 16:279–85.

Scholl, T. O., R. Karp, J. Theophano, and E. Decker (1987). "Ethnic Differences in Growth and Nutritional Status: A Study of Poor Schoolchildren in Southern New Jersey." *Public Health Reports* 102:278–83.

Schwede, L. and M. T. Salo (1991). "The Shelter Component of S-Night." Pp. 115–

20 in *Proceedings of the 1991 Annual Research Conference, Bureau of the Census, Arlington, Virginia, March.*

Shah, C. P., M. Kahan, and J. Krauser (1987). "The Health of Children of Low-Income Families." *Canadian Medical Association Journal* 137:485–90.

Shane, P. (1987). "Public Health Issues of Homeless/Runaway Youth." Paper read at the Annual Meetings of the American Public Health Association (New Orleans).

Shapiro, I., and R. Greenstein (1988). *Holes in the Safety Net: Poverty Programs and Policies in the States.* Washington, DC: Center on Budget and Policy Priorities.

Shekelle, P. G., and J. Kosecoff (1992). "Evaluating the Treatment of Sexually Transmitted Diseases at an Urban Public Hospital Outpatient Clinic." *American Journal of Public Health* 82:115–17.

Shinn, M. (1992). "Homelessness: What Is a Psychologist to Do?" *American Journal of Community Psychology* 20(1):1–24.

Shinn, M., J. R. Knickman, and B. C. Weitzman (1991). "Social Relationships and Vulnerability to Becoming Homeless among Poor Families." *American Psychologist* 46:1180–87.

Shlay, A., and P. Rossi (1992). "Social Science Research and Contemporary Studies of Homelessness." *Annual Review of Sociology* 18:129–60.

Sidel, R. 1996. *Keeping Women and Children Last: America's War on the Poor.* New York: Penguin.

Singer, J. D. (1982). *Diet and Iron Status, A Study of Relationships, United States,* series 11 (publication # PHS83-1679). Washington, DC: U.S. Department of Health and Human Services, National Center for Health Statistics.

Slesinger, D. P., B. A. Christenson, and E. Cautley (1986). "Health and Mortality of Migrant Farm Children." *Social Science and Medicine* 23:65–74.

Snow, D. A., S. G. Baker, and L. Anderson (1989). "Criminality and Homeless Men: An Empirical Assessment." *Social Problems* 36(5):532–49.

Snow, D. A., S. G. Baker, L. Anderson, and M. Martin (1986). "The Myth of Pervasive Mental Illness among the Homeless." *Social Problems* 33(5, June):407–23.

Sobell, L. C., M. B. Sobell, and T. D. Nirenberg (1988). "Behavioral Assessment and Treatment Planning with Alcohol and Drug Abusers: A Review with an Emphasis on Clinical Application." *Clinical Psychology Review* 8:19–54.

Sogunro, G. O. (1987). "Urban Poor and Primary Health Care: An Analysis of Infant Mortality of an Inner City Community." *Journal of Tropical Pediatrics* 33:173–76.

Sosin, M., and S. Grossman (1991). "The Mental Health System and the Etiology of Homelessness: A Comparison Study." *Journal of Community Psychology* 19(4):337 50.

Sosin, M., I. Piliavin, and H. Westerfelt (1990). "Toward a Longitudinal Analysis of Homelessness." *Journal of Social Issues* 46(4):157–74.

Special Committee on Aging (1978). *Single Room Occupancy: A Need for National Concern.* An information paper prepared for the U.S. Senate Special Committee on Aging. Washington, DC: U.S. Government Printing Office.

Spurlock, C. W., M. W. Hinds, J. W. Skaggs, and C. E. Hernandez (1987). "Infant

Death Rates among the Poor and Nonpoor in Kentucky (1982 to 1983)." *Pediatrics* 80:262–69.

St. Peter, R. F., P. W. Newacheck, and N. Halfon (1992). "Access to Care for Poor Children-Separate and Unequal?" *Journal of the American Medical Association* 267:2760–64.

Stagner, M., and H. Richman (1985). *General Assistance Families*. Chicago: National Opinion Research Center.

Staley, S. (1992). *Drug Policy and the Decline of American Cities*. New Brunswick, NJ: Transaction.

Stark, L. (1987). "A Century of Alcohol and Homelessness: Demographics and Stereotypes." *Alcohol Health and Research World* 11(3, Spring):8–13.

Stark, L. (1992). "Counting the Homeless: An Assessment of S-Night in Phoenix." *Evaluation Review* 16(4):400–8.

Stoner, M. R. (1983). "The Plight of Homeless Women." *Social Service Review* (December):565–81.

Stonich, S. C. (1991). "Rural Families and Income from Migration: Honduran Households in the World Economy." *Journal of Latin American Studies* 23:131–61.

Streeten, P. P. (1989). "Global Institutions for an Interdependent World." *World Development* 17:1349–89.

Study Group on Homelessness (1993). *Homelessness: Social Cooperation in Europe*. Strasbourg, Germany: Council of Europe, Publishing and Documentation Service.

Sullivan, P. A., and S. P. Damrosch (1991). Pp. 82–98 in "Homeless Women and Children." In *The Homeless in Contemporary Society*, edited by R. D. Bingham, R. E. Green, and S. B. White. Beverly Hills: Sage.

Susser, E. S., S. P. Lin, S. A. Conover, and E. L. Struening (1991). "Childhood Antecedents of Homelessness in Psychiatric Patients." *American Journal of Psychiatry* 148:1026–30.

Taeuber, C. M., and P. Siegel (1991). "Counting the Nation's Homeless Population in the 1990 Census." In *Enumerating Homeless Persons: Methods and Data Needs*, edited by C. M. Taeuber. Washington, DC: Bureau of the Census.

Tessler, R., and D. Dennis (1989). *A Synthesis of NIMH-Funded Research Concerning Persons who are Homeless and Mentally Ill*. Washington, DC: National Institute of Mental Health.

Thompson, F. E., D. L. Taren, E. Anderson, G. Casella, J. K. J. Lambert, C. C. Campbell, E. A. Frongillo, and D. Spicer (1988). "Within Month Variability in Use of Soup Kitchens in New York State." *American Journal of Public Health* 78:1298–1301.

Timmer, D. A., D. S. Eitzen, and K. D. Talley (1994). *Paths to Homelessness: Extreme Poverty and the Urban Housing Crisis*. Boulder, CO: Westview.

Torres, R. A., P. Lefkowitz, C. Kales, and P. W. Brickner (1987). "Homelessness among Hospitalized Patients with the Acquired Immunodeficiency Syndrome in New York City." *Journal of the American Medical Association* 258:779–80.

Tucker, W. (1987). "Where Do the Homeless Come From?" *National Review* 39:18.

Tumin, M. (1964). "Competing Status Systems" In *Development and Society: The Dynamics of Economic Change*, edited by D. Novak and R. Leachman. New York: St. Martin's.

United Nations (ECLA) (1989). *Report of the Economic Commission for Latin America*. New York: Author.

U.S. Bureau of the Census (1993). *Poverty in the United States (1992)*. Current Population Reports, Consumer Income, Series P-60-185. Washington: U.S. Government Printing Office.

U.S. Bureau of the Census (1994). *Statistical Abstract of the United States*, 116th ed. Washington DC: U.S. Government Printing Office.

U.S. Bureau of the Census (1997). *Poverty 1996: Poverty Estimates by Selected Characteristics*, pp. 60–198. Washington DC: U.S. Government Printing Office.

U.S. Conference of Mayors (1986). *The Continued Growth of Hunger, Homelessness and Poverty in America's Cities: a 25-City Survey*. Washington, DC: Author.

U.S. Department of Commerce News. 1991. "Census Bureau Releases . . . " Press release announcing S-Night results, April 12.

Vernez, G., M. Burnham, E. McGlynn, S. Trude, and B. Mittman (1988). *Review of California's Program for the Homeless Mentally Disabled*. Santa Monica, CA: Rand Corporation.

Vicic, W. J. (1991). "Homelessness." *Bulletin of the New York Academy of Medicine* 67:49–54.

Wadsworth, M. E. (1988). "Inequalities in Child Health." *Archives of Disease in Childhood* 63:353–55.

Ward, B. (1962). *The Rich Nations and the Poor Nations*. New York: Norton.

Weitzman, B. (1989). "Pregnancy and childbirth: Risk factors for homelessness?" *Family Planning Perspectives* 21:175–78.

Wilton, K. M., and J. Irvine (1983). "Nutritional Intakes of Socioculturally Mentally Retarded Children vs. Children of Low and Average Socioeconomic Status." *American Journal of Mental Deficiency* 88:79–85.

Winick, M. (1985). "Nutritional and Vitamin Deficiency States." Pp. 103–8 in *Health Care of Homeless People*, edited by P. W. Brickner, L. K. Scharer, B. A. Conanon, A. Elvy, and M. Savarese. New York: Springer.

Wolber, G., W. F. Carne, and R. Alexander (1990). "The Validity of Self-Reported Abstinence and Quality Sobriety Following Chemical Dependency Treatment." *International Journal of Addictions* 25:495–513.

Wood, D. L., R. A. Hayward, C. R. Corey, H. E. Freeman, and M. F. Shapiro (1990). "Access to Medical Care for Children and Adolescents in the United States." *Pediatrics* 86:666–73.

Wood, D. L., R. B. Valdez, T. Hayashi, and A. Shen (1990). "Homeless and Housed Families in Los Angeles: A Study Comparing Demographic, Economic and Family Function Characteristics." *American Journal of Public Health* 80:1049–52.

Wood, D. L., R. B. Valdez, T. Hayashi, and A. Shen (1990). "Homeless and Housed Families in Los Angeles: A Study Comparing Demographic, Economic, and Family Function Characteristics." *American Journal of Public Health* 80:1049–52.

Wright, J. D. (1988). "The Mentally Ill Homeless: What Is Myth and What Is Fact?" *Social Problems* 35(2, April):182–191.

Wright, J. D. (1989a). *Address Unknown: The Homeless in America.* Hawthorne, NY: Aldine de Gruyter.

Wright, J. D. (1989b). *Correlates and Consequences of Alcohol Abuse in the National "Health Care for the Homeless" Client Population: Final Results.* Washington, DC: National Institute on Alcohol Abuse and Alcoholism.

Wright, J. D. (1989c). "Homelessness Is Not Healthy for Children and Other Living Things." *Journal of Child and Youth Services* 14:65–88.

Wright, J. D. (1990a). "Poverty, Homelessness, Health, Nutrition, and Children." Pp. 71–103) in *Homeless Children and Youth: A New American Dilemma,* edited by J. Kryder-Coe, L. Salamon, and J. Molnar. New Brunswick, NJ: Transaction.

Wright, J. D. (1990b). "The Health of Homeless People: Evidence from the National Health Care for the Homeless Program." Pp. 15–31 in *Under the Safety Net: The Health and Social Welfare of the Homeless in the United States,* edited by P. W. Brickner, L. K. Scharer, B. A. Conanan, M. Saverese, and B. C. Scanlan. New York: Norton.

Wright, J. D. (1991). "Health and the Homeless Teenager: Evidence from the National Health Care for the Homeless Program." *Journal of Health and Social Policy* 2(Spring):15–35.

Wright, J. D., T. L. Allen, and J. A. Devine (1995). "Tracking Non-Traditional Populations in Longitudinal Studies." *Evaluation and Program Planning* 18(3):267–77.

Wright, J. D., and J. A. Devine (1993). "Family Backgrounds and the Substance-Abusive Homeless: The New Orleans Experience." *Community Psychologist* 26(2):35–37.

Wright, J. D., and J. A. Devine (1994). *Drugs as a Social Problem.* New York: Harper Collins.

Wright, J. D., and J. Lam (1987). "Homelessness and the Low Income Housing Supply." *Social Policy* 17(4, Spring):48–53.

Wright, J. D., P. H. Rossi, J. W. Knight, E. Weber-Burdin, R. Tessler, C. Stewart, M. Geronimo, and J. Lam (1987). "Homelessness and Health: Effects of Life Style on Physical Well Being among Homeless People in New York City." Pp. 41–72 in *Research on Social Problems and Public Policy,* Volume 4, edited by M. Lewis and J. Miller. Greenwood CT: JAI.

Wright, J. D., and E. Weber (1987). *Homelessness and Health.* Washington, DC: McGraw Hill.

Yates, G., R. MacKenzie, J. Pennbridge, and E. Cohen (1988). "A Risk Profile Comparison of Runaway and Non-Runaway Youth." *American Journal of Public Health* 78(37, July):820–21.

Zee, P., M. DeLeon, P. Robertson, and C. H. Chen (1985). "Nutritional Improvement of Poor Urban Preschool Children: A 1983–1977 Comparison." *Journal of the American Medical Association* 253:3269–72.

Index

233

8

Second Wife: Eleven Poems

Helane Levine-Keating

Second Wife

We are walking on the beach
well past the sand bar
to be alone.
Behind us a following wind.
You walk lower, closer to the water
to even our sizes.
Under my tan
first traces of smile lines.

You are broad,
a tall man with thin legs.
Two tall, thin-legged children
lounge on the blanket we have left.
Like you they have tawny hair.
They are in your keeping.

"Second Wife" (originally titled "The Stepmother") and "Stepdaughter 19" (originally titled "Stepdaughter, Nineteen") both originally appeared in *Pudding* issue 6, vol. 2, no. 2 (1982), and appear courtesy of the author. © 1982 Helane Levine-Keating. Other poems © 1988 Helane Levine-Keating.

Perspectives: Stepmothers

You come here every summer
to this same cottage, this same beach.
As frisbees cut the air
your children toss memories
back and forth, some from before my time.
Second daughter in another family,
I recall feeling left out.

The walk back takes longer:
we are now breast to breast with the wind.
The blanket we edge toward is invisible,
all civilization is invisible.
Only the dunes, tenacious as blood ties.

Two Weeks with Your Daughter

i

This is the first morning.
Lean and supple, she and her boyfriend arrive,
striding into this familiar cottage like heroes.
Handing out bagels as truce flags, I peruse
pure-scrubbed features, trying to connect
her wholesome mysteries with your sleepy face.
Hot tea steams in our eyes,
a lone tear travels down her cheek.
A scant ten minutes into this relationship
and she's warning me she's her mother's
daughter. *He's only my biological father,* she says,
leading with her chin in your direction.

But your father loves you, I offer,
trying on my mother's voice like a tawdry costume.
Why should she believe me?
She has been born again.
I cook the eggs, ask about her home in Iowa.
She talks of Jesus, a man I never learned about.

After dinner she hovers around us, testing the water.
A question here, a hook there. She's got a net and
she's drawing it tighter. At midnight
she makes me divulge my age.
Fifteen years between you! she snickers,
my glitzy gold carriage dissolving into a pumpkin.

ii

She and her boyfriend share a bed but vow they're chaste.
True, she wears no makeup, her bathing suit begins
at her neck. Lunch at the clam shack,
two identical smiles stick to the corners
of their mouths as they confess
they've come here to convert you. In the afternoon
he retires to index his Bible.

Every night they say Grace, holding God in their hands
the way hippies once held acid. At eighteen, they've
outgrown sin. Every night you lecture them
how religion is the cause of war.
This is the argument
both of you want to win.

iii

Claws extended, her fury leaps at you,
the weather-beaten Tom. *Stand up to her,
put her in her place!* I long to shout,
recalling my father's strict voice that bruised
my ears, the red glare that shackled my tongue.
For a moment I respect your meekness.
For a moment I remember why I married you.

For days you pretend nothing's wrong,
gulping vodka after vodka even though
she swears she won't talk to you if you've had a drink.
From across the dune, I watch you pull her onto your lap.
Sunset pinks slowing waves.
Both of you weep.

Like you she's addicted:
you're the fire that burned her best bridge back,
you're the fire she'll have to walk through.

iv

It's clear you're torn between us,
the first daughter and the new wife,
want us both to love you best. Finally
the riptide grabs you full force
as you blast me at dinner in front of your daughter.
The mother in my brain wags a finger at me:
Blood is thicker than water.

Scarlet-cheeked, heaving, I leave the table.
Surely you've confused us—the one who loves you
and the one who hates you. Ears crimson,
humbly she stares at her plate.
I don't want to be a child in this family.

Marching the beach in exile, I'm a screaming
wraith washed ashore in a Wellfleet shipwreck,
heart luffing like a loose sail. Inside
everyone smiles, resuming lobster forks and roles
without the stranger who alters the ritual.
The scent of sacrifice lingers in the air, yellow.

v

The day she leaves is humid; rain clouds hover
over the dunes like dirty white hens.
We snap pictures: your daughter, her dog, her boyfriend,
my cat, you and me. I am frowning,
she is hooded. I know she's glad to go
as she lifts me in her arms,
a head taller than I am.
Distant thunder.

That night the storm comes
punishing the ocean and unlacing my roar.
We pace the dunes getting soaked.
I am trying to reach for you in the ice of
my language, a man who has retreated
from the criticism of women.

Silently you stoop in the rain—
wet, guilty, old heart brandishing its scars.
Lear at last, you hobble to her side too late.

vi

Stiff morning, air hung out to dry like bleached
laundry. As we climb the dune trail
your daughter's face floats before us,
starved, mewling, over and over begging for scraps.

The sun's been up for hours, returning
the sand to a warm carpet. Blankets
dot the beach. Here and there small children
dart and squeal, looking back at their parents
to make sure they're watching them.

Perspectives: Stepmothers

The First Wife Comes to Dinner

I should have worn red flowers in my hair as a sign
designating pecking order. Who sits where when
the first wife comes to dinner? Do the children encircle her,
plump, snug life preservers in an uncharted ocean?

Chafing yet complicitous, brow furrowed like a sailor's,
I worry if the food is fit, the secondhand silverware
polished. I'm dancing for her supper
as if she were captain.

Since no one sits down first, I see
I am also cartographer: my husband and stepchildren
trapped in the rhythm of old shanties. A treacherous
current makes me place him facing her.

Conversation stutters like a small-craft warning.
Slowly we chew our clams, praise the salad dressing.
As her eyes lock silently with mine, she battens down
hatches. Still she won't talk to me.

At last it's time for dessert, a soft sandy shore
for a foundering ship. A relief to fetch tea.
My absence returns them to themselves;
at last they're free in the past.

Then, while children drift lazily off
to other dreams, other rooms, an aluminum chandelier
scans our midnight faces like a search beam.
One lone barnacle child, a girl, hangs on.

Seasons pass: winters of sharp waves bearing
driftwood, iridescent fish glowing ominously
in the night's wake, summers of swift
passionate storms, small boat wrecks.

Stepdaughter, 19

(for Martha Keating)

It is two-thirty a.m.
when the phone wakes me abruptly
Someone whispers your name
an accident at a party

Firecrackers
casually crammed
in a friend's coat pocket
have exploded

You may be hurt
and rushed to some downtown hospital
scorched or charred
the caller explains
It is a dark night
She is uncertain of identity

Clenching my breath
I dial the emergency room
They have never even heard of you
can't reveal if you are blinded
your artist fingers burned

Shawl clutched close like a life preserver
I remember last summer
your sister tossed into a ditch
by a madman in a park in Iowa

These are new feelings
hot maternal fears that choke
make me lie awake
listening for the door latch

Full-blown you burst
into my childless life
It is May
I have just turned thirty

Perspectives: Stepmothers

Stepmother's Nightmare

Her stepchildren are quick to hate
her, her aquiline nose that always looks
snooty, her purple knit dress so skimpy
and queer, the fraying quilt she drags

over their father. Their own queen dethroned,
she is the sequel—a derivative novel
filled with family squabbles and unrequited
love lacking the dazzle of the first.

And now that they have acquired her,
this quintessential hag capable of making
Cinderella squat in cobwebs, nothing
can seduce them. They offer her no

trial, but hiss behind her back.
Brows squinched, they squash their hurt.
For them she's beyond inquisition: no mother
resides within her, only a treacherous whore.

Schefflera

This is the tree
his first wife left him
when she packed the car with kids
and headed west. Tall as a lanky woman
it didn't fit.

See how carefully he tends it—
sponging each foot-long leaf with
warm water, lugging it
each May into the garden,
carrying it back like a trophy
into their bedroom every fall.

For seven years it has sat
next to his side of the bed
stealing space, gobbling light
although his second wife
never waters it.

Now it's so heavy
his grown sons have to help him
lift it into the sunlight. Soon
it won't fit up the stairs.
Then every season, every light
it will overhang them,
an old wedding canopy
shadowing their bed.

Perspectives: Stepmothers

The Visit

Once a week his children come to visit.
Four adult stalks, they look down
at their father, each flaunting his traits:
bushy eyebrows, steel blue eyes,
two with skinny calves, three
with amber hair, four pairs of chiseled
cheekbones. Even with all this

they want, they want.
Half-starved, they nibble
at his hairline. Dark voices
blot his out. He grows smaller.
Like an old man twiddling whiskers,
gravity tugs on his jowls.
Fur sprouts in his ear holes.
One by one his teeth fall out.

Soon he's hardly visible,
a dwarf snoring on the
sofa. His children circle him,
gleeful giants dancing
round a dying bonfire.

The Pregnant Stepmother Attends her Stepdaughter's Wedding

For months I've dreaded this—
driving out to enemy territory
my middle cushioned by pillows,
luncheon at his ex-wife's house,
photos of my husband as a young daddy.

Still not fat enough
to be congratulated, I flourish
my newly swollen potbelly for all to see.
With bravado I boast I'm expecting.
The ex won't acknowledge I'm pregnant.

The minister has no title for second wives,
prays that I'll vanish. My stepson
forgets to escort me down the aisle.
Guests whisper, "Who is she?"

My husband and and I sit in the pew
behind his ex. Church light ignites
tiny hairs on her arm, nuzzles the curve
of her nape. I imagine them making love.

After my stepdaughter is married,
she kisses her Mommy and Daddy.
I want her to kiss me too.
My hands fly to my belly.

The bridesmaids are sympathetic,
complimenting me on the color
of my dress. They're just being kind
and will later talk behind my back.

Perspectives: Stepmothers

Déjà Vu

On the lake a man paddles his canoe
softly pressing the paddle into water.
The aluminum canoe with its mottled repairs
gleams in the sunlight. Its reflection precedes it
in a long black shadow.

On shore a child and woman play, sun shaping
their curls into scalloped gold. They are
watching each other, mirroring each other
as the air slowly warms. When they slip into view
his face softens, its gullies disappear.
Love makes his stomach queasy.
Soon they will run out on deck to greet him.

Now the view changes, though the man still canoes
on the same green lake, the boy and his mother
still sport and woo. The shore is this shore
years earlier, the trees are sparser, thinner.
A different woman waits on shore, four other
children dance around her.
The same sun ignites their heads.
They were his family then, these fallen angels.
Is it love or the memory of love
caroming within him?

Years Later

Years go by.
She is getting older,
her stepchildren are getting older.
They have come to love her
in their own way, they have grown
used to her cooking. Her home
is home to them, her child their brother.
She remembers their birthdays,
they bring her flowers.
For a short while peace
descends on the kingdom.

Just when she has almost forgotten
the curse, forgotten the heritage
passed on to her from stepmother to
stepmother, just when she has almost
sunk like a maiden into the unexpected
feather bed of married happiness,
a new hedge of briars springs up
keeping her from the castle.

Her eldest stepson, now a man,
falls in love with her closest friend.
All that she has gained slips away
like rain on a sloping roof until
once more she is at the beginning,
caught in the misty netherworld of
neither parent, sister, friend.
Once again to speak her mind
means she is wicked, to be silent
means she is false. Once again
there's no one to guide her.

Her stepchildren have never asked
her permission; her best friend
sees no reason to. The moment her birthday
arrives, they prick her finger
with their news. Quickly she ages
before their eyes until she's a hag,
a miserable old witch without a home.

Youngest Stepdaughter's Wedding

The day after her wedding
snow buries the hillsides,
outlines yellowing leaves in white
like ice on a mustache. In the valley
a corona of deep brown horses
rings the corral—their movement slow
against steady snow, the red
hat and red mittens of a curious child.

Next door the newlyweds still sleep
their fire burned low in the fireplace,
the crepe paper canopy over the bed
askew, one blue strip crossing the
groom's shoulder as if he were a fallen
soldier. Lying on the floor by the bed,
a boutonnière of blood red roses.

We stand at the window
pressing our cheeks against cold
glass, steaming it silver then
wiping it clean once again
to see outside snow
burying the hillsides, snow
outlining the aspens' leaves, pine
needles like hairs on a mustache,
deep brown horses stamping and steaming,
red mittens on our small red-cheeked son.

While inside, between us, between
our deliberately casual voices practicing
"Do you think she and *her husband* are up yet?"
I imagine we are so deeply wedded
we are imagining the same scene:
the bride and her groom curled
on their bed for warmth, the fire
banked, the blond corona of her hair
dreaming against his black mustache,
red and blue ribbons of crepe paper
strewn across their shoulders, roses
on the floor by the bed, our daughter.

9

One Step Away from Mother: A Stepmother's Story

Alice Neufeld

I never say I'm Katherine's "stepmother"; being a stepmother means that one's motives are always suspect. A direct "Clean up your room" seems to hum to the Cinderella tune of exploitation. And because I'm not really old enough to be Katherine's mother, I have often felt cast in the equally wicked role of stepsister.

Katherine was fourteen when I, at twenty-nine, became her stepmother. In no time at all, she memorized my wardrobe: "Do you have, like, an oversized shirt I could borrow? I think I remember a blue one." She calls out from the interior of my closet: "Alice, is this *new?*"

"Yes. And I have not worn it yet, and don't really want you to borrow it." My jewelry box is another favorite playground of Katherine's, and no one knows its inventory better than she does. I knew Katherine coveted a heart-shaped pendant I often let her wear, and waited until her twenty-first birthday to buy her one just like it. Her mother always bribed her way out of Katherine's life, and I refused to bribe my way into it.

Katherine was four, in 1968, when her parents separated and joined an urban community of psychotherapists and patients who lived in rent-controlled apartments on Manhattan's Upper West Side. A patriarch-leader, with roots in the Old Left, organized his commune into sex-segregated apartments where ideology was delivered as therapy.

Commune ideology was roughest on the children. They were separated from their parents, assigned therapists, and raised in separate living quarters. Katherine remembers slipping up the "adults only" stairway at night to sneak into her father's bed. She remembers missing her mother. Katherine's therapist was a tactless, ungainly woman who kept insisting that her parents didn't love her: "Liar! Liar!" Katherine screamed.

Steven left the commune. Virginia remained. She broke off all relations with her own parents, as the commune urged, and contacted them only for requests for money. She was a lonely only child, with strong female accomplishments in painting, cooking, and elegant taste.

Divorced, with her four-year-old daughter, Virginia was thirty-five and on her own for the first time in her life. She was shaky, and her unrealized ambitions to become a serious painter drew her to the commune, where her ambition met with opportunities as well as emotional support. Some of the most influential and successful artists of the day were also commune members. Therapy confirmed her doubts about her ability for mothering and she became convinced that Katherine was better off without her involvement.

"Then why did you *have* me if you didn't want to *be* a mother," Katherine accused Virginia over the telephone in my kitchen. She was thirteen, and had been living at boarding school for the past six years. Confronting Virginia about her erratic mothering had become routine for Katherine. I tried to help her grasp the incomprehensible events that led up to her present pain. Blame was uppermost on Katherine's mind, and we fished our way through her past, until Katherine came up with her father, the culprit who had wanted the divorce in the first place: "He must have stopped loving her," Katherine lamented. "What made him stop?"

"People don't stop loving each other," I explained, "but things can happen to make people realize that they don't want to, or simply can't go on living with each other."

"What could have happened?" Katherine kept looking for a catastrophe.

"It's not necessarily one thing that happens, but people changing the way they feel about the things that happen or don't happen. A marriage ends when each partner loses faith in the other's ability to steer to safety."

Nine years ago, Virginia sabotaged our plan to have Katherine live with Steven and me. Katherine was fourteen, and it had been more than ten years since she had lived in a family. I expected some passive disapproval from Virginia and the commune, little else. Our plan, after all, demanded almost nothing from Virginia, who knew that Katherine was unhappy to be so far away in New Mexico where the commune always sent their children to school. I thought, with Steven and I taking care of Katherine's day-to-day needs, Virginia might play the part traditionally reserved for divorced fathers. She could visit with her daughter now and then, and reap the benefits of having a teenaged daughter who was eager to admire her mother's accomplishments.

The ten days before Steven flew out to fetch Katherine from New Mexico were fraught with long-distance phones calls and the exhaustion that comes from having to funnel the fullness of feeling into thread-bare telephone wire.

"She cries and says that she's miserable," Steven explained. "She wants to live with us. That's all she keeps saying."

The headmaster told Steven that Katherine was rebellious and refusing authority. Our home represented far more than escape from school, he reassured us. It was a chance to live with a parent, a chance for Katherine to make a long-held fantasy a reality. "It would be very good for her," he said. Legally, Virginia was the custodial parent, and Steven also feared reprisals from the commune, but the headmaster was willing to take the risk of releasing Katherine in our custody.

"What did Virginia say?" we asked Katherine as soon as she hung up the phone that first day home.

"She didn't say much of anything," Katherine said. As the day unfolded, I grew confident that Virginia would do little to interfere with her daughter's new life. We relaxed. I helped Katherine unpack, and we discussed how we'd make small alterations in her bedroom.

The public schools were first-rate, we explained. Virginia was a snob and had gone to private schools, and Katherine was leery about going to public school. In time, Katherine would grow to trust me, I thought. In time, the love that I felt for his young girl, who had a sweet charm that pretty girls learn early, would ripen into intimacy. There was no point in rushing things that must take their course.

At dinner, Katherine spoke to our sheep dog, Caliban, promising to bathe and brush him so that he might sleep with her. She chided us for allowing the dog to develop the bad manners of begging at the table, and planned to train him.

After dinner I brought some logs in from the garage and lit the fireplace to take the chill out of the living room. Outside, through the curtainless bay window, the dark trunks of oak trees stood upon the bluff that reached toward the water of Long Island Sound. I spoke of my love for the house and the view, then I drifted onto talk about our new family. We changed for bed. Suddenly, the dog scrambled to his feet and barked angrily; the brass door knocker resounded throughout the house.

"Who the hell is that?" Steven said loudly, and then, without opening the front door: "Who is it?"

"Katherine! Katherine!" A shrill female voice: "Give me Katherine! I want my baby. My Baby!"

"Oh my god, it's Mom," Katherine said. From the kitchen I saw the beams of flashlights. There were two people at the front door along with Virginia. A third beam of light moved from the driveway toward the porch.

"She's not alone," I said.

"This is a commune scare tactic," Steven said. "Lock the kitchen door and the porch door. Hurry."

Katherine ran to bolt the two other entrances to the house. I held the dog by his choke collar so that he wouldn't lunge when Steven opened the door.

We had to scream to hear each other over the dog's incessant barking. A flashlight beamed into the living room, and I felt invaded. Any second now, Virginia would come in. Calming her hysterics would take hours, and I tried to brace myself for the long night ahead.

"What do you want with Katherine?" Steven called out. He was stalling; I wished he would hurry, let her in and get it over with. That screeching woman is Katherine's mother, I told myself. Steven was married to her for ten years, you don't have to feel so frightened.

"They're going to try and grab her," Steven said. "I know them. What should we do?"

I was afraid to look at Katherine, afraid to look her in the eye; she would see me wanting to lock her mother out. She'll never forgive me; during some terrible future argument she'll drag out this grievance and say: "You wouldn't let me see my mother!"

"I think Katherine should decide," I said.

"It's twelve o'clock, for god's sake," Steven called to the people outside our door. "Quiet that woman down, will you!"

Katherine followed me into the bedroom, where I felt less exposed. Her brow was furrowed: "I'm sorry, Alice," she said.

"Don't worry about me, Katherine. If you want to talk to your mother, it's all right."

"Katherine?" Steven asked.

She hesitated, and then she said: "Well, I think she's being very rude, coming here like this at midnight." I waited for more but there was no more. Of course she was being rude. Was bad manners a good enough reason for turning one's mother away?

"Does that mean that you don't want to see her now?" I asked.

"Yes."

"Come back in the morning, Virginia." Steven opened the door a crack, positioning his weight behind it so that he could shut it quickly again if he needed to. "Katherine is tired, it's been a very long day. She'll see you in the morning." There were more screams that seemed hollow now, as if on cue. "I'll call the police," he said firmly, "if you don't leave now."

The sound of car doors slamming, then headlights flashing as Virginia drove off with her entourage. Katherine was full of apologies.

"Please, it wasn't your fault," I told her. I felt very sad. Something had gone terribly wrong, a woman who was once loved intimately as wife, and still loved as mother, was now an interloper. By keeping Virginia out, I feared we had somehow permitted a greater chill to enter.

Two weeks went by with no word from Virginia. Katherine broke the silence to telephone her mother and announce that she'd begun to menstruate: "So what do you want me to do about it?" Virginia responded. Katherine lay crying on my bed: "A girl wants her mother at a time like this." Even before I became her stepmother, I was showing her how to insert a tampon and giving her Tylenol and a heating pad.

For most of Katherine's life, Virginia had been a mother by long distance. Twice a year she saw Katherine for one day when she bought Katherine clothes and took her to the dentist and doctor for checkups. Katherine blamed the commune for coming between them. She remembered how her mother always made "perfect sandwiches, no lettuce or anything ever spilled out over the edges."

"It's been almost ten years. Virginia must need the commune to have remained with them for so long," I said.

Katherine resisted going to school. We talked endlessly, cajoled, and insisted, unsuccessfully. She complained of cramps. The doctor said that she was constipated. The girl was holding back, waiting for Virginia's approval.

After the third week, Virginia telephoned: "You have two weeks to return to boarding school. If you don't, I will wash my hands of you entirely. I will never speak to you again or have anything to do with you."

"How did she sound? Katherine, were these words part of a larger conversation?" I asked. "Did she give any reasons, make any arguments for taking such an extreme position?"

"No. It was strange, she sounded, like, it was as if she was reading a statement, as if she was reading something that was written down."

"If you ignore the threat, Virginia will give in," we told Katherine, but she was not prepared to take the risk. We did not blame her. She never gave herself a chance, and there was no doubt in my mind that Virginia had exploited whatever fears Katherine may have had about living with us. We would still be here, we reassured Katherine. The door was always open.

The day Katherine flew back to New Mexico, the house was filled with her absence. The late April sun poured into our bedroom and the light seemed mercilessly bright to shine so clearly upon so much emptiness. I closed the blinds, and Steven and I lay down on the bed without touching. We slept like mourners, robbed of a future.

Katherine finished high school in New Mexico. We saw her summers and during winter and spring break. Virginia continued to spend a total of two days a year with Katherine, but Katherine never asked to live with us again. Whenever her daughter demanded more of her time, Virginia bribed her way out of Katherine's life, encouraging Katherine to befriend wealthy schoolmates and visit with them on school holidays. Virginia would pay the plane fare for Katherine to fly to California or Hawaii. Katherine considered herself lucky compared to two other boys at her school who also had commune-member parents: "They *never* get to go home. Not even for *one* day!"

Our house was never really home for Katherine either. She presented herself as a sophisticated traveler who was dropping by for a visit. Her attention seemed focused elsewhere, her talk was of the places she had just come from or was about to see. "Why aren't we rich?" she asked once after enumerating the numbers and styles of luxury cars parked in the driveway of a wealthy friend's house. "Why don't you write a best-seller, Dad?"

"I always think I *am* writing a bestseller," Steven quipped. Virginia sometimes boasted of the personal deprivations she had undergone so that Katherine could have her hair "cellophaned" at Bloomingdale's salon. She provided Katherine with credit cards to all the exclusive department stores. I knew I had something else to give Katherine; if it didn't come wrapped in a box, Katherine wasn't interested.

She remained peculiarly uncurious about our lives and refused invitations to be with us and meet our friends. "I have to do laundry, and pack," she said. It was as if we didn't count. It was Virginia she wanted, if she wanted anybody, and Steven and I spent most of our time futilely trying to heal the wounds of rejection Virginia inflicted on her, again and again. We lived sixty miles away from Katherine's mother, but it might as well have been six thousand for all the times she refused to see her when her daughter was home for an extended stay.

One Christmas, Steven, Katherine, and I made a special trip to the world Trade Center rooftop restaurant where one of Virginia's paintings—a large ball of yellow flame—was installed. The three of us sat at a table for four, awkwardly celebrating Virginia's prosperity in her ghostly absence. Katherine was full of pride in her mother's success, and Steven and I were happy for her. Why Virginia was not in our place where she belonged was a mystery to us. In bed, Steven and I joked our way out of despair. "Did you notice how Virginia's canvas resembled the burning bush in Cecil B.

De Mille's *Ten Commandments?*" Virginia remained a remote god, an illusion at whose altar Katherine had come to worship.

Occasionally, Katherine condescended to go clothes shopping with me; she had never heard of Abraham and Straus, and I felt like I was taking her to Mars, for all her hesitancy and the wary way she eyed the clothes racks. When she found something she liked, it was as though she discovered there was life on other planets after all, and I watched her lose herself, momentarily, in the mirror of the department store dressing room.

Her satisfaction was short-lived, however, and inevitably, in the car on the way home, she suddenly remembered that there was something else she absolutely needed to have. Her visits became a litany of "buy-me's" that Steven often encouraged by refusing to say no. Her bathroom was cluttered with bottles of hair conditioners, moisturizers, and massage gels made with extracts of fruits and vegetables: olive, aloe, coconut, honey, almond, lemon, lime, and ivy. I gathered up the bottles Katherine left behind: "Maybe we could donate these to the female population of a small Balkan republic and deduct it from our taxes," I told Steven.

The cost seemed staggering, but I approved when Steven bought "Pretty Boy" for Katherine's fourteenth birthday. As quarterhorses go, he was modestly priced, and there was no charge for boarding the horse on school grounds. We paid for expensive tack and horse blankets.

Weekdays, Katherine awoke at 5:30; by 6:00 she had mucked out his stall and fed Pretty Boy. As Katherine's "family," we memorized Pretty Boy's genealogy and celebrated his birthdays. Nights when she was home for a visit, she had nightmares about forgetting to feed her hungry horse. When she was gone, we slept soundly, knowing that Pretty Boy was absorbing a measure of healthy teenage passion that might otherwise have been squandered on drugs, sex, or fast cars.

At seventeen, Katherine was still embarrassed to have me fill in for Virginia. She wanted to be "normal," to have a "normal" mother-daughter relationship, and Virginia continued to frustrate those ambitions: "Let Alice take you to the gynecologist, if she's so great," Virginia told Katherine. I was relieved to be the one to discuss birth control with Katherine and to take her to my doctor. Though I didn't fit the "normal" picture either, there were advantages to my big-sister age and attitude. We took care of that business without the *Sturm und Drang*. By boarding-school standards, Katherine was a "late bloomer," and I respected her privacy, sensing that her first sexual experience grew out of the need to see herself as "normal" and womanly.

I was touched by Katherine's craving for the ordinary domestic experiences that girls her age took for granted, and prepared feasts of mundane rituals. She loved having a boy "come to the house to meet her parents." I minimized my youthfulness and appeared very matronly: "Take a sweater, just in case it gets cold later," I advised her. Steven combined just the right balance of *Father Knows Best* humor and paternalism.

We saw Katherine regularly when she came east for college, and added the celebration of all holidays to her repertory: pumpkin seeds were dried and roasted for Halloween, the apple pie was deep-dish Dutch at Thanksgiving, and for late winter nights after New Year's, the Droste's hot chocolate was capped by a cozy Campfire marshmallow.

When Katherine learned that I was pregnant, however, she thought that I'd gone too far: the age difference between siblings was too excessive to be in good taste; by any "normal" measure, Steven was too old to be dandling anyone but his grandchild upon his knee. I was definitely jeopardizing the dignity of our family in the halls of normalcy.

Babies also frightened Katherine. In spite of my encouragement, she refused to hold Natasha, and there was little I could do to mitigate her uneasiness around diapers. The gurgles, the cooing, the toothless gummy smiles and kisses left her cold. She wondered at my involvement and envied Steven's delight as well. "I love music boxes too," she once told Steven when he bought one for the baby; "buy me one too, Dad."

At eighteen, Katherine began to search through the cardboard boxes in the basement where we stored many of her belongings. "The one thing about Virginia, she really knows how to pack things carefully," Katherine said, with seemingly earnest gratitude, as she removed layers of tissue paper and relived her childhood: "I liked to collect things," she said. There were china rabbit and duck reproductions of Beatrice Potter characters, sterling silver cups and spoons, a large carton of doll-house furniture, and framed watercolors of farmyard animals that Virginia had painted for Katherine's bedroom. Sweaters with lace collars were spotless, wrinkle-free. "I had a lot of other really nice toys, antique dolls with porcelain faces, but I broke a lot of things, and spoiled them."

"You were probably too young for those delicate toys," I said.

"Then I became a real pris, you know, prissy."

Katherine never tired of the ritual admiring of the things that represented her childhood. She reiterated Virginia's love for artifacts. I imagined Katherine had learned to bathe in that love for things and to steal some of it for herself. The prissy girl makes herself into a doll; Katherine liked Natasha best when I dressed her up like one.

"Make her put her clothes on," Katherine said, when Natasha was three and fond of running naked through the house.

Natasha learned to knock at Katherine's door: "Can I come in?"

"No."

I tried to distract and console Natasha, and restrained myself from charging into Katherine's room and beating her to a pulp. But Natasha was resourceful, and slid pictures under her door or taped them onto the outside, refusing to take no for an answer. At the dinner table, Natasha pursued Katherine with food offerings.

"I'm on a diet," Katherine said.

"Well, when are you going to stop being on a diet?"

"When I'm skinny."

And then, daily for days afterward: "Are you skinny yet, Katherine?"

"Do you think I could take Natasha with me sometime to meet Virginia?" Katherine asked me one day; I hesitated.

"Natasha is my sister, after all," Katherine said in explanation, "and I talk about her so much, you know, I'd like Virginia to meet her, so she knows who I'm talking about."

"Of course." I felt rather ungracious and guilty.

"Me and Katherine, we have the same daddy," Natasha announced, "but we don't have the same mommy." Steven and I were waiting downstairs while Katherine took Natasha to meet Virginia. We stopped at Virginia's so that Katherine could load our car up with Virginia's paintings. At fifty, Virginia was giving up her studio, twenty years of work, and becoming a computer programmer.

During that visit, Natasha played with Virginia's pet poodle while Katherine gathered up the paintings she wanted.

"How did it go?" we asked afterward.

"Fine," the sisters agreed, like coconspirators, from the back seat of the car. Later, Katherine said that her mother had found Natasha to be smarter than she had expected. What had she expected? I wondered.

I surveyed the basement in search of a safe dry area to store Virginia's paintings. In the fall, Katherine would take some of them back to college for her junior year. In summer, the cesspool sometimes overflowed from Katherine's interminable showers, and I stacked the canvases high off the cement floor; we can't have Virginia's *oeuvres* floating in shit, now can we, I muttered.

There were a number of paintings of room interiors viewed from bizarre angles: a corner where the ceiling met the wall or a floor. Flooded with light, they illuminated the lonely way rooms withhold shelter. Katherine's favorite was a painting of the three antique velvet dresses she'd worn as a child. A shadowy darkness in the holes for the necks spoke to me of Virginia's vision of the girl she once dressed in them.

In high school, Katherine rarely read books for her own pleasure, but she became a serious college student, proud that her professors had read Steven's books, and proud of herself for excelling.

Natasha continued to idolize her big sister, and Katherine became openly affectionate: "I really can have fun with Natasha now." Katherine also felt protective of Natasha, and closed the door on our marital quarrels to comfort the child and receive comfort from her.

Katherine graduated with honors. I don't know what excuse Virginia gave for not attending the ceremony. I took photographs of Katherine and her friends in their caps and gowns. We met her teachers, who offered to write letters of recommendation for her and asked her about her future plans: "I'm going to work for a year, and then I was thinking of applying to law school," she said.

Driving home down the thruway, we asked Katherine when she planned to follow up on the interview at *High Style;* "call me when you're ready to work," the personnel director had said, impressed with Katherine's "enthusiasm and good taste."

"I need a vacation," Katherine said. "I just graduated and you're putting a lot of pressure on me." Changing the subject to a new diet she was eager to start, Katherine read aloud about the danger of mixing proteins and carbohydrates.

A month went by while Katherine ate little, slept late, and complained about being awakened by the noise Natasha made in the kitchen while we fixed the child's breakfast. We pressured her to look for a job. Money was tight. I bought a large supply of Woolite to help her reduce her dry-cleaning bill, and Steven told her to call her friends after business hours. "I want to be rich," she said.

"I want you to be rich too," I said; "meanwhile, economize."

"Katherine wants *you*," Steven said on the telephone from the hospital. "Will you come?"

That morning, Katherine had stumbled into our bedroom with a bruise on her head. She'd been up all night with insomnia and at 6:00 A.M. had decided to go for a bicycle ride to tire herself out. It was steaming out, and she was wearing a sweatsuit and had no food in her stomach; she didn't remember feeling faint, but she had blacked out.

I asked Steven to take her to the emergency room while I got Natasha ready for school. I knew that Katherine wanted me with her, but I sent Steven in my place. I needed to go to the library and seize an hour to do my own work. The summer was precious work time for me, and after a year of full-time teaching, I was determined to stick to a routine.

From the library, I went to the hospital and arranged Katherine's tray with the chicken salad, the vanilla ice cream, and the *Vogue* I'd bought. "I'm starving," she said. An intern came in and asked me to leave while he inserted an IV into Katherine's arm: "It's glucose, nothing serious," he said.

"She can stay while you do it," Katherine said.

"I'll be right back. I want to talk to the neurologist, and get some more ice packs, anyway," I said. The neurologist raised an eyebrow incredulously when I introduced myself as Katherine's mother, but he answered all my questions and admitted that the low potassium level in her blood, the heat, exhaustion, and crazy diet could've explained Katherine's blackout. Still, he wanted to do a CAT scan.

"Her EEG shows an asymmetry—could be normal—but in some cases it's a sign of an obstruction. . . ."

When I returned, Katherine was saying to the intern: "My veins are really hard to find . . . I know, I just know it's going to hurt." The intern was turning Katherine's forearm this way and that.

"The last time I needed an IV was when I had my tonsils out, and they stabbed me ten times, I'm not exaggerating, before they got it in. My arm was sore for weeks afterward. Really."

"Oh." The intern blushed, a mustache line of perspiration wetting his upper lip. Katherine's chatter wasn't helping.

"Wait a second," I said. "Let's have some positive thinking, that's the first thing. This is *not* going to be one of those ten-stab tries."

"That's right." The intern smiled up at me gratefully.

"Can you see what you're doing?" I asked. His body blocked out the available light as he leaned over Katherine to search for a vein. "Let's put a little light on the subject." I walked over to the bedside and turned on the overhead fluorescent light so that the area around her arm was lit up, and I could see for myself the blank map of her arm as I held out my own for comparison.

"Too bad you can't give me the IV," I said, holding my arm next to Katherine's for the intern to use as a guide. "Don't look," I told her; "look away." The intern was about to make his first try. She turned her head and he did it on the first try.

I moved over to be near his tray and handed him strips of adhesive tape to keep the needle in place. "Do you need any assistance, doctor?" a nurse said when she saw me working.

I arranged Katherine's bathrobe around her shoulders and helped her into the wheelchair, rolling the IV stand next to her while the intern steered toward the elevator and left us downstairs to wait for the CAT scan technicians.

"Some of these interns are good-looking," I told Katherine. "Take advantage of your stay and meet a rich doctor," I teased.

Katherine seemed cheerful as she lay down on the narrow strip and slid her body back so that her head lay between an opening in the great cylinder that scanned the brain. I petted her leg. "See you in a bit." The technicians said I'd have to leave. Outside, in the drafty hallway, I smoked cigarettes and stared out the window into the solid cement courtyard and an overcast sky, a fitting backdrop of bleakness.

Katherine had telephoned her mother but Virginia did not return her call. "I'm so mad," Katherine said. "She had someone else call me—a complete stranger, a commune member called to ask me how I was feeling. The person said that Virginia was too busy to call, but that she was really worried about me. That's such bull. 'If Virginia's so worried about me, she can call me herself,' I told the stranger."

The CAT scan control-booth door was open, and I overheard the technicians talking and listened for some allusion to Katherine's condition. I tried to reassure myself: there was nothing wrong with Katherine that three healthy meals a day and a good night's sleep would not cure. The diet that had weakened her was Virginia's idea. Virginia did not come to Katherine's graduation. Virginia did not return Katherine's phone call. No matter what I did, Virginia was there, pulling the rug out from under our lives; it was my job to pick up the pieces and dust people off. But this time, something might be seriously wrong. . . .

The next day we found out the CAT scan was negative. I got Katherine back on her feet. The doctor said she could expect to have headaches for some weeks. It was hard to make Natasha be quiet around Katherine. Then, the child got chicken pox and, because Katherine had never had them, the house became divided into two quarantined halves. I ministered cooling compresses to Natasha's itchy body and then inspected Katherine, who suspected every vague redness on her body to be incipient pox. Meanwhile, Katherine hoked up excuses for not following through on her job interview: "I need a resume." We spent days helping her write one. On high-quality paper, she had one hundred copies printed. "Looks very professional," she said.

"Yes," we agreed, though she never got around to mailing any out.

It was July. Steven and Natasha and I were to go off to Vermont where Steven was teaching at a summer workshop. Katherine was going to stay behind, commute on the train to Manhattan, and job hunt.

"Virginia says I can stay over in a spare room in the commune apartment while I look for work," Katherine announced.

"Perhaps you'll get to see more of Virginia, and to do things together," I said, but Katherine denied the plan had anything to do with her yearning for a mother: "It's just for convenience," she declared.

We were away for two weeks, when Katherine telephoned us in Vermont: "She was very upset," Steven explained. "She was crying. She's taking the bus and will be here tomorrow."

"I wish *you* were my mother," Katherine wept.

"No you don't," I said, realizing that I wasn't speaking my mind clearly. "I just mean that our relationship would be different if I were your mother." I thought of my mother and myself, and how the intimacy between us could be stifling at times. With Katherine, I was always bridging the distance between us. I had to choose my words carefully to make certain she understood me.

"How would it be different?" she asked.

"Oh, I'd probably be more demanding and more critical of you if you were my daughter, you know, more like the way my mother is with me."

"You would?"

I nodded. Katherine had no awareness of my restraint. Didn't she feel how we handled each other delicately, as if we could not sustain the nasty verbal blows intimates hurl at each other when they're in pain? But it was not our relationship that now made Katherine weep and run away. Virginia was "acting weird." I wanted to know more. Katherine told Steven some details about Virginia's drinking and constant use of tranquilizers.

"Tell me," I said, "do you think that Virginia was always so 'strange,' as you say, and that you just saw her now clearly for the first time?"

"I don't know. Maybe. I'd say something about myself, and it wouldn't register, she'd just start talking about herself, and go on and on. It was like I wasn't there. And when I withdrew, she didn't even notice. It was awful. I was embarrassed to be seen with her in public. She thinks a shopkeeper she met once is a friend."

On a number of occasions we had suggested Katherine might benefit from talking to a therapist and now I suggested it again. In college, she had been in therapy for a couple of months. "Do you think you'd like to talk to your therapist now?"

"No. I just cried all the time, so I stopped going. He'd just say . . . he was so sympathetic and understanding that he just made me cry all the time. I felt so bad. I like talking to you," she said.

"Have you met Steven's daughter? This is Katherine." In Vermont and later back home, Katherine now got a job, made friends with our friends, hung out with Steven's students, and threw herself into our lives as she had never done before.

"I wish that when you introduced me to people you'd say I'm your daughter too, and not just Steven's," she said.

Katherine wanted a second chance. She wanted me to be the mother I had offered to be when she was fourteen and had come to live with us. Only now she was eager to let go of Virginia and cling to me.

Steven went away as visiting professor to California for six months and Katherine stayed behind with me and Natasha. In my absence, Katherine was "the adult" with Natasha, but when we were all together, she became a child again. After my long and tiring working day, I'd pick Katherine up at her workplace: "I want to sit up front," Katherine complained. Natasha protested against the back seat.

"What difference does it make?" I tried to get Katherine to humor Natasha.

"I'm embarrassed to have people see me getting into the back seat," she said. Who notices? Who cares? I wondered. Sitting in the back seat of the car made Katherine feel like a child; up front, next to me, she was masquerading as an adult.

Katherine began to sink under pressure. Virginia was fifty and nowhere. She left the commune. Eighteen years after her separation and divorce from Steven, she telephoned and told me: "I'm so tired of being angry. I don't even hate Steven anymore." In her little-girl's voice she once asked Katherine for money and Katherine wept, complaining to me: "She wants *me* to take care of *her!*"

Before it was too late, Katherine hastened to get away from Virginia and applied to a highly competitive graduate school program on the West Coast. Thinking that her life would begin in graduate school, she refused the advances of young men and women at the electronics firm where she worked as a receptionist.

"You've got to live in the present too," I urged.

"The men at work just think I'm an airhead, a Valley girl." Other girls did not share her ambitions and dissatisfactions.

On weekends, Katherine wanted to be my sidekick, to go to the movies together and to eat out in restaurants. I couldn't do anything on my own without feeling I was abandoning her. She planned to spend the four-day Thanksgiving weekend with friends from college, and I circled the date on my calendar, like a prisoner awaiting parole.

She was rejected from graduate school and began to oversleep mornings and miss work. I worried about leaving her home alone all day with no distractions from her cares. She was home for three weeks: "I don't care if they fire me." She sulked, feeling robbed of a promising future. "It isn't fair!"

"No, but the sooner you stop lamenting over the unfairness of life, the better off you'll be."

"But I'm so ignorant! All I wanted to do was learn, and they're not *letting* me!"

"Not letting you learn? No school has such power. There are many ways to learn. If you're 'so ignorant,' as you put it, then you're in an ideal situation, in a way, because almost *anything* you do will teach you something new."

I could tell this conversation was about as comforting to Katherine as a bed of nails. Evenings, she withdrew into her bedroom. She ate dinner alone, and I worried she wasn't eating properly.

"Have you spoken to Virginia lately?" I asked one night.

"Yes. Some woman is letting her share a tiny apartment, and Virginia had to give away her dog. It's so sad."

Two days before Thanksgiving, Katherine felt sick.

"Perhaps you'd better come with me to my mother's," I said.

"No. I want to see my friends over the weekend and if I come with you, I'll miss them."

On Saturday she telephoned my mother's apartment: "When are you coming home?" she cried. Her friends wouldn't drive out to see her. She was feeling too ill to travel. On Sunday I had plans to go to the museum. I telephoned a good woman friend and she said she'd take Katherine over to her house.

"I'll be back Sunday evening," I told Katherine. She didn't hide her disappointment and I didn't explain myself.

Steven came home before Christmas. By New Year's Katherine was re-solving to become more social. She took a TV production course, made new friends, and felt confident enough by May to take the funds Steven had set aside for her further education and move out to California to live with her old friend Carol.

Perspectives: Stepmothers

The phone rings at 12:30 A.M.

"*I got a job!*" *Katherine sings over the wire.* "*It's not a career, but it's fun, that's okay isn't it? I don't want to be doing it when I'm twenty-five, but it's okay for twenty-two, isn't it?*"

"*Yes, it sounds just fine for twenty-two.*"

"*I can't wait for you guys to come and see our beach house. It's small, but terrific, so . . . California!*

On my birthday Katherine wrote to me: "Thanks for putting up with me when I couldn't put up with myself. I love you very much."

I love you too, Katherine. *Bon voyage!*

10

The Envious Heart

Helane Levine-Keating

> Then her envious heart had rest
> so far as an envious heart can have rest.
> —*The Brothers Grimm, "Little Snow White"*

Apples are the fruit of autumn
the season I detest. That was when
he married me, never letting on.
He said she was simply a girl,
a thin thing with straight hair.
He said he rarely saw her
although she was his daughter.

You are my only queen, he said.
Look in this mirror—
it is yours.

I look, but all I see is
her sneering face, her wide lips
mimicking mine. Instead of a little girl
there's a woman not much younger than myself.
When they're together she's his queen,
that black-eyed slut, calling him Daddy
with her bone-dry lust, looking
over her shoulder at him
till he turns from me, transfixed.

Perspectives: Stepmothers

She'll stop at nothing,
making him tell her stories
about her mother, the same ones
over and over. How can I
cover my ears?

Now everywhere I go
voices whisper
proclaiming her loveliest.
Who remembers my beauty?
Each night beneath his body
her shadow erases me.
In my mirror I am invisible.

Mothers

11

Only My Favorite Mommy

Sheila Alson

I have not gotten beyond the adjustment period yet. It is entirely possible that the adjustment period never ends, and I am here thinking about the beginning of the constant reshuffling that will occupy the rest of our lives. This is the story of one particular mother's experience with her children's acquisition of a stepparent. The mother is me. These are the particulars of my life.

Steven and I were much better at divorce than we were at marriage. At twenty-five, when I married him, I knew I was marrying my future children's father. Through the personal earthquake of divorce we controlled our deepest urges to punch and counterpunch so that we could maintain amicability and continue co-parenting our two children. We have joint custody, which means that Alex (five) and Amy (ten) live with each of us half the time. They have two homes.

During the postseparation period, when no new love had yet come to fill in the spot that divorce had vacated, Steven and I spent much time on the phone and in each other's houses. We were friends, but with the definite lack of ease that our joint history had given us. Our children remained the best effort between us.

Then Steven decided he wanted love in his life—not an unreasonable request—and Joanne appeared, with her fourteen-year-old daughter, Susan. A few months later they rented a house together around the corner from me. The following are entries from a journal kept during the time of transition.

Alex called yesterday and left a message on my machine. "I love you and miss you." Relief that he misses me when he's at Steven's house. He wakes up in the morning on the days when he's with me and asks if he can go to Daddy's today. I wonder why he's not satisfied here. I am even-tempered with the kids most of the time. Maybe I'm not paying enough attention to Alex when he's here. All my domestic instincts come out when the kids are around. I seem able to clean house only when they are at home with me.

There's something going on at Steven's house that draws Alex. It's Joanne and Susan—the new family.

Alex comes into bed with me in the middle of the night. It's a big, empty bed and I welcome his warm little body snuggling up to me. He crawls into bed with Steve at his house, but now it's not "Daddy's bed." It's "Daddy and Joanne's bed." He snuggles between them the way Amy used to snuggle between Steve and me until her newborn brother took her place. But Alex has no baby to take his place in bed and it's up to us to wean him away from that. It's time. It's more than time. He's almost five years old. Maybe now that Steve will have a permanent bed partner he'll agree that it's time. We have to show a united front on this.

AMY *(message on tape):* Hey, Mom. You already know my name and you'll see me tomorrow. Just called because I just need to talk to you about something you already found out about. Clue—having to do with me moving with another person besides my family. Goodbye.
ME *(calling back):* Do you want to talk about your message now?
AMY: Not while Alex is still awake. Daddy didn't tell him yet. He says Alex will be so excited, and it will take a while before he and Joanne find an apartment.

Alex woke up next to me this morning and said, "I had a dream I was riding a magical horse and it was not scary and it took me home to Daddy's house." He wrapped his warm body around my arm and hugged it. "I love you, Mommy."

I had the flu yesterday. I'm recovering today in bed. Alex watched TV all afternoon but after a few hours he demanded my attention and presence downstairs so I dragged myself into the living room and read a few books to him.

I asked Steve for help but he is not interested in helping me any more. When the kids are with me, it's for me to deal with. I asked Amy to go to the store and pick up a few items and something for each of us for dinner.

She's being very helpful. She even put Alex to bed. But she's still only ten years old and can't hold herself back from fighting over her possessions with her brother.

She's afraid to fully open up to me about her feelings about her daddy and Joanne. She knows how sensitive I am about it. She says she doesn't want to live with someone she doesn't love and she doesn't love Joanne.

ME: Is it Joanne herself, or is it just living with anyone? Do you like Joanne?

AMY: She's nice. It's not Joanne. The only thing wrong with her is she's around too much. It's never just the family any more. She's always there. You know those tickets to Alvin Ailey? Well, last week Daddy said Susan decided not to go. I didn't even know that they were going in the first place. And they're going along to the celebration dinner Daddy promised me for my performance.

ME: Do you get along with Susan?

AMY: Well, yes. She's okay.

ME: She'll be like your older sister now. You get to have an older sister.

AMY: Well, yes, but I never thought she would be a teenager. I mean, she'll be going out with boys and everything. Alex will be thrilled. He's really into Susan. He really likes Joanne, too. Daddy says Alex needs a mommy in every house.

ME: Are you jealous that Alex likes Susan?

AMY: Yes. I am. I'm afraid he won't think I'm so special anymore.

ME: You'll always be his Amy. You'll never be replaced.

AMY: Neither will you, Mommy.

Can't find the way to deal with Amy any more. Maybe she just needs to fight and I'm the only one she can fight with. But it drains me. The adjustment is so hard for her. She likes Joanne. She wants me to like Joanne. I do think Joanne is probably a very nice woman, but it's still hard for me to adjust.

I think my daughter's adjustment is linked to my adjustment, but she has her own problems as well. She says she doesn't feel at home with Steve and Joanne because Joanne does not feel like part of her family yet. So she can't get hysterical there and throw tantrums when she's frustrated because she's embarrassed in front of Joanne and Susan. So she saves it all for me and she blows up at the least little thing. She's constantly on Alex's case as Alex is also on hers.

I notice my father's books consist of western novels, *Prevention* maga-zine issues, and Masters and Johnson's *The Pleasure Bond*. My father and his new wife are at the Ramada Inn while Joe and I are using his apartment for the first day of our weekend in Florida together. Joe is out running.

If there's anything to work out here, it's the past in the present—replacement and loss. For most of us, when we marry we place our trust in the illusion that we can build our family around us and take refuge in it. For me, the illusion has gone. I stepped out of the refuge. With all the analysis and conviction I have concerning the demise of our relationship, I am still bewildered. I have left behind an essential and dear part of my-self, a self who still needs the illusion. The way one's phone number be-comes one's name, when I gave away the family phone number to my ex-husband, I gave away my name. Tuesday, when I dialed that name of ten years, it was his new partner's voice on the machine. It said, "This is the home of Joanne and Steve . . . ." Someone else had stepped into the il-lusion, taking the place I had left.

I left the message I meant for him. "I am doing book orders for Alex's daycare, so if you see any money or order forms in his pouch when you pick him up this week, leave it there. It is for me."

I left for vacation.

I thought I would just push these feelings away, but the necessity of writing this article puts the title "Stepparenting" on the top of the page and pushes the issue to the forefront. Joanne is the stepmother of my chil-dren and the new partner of my ex-husband. This is a new situation and we have not yet settled into any modes. We are just reacting. I know none of her reactions. I know only my own and the reactions of my children, at least those they share with me.

I am away on vacation and I call up my children. Amy answers and she is excited to hear from me, but Alex, Steve, and Joanne are out. She insists on calling back when they get home so Alex can have the opportunity to talk to me, too. When she calls back an hour later, Alex won't come to the phone. Amy is mortified and says her brother is rude and he must come. I tell her, "No. No. It's okay," but she persists.

Finally, Alex gets on the phone and whines, "Hello." I am stiff in my voice and ask him how he's doing. He answers, "I didn't want to talk to you because I want to watch the movie with Joanne and Daddy."

I say, "It's okay, Alex. I love you."

He says, "Who else would you like to talk to?"

"Put Amy back on." Amy by now hates him for acting that way to me, but I try to assure her I understand, and do understand that this five-year-old does not feel the significance of the 1,500-mile distance or the subtleties of adult insecurities, but sometimes rationality has nothing to do with the way we react. After I hang up the phone I cry.

Last night Amy said she was feeling better about Joanne, but she still feels jealous.

ME: Jealous of what?

AMY: Of Daddy and Joanne. They're always kissing.

As Steve dropped Alex off he gave me the latest report on Alex's nighttime habits. He spent every night in his own bed, but he put up a big fight and cried every night. He only went to sleep, finally, when Steve yelled at him.

So, at 12:00 P.M. Alex woke up as usual and started to come into my bed. I was already asleep but woke. I gently picked him up, put him down into his bed and lay down with him.

He would not settle down. He cried the whole time. "Mommy, I need you. I can't go to sleep without you. I want the wall to fall down between our room so I won't have to sleep alone."

I finally left him in his room crying. He came into my room hesitantly a few times and ran back into his own room. Back and forth. It was almost 1:00, and I was tired, and he was crying. He came into my bed, and I said he had to leave. He was crying so bitterly I wanted to hug him, and he said, "It's like you don't love me." I said I love him. I hugged him and gave in.

ALEX: Don't do that to my favorite mommy.

AMY: She's your only mommy.

ALEX: She's my favorite mommy.

AMY: She's your only mommy.

ALEX: She's my only favorite mommy.

AMY: She's your only mommy.

ALEX: She's only my favorite mommy.

AMY: Only your favorite mommy? Only? She's the only mommy you have.

AMY *(to me)*: You're mine, no one else's.

ME: What's this *mine?* I'm yours. Can't you share? You can't share people? You're mine, but I share you with Alex. And I share you with Daddy.

AMY: I'll share you with Alex but with no one else. You can share me with Alex and Daddy but with no one else.

ME: But I share you with the world. I share you with your friends who you love and your friends who you don't love and with your grandparents and aunts and uncles and your teachers and the friends of your friends.

AMY: My teachers don't have me.

ME: I share you with the world.

ALEX: And with Joanne and Susan.

Amy writes a story for school, a play in which the mother character is saintlike in her capacity to understand; there's a scene at her father's house: the father and his girlfriend smooching at the table and the ten-year-old girl character going up to her room to cry.

After writing the story, Amy is afraid that if her daddy sees this play his feelings will be hurt because the daddy in the play walks away helpless in the face of his daughter's crying.

I could tell Steve was annoyed when I reported to him Wednesday morning that I was weak and let Alex stay in bed with me. But I said I intended to keep him in his own bed. At least at his house, Steve said, he would get the message clearly.

Amy says she is like a baby. She needs attention all the time like a baby, to be watched and checked in on all the time to see if she's all right. She says she needs to receive constant attention, just like Alex and Susan.

I think the story of the birthday dinner epitomizes my own conflict. It's interesting to me that the whole birthday interaction never made it to the journal. It is only in retrospect that I can record the story.

My kids were born on the same date five years apart. This coincidence of planet alignment fills me with respect for the day, February 24, a day that I consider not only their birthday, but my day of birthing.

Immediately I ruled out the possibility that Joanne could attend their birthday parties. The move was only a few weeks old at the time, and my emotions were on edge. I didn't want to put myself through the strain of having to push down tears while trying to run two consecutive children's parties. So, by fiat, I said I didn't want Joanne to come, and I wanted the parties to be either at my house or in a neutral place. (To date I have not gotten past the front door of their house.) Steven said he understood, and that Joanne would understand, too. But the kids did not understand.

Alex said he wanted Joanne at his party, but accepted my decision with the same consternation he uses when I tell him he can't have another cookie. Amy, who has found the joint gift of words and volume with which to torture her parents, screamed and yelled that it was *her* birthday and she wanted to celebrate it with all the people she lived with. As is our style of combat, I countered her high pitch with calm explanation. I can remain rational if she does not hold out too long. Luckily, this time, there was no need for my own hysteria. I told her, and I still hope it will be true someday, that I will soon get used to Joanne's presence in their lives, but now it makes me feel sad because it reminds me of the good things I gave up when her daddy and I decided to get a divorce. Soon, I said, I hope we will all be friends, but it hasn't happened yet, and I don't want to feel sad on my children's birthday. Amy responded to that explanation, and the issue was dropped for the moment.

Round two began when Amy realized that though the parties were Sunday, their real birthday was Tuesday, a day that the children are normally with Steve. On Tuesday she wanted to have our traditional family dinner for their birthday with everyone. We should all go out to dinner together, all around the big round table in the Japanese restaurant. "I thought we dealt with this already," I said. "I'm angry that you're bringing it up again."

"This is different. It's the day of my birthday and you won't let Joanne come to the party. I want to have a chance to celebrate it with her. You're my mother and I want to celebrate it with you too."

"So after school you and Alex can come to my house and we'll have a snack together. Then you can leave and have dinner with Joanne and Daddy."

"You say you want me to feel comfortable with Joanne and accept her as part of my family, but you're making it so hard for me by not even eating dinner on our birthday together. I think if you can't even be in the same room as her, I feel guilty for being friendly with her, like I'm deserting you."

How did this ten-year-old learn to say such things? I panicked, started to scream at her, then disallowed the conversation. I needed time to think. I promptly ran to the experts, the women who are the mothers-in-arms in this parenting endeavor—my friends. I got as many opinions on what to do as I have friends, each feeling very strongly about this issue. There were two basic tendencies: (1) Listen to the clear needs of your child; you are the adult. (2) Listen to your own needs; the child will survive and will benefit from a mother who clearly states her own needs.

The date was drawing near with no solution, so I attempted a modified version of the original all-evening celebration. I proposed, "I will meet you and Daddy and everyone else in the restaurant at 5:00, and we'll all eat together. Then I will leave for my class."

"But I don't want to open my presents in the restaurant. I want you to come over to Daddy and Joanne's house before the restaurant so I can open all the presents at the same time."

"Don't push it, Amy. I said what I would do. I won't do any more." We hung up, still furious at each other.

The next morning Amy called with another proposal. "Daddy suggested that Alex and I go over to your house after school and we'll open presents from you there. Then you, Alex, and I will meet Daddy with Joanne and Susan in the restaurant at 5:00. We can all eat, then you can leave."

"Okay." Relief.

Tuesday comes. Already by 3:00 I have a headache. I rush around after work to wrap the presents for my kids before they come over. They come through the door with smiles and hugs and open their presents. An idyllic family scene. Gift wrap spread all over the floor and presents immediately played with. At 5:00 the three of us pile into the car. As we are parking in front of the restaurant I see my ex-husband with his new partner and her daughter drive by on their way to a parking spot. My stomach is about to drop out of its abdominal cradle.

We enter the restaurant first. I choose the big round table in the corner and seat myself with my back against the wall—the best defense. My kids sit across from me, but I ask them to sit next to me, one on each side. We wait for the others.

Joanne seats herself directly across from me, her daughter on her right, Steve to her left. We are all smiles and chatter. I immediately notice her sweater. "I have the same sweater," I say. "But, come to think of it, I haven't seen it in a few months."

"This one's not yours. It's mine." This she says with a giggle.

"But I just mean that I must have neglected to pick it up from the dry cleaner. Of course that one is not mine."

Joanne wants to order the eggplant appetizer, but Susan and Steve hate eggplant. So she asks if I will share it. I'm not crazy about eggplant, but what the hell. Share children. Share eggplant.

The eggplant is poorly prepared and Joanne is apologetic. I don't eat it.

Steve and I fill up the air with conversation about the evils of the board of education, the employer we both have in common. With animation we take turns explaining the ins and outs of working for a bureaucracy to Joanne. This is a bond between us—a safe, impersonal bond.

Amy sticks close by me during the meal, holding my hand and following the conversation. Alex quickly develops a close relationship with the waitress, and, as the restaurant is empty, she plays games with him in the aisles.

Only twice during the hour do I feel close to tears, but each time I manage to turn my head and push it back down. By the time the hour is over I have a massive headache, but the hour does end, the headache goes away with a good night's sleep, and I am still intact, telling the story.

To date I have not made much progress on the issue, but I am working up the courage to ask for a tour of the new house. I am now involved in the beginnings of a new relationship and will soon have to deal with the difficulties of stepparenting from new angles—his relationship with my children, my relationship with his child, his relationship with my ex-husband, my relationship with his ex-wife. My father's marriage is probably breaking up. My father and his wife are both feeding me their gripes about each other, and my own mother is dying to hear the details from me. Should I tell?

12

A Rainbow Family in the Deep South

Yandra Soliz

Dear Ms. Maglin,

I read your stepfamily article in *Ms.* magazine February 1985. I wanted to share a few things with you about my own unusual little family.

My name is Yandra Soliz and I live in an Air Force town in middle Georgia. I am forty-four years of age and am Spanish and American Indian. I live in a blended interracial family and as such we are unusual in many ways. Living in a blended family is a unique experience in itself, but when the blended family is composed of multiracial members, it becomes even more complex. The stresses of daily life are compounded tenfold. . . .

I was born and raised in Texas in 1941. We were poor, of course. Not destitute. Just regular poor. I've experienced racism since I was a child. We were patronized, exploited, and made to feel like second-class people. My life has been one of severe hardship, deprivation, and isolation.

I left South Texas at the age of sixteen and went to El Paso to live with an aunt. There I met an Army serviceman, married, and went to live in the huge metropolis of New York City. I lived there for seventeen long years. My life there is another story. . . . The fast pace and violence of the city shocked and frightened me. But I also loved New York; all was not negative. I found out that being dark I was classified as Puerto Rican by everyone except Puerto Ricans. . . . I left my husband after seven long years of enduring physical and emotional abuse. I had two young children who were part Indian and part white. Then I met a black West Indian and

This letter is actually created from two long letters sent in February and March 1985.

had a very beautiful baby girl from that relationship. She is my youngest and her name is Yolanda.

I left New York in October 1978 and went back to Texas. It was a bad mistake. My young daughter experienced blatant racism and it broke her spirit. She had not experienced it before in New York City. She had gone to an inner-city school with multiracial children and now she was in school with children whose parents were rednecks and Mexicans. . . . It was not easy for my daughters and I in Texas. . . . I left Texas in June 1979 and went to live in lovely Oregon. For the first time in my turbulent life, I settled into a stable and quiet routine. I had a good job as a hospital ward clerk and I made many friends.

In May 1983 I answered an ad in a pen-pal singles column. The newspaper had made an error and I wrote to this man, thinking that he was from California. . . . When his glowing letter arrived from Georgia, I was stunned! He seemed like the perfect man for me, but the state of Georgia became a serious thought in my mind. I was well aware of the powerful racial dynamics which were inherent in the South. . . . I kept the letter for a whole month in my closet. Twice I would begin to write and then threw the unfinished letters away. To make a long story short, we began writing and quickly fell in love.

We were married in December 1983 after a whirlwind of ten days in October of the same year. I met all his grown children and his young son, who was then twelve.

I began my new life in Georgia in December 1983. My husband is a very caring, tender, gentle, and sensitive man. . . . It is hard to believe that he came from harsh, severe poverty in the mill country of North Carolina. His family was a rough, poor group of people and they were classified as poor white trash. He left home at a young age and joined the Army Air Corps. His attitudes toward people and the world at large are not those that his parents or grandparents had. He has truly evolved. . . . He has totally accepted my fifteen-year-old daughter, who was fourteen when we married.

Our family consists of my husband Robert; myself; Mark, Robert's son, who is fourteen; and Yolanda, my daughter, who is fifteen. I would consider us lower middle class. My husband is a retired Air Force sergeant and he has a very good job with a prominent law firm as a legal assistant and title researcher. He is considered one of the top in his field in Georgia.

Now to the nitty-gritty part of my story. . . . first of all my daughter and Robert's son are two different people. My daughter is shy, quiet, and very withdrawn. She is paranoid about white people and clearly distrusts them. She is angry at me for having married and placing her in a blended mixed family. . . . My marriage and new lifestyle have greatly affected her. We've always been close and she had our little duplex in Oregon all to herself while I worked evenings as a medical hospital clerk. Our lives were set and we were happy together. But now, she resents sharing the bathroom, etc. She resents living in a multiracial family. She is very unhappy at her high school. The black girls at her school question her mercilessly about her color, her background, her family. . . . She comes home all stressed out. . . . She suffers from bouts of abdominal pain and tension headaches. I ache for this child of mine and have bouts of guilt over her unhappiness.

Yolanda speaks to my husband Robert, but only occasionally. She admits to me that he's a good man. She compares him to the white father on the television program *Different Strokes*. She knows very well that he's very good to me. Robert really loves Yolanda and realizes that she needs help. But she refuses to allow him to even be a friend to her.

Robert's son is outgoing, personable, and friendly. He's a good-looking youngster and very much like his dad. There is no malice or hatred in his heart. He tried to make friends with Yolanda from the very beginning, but she would have none of it. Yolanda will simply not speak to him. So now he avoids her as well. They are like two boarders living in the same house, that's all. It is so strange. However, things are changing; Yolanda is beginning to communicate with Mark more while withdrawing more from Robert.

Mark has caught some flak at his school for having a black stepsister. They use the derogatory word. He has stopped bringing his friends over to the house and I'm sure I know why. . . . Now, as for me and Mark. At the beginning of my marriage to his father, we really hit it off and became friends, but at this point, he and I are no longer friends. There is a rift between us now. We are not ugly to each other, but there are occasions when the anger and the hurt surface. His father is caught in the middle.

My husband and his son have a good relationship. It is hard on Robert because Mark is an active fourteen and Robert is fifty-six. Mark literally engulfs him with affection and clings to him. His mother died when he was only five. After that, his first stepmother was a cruel woman who physically and mentally abused him. And now me. He has been through a lot of changes, just as Yolanda has. He loves his father and somewhat resents me and sees me as a threat. He feels that Yolanda gets away with a lot of things and he doesn't. My parenting is different than Robert's and that has caused problems. I am very liberal and permissive with Yolanda whereas Robert is a fair disciplinarian.

Mark spends every weekend with his older sister in another town close by. There is a strong bond between them and I strongly sense that they talk about Yolanda and I. They think we're weird in our ways. I am very hurt for I know for a fact that he told his older sisters that my daughter ate all the food in the house, etc. Also he told them I had his father wrapped around my finger and that I cooked only TV dinners. Things like that. He wants to go to live with his sister, but Robert won't let him. . . . Then there was a misunderstanding over a phone call my daughter answered from my husband's older daughter. There were some accusations and hurt feelings all around. Well, at that point, I went into my Indian shell and have been there for a long time.

There have been many cultural and ethnic differences between his children and I. They are a very family-oriented group and my daughter and I are not. Holidays are not that important to us, but they are to them. Furthermore, my husband is a very precious, kind, generous man and before I came along was always helping his daughters financially, especially two of them. My husband has paid all the insurance and bills on a mobile home he gave to the youngest daughter and we are heavily in debt. I do not feel it is fair to my husband and to us, his family. I could have begun college with that money. This whole matter has left me feeling resentful and antagonistic toward his daughter. I feel Robert has placed her before us, his family.

I will not go to Robert's children's homes. . . . They're nice enough and I know they like me, at least for their father's sake. . . . it is hard for me to go to his grown children's homes and hear racist words and slurs used loosely by their husbands and wives. . . . I do not wish to sit there and smile frozenly as this goes on. . . . Last year my husband went alone to their homes for Thanksgiving and Christmas. I stayed home with Yolanda. However, this happened initially when we were first married but as time went on, I accepted them a little more and felt more comfortable around them. There is one daughter in particular whom I really like and respect. . . .

There are the usual problems of finances and other normal things in our marriage. And there are other problems in our marriage having nothing to do with race or our blended-family status. I tend to have mood swings and bouts of depression. My husband says I am like a chameleon, never the same.

I would like to get on with my life and learn all that I can. My husband and I are presently in an interracial family support group in Atlanta. I am attending evening college classes and hope to pursue a career in the human service area. I will close my story now. Even though I wrote it in parts, I find myself weary and emotionally drained. I struggle hard with my complex and ambivalent feelings and thoughts. I wanted to write about my life, as it has been unusual and very different. I consider myself a true survivor.

Sincerely,
Yandra Soliz

13

The Step-Wedding

Wilma Wolfenstein

From time to time in every family's history there occurs a milestone, a major event that marks a critical change in the family life cycle. In this account of my daughter's marriage I shall describe, from my personal perspective, the unfolding of the wedding preparations, the occasion itself, and its aftermath, against the background of an exceptionally complicated family network (Figure 1).

Most families, according to the psychiatrist Jack Bradt, pass through nodal events mindlessly, "unaware of the exquisitely sensitive possibilities of disturbance and the complexity of meaning of such events in the multigenerational system of some families."[1] Edwin Friedman, family therapist and consultant on family life, views "periods surrounding rites of passage as 'hinges of time' . . . [when] family relationship systems seem to unlock." He discusses "how family process operates at emotionally significant moments of life cycle change."[2] The story that follows tells what happens when the bride's two families, long out of contact, are drawn temporarily into each other's orbit by the marriage of a mutual daughter.

A Little Background

My daughter Laura had gone to college on the West Coast. After graduation she remained there for several years, struggling to find her way, to find herself, during the unrest and social ferment of the 1970s. A gestalt group provided anchorage for a while; the feminist movement surely had a permanent impact on the course of her life. From my home in Ohio I tried to stay in touch despite the miles between us. Although I refrained from probing, I did sometimes wonder how I, as her mother, fared in whatever assessments went on.

Figure 1. Genogram of Members of the Step-Wedding: Laura's Family

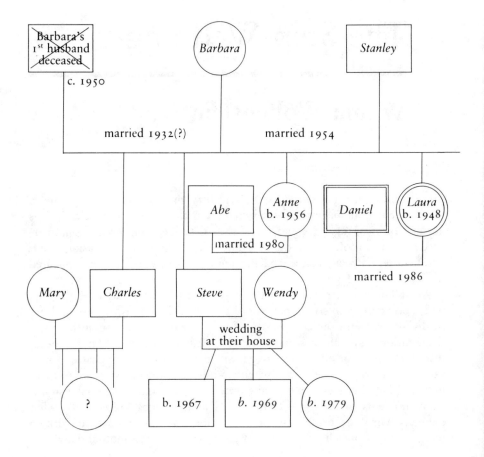

Note: Italics indicates family member present at wedding.

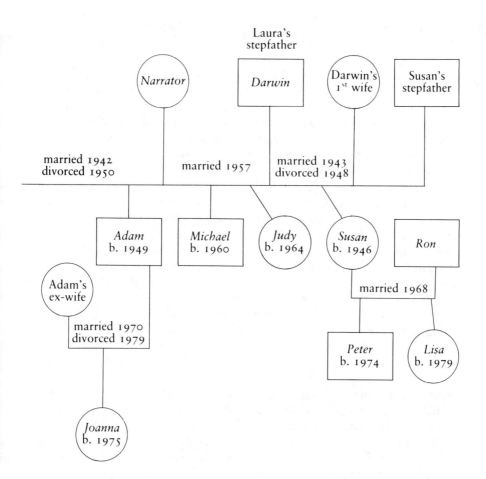

Perspectives: Mothers

My daughter was not yet three, my son Adam only one year old, when I separated from their father. As vital as this step was for me, I have never overcome a certain uneasiness over the possible hidden and subtle effects on the children of that early separation from their father. I moved with Laura and Adam back to the Midwest town where I had grown up. Their father came from time to time, and later they visited him annually on the West Coast where he settled with his wife, Barbara, his two stepsons, and the new baby of the remarriage. With nearly a continent's breadth dividing the two families, my role as primary parent was reinforced. Moreover, this was the era before the invention of joint custody.

By the time I remarried, Laura was nine and Adam seven. The children and I joined Darwin in the Ohio city where he was employed. Quite soon a more dramatic change confronted us: my husband's work took us abroad for an entire year. And so the process of consolidating as a stepfamily took place against the backdrop of a foreign land: one adventure within another. Laura adjusted with ease, just as earlier—and later—she accommodated smoothly during the repeated visits with her father's family. During those summer trips Laura became friendly with all members of her father's family, including his wife, Barbara, Barbara's two sons, and little Anne. I have always taken a certain pride in Laura's talent for moving so gracefully within the intricate family system in which she found herself.

Much later, as a young adult, Laura would sometimes tell me that she was not "hung up" on finding a husband. I supported her resolve to develop a firm sense of herself before making that fateful move. From personal experience I couldn't have agreed more. Was she warned then not only by feminist doctrine but also by her mother's example?

Eventually Laura decided to pursue her education. She enrolled in a graduate program in a Michigan university. After obtaining her degree Laura at last found the kind of fulfilling work that had eluded her for so long. It was not until she was well established in her profession that Daniel entered her life. At a distance I followed the evolving romance as it became increasingly clear that here were two young people ready to settle down together. When they announced their engagement my husband and I were delighted to welcome Daniel into the family.

Planning the Wedding

Laura and Daniel set the wedding date five months ahead and together they devoted serious thought to its planning. From the start they wanted

114

family to be present. Daniel's parents and other close relatives live in southern California; Laura's father and stepmother had recently moved to that region. During her own years there Laura had grown very close to her stepbrother and his wife, Steve and Wendy. Laura conceived the idea that Steve and Wendy's home in the canyons would be a perfect site for the wedding. They agreed. Silently I surrendered my secret dream of her wedding at the fireplace of our Cleveland home. After all, nearly all family members—with the exception of my husband, myself, and our two mutual children—reside in the vicinity of southern California.

Through Adam, my older son who also lives in that area, I gathered that my former husband and his wife, Stanley and Barbara, should not be expected to participate actively in the forthcoming wedding. At the time Laura and Daniel announced their engagement they had rejected her father's request for a traditional Jewish ceremony; hence, according to my son, Stan and his wife would be taking a back seat, so to speak. What an odd twist! The wedding would be in his stepson's home; but if Stan and Barbara were to be passive onlookers, it seemed clear that my husband and I would be principally in charge of the affair. And so across the continent I began the task of contacting caterers, consulting at each step with my daughter and Daniel, who as a modern bridegroom wished equal input into the decisions.

At the same time I felt impelled to take on another mission: to bring Stan and Barbara, if possible, into a more active and positive mode of participation. They had moved to the Coast some thirty years earlier while I had remained in the Midwest. Face-to-face contact between us had been rare, and there was virtually no written communication since our two mutual children had grown up. Friends asked me repeatedly in the weeks before the wedding whether I was feeling tense or apprehensive in view of the forthcoming mingling of the families. The truth is that I found myself eagerly anticipating the wedding as a very special "happening." Although a first marriage for the principal parties, I envisioned it as a "step-wedding," with three sets of parents offering their good will to create a memorable and meaningful event. That one set of parents would be only reluctantly present in the background seemed contrary to the spirit of the occasion.

In my fantasy everyone belonging to this extended family should be delighted to celebrate this rite of passage together. Surely the bride's two sets of parents were safely past the first raw stage, when disagreement over some issue concerning the children used to erupt periodically, causing temporary skirmishes between us. And so it was in a genuinely benevolent frame of mind that I broke the long silence and wrote to Stan and Barbara expressing our enthusiasm about the approaching marriage:

I know you are disappointed that they do not wish to have a rabbi perform the ceremony. However, I feel that it's their wedding, and it's their right to plan it as they choose. What I find wonderful and moving is that they're placing such importance on having family members present—siblings, half-siblings and "steps." Maybe it's even a tribute to both sets of parents that Laura feels not only comfortable but enthusiastic about including this whole odd assortment of relatives. . . .

About a month later came the following disconcerting reply to my peacemaking initiative:

For two avowed Jews not to have Jewish content and tradition in their wedding ceremony spotlights by default their missing Jewish background, which aside from religion, represents a civilization from which has come the ten Commandments, the day of rest, the Golden Rule, struggles for freedom against slavery as embodied in Chanuka and Passover, the supreme court (Sanhedrin), the idea of a universal god (suggesting equality for all people), etc., etc. . . . True, we are disappointed.

Enclosed in the same envelope was a copy of a Miss Manners column. Marked for our attention was a letter from an engaged couple who stated that, as nonpracticing Catholics, they felt a traditional ceremony would be inappropriate. However, both their families were devoutly Catholic. A further complication: the respective sets of parents do not get along. Wouldn't it be better, the couple asked, to marry in private? If the troubles would outweigh the pleasures, Miss Manners replied, then by all means elope!

I absorbed the message in the letter and its appended clipping in a state of disbelief. Was I naive then to have expected at the very least that Stanley and Barbara would come through with some expression of warmth and caring toward Laura and Daniel? The total absence of any such sentiment stunned me into silence for several weeks. Finally I persuaded myself to compose an answer:

Thank heaven Laura and Daniel did not follow Miss Manners' advice and decide to elope. How sad to be exchanging vows in some sterile ceremony in a judge's lonely chambers.

I confess to feeling wickedly gleeful over this sly innuendo to my own ill-fated marriage to Stan, which took place by coincidence in the same city where Laura and Daniel now live. Even now, in images more vivid than I care to retain, I can still see the judge's "lonely chambers" and still recall the impersonal procedure. But now my letter continues, as if to offset my mischief I must offer token amends:

> I confess I too would have been happy if they had chosen a rabbi to officiate. But far more important to me, and more auspicious for their future together, is the fact that they are both highly and happily involved in planning the wedding, and are in accord.

And I close again with the plea that, since Laura wants us all together, the best gift we can give her is to make this a truly joyous occasion.

At Thanksgiving Laura and Daniel came to spend the holiday with us in Ohio. It was from our home that Daniel called his parents to schedule a date for us to meet them. His parents decided to host a dinner that would include Daniel's sisters, brother-in-law, and nieces. This would be on Thursday, two days before the wedding; Daniel and Laura would have arrived by then.

During the final weeks I gathered from Laura that her father was contacting her more frequently. Perhaps his attachment for her was drawing him inevitably into more active participation in the coming festivities. About two weeks before the wedding Laura phoned to say that she had just spoken to her father. In a voice that betrayed a distinct note of anxiety, she said they had discussed the question of how to program the evening before the wedding. Laura and Daniel had proposed gathering at a restaurant, including on this occasion all three sets of parents and a few other guests. Her father argued vehemently against this suggestion for Friday, insisting that such a get-together should be held on Thursday. He seemed unable to comprehend that Thursday was set: that was to be our opportunity to meet Daniel's relatives. Although Stan and Barbara had already met them, and indeed had seen them socially on a second occasion, Stan was objecting strenuously to being excluded on the date that was set aside for Darwin and me to be introduced. Upset by her inability to get through to her father, Laura wound up our conversation saying, "Mother, I just wish you'd call my father and talk to him directly." I promised to think about it and we said goodbye.

The instant I put down the receiver I was dumbfounded: I recognized this as the classic plea of the child of divorce to be removed from the middle. In the stepfamily group that I cofacilitate, we are constantly warning participants to beware of using their children as go-betweens. Yet I was caught unaware and unprepared: the last thing I wished to do was initiate a call to my former husband. I had only just managed to answer his "contributions-of-the-Jewish-people" letter. On the other hand Laura and Daniel had been so competently planning step after step of the wedding and were so cooperative as I consulted them about the caterers. This was the first sign of stress to come to my attention. Hard as it was to practice what I preach, I forced myself to gear up and make that call.

What a muddled conversation we had, Laura's father and I! Yes, he supported the idea of a general gathering, but on Thursday. He and Barbara would be happy to have a potluck at their place. Laura was definitely on target in telling me that he was not registering the information about our prior engagement. The call ended with nothing settled.

In the end he got his way. Somehow Wendy and Steve, in whose home the wedding would be, assumed the role of third-party interveners and persuaded Laura and Daniel to go along with her father's scheme. This necessitated rescheduling our date with Daniel's parents to an evening earlier in the week, prior to Laura and Daniel's arrival.

It began to look as though I was achieving my aim: Stan and Barbara were indeed taking a more active part in the wedding activities!

The Week of the Wedding

We arrived in Los Angeles nearly a week before the wedding, just in time for our granddaughter's birthday party. Lisa is the child of my stepdaughter, Susan; and yes, Susan and her family also reside in Southern California. Our family is vastly extended in every direction in terms of its genogram but geographically it is almost entirely concentrated in Greater L.A. Susan also had a role in wedding preparations; she played intermediary for the bridal pair in locating the three musicians who provided the baroque musical background.

The following evening—according to the New Plan for meeting each other—Daniel's parents took us to dinner. Although they were impeccably discreet, I sensed they were more than a little chagrined at having to revise their party plans. As it turned out, however, our evening together was very enjoyable, and we probably got more thoroughly acquainted as a foursome than we would have in the larger family group as originally planned.

In midweek Laura and Daniel flew in. And on Thursday Stan and Barbara entertained at their home by throwing a potluck dinner. I even managed, in the kitchen of our transient apartment, to put together a pasta salad; every guest brought a contribution. The potluck affair provided an opportunity not only to meet Daniel's other relatives but also to renew acquaintance with Laura's other parents and her various step-relatives, some of whom I had not seen for over thirty years. (Indeed, some of the younger generation I had never met at all.) I suspect that this odd, informal party did after all set the tone for a more relaxed mingling of the guests at the wedding.

During the evening my former husband approached me with an offer to share some of the wedding expenses. He had previously accepted the assignment of seeing to the floral decorations, since that had to be arranged in advance. But all other costs—for the caterers, the musicians, the cake, the chair rental—were being assumed by my husband. My suggestion to Stan was that he might cover, if he wished, those items other than the catering, which was a major charge. The matter was left dangling.

At last the day of the wedding arrived. As we wound our way up the canyon to the attractive home of the wedding hosts, I was in high spirits. Assembling together were about forty-five people, nearly all of them relatives on one side or another, all mixing amiably and with apparent ease. I stopped in the kitchen to check details with the caterers, then circulated among the guests until it was time for the ceremony.

Selecting a judge had been a major item on Laura and Daniel's prenuptial agenda. In due course they chose a family court judge who presides daily over cases involving domestic dispute, marital breakdown, contested custody. For his spiritual comfort, Laura and Daniel learned, he needs from time to time to perform a happier sort of judicial function. Now that the moment drew near, the judge motioned to us to find our seats as he himself moved toward the fireplace. Without fanfare Laura and Daniel entered and took their places facing us all. Alongside the bridal pair, solemn and poised throughout, stood my ten-year-old granddaughter, Joanna, Adam's daughter, the sole attendant and bearer of the rings.

In a sentimental daze I listened to the judge's opening words. Then, making a supreme effort to blank out the fragmentary memories of Laura that were crowding my mind (Laura as a smiling infant, a curly-headed toddler, a newly fledged teen testing her wings), I concentrated intently on my son-in-law's statement explaining the couple's values and ideals. Next, my daughter read a tender poem describing the gradual, irrevocable growth of love and trust. But the real surprise came when the judge introduced into this civil service two symbolic rites borrowed from traditional Jewish ritual.

Entranced, I watched as the bride and groom in turn sipped wine from a single goblet. A little later, as the bridegroom lifted his foot to stamp on the glass in that dramatic gesture intrinsic to Jewish weddings, I knew that both these symbols spoke to a part of myself that still seems to survive beneath my more overt, nonpracticing Jewish self.

The judge pronounced the couple man and wife, marking an end to the formalities. We all rose, gathered in groups, drank toasts, and eventually queued up for the buffet supper. Wandering among the company, feeling privately amused by my rather ambiguous role as hostess-guest, I even had a pleasant chat with Barbara, who seemed after all to be more or less approving of the ceremony. (But why was she wearing black?)

At one moment someone discovered that the five children—who, for my husband and myself, are "his, hers, and ours"—were all clustered together, and a photo was taken. It had been years since these five had been on one spot; ironically here they were on the turf of Laura's other family.

Once more Stan approached me, suggesting that he would like to cover some portion of the wedding expenses. Since I had been dealing over a long period with the caterers, I again told him that I felt Darwin and I ought to be responsible for that principal expense; however, if he wished to take care of the other items I would let him know the breakdown later. Talking business at the wedding seemed somehow inappropriate.

The Aftermath: A Sour Note

Following our return home I sent Stan and Barbara a friendly note, expressing pleasure with the wedding, thanking him for seeing to the floral arrangements, then itemizing the charges for the musicians, the cake, and the chair rental. The sum of all these costs, including the flowers, amounted to considerably less than half the caterers' bill, "and," I wrote, "if you wish to take care of those extra costs that would be very nice."

A week or so later we received a short letter from Daniel's parents. Here are the opening words:

> Stanley called last night to inform us that we should send you a check for $285 to cover the music and the wedding cake. This we gladly do.

Although they graciously claimed they had wanted to help with the plans and the expenses from the beginning, I was nonetheless unspeakably embarrassed and shaking with anger. My husband shared my outrage at this turn of events, and I wrote back to that effect, returning their check. I explained that the list of expenses I had sent to Stanley was in response to his repeated offers to share with us, and that I was mortified that he would try to pass on a portion of those costs. After receiving my letter they telephoned, confessing that they were unprepared for the awkward position they found themselves in. Despite some mutual embarrassment, I felt the incident forged a link between us.

Meanwhile a letter came from Stanley, praising the wedding, then reporting that he "had approached Daniel's mother and she had agreed to take on half the extra cost." He enclosed a check for $60. That, added to the florist's fee, plus the charge for mailing some wedding gifts back to the couple's home, would add up to *his* half of the extra costs.

What I did then was to compose the angriest letter I have ever written and addressed it to Stan:

> When you offered to share the wedding costs with us, I took you at your word. I assumed that, as joint parents of the bride, you honestly wished to honor some portion of the financial obligation. I was shocked and mortified beyond belief to learn that you took it upon yourself to ask Daniel's parents to send us a check, after indicating to me that *you* wanted to take responsibility! That was, to say the least, unseemly (meaning, "improper, inappropriate, not in keeping with established standards of taste") and in fact both Darwin and I felt humiliated and angered, and naturally returned the check.

I added that I was sorry for needing to write such a harsh letter, closing redundantly with the following:

> But there are certain guidelines of taste and propriety that should not be crossed, and you have crossed them.

I returned this check also, by now not only finding it tainted but also deeply regretting that I had not rejected Stan's offer straight away.

Perhaps two weeks passed before the high point of this correspondence was reached. This arrived in the form of a seven-page handwritten letter from Barbara. It was addressed to both Darwin and myself but was clearly targeted for me.

> It is with Stan's permission that I write. There are matters which I feel need airing among us. I . . . was amazed that after all these years you still bear so much hostility toward Stan. Stan of all people could never be guilty of the guile, duplicity, and insensitivity you have attributed to him. It is almost inconceivable that anyone could write such a letter to him.

Continuing, Barbara rebukes me for my "failure to encourage any kind of social relations among ourselves" during our occasional visits to their community:

I can see in retrospect that the decision to remain apart and distant was apparently intentional and purposeful and not innocuous. . . . You never addressed yourself directly to me nor even acknowledged my existence nor my role in your children's lives. I never let this prevent me from trying to make a warm and welcoming environment whenever your children came to stay with us. . . . The summers and vacation time Laura and Adam spent with us sometimes placed a heavy burden physically on me. I remember one particular summer when Anne was born. I had just returned from the hospital when your two children arrived for the summer. My two boys were also home and the care and feeding of all took its toll on me. [The end of summer] found me hospitalized and I was forced to stop nursing Anne at the critical time of three months. But it was important for Stan and the children to have their time together and I did not complain.

Frequently they [Laura and Adam] came camping and traveling with us—all five of us crowded together. This was no great vacation for Stan and me since we were both coming from stressful jobs. But again no complaints.

Arriving at last at the current situation, Barbara berates me for not consulting them at an early stage so they could play a role in planning the wedding. A bit further on, however, comes this incredible contradiction to the "regret" at not being included. If only we had been in touch, she writes,

we could have told you that initially when Laura and Daniel made a very special point about it being "their" wedding, and that in a sense they were discouraging any interference, we were delighted. In spite of the fact that they chose a judge instead of a rabbi, we were happy that these were two mature people making a mature statement. *It freed everyone from the responsibility of planning, executing, and paying for the wedding.*

Finally, in a turnabout, Barbara ends with the hope that we can put the past behind us. Alas, that conciliatory gesture at the tail end seemed hardly enough to cancel out the foregoing pages. Normally when someone says there are matters that need airing, I applaud. In this case, however, I managed to get hopelessly hooked by the tone of righteousness, resentment and blame that pervades this astonishing letter. I wanted desperately to be finished with the whole unpleasant business. How was I to respond? I felt at the time I must not get tangled up in a point-by-point rebuttal: there was far too much overlay of emotion to pretend to be logical. I declined as well to play the part of one accused: I was not going to defend myself (ourselves) against the leitmotif of reproach throughout. Nor was I in the mood to placate. My reply, I fear, was unkind as well as terse:

> It is true that I was extremely angry when I last wrote, but far from true that I "still bear so much hostility toward Stan." My anger relates strictly to this specific episode. I'm afraid I made a grave error at the time of the wedding. My mistake was to believe that Stan was offering in good faith to share some of the expenses. How did we get from those offers to Barbara's seven-page recounting of family history?

It was with a sense of closure and relief that I mailed this letter, the final word in the series of exchanges reported in this account.

Epilogue

More than a year has passed. I find myself reflecting in a more somber way on this sad dénouement. The sense of closure and relief did not last. Although the anger that Barbara's letter stirred up in me gradually subsided, the episode at times still haunts my thoughts. What is most remarkable is how Barbara and I—so many years after the "visitation" era, so very long after the "official" connection between our two families ended— inevitably slipped back into our respective roles.

I recognized Barbara's letter instantly as a classic stepmother's lament. In insisting that she welcomed my children warmly and accepted their visits uncomplainingly despite their burdensome nature, Barbara captures the mixed feelings of a multitude of stepmothers everywhere. And in declaring her resentment of my attitude she is speaking also for innumerable stepmothers who see in the biological mother an archenemy impeding the stepmother's sincere need to have an impact on the stepchildren's lives. In essence, Barbara's letter parallels what I found in my interviews with stepmothers (for my master's degree) and what has been borne out also in the support group I colead: the tendency in many stepmothers to have strongly ambivalent feelings toward their stepchildren and to be harshly judgmental toward the biological mother.

However, this understanding in no way prevented me from reacting (decades later!) with a kind of instinctive protectiveness toward "my" children. Barbara's letter left me bristling with righteous indignation, fiercely defensive with respect to my children, my values and beliefs, myself. Familiar as I am with stepfamily dynamics, I am still wondering why it took so long to rise above the anger this letter aroused in me. After all, I colead a support group for adult partners in stepfamilies. It is my function, my specialty, to help people understand more clearly the complications and intricacies of stepfamily relations. I have always prided myself on the ability to see everyone's point of view. I know I possess a strong capacity for empathy. I think of myself as a mediator and peacemaker. I know perfectly well that a major issue for stepfamilies is that of dealing with the biological parent outside. Aside from all that, I am a stepmother myself! Yet, as this post–step-wedding drama unfolded, there I was, along with Barbara, playing out *my* assigned role among the cast of characters. While my final written reply to Barbara was brief, perhaps even insulting in its restraint, internally I was mirroring the same emotions of righteousness, resentment, and blame that I could not abide in her. When the ashes settled there was no mistaking the stark truth: I had followed the script and I was *not* above the fray!

Sometimes in my imagination I find myself composing a more substantive answer to Barbara's letter than the one I actually sent. One of my imagined versions would be closer to what she may have expected—a reply to her allegations one by one. For example, in response to her reproof that I never encouraged social relations between our two families, I would quite agree, stating that we felt, Darwin and I, that it was enough to permit the children to build as close a relationship as they wished without all of us having to interact socially. I would also point out some contradictions: for example, how in her letter she reprimanded us for not involving them early in the wedding plans, then in a later page claimed that we were all absolved of any responsibility for the wedding since the couple insisted on designing their own ceremony.

If I were to write in a more sympathetic mood my fantasized letter would take on quite another tone. I would certainly comment on the ill-timed visit of my children that followed far too closely the birth of her baby. I might confess that I too would have been upset had visiting step-children intruded so soon into that sensitive period when I was trying to establish a bond with my newborn infant. I might even add how ironic it is to recall my reluctance to send the children off for that visit. I did so only because—as she pointed out—this was necessary for the sake of their relationship with their father.

In yet a different state of mind, a more dispassionate one, I might write the following:

> It has taken me a long time to digest your letter, to screen out those parts that offended me and to examine the rest with any degree of objectivity. Before the wedding I actually believed that all the old

issues between us had died. Is it not incredible how the wedding unearthed old bitterness and resentment that one would have thought buried forever!

Notes

1. Jack Bradt, *The Family Diagram: Methods, Technique and Use in Family Therapy* (Washington: Groome Center, 1980), p. 23.
2. Edwin Friedman, "Systems and Ceremonies: A Family View of Rites of Passage," in *The Family Life Cycle,* ed. E. A. Carter and M. McGoldrick (New York: Gardner Press, 1980), p. 430.

14

Daisy Chain

Morgan David

My ex-husband, who simply liked being married, regardless of the details, remarried immediately against all advice. His new wife and I often have to speak on the telephone, although we've never met. We operate in a no-man's-land—the world of divorce. Should we meet, do we turn our backs, or greet one another? Do we understand, are we soul sisters or mortal enemies? Were we stranded on a desert island, survival would force friendship and we would be sisters. Family, survival, intimacy, and distance; how very strange life is!

Now we are constantly reminded of what takes place offstage—a new VCR or computer, health problems, every fight, telephone spat, or piece of good news is telegraphed in conversation as the children straddle two houses only several miles apart. Often the combined happenings of the two families seem a soap opera. After oceans of pain, there is now often a chuckle over their lost keys or negotiations over decorating.

Sometimes, there are the inevitable inner comparisons, as if she were another, shadow, self in another corner of my life. She's sick—how sorry I am—and how glad that it's not me. She's bought a Lincoln Continental—would that I could. She's fighting with him—how well I know how easy that is. He puts her down—I'd like to give her some advice, she doesn't have to take it.

Sometimes she's so good to the children I want to call up and complain for fear she'll steal their hearts. Sometimes so harsh with them I want to picket. You have to be quite strong to deal with a shadow self with equanimity.

Complicating things still further, his new wife also has two households.

This is an excerpt from a story of the same name.

The daisy chain stretches farther, and still farther. Down in New York, on the estate where she spends half her time, there is another family; three children, four dogs, a maid, and a cook. How fragmented she must feel, the way I felt when we were "birdnesting" and shunting back and forth to the house in rotation, so the children would not be disrupted. How tired she gets—I know so well how that feels—sometimes so tired she even fails to return. . . . Solid lines become broken lines in sketching our family.

Stepdaughters

15
Lizzie's Axe

Helane Levine-Keating

> Lizzie Borden took an axe
> And gave her mother forty whacks
> When she saw what she had done
> She gave her father forty-one!
> —After an American murder trial of the
> 1890s in which Miss Borden was acquitted
> of murdering her father and stepmother

So you want me to admit it?
Say that I sneaked into my stepmother's bedroom,
the small hatchet tucked in my sleeve?
Describe how she looked at me before she noticed
the axe—disdain dripping from her lips
like sweat? how her corset hung open,
unable to contain two hundred pounds
of puce flesh? Or how amazed she was,
groveling before me, tongue
lolling like a dog's?

And you'd like me to recount
how I spent the hours between their deaths
while the maid washed windows.
Did I rinse out my blood-speckled hose,
did I burn my dress?
When I went down to the cellar
to soak my menstrual rags
was I plotting to murder him too?

How could a woman kill her own father?
Did I hate him so, my father the undertaker—
hate the way he hated
to smile, hoarded money, bought his fat wife
houses? How long do you think
I watched him snore before I struck
him lying on the sofa, axe
clanging as it cleaved his skull,
hissing as it scooped out his eye?

And would you like to come away
from me muttering "Poor Lizzie,
they were so mean to her,
they had it coming," or
"Vicious Lizzie, demon murderess"?
But you don't want the truth.
You're like his wife, just wanting
someone else to point a finger at
so you don't have to look at yourself,
blame yourself for those you murder daily.

16
Mementos

Kathy Chamberlain

Just as Lois is about to leave for the mall, she hears a banging on her front door. She doesn't need anyone to tell her who this must be, making such a racket. Of all cities in the country, why does her stepdaughter have to live in Los Angeles? Lois has never understood what this connection is supposed to be about anyway, or what it is that Samantha wants from her.

Lois opens the door and sees Samantha, a blowsy blond, standing there in an ankle-length, rainbow-colored dress with flowing sleeves. She has on a necklace of wooden beads, each one differently carved, and an armful of clunky wooden bracelets.

"I was about to go to Bahia Blanca," Lois tells her.

"But you can go shopping any old time." Samantha is winding a strand of hair around her finger. "I just had a terrible experience—feel sorry for me! The guard in your security booth refused to let me in because I wasn't on some crazy list. It took ages to convince him I wasn't a cat burglar."

"If you had phoned me first, you would have been on the list," Lois points out. "You're thirty-eight years old if you're a day, Sam. You might start acting like other people." She smooths her powder-blue silk blouse and her tailored navy slacks.

"I can't call first," Samantha says, waving her arms as she moves into the living room. (With all the strange jewelry and her long flowing sleeves, she looks to Lois like a foreign woman, right out of the pages of *National Geographic*.) "I can't call because I'm never sure when I'll be in the area. Although today I did drive down on purpose, since there's something I want to ask you. You're looking especially thin, Lois. New slacks, I see."

Samantha spreads herself over a chair near the patio doors and puts sandaled feet on an orange tweed footstool. Lois sits across from her stepdaughter, on her green cut-velvet sofa. Her whole decor is beige, orange, and forest-green—beige carpet and walls, orange and green furniture. A custom-built cherrywood box with interior lighting holds her collection of figurines.

Samantha leans over Lois's glass coffee table and fingers everything on it, the collection of catalogs, the crystal ashtray. She picks up a praying hands statuette, then puts it down so hard it chinks against the glass. She holds up a pamphlet for widows and reads the title in a loud, disbelieving voice: "'What to Do When He Goes'!"

"People have to think of these things," Lois says. "*I* certainly did. And how's business?" she adds, for something to say.

"I don't know how Renzo and Wick's business is and I don't care. I'm bored, Lois. You're looking at the world's greatest expert on ad copy for bathroom fixtures. If it weren't for the paper I don't know what I'd do."

Oh no. Lois will not be drawn into any talk about that newspaper. In her spare time Samantha writes for some "antipoverty" tabloid, published in some peculiar place called Venice where Lois has never been. With difficulty, she has managed to keep this and other information about Samantha (the divorces, the suspicion that she has boyfriends of all colors) from the fine people she has met since beginning her new life here in Par-A-Dise Hills Estates.

Everyone else's youngsters lead such respectable lives, Lois thinks as she watches Samantha (why is the girl so restless today?) get up and peer into the custom-built box. Everyone else's youngsters are chiropractors or cardiologists, or work for large corporations like John Deere. They are homeowners and married, and live nowhere near Los Angeles but in places like Boise, Ann Arbor, Omaha, Moline. And this hobby! Doesn't Samantha know "antipoverty" is out of date? You never hear such terms any more. Which means that impossible era is, thank the Lord, long over.

"I'm hungry," Samantha announces, parading without ceremony into the kitchen alcove. "There's never any food in your fridge. Carrot sticks . . . Lois, you eat like a bird. Maybe I'll bring a ham next time I come."

"You can have some carrots but don't leave the door standing open like that. Can I get you a glass of ice water?"

"No thanks." Samantha wanders back into the living room, wanders over to the glass patio doors where she pulls aside the drapes. "Another Mercedes—look," she says as a slate grey sedan eases into the driveway opposite. "This place is full of them. You won't mind if I'm blunt, Lois?" She scoots up the orange tweed footstool and sits down on it, close to her stepmother. "The longer I'm in therapy, the more I'm convinced we should just say what we mean straight out. And I want to say that retirement villages are depressing, Lois—they are creepy. Haven't you noticed that these shiny metal cars with their plush interiors look just like . . . coffins on wheels?" She whispers the last words as if she were telling a ghost story to an eight-year-old. Huge blue eyes, waving hands, scary voice—all demanding "pay attention to me." Lois sits as far back on the sofa as she can.

"It's like these big sleek cars are purring down the streets looking for their next victim. Even though everything here is all shiny and spotlessly clean, Par-A-Dise is gloomy, Lois, this is my point. I'm missing South Dakota lately (something new for me) and I'm thinking, after living in that wonderful roomy old house on Maple Lane I don't see how you can stand this kind of place."

"Death doesn't frighten me," Lois says, "if that's what you're getting at. I even have my plot picked out back in South Dakota. Right next to your father." She watches Samantha closely to see her reaction. Samantha is playing with the praying hands, turning the statuette over and over.

"Of course I bought it mainly for its real estate value," Lois continues. "And as far as Par-A-Dise is concerned, I'm only sorry you can't appreciate it. It offers a quality of safety you don't seem to understand."

"If you think Par-A-Dise with all its barbed wire and stone fences is safe, Lois, then answer me this: why do you and your friends carry around those nasty little weapons? The pocket mace, even pistols I bet, like the one the President's wife flashed on TV. Did you *see* that?"

Lois, with her long-standing admiration for the First Lady—even a certain resemblance to the First Lady—resents this remark. It never fails to amaze her that someone like Samantha who has been handed such advantages understands so little.

Samantha lifts an arm and jiggles her wooden bracelets. As they fall, one by one, to her elbow, she says, "You and your friends, you people who live in these walled-in places, are turning a natural fear of crime in the cities into full-blown paranoia. You who have nothing to fear carry pistols. You suspect every visitor. Par-A-Dise doesn't allow children or pets. Your motto could be 'Never trust anyone under fifty'! I had to say this, Lois, for your own good."

"If we have nothing to fear it's exactly because we take precautions," Lois manages to say—but she feels Samantha is getting the upper hand. "And I heard what you said about the house on Maple Lane. It was big, all right, the largest house I had ever seen, but it was hot in summer and freezing in winter. And that town, believe me, is not the pleasantest place to live if you've buried two husbands. Incidentally, if you're going to stay much longer, I've got to run upstairs and tell Beverly Marston she'll have to go on to Bahia Blanca by herself. I was supposed to pick her up ten minutes ago. This may take some explaining."

"Go ahead and talk to her," Samantha says. "There's still something I want to ask you, so I'll wait out on the patio."

Lois lied. She hopes the good Lord will forgive her. She and Beverly have no plans to go shopping this afternoon. In fact, at this very moment, Beverly should be at LAX picking up her sister who has flown in from Duluth.

Lois simply had to get out of the condo, couldn't take it one more minute. Pushed right out of her own home, that's what it amounted to.

She sees her baby-blue El Dorado, shiny, immaculate, sitting in the carport. She opens the door, slides in, and leans her head against its padded steering wheel.

Those clunking bracelets and all that moving around, saying terrible things. Lois had wanted to scream.

It had always been that way when Samantha visited. When Lois married Lew Gresham, she hadn't realized what she was in for, in more ways than one—but she definitely hadn't taken into account his offspring. Samantha was grown already and no one could accuse Lew of being overly involved with her, but whenever the girl had come to see them, about once a month when they were first married and Samantha was teaching kindergarten in Minneapolis, Lew was mesmerized.

He didn't say much—he never was a talker—but his eyes followed his daughter constantly, wherever she went, and Lois always felt erased, pushed out, and somehow in the wrong.

Just as she is feeling now. She looks at her smooth blue dashboard and traces the edge of the speedometer. No one can say she hasn't put herself out to do something about Samantha, to have some influence over her.

Lois tried three or four times to explain a little about her own background so that her stepdaughter, who was forever making crybaby remarks about the poor, could discover what life had been like in the days before everyone was on the dole. It was for Samantha's own good.

Once, soon after Lew died, Lois had made the effort, even though nothing was more painful than to go digging up awful old memories. She had talked of the years when she was a child bride, married to Howard Fremps, who never had been able to make a decent living from the farm. The days when she had to wear dresses made from feed sacks stitched together.

And she talked about the worst time of all. It had come during that coldest winter, the winter it was so cold she got frostbite on her fingers from hanging the clothes on the clothesline out back. It was then that the doctor who came through every few months had told her the news: she would never be able to bear children.

"You young people," she had said to Samantha, "you have no idea what life is all about. Not the faintest idea. When the doctor said to me, 'You will never be able to have children, Mrs. Fremps,' I minded, let me tell you. I minded very much. But in time I came to accept my condition. And finally, I want you to know, I realized something very important." Here Lois paused until Samantha finally asked, "What? What was that?"

And Lois lowered her voice, because it was a religious feeling she had about this: "God knew what he was doing when he didn't let me have children. Because I hate them. All of them. It was years before I understood that *God knew what he was doing.*"

She stopped to let this sink in, but Samantha just sat there, her bosom heaving, her mouth half open, not saying a word. Then she began to cry, and Lois actually had to ask this grown woman to use a hanky because she needed to blow her nose.

What's more, while sniffling into the tissue Lois had given her, Samantha stuck out an elbow and knocked over a figurine sitting on a glass end table. It was a statuette of an Alpine girl in a pinafore. It broke into several pieces.

Damn the girl's clumsiness and largeness and noisy accusations, thinks Lois, getting out of her car. She doesn't have to put up with this for one more minute. Indeed she does not.

Samantha is doing stretching exercises, dangerously close to the cherrywood shelves that hold the Hummel figures—bending to the left, bending to the right.

Lois knows it is her Christian duty to make an effort with Lew Gresham's only child, but no one ever said she had to do it in her own living room. "Why don't we take a quick trip to the mall," she says, "before you go home."

"Me go shopping?" asks Samantha. "Lois, you never learn. I don't need anything from there. I have to leave soon anyhow. While you were gone, by the way, I figured out something that's been bothering me about your place, what's missing, I mean. There's nothing personal in this room."

Lois is shocked. "What are you talking about? My crewel pillows, the figurines . . . "

"No, no. Not knickknacks. I'm talking about old photographs, letters . . . I don't know—mementos."

Lois is holding herself rigid but manages a little laugh. "Oh, those silly old things. They're all in boxes in the cellar back in South Dakota. I wanted everything here to be brand new."

"You don't even have that snapshot of my *father* in his fishing hat?" Samantha's voice is rising. "I was going to ask you for it. That was my reason for coming here today! There, I finally said it. I don't know why it took me so long to get this out. I just reached the point in my therapy where I can admit how much I need my father—or anyone, I mean anything connected to him, any reminder of him. Dad's Eagle Scout badges, his stamp collection, his Bronze Star—I was going to ask you for those things, too, Lois. Where exactly are the boxes?"

"Stored somewhere in the cellar."

"I don't know what you mean. The house on Maple Lane was sold."

"I'm just not interested in all that awful old stuff now that I've moved out here. For land's *sake*, Sam. Forget about it."

"It's easy for you to say. You and Dad weren't married that long, but he's been my father for my whole life."

"No, not married that long." Lois takes a step closer. "Hardly married two seconds when you consider that I spent years acting like his private nurse before the cancer finally killed him."

"Where are those *things!*" Samantha's voice is close to a scream.

"I burned them," Lois says, sitting down. "And took the ashes to the dump. And where were you, may I ask, when I spent months sorting through mounds of junk by myself? Besides, I thought you had taken everything you wanted already."

"They're *gone?*"

"Gone."

"You definitely didn't save the picture of him in a fishing hat?"

"Awful old picture. Made him look like a hobo. I remember throwing it out. Surely you have other snapshots."

"But that's the one I took with my Brownie box camera, the time he took me someplace for a whole weekend. We went to the Jimmy River to look for trout. I've been remembering he did do some nice things with me."

"And I was supposed to know all that? I ask you."

"I don't know what to say to you," says Samantha, wrapping her arms tightly about herself. "It's like you destroyed part of my father, took a piece of him away."

At this something inside Lois explodes, and in the white heat of explosion, things seem to light up around her—the carpet, the walls, the sofa she is sitting on, the drapes at the side of the patio doors, even Samantha—and Lois thinks she can finally see what Samantha has been up to.

"*Do you want,*" Lois begins saying—and feels an odd power in her tone, because Samantha jerks her head around as if Lois had compelled her to do it—"do you want me to have your father *exhumed* and buried on the other side of the cemetery with your mother? That's what you're after, isn't it? Now I understand. You want me to dig him up. You and the whole town always thought your father should have been buried with your mother, and that I should go to lie with Howard. That's what you have been thinking all along. That's what it is that you want from me."

Samantha is looking shocked, confused. "No, I . . . have him moved? After all these years? Myself, I think cremation—*no,* I don't want him moved after all this time. Christ, it's never occurred to me one way or the other." She covers her face for a moment with part of her sleeve, then says in a voice that can hardly be heard, muffled as it is by the sleeve, "Dad was such a fine person in some ways."

"A pillar of the community," Lois says, "before he became ill." She tries to think of something to add. "If he were here today and could see what you have done with your life . . . " But it is all she can do to keep her hands still by folding them on her knees. She does not have energy to continue.

Neither, it seems, does Samantha, who has begun to go through motions of leaving. Lois watches Samantha adjust the shoulders of her rainbow-colored dress and search about as if to make sure she hasn't left anything, even moving the orange tweed footstool a few inches, perhaps to see if a bracelet has fallen off and rolled underneath. Then she heads for the door. Before it closes behind her, Samantha turns to take a last look at Lois, who is sitting very straight on her cut-velvet sofa.

17

Stealing Clothes from My Stepmother

Alison Townsend

It wasn't fashion, but you
I wanted, all those times
when I crept,
a thief at fifteen,
into the sweet, steamy
heat of your
dressing-room closet.

It was to be like you
that I tried all your clothes on,
slipping the silk
with its French lace
over my skin like affection,
magic that could transform me—
the "daughter"
who was not
your daughter—
into something other
than what I was.

It was to get close to you
who never permitted closeness,
that I sneaked jackets
out for the evening
and wore them to concerts,
or "borrowed" a blouse

and returned it the next day,
the half moons of alien sweat
beneath each armpit a sure
guarantee of my capture.

There is no escape.
It is all that you gave me.
I am like you,
but with shifts
in the colors and fabric.

But you would never have
guessed this from the way
we stood screaming, the
simple fact of our competition
raised between us,
definite as a clenched fist
or the hand
which struck my face,
slapping the skin
till it burned
with the weight
of what lay,
never said
under all of my forays
among your most private
possessions. What might
have been stopped,
or even accepted,
if I had been your blood daughter.
If you had loved me.

18

The Woman and Her Past

Berenice Lopez

Dedicated to Freddy Lopez and my four children

I never really lived with my mom after my eighth birthday. Mom remarried. My brother, Leon, was placed in a boarding school in Santo Domingo. I was placed with my mother's mom, Grandma Maria. My childhood was a nightmare. Without anyone knowing, I was molested by two uncles. I couldn't tell my mother; she only had eyes for her new family. Grandma Maria never believed children. She said they spoke only lies; they liked to invent things. (I can talk about this now thanks to the help of many people who cared; then I suppressed my pain.)

Coming back to the past, Mom took me to her house on and off—whenever she remembered her other children. Every time I went with her I was miserable. Mom talked about my father, and her husband would join in with bad words toward him. I felt quite bad about this, especially since at the time I thought Dad was great.

My stepfather never disrespected me although he did hit me. One time he threw soup on my body. I told him to stop. The thing that hurt the most was Mom had a smile on her face and just told me, "You deserved that." I began to hate my mother and what she represented at the time.

Grandma Maria fought to have me with her. By this time I was ten years old. I was already blooming. This was when I fought with my uncles so they wouldn't hurt me. I had to lock myself in rooms and I wouldn't come out until another grownup came to the house. I hated Grandma's house, but I hated my mother and her husband more, to the point that I would rather lock myself in rooms and even be so scared that my whole body was as stiff as a dead person.

I couldn't write to Dad; his wife would take the letters. Plus I knew from Leon, who was then living with them, that she hated us and mistreated him to the maximum. I asked myself, "Who can I turn to?"

The molesting and rape stopped at the age of nine and a half. I made it stop. They tried again at ten but I threatened to tell my mother. However, I didn't say anything because I didn't want to be thrown out on the streets; I didn't want to become a prostitute. At the time I thought that would happen to me if I told and that I would get the beating of my life. You see, Mom had time to take a cab and beat the hell out of me when Grandma Maria called her and said I did something bad, but for nothing else. My stepsister and stepbrother were Mom's pride and joy.

Well, years passed. When I was sixteen, Mom moved in with her husband to Grandma Maria's house. I stayed with Mom. We built sort of our relationship but still it wasn't a strong one. She would ask me why I didn't give her love, but I didn't know how to. Her husband was treating me a little better but still he had his reserves and I also put my distance from him.

We lasted two years together. Mom and my stepfather moved to New Jersey and I chose to live in New York with the mother of my father, Grandma Gregoria. She was and is my true mother and the most important person in my life.

At eighteen, I went to Santo Domingo for summer vacation. I went to Grandma Maria's house. She lived by herself but she was the same, a woman who was a racist, a critic to my brother and myself. I was mistreated by her so I went to stay with my father. My stepmother had a big fight with him so she could kick him out of the house and I would have to leave also.

After returning to her Grandma Maria's and being beaten, Berenice went to a friend of her mother's and received some comfort. Afraid to reside with any of her family, Berenice got married; however, her husband rejected her because she was not a virgin. After being treated "like dirt" for some time, Berenice tried to commit suicide.

My mother and father found out what had happened [the rape] to me and they, as never I had seen them before, hugged me and kissed me. They asked me to forgive them for not being there for me when I needed them and for not defending me from those men who hated me. My outside said "I do forgive" because who am I not to forgive my parents, but my inside said "never." My stepfather didn't pay attention to me, even then. I thought someday he would care, care enough to say how sorry he was for what happened to me. I asked my mom what he had said of my problem. He answered her by saying, "Thank God it wasn't my baby Martina, anybody but her."

Since that day, I learned I could never dream of having a real father, for my father who created me was never home and my stepfather just didn't give a damn.

19

"Whose Side Are You on Anyway?" A Stepdaughter Ponders the Unanswerable

Reminiscences by O.C.
Edited by Yvonne Stam

There are whole periods of time when it seems as though my family has always been together the way I know it now: my mother, my stepfather, my brother, and me.

But then something will happen that will take me back to the time when I was seven or eight, the years before my mother married Edouard.

I suppose that must have been an especially sensitive time in my life because the memories are most vivid when I'm feeling down or a little unsure of myself.

I must have known that Edouard and my mother would get married. For about a year, he spent lots of time with us, and I could see that my mother was happy about this.

As for me, when I first met Edouard, I felt, well, threatened. I wasn't very nice to him. I can admit now what I'm sure I didn't then. I was jealous. The truth is, I felt that way about most men that came into my mother's life. But after some time he turned out to be a lot of fun and we shared a lot of good experiences together. He was very creative and so was I. We started a lot of projects together and completed some.

I remember going to the beach and things like that. I enjoyed his companionship sometimes. He was a very interesting and artistic person.

It's funny that even though I was so young—eight years old only—I had some appreciation of these qualities. Maybe it was because of how different he was from my mother.

My mother was more of an intellectual; he was more of an esthetic person. I remember making tape recordings and making candles with him. I had a bottle-cutting craft set that I liked working on with him.

It was good to have someone to do these things with. It was a kind of play . . . doing fun things that my mother never seemed to have time to do with me. But, for all that, I still felt uneasy and couldn't feel totally happy about Edouard's being with us. It seemed that something was going to happen, something that I wasn't going to like.

I'm fairly sure now that this uneasiness had much to do with how I felt about my mother. Even now, it's not hard to recall how *possessive* I was of her. Really, I just didn't like the idea of her being close to anyone other than me.

So, even though these were fun times with Edouard, the resentment never quite went away.

I guess this is understandable because of how my life had been up to then. I remember spending most of my younger life with my mother—just my mother and me. And any time somebody else came into the picture that my mother seemed to like or even care about, he was in for a hard time from me.

At some level, I was aware of my behavior. I sometimes would feel kind of mischievous, and there were times when I wanted to get close to people my mother liked, but this never happened easily.

That's probably the main reason why I was not happy about the idea of my mother, Edouard, and me teaming up as a new family. I worried about how my life might change, and it surely did.

For one thing, Edouard came from a large family. His mother and father and several brothers and sisters had come to our city as immigrants several years before. Once he and my mother got close, we started spending lots of time with this family. Every holiday, every birthday, every occasion that arose was an occasion to celebrate with them.

These family celebrations were something of an alien experience for me. This is probably because Edouard is from the Caribbean; my mother and her family are black Americans. Edouard's family seemed quite different from American families in the ways they interact and the ways they extend themselves to each other. On the surface, at least, these people seem to be a lot closer than people in American families.

My mother's family was small by comparison. There was my mother's sister, my mother, my grandmother, and my grandfather, and me, of course: five people in all.

I have so many good feelings about my mother's family and how much they loved me. I mean, I was everything to all of them, it seemed. I was the center of attention, the "little princess." I felt very special whenever I was around them.

I don't think I was prepared for how culturally different Edouard's family is. The first hurdle I encountered was with their language. Half of them didn't speak any English. This was the main reason I came to dread those family get-togethers. Who could forget the endless chatter in a language I didn't understand?

After Edouard's brothers and sisters married, the decibel level rose, what with all the crying babies and toddlers running all about. But that came later.

At first, there was only one other child besides me. There was always a crowd of adults, though. The language was different; the food was different; the music was different from anything I'd known before. I really didn't feel a part of any of it.

It was really not their fault that I felt so left out. As I look back, I can see that Edouard's family tried hard to be warm and friendly to me. But something was missing.

That was before he married my mother. After they got married, we three didn't get off to a good start at all. Most of the conflict, it seems, was circular—conflict between my mother and him about me, and between my mother and me about him.

I was only about ten years old. But I was aware that we were all going through a bad time. For one thing, my mother was constantly being put in the middle of arguments between Edouard and me. What made it so bad was that Edouard and I didn't communicate well at all. He spoke English well enough. That wasn't the problem. What I remember most about this period were the *complaints*. Edouard had complaints about me; I had complaints about him. It's not clear what all the anger was about, but things often heated up and boiled over very easily.

What didn't help was that Edouard had a bad temper. And he thought I was spoiled—a brat. I'm sure of this. It wasn't hard to find things about him I didn't like.

Both sets of complaints always fell on my mother. She had to hear it from both of us, sometimes at the same time!

This was probably unfair to her, unconsciously demanding that she play the mediator. But if she hadn't played that role, I'm sure something disastrous would have happened.

Once my mother stepped in between us, I knew I had the advantage over Edouard. Unreasonably, I suppose, I felt that she should always be on my side. The strangest thing about all this was how important the outcome was for me. You know, if I had had a different sort of mother, if I'd had a mother who always took *his* side, I don't know how I would have coped with it.

Now that I am an adult and I look back on it, I can see how all this contributed to their ruined marriage. You never know. Maybe their marriage would have worked better if she had taken his side more. I'm sure it must not have been easy for her.

But who knows? Even if I had not been in the picture, I wonder if they would have been able to make a go of it. I said that he had a very bad temper, and at times he was totally unreasonable.

It's easy to see now how the fights between Edouard and me led to fights between the two of them. But all I cared about at the time was that my mother loved me. And I needed to test this love. Her marriage to Edouard must have left me insecure about this. In some ways, I guess I demanded to be shown that she considered being my mother more important than being Edouard's wife. It's possible that he was putting her to this test also.

There are times now when I think of all this and I feel a little guilty. I hope I'm not deceiving myself, but I feel that my mother was not really manipulated out of the marriage. They broke up after about eight years. Leaving was, after all, her choice. My mother has always been a strong person. She made her own decisions just like she created her own options. I'm sure she did what she felt was right—just like she did when she decided to have another child at a late time in her life.

My mother was in her late thirties, and I was twelve, when she told me she was pregnant. And once again, I felt jealous. I clearly recall feeling that way, maybe even a little more than when my mother had gotten married.

I can laugh now when I think about how I took the news that I would have a brother or sister. Very simply, I did not want my mother to have another baby. There were both rational and irrational feelings about this. After all, I had spent all those years being the only child, and the only grandchild in my mother's family. And losing all that to another baby— all the attention and God only knows what else—really had me upset.

It's easy to speculate on what some of these other losses involved. Edouard and I were getting along a little better than at first, maybe twenty-five percent of the time. And I was beginning to get more comfortable with his family.

It is hard to put my resentment about the baby into words. I guess you could say that it had something to do with the idea that my mother was having this baby with *him*.

But just before the birth, a cloud seemed to lift. I suddenly found myself looking forward to the event.

And I remember when my brother was born. It counts as one of the most significant events of my life. As luck would have it, I was suffering from a bad flu that had thrown me into a delirium the same night my mother went into labor. I'm a bit hazy on the details. All I know is that I went to stay with my grandparents; and when my mother was to come home with my brother, I was still too sick to be around the baby. I was so heartbroken about not seeing him that my mother sent for me anyway.

I got my first look at my brother, J. R., with my mouth shielded behind a surgical mask. Edouard has an exaggerated fear of disease that is not unusual for people who come from the tropics. But even he felt sorry for me and allowed me to hold J. R.

I loved my brother from that moment on. It's amazing how not one unhappy thought remained in my mind that day, and I cannot recall ever thinking again that the baby would change my relationship with my family. It seemed I had overcome the fear I'd always had of sharing my mother.

There were other changes. True, I was getting older and the relationship between Edouard and me was maturing. But after J. R. was born, a distinct change occurred. Edouard and I seemed to care more about each other. We still argued, but a new kind of bond seemed to have formed.

The way I see it, this had everything to do with my brother. Edouard saw how much I loved J. R., how much I loved taking care of him. And that made things a little easier between us. For the first time, we were really a family, I thought.

Not long after, my mother and stepfather bought a house and we moved to the suburbs. I wasn't happy about leaving my friends, but my mother explained that I would have a better life outside the city.

The move to the suburbs probably caused us to pull together as a unit more than before. After all, we were two hours away from all our relatives, and we didn't see them nearly as much as before.

One thing that was kind of awkward was deciding how to describe Edouard to my new friends. For the first time, I began to consider calling him "Dad." I hadn't seen my natural father for so many years that he virtually did not exist for me. Anyway, I didn't worry about this too much. When it came time to introduce Edouard to anyone, I simply said, "This is my brother's father," conveniently resolving what otherwise would have been a sensitive issue for me.

J. R.'s existence made something else easier. My mother's marriage to Edouard was both cross-cultural and cross-racial. Edouard, you see, is white-skinned, while I am dark. Being able to say he was my brother's father circumvented certain other questions rather neatly.

I remember, though, that Edouard was not a radically changed person even though we got along better. His complaining had become commonplace in our life. But the quality of his complaints changed. He and my mother had lots of conflicts, but now I seemed to be removed more and more to the sidelines of these arguments. Edouard has an Old World, macho attitude about family, and he and my mother had lots of fights over my brother.

I've heard that conflicts over child-rearing practices are among the most common marital problems. This now became the central problem in the household. Edouard behaved toward me like lots of other fathers of teen-agers. He criticized constantly—criticized my clothes, my choice of friends, the usual. But arguments over my brother now took center stage. Edouard scrutinized everything—what J. R. ate, how he was dressed, what toys he played with. He held my mother strictly accountable for everything imaginable.

I don't know if this was something new. It certainly seemed so to me. Maybe these are some of the same issues that they had struggled with about me. I'm not really sure.

This again raises the question in my mind of whether their marriage's failure was inevitable. I tend to think that their conflicts, over children at least, would have been the same, no matter what child was involved.

All this seems so long ago. Now that I'm in my mid-twenties, I don't look back on all this with bitterness. I find that I truly like Edouard. I don't resent him, which surprises me. In fact, I'd even say I have a love for him. And it's odd, he talks about me now as if he wants me to feel as if I'm his daughter, something I never thought he felt in the past. That he expresses this to me now amazes me. I never thought he loved me or cared. You know, I interpreted his harsh attitudes totally differently back then. But now I see that this is just the way this man loves.

I'm sure I've gained lots that's positive from this stepparent/stepdaughter relationship. I can start by saying that I've gained him—Edouard. I like him so much more than when I was living with him. Not that I feel I need to seek out his company often. But he's my brother's father and someone that I spent many years of my life with.

I cannot, however, escape the negative associations. Maybe the relationship I had with him, the constant bickering, has affected my relationships with other men. I don't like feeling this way, but it's possible. I'm a strong woman, though, and I may, in fact, have gotten a lot of strength from that situation. I have learned how to stand up to difficult situations and never fold. I am quite a determined person who does not easily back down from anything. That's one side of the coin. The other side, however, is a certain rigidity in my disposition. I am somewhat inflexible, I guess, and difficult to please, traits that I'm sure became entrenched as a result of some of my family experiences.

When I look at stepfamilies in general, I am not convinced that mine turned out all that badly, though it's a situation I would not care to face again. You know, I really wouldn't want any children I might have in the future to go through this. And I cannot imagine that I would welcome being a stepparent myself. It's too problematic, too strained. Here you are, an *outsider,* trying to wedge yourself in between a parent and child—two human beings that just cannot, I feel, have a stronger bond. Is that anything but a no-win situation? There're all these feelings of disloyalty, and somebody's bound to get the short end of the stick.

In spite of that, if I had a child and my marriage broke up, I can't say that I wouldn't get married again. I guess I believe it's better to have a stepfather than no father at all. Should this happen, I know I'd be coming into the stepparenting situation better prepared. Because of what I've experienced, I'd know what to look out for and what to expect, but I'm not sure that would guarantee me success.

20

The Mother Who Is
Not the Mother But Is

Alison Townsend

The mother who is not the mother but is. The words wake me. They lure me from sleep like a fish hooked in water and then reel me, slowly but deliberately, in. In from a dream of my stepmother, Shirley. In from a memory of standing alone on an open shoreline, many years and miles away from her, and listening, listening, listening. Tilting my head to catch whatever it was I seemed to hear circling in the salt spiral of the waves as they hurled themselves, moon-driven and unavoidable, toward the crumbling brown bluffs of a far southern California beach. Over and over again I heard the words, *My mother, my mother.* And then: *The mother who is not the mother but is. Is, is, is,* until the tone shifted from a whisper of swirling sand to a roar and the waves were singing—no; the waves were screaming—not about my own, gone, dead-from-cancer-at-too-early-an-age mother, but about Shirley, *the mother who* (the waves told, the waves *tell* me) *is not the mother but is.* Is all I have to call mother now, this woman who stood (who stands yet) apart from me on the rose-carpeted stairway where we first met, always higher up than I am, always frowning and stony, her arms folded severely, inflexibly (for they will not, they will never embrace me) across her frozen chest. This woman. The *mother* who, it is true, is *not* my mother, but whom I have called "Mom" now for over twenty years. I turn, rising, surfacing for real now from the blue depths of sleep into the shock of clear daylight. But the dream echoes: *The mother who; the mother who is; the mother who is not but . . . .* And I sit up, knowing that somewhere deep inside me I must acknowledge this. Must clarify my tangled thinking about her with this message of moon and waves and salt.

The mother who is not the mother but is. The Stepmother. The blame. The pain. The guilt. The pardon. I must scrub floors each day after school. I must have my braids cut. I must wear different clothes, must act differently than who I am when I am being most myself. Must not ever be *that* self or this woman who forgets birthdays, forgets Christmas, forgets all the small details of loving and giving for years at a time, but who calls me suddenly, late on a spring evening after receiving my last letter to say, *Something's wrong. Something's bothering you, I can feel it between the lines here. You're unhappy. Tell me what it is.* And how we talk then, our voices flowing easily in and out of one another as if we were, in fact, related bodies, beings who recall a time when I floated, we walked as one. As if I, who am not her daughter, who will never *be* her daughter, am more her daughter than if we were related by flesh and dreams and blood.

The mother who is not the mother but is. So many years withdrawn from me, withdrawn from us all, with her migraines and rages. Psychiatrists and Valium. Her hatred of self and others. The always empty refrigerator. The locked door that kept us out of her sight like spies tiptoeing through the enemy territory of the silent house, silent because her "nerves" could not withstand noise. Could not withstand children or cookies or homework or ball games or even friends who slept over. Could not withstand the thought of us, growing up like resilient weeds all around her, constant intrusions on her hothouse consciousness.

The mother who is not the mother but is. And what is *my* inheritance? What is my legacy of trust or confidence? In another poet's words I used to dream of "some infinitely healing conversation" that could take place between us.[1] A conversation that I know (but only lately) will never happen. Will never take place as richly and completely as I have imagined, but only partially and in small sharp pieces, the way our lives together have been partial, me grown up now and living on the West Coast, she divorced from my father, living in a Midwestern city that is strange to us both and finding what she calls her *first real happiness* after an act of betrayal. An escape from the marriage she so hated with my father, to live freely and out in the open with her lover, a married man.

Shirley. *The mother who is not the mother but is. Is* in some way I cannot ever fully decipher. Shirley. The woman who asks, when I tell her I'm writing a novel based on my girlhood and adolescence in North Salem, *I'm the wicked stepmother, aren't I? Go ahead; you can tell me the truth. I can take it. At this point I can recognize myself for what I really am.* I laugh and deny it, of course, all the while thinking in the back of my mind about Thomas Wolfe and how he could never go home again after writing that novel. But there is no home in North Salem now, there will never be a "home" again, the odd and defiantly *un*blended combination of people I call "family" scattered like seed pods to all four winds.

Because it is true, of course. She *is* the wicked stepmother. She *is*. And, as much as I may dream of that conversation with her, I can't forget the neglect. Can't forget the abandonment, the distance, the scoffing, the sneering, the litany of venom she spilled upon me like acid falling downward in the place of nurturing rain. Can't forget *or* forgive, so that when I describe her to my friends now, there is nothing I can do but laugh bitterly and refer to her as the woman who sabotaged my girlhood. The enemy I clung to even as we lived in a state of guerrilla warfare, her cunning pitted against the desperation of my youth.

Yes. She *is* the wicked stepmother. And I am Cinderella sitting in a bed of ashes, not ever completely knowing that the possibility of transformation is something I hold within myself. But she is also the opposite of wickedness inside me, appearing once in a dream of uncontrolled burning to pull me into safety from the blazing wreck of a car. Pulling me to safety and then whispering fiercely in my ear, *Are you crazy?! Don't you want to live? To write? To see things?* Whispering as if she was the voice of fire itself and all the while brushing ash from my body as roughly as any mother animal. Brushing me off and then pushing me from her abruptly with *There, you don't need me! You're grown up now. You always have been. Go take better care of yourself!*

Shirley. And the word *care* torn from a dream's code as if it could make up for something, as if it could be the name of *the mother who is not the mother but is. Is,* even in her dark aspect, which I recognize as Hecate or Kali, the black side of the moon's pure light. The other side of myself in her mystic Welsh stubbornness, even in her obvious victimization, the victimization that tortured and abused me in its turn. *The mother who is not the mother but is. Is* the break in the cycle. *Is* against her will and ability, perhaps, but who tries now, in her own unreliable way. Who says, with a note of sorrow I have never heard before echoing in her voice, *It wasn't you I was mad at all those long years, Alison. It was your father. It wasn't you.*

The mother who is not the mother but is. Is as spontaneously and unexpectedly as the blue-and-white striped shirt I put on this morning, thinking, *Shirley*. Thinking, *I learned about this from Shirley's impeccably good taste.* That taste and how it is imprinted upon me whenever I choose furniture, clothes, food, fabric, even the uncut pages of a fine old book. Her taste, which merges with my own even more deeply than that of my blood mother's, though I carry her values also in that bright red stream. Shirley, guiding me and helping me without my knowing it. Shirley, confusing me and leading me astray, our bodies utterly dissimilar and yet related through the common fact of being women and having bled together at the same time for all the years I lived in her house. Related too, through every woman's hope for her daughter (*even* the daughter who is not the daughter). The hope that she have something more. Something better, like those words she once uttered to me in high school, forbidding me to take typing classes because she didn't, she *did not, and did I hear her?* want it to be too easy for me to fall back on secretarial skills if all else failed.

Those words, spoken so harshly, and yet with something like care not far behind them. And me, her forever embarrassing stepdaughter. The one who didn't even know how to gracefully accept the Barbie doll she gave me on our first birthday together. The Barbie doll I had wanted so badly but that my own mother had pronounced, *Vulgar. Not an appropriate plaything for nice little girls.* Shirley. And what she did or did not give me, the scratched record of conversations that could have been between us still skipping inside my head though we are on track together now more frequently than not.

Shirley. *The mother who is not the mother but is.* Is both rejecting and accepting, stumbling and human, as I am, as we both are, everything sharp and awkward between us born during that first year together, she silent and me stubborn, refusing to call her "Mommy" for at least six months. To recognize her by the name of my real, my rapidly slipping away, my forever dead mother; though my siblings Steve and Jenny jumped into it as easily as water, seeming not to remember that there had been anything, had been *anyone* before. Before Shirley and her battered old Ford smoking to a start in the driveway of the new split-level where we all so suddenly lived together in that family that was not a family but was, is.

I look back. It is a hot day. A trip to the beach. From the back seat I reach forward, touch the nape of her neck shyly, stroke her hair and say, *You're pretty, Mommy. You're pretty.* I say her name that is not her name but is and she turns, her tears spilling salt and flowing like the word *ocean* or *mother* into a new country. A place of possibility. A memory saved out from among all the other memories of *the mother who is not the mother but is,* and the daughter who recognizes it. Recognizes it and would swim the English Channel, or an entire ocean if she had to, simply for the occasion and what passed between us in that moment, in the falling of those brief, those bitter, those completely unbidden tears.

Note

1. Adrienne Rich, *Of Woman Born: Motherhood as Experience and Institution* (New York: Norton, 1976).

21

Name and Shelter Made Me Homeless: Notes from an Interview with a Latina Stepdaughter

Elisa Davila

This is my translation of an interview done in Spanish during August 1987 with a Latina stepdaughter who prefers to remain anonymous.

She was obviously affected both in a positive and negative way by the experience of being a stepdaughter. She has become a very open, ideologically liberal, and modern woman in the way she sees the world and in the way she is bringing up her own daughter. I use the term *modern* to indicate feminist, since that is the word she prefers to use when comparing her ideas and experiences to those of her mother, sisters, and other relatives.

The alienation and denial she suffered as a child and as a young woman make her a strongly quiet (sometimes very stubborn) and courageous woman. She is the first person in her family to graduate from college, and she has set an example to her "three families." Even her own mother, who did not have more than a few years of primary education, is talking now about the need of "la negra" to go to graduate school.

She has become more accepting of different lifestyles and of different family units and arrangements. She left her husband when her daughter was only two years old, moved to another town, and began attending college and raising her child on her own against the wishes, demands, and impositions of her ex-husband and her family. She may suffer more for being illegitimate and black than for being a stepdaughter. Yet the fact that she is a stepdaughter has given her deep insight into family relationships.

The terms *hijastros* (stepchildren) and *padrastros* (stepparents) are not in the active and everyday vocabulary of Latinos. Other words, however, such as *ilegítimo* (illegitimate), *madre soltera* (single mother), *madrina* (godmother), *abuelita* (grandmother), *adoptivo* (adopted) are more widely used and reflect the importance that the relationships they connote have in our culture. The extended family is still the institution that maintains the cohesiveness of the society and supports the members of the family groups in different ways. Children are, for the most part, more used to going to live with aunts, grandmothers, cousins, or other relatives when there are major changes in their own families such as the death of a parent, separation, divorce, a new marriage, or a new partner in the household.

Stepdaughter by Default

This is not an easy account. I was born dark, *chola*,[1] illegitimate, and poor. I was the second child of a strong, passionate *limeña*[2] and a handsome, well-mannered sculptor. He was the grandson of a black woman; his race did not match his class or his talent, and it was just his color that he passed on to me. I inherited the darkness of the skin and all the extrinsic disadvantages of being dark in a racist society.

I love my father and his smile. When he smiles, it is like a half moon shining from ear to ear against the dark roundness of his face. But smiles were not enough to feed two daughters, or to isolate them and their mother Tina from the disgrace of concubinage and the stigma of illegitimacy.

My mother married Andy when I was three years old. She did not love him, and she has never really loved him. Living in a paternalistic hierarchical environment, she opted to marry a man she did not love in order to secure for herself, and for her two daughters, a place in the communal structure of that society.

Although Peruvians are traditionally Catholic, my mother did not marry in the Catholic church. Although about 30 percent of low-income women from the poor class never marry (they prefer to have one or several common-law relationships, which give them more freedom), my mother was very conscious of the need to have a legal marriage, for security, protection, and class mobility. This is, at least, the way she rationalized it and explained it to me.

Yet there was another, stronger reason for her marriage. It is one that she has just begun to openly accept and talk about. Erasmo (my father) had another woman and he was going to marry her, leaving us to a darker fate. My mother had to keep her own honor and her pride safe. Like many other women in a similar situation, she felt that she needed to protect her own pride, to immerse her own pain in other waters, and never allow a man the empty victory of leaving her behind.

And so it was. A private affair, an intimate betrayal both condoned and repudiated by society brought me to this world and placed me later in a stepdaughter/stepfather relationship.

"Daddy" Does Not Mean Happiness

At three, what can one remember? Maybe some colors, smells, undefined sensations, and a secure, warm grasp by your side. Yet I just barely remember another hand reluctantly helping me down the steps, and a harsher voice demanding that I call him "Daddy," a word that I could not connect with his face.

I spent a very unhappy childhood. New children were born, among them a boy who became the center of the household. I grew skinnier and darker with a fear of talking and a longing for a father and for leaving my own home. At thirty, I still have difficulties talking, and still do not have a home.

My stepfather saw me as an intruder, an obstacle to his own happiness and the security of his relationship with my mother. She would let my father take me out two or three times a month over the objections of her husband, Andy, and Bertilda, my father's wife. She (Bertilda) also disliked my presence and also saw me as an intrusion in her life. She was so jealous of my presence that she forbade my father to give me anything. I never enjoyed the happiness of opening a gift from my father in the presence of others. I felt that I was the cause of internal tensions in the two households. I was the sharper edge of two parallel triangles connected at one end by me (see Figure 1), or the center of a quadrangular relationship with two insiders connected by blood and affection, and two outsiders con-

Figure 1.

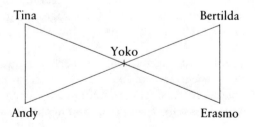

Figure 2.

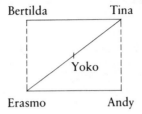

nected by jealousy, insecurity, and distrust (see Figure 2). Life was upside down from whatever angle you looked at it.

My mother worked during the day, and Andy stayed home (he worked at night) taking care of the children and doing the traditional chores of a woman. By age seven, I had developed a serious case of nervous asthma, which Andy used to isolate me from my other sisters and brother. He claimed I had a contagious disease and did not want his own children to acquire it. Alone in my solitary childhood, I resented that man who demanded to be called father, but who used his diminished male power to victimize me for his failure to possess my mother entirely.

Being humiliated at home and at school, I began to understand the real meanings and connotations of the words *la negra, chola,* and *papá*.[3] The semantics of that grammar used to establish blood relationships, race, and class differences entered very early in my silent vocabulary of pain. The opposites in language were just symbols and reflectors of the opposites and distinctions in life. Duality and opposition, love and hate, white and black, poor and rich were the constant rulers and opponents of my childhood.

Affectionate Pretense to Cover Up a New Word: Sex

By age twelve, I had become quite mature and attractive. My own metamorphosis played a trick on "Daddy." The ugly, asthmatic intruder had become a good-looking *mulata* whom he began to secretly desire. At first, it all seemed like just new affectionate games, big unusual hugs, intentional looks and words that surrounded me in a dangerously sensual environment. His previous distance and disdain gave way to new forms of behavior in the afternoons when my mother was not at home. He used to take me into his arms, hold me tightly, and throw me in bed, rubbing his whole body against my legs and breasts. Shock and fear plunged me into deeper silence and an intense desire to run away, to escape. The opportunity came one day during a rage when he hit me with a cooking pan and I ran away to my father's house. I returned to my mother's home after two weeks of pleading by her, and after a forced agreement with Andy to never touch me again.

Since then, a recalcitrant silence and mutual mistrust have kept us apart.

Today and Looking at Tomorrow

Both families came to this country. I married just to escape that environment, gave birth to a girl, divorced, and fell in love again. Soon, my own daughter will be in turn a stepdaughter. She will be a new pointed *arista* of a new inverted triangle. I feel sorry for her, and I am afraid for her, for myself, for the new man in my life. Would it be better for her? How can I predict? As the poet said, "In a moment there are visions and revisions which a minute can reverse."[4] From a wasted land, a wasted youth, would it be possible to bloom again?

Life has made me more accepting of people and of different relationships. I am also more critical of society and its institutions, particularly those that force women to marry as a means to avoid collective repudiation.

It is of course ideal to have a family with a father and a mother, but it shouldn't have to be a disgrace to be a single mother. Children do not ask to be born. Society, particularly women, should have provisions to accept them and to sustain those born to unmarried couples.

Stepchildren frequently experience traumatic and solitary life. It is often difficult to accept the new person in your parent's life. Now that I am older, I have finally developed a good relationship with my stepbrothers and sisters. We share more, and I sympathize with their fears and insecurities. On both sides, they also resented the attention I received from my mother and my father. We talk to each other more now, and we have discovered that we were all solitary and unhappy. We were cruel as children and young adults without knowing it. There were no role models for any of us to follow then, and there are not many now.

I can detect already in my daughter's eyes a vague reflection of my own look at that age. Her questions make me question my decision to marry again. How much longer do I have to deny my own happiness? What would be the best thing for her?

We will be taking part in a new act of a life's drama, one that doesn't have a writer's plot or vision, only characters and players.

Notes

Acknowledgments: I would like to thank Professor Linda Greenow (department of geography, SUNY New Paltz), who has written about market women in Peru and has lived in Mexico, Peru, and Bolivia. She kindly read this manuscript, made suggestions, and helped focus the question within the Latin American context.

1. *Chola,* a perjorative word used in Peru to refer to Indians, and mixed-blood children. The technical word is *mestizo.*

2. *Limeña,* a woman from Lima, Peru.

3. *La negra,* the black one; *papá,* Spanish for "Daddy."

4. This is a paraphrase of a line from T. S. Eliot's "The Love Song of J. Alfred Prufrock."

22

When East Meets West: Second Mothers and Abandoned Daughters

Shirley Geok-Lin Lim

As a writer, I have written on many topics. Turtles, crocodiles, shells, pianos, birth, death, insects, swimming pools have all appeared in my poems; and my short stories have mothers, fathers, farmers, teachers, blind men, drunk men, and all kinds of other characters. But I have never been able to draw upon the most traumatic experience in my childhood, my mother's abandonment of my family when I was eight and my unhappy isolation in my father's second family. The most painful of life's raw deals, the stuff that psychologists make hay of, is too close to home, to the damaged heart, for me to pick up.

But where the imagination cannot venture, a factual autobiographical piece may work. Hence I find myself submitting my unworked confusions, my still outraged self-pity and sitting-in-a-corner whining to a sociological perspective and making more sense out of all those sad years than I had ever intended.

My parents were Westernized Chinese Malaysians in a small town in Malaysia. He was a shoestore manager. Every month crates of canvas shoes, shiny men's leather shoes, and ladies' dress shoes arrived from England. This was in the 1940s and early 1950s before capitalism went east and began cheap production in Hong Kong and Taiwan. Only the middle-class and well-to-do shopped at Bata's then. The status conferred by wearing a pair of Bata shoes in our little town was somewhat akin to that given today to a pair of Guccis in Manhattan. She was English-educated, a minority among the townswomen who were either uneducated or had received a few years of Chinese education. When she was a young girl in the

1920s in Malaysia, access to an English education was limited, first by the small number of schools and teachers, and second by the dominant cultural ideology that girls intended for marriage were never intended for schooling.

I remember them as a couple who would have felt at home immediately in an American town. They loved the movies, and through my father's business connections they caught every movie that came to town. With two movie houses carrying English-language movies (and three others specializing in Mandarin, Cantonese, Tamil, and Malay movies), they were steeped in Hollywood lore. Our home was filled with filmstar pinups. Signed black-and-white photographs of Clark Gable, colored pictures of Errol Flynn in swashbuckler costumes, the very young Debbie Reynolds, even Francis the Talking Mule were familiar icons. My father, an avid reader, subscribed to movie magazines and a host of other Western periodicals. I remember studying immense Buicks and Oldsmobiles in the pastel advertisements of the *National Geographic*. And there was the phonograph, a crank-up box with a trumpet-shaped sound piece from which came the nicest music: "The Indian Love-Call," "Oh Rosemary," "The House of Bamboo," "Mockingbird Hill." My father loved to yodel, and he always sang while he took his shower. He had a little ukulele and he would strum it hard when he sang to us, which he continued to do until my second mother straightened him out.

Was ours a typical Chinese-Malaysian home in 1950? The description is nothing like the stereotypes that prevail even today of life in Asia, or life in the so-called Third World. We were middle class enough that my father drove a car, a Hillman. We had a refrigerator, a maid, and a tutor for unsuccessful Mandarin lessons. We ate ham occasionally for breakfast and spent Sundays on the beach reading the Sunday comics. I especially liked the Phantom with his purple bodysuit and black mask; my brothers preferred the Lone Ranger and Tonto. We spoke English in school and at home, and we read the movie magazines and Junior Classics comics. Yes, perhaps we would have all adjusted easily had we been lifted miraculously to Dayton, Ohio.

But we also felt miraculously at home in Malacca. Malacca was then one of the many outposts of the British Empire, having been taken from the Dutch in the eighteenth century, who had taken it from the Portuguese in the sixteenth century, who had taken it from native Malay rulers in the fifteenth century. Various shrines, temples, and churches still testified to the layers of cultural domination through the centuries: holy *kramat* (malay royal burial ground), ornately carved Chinese temples, a ruined Portuguese cathedral, a handsome red-stoned Dutch church converted to an Anglican parish. Asian and European stood together architecturally, and their dead lay under inscriptions of a myriad languages. Malacca provided historical models of cultural comminglings and hybridization that nurtured a spontaneous and embedded pluralistic consciousness. There were enough middle-class English-educated and Westernized Chinese Malaysians in our little town that we did not grow up with a sense of being cultural freaks. In the evenings my father drove us in his Hillman to the best ice cream store and we would sit in our nice clothes shoveling quick-melting corn ice cream into out mouths and keeping our eyes opened for other children, school friends, just like us.

Of course it was expensive to maintain an increasing family in a middle-class style. Ever an optimist, my father borrowed an enormous sum when his lifelong friend, the town's pawnshop owner, guaranteed him a 500 percent return on investment. In this Western-style story of greed, the pyramid inevitably broke down and we suddenly found ourselves destitute.

Now, in a traditional Chinese family, no one can ever be totally destitute as long as there are other relatives with something. It was proper and natural for my father to move his entire family into my grandfather's house. A large rambling building with many dark and small rooms on the second floor, the ancestral home was already shelter to the families of my grandfather's first, third, fourth, and sixth sons. Some families had two or three bedrooms, depending on the number of children. My third uncle had eight children, and they had three bedrooms. With four boys and a girl, my parents were given two rooms. The first floor of the ancestral house, however, was common property; we all shared the altar room, the courtyards, the receiving hall, the kitchens and bathrooms, and so on. As an individual family we were very poor, but as an extended family we still had family dignity and standing.

In the objective light of hindsight, it is clear to me that my mother found herself moved from a Westernized family structure with the private and autonomous pleasures of the middle class suddenly and violently to the traditional Chinese extended-family structure, with its absence of privacy and its rigid hierarchical placement of individual members. As the wife of the fifth son, her position in this tribal organization was among the lowest. Only sixth uncle's first and second wives ranked lower than she did. Moreover, as the wife of a failed son who had spent his patrimony, she had lost whatever "face" she had gained from his earlier business success. Even more than noncareer wives today, the Asian woman's status was (and continues to be) inextricably tied to her husband's job and social position.

In the female household her English education was held against her. The women, my aunts, were almost wholly Hokkien speakers. My mother, of assimilated Chinese background, was originally a Malay speaker who had chosen to become fluent in English, as it was the colonial language of prestige. She also spoke Hokkien (the most popular of the Chinese South Seas dialects) and Teochew, her parents' dialect. It was her very linguistic multiplicity that made her different from her conventional sisters-in-law and that, she realized, would permit her access to employment whereas they were necessarily unemployable. Language skills brought her future freedom, but they also led to her dissatisfaction and displacement in the narrow domestic sphere that my aunts ruled. Brought face to face with that other Asian reality, that seemingly regressive conservative Confucianist world of the Chinese partriachal extended family, my mother was a kind of Nora trapped not in a doll's house but in the dark shabby rooms of the ancestral home.

No true-born Chinese woman would have shirked her duties at this point. With five sons, a daughter, and a husband still employed, although at a much reduced salary (my father, forced to give up his store, had found work as a poorly paid shoe salesman), her path of scrimping, saving, and caring for us until such time as her sons would be able to go out to work and support her in their turn was foreordained in Chinese culture. Every woman lucky enough to be married and with the tremendous good fortune of possessing five sons might perhaps have complained about the hard knocks of poverty, but she would have submitted to her fate.

We were Westernized in taste, but there was never any doubt that we were Chinese in tradition. Until the business losses, we enjoyed a kind of bicultural ease that allowed us to respect our elders, to observe the elaborate rituals of ancestor worship, and to think simultaneously in diametrically opposed ways without any sense of strain. We studied the laws of physics, yet maintained our profound belief in spirits without a pang of skepticism, just as we continued to enjoy salted apricots after having been introduced to Cadbury's chocolate bars. It did not appear then a matter of either/or but of both together at once.

But the retreat to my grandfather's house was a return to a largely monocultural and Asian society. The large house was dominated by the altar room with its huge teak and mother-of-pearl—ornamented two-tiered altar table. Grainy black-and-white portraits of my grandfather and grandmother were mounted above the table, and an enormous brass urn full of joss ash usually contained a stick or two of burning joss. We children called our elders by their respective titles in terms of their birth rank in the extended family. Uncles, aunts, and cousins of higher rank than us received honorific titles; they in turn addressed us with lower titles. Oldest son of number-three uncle, therefore, was a highly esteemed individual, regardless of his actual lackluster school performance, while second son of sixth uncle was to be ordered around or ignored. The men left the house each morning, and the women cleaned, washed, and cooked the meals.

My mother had escaped the narrowness and tedium of Chinese social life through my father's short-lived wealth; she had had an independent household; had, in fact, always helped with the shoestore and waited on customers herself. It must have appeared to her that she had suddenly stepped back a century to a social world where women were confined to their husbands' ancestral house and to the grinding boredom of domestic work. There is a nostalgia in the contemporary search for cultural roots that romanticizes the actual oppressiveness of long-stagnant social structures, especially the oppressive positions of women in patriarchal and tribal societies. My mother was a new woman who, having once tasted Western middle-class pleasures, could not adapt herself to the traditional bonds and bondage of the Chinese extended family. Perhaps all those glittery scenes from slick Hollywood shows preyed on her imagination; perhaps the Western ideology of the individual and the pursuit of happiness in now long-forgotten movies such as *Annie Get Your Gun* and *Back Street* had steeped her dreams and weakened her cultural and maternal roots. When she fled the old mouldering house and the small town, it is instructive that she went to the big city two hundred miles away, the largest and most Westernized urban center at hand—Singapore, home base to the British army and navy, temporary port to every wandering sailor, and shopping paradise to Southeast Asia. Like Nora, she found a duty to self more sacred than duty as a mother or wife. She chose the life of freedom and individuality long before Betty Friedan woke up from her suburban sleep.

My mother's abandonment left her children with no protection in an Asian society. While my father's financial fecklessness embarrassed us all, my mother's unthinkable flight put us beyond the pale of acceptable society. Under the judgment of stern Chinese morality and Anglo prudishness, stained by our parents' sins, we became invisible in the town. Where once we went as a family to visit other families, we were never to venture out as a family again. My brothers and I were like wild animals, fending for ourselves, making strange liaisons with other children outside the familial circles. Occasionally when a classmate's parent met me hovering outdoors, an expression of pity and recognition would creep under an abstracted blank smile. No one asked me about my father or my mother. From notable citizens they had become worse than nobodies, both social disgraces to be uncomfortably ignored. It was almost inconceivable that we were still living in a small community surrounded by my father's childhood friends, my mother's bosom companions. Our situation was closer to that of migrant workers who had put up a shack on the wrong side of the tracks.

When my father finally took a second wife a year later, I was delighted. Finally, I thought, I would have a mother who would sew me dresses, cook regular meals, and give me affection. Under the influence of my English education, I thought of her as my stepmother. I hoped for love from her, and when I saw only indifference, it was easy for me to cry and think of Cinderella and her cruel stepmother. I was an impressionable eight-year-old, and Western fairy tales were more vivid to me than my daily life of suffering and hunger. Thus, for years I have seen my father's second wife, based on Western models of stepfamilies, as the stereotypical wicked stepmother. Didn't she have my puppy destroyed? Didn't she complain of my behavior every night to my father? Didn't she have me in the house and not say a word to me for months at a time? The list of hurts and wrongs extends deep into the night.

But again in hindsight it is clear to me that my father's second wife had never set herself up as a second mother. Her social models were completely alien from mine. Chinese-educated, she was as unfamiliar with the witchy stepmothers in *Cinderella, Snow White,* or *Babes in the Woods* as I was with the Confucianist ideal of the good woman contained in the Analects. She did not see herself as a stepmother whose role was to replace my mother's absent attentions. She would have been morally revolted by the notion of stepmothering as an active taking on of maternal duties for children belonging to one's husband's first wife. To do that would surely be to overstep the proper boundaries between social unequals.

My father in fact had never legally divorced my mother, and had married the second wife outside of British civil law. They had married under traditional Chinese custom, with the exchange of gifts and the tea ceremony kept to a minimal ritual as the groom's parents, my grandparents, were both dead by now, and my father's second wife had only a mother and brother as living relatives. She was his second wife; her duty was to him and to the second family they would have. We were still the children of his legal first wife, and it was only because the first wife had chosen to abandon her children that the second wife was compelled to care for them.

In traditional Chinese society, a man was allowed to have as many wives as he could maintain. If he married each wife in Chinese custom, he was legally recognizing his financial and social obligations to each, without giving up the claims of the previously married ones. Thus, it was possible for a man to have four wives, if he could maintain support for them and if through the ritual ceremony he recognized their legal claims on him. Every child born out of these relationships was legitimate and could claim an inheritance. But the first wife had the highest legitimacy. Her children, especially her sons, were always seen as the first heirs, and her legal rights over the claims of the other wives were always upheld under Chinese law.

Because of the legal disadvantages involved in apportioning the rights of second- and third-wife families, Chinese women preferred to be first wives even though husbands usually were more sexually bound to second and third wives. And it was usually the very rich Chinese man who had two and three wives. The average man, it was generally known, had mistresses who received no social standing and were fairly expensive, but not as expensive in the long run as keeping a second family. Of course, if a mistress presented a man with a child, especially a favored son, the chances were that the man would legitimize the relationship by making her a second wife.

My father, perhaps to evade the expenses of a legal and difficult divorce, most probably so as not to disinherit the claims of his children from the first marriage, chose to remain a Chinese in his second marriage. It was to his advantage to abandon the proprieties of Anglo-Malaysian society, based on British civil law (and in which his actions had already made him a pariah) to return to the more flexible marital organizations of Chinese custom. As a bankrupt businessman beginning a new career as a legal aide (he was called a petition writer then), it was unlikely he would have been able to attract a Westernized English-educated woman to be his second wife. He married a young uneducated Chinese woman of low social origin intended for life as a domestic maid, to whom the position of a second wife to such a man was still a social step up in the world. She neither read nor spoke English, observed the ancestral worship days of her husband's parents religiously, was satisfied to clean, wash, and cook daily, and had no ambitions beyond raising her own children to successful adulthood. Never having known a middle-class, Westernized life, she had no yearnings for individual expressions of private pleasures. She was devoted to my father and did her duties in caring for our meals and clothes with remarkably little resentment. We always remained for her the children of the first wife, and she made no attempt to reach us emotionally.

Had our mother remained with us, that social arrangement would have been meaningful. She would have provided us with the affectional bonds we needed. Children of first and second wives did not normally see themselves as stepchildren but as separate families with the same father. Their mothers defined their legal and familial identities. But our Westernized mother was working as a salesgirl in the largest department store in Singapore, while our Chinese second mother was caring for our physical needs at home. In our personal lives, the disparate cultural elements of East and West were disrupting our emotional and psychological selves, and the usual misery rising from the core of helplessness, which is the essential sensation of childhood, was compounded by these larger social forces of Asian modernization.

All stepfamilies have problems of adjustment, of individual resentments, losses and gains. My childhood, however, was spent in a cultural limbo between Western and Oriental values and ways of experiencing. It has taken me all these years to recognize the sharply ethnocentric character of my second mother's behavior toward her husband's first family, thus releasing me from the futile cycle of blame and hatred. It will take me a longer time to forgive my Westernized mother for acting on her ill-learned notions of liberty and the pursuit of happiness. Surely between the overwhelming needs of children for stable and nurturing mothering and the woman's emerging sacred duty to herself, some kind of balance and harmony can be struck, a balance beyond ethnic differences, beyond cultural divergences, to a universal feminist principle.

Had I been myself less influenced by Western ideas of individual happiness, I probably would have been less intensely miserable. Had I been a Chinese-educated girl, I would have taken my place beside my stepmother in the kitchen to help her cook those enormous meals for a huge family; I would have cleaned house and done the laundry in preparation for the time when I too would be a wife and mother with these responsibilities. Instead I was a little English school scholar, my sex in no way interfering with my ability to win academic prizes and scholarships. I sought escape from the drudgery and prisonment of marriage through my studies, determined never to marry, never to have children, always to be economically and socially independent, an ambition unthought of for women in traditional Chinese society.

My mother had led the way. I followed, beyond Singapore to New York. But my second mother's domestic devotion, unvalued then, has also followed me. In my pursuit of career and prizes, I keep stumbling over Asian pieties: the husband and son first, the family as supreme value, the woman for housework, ancestor worship that keeps pulling me back eastward, away from America. Both East and West have perfidious values; both have ideologies that energize me. I will just have to make the best of these collisions in my life.

23

What Really Is a "Normal" Family?

Erin Marie Hettinga

My family. Strange—well, you could call it that, but I like to think of it as different and unique. My mother, my eighteen-year-old brother, and I moved to California from Iowa. We did this so we could live with my stepfather. We are all white, but my stepfather is black. Also living with us is my stepfather's granddaughter. She is ten years old and also black. I refer to her as my younger sister, yet she really isn't. Many white people in this country believe my family is abnormal and strange, but I don't. I don't remember when it was no longer strange; it could have been before or after Tameka's arrival.

My stepfather, Charles, lived with us in Iowa for two years, and for the second year his granddaughter, Tameka, lived with us. The adjustments of having a little girl around twenty-four hours a day were tremendous. I was so used to doing things around the house by myself. Though she may be helpful, she can also be harmful. She is very interested in most everything I'm involved in. I love the attention, but sometimes it becomes over-whelming.

I remember that I never would refer to her as my little sister when she first lived with us, and I know that she wished I would. I always said she was Charles's granddaughter who lived with us. Now I have gotten so used to her that I do call her my younger sister. One reason is that it is so much easier to say than "my stepfather Charles's granddaughter." There are some situations that can be really hard to cope with. One of them is that when my friends come by, they always comment on how cute or polite Tameka is. I know this is not always true. She can become a real devil if she wants to, but aren't most little kids?

So many incidents pop up unexpectedly about my family. Once after a track meet, a friend of mine who is black and on the boys' track team was bringing me home. He was worried what my parents would think if they looked out the window and saw a black boy bringing home their blond daughter. When I told him that my stepfather was black, he didn't believe me. I had to show him a picture to prove it. Now we are always joking about that day. I have another friend who just had her house redecorated in art deco colors like peach, lavender, and mint green. Whenever she comes over to my house, she always comments on how she wished that there were a room in her house, like our whole house, with African statues in it. This is interesting, because sometimes I wish that my house could be more like hers.

There is one holiday that reminds me of a United Nations meeting. This is Thanksgiving. It used to be held at Charles's house in Davis, California. Now we have it in Sacramento, at our friend Barbara's house. The reason that it reminds me of the United Nations is that Barbara is Japanese, Charles is black, we are white, and the rest of the group is a mixture of Chinese, Filipino, Chicano, and American Indian. The dinner menu includes sushi and rice balls for appetizers. Then we have goose, turkey, and southern baked ham, which our friend Rich will be happy to know is the best of the three. Rich always travels from Chico, California, with his cooked ham in a backpack. The meal always ends with my mom's cheesecake and sweet potato pie. I forego the sweet potato pie because I haven't learned to like it; I prefer pumpkin pie any day.

My stepfather, Charles, has taught me about life and about living. He is always ready to help with history homework, fixing my bicycle, or just talking when I need someone to talk to, unless, of course, he is the middle of some crisis like cleaning up his own paperwork. It seems that whatever any of us do wrong, Charles can always think of a lesson to be learned from it and he is always looking on the bright side.

At the age of sixteen I have already lived through experiences that most people only read about.

Shortly after I wrote the above comments about my family, my stepfather died of cancer. My family life has gone through drastic changes. Tameka is no longer living with us, and so many people might think that I now have a fairly normal life. Yet how could it be normal without Charles? Though he was my stepfather, he was really my father for four years. I loved him, and I miss him so very much.

Stepgrandmothers

24

I'm My Own Stepgrandma

Juanita R. Howard

In 1962, at the age of thirty-four, I found myself, a black woman, trying to reorganize my life and manage some overall coherence. I had been separated from my first husband for about a year and had rather reluctantly decided to share my mother's home. I had no children and was planning a divorce.

I was also studying for my master's degree in counseling at Columbia University. And, simultaneously, after approximately eight years as a counselor in the New York City daycare system, I had resigned and was accepting a new position as a probation officer in the family court system. I could not know then how providential this move would be, because it was on this new job that I met Guy, my present husband. Since his responsibilities included processing new cases as they were brought into court, I consulted with him almost daily. Over a six-month period, we became better acquainted, and quite often we would find ourselves together in the staff lounge laughing and joking with other colleagues over a game of cards. During those times, I learned that he had been divorced for five years and had an eleven-year-old daughter, Kay, who lived with her mother.

The sadness and tension in Guy's voice made me aware that the divorce was very emotion-laden and freighted with structural animosities on both sides. His displeasures with the situation were amplified by the court order requiring him to pay alimony in addition to child support, even though his ex-wife was working at the time. Despite the bitterness, his ex-wife did permit his daughter to visit with him every Saturday. This had been an established arrangement for over five years. My stepdaughter-to-be was less than enthusiastic about me when we first met. Given the circumstances, I understood her discomfort.

During the three years that we dated, I always waited to be invited to go along on their Saturday visits, which entailed going to museums, shopping, or just walking around the city. I consciously made every attempt to react appropriately, saying the right thing and basically trying to be perceived as not unduly interfering. Of course, with little knowledge of Kay and less about the relationship between Guy and his former wife, my attempt at balance was very difficult. Mistakes were made. One day when the three of us were walking along Central Park, I attempted to lock arms with Kay and she pulled away. I knew there was a lot to be done to develop this relationship—timing is all.

In 1966, after my divorce was final, I married Guy and so became a stepmother. There was cautionary irony since both of my parents had remarried when I was about eleven years old and I found myself with a stepfather and stepmother. Although I used to brag to my schoolmates that I had two sets of parents, the reality was less than emotionally comfortable. My father tried to maintain his expected role, but had never managed to do so anywhere near satisfactorily. And before her remarriage, my mother in her turn was bitter over what she saw as her loss of my father to another woman. The relationships were painful for me, and my family involvements were at best the source of one embarrassment after another. Although my mother's bitterness and anger did not distill in me, I nevertheless felt uneasy with my stepmother—a feeling that, to the present, has never quite left me.

I also became the new daughter-in-law. I'm happy to say that from the beginning I have enjoyed a wonderful relationship with my in-laws. I have never felt a hint of reservation or anything other than amity toward me. My mother-in-law is still in civil contact with her former daughter-in-law, but we are careful to keep comments about her very general, for the most part.

After my marriage, I found that my stepdaughter was a bit more receptive to my overtures. Knowing that I am an academic, she sought advice about her school work. Unfortunately, she and her father were often locked in emotionally unproductive battles over her problems with mathematics. Most of those times I found myself moderating the terrible heat they generated. I realized that there were a lot of subsurface feelings between them being played out in those confrontations, something that I hoped I could productively channel. However, she spent the balance of her high school and early college years in New Orleans with her maternal grandparents, and our contacts with her were basically by phone or during short visits for holidays or some part of the summer vacation.

While attending college, however, Kay fell in love and decided to marry. The wedding took place in New Orleans. Her mother and maternal uncle attended. Her father and I did not. Although we never asked, we assumed our presence would have evoked too much tension. Consequently, we never physically met our son-in-law and only spoke to him on the phone a few times.

One year later our grandson was born. It is very difficult to describe the humbling joy that we all felt. There were many phone calls, and pictures were sent. He was beautiful. Visits were tentatively planned. Tragically, however, our grandson died, a victim of sudden infant death syndrome. It was a totally emotionally dislocating experience for us all. My husband's grief, in particular, was wrenching. And how could it be relieved, given the geographical and even greater emotional remove?

However, within the year, a new grandchild was on the way. Unfortunately, the accompanying news was that Kay and her husband were separating. She returned to her maternal grandparents' home. Working part time, she awaited the birth of her child.

Throughout all these years, my husband was the primary means of his daughter's economic support. He paid her tuition, sent her an allowance, and supported her financially in whatever other ways were required. He continued this support while she and her husband were students, including the continuing expenses for her education. When she took leave from college during her first pregnancy, he, in addition, was obliged to provide for her many financial "emergencies." He also felt obliged to provide for her even more frequent emotional crises with personal advice, which apparently she almost always rejected. As for me, my role with my stepdaughter changed to some degree, from academic adviser and part-time mediator to confidant, even while she was away.

On December 2, 1979, our second grandchild, Rachel, was born in New Orleans. This totally happy news was somewhat modified by the reality that my stepdaughter's marriage in the meantime had terminated. Now all the problems of single parenting had to be considered. Fortunately, Kay's grandparents were physically and mentally able to provide the immediate housing and emotional support that she and the baby needed. They had a place to live and my husband continued his financial help. His ex-wife (who was now remarried) began making plans for her daughter and new grandchild to return to New York and share an apartment.

This meant that my stepdaughter and her child would be in New York. The process of reestablishing relationships would begin again but with an added dimension—a grandchild. The reality of this new family member was joyous! My husband was excited. We had pictures of the baby and the anticipation was unbearable.

My anticipation was also anxiety-laden and generated a million questions. Paramount among them was whether I, after all these years, qualified for consideration as a grandmother. After all, the baby was coming to her "natural" grandmother. There were already the years of being a step-mother, all those feelings of being left out of the important times. Would the new configuration leave me yet another generation removed from important events?

They arrived in New York February 1980, and were met at the airport by the "real" grandmother and her husband. Over the next few days, we talked with Kay by phone and arranged to pick her and the baby up on the weekend for a Sunday visit.

On that Sunday morning we arrived at their apartment building at approximately 9:30 A.M. My stepdaughter was in the lobby, holding a white bundle in her arms. My husband went into the building. I could see him kiss his daughter. He picked up a carryall that contained the baby's diapers, etc., and they walked toward the car.

I actually didn't know what to expect. As they approached the car, I opened the door to greet them. Before I could get out of the car, Kay thrust the bundle into my arms. "Here," she said. "You might as well get used to it." We all laughed as she and my husband got into the front seats. As we drove away, I sat in the back seat with Rachel in my arms. I looked down into her face and a feeling engulfed me that I could not explain. I had never had a child and, although I had worked around children for over ten years and become attached to many, I had never been intimately involved with a child. The birth of our granddaughter was to have a tremendous impact on our lives, in general, and my husband's and my life in particular.

It was a strange but deeply gratifying day. Kay was obviously experiencing a deep depression over her separation and anxiety about her plans for the future. She and her father talked about her feelings, while I spent most of the time tending to the baby's needs. Of course, not having ever actually raised or physically cared for a newborn, I was apprehensive about all that had to be done. I listened to and wondered about every sound that Rachel made. I was given a lesson in the quick technique of changing a diaper. I had been around my friends' babies, and even engaged in feeding and diaper changing. But this was different. I was so self-conscious. And in light of the many statements about how Rachel's natural grandmother just whipped through these tasks (not said maliciously, I think), I decided to do what I thought I could do best: follow directions.

I had been in the process of improving my photographic skills, and on this first visit I began taking pictures of Rachel in every conceivable pose and situation, a practice I've continued.

We considered what I could be called by our granddaughter when she started to talk. Since my first initial sounded somewhat like our pet name for her, we tentatively settled on that. But it was not to be Grandmother or Grandma, or "grand" anything. My husband decided that he would be "Papa" because that was what he called his grandfather. We were surprised, however, when we learned that his ex-wife's husband was to be known to Rachel by his first name prefaced by "Papa." That discovery—and my granddaughter's emphatic statement when she was three years old that she "only had one grandmother"—let me know that serious instructions were being given to Rachel. I had never insisted to her that I was her grandmother, although I called her "my granddaughter" when introducing her. When she was five years old, she had begun the process of unraveling and understanding the relationships among the many people in her family. Testing them out, but also playing a game, she would announce that I was her mommy and my husband was her father and she was the baby. Now that she's seven (and a half), she has worked it out. And as our love for each other has grown, I am not disturbed when she says to people that I am not her grandmother but "J.J."

Fortunately, that love has been allowed to grow. I think that all parties' love for Rachel strongly dictated an otherwise absent understanding on all sides—circumstances that made it possible to extend collective nurture and implement plans to the direct benefit of the child.

My stepdaughter had found a job approximately two months after returning to New York. Between her mother and a babysitter, she was able to arrange adequate childcare. For the first two years, visits with our granddaughter were frequent but irregular. But Kay's visits to our house with the baby also got her away from her regular routine. Slowly, our relationships were growing in a relatively very positive way and we found ourselves doing things together that focused on Rachel's enjoyment. About the time my granddaughter became three years old, the visits began to take on a pattern: an all-day Sunday visit, with breakfast prepared by my husband, every two weeks. We showered our attention on Rachel, and on many occasions my stepdaughter would read the newspaper, watch TV, talk with us a while, or take a nap. Sometimes we would go for a drive or stroll through Greenwich Village, SoHo, or Harlem, attend street fairs, outdoor art shows, or visit friends and relatives to show off our granddaughter. In the Harlem community where my husband and I lived, all the neighbors became acquainted with my stepdaughter and Rachel. My status was certainly elevated in the eyes of women I knew, those married with grandchildren and those married but without children.

This new status carried with it many anxieties. For example, I was with my granddaughter in a neighborhood playground. While running, she fell and scraped her knee. I was upset, first because she had fallen and hurt herself (though not seriously) and also that it had happened while in my care. My stepdaughter was visiting us and she was in the house talking with her father. I felt inadequate, ashamed, and frightened that I would not be trusted to take my granddaughter out alone again. My childish but real concern was that her "real" grandmother would question my competence. I felt forever in competition and forever inadequate because of my "step" position.

However, there were individually rewarding moments. For example, while riding in the car on the way to their house, I would sit in the back seat with Rachel in my arms. We would look—no, stare—at each other throughout most of the ride, and then she would go to sleep. Most of the time I would hum a tune and the motion of the car did the rest. Sometimes she would seem engrossed in the light patterns on the ceiling of the car or the reflection of headlights and highway lights flashing by.

Over these years after Rachel's visits, this still continues to be her favorite seating arrangement when we take her home, even though she is now too tall to lie comfortably in my lap. But we try, as the position is still emotionally satisfying. As she grew older and taller, we began to pick out certain landmarks on the streets and the highway, a game we continue to play.

When our granddaughter was about two years old, my stepdaughter decided to continue her college education. The required change in her routine also affected the frequency of their visits, because Kay wanted to spend more time with Rachel on the weekends. We understood and offered no opposition. However, by the time our granddaughter was three and half, the biweekly pattern more or less resumed and has remained about the same. This regular pattern of visiting, however, meant that our plans began to revolve around when our granddaughter would be coming to visit. It was an every-other-weekend arrangement, to which we were all becoming accustomed. This was fine for my stepdaughter and for my husband. But it presented a few concerns for me. Several vocational changes had taken place for me and my husband. He had become an administrator and I had completed my doctorate and become a college professor. Each of our positions involved attendance at professional meetings. However, his meetings were generally during the week and usually during working hours. But many times the meetings that I needed or wanted to attend frequently fell on those weekends that my granddaughter was due to visit.

The first time this occurred, I didn't know what to do. What I did was resent the fact that I had to make that decision. Then I felt angry that I would have to deal with my husband's disappointment, and angry because the interposing event wouldn't be as important to him as it was to me. There was also our granddaughter's disappointment. At the age of four and a half, she looked forward to seeing us at the usual intervals.

But of course it worked out. My husband had already recognized that my involvement in academic and artistic activities imposed certain responsibilities and would have to be taken into consideration, along with our social life. When our granddaughter was younger, we were able to skip a weekend when neccesary. But when she was old enough to understand schedule alterations but not appreciate why they had to be made, I became concerned that she would feel rejected.

We also recognized that as our granddaughter was getting older, my husband would leave more of her care to me, in terms of reading stories, playing games, and so on. At first I resented not having a chance to take a nap or stop for a moment. I realized that I hadn't established a routine that included rest periods for me. Usually, while Rachel was napping, I was preparing for dinner. Or I had let her play too long and everything had to be concluded in a hurry, leaving me exhausted when we returned from taking her home. I was trying to do too much again. Trying to be the "perfect" stepgrandmother. I also realized that my husband was very cooperative, that most of my exhaustion came from tension and from "talking too much."

My main concern between the three- and four-year-old periods was discipline. In these seven and a half years I have physically disciplined my granddaughter only once. I've frowned, I've shaken her arm and raised my voice (not often), but I've never spanked her. I feel proud to be able to say that, because in the black community "spare the rod and spoil the child" is a sincere belief. But I have talked a lot, explaining and reasoning with her—so much so that my stepdaughter has stepped in to remedy the situation in the way mothers do.

I believe that my relationship with Rachel began to deepen during her weekend visits with us because that was when we really began to be on our own with her. In 1983, we moved to a new apartment and she began to spend every other weekend with us alone. Within our first year there, she had accumulated many books and toys that were kept in a special place in the den/library. So when she stayed over on "her weekends," she and I shared the hide-a-bed in the den. This meant that when we woke up on Sunday mornings, I could read her a story, play a game, or talk about whatever interested her without disturbing Papa, and he could start breakfast without disturbing us.

I had never slept with a small child—or any child, for that matter. I can tell you that sleeping with this particular four-year-old was an experience. She either pulled the covers or tossed them off, threw her legs over me, and woke up early. And I spent many nights covering her up or trying to cover myself. Now that she's seven and a half some of that has changed. She is a little less restless and I have learned to sleep a little deeper and longer. And once my husband arises, she gets up and talks with him. During those talks he gets her washed and helps her brush her teeth, and she'll read one of her books or watch a favorite video. But mostly, she comes to see if I'm awake and ready to get up. If I'm not, she'll talk to me until I give in.

"Sleepover" is a time of "getting to know you," which includes many things. You get to know yourself. You want to be the grandmother, but what does that mean? Yes, there is some permissiveness. Your stepdaughter says, "You let her do things that she doesn't do at home." Or, "I don't let her do that: she knows better." So who do you please—yourself, the mother, the child? And what about Papa? Well, Papa and I talked about discipline, controls, and limits. Although I sometimes let Rachel express herself too much, we have struck a fairly good balance. We found that a better balance was maintained when she visited alone. Our house became her house, sometimes a Disneyworld. And our trips became, and are still, special. And I felt that all my efforts had paid off the first time I heard the words "I love you, J.J."

What I have come to realize is that my role has become more defined as my relationship with Rachel has become more meaningful and secure. Our relationship has influenced the relationship between my husband and his daughter. She has observed him with her child, playing, hugging, kissing, talking—a role she had never seen him perform and did not remember from her own childhood. Her marital and parental experiences have made Kay see her father from a different and more positive perspective. His role as grandfather (he looks too young to be a grandfather!) has also elevated his status in her eyes.

The second significant event that helped me feel more secure in my role was the time my grandaughter cried when I attempted to leave the apartment to attend a meeting. But the third event, a year later, was more satisfying: she waved goodbye and returned to her drawings when I left to attend another meeting. I learned from that that neither a child nor an adult has to be engaging you every moment as an expression of love. That usually happens when one feels love is being withheld.

My granddaughter has brought me a great deal of happiness. She has made me reevaluate my feelings and ideas about love. She has established for me a more definite role in relationship to her "real" grandmother and my stepdaughter.

Recently, Rachel asked me if I loved her and I said, "I do." Then she wanted to know if I would love her forever, even after I had died and gone to heaven. I said I would—and I will.

25

From Dutiful Daughter to Stepgrandmother

Judith Hocking Higgs

I grew up in the northern panhandle of West Virginia in the 1940s and 1950s, a time when "stepmother" was something Cinderella had. In my neighborhood, everyone had one mother (who stayed home), one father (who went to work), two to four grandparents, and seven or eight siblings. There were few divorces and fewer second marriages. Upon graduation from the Catholic high school, my friends and I followed the expected patterns: some went to college, most got married, while a few of us entered the local convent to begin our lives in the ministry of teaching or nursing.

After spending thirteen years in the religious community as a student and then a teacher, I requested a dispensation from my vows and was married at thirty-two to a widower who was father to fourteen offspring. His oldest son was six months younger than I; the youngest, a daughter, was twelve.

The children at home (four at the time) needed a mother, and I was excited at the prospect of my readymade family. I had known several of the younger children from school and from the folk choir at church, and genuine affection had grown through the years. I looked forward to the challenge of organizing a household where hundreds of dark socks were stored in one large dresser drawer for all the boys to use. I knew I would have to learn to cook, but I thought I could do better than "hot dogs, baked beans, and potato chips"—their usual fare. I didn't want to just care for the children as a mother would, I wanted to *be* their mother. After the honeymoon, however, real life would finally begin . . . and it's taken over ten years to recover. My years as a dutiful daughter and a celibate sister taught me how to keep house, pray, teach, write, balance a budget, counsel my students—but nothing prepared me to be a stepmother.

After our June wedding in 1975, the first ten months of our marriage were spent in the big turn-of-the-century home on 36th Street in the North End of Parkersburg, West Virginia—the home where most of my husband Harry's children had been born and reared. It was the year of firsts for our new family: our first (and only) canoe outing down the Little Kanawha River; our first family vacation (a weekend trip to Columbus, Ohio); our first preparation for a new school year; our first Thanksgiving and Christmas.

We had fun-filled times and normal family hassles. I learned to cook; the children taught me where the broom was kept and which socks belonged to whom. The family handled my novice attempts in the kitchen with politeness and tolerance—except they refused to eat bread pudding and summer squash with stewed tomatoes. (Could anyone blame them?)

In September of that first year, my younger sister (who had stayed with us for the summer) went back to college, and it was a busy time for the rest of the household. Tom began his senior year in high school; Don left to board at a preparatory seminary; and Ann began her career at Hamilton Junior High. In a few months, David joined the Navy, and I went back to work part time at the local community college.

By Christmas of the first year, I knew what I wanted Santa to bring—a new house where there were no ghosts, my own home, a smaller house to fit our family of five. I wanted to determine where the broom was kept. I wanted to arrange the furniture and to live in a home that reflected my taste and color preferences. Within two months we had found the place, a story-and-a-half bungalow with four bedrooms. The new house was in the same school district, not far from the "old" neighborhood. It was perfect!

We moved in March 1976—the same month that the adoption was finalized. Harry and I had gone to court to petition my adoption of Don and Ann. (Since Tom had turned eighteen, he had not been included in the process.) The dream Harry and I had shared had come true. Although he had been very close to the younger children since his first wife's death, Harry wanted them to have a mother to care for them, to protect them, to be with them if something untimely should happen to him. So I now had not only a wonderful husband but two enthusiastic children. I was so thrilled when we received their revised birth certificates listing "Mother: Judith Hocking Higgs." Don and Ann bought me a terrarium, and the four of us went out to dinner to celebrate.

And then . . . "all hell done broke loose, honey!" The honeymoon ended. The party was over. Our neat world turned upside down. Nothing in our experience prepared us for the painful reversals of the next months and years.

The older children were hurt and appalled that we had sold the old family home. This was natural, since it was a great part of their childhood memories. It was the center of their "remember when" stories, the place where they grew up. It was the home where their mother lived . . . and died. It was the home where their Grandmother Higgs had lived with them until she went to be cared for in a nursing home. It was the home where Danny, their younger brother (Don's twin) had lived, and died of cancer at age twelve.

When we moved, some of the older siblings visited us. A few dropped in frequently. It has taken some of the others years to be comfortable in our home. I tried not to take their discomfort personally, but attempted to play the role of hostess/mother/cook at our family gatherings.

It was the adoption, however, that caused the greatest upset with the married siblings. They felt disapproval, confusion, resentment, maybe rejection. Perhaps their unresolved grief for their own mother's death, only four years previous, became mixed up with negative reaction to my desire to be a mother to Ann and Don. Even though I had developed personal relationships with most of them, I still cringed at being introduced as "my stepmother" or at receiving gifts addressed to "Dad and Judy." Wasn't I ever going to be more than "Dad's wife" or "Judy that lives with Papaw"—to quote Krista, granddaughter number four.

After our move and the adoption, my relationship with Don grew much as I had hoped and expected. A serious reversal, however, took place in my relationship with Ann, who was then thirteen. While I wanted so badly to be her mother, to teach her, and to model for her, she began to reject and oppose those efforts. She was reflecting the negative feelings of her older siblings, and at the same time struggling in those early teen years to find her own identity, and the "old" family seemed to become everything to Ann. The "old" family was an ideal one, and perhaps existed only in her imagination.

She called me "Mom" when we were alone and "Judy" when any other member of the "old" family was present—as she does to this day. She would act indifferently to gifts and clothes I bought for her. She began to resist with silent stubbornness the way I expected things to be done in the house. Later the quiet battles grew into screaming and mean arguments, with Dad, ever the peacemaker, trying to bring back calm and resolution.

The hurt and the pain came to a climax during the third Christmas we spent in our new house. I had begun working full-time, and we had extra money to spend on gifts, so I was determined it would be a special family

Christmas. We bought presents for everyone, decorated the house, invited all the in-town children and grandchildren for a Christmas Eve celebration. Laughter and chatter filled the house as Christmas songs were played on the stereo, and everyone enjoyed holiday snacks and drinks.

The small children tore into their gifts with much gusto and delight. The last gift to be presented—no, the second to last—was a guitar for Ann, resting in its red velvet-lined case. I foolishly thought that the expensive and special gift would somehow mend our relationship, that she would appreciate my motherly gestures. It was not to be.

In the midst of the merrymaking, Ann presented me with a letter and asked me to read it aloud in front of the family. I read it only once—and silently—but I have remembered the heartbreaking words: "Dear Judy, I hope you will understand, but I can never think of you as my mother, for I loved my own mother too much, and always will." I left the room and the celebration without responding.

Some years and many counseling sessions later, I began to deal with my frustrated ideals of motherhood. I learned much about myself as a woman, and began to be reconciled with what my role would be and would never be. While I was a member of a religious community, my identity was defined by the vows of poverty, chastity, and obedience. I knew who I was, a celibate person living in a community of women, dedicated to service. I lived by the Rule; there was little room for self-direction, self-interest, or self-development. A "good" sister had few possessions; she thought of others first; while she suppressed her sexual instincts, the good sister loved everyone, but she was a "special person" to no one. Unlike some of my restless peers, I embraced this way of living my womanhood. I was quite happy and committed to the celibate lifestyle.

After a semicloistered novitiate experience, I spent several years in college and in graduate school. I completed a master's degree and began teaching English at a new community college in Parkersburg, a hundred miles from our Wheeling motherhouse. In the late 1960s and early 1970s, many changes occurred in our community and in our church. I dressed once again in street clothes, and I became newly aware of myself as a feminine individual. I began to realize that I wanted to be a "special" person to someone . . . and then I met Harry.

After we married, my identity as a woman changed, as would be expected—dramatically. My life was no longer guided by a rule but by my expectations of what the "good" wife and the mother was to do. I would have described my role as that of Mrs. Brady in the television series *The*

Brady Bunch. She was the all-loved, all-loving mother of an active brood, the perfect mother and stepmother. She taught wisely, fixed broken toys and broken hearts, solved all their problems, and ensured that everyone lived happily even after. She was the object of adoration and respect of the entire household.

I soon learned that this ideal existed only in the realm of situation comedies. Although I worked hard at organizing our household and at establishing relationships with my husband's children, I began to realize that Mrs. Brady I wasn't. Harry and I began counseling with a psychologist who was interested in step-relationships. Through counseling, Harry and I learned to readjust our expectations of my role as mother to the children. We accepted the fact that, despite our good intentions, my role was different than we had predicted. As our understanding grew, I became aware that I need not depend on the response of others to find out who I am. I am a self-directed individual, and I am very much responsible for my own happiness and peace of mind. I have learned that Ann's positive response is not necessary to my fulfillment as a woman. I have begun to come to terms with my role as a stepmother, AKA Dad's wife.

As a stepmother, I am a friend to my husband's children, now all adults. I am a significant person in the lives of some of them. Carol is one of my best friends. I have been with Pete and Steve through personal crises, and they have done the same for me; Matt is close to me; he is the most like his father. Jim is my financial adviser; Tom was the first one to send me flowers on Mother's Day. Don is my joy and, at times, my frustration. I have been their listener, their coach, their support, their critic, teacher, sister, mother, resource, and grandma to their children.

And what about Ann? Ann moved out of our house the week after she graduated from high school. She lived with one of her brothers until she was married several years ago. I helped to plan her wedding, and as a Catholic deacon, her dad was the church's witness to her marriage vows. Over the past years, my relationship with Ann has become less strained and more peaceful. Past hurts have healed, and we can enjoy each other's company and caring concern of one woman to another. She is soon expecting her first child, and I look forward with great anticipation to the new baby.

In fact, one of the happiest facets of my newly found identity of stepmother is that of grandmother to the younger third of the Higgs grandchildren. Having grown up in a big family, I have always felt that babies and young children are a joyful part of family life. Our grandchildren have provided the opportunity I missed as a celibate adult to experience the fun and love and laughter that youngsters bring into a family. Since Harry and I were married, seven babies have been born, two children were adopted, and two new ones will soon be born into the family. To the young children I *am* "Grandma," for I'm the only Higgs grandmother they have known, and I love it. My relationship with the grandchildren warms my heart and has touched an instinct of motherhood that was dormant during thirteen years of religious life and frustrated in the legal imposition of parenthood by adoption.

I revel in buying Cabbage Patch Kids for brown-eyed Mandy and taking Brian and Doug for a Saturday treat at the local pizza place. I love getting Happy Grandparents' Day cards from Melissa and Crystal, and sharing my ladybug collection with Sarah Josephine.

My heart aches with joy when I remember how little red-haired Carrie raised her arms to "Mamaw" to be lifted up the step into the dining room. Two weeks later Grandpa and I waited in the hospital corridor during her surgery for a congenital heart defect. We were there to make the sign of the cross on her sweet face after she died. Even though my name was included in her obituary only as her parents' afterthought, I'll always be the one Carrie called "Mamaw."

Today, being Grandma has become an important part of who I am. I am a satisfied person, a maturing career woman, a happy wife. Harry and I live alone and enjoy each other. We have lived through the past twelve years and have learned much about growing, about the importance of setting goals for ourselves, and about depending on ourselves. No one twelve years ago recognized our unrealistic expectations about the adoption and instant motherhood. Although we had to live through those years of frustration and dashed expectations, together we look forward to the coming decades with delight.

Part II

Stepping Out

26

Choosing Consciousness

Elizabeth Kamarck Minnich

In thinking about being a stepmother, I find that my first impulse is to explore what is hard about it. My need, though, is not just to complain; it is to be understood. I find myself fiercer about the lack of simple personal understanding I get as a stepmother than just about anything else. And for some reason, I start seeking the understanding I crave by expressing my hurt and anger. I don't know why; that is not my style of choice. Perhaps I do so because I am not expected to.

The present stereotype of stepmothers does not seem to be that we are mean, but that we are noble—probably wrong-headedly so. People look at me with something akin to awe when I tell them that I live with three children who were one and a half, nine, and eleven years old when I arrived. I feel often as if what I am supposed to be is tired, but strong and unwilling to show it; exploited by husband and kids, but uncomplaining— a mother, that is, but with the particular suspect nobility that goes with mothering someone else's children. People look at me, standing there saying right out loud that I am a stepmother, and, while they go on smiling and making eye contact, they stop hearing me. I can only guess what goes on in their minds from what they then say, but here is my guess: They wonder about the "real" mother; they assume I mother only part time (not true; two of the three are with us all the time, and the third about half the time); they think the kids' father must be absolutely wonderful (or diabolically clever, or both) or else I wouldn't have taken on so much; they picture me cooking, cleaning, washing clothes and (rightly) can't fit that picture with the me they know; they wonder if I have sold out my feminism, or at least made compromises with it; they assume that either my work or my care for the children is being slighted. One friend, on hearing about the children involved in my then-new relationship, said, "But, Elizabeth, you're so *urban*."

That kind of scrambled perception on the part of friends can be tiring as well as amusing. The problem is that it can close off the possibility of talking about the more constant sensitivities that barely cover real vulnerabilities.

I am vulnerable to the children, with whom nothing can be considered safe or established, and who not only have doubts that I will stay but who test to see if I can be made to leave. I am vulnerable, too, to the world of neighbors and schools and doctors and other parents that children connect us to whether we want to be connected or not. I must deal all the time with assumptions and expectations on their part over which I have no control. If I am not a mother (without prefix), then who can I possibly be and what rights can I have to be concerned for the children? I had serious difficulties getting into the hospital to see our oldest when he had appendicitis. Every time I go to the doctor, dentist, or school with one of them, I have to explain who I am and then wait to see whether or not they are comfortable with stepparents. One teacher regularly looks confused when I arrive at school to pick up the youngest child, and then, not knowing what else to say, calls across the room to him, "Your ride is here." If I'm not a mother, then I'm a ride. Silly, but it makes a difference to the child, and to me, to hear, "X, your mom is here" and "Y, your ride is here" in all sorts of variations, day after day, year after year. And I am vulnerable to the children's biological parents, both of them—whatever the relationship between them, whatever the relationship between me and my parent-partner—because the claims of birth parents have a primacy that a stepparent's do not. The birth parents may be divorced, may have ended any significant personal relationship, but they are the parents and I am always a step away. Relations with in-laws are nothing compared to relations with ex-wives, ex-husbands, ex-parenting partners.

Being a stepmother means *negotiating* relationships, from those with ex's one hardly knows to those with children one loves, and negotiating them constantly. Clichéd though it is, getting through a week as a stepmother is like skating on ice that threatens, but in shifting places, to be too thin. When things are fine with the children, trouble arises because of the ex; when things have settled down with the ex, trouble arises with the school; when there seems to be no trouble, anxiety bubbles up from the psyche: Who am I? Why am I here? Can I do this? And through it all, there is the high tension, the joy, and the fear, of love.

When you move in with someone who has children, there is neither time nor space for a honeymoonlike period, and no time at all for easing into loving the children. No nine months to be expecting, no years of physical care to create the most intimate of bonds. There they are, and there you are, and suddenly, there is to be love between you. But what kind of love? In my experience, being a stepmother means loving the children more than our society expects ("Isn't it wonderful? She's not even their real mother!"), less than we (who usually try too hard) fear the children need, and often both more and less than we can accept because it hurts to love unreservedly when you are always a step away from being the "real" thing.

Stepparenting is nothing if not uncertain. There is nothing given in these relations—nothing of biology, nothing of history, nothing of social conventions and clear expectations, nothing of religion, nothing of any political ideology I know of. Nothing. There are old negatives hovering around the Wicked Stepmother figure, but those seem to the conscious mind, at least, too extreme to constitute a challenge; it is easy to feel virtuous compared to them.

Still, the conscious mind is early revealed as a rather inadequate source of understanding for stepmothers, which is hardly a surprise. Thinking about the Wicked Stepmother image, I have found what I think underlies at least some of the vulnerability in being one, and why I find the role hard. To be as well as to have a stepmother is to experience a radical contingency. To get a Wicked Stepmother, one's mother must leave or die, one's father must remarry, and a new woman must move in. (Obviously, I am starting here only with the culturally admitted stepmother role in which she is a new *wife;* there are lots of other ways for children to have a new significant partner in their and their parent's life.) At base, the stepmother is felt to be wicked because *any* replacement of mother is frightening. I believe the human fear of contingency is starkly revealed in stepmother stories. It is in the fear the child in all of us carries, the fear of loss of mother—which is powerfully mirrored by the fear mothers have of the loss of a child. The stepmother, after all, literally embodies loss. Hers is not and cannot be the body of the child's deepest memories; her simple being there marks its loss.

The contingency that stepmothers live is multifold. We are reminders that children cannot count on having both birth parents with them always and through everything. The stepmother symbolizes the reality of a contingency given in human life and so, I think, frightens all of us—maybe even, maybe particularly, stepparents ourselves. Maybe that is why so many of us find ourselves working far too hard at being mothers. We are trying to make loss all right, for the children and no doubt also for our own childselves.

At the same time, having a stepmother also forces another difficult recognition: mothering is done by particular individuals. When we always have with us the woman who gave us birth, one of our struggles is to individuate her, to remove the person from the magic miasma of her mothering. Until we can see her individuality, we have trouble finding our own, for her status as the Great Mother requires ours as the Child in the mythology constituted not only by the dominant culture within which we live but also by our own most inchoate feelings. The stepmother speeds up that painful but empowering process of separation. The children meet a stranger called "Elizabeth," or whatever, not "Mother." She is unfamiliar, in the true meaning of the word. Children are then forced to know that their mothering comes from an identifiable individual separate from them on whom they are nevertheless dependent.

One way to deal with the fear and anger that all individuation arouses, but perhaps particularly that forced so abruptly, is for stepchildren to find fault with the substitute mother they did not choose. It is *her* individual failing that their parenting is not perfect. That is easier than facing the reality that needs are limitless, that no parenting can be perfect, that we all grow up restlessly yearning for a relation no real human can fill, that we both delight in and resist our separateness. And it is easier to be angry at the stepmother than admit feeling left by the birth mother. Stepmothers make it easy for children to deal with their ambivalence: mother is good, stepmother is bad—or the reverse, which is no more honest or stable a judgment. It is very hard indeed for stepchildren to love their stepmother without an admixture of anger, guilt, or anxiety.

And the love of stepmothers for their new children may also be ambivalent, in part because we share the primal fears of loss of Mother and the frustration of having been imperfectly parented. On top of that which is reawakened as we struggle for acceptance and love, though, there is a further complication.

Stepmothers are thrown suddenly into an experience of a kind of love that is unlike any other. To love children is to love without reasons, because children, who can give us more reasons to love them in five minutes than many adults ever can, and just as many reasons not to love them, call forth a different sort of love than adults. They are always more than they are, tumbling into the future with every fast change as they do. Our love seems to search through any particular way they are at any particular moment to find something more essential to recognize, to anchor in. Their charm is not the reason for the love, it is the invitation for it to go searching for something deeper. But what is there to find that is deeper? It is mysterious and elusive, what we find to love in them through the generic charm of children, but it does have something to do with a particular self. It also has to do with our physical relation to them, to the intensity of bonding that physical touch does indeed establish, and it has to do with their need of us, and with the ways they touch our own deep memories of being so needy, and our own hurts and betrayals as well.

We never love because of reasons, of course, but in the case of children and parents, reasons become patently irrelevant. However, for birth parents that unconditionality of the love for children can at least seem to be anchored, for example in identity: "she is my daughter" is a simple statement of a very, very complex intertwining of identities. Stepmothers, in loving the children, also come to do so unconditionally while always being aware that theirs is a contingent, ever-negotiated relationship with no clear anchor at all.

And as though that were not complex enough, there is often also the "real" parent to contend with, someone who is going to have complicated feelings about this new bonding. More than one stepchild has been told, directly or indirectly, by her or his biological mother that the stepmother is *not* to be loved, not to be trusted, not even to be liked. Such messages are always troubling to the child, who then withdraws from the stepmother, or clings to her, or becomes angry with her. Yet the stepmother may not know where the confusing behavior is coming from. Crucial parts of the child's life taking place in another home (when there is shared custody, or provision for regular visitation) make a difficult relationship even more so. And that, of course, can please the "real" mother, who is living not just with the knowledge that her child has another mother but with her own profound terror that she may lose the child.

To the stepmother, the world says, as she and the children struggle to believe in each other's possible permanence, in each other's care and trustworthiness, "Oh? They're not your *real* children?" To the birth mother, as she and the children struggle with fears of betrayal and loss, the world says, "Oh? Your children don't live with you?"

I love the three children with whom I live. That does not change the fact that at any moment of any day, they and I can be reminded that they have another mother. In their reactions to the letter or the phone call, I am reminded of how deep the old relationship goes—and how much a part of my relationship to them it is. From the perspective of a stepmother, I find it hard to understand how birth mothers can possibly worry about losing their children. I do understand, of course; I would have the same worry were I in their position. But it is also true that I know intimately how strong that bond is. I see it; I hear it; I feel it. And I know that I do not have anything like it, and never will.

I say to myself, " 'Real' mothers are the people who take day-by-day care of children, the ones whose lives are intricately involved with their children, the ones who keep the children safe, who wrestle with their souls and fight with them and love them and try to heal them and give up on them and give in to them. 'Real' mothers," I tell myself, "are the ones who do the mothering." But it doesn't work, and I now disagree with people who try to tell me I am the "real" mother. We have to live in the world we have, whether we like it or not, and in this one, people have one mother. I am not that one. I love, I hurt, I try, I fail, I get angry, I do well and so do they, and I am not the one. Yes, that hurts. Yes, it makes me angry. I *am* vulnerable.

A birth mother can have been out of the children's lives for the majority of those lives, can have not raised the children by her own choice or as a consequence of her own chosen actions, but she remains the one people mean when they ask about the children's mother, and she remains in their lives. Even if she wants nothing to do with the children, she is in their lives, in our lives, at the very least as a symbol with which they and others can conjure the most powerful of feelings: of desertion, of loss, of longing, of anger, of hope, of guilt. It is that reality with which stepmothers live. There is no changing it and it is hard to accept it.

Their birth mother suffers too. I know from noncustodial mothers who are my friends that guilt is a powerful force in their lives no matter how necessary their choice was, no matter how clear they were and are about it. They miss their children, the dailiness of mothering, and they, too, suffer from a kind of social stigma that cuts, and deeply. While stepmothers hear, too often, "You're not their *real* mother?" the "real" mother hears, "You left your children?!" and she cringes.

Nor are these difficulties we each face only our own: we are, in such experiences, pitted against each other. I fear that is almost unavoidable in this world as it is. She fears that her children will forget her, or hate her, and she tries to do what she can to hold on to them even long distance. And then we, the stepmothers, must deal with what she does as it affects the children. It is hard not to resent her efforts; they lead so directly not only to painful emotional upheaval for the children, but to renewed ambivalence about us.

It is possible for her to support the children in coming to love us; it is possible for us to support them in continuing to love her; it is possible for all of us to learn for ourselves that love, even for mothers, need not be exclusive. But it is hard for all of us, and we slip often into far less comfortable, far less admirable behavior.

I feel much more kinship with those who have borne children now than I ever did before I became a stepmother. I am very grateful indeed for the bonds it has allowed me to discover with women with whom I might otherwise have very little in common, and the deepening of my relationship with others who were already friends. We share many experiences, and, through talking about those we do not share, we have often come to know our different situations more clearly.

It is, I believe, in this weave of common and different experiences—including experiences of conflict—that some of the mysteries that still enshroud the real experience of motherhood as personal experience and as institution can be found. My focus on the sensitivities, the vulnerabilities, of stepmothers points me toward a particular set of issues, of course. The works of feminists that seem to me most like those I would like to see about these issues are, I find, those now emerging about sexuality. In parenting, as in sex, the sheer power of the physical, psychological, political formation of who and how we are rises to the surface and confronts us. To carry out an analysis of why we feel as we do with personal as well as intellectual honesty, to try to live according to chosen values is never so difficult as when one's own deepest needs, and so most powerful pleasures and pains, are involved. I have heard parents of all sorts admit their inability to act with their children as they wish they could, as they are quite sure they ought to, just as I know many have (on occasion, at least) wished to reshape sexual desires and pleasures to suit principles more closely. The knot of principle, practices, pleasures, and pains in these areas seems to me to point toward areas in which our thinking is most called for just as it is most difficult.

It is easier to think oneself free of the dominant culture than it is to free one's feelings. Our feelings can betray us. Our feelings are also among our clearest guides and sharpest prods to keep going, to keep working. It is that emotional paradox, as well as all I have said about the vulnerability and contingency of the stepmother relationship, that keeps me thinking about my situation—our situation. Yet often I get stuck.

As a stepmother, I have been badly stuck on the *singularity* of Mother. I wonder where that singularity comes from. I can't get it. It is a social construct, of course, one that appears in all sorts of books and television shows and stories and everyday assumptions. It seems also to be downright religious: there is a depth to the belief that we should all have one real mother who should answer all our needs that defies my understanding of socialization. Birth mothers suffer from it; they feel an almost unbearable responsibility for their children that is utterly unrealistic in the best of circumstances. None of us feels as if we had perfect mothering, and we suffer variously from its deprivation. Why? Where does this craving for something no one has had and no one can give come from?

Is its depth the result of the intensity of physical bonding that takes place before, during, and for a while after birth? Is that bonding really so deep, so primal, that no amount of counterexperience can temper it? Is it the emotional as well as physical bonding that takes place before language, before conceptualization, and so defies any future effort to mediate it? Is it a given of the human condition because of the physical or emotional bonding from birth, or because of some species programming or tribal memories or instinctual provision?

It is hard indeed not to look for some ground for our craving that feels as primal as it is. No wonder we turn to nature, those of us who do not turn to religion for supra-social explanations. But that, of course, lands us in the all-too-familiar nature versus nurture controversy, which has never interested me very much before. It has seemed to me evident that it is logically speaking a chicken-and-egg debate, one that can consume a lot of energy but get nowhere because the unspoken premise (that there was some one thing that came first and that caused what followed) is wrong. "Nature" and "nurture" are names we humans have given different aspects, or moments, of an infinitely complex set of interactions. We create them as separate concepts and then argue about how they relate. A waste of time, obviously. Yet now I find myself wondering whether the singularity of Mother comes from nature or from nurture, and caring passionately about the debate. Against all I know, I seem to want it to be one or the other.

I have long said that those who argue for explanations by nature are really against change. What is by nature, they have told us, must simply be accepted. Whenever we have questioned our lot as women, we have been told that it is "natural" in just that spirit. So what am I doing wondering if the primacy of the birth mother, enshrined within the insistence that there can only be one mother, is based on something "natural"? Perhaps I am trying to find a way to accept it more easily. And if it is by nurture? Then perhaps I could temper the hurt of the present with hope for change.

I know better. With humans we deal always with what has been made from what was given. We can always change, and there are always limits to that change. But now I surely understand better at least one set of reasons why the debate about which things are unchangeable because of nature rages on. For the first time, I find myself craving certainty. I begin to realize the privilege that must have gone into my much more familiar liking for uncertainty, my easy commitments to change.

And I suspect I am not at all alone in being troubled by the idea-passion of singular Motherhood; it has, after all, been used against us all, and that means we know it has some power in the world. If we are the mother of a child, at times the world gives us respect and some power over what is to happen to us, to the child. When I do not tell people that the children are my stepchildren because I want to bask in the illusion, in the acceptance, a mother gets, I am feeling some of that power. If they *were* my "real" children, would I be able to keep myself from accepting, using, even exaggerating the power I can get from claiming the mystery of Mother?

In a world in which we are so powerless, it is hard to walk away from power handed to you, however double-edged. And, of course, the power of the Mother is double-edged as well as severely circumscribed.

We have claimed what power we can get, and we still do so. I have known women to use all the mystique of motherhood they can muster in order to fight for what they want in a relationship, in a community, in the courts. I have seen birth mothers decide to use it to counterbalance the greater economic power the father usually still has, to use it to achieve not only some fairness but even to get revenge. Stepmothers have characteristically seen more of what biological mothers will do when hurt than we want to (I even know of one who tried to persuade her four-year-old son to start nursing again when she felt she was "losing" him). What power they can get by calling this hypocritical society on its supposed reverence for mothers has been used against us as well as against the fathers and the law. And when all efforts break down and decisions about children and who is to parent them under what arrangements are taken to court, however powerless the biological mother may be in that male-dominated system, stepmothers are more so. We have no standing whatsoever, nothing even of the society's hypocrisy to call on. Only occasionally are we considered, and then it is as part of the conditions offered by the father. Does he have a good income? A good house and neighborhood for children? Is there a school close by? Does the stepmother make a good appearance on the stand?

Such scenes are vicious and humiliating for everyone. The mother is on trial. Is she good enough? An impossible, terrifying question: is it possible for any mother to be good enough? And the stepmother is reduced to being an appendage, a condition of someone else's home. Women rarely win in any sense at all. The courtroom reveals the degree to which Mother is a construct not of our own making that continually haunts and continues to divide us.

I am very uncomfortable indeed with efforts, however well intentioned, to play on the power of mothers that derives from a patriarchal culture. Organizations like Mothers Against Drunk Driving and Mothers for Peace make me cringe. I would have been uncomfortable with them on theoretical and political grounds anyway; in addition to other problems, they certainly exacerbate the culturally created tension between birth mothers and other women. Is my opposition to drunk drivers and to war, or that of child-free women, less telling, less valuable, less credible? But can you imagine "Stepmothers Against Drunk Driving"?

But it isn't that I would prefer to be taken seriously as mothers are; the problem is that the terms on which all of us are taken seriously are unacceptable. We are "good women" when we fulfill prescribed functions defined in relation to men and to children: good wives, good mothers, good homemakers. That I hear "Your ride is here" rather than "Your mom is here" simply makes me confront my function as provider of services in a way that is less mystified.

I begin to realize that there is a way in which my peculiarly contingent relation to motherhood is not unlike the relation between being a feminist and being a woman. I am a mother in the mode of stepparenting; I am a woman in the mode of feminism. As a stepmother I cannot forget that I am not perceived as a "real" mother; as a feminist I cannot forget that I am often not perceived as a "real" woman. When I think about it that way, the degree to which both *woman* and *mother* have been defined biologically (that is, as woman's reproductive capacity is defined in a patriarchy, not in any neutral "scientific" sense) emerges with renewed clarity.

I no longer live as sharply with the desire to be a "real" mother as I did in my early years as a stepmother (it has been about seven years now). I am coming to realize that to be a stepmother is to experience what it means to be a woman in the dominant culture in a particularly intense way. To live as a woman is to live as an anomaly in a male-defined system. It is to live simultaneously as an insider and an outsider, as victim and as victimizer, as a category to ourselves and participants in other categories. In a sense, all women are step-humans, living daily subject to all that is prescribed for humans yet denied the status of the "real" humans: the privileged, heterosexual, able-bodied Euro-American men. Our being is contingent on much more than we control, and we feel that contingency in a terrible vulnerability. So it is with being a woman; so it is with being a mother; so it is with being a stepmother. Our states are similar even when forced into opposition, and different even when mutually understood. Most important, each sheds light on the other, perhaps particularly where we encounter the frictions between us.

My feminism, and all my work on feminist scholarship over almost twenty years now, does not solve the confusions with which I live as a stepmother. What it does do is to strengthen me in my ability to live with them, to keep struggling to understand them, to use my angers and hurts and confusions as calls to keep thinking and working. In a sense, both stepmothering and feminism keep me from sliding easily back into the roles for which I was socialized. For that, I am grateful. I would rather be conscious of my situation. As Hannah Arendt said, if we must choose between being pariahs (suspect outsiders), or parvenues (tokens whose loyalties are all with the insiders), it is best to be "conscious" outsiders. That way we can live in the world as it is without yielding to it. It is a struggle to become and remain conscious—neither feminism not being a step-mother has made my life easier. Both have held me to the task of thinking and feeling things through, even when it hurt to do so. But both have also given me moments, however fleeting, of clarity and so of a kind of free-dom, and both have been the source of friendship and love and support I cannot begin to measure.

Having plunged into thinking about what is hard about being a step-mother, I reemerge each time amazed at the complexity, fascinated by what that complexity calls us to understand, and, I hope, more able to avoid any of the easy "solutions." I would not be safer, more comfortable, more powerful, freer if I were a "real" mother or if I were child-free any more than I would be if I gave up my feminism and tried to be a "real" woman. No matter what choices we make or realities we face concerning our sex-ual life, our child-bearing capacity, our desire or lack of it to raise children alone or with others in all sorts of possible arrangements, we do so in a world in which we remain step-humans. Working together, perhaps we can change that world. In the meantime, we can and do find with each other moments of recognition of who we are and how we are trying to live that far transcend in their sharp, sweet reality the false promises of acceptance held out by the old world.

27

Cross-Sex Stepparenting: A Personal Essay

Kathleen Dunn

In the last twenty years there has been a series of revolutions in American families. In 1960 three-quarters of American mothers with children under six stayed at home, while today over half are in the workplace. Further, the growth of divorce and subsequent remarriage of many divorced parents means that today many parents and children are newly experiencing life as part of stepfamilies. According to the Stepfamily Association of America, 1,300 stepfamilies are formed every day in this country, with one child in five living at least part time in a stepfamily. What follows is one person's experience with stepparenting, and my analysis of that experience over a sixteen-year period. It is written with the hope that my experiences and mistakes might help new stepparents.

In 1966 I was separated from my first husband when I was twenty-six and my son, Tom, was nineteen months. I spent the next several years learning to be a single mother, head of a household, and a professional. I was lucky to live in a neighborhood just being built where I was able to meet young couples with children and was accepted into a neighborhood woman's support group that still functions today. This group provided friendship, support in child rearing, important knowledge about the community and school system, and surrogate mothers in case of emergency.

Shortly after my separation, I was also fortunate to get a part-time job as a supervisor of student teachers at a nearby college. I then became involved in the early stages of the women's movement both from my own experience as a single mother and through being asked to teach the "women's" part of a new history course, "Social Forces in American History." The reading I did to prepare for this teaching startled me. As a history major at a women's college, I realized that women—except for a few "great women"—had been left out of my education. From then to today, I have been an active member of the women's movement. By 1969 my part-time work had become full time, and I discovered that I especially enjoyed teaching late adolescents and young adults, helping them to make the transition from student to teacher. I realized that since I did not want to return to teaching junior high students, I would have to get a doctorate, while also earning enough to support my household.

In 1969 I also learned that another professor with whom I had worked on several projects, but had kept at arm's length, had separated from his wife. We began seeing each other shortly after his separation. We were married in late 1971 after Alex had gone through a very stormy divorce. He had separated from his wife just before his only child's sixth birthday. From the moment of his separation, he was determined to get custody of Bill, both because he was sure that he was the better parent and because he feared that his ex-wife's alcoholism and mental instability were bad for Bill. Although I felt empathy for his wife, knowing how important having custody of Tom was to me, I was appalled at his stories of his wife's treatment of Bill.

For the first year and a half of my involvement with Alex, I only heard about Bill, while Alex interacted regularly with my son, gradually assuming the role of father. (Tom's own father has always acted as a beneficent uncle.) Bill is only three months older than Tom, but he was six inches taller, thirty pounds heavier, highly intelligent, verbal, polite, and well behaved. Tom was small, quick, never still, with a high squeaky voice and major problems in school learning to read. In 1971 we held Tom back for a second year in first grade because of his reading problems and in anticipation of our marriage: we thought it best that the two boys not be in the same grade. Nevertheless, I experienced my greatest doubts about this second marriage around issues of parenting and stepparenting. Would Bill like me? He idolized his father and from reports appeared to fear his mother. Could he make room for another person as a parent in his life? How would Tom react to his stepbrother? Would Bill's talents make Tom feel even more inferior or stupid than he already did because of his reading problems, diagnosed by 1971 as dyslexia? Alex was also critical of my parenting of Tom; he felt that I overprotected him and wasn't strict enough with him. Both criticisms had some validity, but that didn't make them any easier to hear, especially since Alex seemed like a perfect father to Bill and was also terrific with Tom.

I wrestled with these issues—complicated by the fact that marriage would not solve financial issues since more than half of Alex's salary was going to his former spouse. I knew that I had to continue to work full time, but also had to enter a doctoral program in order to stay where I was teaching. At the same time, I was participating in the creation of a "blended family." In 1971 we had not heard of such a term, nor did we know much about stepparenting. We had both had difficult first marriages and now wanted to create a strong new marriage and a family. On an almost conscious level, we wanted to believe that our first marriages had not existed.

Despite some doubts, we were married in December 1971; the two boys were seven and eight. I entered a doctoral program, commuting eighty miles weekly to a state university, and continued full-time college teaching. Family life revolved around the twice-weekly visits to Bill, who lived thirty miles away. On Tom's ninth birthday in the spring of 1973, we received a phone call from Bill's mother's minister, asking us to pick up Bill immediately: his mother was in need of hospitilization for mental illness. We did so and immediately filed for custody, which was granted. Our goal at that time was to put together a family as close to "natural" as possible, with both of us striving to be a good parent to each boy. I think that we equated "good" with biological parent, and we did not confront the issue that we were not a biological family.

This goal turned out to be impossible. If we had had more realistic goals or some education in stepparenting at the time, our parenting and marital relations might have been much better. As I look back over the past sixteen years, I see some of the source of our problems in issues related to stepparenting and particularly cross-sex stepparenting, which I think I should have better understood at the time. In my case, the cross-sex stepparenting is between an adult female and male child. There are similar issues, complicated by the way our society conditions gender roles, when the adult is male and the child is female. Over the last fifteen years, because of the women's movement, more women than men may have thought through the meaning of male and female roles in this society. Thus they may have made more explicit to themselves the type of parenting they wish to do and the ways they hope to influence the development of their stepsons. Further, the stepfather/stepdaughter relationship may be complicated by the daughter's sexuality. The general expectation that men are usually attracted to younger women as well as the current explosion of publicity about girls being sexually molested may make a stepfather self-conscious in his legitimate efforts to show affection to a stepdaughter. Nevertheless, many of the issues raised in my story can be applied to cross-sex stepparenting of either stepsons or stepdaughters. Among the issues I found to be especially difficult are the good mother/bad mother syndrome, favoritism, parents' differing values about achievement, the meaning of family, expression of affection, and feminism.

The good mother/bad mother split, which we recognized at the time Bill was first visiting us, rests on the myths of the wicked stepmother and the fairy godmother. (The mythic power of the wicked stepmother is stronger for mothers than fathers, but can be an issue for both.) Did I have to be one or the other, or could I be a person who tried to be a "good mother"? Would Bill need to make me into a wicked stepmother in order to return at the end of a weekend to his mother? To explore these questions—which I did not do then—I needed first to uncover what I meant by a "good mother."

Our images of "good parents" come first from our family backgrounds. My definition of a good mother came in large part from my experience as a daughter of a tall beautiful mother who had died of cancer when I was twenty-three. When I think of her, even today, the first adjective that jumps into my mind is perfect. She ran a part-time business from our home and emphasized family ties, loyalty, and kin helping kin. She frequently confided in me, the eldest, because my father traveled extensively for his work.

My conception of "good mother" was also influenced by the early women's movement. I believed that I could combine family and work as my mother had (although she had extensive domestic help), provided my husband and children shared the domestic chores with me. I knew that I had to provide "quality time" with the boys, though I was unsure of what that meant since I was not particularly interested in playing team sports. (After school the boys most wanted to play, according to the season, baseball, football, basketball, or street hockey with the neighborhood boys.) And I wanted to raise the boys in nonsexist ways to be men who could show their emotions, care for others, and participate in the full range of family work as well as in the world of work. These elements went into my semiconscious definition of good mother. Thus my childhood experiences and my conscious feminist musings shaped my behavior with both boys. Stepfathers, in a situation similar to mine, would also need to work through their own conception of the role of father and their expectations for their stepdaughters' future roles. Even as men learn to nurture more in our society, they must also learn how to help their stepdaughters to be independent and assertive.

In our situation the related syndromes of wicked stepmother and good mother/bad mother split were even more complicated; it took me four to five years to learn the extent to which Bill was being physically and psychologically abused by his mother. It took twice that time to realize the extent to which his father, Alex, had also been so abused by his mother.

This pattern of abuse made it difficult for Bill to relate to me, no matter how much I tried to be supermom. Bill would come for a weekend, eager to see his beloved father, only to have to share him with a new brother and mother who had had him all week. I would try too hard to be a "good mother," falling into common motherly roles by cooking his favorite foods or buying him new clothes because he was embarrassed by his old ones. He would be eager to get the new clothes, but then have a tantrum in the store over some trivial issue. A pattern emerged: a noisy confrontation on some issue, usually shortly before Bill was to return to his mother. Even though we recognized the pattern, and I would resolve weekly not to be drawn into a confrontation, Bill would find a chink in my armor and "push my button." Often the issue would begin with Bill breaking a rule that both his father and I had agreed to enforce. He almost never broke rules when his father might catch him, but rather when I would. The confrontation would escalate until Alex intervened to stop the argument, leaving me angry with Bill, with Alex for not backing me up, and with myself for not having taken quick disciplinary action and then withdrawing from the dispute.

I had hoped that this syndrome might end after Bill came to live with us. It did abate somewhat, but often returned when Bill was preparing to see his mother—and still can today, although we are much quicker at recognizing it and stopping the self-defeating behavior it involves. I think that in the case of any stepparent and perhaps more so with the cross-sex stepparenting, it is especially important for the biological parent to back up the stepparent's efforts at appropriate discipline and setting limits for children. Although I realized that Alex and I had to agree on the rules and limits we enforced, I did not realize the subtle ways that I had become the disciplinarian until both boys were out of high school. Part of the problem was that Alex had had an abusive mother and a passive father and perhaps subconsciously expected women to be "bad mothers." His mother had regimented her children's lives with required music lessons, daily practicing, and noisy lectures if a child did not perform appropriately, while his father watched passively.

Thus Alex supported Bill's refusal to try new things, to practice, or to follow through on projects he had started. While I did not want to force Bill to do something or learn a new skill, I also felt that some initial support could help him see if the activity was really not for him, or if he simply needed perseverance to get past the first threshold of skill. After an initial protest, usually in front of the boys, I would give in to Alex's argument that he wasn't going to force the boys to learn anything they didn't want to. Bill chose to drop art, music, tennis, and skiing lessons although he did have natural artistic and athletic abilities. In organizing the lessons,

I was probably trying to be supermom, making sure that my children had opportunities to find and develop their natural talents as it appeared that the children of my nonworking friends were doing. Tom voluntarily continued with some of these activities, but Bill did not.

By taking on the role of disciplinarian without realizing that I was doing it alone, despite our prior agreement on disciplinary issues, I reinforced the wicked stepmother image. Alex, who did not want to be a parent like his own parents, became actively engaged in the boys' lives. He played the sport of the season on almost a daily basis after school, was a Scoutmaster and Little League coach, and went frequently to high school athletic events. Because we were both on academic schedules, we were often home in the afternoons when the boys were in elementary school. I would sit at my desk, working on my thesis, while Alex was outside playing ball with the neighborhood boys. When they came in, it would be me who asked the hard questions about whether chores or homework were done before watching TV. Now I can see that Alex was avoiding being both passive and absent like his father as well as a disciplinarian like his mother.

Adding fuel to the issue of "good mother/bad mother" was the problem of favoritism. Now I can admit that I always favored Tom. Then I was trying hard not to do so and to be as close to a "natural" mother to Bill as possible. *Favored* is perhaps not the right word, but it is the word Bill used. He knew that he could always get me to give in on an issue when he said that Tom would be able to do it if Tom had asked. Many mothers may have a special bond with children whom they have nursed from infancy, and they certainly have a different and longer history with their biological children. This difference does not stop them (or me) from developing a strong bond with a stepson, but that bond is often not the same as with a biological child. I think also that it looked to Bill as if his father did a much better job of treating the two boys in the same way. However, the usual interaction between Alex and the boys was sports, which all three loved and at which Bill excelled. My interaction was more often around those daily motherly duties of chores, choice of TV program, homework, getting to school on time, or going to bed. If I had analyzed the times in which Bill and I related easily—teaching him to swim, to dive, to ski, to hike, or to drive—I might have realized that a central aspect of our problem was discipline and limit setting. If Alex and I had been better able to share this aspect of parenting, I might have become a person to Bill instead of a "wicked stepmother."

There were also circumstances, which may occur in many blended families, that made it look as if Tom were the preferred child. He had an extended family on his father's side, who took him on vacation trips, gave him presents at Christmas, and helped pay for the private schooling that he received after the age of nine because of his reading problems. Bill's mother's family deserted him, and his father's family was almost totally absent from our lives, while my family was very close. Although my family gradually accepted Bill as a full member of the family, he always felt hurt that he did not have the extended family and opportunities for travel that Tom had. And he was angry that he, too, was not in private school. As a family we should have more explicitly confronted these inequities, which were situational and over which we did not have too much control. It was not enough to explain why Tom got more Christmas presents when they were ten, but we had to keep doing this in different ways for different situations much more frequently as they were growing up. We were successful in getting the members of our own immediate families to treat the two boys as brothers, but we did not do enough from month to month and year to year to alleviate Bill's hurt.

Every couple who has children must realize that each parent has some different values and parenting styles from his or her own family of origin. Part of the struggle of parenting is recognizing these differences, understanding where each person's values and styles come from, and deciding as a couple which values and attitudes are to be passed on to the next generation. This task becomes more difficult for stepparents because another set of parents is also providing input into values and attitudes. In stepparenting it is particularly crucial to recognize different values held by the parent and stepparent and to create a plan for handling these differences. In the area of values, it is very tempting to consider your own values as the right ones, and ones your spouse will obviously agree with. As I look back over our history, I see four values in particular that I held strongly and that were less important to Alex: achievement through hard work, close family ties, outward expression of affection, and feminism.

In the area of achievement, both Alex and Bill have almost photographic memories, retain easily what they have read, write quickly and easily, and have high academic talent. I have always had to work to achieve and have to watch myself that I don't become a workaholic. Tom, with his reading problem, also has had to struggle; he learned to work hard at school and to organize his time carefully to complete assignments. Bill, on the other hand, coasted through high school and a prestigious Ivy League college. From seventh grade through high school, his casual attitude toward his studies was a continual bone of contention between us. Although I knew intellectually why Alex did not want to push him (because of his own childhood experiences), emotionally I had trouble accepting Bill's refusal to develop fully his very real academic talents. Hindsight and therapy help me to realize now that Alex and I should have decided together how much Bill was going to be encouraged to do in school. If I could not accept him when he was not working as hard in his school work as Tom was, or as I was in my teaching, that was really my problem. Instead of being angry when Alex and Bill watched a sports event on TV while Tom and I worked, I needed to respect the different choices we had made and not shape Bill to my image of a "good" student.

In the second area of values, close family ties, I had developed from my upbringing a strong sense of family, which was fostered by the fact that my father and several members of my extended family lived close by. Alex had had almost no experience with family other than his parents and two siblings. His father was one of six children, but Alex had never met most of his aunts, uncles, or cousins. Although he came from an old Yankee family and was always told that he had to live up to the family name, the family itself was missing. In contrast to my frequent involvement with my side of the family, Alex has had little involvement with his siblings or father. Bill has had almost no positive contact with anyone on either his father's or mother's side of the family. Although I overdid my involvement with my family, allowing my father to interfere too much in our affairs, Alex was both jealous of my involvement and critical of me for having this strong value. This criticism showed up in the form of ridicule, which Bill also picked up. It proved easier for me to accept teasing or criticism from a spouse than from a teenager.

My family of origin was easily affectionate with one another. My earliest memories are of my parents hugging. Alex does not easily express affection. Bill has always pushed me away. Even as a child he did not want to be hugged or cuddled in any way. I tended to react to his pushing me away as a statement about his feelings for me rather than understanding that any physical expression of affection made Bill feel uncomfortable. Since I thought that such affection was good and natural, I kept hoping that Bill would come to enjoy an occasional hug or snuggle close while I read aloud in the evenings. Again Alex and I needed to talk through this issue, and together we should have decided if it were necessary to help Bill to become more comfortable with physical affection. Then we could have decided how either to help him to change or help me not to feel that Bill's lack of affection was a criticism of me. We probably would have needed a family therapist to help us work through this issue, in part because this area was entangled in two generations of child abuse of a male child by a mother.

Lastly, Bill and I got into trouble over my feminism. He took every opportunity to demonstrate the superiority of men over women. He loved to say such outrageous things at the dinner table as "There never has been any good woman politician" or "Women are not creative because there have been no great female artists." He resisted doing household chores and did not learn to cook, despite the fact that both Alex and Tom became accomplished cooks during these years of building a dual-career family. In hindsight, perhaps some of his rhetoric was aimed at provoking his father into taking a stand on these issues. I think that he wanted to know where his father stood on women's roles, which were changing so rapidly in the 1970s and early 1980s. Because his father did not like such confrontations, he was usually quiet or stepped in only after they had gotten too noisy, with the focus on the process of stopping them, not on the substantive content. When occasionally he would stand up for my point of view, the argument was usually diffused quickly. Several feminist friends who have sons and intact families reported the same syndrome: one son takes on the mother because of her feminist views while the other son supports the mother. In each case the situation improved when the father agreed to step into the fray and acknowledge that he understood and agreed with the mother's ideas. Armed with this strategy, Alex more openly supports feminist ideas when they arise, which diffuses Bill's attacks; now he rarely challenges me in this area. Issues surrounding feminism and mother/son relationships are complicated and made even more so by stepparenting with its images of the "wicked stepmother"—the tendency to view stepmothers as naturally wrong or evil.

It is very difficult to make generalizations about cross-sex stepparenting because the circumstances of the first marriages, the ages of the children, and the relationships between the marital couple are important variables in establishing fruitful stepparenting relationships. Among the questions a couple needs to consider is the stepparent's role: should the stepparent become parent, aunt or uncle, or close adult friend? Individual circumstances, such as the ages of the children, will help to dictate that answer. In our case, we decided to take on the parental roles because of the physical and psychological distances that the other biological parent had from each boy. Even today, after many difficulties, I would still defend that decision. However, we did not together make explicit, let alone agree upon, what we each meant by mother and father roles. Although I have been a part of the women's movement since its beginnings in the late 1960s and have studied feminism, I did not consciously enough apply its analysis of the roles of mothers and fathers to my actions as a mother and stepmother. So, based on our own family and adult experiences, we each expected the other to act in ways different from how we actually acted. And both of us were hypersensitive to criticism about our own behavior or the behavior of our biological child.

Our failure to communicate led to a year's separation at the time when both boys entered college and to an angry denunciation by Bill that I had not treated him as well as I had treated Tom over the years, and that he had never felt that he had belonged to the family. Two years of therapy have helped us to put the marriage back together in ways that are much richer than before. An occasional family therapy session has also helped us to be better parents to young men finishing college. Clearly both sons are greatly relieved that the family is back together, and they are appropriately working at leaving the family to begin their adult lives.

However, we would have more easily parented both children, had we gone for help earlier. Why didn't we? We did once, but had the bad fortune to begin with a therapist who wasn't right for us, and we didn't know then that it is common to shop for therapists until finding a person who has that indefinable quality that allows both spouses to respect and open up to the therapist. Also, we were both highly trained academics, well read in psychology, with the hubris to believe that we could talk out our own problems. In our case, this was not possible, given the strains of stepparenting, dual careers, and our own inability to perceive immediately and thus control the source of some of our own parenting behaviors. In hindsight I realize that a feminist analysis of the family also might have given us the ability to name the conflicting dynamics present in our family (a woman who works as a professional, but also wants to be supermom; a father who wants to take on nurturing and companionship roles, but not the disciplinary one). Such a feminist orientation helps to make explicit and thus to question traditional roles of mother and father and to focus on more androgynous roles of parents working together to raise children and stepchildren. As a family, we have clarified our views on such issues as favoritism for the biological child or management of discipline and then supported each other in changing our actions in these areas.

In thinking about my experience, I have wondered whether cross-sex stepparenting is more difficult than being a stepparent of the same-sex child. I talked informally with six stepparents, evenly divided between fathers and mothers in cross-sex stepparenting situations; five said that they had better relationships with the same-sex stepchild than with the one of the opposite gender, and one couple didn't think that the gender of the stepchild was an issue. It may be easier to be a stepparent to the same-sex child because gender issues and societal problems of sexism or sexual issues do not complicate the relationship. Although there are problems inherent in any parent/child relationship, as the literature on mothers and daughters suggests, there are also certain commonalities of experience and interests based on gender socialization that can help a stepparent develop a relationship with a stepchild.

Well into the decade of the 1970s and even today, boys and girls are often socialized in different ways. Janet Lever in her 1976 study of fifth-graders found that boys played age-mixed team games outdoors on a daily basis, while girls were more likely to play in pairs or small groups their games of individual skills or imagination, acting out interpersonal relations.[1] A stepfather of boys may more easily join in ball games with the neighboring boys, as Alex frequently did, than a stepmother who does not have such skills. (One stepmother who loves basketball described to me how shooting baskets with her eleven-year-old stepson helped to cement that relationship, although the stepson does not tolerate losing to her as he does to his father.) Likewise a stepmother may see herself more easily facilitating the imaginary games of girls by providing clothes for dressup or support in cooking and crafts.

If and when this still common daily segregation along gender lines during nonstructured play time of children aged five to twelve should be broken down (girls join the pick-up team games and boys join the imaginary games), then stepparents may find it easier to begin close relationships with children of the opposite sex. I was best in building my relationship with Bill when we were sharing recreational activities like hiking, but this activity was infrequent, whereas Alex joined the ball games with his son and stepson almost every day. Our society reinforces and calls "natural" the camaraderie of being "one of the boys" or "one of the girls." As long as we are bombarded with sex stereotypes and "natural" differences between boys and girls from infancy, there may be more initial barriers to cross-sex stepparenting than to same-sex stepparenting. When you begin a new relationship with a child, you remember what you liked best to do as a child and draw on those skills and interests. Given the ongoing sexism of our society, a stepparent may initially have more in common with the same-sex stepchild; "naturally" sharing activities helps to create important bonds between child and stepparent.

However, armed with knowledge of the history and reality of sex-role stereotyping and socialization in this country, a woman with stepsons or a man with stepdaughters might try consciously to join in activities the stepchildren like, even if they feel awkward at them. For example, a stepmother might also join in a pick-up ball game and encourage other neighborhood girls to play. A stepfather with a stepdaughter interested in dance might ask her to help him with stretching exercises before he goes jogging and to join him in this exercise. The challenge is to move beyond gender stereotypes, examining the daily activities and preferences of a stepchild and then finding ways to interact in such a way that a comfortable, loving relationship is developed between stepparent and child.

Parents usually do not consciously analyze interests and gender roles of their own children unless they have particular parenting problems. Such an analysis may, however, make stepparenting easier. If stepparents realize that their unconscious views of gender roles may be interfering with establishing relationships with stepchildren of the opposite gender, they may be more likely to adopt nonsexist ways of relating to their stepchildren.

In blended families where new spouses have decided to take on the role of parents, I strongly believe that a feminist perspective that consciously examines mothering, fathering, and parenting roles may help newly united couples examine their own attitudes, values, and life histories and thus move beyond the traps of traditional mother or father roles. Such a perspective—and for some, outside help—can provide stepparents with an analysis of their own scripts as parents and of common issues that stepparents encounter. Outside help might take the form of a stepparents' couples group, a women's group, or family therapy. Today, unlike the early 1970s, there are local groups and national organizations (such as the Stepfamily Association of America), which are often listed in local newspapers.[2] A neighborhood or local group of couples struggling with similar parenting issues is one of the most helpful ways to gain support and perspective on stepparenting problems. Parenting is perhaps the most complex and rewarding task of our adult lives; stepparenting can be even more so.

Notes

1. Janet Lever, "Sex Differences in the Games Children Play," *Social Problems* 23 (1976): 478–87.
2. Stepfamily Association of America, 28 Allegheny Drive, Suite 1307, Baltimore, MD 21204.

28

The New Family and the Old Ideology

Judith Grant

Non-Marxist feminist theory has been preoccupied of late with "mothering," "maternal thinking," and developing a "feminine ethic of care" (Gilligan, 1982; Ruddick, 1984; Noddings, 1984). It is probably no accident that this trend has gained prominence in the pro-family 1980s. Unfortunately, in the process of reevaluating the role of right-wing women and housewives in feminism, the movement often appears apologetic for its sexual radicalism of the early 1970s (Mansbridge, 1986, pp. 99–108, 128–31, 168), and sometimes even sympathetic to right-wing women. This retrenchment is tragic when we consider that it means we have let conservatives set the agenda in our discussions of the family. This essay is an attempt to move toward a more progressive discussion of it.

In the following I propose that the inordinate amount of attention paid to "biologism" in some feminist theory, as well as in American law and social custom, is the result of the assumption that families are always related persons. In this essay, I want to talk about the impact of this ideological thinking on nontraditional families; that is, those composed of related and unrelated people. In part, my thinking along these lines is rooted in my own experience as a stepdaughter. I think it is clear that at least some of our private, internal problems as members of nontraditional kin systems stem from social pressures to conform to an allegedly natural model of the family that is, in reality, not natural but socially constructed.

The French Marxist feminist theorist Michele Barrett presents a very persuasive case on the tenaciousness of mainstream ideas about the nature of the family. She also shows that there is a relationship between this current (mis)understanding of the family and women's oppression. Barrett sees a connection between the male-headed nuclear family and capitalism. She argues that an "ideology of familialism," left over from precapitalist eras, interacts with the capitalist mode of production to produce the particular family structure currently in existence. We tend to think of the family, she says, as a privatized structure, composed of related people, whose function is to be a haven from the heartless world of capitalist society. But since this description is mere wishful thinking, Barrett says it is better thought of as an ideology she calls "familialism."

Barrett shows that this particular notion of the family is not inherent to capitalism, but originated in a preexisting belief in the domesticity of women, which was incorporated into capitalism only later (1980, p. 176). She dubs this interaction between familialism and the contemporary Western family structure the "family-household system" (p. 211). It is composed, she says, of a social structure, the "household" (p. 210), and an ideology, "familialism" (p. 206). Our ideas about family—what it is and what it should be—can survive because they are reinforced in the economic sphere. Thus, sex segregation within the capitalist labor market and the internal structure of the household serve to buttress one another, and the family-household system has become deeply entrenched in our society. It is, Barrett argues, responsible for women's oppression today.

As Barrett points out, although the family is "popularly thought of as a group of people related by blood, who share the same household," this particular notion is "an historically specific one" (p. 200). According to the ideology of familialism, the family is seen as "naturally based on close kinship, as properly organized through a male breadwinner with financially dependent wife and children and as a haven of privacy beyond the public realm of commerce and industry" (p. 204). Barrett's historical analysis shows that this definition is distinctly bourgeois (pp. 202–204).

I would like to elaborate on one aspect of Barrett's ideology of familialism, namely, the ways in which it is connected to "biologism." When we look at nontraditional families of any sort—two-career couples, stepfamilies, single parents, open marriages—we see that the current biologically based family form is at least partially responsible for the very real problems encountered by those who deviate from what is deemed acceptable, whether they do so out of rebellious choice or an unanticipated fall from middle-class norms.

It is clear that the male-headed nuclear family is, for all intents and purposes, dead. It can no longer be taken for granted that marriages will last a lifetime, that women will marry or reproduce, or that men will be the primary breadwinners. But feminist theory has lagged behind, insofar as it has been based on a mothering role that assumes the traditional family. Most mothering theorists have, by their own admissions, drawn their inferences from the experiences of women who are white, middle class, heterosexual, and married (Chodorow, 1978; Ruddick, 1984). Therefore, even apart from the politically suspect nature of feminist theories based on mothering and male-female difference, there is the empirical problem: there are very few women who fit the profile of the abstract woman presented in many recent feminist theories.

Why have recent feminist theories taken the traditional, and at this point, mythical, family as their starting point? There are several plausible reasons. First, the desire to find an experience common to all women has led feminists to theorize about mothering (Grant, 1987). In so doing, they have mistaken the cultural icon Mother for the reality. In truth, mothers and their circumstances vary as much as women themselves, and it constitutes a methodological error to theorize motherhood, or even femininity, apart from the circumstances that brought it into being. Motherhood as we now know it makes sense as a concept only in the context of a family. But the question of what *kind* of family all too often goes unexplored. Indeed, the mothers most often theorized by recent feminist scholars presuppose a male-headed nuclear family, which actually exists for very few women. In this sense, the mothers in feminist theory tend to be abstractions.

The second reason feminist theorists have been led in this repressive direction has to do with "biologism": the implicit or explicit acceptance of the bourgeois definition of the family as a group of biologically related people. The term *biologism* has most often been used to criticize early radical feminists, like Shulamith Firestone, who were interpreted as having effectively linked women's oppression to their reproductive capacities. I have in mind a broader usage. Biologistic assumptions may be merely implicit in our thinking and still yield normative prescriptions and practices regarding appropriate behaviors for families and individuals therein. Biologism is a reactionary tendency in feminist social theory, as it places an anachronistic "natural" entity at the center of our thinking about families. Sometimes this had led to a mystical treatment of natural motherhood. Adrienne Rich (1976, p. 63) provides an example of the latter in her description of pregnancy. She writes that she experienced the embryo as

> something inside and of me, yet becoming hourly and daily more separate, on its way to becoming separate from me and of—itself. In early pregnancy the stirring of the fetus felt like ghostly tremors of my own body, later like the movements of a being imprisoned in me.

Like the Right to Life thinking, biologism is antichoice. This ideology is institutionalized in laws and economic structures and creates oppressive conditions for women not currently living in traditional families. Theorizing about families from a broader standpoint seems a logical and necessary response to the ideology of biologism.

The circumstances of women's lives in recent decades have themselves constituted a challenge to purely biological definitions of the family. Stepfamilies can be seen as part of a broad challenge to the traditional family. This new structure includes families comprised of lesbians, gays, unmarried parents, and/or other cohabiting adults. Like stepfamilies, these can be made up of both related and unrelated individuals. Examining the situations of nontraditional families illuminates the impact and implications of the ideology of biologism.

Although all families have a different plight on many levels, the situations with which I am most familiar have to do with the intersection of class, gender, and biologism in the context of the stepfamily. Three issues arise at this juncture: men as symbols of power, the stepparent as interloper, and female bonding around absent men.

My own personal experience of the family differed significantly from the traditional model and, I think, reflects some of the complexities to which I refer. My mother has been married three times. I am the child of my mother and her first husband. I have one half-brother (he is the child of my mother and her second husband). My mother and her third husband share no children of their own. I have met my biological father twice since he and my mother separated when I was very young. Perhaps predictably, I feel little connection to him or to the four children he had with his second wife. While I was growing up in my mother's home, our white, working-class, Irish Catholic family underwent considerable economic change. When my mother, unskilled by labor-market standards, could not find work, we were forced onto the welfare roles for six years. Upon my mother's third marriage, our position changed abruptly: we became middle class. This change in our class illustrates the desperate nature of female economic dependence and the familiar reasons why men shy away from relationships with women who have children.

Economically, men are especially powerful vis-à-vis working-class women. Although both female and male workers have limited earning power, the wages paid to working-class women are rarely sufficient to support children. Their choices are often minimum-wage jobs, part-time labor with no benefits, or work in the home supplemented by the state. The higher-paying working-class jobs (construction or skilled labor, for example) go to men. Thus, the single, working-class mother looking for a husband has a quantifiable measure of the powerfulness of men. While single, she may enjoy a certain amount of welcome autonomy over her own life and children's, but there is no escaping the fact that upon remarriage she trades that autonomy for economic security. He who brings in the money wields considerable power.

As a girl I experienced my stepfather as an interloper, partly because of the automatic power he received by becoming part of our household. Without having to prove himself in any way, he simply assumed immediate status as head of our house; his gender and financial status in the public world translated easily to a concomitantly powerful place in the family. There was no doubt in my mind that his power stemmed from maleness and money.

Like most older stepchildren, I met his pseudoparental power with deep resentment. Although my stepfather and I have become friends, at the time I experienced his presence as an encroachment on the bonds between my mother and me. I felt much like the character Eleanor from Molly Hite's wonderful novel, *Class Porn*, who, wittily reflecting upon her own stepfather recalls:

> After sixteen years of believing I was conspiring with my mother against men, or against men in all their brutish aspects, I was suddenly presented with Bob, a fait accompli. . . . It should have been clear sooner that what we had here was a major shifting of allegiances. I was just confused. For a long time I assumed that my mother thought Bob was basically contemptible . . . it didn't really hit me that the standards had changed until the two of them were married. That was when I finally realized that my mother didn't need me any more. It was a bit of a shock: I'd put up with a lot over the years on the theory that she needed me. Now it appeared that what she needed was Bob. [1987, p. 180]

In this passage the stepfather is viewed as an intruder who despoils the mother/daughter bond forged during the period of absent men. The mother's temporary anger at men after her divorce is misinterpreted by the daughter, who has developed considerable proprietary and protective feelings toward the mother. She thought these had been reciprocal, until her stepfather made her feel obsolete. She feels betrayed by her mother, a bit embarrassed at her misinterpretation of the situation, and hostile toward both adults. It is my experience that Eleanor's feelings are absolutely authentic. Hite's passage, and the circumstances of my own childhood, reflect serious changes signaling the need to rethink the biologistic ideal. That is, nontraditional families, including stepfamilies, are encouraged to emulate a chimerical ideal typical family, often with disastrous consequences. My own experience provides a case in point.

My stepfather and I were thrown together partly out of our common love for my mother, but partly because of financial dependence on him. He was expected to support me and I was expected to be grateful. Instead I was furious, and quite probably so was he. Money aside, we were also intimidated by the pressures of role expectations, which were completely out of line with our sentiments about each other. Put simply, we did not want to be father and daughter. I do not think that our lack of feelings had to do with the fact that we were not biologically related. To the contrary, I believe that our constant awareness of our unrelatedness interfered with our abilities to come to terms with each other simply as human beings living in the same house. We resisted our assigned roles but were at a loss for alternatives.

Put in social perspective, this seems directly related to a host of feminist issues: the financial dependence of women on men, the perceived need for two parents (one of each sex), and the fact that the only acceptable familial model is the male-headed nuclear one. My stepfather did not *have* to be in charge, but he was because that my mother and he believed that that was the way "it was." I should have been able to develop my own feelings about him slowly. But again, I felt I had to treat him as my father, and that I had to do so immediately.

The problems faced by stepfamilies are not unique; they are shared by nontraditional families trying to exist in a world full of ideological training that has led us to expect biological relatedness and to have unrealistic expectations about families. But perhaps more than other nontraditional relationships, the stepfamily creates a serious confusion: there are people who theoretically *could* fill the roles of mom, dad, and kids, but who either cannot or do not want to. It is almost the norm for stepfamilies to be characterized by a lack of love and commitment between unrelated people. This cannot be due to insufficient gene sharing. I think this widespread rebelliousness signals the obsolescence of biologism. The ideology no longer fits the reality.

The existence of the stepfamily challenges the psychological expectations we have for families in general, as well as the economic function that they, and the men in them, serve. In real stepfamilies, the loving children who have no preferences apart from their parents' coupled happiness are exposed as mere sit-com plots. In the 1960s such television programs as *The Brady Bunch* and *The Courtship of Eddie's Father* reflected an anemic attempt at coming to terms with the new social reality. Even though the broadcasters had young TV parents dying like flies, leaving widowed characters rather than divorced ones—doing away with messy problems of ex-spouses and rebellious offspring—such shows did attempt to speak to a new experience of single parenthood. But they did so by asserting a blind formalism, telling us that new people could fit into old slots replacing old moms or dads, and that the new associations wouldn't feel much different than the previous ones. In fact, what most of their plots showed us was that children really wanted their parents to remarry and would go to almost any lengths to aid in their courtship or new relationships. Of course, resistance is actually more often the norm.

Family roles in general are oppressive. In traditional families, however, we tend to feel (however wrongly) that we are in control. Stepparents, in contrast, might not parent were it not for a romantic relationship with someone who happened to have children. They are therefore forced to enter a situation demanding a level of love and commitment that feels, and may be, coerced. Stepchildren, in an effort to maintain stability, or perhaps to regain some control in a real or imagined pecking order, may refuse to relate to the stepparent as a parent, or in any way at all. Finally, the biological parent in a stepfamily may, either consciously or unconsciously, collude in stepfamily problems by giving messages that the child's relationship to the new family member is somehow threatening and not sincerely desired. Economically, the stepfather (and sometimes the stepmother) must often provide for people over whom he has no legal claim or deep love. If he chooses to limit his financial support, he risks alienating both wife and stepchildren, thus further damaging the already tenuous stepfamily bonds.

In a broad sense these problems stem from stepfamilies trying to fit into a traditional if mythical mold: the father at the helm, complete with dutiful children and caring wife. In this way the dead biological family weighs like a nightmare on the brains of the living, nontraditional one. The former is well rooted in history and even appears to be the natural mode of association. But we are, of course, very far from nature, and the family has changed significantly.

The predominance of the concept of the biological family is related to its material basis. Until recently, the vast majority of families lived in the same town their entire lives. Now we have become a transient culture; 17 percent of all Americans move every year (*Statistical Abstracts 1986*, p. 14, table 15). We used to work with relatives, both in businesses and in the home. Now we are more likely to work with acquaintances. Marriages used to stay together for a lifetime. Now divorce is nearly as prevalent as marriage. Gender roles used to be much clearer: men worked outside the home and women supplied caring and other labor within it. Now this too can no longer be taken for granted.

Reality has changed; new units of kinship have displaced old ones. So far, instead of acknowledging this, we have chugged along with the same sets of expectations for ourselves and our loved ones. There is, for example, much pressure to get married. The pressure is both economic and ideological. Women who want children need a man for both economic and social reasons. This is more or less true across race and class. Divorced mothers feel the need to marry and provide their children with a "real family." Lesbians must constantly explain their "singleness" to friends and co-workers, as only heterosexual couples are recognized. Under the tyranny of "naturalness," lesbian and single women may find it difficult to adopt. Once married, there is pressure to reproduce, as it is a mark of being adult and of having a "real family." For women, motherhood means gaining access to an elite class of "real women." More and more attention is given to fertility clinics and the issue of surrogate motherhood, while many unwanted children grow up in institutions. This all because of the desire to pass along one's genes and the feeling that one could never love "someone else's" child.

Those who have most often noticed the changes in family structures have done so with trepidation, and have pointed to them as the harbinger of national disaster (Gilder, 1981; Moynihan, 1965). They have usually counseled a return to traditional values and a male-headed household. Others have sought an extreme and individualistic freedom of choice and have been, by and large, antifamily. Barbara Ehrenreich (1983) presents a case in point in her illuminating discussion of the male flight from commitment, which can be summed up as the "Playboy philosophy." Early feminists attacked the family as patriarchal and have been maligned ever since for, among other things, causing its death. Perhaps people on all sides of the political spectrum resist admitting that the family has changed because they fear nothing else can provide the same sense of sanctity. Rarely do we consider the possibility that new kinship systems can provide the same social function—or even a better one.

In a retreat from early feminist positions, which attacked the biological nuclear family as a patriarchal institution, recent feminists have tended to take it as given and have analyzed women's position within it (Dinnerstein, 1976; Gilligan, 1982). This analytic trend apologizes for the perception of feminism as antifamily, rather than elaborating on the fact that the early movement opposed only a particular kind of family. The new pro-family feminism stresses that women should be able to have both a career and a family, maternity leave, daycare, pay for housework, child support—and all these prescriptions would be earnestly welcomed. But it also suggests that maybe abortion is a type of violence against women (Rich, 1976, p. 269) and that we may have something to learn from right-wing women (Dworkin, 1983), propositions that strike at the core of what used to be meant by feminism. Is it really desirable that the biological family is the only one we can offer to feminist women seeking to transform society?

The biological family model legitimates, for example, zoning laws that discriminate against cohabiting unrelated people and thus inhibit the development of alternative living styles. Legally unrelated lovers are hurt financially by a host of laws, including inheritance, which insist that "next of kin" means a biological family member rather than someone with whom one has had a close relationship for years. Single mothers and women in general suffer from gender-based wage differentials that assume a male head of house, and from welfare laws that insist that a man living in the house necessarily implies financial support. Stepfamilies are discriminated against by inheritance laws and by divorce settlements, where former stepparents are not legally entitled to visitation rights. In addition, there is the tendency to assume some pathology connected to people living in nontraditional families. Children from so-called broken homes are stigmatized by school counselors, neighbors, and "real" relatives.

There are problems involved in creating new ways to live with people whose relationship to you has yet to be named. *Spouse equivalent, lover,* or *partner* just don't have the same connotations as *wife* and *husband,* and every child knows that Snow White's stepmother was not the same as her mother. Relatively benign problems are magnified in the face of the message, communicated daily through language, laws, and popculture, that blood is, and *should be,* thicker than water.

The new family points toward both an expanded political practice and theory for feminism. Neither must continue to assume biological kinship. Both should address the concerns of nontraditional families by redefining the family to include associations by choice. Indeed, the birth of this new order is fundamentally connected to women's liberation, but not in the manner some have imagined. We have not caused the demise of the old order, but are ourselves one of its symptoms. Material changes have dislodged now obsolete institutions and created a space for new ones to emerge. The family is one of these. We can take part in the construction of a new reality by ensuring that it is treated as legitimate by the state and society. This means advocating appropriate changes in both laws and attitudes. The current stress on "the family" as understood by those to whom I referred at the start of this chapter deradicalizes the potential of a new structure and reproduces old prejudices.

The radical connections between the new family, sexual freedom, and self-determination have yet to be explored. The value judgments communicated by traditional thinking about families are, however, evident. For example, the refusal to acknowledge long-term lesbian and homosexual liaisons as types of families communicates the attitude that these relationships are immoral. "Real" families are portrayed, in contrast, as keystones of morality. Likewise, there is implied criticism in the refusal of most agencies to allow unwed women to adopt children. In that case, the moral weight of the state is brought to bear on the side of convention. As Michele Barrett points out, there is a perniciousness in the refusal to acknowledge that a particular socioeconomic structure (capitalism) is fundamentally linked to this ideology. Finally, I offer my personal story as a demonstration of the fact that stepfamilies face internal conflicts around role expectations and shifting financial obligations. Under the present circumstances, individuals are literally denied self-determination by virtue of their sexual choices, among which can be included the decision not to marry or to remarry. When our society retains a very narrow, biologically based understanding of the family, even such seemingly mundane choices can place us outside the mainstream.

References

Barrett, Michele. *Women's Oppression Today: Problems to Marxist Feminist Analysis.* U.K.: Verso, 1980.

Chodorow, Nancy. *The Reproduction of Mothering: Psychoanalysis and the Sociology of Gender.* Berkeley and Los Angeles: University of California Press, 1978.

Dinnerstein, Dorothy. *The Mermaid and the Minotaur.* New York: Harper & Row, 1976.

Dworkin, Andrea. *Right Wing Women.* New York: Coward, McCann and Geoghegan, 1983.

Ehrenreich, Barbara. *The Hearts of Men.* Garden City, N.Y.: Anchor Press, 1983.

Firestone, Shulamith. *The Dialectic of Sex: The Case for Feminist Revolution.* U.K.: The Women's Press, 1979.

Gilder, George. *Wealth and Poverty.* New York: Bantam Books, 1981.

Gilligan, Carol. *In a Different Voice: Psychological Theory and Women's Development.* Cambridge, Mass.: Harvard University Press, 1982.

Grant, Judith. "I Feel Therefore I Am: A Critique of Experience As the Basis for a Feminist Epistemology." *Women and Politics,* Fall 1987.

Hite, Molly. *Class Porn.* Freedom, Calif.: Feminist Crossing Press, 1987.

Mansbridge, Jane J. *Why We Lost the ERA.* Chicago: University of Chicago Press, 1986.

Moynihan, Daniel Patrick. *The Negro Family: The Case for National Action.* Washington: U.S. Department of Labor, Office of Policy Planning and Research, 1965.

Noddings, Nell. *Caring: A Feminine Approach to Ethics and Moral Education.* Berkeley and Los Angeles: University of California Press, 1984.

Rich, Adrienne. *Of Woman Born: Motherhood As Experience and Institution.* New York: Norton, 1976.

Ruddick, Sara. "Maternal Thinking." In Trebilcot, Joyce. *Mothering: Essays in Feminist Theory*. Totowa, N.J.: Rowman and Allanheld, 1984.

U.S. Department of Commerce, Bureau of the Census. *The Statistical Abstract of the United States, 1986*.

29

The Strengths of African-American Stepfamilies

Margaret Wade-Lewis

Not long ago a colleague and I were discussing the stepfamily in the African-American community.[1] When we were growing up, he in Florida and I in Oklahoma, there were many family situations that we didn't realize were blended or included stepchildren. The relationships were considered a private family matter, not the business of outsiders. We wondered what had changed.

From my perspective, several changes have taken place. Today more stepfamilies are the result of divorce and remarriage; in the past many more were likely the result of death. Hence today's children gain an additional set of parents, whereas children of the past more often gained a "replacement" parent.

During the summer of 1987 I asked six women about their perceptions of family and stepfamily. They were between thirty-two and forty-two, employed, and from diverse backgrounds. They were raised in Virginia, Alabama, Connecticut, New York, and Panama; today they live in small and mid-sized communities in New York State. Although their economic circumstances and personal experiences differ, they have at least three things in common. They are all African-American, married, and stepmothers. Four are married for the first time. One of these four is an interracial marriage. Although none of them views herself as a feminist, they all have a clear sense of direction about what they want from life, their marriage, and family relationship, and they view their blended family as a source of growth and creative commitment rather than entrapment.

I met these women in a variety of ways. I had known two of them for about ten years. One introduced me to her sister. I met two others through contacts at church, and the sixth at a political fundraiser. They were willing to share with me the intimate details of the challenges and joys they face. We met as strangers, but we parted as spiritual sisters. Our bond is a natural one: I, too, am a stepmother.

Most of these six women recalled that in their childhoods a family was a family, parents introduced children as "my children," and most children, whatever the actual nature of the relationship, addressed parents using titles of respect such as Daddy and Mama. The forms of address may have hinted at step-relationships—Daddy Sam, Mama Annie, Big Daddy, Daddy Two, Little Mama—but always they indicated respect for the station and role of parents. Parents were authority figures, not simply adults of the household.

Among the values that particularly characterize the African-American family are: (1) strong family ties (including strong parent/child relationships with nonnegotiable or unconditional love); (2) well-defined philosophies of child rearing based on traditional African-American values; and (3) strong religious orientation (with or without regular church attendance).[2] These values are no less significant when families involve step-relationships.

Strong Family Ties

The traditional separation of status between parents and children has eroded. Contemporary parents often allow their children to be on a first-name basis with their friends and other adults. Sometimes they call their parents by first name as well. When a stepparent joins the family, the child is often allowed to decide what name is comfortable, and frequently chooses the first name. People outside the family question why the child refers to his or her parent by first name, which leads to the revelation that the family is blended, and often to additional questions.

Today there is also an atmosphere of openness that allows for greater discussion of formerly private family matters. More than one woman I interviewed lamented the passing of the tradition of family privacy. However, they do not believe that the new approach has resulted in the destruction of strong family bonds.

Marjorie married Mark when his daughters were twelve and nine.[3] Commenting on forms of address, she said, "What they call me is irrelevant. It's the respect that is important. They already have a mother. But even if she were dead, they could call me Marjorie as long as they show respect."

She and Mark have had custody of the children since the beginning of their marriage. Marjorie refers to them as her daughters. Her mother views them as her grandchildren, and other family members embrace them as relatives. Mark and Marjorie have decided to have no other children.

A stepfamily does not simply emerge: the bonds must be forged and often be reinforced. Most women said that the early years were the most difficult as new personalities, needs, and priorities were combined into a workable comfort level. They discovered that stepfamilies often start with a honeymoon period, followed by a family crisis. Several of the women discovered that family ties can be strengthened through adversity, such as illness in the family. Paula's situation is such a case.

When Sam and Paula discussed marriage, Sam told Paula about his children. His eldest daughter is Paula's age; his son is a young adult; and his youngest daughter, Tina, was ten at the time. They expected that Tina would spend portions of her vacations with them. Paula's son, James, was seven.

During the second summer of their marriage, Tina came to spend time with them. She and James enjoyed having a sibling near the same age. Paula and Sam were elatedly preparing for the birth of twins in the winter. All was well until Tina developed a serious illness, which required brain surgery. What began as an idyllic summer turned into a tense, unstructured time requiring many adjustments. Would Tina survive? Should the family rejoice over the knowledge of the twins while Sam's daughter's life was in the balance? Was there time for proper attention to Paula's son? How could the new family develop if Sam was preoccupied with his daughter and commuting back and forth over distances to see her at her mother's house?

Tina is now recovering well, the twin sons have arrived, James is delighted to have younger brothers, and Sam is building an addition to their house. Paula feels a good degree of fulfillment. She also feels that she and Tina have developed a more intimate relationship as a result of their constant contact during the illness. Tina is now a young woman of twelve who feels free to ask Paula about womanly issues. Paula treasures these moments. While she does not expect to replace Tina's mother, she enjoys being her friend.

If Tina could live with them all year, Paula would be pleased: "We would be more of a complete family if we had Tina with us because of who she is and because of what she means to Sam."

In the African-American family there is the assumption that children belong to families and that if a man or woman joins a family, it is a privilege rather than a burden to assist in raising the children. Often, however, the process requires major adjustments.

Before Sheena married Walter they had agreed that his three teenage children would eventually leave Jamaica and join them. By the time the first daughter, Amina, arrived, Sheena and Walter already had a three-year-old daughter and an infant son. The challenges were momentous. First, they needed a larger house. Second, Amina assumed that America was paradise and that her father would care for all her needs. Before leaving Jamaica, she gave away most of her belongings, including much of her clothing. She did not expect to attend school although she was still school age.

Amina's brother, Trevor, arrived several years later. At eighteen, he was more prepared to tackle the responsibilities of work and school, and he soon found a job and began pursuing a college degree. He has been a positive influence on his sister. Recently Reena, the third teenager, has arrived from Jamaica and joined the household.

Sheena and Walter have spent the last seven and a half years giving their best effort to raising their children. Both work in blue-collar jobs outside the home. In addition to the three young adults, they now have three young ones, ages seven, four, and two. Finances are sometimes tight. Though Amina loves the younger children, she has not been particularly reliable at childcare. Nor in the early years did she respond cheerfully to advice and direction. Sometimes Walter and Sheena are exhausted by the sheer weight of the responsibility, but they are proud that they are keeping the family together; they would not have it any other way.

Sheena says, "I've grown a lot in this relationship. And I'm sure I've learned a great deal that will help me in raising the younger children when they are teens. . . . If you're going to be a stepparent to teens, you had better know something about teens. They're not all bad, but you have to be flexible."

Billy and Maryemma, who is Sheena's sister, also have six children. When they met, Maryemma was raising an infant daughter and Billy was raising three children: a son who was five, and three-year-old twin daughters. Together, they had two children: a daughter, now six, and a three-year-old son. All the children except Maryemma's first daughter (now nine) are Billy's biological offspring. Both parents work outside the home, Billy in industry during the day and Maryemma in nursing at night. This challenging arrangement requires both parents to give a great deal to the relationship since all the children are under seventeen and still in the household. For example, the two-year-old son spends his days with Maryemma, who sleeps as much as the situation allows. Her sense of purpose makes it possible for her to continue cheerfully, even when she is physically exhausted. "Billy and I work at this situation. I would do it again. In fact, even though I'm tired, when I go to work I feel like I'm working for a good cause. We love children and want to raise them right and send them to college."

Traditional Philosophies

Though children are highly valued and child raising is viewed as a privilege, the children seem to be the single greatest source of tension in these six families. The most harmonious family situations are those where parent and stepparent share similar values about child rearing. In discussions with these women, several traditional African-American values were evident: (1) emphasis on proper respect for parents, elders, and authority figures; (2) reciprocity among family members, reinforced by a strong sense of responsibility to the spouse, the family unit, and siblings; and (3) unconditional love by the parents for the children, love that cannot be cancelled by parent anger, disappointment, punishment, mistakes, or misbehavior. The giving or withdrawing of love as a means for changing behavior is viewed as a negative approach (Noble, 1976).

Five of the women interviewed believe a firm hand is essential in raising children, and that children must be firmly and lovingly guided to understand the privileges and responsibilities of their age group and the appropriate relationship between adults and children. All agree that stepmothers must find creative strategies for keeping child rearing on a positive plane. They believe that African-American children will be more prepared to function in a racist society if they have been strengthened with proper discipline at home. Each one stressed the importance of a coordinated effort between the man and woman in the relationship.

Almost all the woman feel comfortable asserting themselves as strong African-American mother figures. Most do not hesitate to discipline and make important decisions for both their biological and stepchildren. Four feel that the fathers are supportive; two experience difficulty in this regard.

Marjorie and Mark have developed a well-coordinated child-rearing strategy. Sometimes they make decisions jointly; on other occasions Mark defers to Marjorie. He appreciates her willingness to be directive. Because they are affluent, they have been able to provide Mark's children with a variety of enrichment opportunities, including international travel and educational summer camps. Even though they know it would be easier to allow their daughters the freedom many of their peers experience, Marjorie and Mark believe that African-American parents have a special responsibility to practice discipline of the firmest sort and take dramatic stands in certain situations.

When Karen, their oldest daughter, was seventeen, she decided that her parents were too strict and asked to move in with a friend and her family. Mark and Marjorie reluctantly agreed. They decided not to cancel their much-needed vacation; this was not the first time Karen had precipitated a family crisis. Marjorie admits: "I won't say it was the best vacation we ever had in terms of our ability to interact with each other, but we did stay. Parents cannot be reluctant to take a stand. When we returned, the first person we saw was Karen, sitting at the top of the stairs."

Marjorie is certain that her own parents would have objected to the strategy she and Mark employed. However, she believes that if they had begged Karen to stay, or cancelled their plans and treated the situation as a crisis, Karen would have practiced the same behavior on other occasions.

It is not unusual for divorced parents, feeling they participated in the dissolution of a family, to bring a sense of guilt to the relationship with their children. More than one couple has had to grapple with this issue. Ann and Richard have been successful in resolving situations resulting from it.

When Ann and Richard married, her son, David, was twelve and his two sons, Richard Jr. and Ernest, were seven and five. Richard is a nurturing father who enjoys spending time with the children. Ann discovered, though, that catering to their desires, which was Richard's initial inclination, created conflict in the household. Ann attempted to serve as a mediating force by being willing to say no.

During the early years, in his attempts to be reassuring when his sons came to visit, Richard would give them much of his time and allow them to ignore Ann. The younger son was particularly difficult in this regard. He was inclined to call his father to handle his every need, even when Ann was available and willing to help and when his request related to one of Ann's areas of responsibility. After an extremely difficult year, Ann opted not to go on vacation with Richard and his sons. Ten days of being alone with a nine- and eleven-year-old, and perhaps trying never to say no, were quite trying to Richard. The experience underscored for both of them the value of supporting each other in raising their children. From this, Ann notes, "It became clear that I was not the source of the tension, but a mediating force." Since that point, their family relationship is much improved.

The stepmothers who feel they have been the least successful in child rearing are those who see the children only on weekends and holidays.

Camille and John have such an arrangement with his twelve-year-old daughter and eleven-year-old son.

Camille was raised in a nurturing Panamanian family that moved to the United States when she was twelve. She had no second thoughts about marrying a man with children; she herself had been raised in a blended family. But she quickly discovered a significant difference. Her mother had been the biological mother of all the children in the household; Camille as stepmother faced a more difficult acceptance. Children view mother as the nurturer and comforter, and often accept a stepfather much more easily than a stepmother.

Camille feels that ever since she and John began their relationship, his daughter, Renee, in particular, has caused stress by negotiating for primacy with her father. This situation is complicated by other factors in the family life, and by unresolved differences in discipline style between Camille and the children's mother. For example, Camille describes the household in which the stepchildren live as noisy, unstructured, and "too free." The children hear and repeat "grown folks' business." There is no set time for being home, no established bedtime. There appear to be no rules governing such situations as sleeping over at a friend's house. Television watching is unregulated. The children are not taught to respond respectfully to adults or to value gifts they are given by John and Camille.

Camille and John have often discussed these issues, but John believes that adjusting to two very different households is a great deal to ask of the children. So Camille does not feel free to counsel John's children, though she often sees the need to do so. She also fears that her influence on the seven-year-old twin daughters will be adversely affected by the behavior of the older children. Sometimes she feels like an intruder in her own household. On the other hand, one of the major sources of joy in the relationship is her friendship with John. "I love John. He is a hard worker, a good provider and does not hang out. We can count on each other."

Religious Orientation

Historically the church has been a major force in strengthening African-American families. It is not unusual even today, for example, to seek counseling from the minister.

After Amina had been in Walter and Sheena's household for two years, and it was evident that certain concerns would be recurrent, they invited their pastor to their home for a family conference. There it was decided that Amina should live elsewhere in the community. The minister identified two older women from the congregation who would be willing. The one Amina settled upon had, along with her husband, raised five children, all of whom are successful in their personal lives and careers.

Now, two years later, Amina continues to live with the older neighbor, who has become part of the extended family network. Amina is doing well; she has a job and her own automobile and earns the funds to pay rent for her room. She is looking forward to taking courses in night school and to eventually renting her own apartment.

The other women I interviewed have various levels of involvement in church. Marjorie teaches a Sunday school class, shares experiences with her friends from church, and sometimes shares childcare responsibilities with them. Maryemma, Camille, Sheena, and Paula attend church, sometimes with their spouses. Usually they bring their children. Paula describes her relationship with Sam as "an act of faith" because of the difference in their ages. Several of the women attribute part of their success to faith in God and the support of the church and friends who are part of the church network.

Conclusion

How does the African-American community view the stepfamily? Most of the women I talked with believe that the African-American stepfamily has much in common with other stepfamilies. The differences, they feel, result largely from differences in value systems and the racism and prejudice to which African-American are subjected.[4] I agree.

The women interviewed here were particularly appreciative of their husbands as partners in parenting. Paula, for example, agreed to be interviewed on the condition that her husband Sam could also be interviewed. These women emphasized the importance of bonding in parenting because of the powerful impact of societal racism on their families. Several women reported the necessity of dealing with the effects of societal notions about color on their children, a concern of other black stepfamilies as well. This issue emerges particularly in interracial families or in families where some children are much darker or much lighter than other family members.[5]

Each woman concluded that the African-American community views the stepfamily as natural—just another family. This perspective is not new; it is rooted in African and African-American traditions of extended family forms and strong family ties. The stepfamily is an old and time-tested form among African-Americans, evolving in Africa and reinforced by the dislocation of slavery and migration to the cities. In fact, the very survival of the African-American family has depended partly on its ability to form creative and cohesive networks under one roof, often composed of both relatives and nonrelatives (Staples, 1971; Steady, 1981). Adaptability of family roles is one reality for many African-American women that has become an ideal for the women's movement in general.

Notes

1. I prefer the term *African-American* to allude to black Americans' link to the African past.

2. Much research has been done on the African-American family; see Hill, 1971; Nobles, 1976; McAdoo, 1981; Rogers-Rose, 1981. The perspective that emerges from my interviews is one that supports the vitality/regenerative model of the African-American family, which maintains that, despite racism, the African-American family continues to be a bulwark of strength and a source of positive values. This perspective is in contrast to the pathology/deviance model, which maintains that the African-American family is crumbling and riddled with problems largely of its own making.

3. The names of all individuals have been changed.

4. The effects of racism on the African-American family have been well documented; see Steady, 1981; Staples, 1971; and Gary, 1981.

5. Among further issues to be explored are effects of age and class background on African-American women's experiences in stepfamilies.

References

Gary, Lawrence E. *Black Men.* Beverly Hills, Calif.: Sage Publications, 1981.

Hill, Robert. *The Strengths of Black Families.* New York: Emerson Hall, 1971.

McAdoo, Harriette Pipes, ed. *Black Families.* Beverly Hills, Calif.: Sage Publications, 1981.

Nobles, Wade W., et al. *A Formulative and Empirical Study of Black Families.* Washington, D.C.: U.S. Department of Health, Education and Welfare, 1976.

Rodgers-Rose, LaFrances. *The Black Woman.* Beverly Hills, Calif.: Sage Publications, 1980.

Staples, Robert, ed. *The Black Family: Essays and Studies.* Belmont, Calif.: Wadsworth, 1971.

Steady, Filomena. *The Black Woman Cross-Culturally.* Cambridge, Mass.: Schenkman Publishing Company, 1981.

30

Grown-up Steps: Reflections on Two Generations of Stepmothers and Their Adult Stepdaughters

Hedva Lewittes

I am a stepdaughter and a stepmother. I became a stepdaughter at twenty-seven when my mother died and my father remarried. I became a stepmother ten years later when I married Arthur, who had a nineteen-year-old daughter and a sixteen-year-old son. I feel that all my step-relationships have contributed to my growth, and I think that we all have pride in the work that we have done to create our families. I hope that by sharing our experiences I will help to develop new images of roles and relationships within reconstituted families.

In particular, in this essay I will explore the role of stepmother. As a developmental psychologist whose field is adulthood and aging, I am interested in adult family relationships. While the maturation of the bond between mothers and daughters throughout the life cycle is just beginning to be examined, even less is known about stepmothers and daughters. Most psychological and sociological literature on blended families is concerned with the effect of stepparents on young children's mental health. However, I believe that the stepmother can also have an impact on the adult stepdaughter's development. In our relationships, both my stepmother and I drew on the nurturant "mothering" qualities within ourselves but also used the unique position of stepmother. This piece is based on my own memories and observations as well as on conversations that I had with my stepmother, Sara, and my stepdaughter, Jennifer. At various points I have quoted from the tapes of these discussions.

When my relationship with Sara began, I thought of her primarily as my father's wife; I had few preconceptions about what I wanted or expected from a stepmother. We had met only a few times before she and my father got married. I was relieved that he had found someone to take care of him and pleased that he had not married the overbearing, stuffy women that my brother and I feared he might. However, I was frankly more concerned with my new marriage and new life in San Francisco than his. Then, shortly after his marriage my father got sick and with some apprehension, I flew back to New York. I was feeling overwhelmed by my father's illness following so shortly after my mother's death. I was also feeling sorry for myself: my life was being disrupted again.

When they married my father had moved into Sara's apartment; I wasn't sure if I was expected to stay there. I did, however, have a sense that Sara wanted me to come, and when I arrived I found that she was eager to have me in her house. Sara felt that I was part of her family, although she had some apprehensions about how I and my brother would feel about her. She explained:

> You were his children and you were something like my children too. It wasn't the same but something like it. Very similar and that was right away. There was some concern as to whether you would feel that too . . . because you were grown up. In some ways my prior thought was that you wouldn't want me around because your mother had just died. You would object.

To my surprise, within a day of my arrival I felt very much at home. I have only two images of that trip. One is visiting my father in the hospital; the other is of fading winter afternoons spent talking intensely with Sara, sinking into the large soft couch and into the peace of her subtly elegant living room. It was wonderful woman talk. There was no topic; we wandered where our feelings took us, taking time to trace the web of surrounding thoughts and appreciate the details. It was the kind of interaction that I experienced with my closest friends, where the personal boundaries are fluid. Our talking calmed and reassured me. I had expected to be depleted by taking care of others; instead I felt taken care of. From that time on I felt a connection to Sara. Sara had a similar feeling.

. . . that immediate bonding. Yeah, that's the main thing I can feel. It was right away . . . an immediate feeling different than with other young people . . . I felt related to you; I felt maternal.

In our recent conversations, Sara and I analyzed the components of what we felt then. To begin with, we liked each other, as people. Maybe that was lucky. My fantasy is that my father married Sara because she was similar to me. Also, having been made family by the fiat of marriage, we now had the permission, the freedom to create a deep relationship.

I have never thought of Sara as a replacement for my own mother. At the time, when we met, in many ways I didn't want another mother. I had spent years trying to assert my autonomy from my parents. The fact that my mother died just as we were beginning to accept each other made her death all the more painful. Being provided with a stepmother in no way shortened my grieving, stopped my missing the unique way my mother loved me, or ended my internal dialogue with my mother's spirit. But having done a lot of work at establishing my own identity provided a good basis for a new relationship with an older woman. Also, partly because Sara hadn't raised me, because I didn't have to define myself in contrast to her, it was easier for both of us to relate to and accept each other as adults, as separate human beings. As Sara put it:

That's another thing; I felt you were very independent. I related to you [me and my brother] as mature adults. [You] were young but you were mature adults . . . you had all your own ideas. . . . I immediately liked both of you, which I would have done anyway. I related to you. Your personalities were such that I related to you right away.

If Sara had tried to mother me in stereotypical ways, if she had offered to do my laundry or admonish me on correct social behavior, things would not have gone well. But Sara had something else to give. A strong, independent woman, she was a psychiatrist and psychoanalyst and the mother of four children. I had recently become very involved in feminism and was a graduate student striving to develop and balance my work and family life. In some ways Sara was my ideal—not just because she was successful, but because I identified with the fact that she had to struggle in her life. She had been widowed with young children and had dealt with her own illness. So many of her experiences seemed relevant to the problems that I was facing. Being able to be intimate with someone who had gleaned a good deal of wisdom and who conveyed a sense of self-affirmation gave me hope.

When Sara and my father married, I had some fears that my father would be so eager to please her that he would ignore me. Since women usually keep the family together and my mother was gone, I didn't know if either he or Sara would be interested in maintaining family ties. At first, like many newlyweds, my father was very wrapped up in his new relationship. However, they have been together for twelve years now and I can happily say that my father is very much involved in my life and that we have never been closer.

Interestingly, I think that being able to observe from the inside the dynamics of a family other than our own—that is, of Sara and her children—gave my father a somewhat new perspective on the conflicts we had had during my young adulthood. Sara's daughters' lifestyle choices were more like my own than the numerous traditional cousins in my own family. Like me, her daughters had not married and had children when they were young; they too had run off to California to seek their fortunes. Perhaps more important, Sara has served as a good intermediary between me and my father and has also facilitated our becoming more open with each other. She has encouraged him to acknowledge and express his feelings to me and helped to explain and validate my feelings to him. Because my father and Sara are not a monolithic parental unit, my father and I have been able to develop a more independent and personal relationship.

Over the years my interaction with Sara has continued to be enriching. When I got divorced and moved back to New York, their house was a safe place where I felt nourished and appreciated. Sara and I have become intertwined in each other's family. I have an independent friendship with her daughter, my stepsister, who lives in New York, and I am quite close to Sara's son's wife's sister (figure that one out). Recently I attended Sara's cousin's reunion.

So, based on my relationship with Sara, I had very good feelings about the stepmother/stepdaughter relationship. When I began to consider marrying Arthur, I felt positive about the fact that he had children. Indeed, there turned out to be many parallels between Sara's relationship with me and mine with Jennifer.

To begin with, Jennifer and I also responded to each other as people and there was an immediate ease of communication. The first time that Jennifer, Arthur, and I had dinner together, Arthur hardly got a word in edgewise. I felt from her a desire and willingness to connect. As I got to know her, I found many things that I liked about her and that reminded me of myself when I was her age—her sense of humor, her creativity, her insecurities. She was a reflective and caring person.

Even before Jenny moved in, I became involved in helping her. In our conversation for this essay, she indirectly asked me why I had done that. I can't fully answer this question. I'm sure I did it partly to please Arthur, but I also know that I wanted to. Maybe it was because I identified with her, because I resonated to her spirit. At the time Jenny wanted to change colleges. I felt strongly that she was right, that she had a lot to offer and that the school she was attending didn't suit her personally or intellectually. I felt angry that she hadn't gotten the guidance she needed in high school. In addition, as a college professor I had skills and resources to assist her. I was unsure of how to be a stepmother, but I knew how to be a friend and teacher. Jenny also perceived that our interacting around her decision to change schools provided a way to deal with the uncertainty of our roles. This is how she described her early visit to my house:

> I didn't know what I was walking into at the time. I remember it was Sunday morning and every once in a while I would come over for breakfast and Dad would be here and I would feel a little, uh, uncomfortable. I was glad there was something of my life that I could bring in, that I could feel like I had a place.

Helping in this way was also safe because it enabled me to be nurturing without encroaching on Jennifer's mother's territory. I was also able to draw on my experience with Sara. By being an active, competent woman, I could help Jenny to become one as well. As Jenny explained:

> At the time you and Dad got together it was important to have an older woman to connect with. . . . I remember one of the first issues that came up was the fact that I wanted to change schools . . . you were making an effort to be helpful and I appreciated it.

This interaction served as a bridge for me between work and family and helped create a bond between us.

When Arthur and I did marry, I was happy to become part of a family but I didn't really envision myself as mother to his children. For one thing, I didn't really feel old enough to be Jennifer's mother. I was seventeen when she was born and at that time motherhood was not on my agenda. In many ways I related to her more as a friend than as a mother. Once she moved in, I enjoyed having a woman around the house with whom I could talk, reflect, and giggle. When Jenny shared her problems with me I tried to be accepting in the way that I am with my friends. Parents, often because they are so involved and feel so responsible, have a hard time listening nonjudgmentally to their children. I know there were times that

Jenny could be open with me in a way that would have compromised her independence had she disclosed such information to her parents.

However, I didn't involve Jennifer in many of my personal problems, especially certain issues in my relationship with Arthur and my feelings about having a child of our own. I felt that in these areas she undoubtedly had her own strong feelings and self-interest and that this might make it difficult for me to get the empathy and support I needed. I know Jenny appreciated not being burdened with my problems but in our conversation she also indicated that, particularly when I was absorbed with my problems, she sometimes felt excluded from the emotional center of the family—that she had no place.

Before Arthur and Jennifer moved in, I had expected that there would be little opportunity to work out parent-child relationships. After all, John, Arthur's son, was sixteen and lived with his mother in another city, and Jenny was in college and spent only vacations and occasional weekends at home. Needless to say, my fantasy of a readymade family was just that— a fantasy. We had painful and exhausting struggles over issues such as use and care of the kitchen, television watching, and holiday plans. Resolving these problems required change and adjustment on everyone's part. Although there was a good deal of conflict, Jennifer and I were careful with each other. Often we negotiated through Arthur, and most of my overt battles were with Arthur. Indeed, one of Jennifer's suggestions for improvement in our relationship was that I should express my needs directly to her rather than through her father.

A history of our family dynamics would be a book in itself, and I don't feel that I can adequately represent Jennifer's or Arthur's experiences or perceptions. However, a description of some of my conflicts seem relevant to the role of stepmother.

To begin with, like many blended families, when we started to live together we were coming from very different situations. Arthur and Jennifer had long-established patterns of sharing. I had lived alone for quite a while and was accustomed to having control over my own space. I needed an orderly home to cope with the demands and tensions of my work. Often I found myself in the position of challenging unstated assumptions held by Jennifer, Arthur, and sometimes Arthur's ex-wife. I resented having to deal with problems that I felt had been created in a family that was not my own.

The fact that Jennifer was a young adult and was also accustomed to having the run of the house when Arthur was away added to the difficulty. We both liked to hang out and recuperate at home and our ways of doing this interfered with each other. For example, the first weekend that Jennifer came home from college, she planned to have a dinner party for her friends. I objected. Arthur was going to be out and I needed a quiet evening to myself. For both Jenny and myself, the other's responses and behavior were a surprise.

I think that if she had been my own child I would have reacted the same way. What might have been different was that we would have had established ways of communicating about and negotiating such conflicts. Nonetheless, I felt guilty and undermined by the suspicion that I was not acting as I would toward my own child. In this situation, as in many others that arose, the fact that Arthur and I did not respond the same way also created tension. While it is not unusual for parents to disagree about giving to and setting limits for children, after years of being alone with Jennifer, Arthur felt I was coming between him and his daughter. For me, the fact that he expected me to feel exactly the way he did, that he assumed that I would automatically adopt the role of mother, aroused my feminist anger. He was denying my selfhood.

Over time I have come to realize that it is almost impossible to sort out what part of any particular conflict reflects the tensions and role changes that occur in "normal" families and what uniquely comes from being a reconstituted family. However, I have also come to accept that I do feel differently toward Jennifer than I would toward a child that I had raised. As cold as this may sound, I know of several stepmothers who, by insisting that they love the stepchild just like their own, create a situation where resentments are expressed in unconscious and unintended ways and where children feel confused and manipulated by the discrepancy between what they are told and what they experience. For us, I think that acting in concert with my honest feelings and insisting that my needs be considered in creating our family, has worked better in the long run than responding out of guilt. As I explained to Jennifer in our conversation:

> In ways that I couldn't [give] then I set limits and then in ways that I could, I just did. I tried to be very pure of heart. I don't think I did anything out of obligation. And I guess in my head there's a certain aspect of mothering that comes from obligation, that you have a responsibility, that whether you like it or not you've got to do it. And I felt with you I gave in ways that I wanted to.

In negotiating boundaries with Jenny, my prior experience with Sara gave me firm psychological ground. Although Sara and I had never had to face the difficult task of living in the same house, in getting to know her I quickly learned that she was a person with clear limits. Additionally, I did not expect her to feel or act toward me as my mother did. Yet I had survived and prospered in the relationship. Also my feminism and my friends gave me courage to make conscious choices about when and whether I would assume the caretaking role. My friends were invaluable, not only because they supported my right to have rights but because they consistently expressed empathy with and concern for Jennifer.

Looking back, Jenny also felt that good things came out of our process of adjustment. She commented:

> The words I would use to characterize our relationship is sort of happy detachment, which isn't bad. I mean I think almost from the beginning it was accepted that we loved and respected each other and that we could talk about things but we're not really involved in each other's day-to-day lives in a way that a mother and daughter would be. . . . We were both sort of thrown into this relationship and neither of us had any control over the fact that the other one was there. To make the best of it we had to make some decisions that we would have very proper and direct points at which we could get along. I know at least I decided to control what I could control and I think what I could control in some ways was my expectations of you and Dad and what I would get from you and what I would give in return. . . . I know where the limits are. I know what to expect and I'm very comfortable with that. It was really important. And it was more so back when I was eighteen that someone came along and gave that kind of friendship.

Interestingly, for both Jennifer and me the fact that we were "thrown into this relationship" and the unclear definition of roles within our blended family turned out to have positive aspects. We both came to realize that the situation gave us some choice as to how we would relate. I think it helped Jennifer to encounter an adult who had different assumptions and values about how to live and interact. In making decisions about ourselves in the relationship, we both gained a clearer sense of our own identity. Jennifer reflected:

> Dad has the right to do whatever he likes and if it makes him happy I'm going to support it. . . . The fact that I was not going to cause trouble was always really important to me. . . . I was at the point in my life where I was trying to define my personality. I decided I wasn't the type of person to do something like that.

In addition, Jenny, having experienced an unsatisfying relationship with a stepfather (her mother's second husband), had learned like many survivors of divorce that family relationships often need to be protected.

I came into this relationship with more caution. I knew what it was like to have a failed relationship. I knew the cost of not getting along.

In deciding to be supportive of her father, Jennifer was certainly expressing a very adult side of herself. She was able to recognize him and his needs as a separate person. As I had felt when my father remarried, she was relieved that she no longer had to worry about his being alone. But I feel she also gained from his being happy and our becoming a stable family. I valued and supported aspects of Arthur—his unconventional side, his progressive politics, his artistic creativity, and his gentleness—that had previously gone largely unappreciated in their family network. By loving these parts of Arthur, I think I help Jennifer to recognize, love, and respect those parts of herself.

So far this chapter has focused primarily on the past, when Sara and I and Jennifer and I were getting to know and adjusting to each other. To conclude, I would like to explore the present and the future.

The process of talking to Sara and Jenny, listening to our taped conversations, and writing a piece that included their perceptions but basically represented my voice was both stimulating and confusing. While neither Sara nor Jennifer's version of events was radically different from my own, my understanding of what happened and what it meant shifted as I talked with them. In addition to Jenny and Sara's viewpoints, I myself had three different perspectives. I had to integrate my feelings and memories, my recorded interaction with Sara and Jenny, and my analytical observations as a psychologist and writer. In particular, I found it difficult to get an overview of and sum up relationships that were continuing to evolve. Indeed, the process of discussing and examining ourselves had an impact on our ongoing relationships.

With both Sara and Jenny, working on this project was a way to acknowledge our bond. Since Sara's daughter is recording Sara's stories and reminiscences, this was a way for me to document an aspect of the life of someone whom I consider to be quite special. Articulating our experiences has moved us a little closer to feeling like mother and daughter. In addition, I have been working on this chapter during my daughter Leah's first year. Sara is her only grandmother. We share our delight with Leah, and I find myself turning to Sara for advice and support. At this time in our lives, my own and Sara's developmental needs seem to be in sync.

Many of my own concerns are well described by psychological theorist Erik Erikson's model of the adult life cycle.[1] According to Erikson, people in their middle years are involved in the struggle to achieve generativity, which involves the concern with establishing and guiding the next generation and includes productivity and creativity. Expanding on Erikson's ideas, geriatric psychiatrist Robert Butler depicts later life as a time when people strive for a sense of continuity with past and future generations and attempt to fulfill the "elder function," the desire to counsel and pass on what one has learned.[2] Thus, for both Sara and myself, these needs are partly met by relating to each other and Leah. In recent years we both devoted a great deal of time to our careers, and the current desire to redirect some of our energy and become further enmeshed in family seems to be mutual.

As for Jennifer and I, we both liked the idea of collaborating on a creative endeavor. In addition, our conversation gave some closure to the period when we became a family and Jennifer moved from being a teenager to a young adult. Leah's arrival has also been a unifying force. Jennifer has been welcoming and caring toward her, and I get great pleasure from our family gatherings. However, for myself and Jennifer, I think that at this time defining our roles in regard to each other is difficult because we are in a period of transition. As Erikson put it, a young adult is concerned with "transferring the experience of being cared for in a parental setting to an adult affiliation actively chosen."[3] The theories derived from the research of psychologist Daniel Levinson also shed light on our diverging developmental agendas. According to Levinson, youth is a time of exploration and individuation; in middle age, people turn their energies toward settling in and building a solid life structure.[4]

I see my life structure as an intricate web in which my own needs are intertwined with those of certain family members and friends. Although it doesn't come easy, I know that at times I have to compromise my own desires. In order to meet the often overwhelming and competing responsibilities and demands, I have to be organized and efficient. I have to create order and maintain stability. Jennifer is confronted with very different tasks. While at present I am becoming somewhat less engaged in an already established career, she is trying to make a place for herself in the world of work. She needs to explore, take risks and shake things up. She is trying to free herself from some of the constraining voices in her life and assert herself. She faces the scary aloneness of being out there on her own.

Although Jennifer and I try to have empathy for each other's situation, we are often confused and buffeted by these shifting and sometimes contradictory pulls. While conflict over separation is practically a rite of passage for mothers and daughters, these issues seem to effect our step-relationship somewhat differently. On the one hand, because we do not have a history that stems back through childhood, the process is less painful and engenders less rebellion. On the other hand, we do not have that long history to sustain our tie during periods of turmoil. I think that what has helped us to maintain our connection is asserting and accepting that we are part of each other's family. One of the things I have always respected and appreciated about Jennifer is her commitment to our relationship, her willingness to come back and try again. As for the future, I hope that we will reach a point where we will be able to acknowledge, enjoy, and help each other as independent adults and that friendship will prove to be our deepest bond.

Notes

Acknowledgment: My thanks to Sara Sheiner Lewittes, M.D., and Jennifer Pellman for their contribution to and support for this project.

1. E. H. Erikson, "Life Cycle," in *Readings in Developmental Psychology*, ed. J. K. Gardner (Boston: Little, Brown, 1982).
2. R. N. Butler, "Toward a Psychiatry of the Life Cycle," in *Readings in Aging and Death: Contemporary Perspectives*, ed. S. H. Zarit (New York: Harper & Row, 1982).
3. Erikson, "Life Cycle," p. 10.
4. D. J. Levinson with C. N. Darrow, E. B. Klein, M. H. Levinson, and M. McKee, *The Seasons of a Man's Life* (New York: Ballantine Books, 1978).

31

Working-Class Mothering and the Problem of Weaning

Dympna C. Callaghan

In their incisive analysis of the family, Michele Barrett and Mary McIntosh (1982) refer to "the difficult project of reconciling private experience and social need, and of dealing with the ambivalence and contradiction that bedevil the political theorizing of subjectivity," (p. 10)). This is precisely the problem faced by any feminist who seeks to articulate her personal experience and its political implications.

Thus, it is with an uneasy awareness of myriad contradictions that I will attempt to outline some of the personal politics of being a stepparent by oscillating between feminist theory, the dominant ideology of the family, and the point of mundane reality at which these elements converge, particularly in the business of cooking and serving food.

Like most people who strive for a better and different social order, I experience a constant tension between the old tyranny of what a family should be and an uncertainty about how changing patterns of life should be lived. I am ensnared in the "traditional" role of the young woman who marries an older man, and the somewhat untraditional role of stepparent to two people who do not, at twenty-three and twenty, actually require parenting.

It could be that my situation is more common than I realize. Perhaps it is almost as much a staple of American family life as the familiar scenario of young children doing the rounds of various adults to whom they have complex and tenuous relationships in a familial chaos controlled, one fancies, by means of a leather-bound personal organizer. My situation may be seen as merely another chic alternative to the boredom of the traditional family. These are the images that come to mind when one thinks about domestic structures, persistently portrayed as homogenous units admitting little variation. We retain very limited models—stereotypes, in fact—of domestic life. These are the patriarchal blinders that prevent us from seeing the mechanisms of the traditional family structure let alone imagining new ones. With these in place, any domestic structure that deviates from the "norm" can, nonetheless, still be contained.

Given the ideological mystifications that surround everyday living, the recognition that "the individual aspects of oppression and change are not separate from the need for political and institutional change" is crucial (Bunch, 1985, p. 12). My domestic life as a feminist is often a daily struggle for equality within relationships that are frequently unclearly defined. Although there is much to be gained from recognizing that in some way or other I have not conformed to the exigencies of an oppressive social order, it is rarely possible to see my diurnal round as a practical exercise in radicalism. Sometimes it seems like a war of attrition.

As an adolescent in an Irish working-class family in Leeds, an industrial city in the north of England, I could never have imagined myself in my current situation: teaching at an American university, married to a man twenty years older, and a "stepparent" to two grown children only five and eight years younger than I. I certainly had no more idea of being a stepparent than I had of being middle class.

Leeds was a much grimier town then than it is now; a thick, black soot covered all the buildings. Since then, teams of workers have scrubbed most of them with acid, revealing, much to everyone's amazement, white and brown stone. But the areas I frequented most as a child, in that era before conductors yelling "Any more fares!" were replaced by mute ticket-dispensing machines, remain much the same. The center of the city has shifted to the new precinct, but the neglected buildings, like the one in which I took dancing class every Saturday, remind me how grim and confining I used to find this town. It now looks almost foreign to me, made strange and fascinating by time and distance.

When I was ten I had passed an exam that admitted me to a Catholic grammar school, where I soon realized that Leeds, for me, was a totally different place than it was for my newly acquired friends. Their mothers did not buy their fruit and vegetables from the market in sheets of soggy newspaper, but cellophane wrapped from the refrigerator shelves of Marks and Spencers. When I visited the houses of these girls, I was afraid I would say or do the wrong thing—choose the wrong piece of cutlery, or use some half-Gaelic expression that would bring stares and questions from a well-dressed, properly spoken parent. These girls, though Catholic, were born of English parents and were not, therefore, Catholic in the sense that I was

Catholic. They did not say the rosary every night kneeling before the three-bar electric fire and an altar to the Virgin May surrounded with plastic roses.

I thrived on nineteenth-century novels of romantic fantasy, ignoring the rows of bleak, dingy, terraced houses on the way to the library. My favorite book was *Jane Eyre*. Mr. Rochester, as you may remember, is twenty years older than the heroine, and there is a stepchild, Adele. Oddly enough, I had forgotten the age difference between Rochester and Jane until I read the novel again last summer. This time, however, my reading reverberated with Jean Rhys's *The Wide Sargasso Sea,* and with my own experience.

As an adolescent, I dreamed of education as a path from the monotony of working-class life, in which it is impossible to go anywhere or to do anything new because there is no money with which to do it. The annual day trip to Scarborough, the nearest seaside town, was always one of the wettest days in August, the buses were always late, the macintoshes stank of wet rubber, and we drank tea at the bus shelter in the plastic cup-lid of our Thermos. Scarborough, though it offered many pleasures, even in the rain, did not exactly open up the endless possibilities of travel, of escape. It always surprises me that political analysts do not understand why the proletariat is so reluctant to change anything, let alone the status quo. They don't know, or they have forgotten, that in such lives, very little ever changes.

Despite Scarborough, I had a bizarre notion that my life would be a fairy tale. I would do exotic and interesting things,I would read *Paradise Lost* and *The Divine Comedy*. (Indeed I did. I read, I traveled—to Marrakech when I was nineteen on the wages from a summer job as a cleaner.) I would fall desperately in love and live a poignant, passionate life. (And, indeed, I have done that too.)

Social classes after all reproduce themselves through families, through the bearing and rearing of children (Barrett and McIntosh, 1982, p. 43), and so I had no reason to expect that my life would be very different from my parents'. In one sense, of course, I was primed by a grammar school education for upward mobility, and by my father's warning finger at the bus stop early in the morning before school, pointing to girls of sixteen and seventeen pushing their prams to the childminder before a day at the factory or the mill. I was, in that sense, prepared to move up within a field acceptable for women: teaching, the field I have in fact entered. But I was also primed to become a good Catholic mother, not a feminist stepparent.

It occurred to me at twenty-five that I was taking an enormous risk as I packed my bags and three tea chests in my one-room flat in Brighton and came to live with a man so much older than myself. I had always wanted passion, but I feared being reckless. I wondered about age difference. I pondered it excessively. Oddly enough, I did not ponder stepchildren. (I wonder if they pondered me?) I had vague thoughts that his daughter might be a problem. But since my partner's children were eighteen and twenty-one when we married, I did not see myself as a stepparent. I thought that his children would not touch my life. Yes, my adolescent imaginings of the details of my future had indeed been a bit dim.

Sometimes the reality of my transgression alarms the good Catholic adolescent in me: the *third* wife of a man *twenty* years older. I calm myself with the thought that my parents are more than twenty years older than my partner. But there remain these people of six feet three and five feet eight, respectively, who have sprung like sunflowers from my partner's loins, whose mother was murdered many years ago, and whose former stepmother figures in my life every now and again as a voice on the telephone from Georgia. This voice is the echo of my partner's past—in twenty years a man can acquire a lot of past.

I used to think that I didn't have a past, but I realize now that I do. I have a working-class girlhood in Leeds. A crucial element in my past was that I had a mother. Maternal influence is something of which neither my partner nor his children have had much experience. The children lost their first mother in a violent, terrible way; the boy was ten and the girl eight. Their "second mother" left five years later. My partner lost his mother when he was fourteen, after years of chronic ill health; he lost the mother of his children and then the woman he had hoped would replace her for the remainder of his children's formative years. In contrast to all these blank maternal spaces, I have a mother who is, like most mothers, an active participant in the mythology of motherhood. I have a mother whom I love inordinately, who comforted me with "Graw macree my girleen"—Irish words I have never seen written and therefore do not know how to spell. I have a mother who baked at least twice a week: scones, apple pies, jam tarts, and "a sponge" for special occasions. A "plain cook," a "fast cook," a nurturer, a woman of discipline. (Fortunately, my mother had daughters; Irish mothers are notorious for indulging their sons.)

My mother daily fed my father as if he had been deprived of food for a month. He did strenuous work with pick and shovel on construction projects throughout the city, and when he came home his face and clothes were black and he stank of tar and muck and sweat. Once washed and fed, he sank, pale and utterly exhausted, into sleep in front of the television and the aforementioned three-bar electric. My mother, of course, worked too. She had a job as a waitress. She fed people all day long at the Griffin Hotel: barristers, executives, accountants, and the like, a hoard of wealthy ravenous strangers, sophisticated infants crying for my mother's breast.

It is not surprising, then, that many of the problems I encounter with my partner's son revolve around the issue of feeding. As Rosalind Coward points out, "How food is prepared has crucial implications for women in this society, because it expresses deeply held ideologies of provision and dependence" (1985, p. 109). Men of course are thought to be the providers while women are thought to be the dependents whose domestic service is the price of being taken care of. It seems to me that this is a classic instance of ideological mystification since quite the reverse is true. It is men who are utterly dependent on women for everyday survival.

My partner's son grew up the way most men do, expecting that a woman would service all his needs and believing that there is a natural correlation between having breasts and producing goodies from the kitchen. He undoubtedly casts me in the role of mother, and he undoubtedly calls forth the nurturing mother in me. His ideal of womanhood is his grandmother, who dotes on him, spoils him, and most of all feeds him, and his happiest memories are of her kitchen. At first, to find a place in this strange household in a foreign country, I found myself baking, cooking, and being the good Irish mother as a way of being accepted. My partner's son would demand food, only to become sullen and resentful when fed. I suppose I didn't measure up to his all-nurturing grandmother, a woman whose power, at some level, may also have threatened him. I imagine he also saw me trying to fill his cherished maternal space, that of his murdered mother, the mark of his difference from the rest of the unwounded. He both wanted nurturing and resented it.

Not surprisingly, I grew tired and indignant. For a while, it seemed that I was eternally making scones. At twenty-two and showing no sign of ever leaving home, my partner's son displayed clear signs of resenting me as the interloper who was by now refusing responsibility for his stomach. He was the child abandoned by yet another mother, and apparently in retaliation, he became a "vegetarian" who ate only pizza, but was allergic to cheese.

I became for him the wicked stepmother who was coming between him and his father; I was starving him, forcing him out into the cruel, harsh world. Finally, he did get an apartment by himself, but while this eased the strain it did not solve the problems of his expectations of me. In the summer, he moved back in and at twenty-three shows even greater reluctance to leave home.

My partner's son wants me to make up for his lost mothers, a desire made all the more difficult by his father's acute identification with him. My partner sees his son as his own younger, wounded self, an identification he has been able to acknowledge with the help of an analyst.

In trying to deal with the enormous burden of living with two grown men who want me to be a mother, I have come to realize that mothering as we know it in this scheme of things is a vital instrument in the maintenance of patriarchy and in the making of men who dominate women. The table is the site of the worst family battles. War breaks out over tandoori chicken; father and son turn on me when I bemoan their lack of culinary skills, charging that I never change the oil in the car. I point out, with considerable vehemence, the oil is changed only twice a year. "Anyway," I say, waving a large cast-iron frying pan for emphasis, as I turn into a ridiculous parody of women's resistance, "it's not my car. I have a bicycle, which I oil myself!"

With my partner's daughter, I have developed a much better relationship, not because sons are scoundrels and daughters angels (although I have many times been tempted to read the situation in this way) or because I have been, in this instance, more resourceful in evading the role prescribed for me, but merely because I have been able to fall back on another model: sister. I have one sister but no brothers, and I went to an all-girls' grammar school for seven of the most formative years of my life, from ten to eighteen, during which I had contact with no man other than my father. My partner's daughter falls into the sister/close girlfriend mode. At the moment, this causes less pain than my uncategorizable relationship with her brother, but I don't know how viable this model for our relationship will be in the long term. Who can tell what battles lie ahead? Nonetheless, being female in this culture, she is far more independent than her brother and attends college away from home. She is also expected to feed herself, so at least the kitchen is an unlikely battle ground for any future conflict.

Even if I have children to whom I am a biological parent, I cannot and do not want to be a "Mother." Mothers, as we have come to know them, are perfect: mothers feed their children with their own flesh, mothers never yell, mothers love their sons inordinately, they sacrifice their own lives, they are limited, boring, and sometimes they go insane. It is very hard to envision one's place in the world as a woman who does not want to be someone's mommy. No single human being should be assigned all the tasks assigned a Mother. Mothers bear a moral burden of keeping intact the fabric of society. If Mothers don't mother, we are told, children will be drug addicts and anarchy will ensue. If women who have children don't mother in the way prescribed by patriarchy, there is some hope of change, and as feminists we should use this to our advantage. "Don't mother, don't mother," I chant as my mantra, wandering around the kitchen trying to resist the compulsion to serve up food to my partner's son. Then there's the guilt of sending the helpless six-foot-three adult with a football player's physique from the table with "If you want to eat you have to fix your own food." More guilt as he responds, "I only wondered if you had a little extra." I steel myself this time. "If you don't help cook, you don't eat." I'm getting a little better at this all the time.

Did Jane Eyre have these problems of living and communication with little Adele and her charming French accent? I think not. She had servants to cook for her and her disabled husband (he was blind and had only one arm at the finish, you may remember). When we try to escape the tryanny of the traditional, often suffocating "happy" foursome from which we may have come, what price do we pay? What do we bring upon ourselves?

To begin with, the tension involved in male/female relations is exacerbated in the stepparenting situation, where love and power become visible as they cannot be in the apparently "natural" intimacies of the traditional family. Thus, in my case, it's far easier to see these problems of power and gender in vivid technicolor with my partner's son than with my partner, my male, feminist mate.

Yet it is better to struggle with the evils of patriarchal oppression by exposing the flimsy myth of the traditional family than it is to perpetuate it. Interestingly enough, the American antifeminist movement, which puts its considerable energies and resources into "preserving" the traditional family, exhibits enormous distrust of men; after all, men, as a result of "male instinct," want sex without the responsibility of supporting wives and families (Ehrenrich, 1983, p. 147). Thus, right-wing women displace their wariness of men onto feminism, fearing it as a force that, in advocating female autonomy, undermines a woman's so-called right to be supported by her husband. Barbara Ehrenreich points out: "The rights and 'privileges' that the antifeminists believe are accorded to women are, at best, private arrangements reinforced by convention; at worst, comforting fantasies" (p. 146).

Woman battering, child abuse, and incest exist behind that old cheerful facade of the happy family. The right-wing godly women who strive to bring up drug-free, sex-free, sheltered, safe children ripe for salvation will undoubtedly bequeath their children the most grief. Struggling to be ourselves in an honest relationship with those we live with and love is surely better than the hidden violence and misery of living by role expectation.

But what has all this rambling to do with feminist stepparenting and the theoretical rumblings with which I began? To begin with, it has to do with the fact that the personal is political. It has to do with the terrible shock I feel in realizing in this, the twenty-eighth year of my life, that I am not my mother, that I just can't be a mother, that living the way I do requires a new way of thinking, a new way of imagining how lives might be. That new imaging begins with a refusal to endorse the artificial dichotomy between the domestic and the social (Weeks, 1985, pp. 96–120), and a refusal to go on swallowing the lie of the traditional family. Refusing, even in some minor way, to endorse traditional structures after going through the painful process of making those structures visible, must be a step to dismantling the remarkably obdurate institution of the patriarchal family.

It is first necessary to address the way our subjectivity is molded by the patriarchal family, and in this I feel that my level of insight has been greatly increased by psychoanalysis. Both my partner and I have been better able to deal with our situation by regular visits to our respective analysts. I would characterize myself as a generally happy person in a very good relationship, but for all that there are problems in my stepparenting situation that must be confronted with outside help. This necessitates realizing that "family matters" are not necessarily "private," and that the people we live with cannot provide all necessary emotional support. Individual domestic units should not be required to be absolutely self-sufficient, any more than individuals should. In my case, analysis has helped me avoid some of the isolation that I experience through living so far away from my sister, my parents, and supportive women friends.

Therapy is crucial because the problems of domestic life, particularly stepparenting, remain in process for a very long time. There is no instant solution to changing our lives or our society. Long after my partner's son leaves home, I may well experience situations with which sessions of psychoanalysis or counseling could help; for example, what if someday grandchildren come to stay? Sadly, this option is unavailable to those who cannot afford it. At this point we confront the economic foundation of an unjust social structure and its inbuilt resistance to change.

The domestic, the personal, remain crucial frontiers in the feminist transformation of society.

> If redirecting the processes of socialization is to happen, we must then find critical points and strategies for changing family forms and relationships. . . . Since socialization is the growth of a social being, all existing forms of people's relationships can potentially be agents of socialization. . . . Roles are determined largely by family form which defines personal relationships and by class structure which defines economic relationships of groups of people. ["Report of the Bangkok Workshop," p. 29]

In terms of my current domestic circumstances, this means if my partner's son can stop seeing me as a breast and I can stop behaving like one, perhaps we can get along better.

References

Barrett, Michele, and Mary McIntosh. *The Anti-social Family.* London: Verso/New Left Books, 1982.

Bunch, Charlotte. *Bringing the Global Home.* Denver: Antelope Publications, 1985.

Coward, Rosalind. *Female Desires.* New York: Grove Press, 1985.

Ehrenreich, Barbara. *The Hearts of Men.* Garden City, N.Y.: Anchor Press/Doubleday, 1983.

"Report of the Bangkok Workshop 1979, in preparation for the 1980 Copenhagen Women's Conference: Feminist Ideology and Structures in the First Half of the Decade for Women." In *Developing Strategies for the Future: Feminist Perspectives,* edited by Charlotte Bunch and Shirley Castley. New York: International Women's Tribune Center, 1980.

Weeks, Jeffrey. *Sexuality and Its Discontents.* London: Routledge and Kegan Paul, 1985.

32
Reading Stepfamily Fiction

Nan Bauer Maglin

> Little brother took his little sister by the hand and said: "Since our mother died we have had no happiness; our stepmother beats us every day, and if we come near her she kicks us away with her foot. Our meals are the hard crusts of bread that are left over; and the little dog under the table is better off, for she often throws it a choice morsel. God pity us, if our mother only knew!"
>
> —"Brother and Sister," *The Complete Grimm's Fairy Tales*

> But he so much wanted to win Ian over; seeing him embraced by Laura had been unsettling. He didn't want her to have a monopoly on Ian's love. Ian had also been kissed goodbye by Jane; David wondered how she thought of Ian—as a son, maybe, or a stepson, or perhaps just as a little boy who happened to belong to her lover.
>
> —Meg Wolitzer, *Hidden Pictures*

In August 1981 I read *Stepping* by Nancy Thayer; in July 1986 I reread it. In those five years I became the stepmother to three children, two girls and a boy. When I first read the novel, I was just about to enter into this role that then held for me only mystery and a quiet kind of terror; having spent a good part of my adult life wrestling with the image of the wicked mother of my past, I now had to confront the image of myself as the wicked stepmother of the present. Like Zelda in Thayer's 1981 novel, "I always identified with Snow White or Cinderella instead of their stepmothers. I wasn't prepared for this role; I didn't choose it" (p. 9).

After five years of being a stepmother, I am interested in whether I read the novel any differently now. Moreover, stepping, both the book and the experience, has caused me to wonder about the stories we write now about stepfamilies. Western culture has a long tradition of stepmother tales, but are we telling or being told different stories now that family structures have changed so drastically? Myths and fairytales, as Gilbert and Gubar (1976) suggest, "often both state and enforce culture's sentences with greater accuracy than more sophisticated literary texts" (p. 36). For example, the central action of "Snow White" (retitled by Gilbert and Gubar "Snow White and Her Wicked Stepmother") is the conflict of two women: "the one fair, young, pale, the other just as fair, but older, fiercer; the one a daughter, the other a [step]mother; the one sweet, ignorant, passive, the other both artful and active; the one a sort of angel, the other an undeniable witch" (p. 36). Snow White, pure, chaste, childlike, docile, submissive, is "the heroine of a life that has no story" (p. 39) or rather, if she wants to grow up to be the wife and mother, there is only one story to follow.[1]

The fairytale splits the mother into two: the good mother, who is the protector, often taking the form of the good fairy, old woman, or biological mother; and the bad mother, evil fairy, or stepmother, who invariably appears odious, embodying "the major obstacles against passage to womanhood" (Rowe, 1986, p. 212). The queen/stepmother in "Snow White," for example, is a "plotter, a plot-maker, a schemer, a witch, an artist, an impersonator, a woman of almost infinite creative energy, witty, wily, and self-absorbed as all artists are" (Gilbert and Gubar, 1976, pp. 38–39).

This and similar tales sabotage female assertiveness, power, defiance, or self-expression, both by the portrayal of the stepmother and the ends she comes to. For even though the stepmother (or her double, the witch) is powerful and creative, that power is articulated only in evil ways and she is always defeated or destroyed. What these fairytales state and enforce is "the paradigm of women's development in a specifically patriarchal culture" (E. Rose, 1983, p. 209). Tales like Cinderella, for example, "the fairytale most commonly repeated in Western culture, [warn] girls to expect nothing but abuse from women [her stepsisters and stepmother] and teach them to look to men [the prince] for salvation" (Herman, 1981, p. 1). Is that the paradigm under which we still write and live? If the fictions, the stories of marriage, have affected the shapes of our lives, as Phyllis Rose (1984, p. 19) has so perceptively written, so too have the stories of stepfamilies.

As the nuclear family continues to reshape itself through divorce and remarriage, fiction will both reflect and write that reshaping. This article will consider five contemporary extended narratives of remarriage and stepparenting: *Stepping* (1981) by Nancy Thayer; *Happily Ever After . . .*

Almost (1982) by Judie Wolkoff; *Sinking, Stealing* (1985) by Jan Clausen; *The Stepdaughter* (1966) by Iris Bromige; and *The Stepdaughter* (1976) by Caroline Blackwood.

There are more out there, I am sure; statistics would seem to guarantee it. Depictions of the stepmother do exist, as well, in such recent novels as Sue Miller's *The Good Mother*, Alice Munro's *The Beggar Maid*, and Alice Walker's *The Color Purple* and in such contemporary short stories as "The Lost Cottage" and "Family Dancing" by David Leavitt (upper-middle-class divorce and the remarriage of the men), "A Birthday Remembered" by Ann Allen Shockley (a lesbian stepmother), and "A Gift of Grass" by Alice Adams (a stepdaughter's distance from her mother and stepfather). Neither is fiction of the past devoid of stepfamilies. In most, if not all, of these stories, the stepfamilies are formed by death, not divorce, as in "The Bound Girl" by Mary Wilkins Freeman set in 1753 (written in the 1890s), "Tom's Husband" (1884) by Sarah Orne Jewett, and "Oats for the Woman" (1917) by Fannie Hurst.[2]

I chose to discuss these five contemporary novels because at the center of their conflicts is the re-creation of modern familial relations through the replacement of one or more parents. They contain varied narratives of stepfamilies, covering the years 1966 to 1985, and they address their stories to somewhat different audiences: young readers *(Happily Ever After)*, romance readers (Bromige), lesbian feminist readers *(Sinking, Stealing)*, middle-class educated women *(Stepping)*, and "literature" readers (Blackwood). Taken collectively, the five of them create a text against which we can read our own stepfamily stories and in which we can listen for the echoes of Snow White and Cinderella.

We can ask a single question of all of them: Is the stepmother still wicked? That question then breaks down into several others: Can stepmothers do other than abuse their stepdaughters? Can stepmothers like/love their stepdaughters and can stepdaughters like/love their stepmothers? Can stepmothers and mothers get along in some manner? These questions about stepmothers suggest in turn others about the family: Are these stories of "broken" families and tension-filled second families? Are they stories of nuclear families, be they second or first? Or are they stories that deconstruct the dominant discourse and envision different kinds of families? These questions overlay even more basic questions about what a family is, who and what a parent is, and who and what a mother is. While the concentration in this discussion is on the relationship among women (and finally on the relationship of biological mother to stepmother), fathers and stepfathers are in sight as they vary in their exercise of power in the family. Only in *Happily Ever After . . . Almost* is the stepson a prominent character.

I begin with *Stepping* because it is the first book I read and has served as the frame in which I read the other four. As its title suggests, it addresses many of the issues for the stepfamily head on, putting Zelda, the stepmother, at its center with Adelaide, the ex-wife, and Cathy and Caroline, the daughters of Adelaide and stepdaughters of Zelda, on the edges. It is a story of four women in a series of overlapping families.

The situation is that Charlie divorced Adelaide and later married Zelda in 1964; there is fifteen years' difference between Charlie and Zelda; he has two daughters: Caroline, age eight, and Cathy, age six. Zelda's first meeting with the children sets up a persistent pattern: she feels left out, different, alone in the back, extra. Their presence stuns Zelda: they are blond and big boned; she is "dark and small and curly-haired, and alone" (p. 52). Charlie and the girls sit in the front seat, hugging; she sits in the back seat. She is jealous of his love for these two girl children; she realizes that they transform the private adult relationship she has with Charlie. She had never chosen them; she had chosen Charlie. She, a young graduate student, who was not even a mother (and had no desire then to be one), had to compete with Adelaide, their mother, Charlie's ex-wife.

Adelaide's desperation dominates the girls' first summer visit. Adelaide had not wanted the divorce, had defined herself as mother and wife, and could not bear the summers without her two daughters. She would call frequently and "screech"; she wrote long letters of instructions on how to treat *her* daughters. Zelda was trapped in a no-win situation: she wanted to do it right and be a real and perfect mommy and yet she also did not want to be like Adelaide, apparently destroyed by the institution of the nuclear family:

> For a long time, for years, I would not make homemade bread, or talk to women who had children, or keep my kitchen floor shiny. I didn't want to do anything that Adelaide had done. I didn't want to be like her in any way at all. I thought she was a sad, nutty, lost woman. [p. 72]

And Zelda knew she was not the mother (defining this position in very traditional terms): "I couldn't have been their mommy. And I don't believe I ever did things that mommies do" (p. 108).

What she knew was that she was a stepmother and she defined that as "wicked stepmother" (p. 108), sort of the opposite of mother. This is the stepmother of the tales, someone active, a noncomformist, someone who writes her own story; Adelaide up until the divorce had been the conforming, passive mother of the tales. In the tales, however, the mother is dead; in these contemporary tales, the mother and stepmother live side by side, as it were. She, the daughters, and Adelaide all dwell in a condition of "stepping bitterness" (p. 21).

In contrast to the fairytales, the stepmother and stepdaughter relationship is not static; stepmother and stepdaughters go through a thirteen-year process. However, their relationship does not simply get better and better; they never mesh into "a fat new nuclear family" (p. 2). They do gain a history, a context for relating. After about seven years, the girls seem to care for Zelda and Zelda cares for them—especially for Caroline. After a semester of living together in Amsterdam, they had become "a sort of family, that is a group of people connected to each other, sharing a life" (p. 179). However, Zelda becomes pregnant during this time and the relationship turns icy again, like the first summer. The girls, who had just begun to acknowledge Zelda as some sort of mother to them, turn away from her as she becomes a biological mother and as she is in need of some nurturing herself. This is true for the first and second pregnancy. Whereas the girls feel in competition with Zelda for their father, now they also feel in competition with their stepsiblings for him and perhaps for Zelda.

One of the problems in the process of stepping is silence; no one can speak her anger, fears, and needs. For instance, Zelda's pregnancy is never spoken of, even though it is clearly evident. When Zelda speaks to herself, admitting she actively wishes Adelaide dead or passively fantasizes Caroline and Cathy in a plane crash, she is horrified at her ugly desires—not the desires of a mother. When she becomes a mother herself she realizes that even biological mothers fantasize such things. But for everyone in the stepfamily, there does not appear to be the mystique of the natural nuclear family to hold them together if they give voice to negative feelings, although that might, in the long run, have been better: "It might have been better that first year, if the girls could have arrived with whips and sticks and rocks in their luggage, if they could have spent all their time with us hitting us and screaming at us and calling us names" (p. 59). It is hard to speak positive feelings also: "I kept hoping that Caroline or Cathy might say, 'And we're glad you married Zelda. It's been neat knowing her.' But no one mentioned me at all" (p. 162). When the girls become older, twenty and twenty-three, they acknowledge some of the old left-out feelings. And Zelda, at this point, can say that she loves her stepdaughters.

It appears that when they discard the dominant discourse, the relationships work more easily. For instance, after about ten years of summer visits, Zelda says, "I was really happy to see them. I almost cried out of sheer delight. These were my—my what? I had no word for it. Not daughters, not relatives, not friends, but *my* somethings, creatures that I had known for a long time and helped and influenced and cared for" (p. 197). The labels and slots in the nuclear family seem to allow for only limited amounts of love relationships. Again, letting go of the traditional familial name tags seems to open up possibilities. Zelda resolves that "Lucy and Adam and Caroline and Cathy will never be brothers and sisters, but perhaps they'll live as friends. Perhaps they will enrich each other's lives" (p. 173). And Zelda realizes that stepmothers can do different things than mothers (this comes to her at a bar with Caroline in New Haven); they have the possibility of being friends with their stepdaughters.

The biological mother, Adelaide, also is shown as going through a process, although for three-quarters of the story she is portrayed as wicked and destructive to herself, her daughters, Zelda, and Charlie. Adelaide remarries twice and finally secures a job she cares about, but not before a tremendous amount of pain, which appears to Zelda as dominating and determining Zelda's life. At first, Zelda sees only the differences between them: Adelaide is a mother and Zelda wants to be a professional; a generation apart, they have different identities and aspirations. Even the commonalities create separations: they both have to care for Caroline and Cathy; they both were wives of Charlie. An understanding of Adelaide comes for Zelda when she has her own children and she feels like "screeching" in the grips of motherhood. Intellectually Zelda reaches for an alliance with Adelaide: "I've often wanted to feel, in a grand humanitarian way, like her sister; but I'm not her sister. I don't even know her. I've seen her only two or three times in thirteen years" (pp. 5–6).

Both *Stepping* and *Happily Ever After . . . Almost* portray a process that contains good and bad, but both try to present the second family in a positive light. (Since *Happily* is for young readers, it is almost uncomplicatedly positive.) *Stepping* tells the story from the point of view of the stepmother, *Happily* from the stepdaughter's viewpoint. Both contain "evil" biological mothers.

In *Happily*, Judie Wolkoff is rewriting the dominant narrative. In fact, she talks against the notion of an evil stepmother (as well as an evil stepfather), and against the idea that children suffer in the "breakdown" and "disruption" of a nuclear family.

The family, as described through the eyes of eleven-year-old Kitty, consists of twenty-four members. Kitty and Sarah Birdsall's mother (Liz) marries R. J.'s father (Seth); their father marries Linda, who has two children. During the course of the story, both Linda and Liz get pregnant. The girls' dad lives in Croton; their mother lives in SoHo: two different lifestyles are available to Kitty and Sarah. Their father is a Westchester doctor; Linda is a nurse. Their mother is a layout artist and Seth is a photographer. They inherit Jewish grandparents through their stepfather, Seth. And there is R. J.'s mother, Kay, who like Adelaide is portrayed as the desperate (here rich and spoiled) "natural" mother.

The public expectation in the book is that divorce and remarriage can only be bad; it "disrupts" the family and creates a "broken" home, and therefore children suffer. For example, Kitty's friend Minna (the only one who can keep track of all her family) voices this expectation: "Aww, come on Kitty. . . . You don't have to cover for me. You must *hate* Seth! Nobody wants some guy who isn't their father living with them" (p. 7). And Mrs. Worley, Kitty's teacher, queries her on the up-and-coming wedding, disappointed when Kitty would not agree that "sometimes these adjustments can be difficult. Accepting a stepparent isn't easy" (p. 114). Kitty's confidential school folder has the words *Broken Home* added in red after her name. "It looked as if my name were Kitty Birdsall Broken Home" (p. 114).

Both Kitty and Sarah like Seth, their stepfather, and in fact welcome him to the family because they understand that being a single mom was difficult for Liz (she was depressed and harassed during that period). Even more so, they realize that their mother and father did not make good partners.

> The truth is, you *do* want your own parents married to each other. But once you accept the fact that none of you will be happy if they are, you don't necessarily hate whoever else they marry.
> From the start, Sarah and I thought Seth was terrific. Same with Linda our stepmother. She's calm and organized, the kind of person who knows what she's cooking a week before she's hungry. Dad is more relaxed with her than he ever was with Mom, who's been known to forget the laundry for a month if she suddenly got a bug to frame weeds or something. Mom's also moody . . . Dad always stopped talking to her when she got sulky, sometimes for days. Seth talks. And he makes Mom talk. [p. 5]

The book does suggest that there are difficulties in reconstituting or blending families; mainly this involves tensions between the siblings. Kitty and R. J. are both eleven and very different kinds of people. Besides being uncomfortable with this up-tight, smart boy, Kitty is jealous of her mother's patience and apparent affection for him. She always takes his side (p. 54) and never gets mad at him (p. 41). Kitty notices that Seth never gets mad at her and her sister, either. Mom tries to explain the resentment between Kitty and R. J. as largely to do with R. J. feeling threatened that his father was going to live with Kitty and Sarah and not with him, comparing this to how Kitty once felt when her father moved in with Linda and her children, Peter and Shirley. Kitty has already forgotten her own feelings of jealousy towards her stepsiblings.

Not only do R. J. and Kitty work out their difficulties, but an "ex-tended" (p. 146) family is constructed, which includes R. J. in Dad's fam-ily also. When Dad and Linda have a baby, R. J. feels related; when Dad and Linda have the girls over for the Christmas holidays, they include R. J. Looking back, Kitty admits that the saddest day of "all my life" was when Dad moved out; looking forward, she says: "And someday, not so many years from now when you look back and ask, Would I change today if I could? you'll say, No . . . no, I wouldn't. It would mean never know-ing all those new people I love" (p. 215).

Kay, R. J.'s mother, is the only one in this revised family who cannot make it work. Kay is cold to R. J. and critical of him (as a result R. J. is "neurotic" and seeing a therapist); she does everything from giving his guinea pig away to trying to take him permanently to London. When she loses a custody battle (Seth had lost the first court battle when they got divorced) and R. J. runs away, she makes a drunken scene in the middle of the night outside of the SoHo loft. She is the only reason Liz hesitates about marrying Seth: "Oh, Lord, I wonder if I'm tough enough to deal with a woman like Kay" (p. 37).

Kay, like Adelaide, retains the title of mother, yet has great unease about competing with another woman who also is now called (step)mother and has the marriage and the man. Both *Stepping* and *Happily* seem to blame these two women, portraying them as neurotic, rather than somehow showing that they are not the problem. The problem is structural—that the nuclear family is embedded in our social life (and here I mean every-thing from our psyches to our economy) in a way that this new form is not. These books imply that Adelaide and Kay are just not good enough wives and mothers, not good people; they should be able to adjust to the changes in their relationships to their children. In rewriting the stories from the stepmother's and the husband's perspective, the character of the wicked first mother/wife is being created.

Susan Rubin Suleiman, in her paper "The 'Other Mother': On Maternal Splitting," suggests that the inability of mothers to acknowledge "the pos-sibility that they are not the only ones on whom the child's welfare, the child's whole life and self depend" is more than psychological. Because "we live in a society where divorce is rampant, where the old presump-tions no longer hold, where mothers feel increasingly threatened *as moth-ers*, financially, emotionally and legally" (pp. 22–23), mothers feel too vulnerable to let go.

Sinking, Stealing also has an evil biological parent; this time it is the father: Clausen, more than the other writers, looks at the social construc-tion of families, although according to the demands of the genre the action still revolves around personalities. The central struggle is one of custody:

Josie and Rhea had lived together as lesbian lovers and partners for five years, raising Rhea's daughter, Ericka. When Rhea is killed in a car crash, Daniel, the biological father and Rhea's ex-husband, moves to take Ericka (now ten) full time and include her in his remarriage family, which consists of Brenda, his second wife, and their daughter. During the time Rhea and Josie lived together, Daniel saw Ericka intermittently (p. 58), although more regularly after his remarriage.

Sinking, Stealing explodes the definition of mother by taking it beyond the "simple" opposition of stepmother and biological mother. In this tale, the biological mother and second mother (or stepmother? what is the word?) live together; Brenda is another (official) stepmother who calls herself Ericka's mother when Rhea dies; Brenda's mothering of her daughter Leah and stepdaughter Ericka is sustained by Nilda Campos, the housekeeper, who cares for Brenda's kids instead of her own children. Can she be called a third stepmother or surrogate mother? Or can all four be called mothers?

The question of who and what a mother is begins before Rhea dies. When Josie and Rhea move in together, both between themselves and for Ericka the question of Josie's role is crucial. Josie says that Rhea used to tell Ericka:

> "You have two mothers." That was an error, of course. I might be many things, might wake with her in the night and guard her play and comfort hurts and read monosyllabic books and praise her and scold her and make her eat vegetables—but children do not have two mothers. Anyone knows that. . . . So we got it settled: I was not her mother. But neither was I nothing. [p. 21]

When Rhea dies, Josie has no official or legal standing; she has no legal name, "I'm nobody's mother" (p. 21), nobody's relative. But she had parented for five years and a name, "Flommy," had evolved for her position, a name whose meaning now only Ericka and Josie understand.

While joining a family already constructed is not easy, as Zelda *(Stepping)* also found out, it is simultaneously easier and harder to join an all-female family:

> Certainly it made things easier that she [Ericka] was so young when the three of us started living together. Even so, the divorce upset her, and she was jealous at times of my claim on Rhea's attention. As I struggled to insinuate myself into the mother-daughter nexus, there were moments I felt like a hapless organ transplant besieged by an indignant swarm of antibodies. In the end, all three of us were lucky, for by the time the dust of an almost ritual confrontation had settled, Ericka and I had discovered we rather liked one another. [p. 157]

As "official mother," Rhea was always secure in her identity; like Zelda, Josie has no "natural rights" in the role. She takes it on uncomfortably. But whereas the outside world has a name for Zelda once she marries Charlie—*stepmother*—Josie's relationship with Ericka is invisible. A co-worker asks Josie why she appears so down. Josie tells of the imminent loss of Ericka, who is "almost like my daughter." But of course no one can really believe this (p. 94). Gina then asks if Josie ever thought "about having your own kids."

Upon Rhea's death, Josie is catapulted into the position of mother (p. 61) whenever Ericka and Josie are together. When you are in the stepparent position, as Josie was, you can always defer to the biological parent when things get too hard: Here, she's *your* child; you take her. And the child can always ignore the stepparent, appealing to the authority of the biological parent. This is no longer possible for Josie and Ericka. Whereas Josie wrestles with this hard commitment, Daniel has to wrestle with neither his nor Josie's position, given his "natural rights": "But I *am* her father, after all" (p. 82). Against Daniel's biological stance, Josie asserts a social definition of parent: "The point is, I've *raised* Ericka. I've lived with her for well over half her life—much longer than you, in fact. You don't suddenly veto that, cancel it, make it disappear" (p. 82).

But he does decide to cancel it, first by limiting Josie's time with Ericka, using her rather as a glorified babysitter, and then by deciding to move to Cleveland, where he has been offered a good academic job. Josie is not a professional, but a musician and an activist who supports herself through any kind of labor. She cannot afford to follow them. Daniel makes it clear she is not invited anyway.

The only way Josie can maintain any relationship with Ericka is to "kidnap" her. Their trip cross-country, which ends in Oregon, is sadly ironic. They are finally mother and daughter: Laura and Cindy Cole. Cindy/Ericka calls Laura/Josie "Mom." To avoid suspicion they live a Middle American family life: "I've reverted to all-American menus here: no tofu, but meatloaf, fried chicken" (p. 242). Josie works swing shift at Dexter's Do-nut Depot; they have little time together (and little money), cooped up in a one-room apartment. Hiding, lying, anxious of being discovered, they can have no friends, no women's support network. It is hard to be loving under these conditions. In order to have a relationship, their old relationship has to be denied. Josie is no longer Rhea's partner and Ericka's Flommy. "I used to be Rhea's lover. I used to be a musician. I used to be from Brooklyn. I used to have politics . . . I used to attend meetings. I used to have ambitions. I used to read books. I used to love women" (p. 249).

Although Ericka agreed to flee with Josie, she really wanted everything to remain as it was: having an upper-middle-class family with Daniel and a nontraditional one with Josie. Her diary expresses her feeling that no one really wants her (p. 174). They begin their trip west in high spirits as outlaws, but they end in a defeat already foreshadowed in Josie's question, "But what happens when she [Ericka] finds out I'm not her fairy godmother?" (p. 123) Daniel will not compromise, as Josie had hoped. The only solution is to return *his* daughter and suffer the consequences. Yet this story has a fairy godmother. Summoned by Ericka to save her "stepmother," Rhea's mother, Belle, unexpectedly opposes the natural rights of the father and supports her daughter's lover's claim to her granddaughter. Ericka can go back to calling Josie "Flommy" (p. 269). Using political skills honed in the 1930s, Belle, we expect, will work out a shared-custody arrangement.

To the question of what and who a mother is and what a stepmother is, *Sinking, Stealing* shows that the answers are not produced by emotional truths but by a legal system that supports the interests of the patriarchal state and family. Similar to the denouement in the 1986 novel *The Good Mother,* the story (without Belle's intervention) would have ended with a nuclear, heterosexual family and a nonsexual or antisexual mother. In *Stepping* and *Happily Ever After,* the courts were called in and supported the biological father (although not initially in both cases). The contest, both times, was between the biological parents, however. *Sinking, Stealing* asks, what are the rights of the stepmother, of the lesbian stepmother? Although the stepmother has no voice in such a legal contest, she is a legal entity. The lesbian "stepmother" does not exist.[3] Whereas Rhea and Josie and Ericka had been moving toward a redefinition of the family and the notion of motherhood and daughterhood, without the "natural" mother, all the women take their definitions or nondefinitions from their relationship to Daniel. Relationships between these women under these circumstances are unthinkable, even for Josie, who likes to think about the possibilities of sisterhood (p. 22).

In *Stepping* and *Happily,* divorce, not death, is the agent of the dissolution of the family. The new or subsequent family is reconstituted or blended, consisting of adults and children from the first and second families. In *Sinking,* divorce and death are the agents of change; the new family/families consists of adults and children from the first and second families. In the next two books we will look at, the adults from the first family disappear entirely, either because of divorce, death, or incarceration.

The Stepdaughter by Iris Bromige and *The Stepdaughter* by Caroline Blackwood have several similarities yet are entirely different. In both stories the stepdaughter is left with the stepparent without the mediation of a biological parent. Both stories work off versions of the Cinderella legend:

The Cinderella story warns little girls that it is dangerous to be left alone with a widowed father, for the widowed father must remarry, and the daughter's fate depends upon his choice of wife. In some variants of the tale, the daughter suffers because the father replaces her mother with a cruel stepmother. In others, the daughter suffers because the father wishes to marry her himself. [Herman, 1981, p. 1]

In the Blackwood tale, the stepdaughter, Renata, is left alone with her stepmother by her biological father, who deserts the family; only later do we learn that he is not her "real" father. In the Bromige tale, the adult daughter is left with her stepfather when her biological mother dies.

The Bromige book is in the genre of the popular romance: the main plot concerns Bridget's mistaken attraction to the "bad" Felix and her ending up finally with the "good" Robert.[4] The stepfather/stepdaughter relationship is used in the beginning to establish Bridget as alone and vulnerable, near money but financially needy (that is, her stepfather has money but is not generous). In some of the versions of the old folk tale, of which Cinderella is just one variation, the girl who has lost her mother and is persecuted by an incestuous father runs away (Hirsch, 1968). In Bromige's tale the girl who is treated like Cinderella does not run away; halfway into the tale the stepfather dies.

The background to Bridget's story is this: Bridget's father, Paul, was killed in the war. He had seen Bridget only once, when she was an infant. Her mother, Lorna, then marries Owen (part of the wealthy Rainwood family), who loved her before her marriage to Paul. Lorna, still terribly in love with Paul, agrees to marry Owen because she needs financial assistance in raising Bridget; Owen agrees to care for "Paul's child." When Lorna dies, Bridget, although she is an adult and has a challenging part-time job writing and could develop that into a full-time job, remains with Owen as his "housekeeper." She cooks and cleans for him. She does not leave home because she feels she owes him something (p. 132), and Owen keeps her in this position. On the one hand he appears to be the cruel stepfather, bitter about not having his own daughter or more likely not having his wife, her mother (p. 83), and making Bridget pay for this; on the other hand we learn after his death that he had married Lorna hoping she would grow to love him. Whereas Owen and Lorna gave the appearance of husband and wife and Owen supported Lorna and her daughter, he was in great despair over the failure of the marriage. Bridget therefore represents to him both his inability to love and be loved and is the only link to that love.

Bridget is not particularly angry about being a servant, nor is she particularly distressed by being left nothing in his will, although it is clear that she is in a crippling position. She would have liked not dollars but "message of a good will, some indication that I was a little more than an unpleasant duty thrust upon him" (p. 173). Bridget does not see Owen as being really evil, and neither does the reader. Perhaps this is because he does not resonate within a tradition of an evil step*mother* who mistreats poor Cinderella and makes her do all the housework; or perhaps because the incestuous-father version of the tale has not had the kind of power as the Cinderella version precisely because it is not told to young girls by our culture.[5] All the research indicates that it is stepfathers, even more than fathers, who are likely to abuse daughters; Diana E. H. Russell has found that "women who were raised by a stepfather were seven times more likely to be abused by him than women who were raised by a biological father" (p. 234).[6] Perhaps a new script for contemporary fiction will be the evil stepfather.

It is left to Caroline Blackwood to tell the stepmother/stepdaughter story in its most primal and terrifying form. Told from the stepmother's point of view (the text is a series of letters in J's head to herself), it is a story of desertion, loss, and dependence. Arnold, husband of J and father of Renata, away on a business trip, writes and informs J that he is not returning home. He will continue to send money to support their plush Upper West Side apartment and J, but that is contingent upon letting his daughter stay in the apartment. The husband/father abandons the wife and daughter. Left are the stepdaughter (age thirteen) and stepmother, who never had a relationship to begin with. In fact J finds and has always found Renata to be repulsive: "I find Renata to be very ugly. I am therefore in no way jealous of her beauty, but in other ways my attitude towards her is much too horribly like the evil stepmother of Snow White. The girl obsesses me. All the anger I should feel for Arnold I feel for Renata" (p. 13).

Renata, "this ungainly and unhappy girl, who has survived the debris of her father's former two marriages" (p. 14), is motherless (her biological mother has been institutionalized—another crazy mother) and now fatherless. The two women are trapped in the apartment: Renata bakes instant cakes and eats them, getting even fatter and sloppier; J sits, fuming, paralyzed, unable to paint, only able to act out the cruel stepmother role. J realizes it is unlikely she can remarry with Renata in the household, yet she cannot survive without her, needing the custody payments and the New York apartment.

There are other women in this story: Sally Ann (J and Arnold's four-year-old daughter); Monique, the French *au pair* girl, who J also does not talk to, and J's feminist friends, who want to "champion her cause with much more ferocity" (p. 47) than J can feel: she just wants to be left alone.

They are peripheral to the central story, which is about the ties that bind a stepmother to a stepdaughter. The story goes one step further than the Cinderella tale; rather than marry a cruel stepmother, the father abandons his daughter *to* the cruel stepmother, both emotionally and physically.

Renata is every stepmother's fear; J is probably every stepdaughter's fear; and the situation of being tied to each other not out of choice or birth but out of dependence is horrible. We see Renata through J's eyes and she is despicable; we are not sure if this is entirely true. We begin to get some hints of another story, which gives more agency to Renata but no more attractiveness. In the end, Renata disappears, immediately after J finally speaks to her. (Up until then, all J's hatred and anger is voiced internally; between stepmother and stepdaughter there are no words; J is so hostile she cannot speak; she does to want to utter any words that would suggest a relationship, the possibility of closeness.) J intends to tell Renata of Arnold's abandonment and that Renata will have to move out. She learns that Arnold had already told Renata that he was moving to Paris for a young woman and that Renata herself has decided to leave. Renata expects no commitment from her stepmother, even less after she tells her the truth: Arnold is not her biological father; he was forced into marrying her mother believing that Renata was his and he left Renata's mother when he discovered the truth. When Renata's mother was institutionalized, he brought Renata to New York to stay with J and himself, even though he had not seen Renata for many years. Apparently as stepfather he felt some obligation. Renata knows she cannot go to her stepfather or stay with her stepmother. Because Renata is no one's (and especially not Arnold's), J now wants Renata to stay. Even though the offer is too late, the story suggests that by making the move toward Renata, perhaps J can mother herself—and also Sally Ann, who has been neglected in all this. Because J was unable to become the mother to Renata as socially expected, J had such feelings of inadequacy that she "felt neither fitted nor inclined to play the role of a mother to anyone" (p 21).

This novel is most serious in examining the psychological merging of mothers and daughters (read *stepmothers* and *stepdaughters* for these words also), the dependent position mothers and daughters have in relation to husbands and fathers, and both their potential sisterhood and their potential competition as a result of their identical positions. There is another parallel here; Renata notes that J's behavior is identical to her mother's behavior when she was abandoned by Arnold (p. 66). But J is outraged by being identified with the "crazy" mother; moreover, in the past J has suspected that Renata's mother is not some insane alcoholic or paranoid nymphomaniac, as she has been led to believe, but that she is actually cruising the Caribbean with a tall, dark man. "Tired of the dreary and unrewarding day-to-day task of bringing up her unprepossessing daughter" (p. 34), she invented her breakdown to foist her daughter on Arnold, who would then foist her on J. However, the reader is fairly certain that Renata's mother is *not* cruising the Caribbean. *The Stepdaughter* portrays two women so debilitated by the family, so locked in a box by the father, that their only sisterhood is one of victimhood: like Renata's mother, all the women can become madwomen in the attic, evil/crazy stepmothers and mothers. We are left with J obsessing about where Renata is, presuming Renata is walking motherless on the "savage streets" of the city (p. 96). This is not a script to escape Cinderella's tale.

The study *Divorce and Remarriage: Problems, Adaptations, and Adjustments* (Albrecht, Bahr, and Goodman, 1983) summarizes the problems social researchers have found for the "remarriage family." Such a family "lacks much of the shared family experience, the symbols and rituals that help to maintain the psychic boundaries of the first marriage family. . . . It is coming to be generally recognized that the structure of remarriages poses adaptation problems for the partners for which earlier socialization in the nuclear family provides an inadequate role model" (pp. 143, 142). Given no symbols or model, each family is left to devise its own solutions and rules in these complex relationships.[7]

The five stories discussed in this essay indicate that at least in fiction there are now images and models for the remarriage family. Narratives of remarriage and stepparenting *are* being written. They revise the prevailing stories of stepfamilies, the Cinderella/Snow White tale; they explore the constrictions of the nuclear family and the complexities of the reconstituted family. The five fictions look at the stepparent/stepchild relationship. In *Happily* that relationship was less problematic, perhaps because the step-relations were cross-sex relations. (Kitty and Sarah get a stepfather and R. J. gets a stepmother.) In Bromige's *The Stepdaughter,* the relationship was problematic precisely *because* it was a cross-sex relationship. (Bridget is alone with her stepfather.) *Stepping* and the Blackwood story ask if the stepmother and the stepdaughter can get along, can become friends, can love each other, can form a family. In *Stepping,* Zelda and the two girls do become a family of sorts, whereas in Blackwood's *The Stepdaughter* Renata runs away from her stepmother. *Sinking, Stealing* and *The Stepdaughter* (Blackwood) are parallel in removing a man from that formation, although a man wants to separate the two women in the former story (Daniel plans to move, taking Ericka from Josie) and in the latter it is a man who wants to control the two women even if he is not present (Arnold is in Paris, leaving J. and Renata together). Ericka, however, is an appealing articulate stepdaughter; Renata is not. Caroline and Cathy *(Stepping)* are also appealing, although they are not always pleasant. Josie *(Sinking)* and Zelda *(Stepping)* are appealing as stepmothers in that they struggle with their identity; J *(Stepdaughter)* is not. But perhaps the issue is not the character of individual stepmothers and stepdaughters but the nature of the family structure.

All these fictions, each in various degrees, engage in a discussion begun by feminists on the nature of the mother/daughter relationship, extending this to the stepmother/stepdaughter bond. At the center is the question of who and what a mother and a stepmother are. In these five novels, the mother and stepmother exist side by side.[8] The question Rhea and Josie *(Sinking Stealing)* confront is: Are we both mothers? The question Zelda *(Stepping)* asks is: Am I a mother if I am their stepmother, if I do not act like their mother [Adelaide], if I do not act like a mother?

Some of these five fictions, working with the diametrically opposed images of mother and stepmother, write the biological mother as not a good mother. She is a bad mother; she is a cruel and wicked mother; she is a crazy mother. That is true of Adelaide in *Stepping,* of Kay in *Happily Ever After . . . Almost,* of Renata's mother in *The Stepdaughter.* These fictions find it hard to conceive of two mothers, much less two mothers who might be "sisters." Early in the women's movement, sisterhood seemed an ideal easier to obtain than now.[9] A letter to *Ms.* (February 1986) describes the problem: "The *other* woman is more likely to be a student in my women's studies class or a colleague in the local peace group. . . . Surely you can show us how feminism can help us work together." In these fictions, the other woman is the other mother.

One of the ways fiction works toward an answer is to rename position/ function/identity: Zelda is "friend" and Josie is "Flommy."[10] Kin terms from the nuclear family clearly are not adequate as a model, nor is the form of the nuclear family itself. Especially in white middle-class families (and these are the families of these fictions), "few people are authorized or feel free to participate" (Stack, 1974, p. 85), so that one is either mother or not mother. In some black working-class families, as described by Carol Stack (p. 83) and others, several people carry out the roles and tasks of mother; they are provider, discipliner, trainer, curer, groomer. The name and slot of "mother" does not belong to one person so the mother/stepmother opposition may not be as operative. Unlike the white middle class, certain groups (cultures and classes) do not have "the ideological and normative emphasis on the isolated nuclear family" (Stack, p. 155).[11]

Zelda *(Stepping),* trained in the nuclear family, can only imagine herself as different from and in competition with Adelaide. However, after thirteen years as stepmother and several years years as mother, caring for the stepdaughters and her two children, Zelda, writing in her journal, voices a desire. Although it is said ironically, we should take it seriously, for it is here that Zelda begins to move beyond the separate and nucleated families and toward a fantasy of a new family form, an extended family with both mother and stepmother in it:

> A curious thought: I've spent so much time in my life the thirteen years I've been married to Charlie taking care of Adelaide's children. I really tried my best to keep her children healthy and happy when they were with us, and I still care about their happiness. Wouldn't it be only fair for Adelaide to repay me, to take my children off my hands for a while? Oh, wouldn't it be heaven if she could repay me a bit, if I should ship Adam and Lucy off for a week. . . . Margaret Mead, let's redefine "extended family"! [p. 7] [12]

Other feminists are rewriting the family, both in fiction and poetry. Feminist science fiction envisions new family forms, often completely without men. But whether with or without men, the nuclear family is never the basic reproductive and socializing unit of society. The utopian fictions of Joanna Russ and Marge Piercy, for example, open up the relationships between mothers and daughters; there are many mothers, and mothers and daughters are tied by neither biology nor economics. [13]

Other writers have turned to the dominant myths and tales of our culture, rewriting them to "review, revise and reinvent them in the service of women" (E. Rose, 1980, p. 220), so that the divisions between women (the mother and the daughter, the stepmother and the mother), designed by men, are healed. [14] Poet Olga Broumas's Cinderella wants to return to the "my sisters' hut"; she does not want to remain "apart" and "estranged" from her stepsisters any longer. Broumas's Snow White declares she is returning to her mother, the stepmother, the queen. In the version told to Zelda and the rest of us, Snow White, now a young queen, watches the wicked queen "put on red hot shoes, and dance until she dropped down dead." In the feminist rewriting of Snow White, we discover, as Ellen Cronan Rose (1983) puts it so deftly, that "the wicked stepmother with her fatal apple is really the fairy godmother, who brings Snow White the knowledge of her female identity" (p. 220). While it is true that feminist fairy tales are being rewritten so that esthetically and ideologically they are closely related to "feminist demands for gender rearrangement and equality in the family and the work place" (Zipes, 1986, p. 32), it is also true in Zipes's collection *Don't Bet on the Prince* that there are still wicked stepmothers. For example, in "Moon Ribbon," a Cinderella story,

Sylva saves herself without male assistance. With a silver ribbon from her matrilineage line, she leads her stepmother and two stepsisters down "silver-red stairs" to hell. Sylva is no longer the passive heroine who is totally male-identified; however, this women-centered tale still retains a cruel stepmother and two mean stepsisters; there is the good (dead) mother who returns in the form of a "sister" spirit to guide the daughter and there is the bad (step) mother who is "mean in spirit and meaner in tongue" (p. 81).

The five stepfamily fictions examined here do not fully heal; neither do they project utopian futures. They dwell on the complexities of stepfamilies, exacerbated by the patriarchal heterosexual nuclear family and its support in law and in our psyches. Nevertheless, they do not simply tell the old tale; in these the stepmother, the actor, often triumphs and always survives. Still, the old dualities are maintained; evil now resides in the biological mother. The harder tale to tell—bonding between women, the sharing of mothering, and the degendering of mothering—has yet to be written.

Reading and rereading these novels and now writing about them consoles me. My difficulties as a stepmother are not mine alone. Even fiction finds it hard to envision new scripts for stepfamilies. We are, nonetheless, working on them.

Notes

Acknowledgments: I want to thank Chris Suggs and Marianne Hirsch for their close and helpful reading of earlier drafts of this essay, and Daphne Joslin and Susan O'Sullivan for suggesting two of the novels I discuss.

1. Although I mention only Gilbert's and Gubar's readings of the fairytales, I also rely on several other feminist critics: Marianne Hirsch, Judith Herman, Ellen Rose, and Karen E. Rowe.

2. Two novels that could be included in this discussion are *Hearts* by Hilma Wolitzer and *Hidden Pictures* by Meg Wolitzer; see note 3 for a brief discussion of them. *The Stepdaughter* by Caroline Blackwood won the David Higham Fiction Prize for the best novel of 1976. I have not included Rosellen Brown's *Civil Wars* since it is not strictly about a stepfamily as we have limited the definition for this book. What is needed is an annotated bibliography of the fiction of stepfamilies.

3. The feminist analysis of the role of the woman (wife, mother) in the family, the function of the patriarchal nuclear family, the institutionalization of heterosexuality, the relationship of mothers and daughters, and women's reproductive rights, an analysis that began in the 1970s, has today taken on new urgency, both because of new texts and because of legal and state interventions. Some of these include

Phyllis Chesler on custody, Leonore Weitzman on divorce, Sue Miller on sexuality and motherhood, and Margaret Atwood on the state control of female reproduction (all in References), and the 1986 report of Attorney General Meese's Commission on Pornography and the recent Supreme Court decision on sodomy.

In contrast to *The Good Mother* and *The Handmaid's Tale*, *Hidden Pictures* (see note 2) seems to be written out of the optimism of the 1970s, when alternative visions of family seemed possible. It is a narrative about two women, Jane and Laura, raising Laura's son Ian in the Long Island suburbs. Laura's ex-husband, while uneasy about the arrangement, is never openly hostile. Ian, given the choice to live full time with his father and his second wife (his stepmother) and their soon-to-be-born child, chooses Laura and his stepmother Jane. The struggle, given the conventional heterosexual model in the suburbs and the lack of alternative models anywhere, is to figure out how to live as a family. At one point Laura calls Jane her sister; at other points Jane is simply absent from public events. Jane wants to make their life easy, but she also wants to be acknowledged—but as what: "I'm not sure. . . . As your lover, I suppose, but also as part of your household. As someone in Ian's life" (pp. 205–6). In the course of the story Jane evolves from not-mother to sort-of-mother ("even though I'm not a mother[,] I worry about things, the way you do" [p. 206] to a decision to be an activist, out-of the-closet mother: "I feel like throwing myself into everything. I feel like becoming Ms. PTA with you" (p. 291).

Hearts is also optimistic in the end. Linda, after only a six-week marriage, is left with a thirteen-year-old stepdaughter when her husband, Robins' father, dies. They travel cross-country together: Robin planning to get back at her mother who had walked out and disappeared when Robin was five, Linda planning to leave Robin with her mother since she has no interest in stepmothering. By the end of the book, Linda and Robin choose each other or at least feel bound to each other: "You can become a family by the grace of accident and will, . . . we have the duty to console each other as best we can" (p. 323).

4. Janice Radway's *Reading the Romance* and Madonne M. Miner's "Guaranteed to Please: Twentieth-Century American Women's Bestsellers" are useful here in analyzing the power of this genre and in reading it outside the heterosexual romance plot. Miner, for example, reads several bestsellers as daughters' stories about their relationship to their mother. The Bromige novel contains a sisterhood story that appears to be more satisfying to Bridget than either of the relationships with the men. This plot is suggested (pp. 149–55) and then abandoned in favor of the conventional one.

5. Besides the references I have already made to articles that discuss how fairytales enforce "culture's sentences" (Gilbert and Gubar, p. 36), two others critique Bruno Bettelheim's Freudian reading of fairytales: Kay F. Stone, "The Misuse of Enchantment: Controversies on the Significance of Fairy Tales," and Jack Zipes, "On the Use and Abuse of Folk and Fairy Tales with Children: Bruno Bettelheim's Moralist Magic Wand." Stone, through analysis of the literature and a reader-response survey, agrees with the feminist position that fairy tales are "problem-creating stories," not "problem-solving," as Bettelheim claims. Zipes explains that

Bettelheim has no awareness of either the codes in the tale (he sees them as time-less, rather than with a knowledge of history and archeology) or the codes in the reader (he sees all readers as one, rather than a group of individuals who have a sex/gender, an age, an ethnicity/race, and a class). Zipes suggests "that the ideolog-ical and psychological pattern and message of Cinderella do nothing more than reinforce sexist values and a Puritan ethos that serves a society which fosters com-petition and achievement for survival" (p. 173). Add to this the new understand-ings we now have (according to Beverly Lyon Clark's review of *Favorite Folktales from Around the World*) that the Grimm brothers tampered with the folktales, changing mothers to stepmothers. She gets her information from Maria Tartar's "From Nags to Witches: Stepmothers in the Grimms' Fairy Tales," in *Opening Texts: Psychoanalysis and the Culture of the Child,* ed. Joseph H. Smith and Wil-liam Kerrigan (Baltimore: Johns Hopkins University Press, 1985. The issue of tampering is tricky, as Clark says; much depends on who made the change; also, if the so-called tampered version becomes established with hearers and readers, then that is the text to be reckoned with by analysts. For a cross-cultural compar-ison, see Marian Ury, "Stepmother Tales in Japan."

6. Russell looks at class and race/ethnicity differences in biological father and stepfather abuse of daughters in her survey of 930 women and finds differences in the rates. She finds fewer stepdaughter victims in the upper middle class. She finds that Latina women are "slightly overrepresented as victims of both biological fa-thers and stepfathers, that 1.1 percent of Afro-American women are abused by their biological fathers compared to 3.3 percent who are abused by their stepfath-ers. . . . No Asian, Filipina, or Jewish women were sexually abused by either a biological father or a stepfather. The statistics for Afro-American women presum-ably reflect the fact that stepfamilies are more prevalent among Afro-Americans than whites" (p. 249). Russell also notes that mothers in stepfamilies work outside the home more, and speculates on how that relates to stepfather abuse of step-daughters. She suggests that working outside the home does not put daughters more at risk, but rather gives the daughters assertive models and allows the mother the economic freedom to leave the abusive husband. All this needs further research and analysis; it is a good beginning.

7. "The Presentation of Stepfamilies in Marriage and Family Textbooks" by Jeanne Nolan, Marilyn Coleman, and Lawrence Ganong parallels my study of how stepfamilies are presented in fiction. The authors examined twenty-six introductory marriage and family textbooks, and found that they presented limited information on stepfamilies. "There is a subtle, deficit model applied to stepfamilies as indi-cated by little discussion of successful functioning, a predilection toward discussing stresses and a greater than usual incidence of giving recommendations" (p. 565).

8. Susan Koppelman in an excellent introduction to her *Between Mothers and Daughters: Stories Across a Generation* seems to have found otherwise in the short stories she includes. The question of whether the mother is the biological parent of the child or the woman who brings her up, Koppelman says, "doesn't seem to engage the imagination of women who write short stories for women readers. None of the surrogate mothers [grandmothers, stepmothers, older friends, lesbian part-

ners] represented in this collection wonders for a moment whether she is more the 'real' mother than the biological mother" (Introduction, p. xxv). In many (but not all) of the stories in her collection, the biological mother is no longer alive. This may account for our different readings.

9. See Jane Flax, "The Conflict between Nurturance and Autonomy in Mother/ Daughter Relationships and Within Feminism," for one of the first discussions of this problem.

10. In the popular 1986 movie St. Elmo's Fire, the stepmother was renamed "stepmonster."

11. See Stack, passim, but especially pp. 79–89. Raymond T. Smith ("The Nuclear Family in Afro-American Kinship") and Niara Sudarkasa ("Interpreting the African Heritage in Afro-American Family Organization"), for example, both suggest, looking back to African origins and to present Afro-American context, that we cannot read white middle-class stepfamily issues onto black families. Sudarkasa states that for the "African extended family, marriage dissolution did not have the ramifications it has in nuclear-family systems. Children of a divorced couple were usually brought up in their natal compound (or by members of their lineage residing elsewhere), even though the in-marrying parent had left" (p. 43). Smith, looking at the Afro-American family, describes a black man as supporting a woman and her child whether or not they are "his." This issue is not significant in terms of his relations to them, so "there is no image of the wicked stepfather corresponding to the wicked stepmother" (p. 66). See also Susan Tolliver, "20/20 Vision," and Barbara Omolade, 'It's a Family Affair." The wicked stepmother does exist in African folktales; see the tale "The Black Cloth" in Bernard Dadie's collection of the same title. Thus I am not sure whether the "wicked stepmother" has much weight in Afro-American culture. See also Robert Staples and Alfred Mirande, "Racial and Cultural Variations among American Families."

Besides looking at cultural difference, class difference might be informative. For instance, Cherie Burns, in Stepmotherhood, says, "Studies show lower income families have better stepfamily relations because they are more accustomed to taking in extra family members" (pp. 142–43). In All American Women, Johnetta B. Cole points out that "the children of the rich and the children of the poor are often cared for by individuals other than the biological mothers" (p. 11). For the rich it is nannies, for the poor it is a "network of kin, neighbors and friends" (p. 11). Thus for a child of the rich or the poor, the addition of another mother/parent may have different meanings than it does to the middle-class child.

12. Note that the ending of Happily Ever After . . . Almost implies that Kay, the biological mother, may actually learn to live and participate within the reconstituted, extended family.

13. For thoughts about utopian fiction and motherhood, see Susan Koppelman, Between Mothers and Daughters, pp. xxxi–xxxii, Sally Miller Gearhart, "Future Visions," and Susan Lees, "Motherhood in Feminist Utopias." See also Marlene Barr, Alien to Femininity.

14. Rachel Blau DuPlessis, in Writing Beyond the Ending, describes two related ways of rewriting or revising dominant myths. Either there is a "displacement of

attention to the other side of the story, or a delegitimation of the known tale, a critique even unto sequences and priorities of narrative" (p. 108). The writers discussed in this essay use displacement as a writing strategy; the voice and the identification are given to the other side—the stepmother. Snow White and Cinderella's stepmothers' side of the story is told.

References

Adams, Alice. "A Gift of Grass." *Beautiful Girl*. New York: Knopf, 1969.

Albrecht, Stan L., Howard M. Bahn, and Kristen L. Goodman. *Divorce and Remarriage: Problems, Adaptations, and Adjustments*. Westport, Conn.: Greenwood Press, 1983.

Atwood, Margaret. *The Handmaid's Tale*. Boston: Houghton Mifflin, 1986.

Barr, Marlene S. *Alien to Feminity: Speculative Fiction and Feminist Theory*. Westport, Conn.: Greenwood Press, 1987.

Blackwood, Caroline. *The Stepdaughter*. London: Scribners, 1976.

Bromige, Iris. *The Stepdaughter*. Leicester, Engl.: F. A. Thorpe, 1966.

Broumas, Olga. *Beginning With O*. New Haven, Conn.: Yale University Press, 1977.

Brown, Rosellen. *Civil Wars*. New York: Knopf, 1984.

Burns, Cherie. *Stepmotherhood: How to Survive Without Feeling Frustrated, Left Out or Wicked*. New York: Times Books, 1985.

Chesler, Phyllis. *Mothers on Trial: The Battle for Children and Custody*. New York: McGraw-Hill, 1986.

Clark, Beverly Lyon. "How the Toad Won the Race with the Donkey." Review of *Favorite Folktales Around the World*, edited by Jane Yolen. *New York Times Book Review*, January 25, 1987.

Clausen, Jan. *Sinking, Stealing*. Trumansburg, N.Y.: Crossing Press, 1985.

Cole, Johnnetta B., ed. *All American Women: Lines That Divide, Ties That Bind*. New York: Free Press, 1986.

The Complete Grimm's Fairy Tales. New York: Pantheon Books, 1972.

Dadie, Bernard Binlin. *The Black Cloth: A Collection of African Folktales*. Amherst: University of Massachusetts Press, 1987.

DuPlessis, Rachel Blau. *Writing Beyond the Ending: Narrative Strategies on Twentieth Century Women Writers*. Bloomington: Indiana University Press, 1985.

Flax, Jane. "The Conflict Between Nurturance and Autonomy in Mother/Daughter Relationships and Within Feminism." *Feminist Studies* 2 (June 1978): 1971–89.

Flynn, Elizabeth A., and Patrocino P. Schweickart, eds. *Gender and Reading: Essay on Readers, Texts, and Contexts*. Baltimore: Johns Hopkins University Press, 1986.

Freeman, Mary Wilkins. "The Bound Girl" (1890). In *Women Working: An An-*

thology of Stories and Poems, edited by Nancy Hoffman and Florence Howe. New York: Feminist Press, 1979.

Gearhart, Sally Miller. "Future Visions: Today's Politics: Feminist Utopias in Review." In *Women in Search of Utopia: Mavericks and Mythmakers,* edited by Ruby Rohlich and Elaine Hoffman Baruch. New York: Schocken, 1984.

Gilbert, Sandra, and Susan Gubar. *The Madwoman in the Attic: The Woman Writer and the Nineteenth-Century Literary Imagination.* New Haven, Conn.: Yale University Press, 1976.

Herman, Judith Lewis. *Father-Daughter Incest.* Cambridge, Mass.: Harvard University Press, 1981.

Hirsch, Marianne. "Ideology, Form, and 'Allerleirauh': Reflections on *Reading for the Plot.*" *Children's Literature* 14 (1968): 163–68.

Hoffman, Nancy, and Florence Howe, eds. *Women Working: An Anthology of Stories and Poems.* New York: Feminist Press, 1979.

Hurst, Fannie. "Oats for the Woman" (1917). In *Between Mothers and Daughters: Stories Across a Generation,* edited by Susan Koppelman. New York: Feminist Press, 1985.

Jewett, Sarah Orne. "Tom's Husband" (1884). In *Women Working: An Anthology of Stories and Poems,* edited by Nancy Hoffman and Florence Howe. New York: Feminist Press, 1979.

Koppelman, Susan, ed. *Between Mothers and Daughters: Stories Across a Generation.* New York: Feminist Press, 1985.

Leavitt, David. *Family Dancing.* New York: Warner, 1983.

Lees, Susan. "Motherhood in Feminist Utopias." In *Women in Search of Utopia: Mavericks and Mythmakers,* edited by Ruby Rohlich and Elaine Hoffman Baruch. New York: Schocken, 1984.

Miller, Sue. *The Good Mother.* New York: Harper & Row, 1986.

Miner, Madonne M. "Guaranteed to Please: Twentieth-Century American Women's Bestsellers." In *Gender and Reading: Essay on Readers, Texts, and Contexts,* edited by Elizabeth A. Flynn and Patrocino P. Schweickart. Baltimore: Johns Hopkins University Press, 1986.

Munroe, Alice. *The Beggar Maid: Stories of Flo and Rose.* Harmondsworth, Middlesex, Engl.: Penguin, 1980.

Nolan, Jeanne, Marilyn Coleman, and Lawrence Ganong. "The Presentation of Stepfamilies in Marriage and Family Textbooks." *Family Relations* 33, no. 4 (October 1984):559–66.

Omolade, Barbara. "It's a Family Affair: The Real Lives of Black Single Mothers." *Village Voice,* July 15, 1986.

Radway, Janice. *Reading the Romance: Women, Patriarchy, and Popular Literature.* Chapel Hill: University of North Carolina Press, 1984.

Rose, Ellen Cronan. "Through the Looking Glass: When Women Tell Fairy Tales." In *The Voyage In: Fictions of Female Development,* edited by Elizabeth Abel, Marianne Hirsch, and Elizabeth Langland. Hanover, N.H., and London: University Press of New England, 1983.

Rose, Phyllis. *Parallel Lives: Five Victorian Marriages*. New York: Vintage Books, 1984.

Rowe, Karen E. "Feminism and Fairy Tales." In *Don't Bet on the Prince: Contemporary Feminist Fairy Tales in North America and England*, edited by Jack Zipes. New York: Metheun, 1986.

Russell, Diana E. H. *The Secret Trauma: Incest in the Lives of Girls & Women*. New York: Basic Books, 1986.

Shockley, Ann Allen. "A Birthday Remembered" (1980). In *Between Mothers and Daughters: Stories Across a Generation*, edited by Susan Koppelman. New York: Feminist Press, 1985.

Smith, Raymond T. "The Nuclear Family in Afro-American Kinship." *Journal of Comparative Family Studies* 1 (January 1970): 55–70.

Stack, Carol. *All Our Kin: Strategies for Survival in a Black Community*. New York: Harper & Row, 1974.

Staples, Robert, and Alfred Mirande. "Racial and Cultural Variations Among American Families: A Decennial Review of the Literature on Minority Families." In *Family in Transition*, edited by Arlene Skolnick and Jerome Skolnick. Boston: Little, Brown, 1980.

Stone, Kay F. "The Misuses of Enchantment: Controversies on the Significance of Fairy Tales." In *Women's Folklore, Women's Culture*, edited by J. Kalcik. Philadelphia: University of Pennsylvania Press, 1985.

Sudarkasa, Niara. "Interpreting the African Heritage in Afro-American Family Organization." in McAdoo, Harriet Pipes, ed. *Black Families*. Beverly Hills, Calif.: Sage, 1981.

Suleiman, Susan Rubin. "The 'Other Mother': On Maternal Splitting." Forthcoming article in *Signs*.

Thayer, Nancy. *Stepping*. London: Sphere Books, 1981.

Tolliver, Susan D. "20/20 Vision: A Perspective on Women's Changing Roles and the Structure of American Families, Past and Present" *Frontiers: A Journal of Women's Studies* 9 (1986): 27–31.

Ury, Marian. "Stepmother Tales in Japan." *Children's Literature* 9 (1981): 61–72.

Walker, Alice. *The Color Purple*. New York: Harcourt Brace Jovanovich, 1982.

Weitzman, Leonore. *The Divorce Revolution*. New York: Free Press, 1986.

Wolitzer, Hilma. *Hearts*. New York: Farrer, Straus & Giroux, 1980.

Wolitzer, Meg. *Hidden Pictures*. Boston: Houghton Mifflin, 1986.

Wolkoff, Judie. *Happily Ever After . . . Almost*. New York: Dell, 1982.

Zipes, Jack. "On the Use and Abuse of Folk and Fairy Tales with Children: Bruno Bettelheim's Moralistic Wand," in Zipes, *Breaking the Magic Spell: Radical Theories of Folk and Fairy Tales*. Austin: University of Texas Press, 1979.

Zipes, Jack, ed. *Don't Bet on the Prince: Contemporary Feminist Fairy Tales in North America and England*. New York: Metheun, 1986.

Part III

Transforming—Both Within and Without

33

Lesbian Stepfamilies and the Myth of Biological Motherhood

Connie Miller

Jan Clausen's 1985 novel, *Sinking, Stealing,* is about a relationship between a ten-year-old girl, Ericka, and her lesbian stepmother, Josie. Ericka,
her mother, and Josie had been living together for years when the mother
was killed in a car accident. The result, of course, is that against Josie's
protests, Ericka goes to live with her father, Daniel, his second wife, and
their new family. A conflict between Josie's demands for more time with
Ericka and the limits of Daniel's "liberal" tolerance for their relationship
creates the book's action. Because I also happen to be a stepmother who
has lived with a child, now ten, and her mother for several years, I read
Sinking, Stealing with a powerful sense of recognition, delight, and even
relief.

However, I found some things about *Sinking, Stealing* uncomfortable.
For one thing, even though nothing less extreme than running away would
have gotten Daniel's attention, Josie and Ericka's decision to board a bus
during one of their regularly scheduled visits and travel across the country
under assumed names seemed to me an unrealistic form of protest. I began
to understand my discomfort when I realized that the sense of recognition
I experienced had little to do with Josie and Ericka's protest against the
dominating influence of the child's father—the power that straight fathers
have over their lesbian ex-wives is too familiar to be surprising—but with
their freedom from a more complex oppression, one that it is difficult to
find the courage to name, let alone resist.

Clausen, I believe, had to get Ericka's mother out of the way for two
reasons: not just to demonstrate, as she does with painful clarity, the lack

of social support that lesbian stepmothers receive, but also to portray clearly the strength and importance of the relationship Josie and Ericka shared. What I recognized in *Sinking, Stealing,* what gave me such a pronounced sense of relief and delight, was an acknowledgment of the love that can exist between an unrelated adult and child who have worked hard to learn to share their lives. Acknowledging the power of this simple reality is much easier when the relationship is unencumbered by the dominating force of true motherhood.

I am not saying that I would like my lover to be out the way; life without her seems unimaginably lonely. I am also not saying that I would like to be my child's—or any child's—biological mother. Nor am I implying that the family life that the three of us have developed over the years is troubled. On the contrary, our success in forming a nontraditional family gives me the courage to challenge a much-revered institution. It was not the mother as a person, after all, that Clausen needed to eliminate to show Josie and Ericka in a powerful light; it was the institution of motherhood that the person embodied, an institution that places damaging limitations on the relationships between children and all the adults who participate, or who might participate, in their nurturing.

Emma, my lover, and I, and Emma's daughter, Sally, have been living together for eight years, since Sally was two years old. From the beginning, I wanted to develop a separate and significant relationship with Sally. In the same way that those eight years have increased my commitment to my relationship with Emma, they have increased my commitment to Sally, but the two relationships are quite different and not necessarily interdependent.

I sometimes picture our situation as a triangle. As one point on the triangle, I am directly and separately connected to both Sally and Emma. In addition, while not directly connected to it, I am faced with and intimately affected by the side of the triangle that represents the relationship between Emma and Sally. When we all began living together, that side of the triangle was a disproportionately long line. But over the years, as I participated in Sally's care, expressed my own personality and needs, and spent a year and a half, while Emma worked nights full time, functioning basically as a single parent, the sides have become much more equal. Each side of the triangle is different, and each of the three points is left out in some ways: Emma and I are lovers; Sally and Emma share relatives, an interest in and talent for art and crafts, and a nurturing physicality; Sally and I share a kind of humor, a basically chicken-hearted approach to life (we are both, for instance, afraid of skiing), and a belief in the value of independence. But the triangle as a whole functions best when all three sides are about the same strength.

I have always needed to be out as a lesbian among friends and at work, I have had the luxury of working in environments where academic liberalism makes open objection or hostility virtually impossible. Most people with whom I socialize and work know quite a lot about my living situation, and I have actually experienced less overt resistance to my sexual preference than to my relationship with Sally.

For instance, when Emma was working at night, a colleague and I were having lunch. She was considering having a child, and our conversation turned to children. She knew that Emma's schedule made her largely unavailable, she had visited our house and seen me interact with Sally, but still she expressed disbelief that I had much involvement with Sally. Perhaps she assumed, like many of Emma's co-workers, that Emma was lucky to have found a free full-time babysitter, probably some frustrated kid-lover that couldn't have a baby or that no one wanted to marry.

The particular institution where I am employed is highly pressured. People work extremely hard and often very long hours and have demanding research and publication commitments. At a seminar recently, a group of women employees made the observation that no women on our staff had children; the implication was that the demand of the job prevented a demanding home life. I protested: "But I have a child." "No," a woman beside me said, dismissing me totally, "that's not the same." At a recent social event, a very good woman friend of ours, during a conversation on children, introduced Emma as Sally's mother, and ignored me.

Homophobia may, in part, account for these responses. Also, the fact that culturally unacceptable situations have no names effectively operates to keep these situations invisible and unviable. I believe, however, that these responses to my relationship with Sally occur primarily because of an unwillingness or inability to grant that relationship any significance. None of these women has children of her own, and yet they all seem defensive, almost like members of an elite club intent on restricting membership. If caring for a child almost single-handedly for an extended period of time and participating in a primary way in the child's life for eight years do not constitute mothering, it is difficult to understand what does.

Throughout the eight years that the three of us have been together, I remember only two people who have actively given recognition to a meaningful relationship between Sally and me. One was a colleague at work, an aunt who has well-developed relationships with her several nieces and nephews. She commented that it must have been difficult being a single parent while Emma worked at night. The other was a woman who had recently left a marriage in which she was stepmother to her ex-husband's two children, with whom she was desperately struggling to maintain some sort of relationship.

Biological motherhood is not the equivalent of, or a prerequisite for, nurturing or mothering children. The institution of motherhood, however, has created a myth that defines giving birth and mothering as two sides of the same coin, each essential to the other's existence. Cultural enforcement of this myth has resulted in strongly held misperceptions that damage the potential of both biological mothers and children to develop as fully as they can. These misperceptions form a sequence that goes something like this: All women find primary fulfillment in bearing and raising children. Biological mothers, therefore, have fulfilled their destinies and found contentment. They know, by nature, what is best for the children they bore. Women who have not had children of their own are unfulfilled, are in some way unnatural, and do not have the same gut-level sense about children's needs. Only a biological mother can provide her child with the nurturing and love so essential to the child's well-being; only she would want to. The biological mother is all to the dependent, needy child, and therefore she must sacrifice her own self-fulfillment in order to guarantee the child's. With the biological responsibility comes the biological "right" to determine what is best for the child.

The myth of motherhood is undoubtedly responsible, at least in part, for the urgency with which adopted children who have been kindly nurtured and appropriately cherished seek their "real mothers." But the major tragedy caused by this cultural sequence of misperceptions is the bond of total dependency it engenders between a biological mother and her child, a bond of dependency that has been given the name of familial devotion. In a society that has allowed women few outlets for production besides reproduction, their possessive dependency on their children comes as no surprise. And for women, this experience of production through reproduction has provided the self-respect they needed to positively transform their lives. However, even biological mothers who are deeply involved in careers, relationships, or creations are rarely willing to share what they feel is their right and their responsibility to decide their children's fates.

The bond of dependency damages biological mothers as much as it does children, who learn to connect dependability with being essential and with coming first. Mutual dependency denies to both biological mother and child the opportunity for reciprocity, for a relationship where the mother's needs are as valid as the child's, where the child's ability to give is encouraged as strongly as the prerogative to receive. According to the myth of motherhood, a woman who offers a child reciprocity will appear less loving, both to the child and to other adults, than one who unilaterally offers to provide nurture and support. Barbara Macdonald, in her speech at the

1985 National Women's Studies Association conference in Seattle, made painfully clear the potential harm that the mother-daughter bond of dependency does to mothers, and its ageist implications for all women:

> The source of your [younger women feminist activists] ageism, the reason why you see older women as there to serve you, comes from family. It was in patriarchal family that you learned that mother is there to serve you, her child, that serving is her purpose in life. This is not woman's definition of motherhood. This is man's definition of motherhood, a male myth enforced in family and which you still believe—to your peril and mine. It infantilizes you and it erases me.[1]

Macdonald explains that her focus—mother's oppression by daughters—reverses the more commonly expressed theme of daughters' oppression by mothers. From my perspective, the two oppressions are most usefully viewed simultaneously: the root from which they both grow is the bond of dependency enforced by the cultural myth of motherhood. This same root produces an additional oppression: the denial that mutually nurturing relationships between children and women who are not their biological mothers have any significance. This denial constitutes another form of erasure.

Biological motherhood as an imperative is as powerful as heterosexuality. Both have been thoroughly institutionalized in ways that represent narrowly restrictive cultural definitions of normal and appropriate behavior. The risk of mothering in a noninstitutionalized sense (lesbian mothers, mothers who give up custody of their children, lesbian stepmothers) resembles the risk involved in coming out, and results in the same grating mismatch between inner realities and external imperatives.

The extent to which the family that Emma and Sally and I have formed is able to succeed depends directly on the extent to which each of us is able to risk resisting the external imperatives. It is this resistance that keeps the sides of the triangle equal in strength. By standing back enough to allow Sally and me to develop an intimate and unique connection of our own, Emma has taken the enormous risk of sharing what the myth of motherhood sees as her territory, without any guarantee that, once shared, it will continue to be supportive of her. By investing in my dependability, in spite of the fact that no blood relationship ensures a continuing connection, Sally has risked equating love with reciprocity. To make our connection concrete, she has even added my last name to the long list of names that are her own, a list she has transformed into a rhythmic chant and even taught her friends. By demanding that my relationship with Sally has a value that is different from but equal to the value of Emma's relationship with her, I have risked rejection. I have also risked by letting go of a sense of independence that I imagined was essential to my survival, a letting go that offered no guarantees of a better future.

Since so little support for these risks comes from outside our family, and since we have all absorbed and continue to be confronted by the cultural definition of the institution of motherhood, the process of risking is ongoing. I sometimes lose faith that Sally could value our relationship and I pull back, undoubtedly helping to confirm my culturally defined undependability. I respond with insecure defensiveness to implications that I am a less important member of the family we have formed, undoubtedly helping to confirm my unimportance. When the woman at the seminar refused to recognize my mothering, I had to struggle very hard not to believe that she was right.

Emma's priorities still determine (to too great an extent, I believe) decisions about Sally's actions and behavior. One example involves homework. Sally is involved in an accelerated program at school and so has quite a lot of homework. She can't concentrate when Emma and I are talking or when the 6:00 news is on, so I suggested—sometimes insisted—that she do her work in her room. No policy was ever established, however, until *Emma* decided it was necessary, because of a note from Sally's teacher on her report card. My opinions can still too easily be discounted or ignored. Sally frequently gets messages, inside our family and out, that my priorities don't have to be seriously taken into account. When she operates according to these messages, she erases as much of herself as me.

But in light of the sheer force of the cultural imperative of biological motherhood, where Emma, Sally, and I fail and where we remain afraid to risk is less remarkable than where we manage to succeed. For in our lives, as in the lives of many lesbian stepfamilies, the biological mother is not out of the way. No bus trip like the one Josie and Ericka took, to however distant a city, and no assumed names can change the compelling reality of biology. The power and significance of my relationshp with Sally must be recognized in the context of the family we three have formed, a family whose existence depends on the ability of each of its members to experience self-respect and delight. All lesbians continuously struggle against the ominous potential of straight male power. Lesbian stepfamilies, however, must resist an additional and no less ominous force; the myth of biological motherhood. When any one of these lesbian stepfamilies succeeds, it serves as a model for a whole new definition of family, motherhood, and dependability.

Notes

1. Barbara Macdonald, "Outside the Sisterhood: Ageism in Women's Studies," in *Women and Aging,* ed. Jo Alexander et al. (Corvallis, Or.: Calyx Books, 1986), p. 23.

34

Less Than a Mother—
More Than a Friend

Barbara Drucker

They were five years old and they were twins. Side by side they sat, silently watching me as I moved about the kitchen preparing lunch. As I worked I realized I had no idea what they liked to eat. I was going to have to ask them how they liked their sandwiches and what they wanted to drink. They were my new stepdaughters and I was feeding them for the first time.

"I ought to know what kids eat," I thought. "After all, haven't I been feeding my own for all these years?" The twins' identical faces reflected my own anxiety and uncertainty. I wanted to love them, wanted to care for them, hoped to be accepted by them, but I didn't know how. Did being their father's wife equal being their mother? Was I supposed to "mother" them?

Raising my own children to their teen years did not prepare me for being a stepmother. My years as a biological mother had been full of tension and emotional involvement. I had felt responsible for not only their physical environment but also for their psychological development. What they became as adults would reflect on me and show how well I had done my job as a mother. It was hard to separate myself from who and what they were. On reflection I think that the experience of being a stepmother brought me new insights into what being a mother is all about.

As a stepmother, I was able to indulge in the physical part of "mothering" without the same emotional involvement. Caring for the twins was "acting" the part of mother without my self-image at stake. On this first day, however, I was the "mother" because mothers are responsible for lunch. They were two hungry little girls, and at five you don't care who fixes the peanut butter and jelly sandwiches and chocolate milk. It turned out they wanted bologna.

We all survived that first meal. Their visits became routine and lunch or even dinner was no longer a problem. Caring for them, mothering them, was relatively easy. They were polite, quiet little girls, and there seemed to be little evidence of sibling rivalry between them. They amused and comforted each other and therefore didn't make the kinds of demands I was used to hearing from young children.

This spirit of cooperation may have developed because the twins had lived with their mother and their grandmother since their parents' divorce. Interestingly, the grandmother, a widow of many years, had also raised her children alone. The twins' home represented two generations of parenting without a father present. As the stepmother I was yet a third female influence on their behavior. It is possible that the absence of a male role model on a daily basis allowed the girls to develop a behavior pattern of cooperation rather than competition. This pattern of cooperation also became part of the relationship I had with their mother. During their teenage years she and I became the ones to make the plans for the times the girls spent with their father and me. As she and I had always done the social planning for our individual families, it seemed natural for us to coordinate plans for weekends and outings. It also became clear that we had no fight between us. More important, we had the best interests of her daughters as a common ground. We developed an odd sort of kinship as dual caregivers. We did not and could not become friends, but we shared information and concerns about the two growing girls. We naturally saw different sides of them as they reacted to our separate households. Sharing this helped to broaden our understanding of them as people. We, the mother and I, eventually developed a respect for the role each of us played in the twins' growth. With the added influence of their grandmother, they had three women to identify with and to look to for help in the complex task of growing up. They had their father and eventually a stepfather, but in a very real sense they were raised by women.

When they became teenagers, my relationship with them had little of the usual parent-child conflict common to that age. My reactions to their rare acts of rebellion were tempered by the knowledge that ours was a loving but limited connection. They would be going back to their mother when the weekend was over. She was the one responsible for their development, just as I had been responsible for my children. I also had the advantage of experience; because I had already raised three children I knew that even their worst behavior would eventually change. I could remain calm and enjoy the separation from mothering that kept me from agonizing over them.

We shopped for clothes, chatted about movies, and had long conversations about boys and the facts of life. I was becoming a friend rather than a mother. The "friend" part of our relationship became more evident when their first year in college brought two major changes. The first was a crack in the twinness they had always shared. Choosing different colleges finally afforded them the chance to be separate individuals. The other change reflected the female bias with which they had grown up. They both attended colleges with strong feminist communities, allowing them to pursue studies and off-campus activities related to women's issues. They began to learn who they were as women and as individuals, no longer paired together as "the twins."

My growing awareness of them as individuals forced me to view them as new people. Actually we were all "new people." I was returning to college after a thirty-year lapse; they were entering for the first time. We shared the excitement of learning and reading and paper writing. We compared ideas and books and teachers. We were contemporaries in spirit. We all seemed to discover feminism at the same time and rejoiced and reveled in our freedom of expression and thought. It is hard to remember who discovered what first. It was as though each of us came upon feminist ideas independently and then found out that the others shared them. We wrote letters and talked on the phone and entered into a sort of sisterhood in which age differences had no importance. It was all very exciting.

With this excitement, however, there came conflict at home. As the twins took in new ideas about women, their father became the "bad guy." He represented the male authority figure that they were rebelling against. He was also the man I had loved and married. Because I was older and had the benefit of experience to temper my judgments, I became the mediator and tried to keep peace. It was hard. At twenty, life is so all or nothing. They were finally having their rebellion.

They finished college. They traveled and experimented with different lifestyles and eventually arrived at different answers to their growing awareness of who they were. These postcollege years also ushered in a difficult period for all of us. Faced with the stress of entering the real world of rent and car payments and job hunting, one of the twins became ill. She asked for and then rejected help from all her parents. Once again I became mediator. I was connected and concerned and at the same time able to maintain the objectivity that allowed me to reason with her father *and* her mother *and* her. Because I was close but emotionally outside the problem, they listened, and she has retained a close connection with all of us while working out her problems on her own.

It was also at this time that the other twin decided to tell us of her decision to live openly as a lesbian. She had realized that this was her sexual orientation during her last two years of college but had chosen not to tell her family until she was living on her own in San Francisco. She had shared this aspect of her life with her sister and had found a supporting circle of friends, both in college and later in San Francisco, but the decision to tell her parents was evidently a difficult one. She told me about it when visiting with us after she had been in California about six months. She came to me for help in telling her father because she didn't know how he would react. She was afraid he would be either hurt or angry or both. Her mother's reaction had made her wary of parental acceptance, but because we had a history of shared feminist ideas she felt that my response would be different. I welcomed her honesty and openness and tried to be open and nonjudgmental in return. Together we approached her father and were comforted by his understanding, even though he could not offer his complete acceptance.

Our discussion in preparing to tell my husband/her father gave me the opportunity to examine my own feelings about lesbianism and about having a lesbian daughter. I realized that they were and still are ambivalent. Because our society is heterosexually dominant, and as humans we live most comfortably within the social norms, I wished that she had found a heterosexual orientation. I was concerned that she would have problems in a society that would have reservations about accepting her. I worried that she would not be allowed to develop to her full potential because of what many would perceive as an aberrent lifestyle. I applauded her courage, however, in being true to herself and hoped it would give her lasting happiness.

Reflecting then on my almost twenty years of stepmothering, I see that it has afforded me the opportunity to develop a relationship with my stepdaughters that is less than a mother but more than a friend. With my own children there is a deep biological bond that causes real and unreal expectations to cloud our perceptions of each other. Complete honesty and communication are almost impossible. Even as adults, to them I am The Mother, forever in charge of lunch. With my stepdaughters I am freed from the biological bonds and am also freed from preconceived ideas of how my relationship with them is to be. I find I can be more myself with them than with my own children. They do not resent my advice because it doesn't carry overtones of parental disapproval. I can give criticism without the fear of alienating flesh and blood. Love is not compromised by feelings of suffocation. I am the buffer between them and their biological parents that often averts a real breakdown in communications. Stepmothering provides me with the opportunity to take on an honest yet intimate role with someone in another generation.

Many women have had the experience of stepmothering. We have been portrayed as everything from the wicked stepmother of fairytales to the younger-then-stepdaughter soap-opera version. Most of us are neither wicked nor glamorous. We are mothers trying to have a caring loving relationship with our stepchildren. My experience has given me a broader understanding of what mothering really is. It is more than lunch and clean clothes and discipline. It is sharing and growing together so that the relationship includes love and care and friendship. I am happy that my stepdaughters are also my friends.

35
Step-by-Step Parenting

Dee, Wendy, and Viivi-Ann Shirley

This interview took place on a spring afternoon in 1985. Gathered around an oak table in a large Midwestern kitchen, the three of us were participating in an effort to tell the story of the building of a family. On the wall over the table was a large charcoal collage of Virginia Woolf, and on the refrigerator were many postcards of sharp and sassy women, women striding over rocks, smoking, giving speeches, celebrating. As we talked, the phone rang, dinner simmered on the stove, and the late-afternoon sun began to slant through a small stained-glass farm scene, throwing streaks of red, green, and yellow light across the floor. Scuffs, nicks, a clutter of lists and messages, an array of small and large jackets hanging on hooks: clearly this was a household, a house holding a family.

Like many other such families, this one began with a love affair between two people, one of whom happened to have a child from a previous marriage; unlike many other such families, however, this one was headed by two women. A "lesbian" family. Because lesbian mothers continue to suffer custody challenges and children of lesbians continue to be subject to harassment, there are few public records of lesbian mothering and even fewer accounts of lesbian co-mothering. This silence can make an already problematic process immeasurably, and perhaps needlessly, lonelier and more difficult.

Across the eight years of this alliance, the child had turned into a teenager, the adults had grown warier and perhaps a little wiser, and, in the process, somehow a family had formed. Our hope is that the experience we explore in the interview will prove helpful to others. Among other issues, we particularly wanted to cast light on the following questions: What are the factors that transform a federation of adults and children into a family? What factors block or hinder the process? And how much difference does sexual preference make?

One obvious difference is a sad but predictable awkwardness in naming names. Since the choice touches lives beyond our own, particularly the lives of the parents that cared for us and the child under our care, two of us have decided to use first names only. Dee is a teacher in a large Midwestern university; Wendy is a former professor who at the time of the interview was retraining for a career in social work; and Viv Shirley, then Wendy's practicum colleague serving here as a kind of moderator, is now a therapist working in a family service agency.

VIV: Nobody has agreed on what to call families like yours: stepfamilies, blended families, remarried families . . .

DEE: And all those terms have ramifications. I mean, *blended families,* that would be like mixing water and wine: it implies there should be no boundaries, no demarcations.

VIV: Yes, they're all judgmental terms.

DEE: *Step*—what would that be? One removed?

VIV: Sure.

WENDY: Well, in our case, one removed from the norm. I like that better than *blended. Blended* is like the democratic ideal, the melting pot in which all the different groups in the country homogenize. I think there are real problems with that notion because it obscures the differences, hides them, and makes them invisible.

DEE: As a lesbian family, it's not easy for us to obscure our differences.

WENDY: But those two words don't usually even go together, *lesbian* and *family.* I mean *lesbian mother* was enough of a freakout: how can you be a lesbian and a mother? And *lesbian family,* what would that be? Because Ellen, who had just turned fifteen, is pursuing her own life in a very strictly, happily, and typically heterosexual fashion.

DEE: Maybe *stepparent* means step-by-step, gradual.

WENDY: Yes, it's so . . . gradual.

VIV: Whatever term you use, you obviously now think of yourselves as a family unit. When did that begin?

DEE: I think the first question was how Wendy was going to see Ellen in the group of us, the three of us. At first Ellen was just my child; she came along to the farm when we moved there because that's where she lived—with me.

WENDY: Well, it took a long time. Dee and I got together in April 1978. I lived on a farm, Dee lived in town with Ellen, and Dee and Ellen moved to the farm in August.

DEE: Ellen at that point would have been eight. I remember a tremendous struggle in the first years over what Ellen's place was to be, a struggle in defining Ellen's relationship to Wendy. Was she like a sister? Just a kid? A friend? She certainly didn't seem to be a daughter, even a stepdaughter.

WENDY: Yes, it was hard to define. After a while we agreed on a sort of minimal statement: that Ellen was a child and I was an adult woman in the house—

DEE: —who therefore could say—and this was a struggle for you—"Pick up your toys" or "I don't want your little animals in my study."

WENDY: I felt invaded. I didn't know how to protect myself, how to say no, and I was also jealous because Ellen and Dee had an alliance that was hard to find my place in. Dee would say to me, Dee would say to both Ellen and me, in fact, the same thing. She said to Ellen, "I need another adult in my life, and that in no way replaces you," and she said to me that these were not competitive but parallel lines.

VIV: [to Dee]: So you *knew* that they were competing for you?

DEE: Oh, they were. That was very difficult, very hard. In those first years I remember a kind of loneliness. I wanted very much to have another adult who cared deeply about Ellen: who she was, how she was doing in school, how she was growing, someone who had all the tender memories, all the concern for her that I did, and of course, there was no way Wendy could do that.

WENDY: Well, I felt some tenderness, but I also felt anger. It wasn't that I was unconcerned with her or didn't find her interesting and compelling. I was angry that I wasn't getting more time with Dee, that Dee would go to school in the morning and work, and come home, and then because Ellen was little the early evening was given over to her. There was dinner with her where we listened to her little chatter, which did not interest me a whole lot [general laughter]. Dee had a way of talking with her that was a pleasure for both of them, but I couldn't exactly find a way. That was dinner, and then after dinner until nine was time with Ellen, putting her to bed, reading her stories, and so on. And then at nine, nine-thirty—

DEE: —I'd go to work, usually, prepare classes—

WENDY: —Dee would go to work. She had tenure coming up. I felt like, "Wait, what about me? when can I have time?" but I felt it was illegitimate to be fussing about that because the reply was, "This is my child, this is my daughter, it's my responsibility to take care of her," and I didn't know how to say in a way that could be heard through my anguish, that there was a readjustment that needed to be made. I didn't now how to name it or what the process was.

VIV: So, "Let me in also." You felt like an outsider and you wanted in.

WENDY: Yeah.

DEE: In the three years we were at the farm the weeks would go by in four seconds. Ellen would be with us all week and then with her father from Friday afternoon to Sunday afternoon. And what that meant was that we could be a couple on the weekends, which was wonderful—very intense, very close. Since we were out at the farm we had a sense of being in a kind of retreat together. And then Sunday afternoon Ellen would be dropped off at the laundromat where we did the family wash. Mostly you [Wendy] would come, right? And that would be the time we would reconstitute ourselves as a group.

VIV: Okay, but you're using the words *couple* and *group*. You're still at this time not thinking of the three of you as a family unit?

WENDY: No way.

DEE: No. That's right. It seemed fairly schizophrenic.

VIV: How do you mean that?

DEE: Well, it was split.

WENDY: The two worlds were very dissociated.

DEE: And then we'd go back into the week mode.

WENDY: And I'd feel left out again.

VIV: *[to Dee]:* And how did you feel all this time?

DEE: Busy—very busy. *[General laughter.]*

WENDY: Pulled, pulled as well. Torn.

DEE: Somebody told me once that a person can do two things well but it's very hard to do three things well and so generally what you end up doing is, like a juggler, handling two things and tossing the third up in the air. During the week what would often happen was that I would do Ellen, because she was always very immediate, and I would do my work, which always seemed very pressing. And then on the weekend, I'd be with Wendy and my work, and, of course, that's why you felt left out.

WENDY: And that was further complicated by the way in which, in every family, the child can be brought in as a subject for dissension and discussion, triangulated on, in our jargon, when there are conflicts between the adults. And that year when you moved to the farm, I was on a fellowship. So I was not teaching. And I was not at all ready, prepared, in the right place, to be without more routine. I felt a lot of anxiety.

VIV: Because you had been used to a structure, and all of a sudden in your professional life you didn't have that structure any more—

WENDY: —and these two people were in my house—

VIV: —and you didn't have a private structure either. How about Ellen? How was she behaving during this time?

DEE: She's always been a really wonderful kid.

VIV: Okay, so now we have that out of the way. Tell me what wonderful way she was behaving.

DEE: She liked being at the farm. She loved the animals. The farmer we rented from kept pigs and there were cats and—
WENDY: —secret places—
DEE: —lots of secret places where she could set up tiny households.
VIV: Was that something different for her?
DEE: No, she had always had places where she would take her things, her little plastic animals and her teacups, and make little households for herself. She'd wander busily around outside. She helped in the garden and fed the garbage to the pigs. She loved to do that.
WENDY: She was so cute.
VIV: Did you recognize that at the time?
WENDY: Oh yeah, I really thought that she was wonderful. And she apparently made the transition to including me very quickly and without much fuss. When we first met and I came to Dee's house, she had a book of riddles and she would test me time after time with those riddles. I'm as good at riddles as I am with crossword puzzles: I can't do them, I'm impatient, and I couldn't do her riddles. Finally I just said, "I can't do these any more with you because they make me feel so stupid, they make me just feel terrible," and she said, "Oh, really? Oh, I didn't know that. Well, we won't do them any more." And that was the end of it. She didn't test, she didn't pout, she didn't complain, she was very—
VIV: —delighted to know that you felt stupid. [Laughter.]
WENDY: And I was in a one-down position for the rest of my life!
VIV: Sure, you gave it to her.
WENDY: So I felt guilty: here was this eight-year-old doing apparently perfectly well, and I was just beside myself.
DEE: Of course, all this time I was very invested in Ellen being okay, in seeing her—and having Wendy see her—in a positive light. No doubt this blinded me to all the ways in which she *wasn't* perfect, and that must have exerted real pressure both on Wendy and on our relationship. But Ellen did seem to go along fairly steadily at school. She had lots of friends and was always tremendously affectionate.
VIV: With Wendy also?
DEE: Wendy, would you say she was affectionate with you at the beginning? I think she was more polite with you.
WENDY: She was more polite, yeah.
VIV: So, like you say, she didn't do what you call misbehaving.
DEE: No, she didn't.
VIV: Tantrums? Anything?
DEE: No.
WENDY: Well, one thing she was doing was wetting her bed. That was a real concern to both of us.

DEE: She had a series of urinary infections. They started before the divorce, and they would recur.

WENDY: And I thought that they would probably stop when we all settled down as a new and secure home base for her. And in fact within less than a year they spontaneously ceased.

VIV: Then maybe within a year Ellen felt a sense of unity?

DEE: She had a lot of changes to cope with. In 1976 and 1977 her father went to Los Angeles, so during that year I was her sole parent. And that year went well. We made a little house and we made a bond. Then Wendy came along and at the same time her father returned with a woman he had met in Los Angeles.

VIV: He had somebody else; you had somebody else, oh hoo.

DEE: No wonder she made little houses for herself!

VIV: You bet she did.

DEE: I remember times at the farm when she was very sad. She had a cat named Scissors, which she and I got after the divorce. She really loved him. He was just a little gray thing, and he got run over while we were at the farm. It was while Wendy was in France, and Ellen and I were out walking and a car came, really fast, and hit him. Now and then she would cry, and when I asked her why, she would say, "I'm crying about Scissors." Scissors stood in for loss and what she meant was "I'm feeling lost" or "I'm feeling a loss." The car struck him and vanished into the night, and that must have felt as sudden and seemed as random as all her other losses.

VIV: How long after you two moved to the farm did Scissors die?

WENDY: They moved in in August; I must have gone to France in October.

DEE: And that period between August and October was very tumultuous. We had a hard time living up to the hope that moving in together represented.

WENDY: So I left for Europe very unresolved and had a terrible, terrible trip.

VIV: [to Wendy]: Did you run away?

WENDY: Yeah.

VIV: Because of . . . not being included?

WENDY: Yeah, and feeling unsure and disoriented by this change. I felt very positive things and I felt very negative things. And my ambivalence frightened me. It always does.

VIV: What were you ambivalent about? Your commitment to Dee?

WENDY: Yes, of course, because although Dee wasn't my first woman lover, she was the first woman I'd considered making a commitment to. Up until she moved to the farm, it was a great romance, which I had, up until that time, been very good at. You know, impossible people, short romances, great affairs—and here I was in a completely different situation. So I was ambivalent about that. And when I told my parents that Dee had moved in, they responded in a very hostile, frightened, even brutal way. Surely I wanted more separation from my parents than I had had, and perhaps this was one way that I was going to begin to get that, but their response was just overwhelming. So I felt very frightened and guilty and concerned for myself. And some of that has continued for us. You know, we've lived together eight years and my parents have not budged from their initial stance. There's been a real change with Dee's parents and this spring we were invited, the two of us, down to their house for the first time, but the fact that my parents are so negative and frightened and had such different expectations for me weighs on me, and they certainly have never acknowledged Ellen as part of my life.

VIV: So Ellen does not have your parents as grandparents.

WENDY: Not at all.

DEE: Ellen doesn't exist for her parents.

WENDY: Neither of you exists.

VIV: What about your sisters? Does Ellen consider them her aunts?

WENDY: No. No, she doesn't. I recently talked to my middle sister, who moved here two years ago. I said, "A while ago you said something that really hurt me; you said Ellen would never be a real niece to you. You can't imagine how much that hurt." And she said, "Well, look, in the two years we've been here she's come to our house two times. She never talks to my husband. When I try to make conversation with her, sometimes she responds and sometimes she doesn't"—

VIV: —that doesn't sound like Ellen—

WENDY: —"how do you expect me to feel toward her as a niece?" And I said, "Well, if you feel you've extended yourself that way and that's your experience, I guess I understand." But I was still hurt that we didn't seem to have more of a family with them.

DEE: I think Ellen's response to your sister is partly rage at your whole family, which I also feel.

VIV: All right, so?

WENDY: So, one factor is that we don't have an extended family—

VIV: —and this is a function not of being a stepfamily but of being lesbians?

DEE: It's complete homophobia on the part of Wendy's parents, and her sisters feel a lot of loyalty to their parents.

VIV: Sure, they're probably very torn. And Ellen is in the middle of that where they're concerned. It's through Ellen that everybody expresses fairly overtly that they disapprove, that you and Ellen are not part of their family.

WENDY: One of the most wonderful things about our trip to see Dee's parents was the way I felt free to talk about Ellen as my child. They recognized my part in her life and we laughed about being parents of a teenager. That felt just great!

VIV: Is that a new experience for you?

WENDY: Yeah.

DEE: Yes, having that other familial layer. I imagine that if we were a "normal" heterosexual stepfamily, the layers would integrate themselves: Wendy's parents would be "real" grandparents and my parents would get to know her parents, and everyone would know that Wendy has some responsibility for Ellen. But that recognition has come only in the seventh year of our relationship, and only with my parents.

WENDY: Yes, but I know of other stepfamilies where it doesn't work out easily either. I have a client whose mother won't treat his wife's daughter, his stepchild, as one of the "real" grandchildren: she plays favorites, gives different toys to the stepdaughter, and really interferes in their notion of themselves as a family.

VIV: I think that is an area where "step" is very fuzzy. There aren't any norms.

DEE: But in our experience, when Ellen's father remarried, Ellen got a stepmother, someone to whom she gives Mother's Day cards, for example, someone who does much less of the mothering than Wendy does but is legally and structurally a stepmother. And Ellen got another set of grandparents. She's the only grandchild on that side, and those grandparents write her, send her presents, expect her to come to Passover, really see her very much as part of their family. Where we, because we are lesbians, have had to struggle to find a form for our family, theirs was readymade.

VIV: When were you divorced?

DEE: In 1976.

VIV: So you were a single parent for two years before you moved to the farm, and then you were still the sole parent? When did that change?

DEE: I think it began to change very gradually. In my sense of it, the first indication was when Wendy felt free to say to Ellen things like "Pick up your toys" or "Go to bed now." When you began making gestures that were—

WENDY: —that were parental—

DEE: Yeah. Paradoxically it was not when you began to include her, which you did right away, but when you began to be able to exclude her, to say, "Now I don't want you here."

WENDY: In other words, I drew a boundary.

VIV: Was that a parental feeling or was that recognizing your rights as an adult person?

WENDY: Well, first it was rights, but then it moved into the parental.

VIV: How do you distinguish between the two?

WENDY: Well, if it were rights, I would do it for my own benefit: I want more quiet, I want this, I want that. If it's parental, it's also an interaction with whatever Ellen's doing at that point, whatever she may be needing, so my consciousness is split when I'm parental. It's more single-minded when it's my personal rights.

DEE: Yes, in that sense your first gestures toward being parental with Ellen occurred when she was sick, when she had a cold. I'm the kind of person who always goes to work when I'm sick. I keep going—

VIV [to Wendy]:—and you make chicken soup.

DEE: That's right, exactly. I would want Ellen to go to school if she didn't have a temperature, and Wendy would intervene on her behalf.

VIV: Did that cause friction between the two of you?

DEE: No, it didn't, not that I recall.

WENDY: No.

DEE: I was glad there was a kinder person, someone to pamper Ellen, to feed her chicken soup and let her stay home.

VIV [to Dee]: You said earlier that at the beginning you wanted another adult to share in Ellen's parenting. So when Wendy began to do that, was that the crucial change?

DEE: Yes, that was very moving to me.

WENDY: It took us some time to understand each other's position. When I began to really want a child of my own and think about how we might raise it, Dee said, "Well, you would have the primary responsibilities, but I could help with the cost." Then I began to feel like, gee, what I really want is for us to be two parents. I began to feel from the other side the loneliness and the sadness Dee had felt.

DEE: How we were with Ellen at first was very separate. She was my child, and she was someone that existed in your living space.

VIV [to Wendy]: Do you remember when your attitude about that changed? Was it when you began to do the chicken soup? when you began to have some sympathy for what it felt like to be the sole parent?

WENDY: Those were important, yes. Another thing was my own examination of what was going on for me in my inner world, why I was in such a rage. I got a sense—and I *would* think this with my Freudian background—I got a sense of the way in which Dee was the mother and Ellen and I were both children—

VIV: —tugging at her skirts—

WENDY: —and it was like with Mom. It was back to that rage you feel when your mother's attention has to be shared with the other children. In fact, actually, I hadn't experienced that very strongly as a child. It came up, as Freud describes it, when the new circumstance sparked connections with the situation that gave rise to it. With Ellen it was as if I experienced consciously what I must have felt unconsciously very much earlier. That was painful work to be doing, but it proved helpful.

VIV: So, Dee, how did things change for you?

DEE: The thing that happened to me was that gradually as Wendy took more responsibility for Ellen I didn't have to always be supercompetent. I had tried to be the right kind of lover, the right kind of mother, the right kind of scholar and teacher. That's why I say I was busy, and it must have been obnoxious. I was trying to be perfect, and as Wendy began to take more responsibility for Ellen it was possible for me to be more human. I didn't always have to be in control. Some of Wendy's first bonding with Ellen, in fact, occurred when I would get upset and Ellen would talk to her and they'd cope and laugh and carry on.

WENDY: That's true. And that has continued. When there are rough moments with Dee, or between Ellen and Dee, or between all of us, Ellen and I eventually have some discussion about what's going on and what can be done.

DEE: Maybe one thing that we ought to mention is the lesbian parents' group. In 1979, we formed a lesbian parents' group with some other women in town. There were both single mothers and couples who were raising children jointly. The group was very important for all of us.

WENDY: And the kids came. They all went out together, bowling or to the movies, while we talked.

DEE: That was the place, the very first place, that you got acknowledgment for the difficulties of your position.

WENDY: The nonbiological mothers had a real kvetch session.

DEE: I remember the kvetching, but I also remember you speaking very perceptively and caringly about Ellen and how that made me feel the two of us as a parental team.

VIV: What about now? You both refer to Ellen as your child. What would Ellen say? Does she have two parents?

WENDY: I don't know what she would say if you asked her exactly that question. I know that an occasion for her to express herself on this came about with her grandparents when there was a big fight in Dee's family two years ago. Essentially Dee said to her parents, "I want you to include Wendy. She's part of Ellen's and my life, our family. When you send us oranges, address them to Wendy, too. She also eats in our house!" [*Laughter*]. They blew up, and there was a terrible scene. Ellen later wrote them a letter saying that I was as much a part of her family as her stepmother. It was a very wise and loving letter, and I think it had a real impact on their eventual turnaround.

VIV: Okay, so she acknowledges the two of you as parents? She refers to you *[Dee]* as her mother. How does she refer to you?

WENDY: Wendy.

DEE: But she's always called me Dee. Always, from the beginning, she called me Dee and she called her father by his first name. So that hasn't been a linguistic marker.

VIV: So, Wendy, this afternoon you've been saying that you feel like Ellen's parent or stepparent, but, as you talk, I have more the sense of an older friend, something in between a friend and an aunt and a mother, something very unique.

WENDY: Well, the way in which I'm not a parent is that I feel free, Ellen and I both do, to ignore each other, to go out of relationship with each other. And we have times, they can last for days, when we just are in separate worlds: we don't check in with each other, we may not even talk. And that's not something Dee can do or allows herself to do. But I can and do, and Ellen does.

DEE: I feel that if I fell out, you know, went into my own world, it would be a violation. I don't feel I can do that. I never have. But I do feel freer now to be preoccupied with, say, my writing, because I know that Wendy will pick up, and she'll be there.

VIV: Yeah, but the ultimate responsibility is still yours and it is not *[to Wendy]* yours.

WENDY: Well, I know what you mean, but I'm not sure that's exactly true. We wrote a will, for example, in which we said that if Dee should die and Ellen and I survive I would become Ellen's guardian, which means she could live with me until she goes to college and I would be the executor of her finances. Now I suppose if that happened, Ellen's father would claim her and there's no way I could fight him for that, but—

DEE: —but we set up specifically so that Ellen could choose. We named Wendy guardian so that if Ellen wanted to finish high school here, rather than move to the town where her father lives, then she could.

WENDY: And if Dee dies, I want her . . . I feel that I want to see her through whatever it is that her life is going to bring.

VIV: Are there still times, Wendy, when you feel on the outside?

WENDY: Uh-huh, there are.

VIV: Frequent or infrequent, what would you say?

WENDY: Infrequent.

VIV: Dee, do you ever feel left out in regard to Wendy and Ellen?

DEE: Well, nothing like the exclusion Wendy has experienced, but recently I have felt more distance. One difference is that for me it's mixed: when I feel left out, I still feel glad that Wendy's bonding with Ellen. And it's probably also more voluntary: when I feel left out, often it's because I've taken some step into my own preoccupations—

WENDY: —or when you go out of town. We have a great time—

DEE: —they love it when I go away! *[Laughter.]* I think that there are ways in which Ellen has real affinities with Wendy, affinities that she doesn't have with me. And that's wonderful for her.

WENDY: Tell me the wonderful things she has that are like me.

DEE: A messy room. *[Laughter.]*

WENDY: That's what I most complained about! When we got together and I saw the way Dee let Ellen keep her room, I thought, "Jesus Christ, that's incredible. It's a pit up there." And Dee explained that no . . . well, yes—

DEE: —it *is* a pit—

WENDY: —that it's her room; it's her private space. She would get Ellen to clean it up once a week or once every couple of weeks. She's real lenient about that.

DEE: My one rule was that there had to be a path to her bed, so I could get there to read her a story.

WENDY: I'd never seen a mother treat a daughter that way. What do you mean she has her own space and her own . . .? That was like a miracle to me. It was moments like that that made me realize why I was brought to these two people. You know, to be able to see a different kind of family and to think of family relationships differently.

DEE: I think there were some things Ellen and I did that were enabling for you. For the first how many years, it was probably two or three years, you felt you couldn't close the door to your room and be by yourself.

WENDY: You couldn't in my family.

DEE: We come from very different kinds of families. In my family, it was just fine to go to your room and close your door, and that's how it always was with Ellen. I think the way that we were with that finally allowed you to begin to try that, going to your room and closing your door.

VIV: And maybe you left yours open a little more?

DEE: Yes!

WENDY: But just the fact that there were boundaries in this family, distinctness and privacy. In my classically Jewish family, it was very, very different. Being with Dee and Ellen, at first, was like being in a foreign country.

VIV *[to Dee]:* Do you suppose that was difficult for Ellen? She'd been used to you and her father and here's somebody else from a different culture, different lifestyles, different observations, different rules, different expectations.

DEE: Maybe, but in the first years I think I assumed that because I remained for Ellen, things stayed stable for her. If Wendy had other ways of being, that was how she was, but things hadn't changed between the two of us.

VIV: Well, they *had* changed. There was another person in your life now, so of course things had changed between the two of you.

DEE: But I guess I felt so much her anchor—

WENDY: —or she was so much yours—

DEE: Oh, yes.

WENDY: That's another thing. I think she was your anchor in some way, more than your relationship with her father or with your parents had been. In the time we've been together, she's gotten older, of course, but our bond has allowed you to free her from some of her anchoring function, don't you think?

DEE: That's true.

VIV: But I wonder what she was feeling with these two systems coming together. Do you think they caused her a lot of confusion? Let's take holidays. How were they celebrated: your way or your way or did the two of you blend them?

DEE: A good measure would be Christmas/Chanukah. When I left my marriage, Ellen and I didn't celebrate Christmas ourselves. One year she'd be with my family, the next with her father's. And of course when it was at my family's, Wendy wouldn't be invited. Our first family ritual was when we started celebrating Chanukah, the year when—

WENDY: —when we bought a menorah. As a family.

DEE: And that's our holiday now with each other. We make presents for our friends, decorate the house, get out our menorah, and light one candle every night, and each person opens one present each night.

WENDY: There's so much discussion behind the scenes: Ellen and I plot what we'll get for Dee, Dee and I cabal about what we are going to do for Ellen, and there's great glee in it all.

VIV: In a lot of ways this was a different celebration for Ellen?

DEE: For both of us.

WENDY: It was different for me too. I brought in the Jewish ritual part, the Hebrew prayers, but there were spiritual aspects we all added.

VIV: So you made your own, and yet it had enough commonality with what Ellen was used to that it was a nice blend.

DEE: It feels like our chosen holiday. That was 1982, the year we had in Boston all together.

WENDY: That was also the year that Ellen came to live with us full time, as she has ever since, because her father moved out of town. There was a transition to be made to living all together full time. Not having the weekends to ourselves—

VIV: —and up to that point the weekends she was with her father. Oh wow!

WENDY: We were nervous about that; we didn't want to give up our weekends and certainly feared that things might go back to being rough and scary like in the first period.

DEE: We had so privileged weekends as our time together.

VIV: So, the two of you had your couple time when Ellen wasn't there, and you still did not feel that if the three of you were together you could say, "Ellen, you're a child and now it is our adult time"?

DEE: We never learned to do that at the farm; I don't think we ever had.

WENDY: I think, in fact, that's what our fights were about, though at the time I couldn't see it.

DEE [to Wendy]: Remember that family therapy course you took one summer? There was a diagram in which there was a heavy line between the couple as partners and the children—

WENDY: —and a permeable line between the couple as parents and the children. And I realized that we hadn't yet formed a boundary around our alliance as partners. And that was part of what had been going on: the struggle and the pain and the resentment.

VIV: Sure.

WENDY: I am a person who can be comforted by theory. [Laughter.]

DEE [to Wendy]: You have really given us so many gifts, and that one— my learning to separate the couple from the mother and child bond—that was very important. It was a real shift for me, to honor that line.

VIV: From the limited knowledge I have about stepparenting, I have not heard you two say an awful lot, except for the grandparent issue, that is different for a lesbian couple.

DEE: I think the major difference is all the additional stress a lesbian family faces. There was nothing in place to make things easier for us and much to pull us apart. Both our parents would have been happy to see us fail; there was no slot, no label or role, for Wendy; and all around us there was plenty of everyday, garden-variety homophobia, the kind of thing that put Wendy's job in jeopardy.

WENDY: Yeah, that hit the fan after Dee and I got together too.

DEE: But, you know, when we lived out at the farm we really had a portion of the world all to ourselves. It was a place to constitute ourselves by ourselves without people watching. It was a safe place, a magical place.

VIV: You were insulated. When you moved to the farm, you were moving out from under some of the stresses.

DEE: That's right. But one of the happy points in the history of our family was our move into town after three years. It felt like a risk, but it was also an extension, an integration. We're very close with the people around us now, but I remember part of the fear of moving into town was wondering who our neighbors would be, what their reactions to our family would be . . .

WENDY: What would the repercussions be for Ellen? There have been a lot of discussions with Ellen over the years about the difficulties it might create for her to be living in this kind of family, and I know there are ways that's been a stress for all of us. It's hard, for instance, when she has friends overnight. We used to not to sleep in our bedroom together; now we do but lock the door, but Dee doesn't sleep well and gets up real early. My way of dealing with it is to become angry and withdraw.

DEE: I think one of the things that happens is that because Wendy's not a man it's impossible for Ellen's friends to perceive her as a stepparent. They would know what to do with you if you were a man—

VIV: —that's right—

DEE: —but they have no idea what to do with another woman in the house. In Boston the first two or three times Ellen's friends came over, Wendy happened to be either ironing or cooking. Ellen would say, "This is my mom, this is Dee, and this is Wendy who lives with us and she's kind of a relative," so Wendy started calling herself "the slave cousin." *[Laughter.]* There's no way Ellen can explain who Wendy is—how exactly we are "related"—without going into our private life, and because that engages public stereotypes, it is a very fraught subject. If you have a preordained social position, that may put a certain pressure on you but it at least supplies a way for people to understand your importance to the whole structure. Wendy hasn't had that, and that's been rough.

VIV: But Ellen does have friends over?

WENDY: Oh, yeah. When we've talked about this with Ellen, Dee and I have said, "Look, this is your house and we want it to be comfortable for you; whatever we need to do, down to taking things down off the icebox, to make it comfortable for you to have friends here, we will do. Period." And so she said, "Thanks." And when friends were coming, she would go over to the icebox and take off—I mean she went down to the poster for a women's studies lecture series one time. Again, I felt, this is my house, this is my refrigerator! But I stood behind what I said, and I do. There's a parent for you. *[Laughter.]*

DEE: But it makes you feel very beleaguered when you have about you several rings of possibly hostile people who are, at the same time, so important to your family's emotional life, people like Wendy's parents or Ellen's friends. That's been hard for Ellen.

VIV: I expect it has. And even more so now than earlier, because at her age right now, as I recall it, one of the *really* important things is to be just like everybody else.

DEE: Although, you know, it seems to me she is fairly peaceful with it right now. Surely there are some of her friends that know, including a couple of the boys she's dated who are children of my colleagues, but I suspect that nobody wants to talk about it because then they'd have to deal with it—

VIV: —that's probably right—

DEE: —but it seems to be okay if they don't. Wendy, another gift you've given us is a way of being comfortable with being an outsider. As a Jew, you grew up knowing there were people that would hate you.

VIV: So you had some skills to be in the minority?

WENDY: The irony. And the wit. And the . . .

VIV: The plain old survival skills.

WENDY: And I must say, I've felt that was something I was giving to Ellen. She didn't have the luxury of being Jewish or of being a person of color, because there *is* a luxury when, from that position, you can see that the norm isn't simply given, "natural." You see that it can be changed, made better. You get another take on reality. I've never felt she would be damaged by that lesson.

VIV: Is there anything else you'd like to add?

DEE: I think the only other thing I'd mention is gratitude for having a co-parent during Ellen's teenhood. Now that she's fifteen, it's a completely different kind of parenting than when she was eight. And I really feel like we're in it together, particularly in the last two or three years. Even more so this year, when there are all kinds of issues that need to be discussed and I really feel that I have what I didn't have when I moved into the farm, which is someone to talk to about Ellen who had Ellen's best interests at heart.

VIV: You don't feel alone?

DEE: No, I absolutely don't feel alone. Any of the problems that come up or any of the hard decisions Ellen has to make, there are three of us to deal with them.

WENDY: And now I feel that there are areas of parenting that I'm very good at, so that I'm really able to help out and even lead the way in some instances. This is a good age for me, Ellen's adolescence. It could be that here's the advantage of not being the biological parent. In terms of the separation issues, it's less intense for me and—

VIV: —so maybe you can model something for Dee—

WENDY: —I feel like I don't get stuck too often. It's working out very well between the three of us. We're living very peacefully.

DEE: But it has been so gradual, so gradual that as you can tell it's hard to find the relay points.

VIV: Why in the world wouldn't it be gradual? Life is.

WENDY: Well, the expectations are not that, though.

VIV: But I think that is the nature of stepfamilies. Anybody that thinks just because people unite, there'll be this instant family, that is a real crock. [*Laughter.*]

DEE: We at least didn't have that irony. We had what felt like a wholly uncharted terrain.

VIV: So, you were exploring, pioneering, step by step.

36

My Wife-in-Law and Me: Reflections on a Joint-Custody Stepparenting Relationship

Sarah Turner

Every two weeks my fifteen-year-old son loads his collection of three hundred comic books into two long cardboard boxes constructed for this purpose. These two boxes, together with his own and his eighteen-year-old sister's duffel bags and stereo boxes, get brought down to the car, and I take this cargo over to their father's house, about a half mile away. Two weeks later, they and their belongings come back to me. My husband and I separated seven years ago, after almost a year of intense and painful discussion. In retrospect, those discussions seemed to have paved the way for a fundamental renegotiation of our relationship, from husband and wife to co-parents. Even then we realized dimly that because of our children, our relationship would always be around in some form. Thus we were able to construct an amicable divorce based on a basic agreement over two major points: money and custody. He, because he was able, would support the children's major expenses. And, perhaps equally as important, we would split their time with us half and half; neither of us was willing to have any less than half time with our kids, and each of us respected that wish in the other. Two years later, he remarried, and he and Ann subsequently became the parents of Sam, a two-year-old from El Salvador, who is now four.

I want to begin this chapter by acknowledging the importance of a basic fact: the major and often crippling difficult issues raised by disagreements over money and custody have not happened to us. There are three reasons for this, I think. For one thing, we were able to leave behind us, at least operationally, the mutual emotional entanglements that often persist after the relationship is officially "over." We were able to put aside issues of blame, guilt, recrimination, and the like at least partly, I think, because we had talked the whole relationship through already (even though, as I now know, the story of my marriage, like history, rewrites itself with each new development in my own life). Second, Jeff has always had the view that he is and should be an equally involved and responsible parent—until recently, a relatively unusual stance for males in our society. The importance of this equality cannot be overestimated, because it has given us a grounding of common involvement and trust. Third, he, through his family, has the financial resources to provide generously for our children, without anyone having to sacrifice. While I think it would be ideal if we were equal in this respect as well, the fact that his sense of responsibility has exactly matched his abilities to provide has made the potential conflicts in the financial area almost nonexistent.

These three factors—emotional distance, equality in co-parenting and financial security—are important not only in themselves, but also because without them tremendous confusion can occur in people's interpretation of events. Emotional entanglements can play out in financial tugs-of-war, and inequalities of parental time are often exacerbated by financial dependencies (as in the case of the wife who has both less money and more childcare responsibilities). In our case, in sum, we were able relatively easily to come to a basic agreement about the form that our joint-custody lives would take. And in that sense we were able to set up two households with a basically compatible value system. My ex-husband and my "wife-in-law" have constructed a home that I am more than happy to have my children live in. I trust them implicitly and have absolute confidence in their judgment and concern. I expect that they would say the same for me. I am describing, in some ways, the best possible scenario.

However, the issues and feelings that have surfaced for me over the years, even in this situation, seem to be revealing and useful to describe. The very fact that ours is at bottom a healthy arrangement means that I am able to step back occasionally and reflect on some of its fundamental dynamics, dynamics that perhaps all co-parenting situations share to some degree. I am mainly going to write about my relationship with Ann, my "wife-in-law." Much of what goes on is negotiated by the two of us. It is Ann and I, rather than Jeff and I, who have tended to arrange schedules, doctors' appointments, and so on, although over the years those roles have declined as the children have begun to make their own plans. It is we who

have the overlapping roles of mother—two people on one base, as it were—
and we who sometimes get in each other's way. In terms of these issues,
then, we can ask several questions. How do two women, united and
at the same time divided by the same set of relationships, make sense of
this situation? How can they construct their own relationship? How
can they both make meaning out of their situation, so that they can derive a sense of efficacy and control, and be able to explain to themselves,
and sometimes to each other, what is going on (as well as, of course, to
Jeff)?

Thinking about specific issues that have come up for me, I find that
several themes keep emerging, which I want to list, illustrate, and analyze
from a feminist perspective. I will then conclude by suggesting ways that
feminists can think about and deal with such co-parenting situations in
general, so that the feelings, goals, and well-being of all concerned are
fostered best. These themes, which are obviously related and occur in no
particular order, are:

- The issue of a third person sharing the intimate daily life of your
children.
- The construction of a required intimate relationship with someone
you don't know at all, a woman who is "just like" your friends in many
ways but who situationally cannot be your friend.
- The mutual invasion of familial boundaries of time and space, so that
decisions that have been intrafamilial become contingent on two families.
- The necessary interplay between rules (such as two weeks here and
two weeks there) and relationships (how the exceptions get constructed
and allowed), and the complex interactions that take place in the journey
back and forth between rights and responsibilities, to use Carol Gilligan's
(1982) formulation.

Dealing with Your Children

The first and most obvious issue is the fact that someone else is sharing
the intimate role of parent to your children. As the "birth mother" I know
that my perspective is different in important respects from that of the father, or the stepmother, or a stepfather. I feel this issue most strongly when
Ann, who is extremely concerned about the welfare of my children, suggests music lessons, or less TV time, or more attention to course selection

in high school, or more carefully constructed teenage summer plans. My immediate reaction (less so as I have come to understand this more) is anger at the intrusion and a profound guilt that I, the real mother, did not think of it. I think, "How dare she suggest he needs to do more homework or watch less TV? Is she impugning my role as a good mother? Well, actually, I am lazy about these things. They are lucky to have her. Why do they need me anyway. But, after all, how dare she . . ." and so on.

This particular scenario is exacerbated by the fact that indeed Ann is a careful and thorough planner who thinks of things that neither Jeff nor I would have thought of, and in this respect is a more organized parent than either Jeff or I. But Jeff as the *father* has never been expected to arrange music lessons. So my attitude becomes, from a feminist perspective, a complicated issue. Why, given that Jeff and I are both slightly cavalier parents in these respects, should I be the one to feel guilty and not him? Why do many (not all) conversations about the children's activities occur only between her and me? Once, several years ago, who I said I wanted to talk to Jeff about some activity, Ann became hurt and Jeff became angry. "She felt you didn't trust her," he said. I said (and felt), "But you are the other parent."

On the other hand, there have been episodes in which have a co-mother around has been very supportive and useful. She and I agree about matters of teenage curfews; we combine sometimes in thinking about how to deal with boyfriends, and she can be a powerful ally.

In sum, there is a deep issue about sharing parenting, one I didn't really fully understand until I got to know the children of a man I have been seeing. I have had eager instincts to give them things or make other efforts to construct a relationship, and have recognized in myself an urge that must be partly about compensating for a feeling of intrusion, of not being their mother. With my own children I have not had to construct a relationship; I have been able to take for granted, in the deepest and best sense of that phrase, our connection to each other. I can be only myself; I have no choice. And them, too. What a task it must be to construct an analogue to that kind of intimacy! No wonder then that Ann was hurt that day. In my attempts to involve Jeff, I was denying her important struggle and accomplishments in relating to my children on her and their common turf. The feminist question here, I feel, is at some level a very deep one, connected as it is to the simultaneous gift and trap that motherhood is for women. I believe we have to learn how to share these kinds of connections with other adults, without giving up or ignoring the particular personal experiences entailed in being a mother.

Transforming

Intimacy as a Required Course

Ann and I have had to learn how to deal with each other's personalities and particularities on a level that is usually reserved for intimate friends and lovers. We are thrown, for example, into making plans together, as in getting the children ready for a trip. She likes them to be organized and packed a day in advance and I don't care that much about preplanning. Once, we had a misunderstanding about arrangements I had made for a particular weekend, plans involving the vacation house (another joint-custody project). I had intended to use the house, and when my plans fell through I failed to let her know. She would have gone up there had she known it was free, but I didn't know about her anger and disappointment until I called her up on a completely different matter. She had been upset for several days. As I recall, we had an interesting conversation at that point about our different personality styles: my spontaneity and her careful planning. "When I'm upset," I said, "I want to deal with it right away, get it over with. I can't believe you were mad and I didn't know." She said she had been trying to deal with her anger on her own, that she, in turn, could not believe that I had failed to let her know that I wasn't going to use the house.

The point here is twofold; one, the most obvious, is the sudden intimacy of people thrown together by a situation central to both of their lives. The other is that, like many women, I construct relationships with other women quite easily. Particularly in my life as a women's studies teacher and professional, I am accustomed to making the personal political and the private public; I am comfortable and familiar with mutual self-disclosure. Yet, also like many women, I am more comfortable with connection than with conflict, more comfortable with commonalities than with differences. Here, in a closeup situation involving two people with a lot in common, we cannot easily be forthcoming with each other. The things that unite us also divide us. We are never going to be close friends because the situation imposes on us inherently different perspectives on the same events, people, and the situation itself. Whether, without our common situation, we would become friends, is not at issue here. (We have close mutual friends, and some say we would and others say we wouldn't.) What is at issue is the construction of relationships across inherent differences and conflicts. How can we get there from here when, as sometimes happens, I don't get the vacation house precisely because they do? Perhaps the feminist approach is to acknowledge and compare the different perspectives, and allow the resolution to occur over time, and one episode at a time. We cannot usefully either fail to acknowledge the conflict or expect it to be resolved once and for all.

Boundaries of Time and Space

When my children are at their father's house, I seldom call them up, except (as happens quite regularly) when I want them to come over for dinner in the middle of the two weeks. When they do come for dinner, they leave at about 8:30 "to go home and do homework," and I feel a pang similar to that which I feel when I drop them off every four weeks. These experiences feel like a draining off of an important part of me; but each time, once I am alone and have gotten used to it, I construct a life as a single person with work, friends, and a social life quite easily. The loss of my children for two weeks out of every four is like some kind of minor but consistent hole, or hiatus. I am aware of their absence, like a missing tooth, but, like a missing tooth, it's not exactly painful. As I said, this degree of comfort has a great deal to do with my basic trust in their other home situation.

On the other hand, when my children are with me and Ann calls for babysitting or some other plans, I sometimes experience this as an intrusion. I cannot say that I don't want them to babysit for Sam; that's their decision. I certainly don't interfere with their other babysitting plans; after all, it's a chance for them to earn money. But in these instances I sometimes feel as though the other family's life is spilling over into and onto mine.

Similarly, the vacation house: I have visiting rights to the house, built by both of us and now owned by Jeff. Jeff and Ann are very generous; basically I can go there whenever they don't want to. And we divide time at the house during summers and Christmas vacations more or less equally. But Ann was, reasonably enough, eager to redecorate the house on her terms, to her eye, and when I first saw the new curtains in the living room (bought to match a rug that I later took back but that Ann had assumed would stay there), I was really shaken up. "No big deal," I told myself, but my space, my ordering of it, and my definition of it, had been violated. (Here again, this felt to me more like an issue between me and Ann, not me and Jeff, who tends to be more neutral about his esthetic environment.)

Each visit to the house now involves for me a minuscule and very subtle reshuffling of china, cloth napkins, different quilts on different beds. These boundary issues, again, entail alterations and shifts in daily life patterns on an almost unconscious level. They have made me at times feel powerless to make assumptions about regularities and continuities in areas that ought, I feel, to be under my control—like when I serve dinner, or go on vacation. I share my space and my time with another family unit.

Am I implying here that people need control over their family lives that they can't have elsewhere? In a way, I am. In our society the home and the private sphere are touted as *the* place where people do have some control over the decisions that affect their lives, since work under capitalism cannot provide this for many people. In this view the family, as haven and indivisible unit, gives solace, individual agency, and personal recognition; it's where you can be yourself. As we know now, "the family" from insiders' perspectives is often a very different experience, and classically the woman has often provided these emotional boons to others at great cost to herself. It thus may be better, in fact, to see even the most successful families not as easy retreats *from* the world but as arenas *in* the world for people to support each other's needs for efficacy and connection. When I am saying, then, that I resent outside incursions into my family, into my own sense of personal space and agency, I do not simply mean that I no longer want to be a sacrificial mother figure, a person who denies her own needs. Certainly I have a lot more power as an individual in my own house than I did when I was married; any single person does. But these incursions, when they take place, lack the crucial tradeoffs of intimacy and decisions made in common for a common goal that a successful family situation provides. To compromise on vacation time in order to be together with a spouse or children, or to preserve a relationship in some way, is different from compromising on vacation time from a distance, because people not included in your own plans demand it.

However, I have learned to say what I want in these situations less defensively and angrily as I have seen that there is a large middle ground to be negotiated between complete control and complete loss of it. In the absence of deep personal connection and a shared common purpose, boundary issues can be negotiated on principles of fairness and compromise (sometimes). And even *with* intimate personal connections, fairness and a sense of boundaries should be respected in families and among intimates more than I suspect they often are. Perhaps intimacy functions both healthily as a cushion, to ease over conflict, but also unhealthily, as a suppressor of conflicts that should occur and be resolved. The question becomes, then, how to foster both fairness and close connections in family life, particularly as the traditional family gives way to many alternative family patterns like ours.

Rules and Relationships

This brings me to the last issue that has come up in my thinking about joint custody, namely the connection, or relation, between rules and relationships. For example, we have some rules, which are extremely useful, about the children's time and what we call "the schedule" of two weeks at each home. As the children have gotten older, they themselves have determined the intervals to be spent at each house; in the beginning, we split the weeks into fractions, because they and we felt that more than three or four days was too long not to see the other parent. Later, at their instigation, we changed first to a whole week at one place and then to two weeks. ("I do *not* want to drag my stuff back and forth that often, Mum.")

There are also times when a parent has a conference or a trip, and the rules need to be bent. I have experienced at such times a semi-desperation when I realize that I am supposed to have the children at a time when I have to be away—or worse, don't absolutely have to but want to. At these times I feel that I am asking Jeff to bend the rules. He checks with Ann (or vice versa) and then gets back to me. Usually, it's fine. When it's not, I have learned that I can negotiate and that a compromise can usually be worked out. (Recently, in fact, we have been in a transition period, where the children have become old enough to stay home on their own. Jeff says, "They don't have to come to my house; they can be by themselves." I say, "But I think they are still too young," and if I really wanted to go away he would have me over a barrel!) However, the issue here was and is one of power and responsibility to each other, as well as one of rules. In this kind of situation, viewed completely rationally, if two people disagree and the rules are on one person's side, that person ought to win. Furthermore, I have often felt like an unequal player in the struggles over these matters. "There are two of them," I say to myself. "They are a whole family. There is only one of poor little me." Thus my misplaced sense of asking him permission to bend the rules.

But what has happened when they wanted me to bend the rules? Actually of course, I have been happy to do so. Underneath the rules, and preserving them, perhaps even making them possible in the first place, is a mutual sense of responsibility and, I have to admit, an equality of power. The rules are a way of organizing the relationship, but without the mutual trust they would not be enough in themselves. As many people in these situations know much better than I, rules don't work if people don't want the relationship they regulate to work. In fact, many such rules regulate

Transforming

relationships that are actually held together not by the rules alone but by inequalities of power. Thus many women have stayed in marriages because they lack the power, economically and emotionally, to leave, and until recently the rules, or laws, enforced the husbands' powers to keep them there. Now, when rules and powers sometimes go in different directions (as in laws about child support), we can see which is more important. Fathers escape support payments because their powers—both economic and political—override the rules.

Relationships of equality may thus need rules to regulate them (whereas in relationships of power rules play a different role). However, if the three of us didn't want to preserve our system, we could spend our time looking for the loopholes and counting up the compromised days and weekends in such a way that someone would always feel mistreated. What feminist scholars (like Carol Gilligan, 1982) have shown us about the importance of a responsibility and caring approach to decisions is important here. It is at least as much the desire and need to preserve our relationships as it is the desire to be fair that allows us our trust in each other's willingness to compromise. My situation is also fundamentally one of equality with my ex-husband; even though he supports the children, I support myself, and we are equally interested in their emotional welfare. Therefore I can negotiate the relationship with him and Ann as an autonomous person. When women lack such equality, relationships of domination tend to cloud and distort our need for connection and our concern with responsibility. We have to please other people, and must try to use rules in place of power when our reliance on the relationship fails. (This can happen with men, too, but I think less often).

Conclusion

I have had trouble with many aspects of my situation of bringing up my children in joint custody with their father and stepmother. I have not liked being told about appropriate extracurricular activities for them, although I have liked help and support about rule setting. I have not liked being personally involved with someone whose concerns, feeling, and interests I cannot share. I have not liked sharing my children's time, the decoration of my vacation living room, my own vacation schedule, although I have often been grateful for my times of solitude, built as they are on the basic assumption that my children were always all right. I have not liked needing "permission" before making some of my own plans.

I think, however, that all these all these negative experiences are relatively trivial. While I still feel them intensely when they occur, I have learned to step outside them later on, and analyze them as possible aspects of more general issues affecting women and men in families today. The new research on women, particularly that of Carol Gilligan (1982) and Jean Baker Miller (1976), has shown that women's lives (in fact, everyone's lives) rest in a network of relationships and responsibilities to individual people as well as participation in the more formal, impersonal, and rule-bound structures of institutions and jobs. When one family becomes two families, the questions of rules, boundaries, arrangements, and the differing goals and purposes of individuals become more formal and explicit, more institutional in a way, even as the relationships between and among the players become more complex. A feminist perspective on such a situation means an acknowledgment of both aspects of the constellation: the need for commonly agreed-on rules and the understanding that emotional connections both support and defy those rules. Thus the mother-child bond is unique and deep, but that doesn't mean that other adult-child relationships that have important and comparable meaning cannot be constructed. If we mothers rest too much on the uniqueness of this bond, we lose both our children as independent individuals and ourselves as fully rounded people, and we deny them other models of good parenting.

Similarly, women are often separated by the same structures (mother/stepmother, mother/teacher, teacher/student, employer/employee, etc, etc.) that bring them together, and we need to acknowledge where those roles need explications and guidelines to help those potentially conflictual relationships be resolved. Finally, boundaries and rules, while necessary in all relationships, probably mean little unless all involved want the relationship to continue. If we prefer relationships based on equalities of power, we are going to have to figure out how to balance such mixtures of rights and responsibilites, impersonal rules and personal connections, in some meaningful way.

In this regard, the question of joint custody with another parent and stepparent bears scrutiny from a feminist perspective, as one construction of the "divorce relationship." Divorces, when there are children, are ongoing relationships that survive, even beyond the children's growing up. We need to think of divorce, therefore, not only as a severing of connection but as a reconnection of different terms. Joint custody and stepparenting carry with them the connotation of joint responsibility and equality. My situation is unusual in that I can presume good will on both sides. When conflicts occur, as they inevitably do, I have the luxury of reflection on the issues that come up. When the situation involves financial hardship on one or both sides, old and unresolved marital hurts, basic inequalities of power, or fundamentally different value systems, the underlying dynamics of trying to construct a situation of fully equal responsibility across two families may become obscured or seem irrelevant. In such situations, the more basic issues may color every small transaction, giving them an inappropriate intensity that makes them harder to negotiate. Furthermore, most relationships in our society are built on power and domination, rather than equality, and so most divorces and many joint custody arrangements are therefore unequal ones.

But I think it is nevertheless possible to discern some approaches that reflect feminist values, even if we can't always live up to them. The first is the recognition of the need for equality. Father and mother and step-mother (and stepfather) should be co-parents, and as far as possible co-responsible for at least the emotional if not the financial aspects of their children's lives. The details of this equality, and the form that it actually takes, may vary, but the principle should be agreed on by all parties. The second factor is the need for rules and guidelines, ones that reflect and capture this equality and at the same time protect people's rights and ex-pectations of fairness. An example from my own case would be the rule of equal time in each household, in which the children have had the right to determine what the length of that time would be.

The third factor, and the one that perhaps best reflects the recent con-cerns of feminist literature, is the recognition of the importance of rela-tionships in people's lives, that each person and therefore each relationship is unique, and that the connections among people are crucial aspects of our experiences of ourselves. I want to be able to incorporate Ann's and Jeff's, and the children's perspectives on the issues, to see the situation on their terms and be mindful of the relations between and among us, even as I work to articulate my own views. The challenge, then, seems to be how to construct relationships of equality that honor differences, that con-nect us across our differences, and yet do not eradicate those differences in the name of alleged universal truths. Joint custody and stepparenting arrangements, ones that connect people across the divisions between two families, are one place to look for these values.

References

Gilligan, Carol. *In A Different Voice*. Cambridge, Mass.: Harvard University Press, 1982.
Miller, Jean Baker. *Towards a New Psychology of Women*. Boston: Beacon Press, 1976.

37
There for Each Other: A Stepmothers' Support Group

Nancy Schniedewind

We were a group of six women whose shared experience of stepmothering brought us together into the support group. Our particular needs at that time were somewhat different. I was editing a book on women's experiences in stepfamilies and eager to have a sounding board for some of my own experiences and ideas. Lee, a seasoned women's group member and friend, trusted the value that such a group could have for each participant. Both of us were interested in applying a feminist lens to stepmothering. Three of her friends—Eve, Ann, and Margaret—and Eve's neighbor, Dana, were each struggling with difficult stepfamily issues at the time. We hoped we could help each other.

Our lives were both alike and different. We all were well educated, most of us working at professional jobs. While not all of us defined ourselves as feminists, we all respected ourselves as competent women. We were white, heterosexual, and between thirty and forty-five. Each had, or was expecting, at least one child in addition to stepchildren. Some of us had stepchildren living with us throughout the year and others not. Having related to our stepchildren for anywhere from five to fourteen years, we were "seasoned" stepmothers. Still, the ongoing intensity of living in stepfamilies brought us together. Our partners were generally supportive of our participation in the group.

My original vision for the group was that we could share our experiences, step back from them, and bring a feminist perspective to them both to better understand and gain greater control over our lives. My expectation was misguided. The intense emotionality of living as women in step-

Transforming

families was all-encompassing for enough of us that providing each other support for immediate stepfamily crises became the primary agenda. Some members were reluctant to believe that any analysis or subsequent writing on our parts could be helpful; the emotional needs of the moment were too compelling.

We agreed to meet for a couple of hours once a month. We shared leadership of the group by relating our experiences, listening with care, and supporting each other. Sharing our stories as stepmothers was our starting point. From our varied life experiences, several themes emerged at that first meeting that remained with us. How do I maintain my own sense of self, my integrity, my feeling of competence, *and* at the same time be a good stepmother? We sensed the system was stacked against us. One member's comment struck a common chord. Here we were, women struggling with gusto in a sexist society to have control over our lives, work, and relationships, and we find ourselves in a situation—a stepfamily—where we have so little control. Our much-sought-after goal of being self-determining woman was on the line. Much of the work of the group was to struggle to nurture our autonomous selves and maintain relationships.

Our experiences as stepmothers shared in the group, our analyses of our experiences, and the insights gained from the group were often very different. When there was a pattern of feeling or understanding articulated by a majority of group members, *we* is used here. This collective form does not imply, however, that each member in the group shared that perception or experience.

Issues Surface

Deep-seated issues surfaced in our meetings over the next fourteen months. As we talked we were often overwhelmed by their immediacy. So many issues, it now becomes clear, were shaped by the hold that the image of the traditional nuclear family had on our lives. Even while some of us embraced a feminist critique of standard family forms and consciously forged alternative living arrangements, the subtle, sometimes unconscious, expectations about the middle-class nuclear family emerged repeatedly.

We became aware, too, of some of the difficulties, in bringing our feminism into our lives as stepmothers to challenge those traditional roles. The relative structurelessness of stepfamilies and lack of definition of our role created in some of us the need for power and stability. We therefore reverted to old family forms. So too, feminism requires communication as equals and many of us did not feel equal as women in our stepfamilies.

Nevertheless through sharing in the group we broadened our awareness, a first step to change.

A theme that kept popping up, surprising us, and making us laugh (and despair!) was the wicked stepmother. We slowly learned that, deep down, we were afraid we were evil. Much of our behavior was motivated by that fear.

This fear played itself out in our relationships to our stepchildren. Some women experienced excessive guilt because they didn't love their stepchildren. "I should love them, I should care about them; in the least I should be nurturing." We asked the question, "What is our responsibility for our stepchildren?" Eve poignantly remembered her sense of overwhelming relief when her father-in-law told her she owed her stepson (his grandson) nothing.

Differences in feelings toward our biological children and stepchildren produced feelings of wickedness. Margaret recounted, "With my own kids I can say no and feel okay. We both know there's love beneath it. With a stepchild it's harder because there's not necessarily a loving relationship there. Even when I give a legitimate no—'No, I won't type that paper for you now at 11:00 P.M.'—I still feel guilty saying no."

We became aware that we had internalized expectations that we should be the "good" mother, the nurturing mother, and that we should give unconditional love to our stepchildren. When we didn't meet these expectations we blamed ourselves, felt guilty, and disliked ourselves. Beneath all this was the influential image of the "normal" family where the mother is ever-loving and nurturing. Some women were paralyzed by feelings of guilt at "not doing enough." One reaction to the guilt we felt at being the wicked stepmother was to distance from our stepchildren. The more we could disengage, the easier it was to avoid facing ourselves as the "bad mother."

Our "wickedness" also played itself out in the dailiness of household living. Our need for a semblance of control became dramatized in what other family members saw as petty matters—keeping the house neat, eating healthy food, limiting phone use, and so forth. We confirmed our self-perceptions of being bitchy and nasty. In a traditional nuclear family the women's arena of power is in the home. We were resorting again, unconsciously, to these old notions. These limiting expectations of women's sphere of influence again trapped us in our evilness.

The impetus to be the "good mother" was particularly strong for those stepmothers who, because of death or desertion, were the only mothers. The myth of the happy nuclear family took its toll again here. The stepchildren often viewed the biological mother as ideal, particularly if they didn't see her often or if she had died. The stepmother internalized even more the need to be perfect, making harsher the verdict of wickedness at not measuring up. On the other hand, those for whom the mother was an active participant in the extended stepfamily sometimes felt the pressure of subtle competition with her.

We learned to laugh at ourselves as fears of our wickedness emerged from our lips again and again. We began to joke about the evil step-mother. Only as we became more conscious could we begin to ask why and then later to challenge and change.

Another common issue that emerged for several group members was that of not being our true selves when with our stepchildren. Eve felt she played a role and became a different person as a stepmother. "I'm not myself when George is in the house. I feel tension." Another member put it this way: "It's such a relief when the stepchildren have gone . . . then I'm my real self again." Lee framed that experience even more broadly: "Feminism is supposed to open doors for women. Stepmothering closes them. Now I'm a stranger in my own home."

For some of us, masking our true selves and withholding feelings was a coping mechanism, perceived as both negative and necessary. Repressing feeling, while it created discomfort, was also safe. It protected us from that lurking fear that to release our powerful, negative feelings was to court household disaster. If family members knew what we truly thought and felt, we believed, the delicate truce maintaining family stability would be broken.

Our sense that we were part of our "real family" when the stepchildren were gone again points out the strength of our desire for a "normal" family, a family of emotional safety and security, a family without stress and conflict. Steprelations evoke difficult feelings and issues, making conflict inevitable. Somehow we suppressed the fact that diversity and conflict are real for most families; we had bought into the ideology of the happy family.

Lack of power was another reemerging issue that aggravated our experience of being trapped. As stepmothers, we felt we had significant responsibility without comparable authority. We bore important responsibilities for raising children and yet weren't taken seriously as a real mother. We were granted small decisions, but the biological parents had the final say about big decisions. We had responsibility with little power, a situation leading to low self-esteem and stress in any institution, family, or workplace. To give, then, didn't pay off. In response we distanced ourselves from our stepfamilies to protect ourselves from worthlessness. This, in turn, produced guilt. A good mother should be there for others. We were caught in a double bind.

We backed off from our stepchildren in a variety of ways in order to protect our own space. We sought physical space: we worked, we found a private space in the house, we got out as much as we could. Psychologically, we kept our feelings in and we refused to be vulnerable. To share our true selves would be giving everything—nothing would be left.

In this situation where we felt little power, the ability to give or withhold oneself became vital for a sense of control. If we gave more time, energy, or care to our stepchildren we could easily become overwhelmed. For some members, the need for power was strong, playing itself in giving or withholding love.

Thus withholding the entirety of ourselves helped us maintain some sense of control, enabled us to hide our anger and resentment, and saved us time and energy. The price we paid was tension, loss of spontaneity, and a constant feeling of discomfort in our homes.

We were trapped again by conventional family expectations. To be a dutiful, "good" mother brought little power and diminished self-esteem. Protecting ourselves by withdrawing provided some power, but brought with it guilt at our distancing behavior and tension between ourselves and our partners. Release would mean acknowledging several truths: the mother could be other than saint or shrew; "real" families have conflicts and not everyone loves each other equally; it is not necessarily healthy for the mother to be the emotional lynchpin of the family; and power and love can be shared in different ways in families. Such notions were far from what we had internalized as females growing up in our culture. Change would necessitate reconceptualizing notions of family and, harder yet, integrating our feelings with that. When we were caught up in the entanglements of these same feelings, such integration was a difficult task.

Tightening the bind even more was competition, another issue connected to the ideology supporting the traditional nuclear family. Through our discussions some of us discovered we were motivated by the traditional notion of the scarcity of love, something we intellectually disavowed. Yet at an emotional level, worrying that there wasn't enough love to go around, we fought hard for what we could get.

Margaret admitted to wanting to get a stepchild "in trouble" with the parent. Lee wanted to see her stepchild fail as a way to retain her own power. Some discovered in themselves behavior patterns that set themselves up with their partner against their stepchildren. Such patterns reinforced their desire to believe that the stepchildren weren't any good anyway. We had bought into the notion that we had to fight for love and because of our "illegitimate" role in the family, we didn't necessarily have our preordained share. The less for a stepchild, the more for us. Our fear left little room for us to embrace the simple message of a song that one of our young children sang.

> "Love is like a magic penny, hold it tight and you don't have any,
> end it, spend it, you have so many, it rolls right over the floor.
> Love is something when you give it away, give it away, give it away,
> Love is something when you give it away, you end up having more."[1]

As stepmothers it might take us a little longer to end up having more, yet we were initially too afraid to question the myth of scarcity to find out. Our ongoing discussions in the group helped us slowly challenge this and other myths, giving us more space to breathe, analyze our situation, and change.

A Structure for Increasing Self-Knowledge

It was through discussion and sharing that we gleaned most of our growing awareness. We did, however, try several specific, carefully structured, experiential activities as ways to deepen our insight. I facilitated one approach, the trumpet model of self-knowledge development originated by Gerald Weinstein at the University of Massachusetts. This strategy helps people pinpoint patterns of behavior that aren't helpful to them, identify the functions the patterns serve, discover the prices they pay, and find alternatives to them.[2]

Discipline was difficult for many of us; we often backed off from disciplining stepchildren, for fear of conflict. Below is an example of analyzing this particular pattern using the trumpet model. We worked with this process individually and then shared our learnings with each other.

The first step is to identify a behavior pattern. A pattern of behavior is a consistent response to a particular type of situation. One member articulated her typical pattern regarding discipline.

- *When I'm in a situation where* I want to discipline my stepchild,
- *I get feelings of* anxiety, caution, self-doubt, fear.
- *What I say to myself is* "Oh, he's going to think I'm a nag?" "Is this worth it?" "Why make a big deal about it?" "Do I want the hassle that may emerge?" "He's not my child anyway."
- *And what I do is* either not give discipline or do it in a cautious way that comes across like asking for a favor.

The next step in this model is to identify the function of the pattern, how the pattern serves a person. What positive benefits does it provide? Some of the functions of the pattern above were identified as:

- Keeps me from being seen as a naggy, wicked stepmother.
- Keeps relations in the house calm.
- Avoids confrontations.
- Avoids talking about long-term responsibility.
- Avoids growing and intense relationships.

At the same time that patterns serve a person, she also pays prices—the negative consequences of a pattern. Prices are also those things she loses out on because of a pattern. Some of the prices of the pattern described above include:

- Keeps me from being a whole person.
- Keeps me from having equal rights in the family.
- Precludes an honest relationship with kids, with spouse.
- Produces pent-up tension and anger, and encourages turning my feelings in on myself.

Beneath a dysfunctional pattern of behavior is a "crusher," a fear about oneself that prevents a person from examining the pattern. The crusher is usually not true, but the pattern protects a person from facing it because she's afraid it is true. Possible crushers of the example above could be:

- I don't want to be their mother. I'm selfish, I want my life.
- I'm second to the kids. In a crunch Paul would back them, not me.
- I'm powerless in this family.

A redirectional sentence is a statement that turns the crusher around. While not necessarily 100 percent true either, the redirectional statement challenges the validity of the crusher and gives a person incentive to change her pattern. Redirectional sentences related to the pattern above might be:

- I can be a good adult role model without being a perfect mother or even a mother at all.
- I'm important to Paul and don't have to compete with the kids.
- I'm a powerful person and can assert myself in this family in constructive ways.

Next, group members help each other brainstorm alternatives, very concrete steps to take to avoid the dysfunctional pattern. Each woman chooses one or two to try out in her life. The group provides support and feedback as members attempt to make these changes. Alternatives to the pattern about disciplining stepchildren included the following:

Transforming

1. Count to ten, be calm, and give an "I" message (a statement express-ing how a particular behavior makes you feel).
2. When an issue arises more than twice, sit down and listen to the child's point of view, share mine, and try to work it out.
3. Get a mediator in tough situations.
4. Meet each week to get issues out in the open.
5. Give stepchild one positive compliment every day.
6. Do something special with the stepchild at least once a week.
7. Initiate a good, personal talk with her every week.

After each member chooses specific steps from the list and implements them, she shares the outcome with the group, evaluates it, and either con-tinues or changes the strategy as needed. In this context of mutual support, women develop greater self-knowledge and take steps for change.

Learnings and Insights

As the group continued to meet, we found ourselves somewhat more able to step back from the immediacy of our emotions and reflect upon our experiences. Surprisingly, this process was encouraged by talking about the stepmothers in our own families.

When we had first introduced ourselves to each other, none of us had identified ourselves as women who had been in stepfamilies. Only in pass-ing did a reference to a stepmother or stepgrandmother appear. Most of our recollections of these women were very positive.

Margaret reflected on her grandmother and stepgrandmother, who, after having developed stable marriages of their own and raised their children, became good friends. Dana disclosed the fact that though she had chosen to live with her alcoholic mother in order to protect her, her stepmother was more of a positive role model for her. Dana remembered that, when young, she had emotion-laden fights with her stepmother in which she'd shout that she wished her father had never remarried. Now, very close to her stepmother, Dana acknowledged how much she has learned from her, renewing Dana's faith that difficult situations can be worked through.

Yet returning to our own immediate stepfamilies, some group members found it hard to maintain a positive focus. When we asked ourselves how we benefited from stepmothering, some felt so trapped they were unable to answer affirmatively. Others, however, could point to satisfactions. They saw their stepmothering having positive effects on their stepchildren, such as engendering a love of the outdoors. Another source of pride was one stepmother's increasing ability to balance her own independent life with her integration into a family. This feminist also saw herself helping to create new family forms that would give all members increased opportunity for both community and full human development.

Some of us began to gain insight that it was by loosening the hold of traditional ideological, psychological, and practical forms of family that we could function most effectively in our stepfamilies and feel most true to ourselves as women. We came to see that we needed to acknowledge and respect different levels of intimacy and commitment with various family members. We considered that such diversity in relationships in our family might be positive—a welcome validation of the emotional reality of our lives.

Upon reflection we discovered that it was in breaking out of accustomed patterns of communication, or even out of traditional family forms and expectations, that we engaged in most meaningful interaction with other stepfamily members and felt most free from self-imposed distancing behavior and subsequent tension. In reflecting on her resistance as an adult to her new stepmother, Lee recollected that real communication began over an issue outside their immediate relationship: their mutual concern about Lee's sister. When they got outside the dimensions of their immediate family relationship and focused on something else, trust grew.

I suggested that to enhance positive relationships with our stepchildren we might pinpoint something that we would like to learn from them and ask them to teach us. While some members found this idea mind boggling, to others it made sense. Such a step broke down traditional hierarchical family relationships and reframed expectations. Whether it be learning about popular music, computers, or young people's resistance to feminism, we wouldn't be responsible to teach and nurture; we would be on the receiving end—vulnerable, open, and learning.

Lee found that when her stepdaughter moved out of the house for a period of time, she could relate to her more easily when they got together. They could focus on experiences that were common to them as women and not as stepmother and stepdaughter. The loosening of traditional constraints, in this case the physical proximity of daily family life and their concomitant roles, created space for common concerns and caring.

Because of personal changes and lack of initiative to reorganize ourselves after a summer break, the group ended after fourteen months of meetings. Ann had stopped coming because the problem with her stepson had been temporarily resolved. Eve had left to have a baby. Efforts at recruiting new members were unsuccessful. We all left knowing we had been listened to and supported, both in the midst of a particular crisis and with the ongoing problems of being a stepmother. Many of us had gleaned

Transforming

insights and practical strategies to make our lives as women in stepfamilies happier. Some of us had come to understand the powerful impact on us of the ideology of traditional family forms and had become conscious that in transcending them we could best integrate our needs for both affiliation and self-determination.

Afterthoughts

Eight months after the last meeting, group members reflected on the step-mothers' support group by responding to a brief questionnaire. We hope to pass on our insights to other women in stepfamilies who also might want to form a group.

In retrospect, we all felt the stepmothers' support group was valuable to us, some more so than others. Members liked sharing their life situations and emotions with one another. We were reassured that our feelings were legitimate and felt relieved that others had similar experiences. Individuals pinpointed other likes: "new ideas," "setting aside time to focus just on stepfamilies," and "some of our more structured sessions with things to try at home."

In looking back, group members pinpointed significant learnings. A majority realized that they could gain both strategies for dealing with step-mother problems and emotional support from other women. Other insights about themselves, their stepfamily relationships, and stepfamilies in general included:

- I learned I wasn't just a bad mother.
- I should do a lot more talking about my feelings with my stepfamily.
- Relationships can be changed with relatively simple interventions.
- Stepparenting is more difficult for women than men because women have been socialized to believe we have to be unconditionally nurturing and loving to be good women.

In thinking about the effect the group had on our stepfamilies, our responses varied. Several members applied some of the ideas generated in the group and developed more positive interactions with their stepchildren. A couple noted that their situations didn't improve, but the group had served as an emotional outlet and bolstered their ability to get through difficult times. One member recognized that she needed more help to deal with her situation and another that her husband and stepson needed to take a more active part in the problem solving. Two members noted that the group had an ongoing legacy: they have problem-solved together about stepfamily issues after the group ended.

Some of the things we didn't like about the group, or would like to have changed, were linked to suggestions members had for other women who might be considering forming a comparable group. A few members were concerned that we didn't set clearly articulated, shared goals with strategies for meeting them. They suggested that others starting groups clarify such objectives and procedures as well as distribute readings for discussion. One member particularly liked those sessions that focused on one prechosen topic. The structured, experiential activities were evaluated positively and it was suggested that there be more. This necessitates having a skilled facilitator who is either a member of the group or invited for those sessions. Some members felt it important to have an agreed-upon method to facilitate the ongoing meetings to provide clear direction and avoid problems, such as one member with a serious problem taking up excessive group time.

Several of us were disappointed by the small size of our group and recommended that others recruit a larger, more heterogeneous group. While not a view shared by most, one member suggested that stepparent partners be invited and that, on occasion, the whole family be included. Another member with a strong religious orientation felt that the spiritual essence of relationships wasn't being addressed.

Members made note of other sources of support for stepmothers they had experienced: reading, consulting with clergy, and talking to other women. The majority found that the group provided as much, or more, support than other avenues they had tried. But while we valued our women's group, we agreed it was important to see the stepfamily as a system and also work on problems concurrently with all family members. We realized that professional help was appropriate in some situations. Our group, however, provided a basis of consistent collective support that was important and empowering for us as women.

Consciousness-raising groups have traditionally been a valuable contribution of the feminist movement to personal and social transformation for women. They encourage mutual trust, responsibility, learning, and change. Ours was both unlike and like the consciousness-raising groups that emerged with, and continued as part of, the women's movement.

Something of a hybrid between a support group and consciousness-raising group, our group was for some members primarily a meeting place to receive sustenance and encouragement. For others it was also a forum for bringing a feminist perspective to our experiences as a way of connecting the personal and political realms. To the extent that we articulated ways that sexism influences our lives as stepmothers, we heightened the critical consciousness of all members. We came to see that our feelings were typical and shared and arose not from our past or psychology but from the nature of societal institutions, particularly the family. Because of differing perspectives and because of the intensity of emotional concerns, bringing a feminist perspective to the discussion was not a goal for all members. A heightened awareness of the relationship between the personal and social emerged, but not as the central focus of the group.

Developing autonomy has been a goal for many women. This sometimes takes the form of separating from dependent relationships with men or demanding more respect and reciprocity in viable relationships. Feminism's message to women, in such cases, is accessible, clear, and relevant. Many women in stepfamilies, including some in our group, perceive their situations differently. Heterosexual women who want relationships with men often encounter stepchildren as barriers. On the surface, then, feminism appears less appealing to some stepmothers. Yet if it is individuality *and* relationship that we seek, feminism offers the best hope for such integration in our lives.

Slowly this became apparent in our group. To different degrees, we came to see how sexist conditioning, ideas, and institutions of our society helped shape us. We began to understand the powerful effect of patriarchal notions of family on our lives. The cooperative structure of the group empowered us personally and collectively. We became more motivated, day to day and in multifaceted ways, to shape new forms of family that are places of autonomy *and* community for all members.

Notes

1. "MAGIC PENNY" Words and Music by MALVINA REYNOLDS.
© Copyright 1955, 1959 by NORTHERN MUSIC COMPANY.
Copyright renewed. Rights administered by MCA MUSIC PUBLISHING,
A Division of MCA INC., New York, N.Y. 10019.
USED BY PERMISSION   All rights reserved.
2. See Gerald Weinstein, *Education of Self* (Amherst, Mass.: Mandala Books, 1976).

38

The Company of Children

Catharine R. Stimpson

> "The great tribal forms of family may be vanishing, but new
> kinship systems flourish all around us."
> —Dorothy Dinnerstein, in "A Conversation with
> Robin Morgan," *Ms.*, August 1978

I want to talk about family. To do so properly, I must be more personal
than I am wont to be. A narrow-mouthed woman, I prefer reticence to
autobiography.

Yet, too many people who talk about family are less candid, less personal, than they ought to be. Reining in fears and desire that will ride
them anyway, they lie about themselves, and hurt us. I think of the man
in Tampa who, in 1981, pleaded "no contest" to charges of sexual mis-
conduct with an eight-year-old girl and a teenage boy. He was, as well, a
leader of a group called Taxpayers Against Kiddy Smut. That boy, that
girl, might have been spared if he had admitted how horribly he wanted
to touch children instead of pretending to be their guardian.

I grew up within a family that was both huge and orderly: one father,
one mother, no stepfather, no stepmother, two brothers, four sisters, aunts,
uncles, cousins, grandparents. My paternal grandfather married three wives,
but he was widowed twice, never divorced. Implacabilities of death, not
flights of human choice, ruptured his monogamies. We picked flowers on
Mother's Day, picnicked on Father's. We were together for car trips, church

"The Company of Children" was originally published in *Ms.*, July/August 1982; reprinted
by permission of the author. © 1982 Catharine R. Stimpson.

services, and Monopoly. We were comfortable, earnest, robust, and loving.

We had an environment in which to survive. The adults had space in which to suggest that their relatively unformed neonates become well-behaved members of society. The neonates had time in which to construct their identities, to stammer out their thoughts, to hammer in their fantasies.[1]

My brothers and sisters are married. Only one has been divorced. I have thirteen nephews and nieces. No doubt there will be more. I have never married, nor ever wanted to, but, when forty, I began to help another woman raise several children. I have taught one to drive, another to play poker, and given another her first Nancy Drew. My love lacks any security of blood, any sanctity of law. So does the anger the kids and I bring up in each other. Without such regulations, I must balance interference, intervention, and interplay. I must earn and cajole authority. My emotions have a free-floating purity, and risk.

I am a creature of tradition. When I shop with a kid, I realize how reflexively people approve of me if they believe my ties belong to a particular old school. The company of children confers an ancient, reassuring legitimacy. Sighting my own gestures, I sigh and sense a mingling of past and present as close as that of salt and flour in bread. When I arrange food, in the movement of my hands are a taste for the esthetic, a bounty, that are my mother's. When I carve meat, in my voice is a spacious affability that was my father's. Listening to a child split hairs about hygiene, I hear a stubborn, frustrated logic that was my own.

Yet, I improvise the new. As I imitate father/mother, I am neither father, nor mother, but adult in a little group that some admire, and others—perhaps even the kids themselves when they rebel—may disdain. Moreover, I must deal out, and with, a culture my childhood never knew. I, who grew up without television, must permit the goofy reruns of "Love Boat." I, who was told about the old sex intelligently, must refer now to sperm banks, Louise Brown, and adolescent diaphragms.

I have, then, both reconstituted and repudiated family history. Through that choice. I have bitten on necessity. For family life demands some giving up. It schools us in limits. A child—smaller, more dependent than adults—learns this. So do those adults who are not fugitives from realism. The family has also set up a curriculum for sacrifice. The feminine form of the Latin word for family meant household servant—before it came to include household, the retinue of a nobleman, persons of common blood or race, or any group that shares characteristics. Being in a family means serving others, especially small, dependent children. For obligation-ridden adults, there is no free lunch, no breakfast, or after-school snack.

Despite my pride in my idiosyncratic, even loony, choice, I am no anomaly. Rather I am part of that social sweep that puts the ego in its place: a demographic trend. So are many of my friends. The houses that hold us are too heterogeneous, too full of permutations, for a patriarchal god and polyester gospelers to bear. In 1970, "family households," in which birth or marriage binds folk together, were 81.2 percent of all households in the United States. In 1980, they were but 73.9 percent. "Nonfamily households" grew from 18.8 percent to 26.1 percent. During the decade, 15,707,000 new households burgeoned. A majority were nonfamily; of the family category, a majority had single heads. I belong to an emerging group, to a statistic on a growth spurt.[2]

People comment on my trend incessantly. As I struggle with ordinariness, with shirts and sneakers and TV, others talk about my group, and the meaning of it all. My tedium, toil, and fun are raw material for public, and published, argument.

Some people are confessional. They write of their own experiences of contemporary family life—of orgies with married couples at conference centers in California canyons; of bitter custody cases; of unions between transsexuals. Still other people are brisk troop leaders of social change. They jauntily tell us how to march through historical and psychic upheaval. One author, for example, issues a manual for divorced men in order to help them heal their suffering from a "FIR Tree" syndrome of "Failure," "Inferiority," and "Rejection."

Still other people are sober academics. Historians claim that the modern family no longer produces goods and services. Instead it consumes them. It may also be refuge from a ruthless, competitive, loveless world, or, for black families, a legitimate source of resistance to the illegitimate racism of that world. Economists announce that it may now take $100,000 to raise a child. Psychologists theorize that such a child, as a baby, first mirrors the inchoate self in a mother's gaze.

Still other people are ideological. A privileged savant of the New Right clamors that I am committing sexual suicide. He announces that men are naked nomads whom nature has made both wilder and weaker than us girls. Men must have a home, with a wife serene within it. If they do not, the species will not survive. A pope replays St. Paul and a dogma of the Christian marriage. Legislators draft a Family Protection Act that would grant married couples, but only married couples, a special tax exemption if they bear or adopt a child. In response to such maneuvers, a man of the New Left tries to reclaim the family for progressive politics, and even to make it central to them. Among other things, he calls for an American Families Day. Answering him, a women of the left wisely reminds him of both visions of community that transcend family or race and visions of morality that affirm "individual desire and imagination."[3]

Because I am a woman who rejects femininity as usual, the feminist discourse has been, for me, the most searching, steadfast, and sustaining. Though feminists are hardly the only people to question the family, they have provoked the most hostile brouhaha. Plato preferred the state to the family, but few censor him. Perhaps our contemporary cultural illiteracy, in which Plato is a sex club, not a philosopher, has its virtues. Feminists provoke that ire because some dare to think that the family in general ought not to survive, and because all declare the health of women to be a prime test of a particular family. Indeed, only feminists—men and women alike—systematically ask if the angel of the home is really happy there, particularly if her actual stance is less that of angel than of Atlas.

Unsentimentally, feminists have documented the unhappy burden of the women, now a majority of wives in the United States, who work inside and outside the home; the inequities of marriage and divorce codes; the horrors of the wife-beating and child abuse that make the home more violent than a factory, highway, or Army boot camp. It has been feminists who have mourned a refusal, in the United States and elsewhere, to fuse domestic life and sexual equality. They have scrutinized the social construction of sexuality that labels a woman's body the agent of the needs of others; that calls female sexuality correct within the heterosexual home, incorrect but permissible outside that home, and damnable and incorrect if lesbian. Feminists—Brownmiller, Chodorow, Dinnerstein, Rich—have mined connecting shafts between patriarchal sex roles within the home and a public life that threatens us all. They have wondered if the fact that women, but not men, are raised to nurture within the home means that men are dangerously incapable of it outside.

Even as feminists skeptically analyze a family that others fancy, they seek to imagine new communities of intimacy. To be a feminist is to move between negation and hope, between estrangement from time present and belief in time future. In her novels, Marge Piercy has conjured up Utopian societies that are harmonious yet egalitarian, sane yet poetic. In feminist theory, Sara Ruddick has asked why men and women cannot practice "maternal thinking," a habit of mind that respects a balance between self and others, between self-assertion and altruism. In sociology, Rosabeth Moss Kanter has listed ways in which we could integrate work and family life. To have significant labor and leisure; to enjoy dependents and dependence while rejecting the filthy luxuries of domination and submission; to be autonomous and communal; to proclaim differences and yet to sing to children—such has been a feminist ideal, at its most dangerous and lovely.

A rule of language insists that the more we talk about a subject, the more we may be trying to hide something. Some people are consciously evasive. The New Right wraps itself in the flag of the family in order to clothe its poling toward political control. Other evasions loll in the subconscious, and we must yank them to attention. As I dwell on homey details, on leftover apple cores and the cost of tube socks, my quest for tidiness and thrift may obscure more taxing questions. How eroticized are some family passions? How much must an adult guardian, with our wariness about repression, still guard against the expression of a sharp tenderness that veers toward desire? Some polymorphous sexuality is perverse. Or, a less fashionable issue, what might one do about a child whom one might not like? Whose presence, because it may too vividly mirror one's own, may be a pang? Or, a more civic concern, how much might being involved with family welfare mask a fear of other struggles, for example, about the welfare state? The lake of the everyday may be tepid, but its rafts are there, its shores known.

The answers to such queries, like the *whyness* of my present life, still elude me. Yet, I am sure that I have tested several forms of dailiness. No one chooses a family of origin. Many of us crawl into our adult arrangements, heedlessly repeating that primal place. Later, we may not select their dissolution. However, we willful plungers in families of transition have rummaged through our past to decide what we wish to preserve. We are defense witnesses for versions of family life.

Some people accuse me of acting unconsciously. My delight in a young boy, they say, represents the rediscovery of a "phallus" I lost in childhood. Buying balloons for a birthday party is compensation for the "loneliness" I felt while a striving, womb-denying, animus-mad career woman.

Maybe the amateur psychoanalysts are correct, but it all seems much simpler and less theoretical. Because I expect to be here for a long while, because I have education and mobility, I see my life as a series of possibilities. Some can be, and were, deferred. I got bored with being with contemporaries. Though aging, I lacked a crucial measure of maturity. Inarticulately, I wanted a new fusion of responsibility and surprise, of routine and shock, of ritual and unpredictability; touches that did not have to be renegotiated at least for a while; jokes that did not have to be explained; and innocence. Though I will pass on little property and no name, perhaps I wished to infiltrate another's memory.

I did not actively seek the children out. Nor they me. Yet my difficulty now is that too many people—both strangers and acquaintances—perceive my politics, my psyche, and my form of parenting as an assassination attempt on "decency." Conservative scorn surrounds me. So does liberal surprise, but I can disarm that. Some days I ignore the conservative scorn, but I would be a fool to forget the burn of my anger, and the sting of my defiance. They are usable weapons.

I have stood, in the morning, telling a child she must drink her apple juice because she needs Vitamin C. She has retorted that she has often ignored her apple juice, and she has survived. Such dialogues are hardly the scripts of postlapsarian sin. Like many of us, I am engaged in an experiment that is trying to write new narratives of love and freedom, of being with children without using them or using up ourselves. I have a national policy for families—as simple, as nontheoretical as a child's need for apple juice. Let no child starve—in mind or body. Let no child be beaten. Let parenters speak their name, and have enough money and flexible public services to do their chores. Then—let me alone. I want privacy, not to hide some viciousness, not to perpetuate a false division between public and domestic life, but because I need the space in which to give texture to a language of love and care that is now gossamer.

Notes

1. Jane Flax, "The Family in Contemporary Feminist Thought: A Critical Review," in the *Family in Political Thought,* ed. Jean Bethke Elshtain (University of Massachusetts Press, 1982), offers a much more sophisticated analysis of the family's links to production, reproduction, and the construction of internal worlds.

2. Andrew Hacker, "Farewell to the Family?" *New York Review of Books,* XXIX, 4 (March 18, 1982), helpfully summarizes recent family developments.

3. Barbara Ehrenreich, "Family Feud on the Left." *Nation,* 234, 10 (March 13, 1982).

Contributors

Contributors

ANDREA STARR ALONZO, an instructor of English at the Borough of Manhattan Community College in New York, is enrolled in the doctoral program in literature at the Graduate Center of City University of New York. She is also working on her first novel.

SHEILA ALSON is the author of two books of poetry, *Fertility in the Desert* (Stonegoat Press) and *Notes on the Olympus Refrigerator* (Unimproved Editions Press), and numerous plays and stories.

CAROL ASCHER is the author of *The Flood*, a novel (Trumansburg, N.Y.: Crossing Press), and *Simone de Beauvior: A Life of Freedom* (Boston: Beacon Press), a critical study. She has received three PEN/NEA Syndicated Short Fiction awards for her stories, and her fiction and essays have appeared in popular, feminist, and literary magazines. She is an editor, with Sara Ruddick and Louise deSalvo, of *Between Women: Biographers, Novelists, Critics, Teachers, and Artists Write About Their Work on Women* (Boston: Beacon Press).

CRISTINE BRYSON (a pseudonym), gainfully employed outside the home, is early–middle aged, a feminist, an activist, and a creative woman.

SUZANNE L. BUNKERS lives, teaches, and writes in Mankato, Minnesota. She is active in a twelve-step program that derives from the AA model.

O.C. is a twenty-six-year-old management consultant with a New York City firm.

DYMPNA C. CALLAGHAN was born in Leeds, England, in 1959. She currently directs the Women's Studies Program at Bowling Green State University in Ohio. Her book entitled *Woman and Gender in Renaissance Tragedy* will be published by Humanities Press (Atlantic Highlands, N.J.) and Harvester Press (Britain).

SOPHIA CARESTIA is the pen name of a cultural historian and freelance writer. She recently married and lives in Brooklyn.

KATHY CHAMBERLAIN, who teaches basic writing and "The Art of the Detective Story," lives on the North Fork of Long Island. She was co-publisher of *New China Magazine*, and her writing has appeared in *Hudson River, Forward Motion, Minnesota Review,* and *Esprit.*

MORGAN DAVID (a pseudonym), a therapist and member of the clinical faculty of a teaching hospital, was married for twenty years and is the mother of three. Both she and her ex-husband have remarried and are now living twenty minutes apart.

ELISA DAVILA is an assistant professor in Spanish and Latin American Studies at the College of New Paltz, State University of New York. Cross-cultural studies and Latin American women writers are her main fields of research.

DEE is a teacher at a large Midwestern university.

BARBARA DRUCKER was born in New York City. She has had two marriages, three children, two stepchildren, and five grandchildren. She has been a medical laboratory technician in a hospital, an assistant teacher/librarian in a local high school, and an interviewer for a longitudinal study on women's feelings about birth control. A college degree at age fifty-three opened up a host of new possibilities: she cannot wait to see what comes next.

KATHLEEN DUNN is a professor of education and human services and department chairperson at Simmons College in Boston. Her areas of research are women's educational and work history in the twentieth century and women college students' cognitive development.

JUDITH GRANT is an assistant professor in the department of political science at California State University, Long Beach. Her research is on contemporary political theory, and she is currently writing a book about feminist theory.

ERIN MARIE HETTINGA, a junior at Claremont High School in Claremont, California, is a member of the varsity track team, Junior Ladies, and Girl's League. She has danced since she was four years old and has recently taken up weight lifting. Last year she was recognized as the out-standing sophomore female lifter.

JUDITH HOCKING HIGGS, a graduate of Wheeling Jesuit College, Mar-quette University, and West Virginia University, loves complicated counted cross-stitching and collecting ladybugs.

JUANITA R. HOWARD, a sociologist, has been on the faculty of Baruch College, City University of New York, since 1969. She specializes in social communication, the black community, and alienation. She is also the as-sociate producer of three award-winning documentary films which focus thematically on black history.

HELANE LEVINE-KEATING at age twenty-nine married a man with four children ranging in age from sixteen to twenty-one. After eleven years of marriage, she has an eight-year-old son, two stepdaughters, two stepsons, two stepsons-in-law, and one stepdaughter-in-law. Her poetry has ap-peared in various magazines and anthologies, including *Graham House Review, Central Park, Embers, The Malahat Review, Pudding, Heresies: A Feminist Journal of Art and Politics,* and the *1984 Anthology of Maga-zine Verse and American Poetry.* She was the 1986 winner of the Andrew Mountain Press Poem-in-a-Pamphlet contest, as well as *Heresies'* 1986 nominee for the General Electric Foundation Awards for Younger Writers. She is a member of the English department at Pace University.

HEDVA LEWITTES is an associate professor at the College at Old West-bury, State University of New York, where she teaches developmental psy-chology and women's studies. She has been the co-recipient of several fed-eral grants in the field of gerontology education and has recently completed an article based on her research on older women's friendships.

SHIRLEY GEOK-LIN LIM was born in Melaka, Malaysia. Her first book of poems, *Crossing the Peninsula* (Heinemann) received the Common-wealth Poetry Prize. She has published a collection of short stories, *Another Country* (Singapore: Times Books International), and her third collection of poems, *Modern Secrets* (Dangaroo Press, London) is forthcoming. She is an associate professor of English at Westchester Community College.

BERENICE LOPEZ, a mother of four children, is presently a community college student.

Contributors

NAN BAUER MAGLIN is an associate professor at Borough of Manhattan Community College, City University of New York, where she teaches composition and women's studies. She has published articles on feminist pedagogy and women's writing in a wide variety of journals and books. Her writing about mothers and daughters in literature and about her own family has appeared in *Ms.* magazine, *College English, Frontiers, The Lost Tradition: A History of Mothers and Daughters in Literature,* and *Between Ourselves: Letters Between Mothers and Daughters.*

GALE MCGOVERN, forty-nine, has spent the last twenty-five years considering how to come out, when to go back in, and how to connect gay and lesbian issues to other social-change issues—racism, Central American, feminism, and AIDS. She lives in New Paltz, New York, and is coming out yet again in this book.

CONNIE MILLER is a librarian, editor, and writer who lives with her family, cats, and dogs in the Midwest.

ELIZABETH KAMARCK MINNICH is a philosopher who works for the Union Graduate School, the Union for Experimenting Colleges and Universities. Her writing has appeared in *Feminist Studies, The Women's Review of Books,* and in anthologies such as *Between Women, Learning Our Way: Essays in Feminist Education, Educating the Majority,* and *Populism Today: The Politics of Empowerment.* Two years ago, she helped found a local branch of the Stepfamily Association of America.

ALICE NEUFELD is a freelance writer who teaches women's studies at a college on Long Island.

DEBORAH ROSENFELT is professor of women's studies and coordinator of the Women's Studies Program at San Francisco State University. An editor of *Feminist Studies,* she is a feminist critic who mostly writes about American women's literature; "benjamin" is her first published poem.

NANCY SCHNIEDEWIND is professor of educational studies and former coordinator of the Women's Studies Program at the State University of New York, New Paltz. She has written numerous articles on feminist pedagogy, educational equity, and cooperative learning. Her recent books include *Open Minds to Equality* (Prentice Hall) and *Cooperative Learning, Cooperative Lives* (W. C. Brown, distributed by Circle Books).

VIIVI-ANN SHIRLEY is a marriage and family therapist for a private nonprofit agency in central Iowa. Her areas of interest within family relationships include gerontology, stepfamilies, and family mythologies.

YANDRA SOLIZ (a pseudonym) is a native Texan now living in the middle of Georgia.

YVONNE STAM is an assistant professor of English and journalism at Borough of Manhattan Community College, City University of New York. Her doctoral dissertation on correlations between black dialect speakers' proficiency at standard English and their attitudes toward "mainstream" American culture was modeled on social psychology experiments performed in French/English Canada.

CATHARINE R. STIMPSON is professor of English, dean of the graduate school, and vice provost for graduate education at the New Brunswick campus of Rutgers University. She was the founding editor of *Signs*, the first director of the Women's Center at Barnard College and of the Institute for Research on Women at Rutgers. She is the author of the novel *Class Notes*, the editor of six books, and she has published over 100 monographs, essays, stories, and reviews.

ALISON TOWNSEND is a poet, essayist, and fiction writer. Her work has appeared in magazines such as *Milkweed Chronicle, Sing Heavenly Muse, Poets On,* and *Psychological Perspectives,* and been anthologized in *Poetry Loves Poetry: An Anthology of Los Angeles Poets* (Momentum), *Women for all Seasons* (The Women's Building) and *Men and Women: Together and Alone* (The Spirit That Moves Us). She currently resides at the edge of the Coast Range western Oregon, where she writes and teaches part time at Linn-Benton Community College. She has held residence grants in writing at Dorland Mountain Colony and has won prizes for her poetry from *Pinchpenny* and the Oregon State Poetry Association.

SARAH TURNER is a pseudonym. The author is an associate professor of education at a small liberal arts college in the East. She publishes in the areas of women and education and feminist pedagogy.

MARGARET WADE-LEWIS is an assistant professor in the department of black studies at the State University of New York College at New Paltz, where she teaches courses on literature and on the African-American women. Previously she has taught at the University of California, Santa Barbara, and the University of Texas at Austin. Margaret's blended family comprises her husband David, Margaret, and three children—Margaret's sixteen-year-old son, David's nine-year-old son, and their seven-year-old daughter.

WENDY is a therapist, consultant, and adjunct professor at a school of social work.

WILMA WOLFENSTEIN obtained an M.S. degree in child development in 1976, her main interest being in parent education. In 1981, she and Gloria Clark cofounded Stepfamilies of Pittsburgh, a peer support group for adult partners in stepfamilies.